Southern African Literatures

Longman Literatures in English Series

**General Editors: David Carroll and Michael Wheeler
Lancaster University**

For a complete list of titles see pages xii–xiii

Southern African Literatures

Michael Chapman

Longman

London and New York

Longman Group Limited
Longman House, Burnt Mill,
Harlow, Essex CM20 2JE, England
and associated Companies throughout the world.

*Published in the United States of America
by Longman Publishing, New York.*

First published 1996

ISBN 0 582 053064 CSD
ISBN 0 582 053072 PPR

British Library Cataloguing-in-Publication Data
A catalogue record of this book is
available from the British Library

Library of Congress Cataloging-in-Publication Data
Chapman, Michael, 1945–
    Southern African literatures / Michael Chapman.
       p. cm. — (Longman literature in English series)
    Includes bibliographical references and index.
    ISBN 0–582–05306–4. — ISBN 0–582–05307–2 (pbk.)
    1. Southern African literatures—History and criticism. I. Title.
II. Series.
PL8014.S63C47   1996
809′.8968—dc20
                                      95–15523
                                        CIP

Set by 20 in Bembo
Produced by Longman Singapore Publishers (Pte) Ltd.
Printed in Singapore

Contents

Editors' Preface

The multi-volume Longman Literature in English Series provides students of literature with a critical introduction to the major genres in their historical and cultural context. Each volume gives a coherent account of a clearly defined area, and the series, when complete, will offer a practical and comprehensive guide to literature written in English from Anglo-Saxon times to the present. The aim of the series as a whole is to show that the most valuable and stimulating approach to the study of literature is that based upon awareness of the relations between literary forms and their historical contexts. Thus the areas covered by most of the separate volumes are defined by period and genre. Each volume offers new and informed ways of reading literary works, and provides guidance for further reading in an extensive reference section.

In recent years, the nature of English studies has been questioned in a number of increasingly radical ways. The very terms employed to define a series of this kind – period, genre, history, context, canon – have become the focus of extensive critical debate, which has necessarily influenced in varying degrees the successive volumes published since 1985. But however fierce the debate, it rages around the traditional terms and concepts.

As well as studies on all periods of English and American literature, the series includes books on criticism and literary theory and on the intellectual and cultural context. A comprehensive series of this kind must of course include other literatures written in English, and therefore a group of volumes deals with Irish and Scottish literature, and the literatures of India, Africa, the Caribbean, Australia and Canada. The forty-seven volumes of the series cover the following areas: Pre-Renaissance English Literature, English Poetry, English Drama, English Fiction, English Prose, Criticism and Literary Theory, Intellectual and Cultural Context, American Literature, Other Literatures in English.

David Carroll
Michael Wheeler

Longman Literature in English Series

**General Editors: David Carroll and Michael Wheeler
Lancaster University**

Pre-Renaissance English Literature

★ English Literature before Chaucer *Michael Swanton*
English Literature in the Age of Chaucer
★ English Medieval Romance *W. R. J. Barron*

English Poetry

★ English Poetry of the Sixteenth Century *Gary Waller*
★ English Poetry of the Seventeenth Century *George Parfitt*
(*Second Edition*)
English Poetry of the Eighteenth Century, 1700–1789
★ English Poetry of the Romantic Period, 1789–1830 *J. R. Watson*
(*Second Edition*)
★ English Poetry of the Victorian Period, 1830–1890 *Bernard Richards*
English Poetry of the Early Modern Period, 1890–1940
★ English Poetry since 1940 *Neil Corcoran*

English Drama

English Drama before Shakespeare
★ English Drama: Shakespeare to the Restoration, 1590–1660
Alexander Leggatt
★ English Drama: Restoration and Eighteenth Century, 1660–1789
Richard W. Bevis
English Drama: Romantic and Victorian, 1789–1890
English Drama of the Early Modern Period, 1890–1940
English Drama since 1940

English Fiction

★ English Fiction of the Eighteenth Century, 1700–1789 *Clive T. Probyn*
★ English Fiction of the Romantic Period, 1789–1830 *Gary Kelly*
★ English Fiction of the Victorian Period, 1830–1890 *Michael Wheeler*
(*Second Edition*)
★ English Fiction of the Early Modern Period, 1890–1940
Douglas Hewitt
English Fiction since 1940

English Prose

★ English Prose of the Seventeenth Century, 1590–1700 *Roger Pooley*
  English Prose of the Eighteenth Century
  English Prose of the Nineteenth Century

Criticism and Literary Theory

  Criticism and Literary Theory from Sidney to Johnson
  Criticism and Literary Theory from Wordsworth to Arnold
  Criticism and Literary Theory from 1890 to the Present

The Intellectual and Cultural Context

  The Sixteenth Century
★ The Seventeenth Century, 1603–1700 *Graham Parry*
★ The Eighteenth Century, 1700–1789 *James Sambrook (Second Edition)*
  The Romantic Period, 1789–1830
★ The Victorian Period, 1830–1890 *Robin Gilmour*
  The Twentieth Century: 1890 to the Present

American Literature

  American Literature before 1880
★ American Poetry of the Twentieth Century *Richard Gray*
★ American Drama of the Twentieth Century *Gerald M. Berkowitz*
★ American Fiction 1865–1940 *Brian Lee*
★ American Fiction since 1940 *Tony Hilfer*
★ Twentieth-Century America *Douglas Tallack*

Other Literatures

  Irish Literature since 1800
  Scottish Literature since 1700
  Australian Literature
★ Indian Literature in English *William Walsh*
  African Literature in English: East and West
★ Southern African Literatures *Michael Chapman*
  Caribbean Literature in English
★ Canadian Literature in English *W. J. Keith*

★ *Already published*

Author's Preface

This study contains my view of the several distinct but interrelated literatures of southern Africa. Selections range from the expression of the stone-age Bushmen (San) to that of modern voices in the independent states. In respecting the capacity of traditions, cultures and forms of literary response to be specific to immediate contexts I suggest, tentatively, points of common reference in countries that, for better or worse, have entangled histories. The countries of the region are: South Africa, Botswana, Lesotho, Swaziland, Zimbabwe, Zambia, Malawi, Angola, Mozambique and Namibia. (See the map of the region on p. xxii.)

Within the individual countries, the borders of which are colonial impositions that encompassed different groups of indigenous people, literatures have tended to be defined and described according to separate linguistic-ethnic units rather than to the entity of the nation-state. In South Africa, for example, we have South African literature in English, Afrikaans literature, Zulu literature, Xhosa literature, Sotho literature and so on, each having its hermetic sets of assumptions, myths and conventions while there is little consensus on how we might constitute a single South African literature. Possibly South Africa, where ethnicity was both encouraged and enforced by apartheid, presents an extreme case of literary linguistic division. The procedure of defining national literatures in multilingual, multiracial countries with troubled histories, however, is problematic, especially as a fundamental requirement of converting groups into nations is lacking in all the countries of southern Africa: namely, widespread, multiclass literacy in a common language. While the conception of a nation is clearly necessary to the entity 'national literature', what is also required is a strong self-awareness among writers, critics and readers that an intelligible field of, say, Zimbabwean literature or Namibian literature, or Zambian literature exits, or could exist. In developing societies in particular, writers would need to articulate whether they actually felt they were contributing to a national literature: whether their interests coincided with so-called national allegiances. Institutions, including universities and publishers, would be expected to air views on the shaping of canons or the compilation of anthologies in relation to educational and cultural goals. Although themes or genres alone are not sufficient to identify a national literature, there should be an awareness of predominant themes and generic preponderance in response to the idea of the nation. Such literary schooling, however, exists only intermittently in southern Africa, and in the present study the question is permitted to remain open as to whether the individual countries may be said to be developing an awareness of national literatures. The larger issue is whether literary-historical enquiry, in countries where nationalisms or at least sectionalisms have led to tension and strife, should be based on the model of the nation (originary, organic in its symbols) or that of the society (institutional and technical in its daily work). Indeed, Flora Veit-Wild in her 'social history' of Zimbabwean literature asks whether 'the term and concept of a national literature has not become obsolete, whether writers and critics in the Africa of the 1990s have not to find new ways and new terms in which to describe the multi-faceted nature of post-colonial experience and writing'.[1]

Whatever way we pursue such arguments, there remains the historical need to give literatures from predominantly African countries their own priorities, and the term 'southern Africa' gains substance in several common subjects and concerns. In the literature of all the countries, there is the shared experience of colonialism in its abrasive, economic form attendant on strong, permanent settler populations. A consequence is the large theme of oppression and liberation with people in Zimbabwe, Angola, Mozambique, Namibia and South Africa having had to resort to bitter struggles against intransigent, white governments. (In this aspect, the character and depiction of southern Africa is closer to that of Ngugi's Kenya than to that of Achebe's Nigeria.) As a result of the colonial presence in all spheres of life, particularly in education, the racial theories, practices and values of Europe have featured prominently in the language and texts of a great deal of the literary response. Above all, perhaps, the transition from traditional to modern loyalties in aggressive, industrialising economies has led, in literature and life, to swift, often desperate disjunctures. Literature from southern Africa is broadly about urbanization, where the old-versus-the new or the rural memory-versus-the city opportunity characterizes forms of expression beyond any stronghold of language, race or nationality.

These initial observations should suggest that while the contours of different literatures in the region will be encouraged to give the study its shape – the title deliberately retains the plural form – I do not intend to follow the general practice in most existing literary surveys and histories of balkanising the literature into discrete ethnic units:[2] units that can be unwitting reminders of the divide-and-rule tactics of the colonial legacy. Instead, I intend to construct the field on comparative considerations. In looking at frontier clashes in early nineteenth-century South Africa, for example, we might want to ask ourselves whether Xhosa literature would have taken the directions it did had there been no colonial settlement in Xhosa space; obversely, whether early South African literature in English would have followed its particular course had it not encountered indigenous people around its early settlements. The questions in themselves are not meant to be profound; we are reminded, nonetheless, that the Xhosa bard and the settler journalist, though divided by language, literacy, race and probably sentiment, were both part of the same story – a story which remains open, of course, to different interpretations. At a time when the intent in southern Africa is to move beyond the conflicts of the past and chart new directions, the potential of the comparative method to investigate the intersections of traditionally enclosed categories seems to be an important function of literary history. Such an approach clearly cannot regard language systems as entirely self-contained, and I wish to thank the publishers for permitting me to step outside the strict designation of the series as literature in English and, in consequence, to be able to focus on what I regard as important works whatever the language of their expression. (The principle of translation is raised in the Introduction.)

Of the countries that comprise southern Africa, the largest and most contentious is South Africa which, in terms of its literary interests, publication outlets and relatively large readership, has virtually subsumed any literary identity there might once have been in the neighbouring states of Botswana, Lesotho and Swaziland. To take just one example, there is a claim to be made for Bessie Head as a Botswanan writer; the compulsion behind her stories, however, finds its force in the racial stigmatisation of her early South African experience. With colonial institutions dating back to the mid-seventeenth century, reasonably advanced economic and bureaucratic infrastructures, and an active publishing scene, South Africa in the sheer bulk of its literary output occupies considerable attention in this study. The next most viable literary culture is to be found in Zimbabwe. Malawi and Zambia have more modest outputs while Namibia is still finding its feet as an independent country. An impressive literature by Angolans and Mozambicans, which was mostly published abroad, characterised the years leading up to the freedom struggles in the late 1950s and early 1960s. Understandably, the output has not been sustained during the lengthy civil wars that in the post-independence period have sapped the energies of the two countries.

All the countries have retained the European language of the erstwhile coloniser as the medium of state communication and, given the existence of numerous African languages, as the medium of national unity. English serves the purpose in the ex-British colonies of Malawi, Zambia, Botswana, Lesotho, Swaziland and Zimbabwe. Portuguese serves the same purpose in Angola and Mozambique. In Namibia, which was colonised first by Germany and subsequently administered by South Africa, English is the language of official practice while Afrikaans is widely spoken. In South Africa, a union of two British colonies and two Boer republics, English and Afrikaans (the latter an indigenised form of Dutch) reflect the roles of Britain and Holland in the colonial history. In addition to the European languages, there are in all the countries strong languages in the linguistic family of the Bantu-speaking people: the classification of the negroid groups in southern and central Africa. As in the past so in contemporary times, it is the indigenous languages, not the European languages, that have enjoyed majority, popular speech in live, oral communication. Predating both African and European people in the region were the Bushmen and Khoi who spoke versions of a click language that is today virtually extinct. In transcribed and translated form the legends, myths and tales of these ancient people may enter discussion as southern Africa's classical literature.

After an Introduction which enunciates the principles of the study, Part One looks at oral traditions in the subcontinent. Part Two examines the literature of European settlement in South Africa up to the beginning of the twentieth century. At this point a colonial literature emerges with some persistence in the other countries, and so Part Three poses the question of when colonial literature becomes African literature in relation first to early activities in Zimbabwe, Angola and Mozambique and then to South Africa's 'continuing colonialism'. Part Four focuses on the demands that have been made on writers in the independent states by the ideals of new nations and the pragmatics of functioning societies. From such a post-independence perspective, Part Five returns to South Africa: the problem of writing in the interregnum – the time between the death of the apartheid state and the birth of a civil society – gives impetus to a consideration of literary activities since the early 1970s. The arrangement of the material is roughly chronological, but I have interrupted the onward momentum to allow for debates concerning the possessions and dispossessions of language, race, identity and power that have characterised life in this part of Africa. In favouring argument over information, I see this study as having educational value in raising issues about the efficacy of literary study in a contentious social milieu. In universities in southern Africa, literary study is still heavily reliant on criteria of description and evaluation derived from metropolitan great traditions. I hope my argument, in contrast, will suggest ways of focusing on the West through African eyes while granting Africa the importance of its own centrality in the region. Clearly, the terms the 'West' and 'Africa' – as I am deploying them here – are not meant to denote essences, but culturally conditioned terms in an argument: terms that in a highly politicised environment can have both semantic and actual consequences in the surrounding life. In receiving and answering the speaking power of texts in a forum of enquiry and debate, the study acknowledges the contribution made to interpretation by the critical activity and by a community of readers. The implication is that we neither reduce the work of the past to its past condition nor read it today as if it were a product of our time, but think of the work as needing us for the realisation of its potential.

With readers envisaged primarily as fellow academics and students, I have selected bibliographical material that in my opinion best serves the construction of university courses on the literature of the southern African countries. In recommending secondary sources, for example, I have chosen stimulating critical introductions that should provide starting points for further study, and articles that raise key issues in the field. Selections have presumed that readers are mainly English-speaking and, in consequence, the General Bibliographies focus on studies written in English, or translated into English, with studies in other languages identified in relevant end notes. Similarly, the entries on individual authors concentrate on English-language contributions or contributions that are available in English translation. Readers are referred outwards, nonetheless, to details of all the literatures of the region. Biographical entries have had to be confined to authors who have important consequences for my argument, and with the General Bibliographies presuming readers who are principally interested in literature, details of other pertinent studies – history, anthropology, etc. – are given only in end notes. (Whereas complete titles are listed in the General Bibliographies, I have not in end notes included subtitles unless crucial as descriptive guides: accordingly, Fishman's *Language and Nationalism: Two Integrative Essays* appears simply as *Language and Nationalism*.) I realise that aspects of bibliographical convenience contradict somewhat the spirit of the book which is to regard as less than rigid traditional disciplinary divisions between, say, literary and political study, or major and minor writers. Restrictions of space, unfortunately, remain a practical consideration. As general sources of historical detail and debate, I refer readers at the outset to the works listed in this end note.[3]

I also refer readers at the outset to an issue that will be raised undoubtedly by the appearance of this book. Current theoretical debate finds cause in interrogations of political/textual authority. Questions or objections, in consequence, are likely to focus on my authority as a white (male) critic to represent, or re-present, others (Others), my authority or competence – single-handedly – to interpret literature deriving from a range of languages and cultures, and my authority or competence to survey the entire subcontinent. Is it not inevitable – the argument goes in summary – that my narrative will betray my race, class and gender, or – to limit what is in danger of becoming a litany – my linguistic, social and educational condition with English ending up not as lingua franca but metonymic master-code? A disquisition could be written on the issue. Indeed, Henry A. Giroux in defining 'border pedagogy' as respecting the notion of difference in a common endeavour to extend the quality of civil life advises critics – and educators – to unlearn their privileged positions, listen to other constituencies, and try to speak in ways that those constituencies can take seriously.[4] The advice at least ties an ideal to a practice. Border pedagogy – as articulated by Giroux – is certainly consistent with the principles of the present study. As I have suggested, I do not offer an encyclopaedic survey, a task best undertaken by a team of scholars; rather I offer a particular view of literary-cultural development and value at a particular point in history. The early 1990s – after apartheid, after the one-party state, after the cold war – still bears the scars of the near past, and of crucial importance in translating experiences is the creation of new channels of communication. In attempting to avoid possessive delineation, I have sought a style of interpretation that may be understood beyond the borders of the specialist journal.

I could not have written this book without insights gleaned from many of my colleagues. In some instances, acknowledgement is explicit; in other instances, I have probably absorbed their thoughts into my own deliberations. For key observations on literary history in southern Africa – the comparative method, translation as cultural intervention, politics as period marker, literature as rhetorical field – I am indebted especially to articles over the years by Tim Couzens, Albert S. Gérard, Stephen Gray, Isabel Hofmeyr, A. C. Jordan, Preben Kaarsholm, Es'kia Mphahlele, Kelwyn Sole and Landeg White. I am also indebted to several scholars for their comprehensive accounts: Ruth Finnegan, George Fortune and Aaron C. Hodza, Albert S. Gérard, D. B. Ntuli and C. F. Swanepoel, C. M. S. Nyembezi, Jeff Opland and B. W. Vilakazi (African-language literature), Jack Cope and J. C. Kannemeyer (Afrikaans literature), Flora Veit-Wild (Zimbabwean literature) and, on Portuguese-African literature, Manuel Ferreira, Russell G. Hamilton and Gerald M. Moser. There are in addition the many excellent articles that, in literary journals in the 1980s, saw the criticism of African literature achieve perceptiveness and purpose. Despite the many necessary borrowings, however, I hope I have offered something fresh and challenging in what is the first study to consider all the literatures – oral and written, in the various languages – of the several countries of southern Africa.

I wish to acknowledge the contributions of translators of texts from one southern African language to another (see p. xxviii), Catherine Dubbeld, Chief Subject Librarian (University of Natal, Durban), who compiled the Index, and Chris Parsons and Suzé Nunes who checked African-language and Portuguese orthography, respectively. I wish also to acknowledge the research funding granted to me by the University of Natal and by the Centre for Science Development (South Africa).

Notes

1. Veit-Wild, *Teachers, Preachers, Non-Believers* (Harare, 1993), p. 310.
   On the issue of nations and literature generally see: B. Anderson, *Imagined Communities* (London, 1983); H. K. Bhaba (ed.), *Nation and Narration* (London, 1990); B. Davidson, *The Black Man's Burden: Africa and the Curse of the Nation State* (London, 1992); J. D. Degenaar, 'Nationalism, Liberalism and Pluralism', in J. Butler, R. Elphick and D. Welsh (eds), *Democratic Liberalism in South Africa: Its History and Prospects* (Middletown and Cape Town, 1987); J. Degenaar, *Nations and Nationalism: The Myth of a South African Nation* (IDASA Occasional Paper, Cape Town, 1987); R. Emerson, *From Empire to Nation* (Boston, 1962); J. A. Fishman, A. C. A. Ferguson and J. D. Gupta (eds), *Language Problems of Developing Nations* (New York, 1968); J. A. Fishman, *Language and Nationalism* (Rowley, 1973); S. Gikandi, 'The Politics and Poetics of National Formation', in A. Rutherford (ed.), *From Commonwealth to Post-Colonial* (Sydney, 1992); E. J. Hobsbawm, *Nations and Nationalism since 1780* (Cambridge, 1990); B. Lindfors, 'Are there any national literatures in sub-Saharan Black Africa yet?', *English in Africa*, vol. 2, no. 2 (1975).

2. See General Bibliographies ii) 'Descriptive, thematic, critical, theoretical surveys', where titles will usually indicate a focus on a specific language or race, or on written or oral literature. *Literature and Society in South Africa*, L. White and T. Couzens (eds), offers 'case study' essays on literature in several languages as well as in both oral and written forms.

3. J. Grace and J. Laffin, *Fontana Dictionary of Africa since 1960* (London, 1991); P. Williams and B. Hackland, *The Dictionary of Contemporary Politics of Southern Africa* (London, 1989); R. Oliver (ed.), *The Cambridge History of Africa*, 3 vols. (Cambridge, 1977); J. D. Omer-Cooper, *History of Southern Africa* (Cape Town and London, 1987); J. Pampallis, *Foundations of the New South Africa* (Cape Town, 1991); C. Saunders, *The Making of the South African Past: Major Historians on Race and Class* (Cape Town, 1988); M. Wilson and L. Thompson (eds), *The Oxford History of South Africa*, 2 vols. (Oxford, 1969, 1971). See also several titles in the Penguin African Library and the series 'Perspectives on Southern Africa' by the University of California Press.

4. Giroux, *Border Crossings: Cultural Workers and the Politics of Education* (New York, 1992), p. 27.

Map of Southern Africa

Countries of Southern Africa

Population, Languages

Angola

(independence from Portugal, 1975)
pop. 10 m.
main pop. groups: Ovimbundu; Mbundu; whites of Portuguese descent; Mulatto (African-Portuguese).
main languages: Portuguese; uMbundu spoken by Ovimbundu; kiMbundu spoken by Mbundu.

Botswana

(formerly Bechuanaland protectorate; independence from Britain, 1966)
pop. $1^1/_2$ m.
main pop. groups: Batswana; Bushmen; whites of British and South African descent.
main languages: seTswana; English.

Lesotho

(formerly Basutoland protectorate; independence from Britain, 1966)
pop. $1^1/_2$ m.
main pop. groups: Basotho; whites of British and South African descent.
main languages: seSotho; English.

Malawi

(formerly Nyasaland; independence from Britain, 1964)
pop. $7^1/_2$ m.
main pop. groups: Chewa; Yao; Chipoka; Tonga; Tumbuka; Ngonde; whites of British descent.
main languages: chiChewa; English.

Mozambique

(independence from Portugal, 1975)
pop. 15 m.
main pop. groups: Makua; Yao; Tsonga; Chopi; whites of Portuguese
descent; Mulatto (African-Portuguese).
main languages: Portuguese; Makua-Lomwe; xiTsonga.

Namibia

(formerly South West Africa; independence from South African control,
1990)
pop. 40 m.
main pop. groups: Owambo (half population); Kavango; Herero; Damara;
Nama; Bushmen; Rehoboth Basters (Afrikaans-Nama
mixed race); whites of mainly Afrikaans descent.
main languages: oshiWambo; Afrikaans; English.

South Africa

(self-governing from Britain 1910; white republic 1961; independence,
1994)
pop. 40 m.
main pop. groups: Zulu; whites of British and Dutch descent who are
now English-speaking South Africans and Afrikaners;
Xhosa; southern and northern Sotho; Tswana; Venda;
coloured South Africans (mixed race white-African or
Malayan slave descent or Khoi descendants); Indian
South Africans (descendants of 19th-century Indian
indentured labourers); Jewish South Africans; large
Portuguese community.
main languages: English; Afrikaans; four major indigenous language
groups Nguni, Sotho, Tsonga and Venda with Nguni
group divided into four main sections of isiZulu (6
million speakers), isiXhosa, siNdebele (of Zimbabwe)
and siSwati (of Swaziland) as well as dialects among
Ngoni of Malawi and Tanzania; and Sotho divided into
sePedi (northern Sotho), seSotho (southern Sotho) and
seTswana (Tswana or western Sotho).

Swaziland

(formerly protectorate, independence from Britain, 1968)
pop. 1 m.

main pop. groups: Swazi; Zulu; whites of British and South African descent.

main languages: siSwati; English.

Zambia

(formerly Northern Rhodesia; independence from Britain, 1964)
pop. 7 m.

main pop. groups: Bemba; Nyanja; Tonga; Lozi; whites of British descent.

main languages: Bemba; English; Nyanja.

Zimbabwe

(formerly British colony of Southern Rhodesia, self-governing since 1923; unilaterally declared Rhodesia by white settler government, 1965; independence, 1980)
pop. 9 m.

main pop. groups: Shona; Ndebele; whites of British and South African descent.

main languages: chiShona; siNdebele; English.

A Note on Racial Terminology, Orthography and Conventions

Bantu is the anthropologically precise description of the negroid (African) people of southern and central Africa. The different groups (Shona, Zulu, and so on) speak different Bantu-related languages. The term 'Bantu', however, has been reduced in South African racial-bureaucratic parlance to a derogatory reference to the non-white, non-citizen kaffir. In the early nineteenth century the term 'Caffre' did not have entirely insulting connotations, and in the 1880s writers like Olive Schreiner were using the term 'kaffir' in fairly neutral, descriptive ways. In the 1950s apartheid terminology loaded the word 'native' with racial distaste. Wherever possible in this study, I have used the general term *African*. 'African', however, needs to be distinguished from 'black'.

Black is sometimes used, particularly in South Africa, as a shorthand reference for all who are not white: i.e., Africans, Indians and coloureds, the last being originally of mixed descent (white and African, white and Khoi, African and Khoi) or of east Indian Malay (slave) descent. In revolutionary politics, the term 'black' may denote a state of psychological and cultural opposition to white authority.

In southern Africa, particularly in South Africa, the term *coloured* is distinguished from 'African', and in signalling discomfort at being driven to use racial terms in pursuit of their arguments, critics have tended to drop the capital C in Coloured (as a rejection of South African racial classification) and either insert quotation marks or pointedly refer to 'so-called coloureds'. In remaining sensitive to the implications of all this, I have decided to use the term without the capital C, without the quotation marks, and without the squeamish 'so-called'.

Afrikaners are the descendants mainly of the early Dutch of whom many were of the unlettered classes. There are also the influences of German soldiers and French Huguenots while initially racial mixing was not discouraged. As many Afrikaners were farmers, the term for farmer (boer) gained a capital B (Boer) as a general description with nationalistic connotations of the Afrikaner volk (people). In black liberation rhetoric, the term Boer is used disparagingly as a synonym for the Afrikaner oppressor.

In the relevant section I explain why 'Bushman' has been preferred to 'San' and, on the related matter of orthography – particularly in the case of African languages – I have respected usages of the time in the author's own text (e.g. Mofolo's *Chaka*), but in the body of the study have attempted to be consistent in using acceptable modern conventions: Shaka not Chaka, Moshoeshoe not Moshesh. When in doubt, I have followed the practice of experts in the field: e.g. Rycroft and Ngcobo's Dingana not Dingane.

Clearly matters of terminology and orthography are highly ideological. In an English context, Zulu people are often referred to as the 'Zulu' or the 'Zulus'; in an 'Africanised' English context Zulu people may be referred to as 'amaZulu'. Zulu people speak Zulu or, preferably, the Zulu language (English context) or, to Africanise the issue, isiZulu, isi being a language marker: isiXhosa, chiShona, siNdebele. It is difficult to be entirely consistent in usage. Major groups such as the Zulu, Xhosa, Shona and Ndebele have long been referred to in the English context as speaking simply Zulu, Xhosa, and so on, and to insist each time on the language marker could seem to be unnecessarily pushing a point. The Sotho group is subdivided linguistically and, in consequence, language markers are usually retained: the language of the southern Sotho, for example, is usually designated 'seSotho', or 'Sesotho'. I have preferred the capital S to identify the group: seSotho. Similarly, seTswana rather than Setswana.

Decisions as to whether to use italic or roman type for certain non-English words also present difficulties. Several key terms, for example, have currency in English in literary-cultural discussion in southern Africa and have not, therefore, been italicised: e.g., assimilado (particular reference to Portuguese-educated elite in Angola and Mozambique), chimurenga (Zimbabwean war of independence), imbongi (Zulu – praise poet), izibongo (praise poem), taal (Afrikaans language), volk (Afrikaner people), ubuntu (sharing humanity – African philosophy).

A Note on Translated Works

In assuming an English-speaking readership I have cited, where there is an English translation of the original work, the English version of the title with a small (t) denoting that I am referring to a translation. When a translated version of a work does not exist or is unobtainable, I have cited the title in the original language with a translation in brackets. Thus we have André Brink's *A Dry White Season*[(t)], but S. E. K. Mqhayi's *Ityala Lamawele* (The Lawsuit of the Twins). The argument should indicate the language of the original text. In the case of works in translation, the publication date is that of the translated edition followed, when the dates differ, by the publication date of the original version. Accordingly, we have Elsa Joubert's *Poppie*[(t)] (1980; 1978). In the General Bibliographies and Biographies I have also kept, wherever possible, to titles in their English translation, but in the Chronology have usually given dates of original publication or (in Drama) performance, and thus titles appear in the original language of composition.

Several texts in English-translation have been cited in the course of the study. The translators are C. Barnard (*Tomorrow and Tomorrow and Tomorrow* tr. the author); W. Bleek and L. Lloyd (traditional Bushman expression); B. Breytenbach (*Judas Eye*, tr. the author and D. Hirson); A. Brink (fiction tr. the author; J. Goosen's *Not All of Us*); D. Brookshaw (M. Couto's *Voices Made Night*); G. Butler (Marais' 'Winter's Night', A. P. Grové and C. J. D. Harvey, eds, *Afrikaans Poems with English Translations*, Cape Town, 1962); J. M. Coetzee (W. Stockenström's *The Expedition to the Baobab Tree*); J. Cope and D. Kunene (poem by C. Bereng, J. Cope and U. Krige, eds, *The Penguin Book of South African Verse*, Harmondsworth, 1968); J. Cope and D. Malcolm (J. Stuart's Zulu source material including Shaka's Praises); A. Dawes (Van Wyk Louw's *Raka*, Cape Town, 1968); A. Delius (Opperman's poems, A. P. Grové and C. J. D. Harvey, above); D. Dutton (Mofolo's *Chaka*, 1931) and D. Kunene (Mofolo's *Chaka*, 1981); C. Eglington (Leroux's *Seven Days at the Silbersteins*); E. Eybers (poetry tr. the author); I. Ferguson (H. Aucamp's *House Visits*); G. Fortune, A. Hodza and S. Mhlabi (Ndebele and Shona traditional poetry; Chivaura, Kimburai and others, C. Style and O. Style, eds,

Mambo Book of Zimbabwean Verse in English, Harare, 1986); M. Friedmann (Schoeman's *Promised Land* and Vilakazi's *Zulu Horizons*); D. Guedes (Honwana's *We Killed Mangy-Dog*); T. Hahn (traditional Khoi expression); C. Harvey (Leipoldt's 'Oom Gert's Story', and Van Wyk Louw's poems, A. P. Grové and C. J. D. Harvey, above); A. Jordan (traditional Xhosa tales); P. Jordan (A. Jordan's *The Wrath of the Ancestors*); E. Joubert (*Poppie*, tr. the author); R. Kavanagh and Z. Quangule (poems by Xhosa poets including Jolobe and Mqhayi, *The Making of a Servant and Other Poems*, Pretoria, 1972); D. Kunene (traditional seSotho praise poems); M. Kunene (*Emperor Shaka the Great*, tr. the author); D. McCutcheon and N. Tshi-kovka (Maumela's *Mafangambiti*); A. McDermott (Xitu's *The World of 'Mestre' Tamoda*); V. C. Mutwa (African myths in *Indaba, My Children*); C. Nyembezi (Zulu proverbs); N. Roets (Leroux's *Magersfontein, O Magersfontein*); A. Roscoe, J. Schoffeleers and E. Singano (traditional chiChewa myths and tales); D. Rycroft and A. Ngcobo (J. Stuart's material on Dingana's Praises); D. Schalkwyk (Schoeman's *Another Country*); I. Schapera (traditional seTswana praise poems); K. Schoeman (*Take Leave and Go*, tr. the author); C. Searle (Mozambican poetry in *The Sunflower of Hope*, London, 1982); A. Small (Van Wyk Louw's poetry in *Oh Wide and Sad Land*, Cape Town, 1975); H. Tracey (Zulu lyrics including songs of Princess Constance Magogo); R. Vaughan (Breytenbach's *A Season in Paradise*); M. Wolfers (Pepeleta's *Mayombe*, Vieira's *Luuanda*, and Angolan poetry in *Poems from Angola*, London, 1979).

Very little southern African literature in English has been translated into the other languages of the region. One may mention C. Nyembezi's translation into Zulu of Paton's *Cry, the Beloved Country*, S. Plaatje's trans-lation of Shakespeare into seTswana and, under the pressures of Bantu Education, several translations of Shakespeare for schools. In such a con-text, Shakespeare is regarded as safely 'European', even safely 'colonial'. This reinforces an apartheid convention of translating apparently non-contentious texts into African languages: accordingly, works by Rider Haggard have found their translators in southern Africa. A more promis-ing development – since the demise of the apartheid state in South Africa – has been the translation into (South African) African languages of Chinua Achebe's novels *Things Fall Apart* (seTswana and sePedi) and *No Longer at Ease* (isiZulu). According to S. M. Serudu, translations of Achebe are seen as a milestone in the literary history of South African indigenous literature. While in a practical sense the translations should provide sophis-ticated models for African-language writers and students, Achebe's novels translated into local South African languages also symbolise pan-African unity. (See S. M. Serudu, 'Reaching out to Africa', *Literator-ACCLLS Newsletter*, no. 1, 1993, pp. 11–12.)

Abbreviations/Acronyms

ANC	African National Congress
COSATU	Congress of South African Trade Unions
COSAW	Congress of South African Writers
FNLA	National Front for the Liberation of Angola
Frelimo	Front for the Liberation of Mozambique
IMF	International Monetary Fund
Kwa	Place of, e.g. KwaZulu
MPLA	Popular Movement for the Liberation of Angola
PAC	Pan Africanist Congress
Renamo (MNR)	Mozambique National Resistance Movement
SADCC	Southern African Development Co-ordination Conference
Soweto	South Western Townships
SWAPO	South West Africa People's Organization
UDF	United Democratic Front
UNIP	United Independence Party (of Zambia)
ZANU	Zimbabwe African National Union
ZANU (PF)	(Patriotic Front) Amalgamation of ZANU and ZAPU as ruling political party in Zimbabwe
ZAPU	Zimbabwe African People's Union

Acknowledgements

We are grateful to the following for permission to reproduce copyright material:

Ad. Donker (Pty) Ltd and the authors for the poem 'Zulu Girl' by Roy Campbell from *Selected Poems* (1981), extracts from the poems 'Storm-shelter' and 'Under Capricorn' by Douglas Livingstone from *Selected Poems* (1984) and an extract from the poem 'City Johannesburg' by Mongane Wally Serote from *Selected Poems* 1982; Mambo Press for extracts from the poems 'Stamping Song' translated from Shona oral trad. A C Hodza, 'Confiding in a Stranger' by Wilson B Chivaura and 'My Home' by Zimunya from *Mambo Book of Zimbabwean Verse in English* ed. C T O Style (1986); J M Meulenhoff by Amsterdam on behalf of the author for an extract from the poem 'The Dream' by Breytenbach from *Judas Eye* (Faber & Faber, 1988); Michael Wolfers for an extract from the poem 'Contract Worker' by Antonio Jacinto, first published in Michael Wolfers, *Poems from Angola* (Heinemann, 1979). Copyright Michael Wolfers 1979.

We have been unable to trace the copyright holder of the poem 'Mama Saquina' by Jose Craveirinha, trans. by Searle in *The Sunflower of Hope: Poems from the Mozambican Revolution* (Allison & Busby, 1982) and would appreciate any information which would enable us to do so.

Introduction
Writing Literary History in Southern Africa[1]

The initial premise of this study is that in the countries of southern Africa the texts of politics have wanted to overwhelm the texts of art: that public events have confirmed a history of domination and resistance, in which ancient charters have felt the intrusion of harsh, modernising forces. This modern pattern begins with Bushmen hunter-gatherers and Khoi pastoralists – the earliest people of the region – having to defend themselves against expanding African groups (the descendants of iron-age Bantu-speaking people) and, from the mid-seventeenth century, against Dutch trekboers (wandering farmers) who spread into the arid interior of what is now South Africa in search of grazing lands for their cattle. (The parched Karoo has symbolic significance in the literature as a place of solitude, a place of physical and spiritual testing.) With the Dutch East India Company having used the Cape of Good Hope as a refreshment station on journeys to the spice markets of the East, white settlement had begun on the southern-most tip of the continent, and just over a hundred years later, in 1795, the British occupied the Cape, set up administrative structures in Cape Town, and, in 1820, settled on the eastern frontier of the Cape colony. This brought colonists into direct confrontation with the Xhosa who experienced the colonial mercantile and military presence on the edges of their ancestral land.

A politics of racial and ethnic conflict has continued to characterise South African history. The indigenous African people (the Zulu, Xhosa and Sotho, to cite the largest groups) were forcibly brought under white control and, after gold was discovered in 1886 in the Boer republic of the Transvaal, Boer (Afrikaner) pastoralists – the descendants of the early Dutch – found their biblical vision of a promised land in the interior of the country rudely curtailed by British-imperialist mining interests. After the devastation of the ensuing Anglo–Boer War (1899–1902), the two white groups – English-speakers and Afrikaners – came together in a union based on segregationist practice. Rivalries continued, however, and Afrikanerdom having mobilised itself, ethnically, as a chosen volk triumphed at the all-white election in 1948, as a result of which the National Party government was able to institutionalise and extend segregationist provisions into the policy of apartheid. In opposition to the entrenchment of white, specifically Afrikaner, privilege and power, and the dispossession of the black majority, the African National Congress (founded as the South African Native National Congress in 1912) continued to mount campaigns of resistance in South Africa and, after it was banned in 1960, from neighbouring states and from countries abroad. Under the pressure of black civil disobedience and international condemnation of apartheid including the imposition of economic sanctions, the South African government in February 1990 unbanned the ANC as well as other liberation movements and began a process of repealing racially-discriminatory legislation. In tough, rancorous negotiations the draft of a non-racial society has begun to emerge, and in September 1993 Nelson Mandela, having spent twenty-seven years of his life in gaol, in his capacity as president of the ANC called on the international community to lift economic restrictions against South Africa. An interim constitution based on democratic principles was adopted in November 1993, and in elections in April 1994 the ANC became the majority party in a government of national unity.

In their centuries-long occupation of the vast territories of Angola and Mozambique the Portuguese, who first stopped on African shores in the fifteenth century, imposed extraction economies on the indigenous people, and myths of racial superiority and inferiority have served to justify a rapacious history involving conquest and the European (settler) requirement of cheap labour. (The contract, or migrant, worker – the Jim who comes to the Joburg mines, or the João who goes to the plantations of São Tomé – is ubiquitous in the literature.) With systematic colonial rule in Angola and Mozambique a feature of the twentieth century, the two countries continued to be developed specifically to satisfy the trade and economic requirements of metropolitan Portugal. In the early 1960s struggles for independence were launched by nationalist guerilla movements, the leadership of which drew heavily on mixed-race and assimilado intellectuals: the one per cent of the population that was supposed to have assimilated civilised, i.e. Portuguese, cultural values but that opposed the Salazar dictatorship with Marxist class analysis as the revolutionary programme. After the overthrow of Salazar in Portugal itself, the new leaders ignored white settler protests and negotiated the independence of Angola and Mozambique with the guerilla movements. With virtually bankrupt economies and, in Angola, a seizure of power by the Marxist MPLA (one of the rival guerilla organisations), independence has brought little of substance to people who, for thirty years, have known almost continuous warfare: first the freedom struggle, then after 1975 ruinous civil strife. Along the way, both countries fell victim to United States/Soviet Union power politics as well as to South African military destabilisation in the form of attacks on neighbouring states that were designed to weaken African solidarity and create client dependencies. In Angola and Mozambique, capitalist/socialist divisions have accentuated ethnic divisions. But with Marxist–Leninism having been abandoned and the demise of superpower spheres of influence, the future promises a slow cessation of hostilities and a stumbling towards a rudimentary civilian life. As in the region as a whole, there is debate in the post-communist climate about the value of World Bank and IMF structural adjustment programmes, in which the advocates of capitalist enterprise are opposed by those who fear a recipe for new elites and little corresponding improvement in the condition of the poverty-stricken majority.

In Malawi and Zambia the paths to independence, which followed African nationalist agitation in the 1950s, can be seen as part of the decolonising phase of the 1960s (the 'wind of change') according to which the industrialised north would continue to administer the south not through the costly and embarrassingly imperialist exercise of colonial administration, but through the business of the market place. Independence came relatively smoothly to Botswana, Lesotho and Swaziland: British protectorates that had avoided being incorporated into South Africa. Since independence Botswana has remained a peaceful and stable multiparty democracy. Lesotho with problems that were exacerbated by South African interference and Swaziland which has long been wracked by royalist feuds, however, have experienced the post-independence problems of struggles among power blocs for scarce resources and, hence, for sole control of the machinery of state. In Zimbabwe and Namibia, independence was delayed by powerful white interests. Like Zambia, Zimbabwe had been opened to colonial mineral exploitation in the 1890s by Cecil John Rhodes' pioneer column. African resistance to what amounted to white encroachment saw the Ndebele and Shona subjected to the violence of Rhodes' modern fire power. White domination was secured by land apportionment according to which the best agricultural areas were reserved for settlers who comprised just over one per cent of the population while Africans were pegged in tribal trust lands. Zimbabwe or, as it was called in colonial times, Southern Rhodesia had been a self-governing colony of Britain since 1923. In refusing to agree to the move towards majority rule, it unilaterally declared itself an independent state in 1965, only to face fifteen years of guerilla warfare and international sanctions prior to capitulating to British-supervised elections which, in 1980, brought the former guerilla movement ZANU to power. Excluding South Africa, Zimbabwe has the most developed and diversified economy of any African country south of the Sahara, and ZANU – which as ZANU (PF) absorbed ZAPU in 1987 – continues to rule amid lively disagreement about its successes and failures since independence. The story of Namibian independence also involves guerilla opposition to white control. With settlers having benefited from South Africa's long and controversial administration of the former League of Nations mandated territory, United Nations-supervised elections brought the guerilla movement SWAPO to power in 1990 as a majority political party under a democratic constitution. Just as the migrant labourer is a leitmotif of the literature so, in literature since the 1960s, is the freedom fighter. In sharp contrast to Western rationalism and its propensity for technological devastation, we have the myth of the resuscitated African community, its ubuntu (or, sharing) forming the core value in an iconography of resistance and revaluation.

Further details of the countries are given in the Chronology and in the course of the study. The point is that it is difficult, in the subcontinent, to separate literary discussion from a social referent when political events have attained the dimension of compelling public narratives. In societies of thin literary cultures, in fact, the art genres of fiction, poems and plays can easily seem to be mere reflections of massive activities in an external history. In granting such a perception its reality in the material circumstances of the region, I have based the present literary history on a social theory in which forms of literature are tied firmly to the event. A consequence is that while the study of literature in the academic or artistic sense may want to remain receptive to the subjective impact of works, social responsibility demands that we attend not only to the richness of cultural heterogeneity but to inequitable distributions of power in economic, educational and literary resources. In seeking to increase understanding of the society and culture, therefore, the critic remains committed to an ethical base: literary activity, including the activity of criticism, is regarded as a social activity concerned with justice. It is concerned with justice not only in the comprehensive sense of what it is to be human, but in its capacity in southern Africa to extend liberties and contribute to the creation of a civil society. As the countries struggle out of divisive pasts, the historian's task is to recover and reconstitute the past in ways that are usable to both current enquiry and future participation in a democratised public sphere. Instead of the past retaining its impenetrability in antiquarian interest, or shedding its impenetrability in transhistorical notions of relevance, the exploration proceeds according to a dialectical relation of past significance to present meaning: the structure of the work is *created* in specific times, places and conditions, but *lives* in the process of its reception. Accordingly, the present study is itself a form of literature which not merely reflects what is in other texts, but which intervenes in the construction of a literary and moral narrative.

That the study should have a function, a design, even a tendency, is consistent with its social theory. The literary history I have offered does not seek objectivity: the cause-and-effect mode of explanation associated with traditional historiography. Neither, in formalist terms, does it seek to privilege a dynamics of literary structure in the replacement of the exhausted device by its defamiliarised equivalent over and above both reference to a world and communication with an audience. Rather, the challenges to both extrinsic and intrinsic history derive from the two not entirely complementary interests of deconstructive textual analysis and a politically conscious criticism. The former insists that all kinds of writing, whether history-document or poem, are texts, that the relation between language and society is analogical, and that facts and truth are determined not by their properties in the world but by discursive practice. The latter insists that we know the society not only by interrogating texts but by experiencing its determinative effects on our lives: that the literary scholar, accordingly, cannot erect literature into an aesthetic object of study in refuge from other forms of cultural practice or social engagement. In short, material forces are not to be wholly absorbed by symbolic needs, but are to retain the external purchase that might make possible action leading to change: in literary analysis, the change involves the interpretation and evaluation of moral and aesthetic perception in relation to a societal claim. The literary impact of a work is thus allowed its pragmatic purpose, and a tension – both problematic and necessary – characterises the approach. There is, at the one pole, a need for a hermeneutics of suspicion: a re-reading of authorities, a questioning of positions, reputations, traditions and influences, as texts are set in contexts of controversy in which terms such as major/minor, functional/aesthetic, the West/ Africa, are held up to discursive investigation. At the other pole, there is the need in societies of severe inequalities for a humanism of reconstruction, in terms of which damaged identities are reassembled, silenced voices given speech, and causes rooted close to home in the priorities of the southern African scene examining itself while it examines its relations to the West.

In procedures of re-positioning alternative or marginalised voices, of course, the critic risks an impasse of race or gender. By assuming a commitment to special black or women's work in which the previously neglected author is perhaps given exclusive prominence, for example, it can become difficult to connect the study to the functionings of the entire society. I have tried to identify interrelationships by locating the concepts 'race' and 'gender' in a politics of power where subjects, values, entire fields of activity, struggle for their centres and by recognising that any mode of enquiry entails the social production of meaning. In fact, a similar principle of engaging with the workings of the society as a whole underlies the comparative method that I mentioned in the Preface. Accordingly, literatures in different languages may be interpreted not as self-enclosed within their own ethnic systems, but as having been influenced by linguistic and cultural interchange in the context of events: events which in the politics of the subcontinent have often been cataclysmic, including the great trek of Afrikanerdom, the national suicide of the Xhosa, and the actions in 1976 of the Soweto youth. In turning textual criticism to referential account, we could say that such events are themselves texts: validations of myths, struggles for the icon, the sign, that have required and, in changing circumstances of reception, will continue to require semiotic interpretation.

In refusing clear demarcation between the text of the book and the text of the world, I am proffering a particular definition of literature. It is a definition that, in literary history, has consequences for the relationship of genre-change to political-change, and for matters of periodisation. I have regarded literature in southern Africa, most usefully, as speech and writing: generally, as rhetorical activity its purpose being to persuade an audience. In this, I am endorsing a long tradition in the region from ceremonies of ritual in ancient African communities to modes of survival such as storytelling among migrant workers in the alien city environment. In both of these instances, the literary sign is held in close correspondence to the event: the consequence is a conception of the content producing the form, and the function lending substance to the aesthetic insight. Similarly, literature attached to settler communities, Afrikaner language struggles, and campaigns of African mobilisation has been characterised by weighty topicality, the turn of the public phrase, and an imperative of communication. The pamphlet or periodical has often had to serve the demand for swift dissemination of information with an appeal to fact and opinion. Of course, the risk of rhetoric in the insidious allure of fine language and the potential of rhetoric to assist in change – truth being regarded not as fixed and abstract but as situated in human conversations – identify the perennial difference and tension between the 'serious' and the 'rhetorical' condition. What is inescapable is the implication of the reader – the critic as well as the public – in the sense-making procedure. If truth may be regarded, rhetorically, as the property of statements, then which statements are valuable, which dubious and for what reasons? Perhaps more fundamentally, in a literary study, which pieces of expression are literature if literature has been cast as functional rather than onto-logical?

As I have intimated, my own social theory should permit any speech and writing to be included in a literary history. Certainly, oral voices as well as written voices should be permitted their say; traditional, popular, and elite voices all need to be heard, and non-fictional forms of expression should not necessarily be regarded as having less insight than the art genres of romantic imagination. Had I remained entirely consistent with my criteria, however, I could have ended up conceivably with a study that subsumed forms of fictional expression under the combined output of history studies, religious sermons, political orations, and so on. In times of social instability the ideas, insights, visions and prophecies of art may not necessarily be truer than those of the document, while the document has the advantage of its immediate interest. It is worth recollecting, in this respect, that the demands of public commitment have led many creative writers in southern Africa – I think randomly of Pringle, Plaatje, Schreiner and Paton – to complement their fictional works with substantial prose commentaries. In pursuing non-fictional forms in literary history, however, one has to consider the expectations raised by convention. The term 'literature' today – in Africa as well as the West – raises the expectation of imaginative expression; and historians, lest they are to be regarded as eccentric or perverse, are obliged at some point to hold on to the view that any discipline tends to distinguish and consolidate itself by the precision of its definitions and conventions: hence, through some degree of exclusivity. Most readers will expect a literary history to focus on the imaginative forms. Indeed, were the literary historian to neglect the novel, the poem and the play, who else would devote attention to these particular configurations of the culture? In entertaining the idea of literature as a range of rhetorical effects, therefore, I have still wanted to devote most attention to the poem, play and story as kinds of discourse distinguished by the concentration of their sensory and experiential appeal in the shaping of consciousness within specific social relations.

According to convention most readers will also expect literary history to focus on elite forms of expression. University study, after all, has entrenched the conception of literature with a capital L. Instead, I have considered not only the elite (the serious novel, the contemplative poem), but the traditional (the Bushman story, the Zulu military panegyric) and the popular: that difficult to define category of hybridised, often opportunistic, often city-bred response that may encompass conservatively inclined religious ritual and politically progressive tracts.[2] Given that some forms are more popular than others, the popular may veer towards the serious expectations of literary culture (city-slick stories in *Drum* magazine in the 1950s) or towards the entertainment of mass-media culture (the TV sitcom or soap). Here, the demands of space taken together with my own competence as someone trained in literary as opposed to cultural forms have led me to devote more attention to the literary convention than to the entertainment convention. Hence, the elite novels of Gordimer and Coetzee are given sanction in a way that Wilbur Smith's adventure blockbusters are not. Another history – I realise – could be written on the signs of southern African culture.[3] Similarly, another history could be written on re-arranged relationships, in literary education, between metropolitan and local texts. Instead of thinking of African booklists replacing Western booklists on syllabuses, for example, we could ask how *Othello, The Tempest, Pilgrim's Progress* or *Heart of Darkness* – texts that have been associated with colonial-African dilemmas

– might most fruitfully be taught in southern Africa. To take the case of Thomas Mofolo's epic *Chaka*: we could identify the influences not only of African oral sources and the politics of the author's day, but the influence of Shakespeare's *Macbeth* which provides a prototype for character and plot. We might go on to ponder whether courses on Shakespeare in Africa should include comparative studies of the Shakespeare and Mofolo texts. I only hint at such re-arrangements while remaining more concerned with the southern African perspective on its own materials.

In granting that notions of authorial genius and artistic autonomy may be qualified by the social context, the aim is not to privilege the base over the superstructure, but to read the literary and historical terrain as a semiotic whole. Consequently, I do not offer an introductory section of intellectual and social trends as a prelude to chapters which, drained of context, account in terms of genre-change for the period's major works. Instead, in minimising the division between the text and the historical event, I have examined each as constituent of the other and have thus reiterated my criterion of literary production itself as a form of social practice: as one of the many discourses that has helped create and affect the consciousness of the society in its attitudes, behaviour and actions. It follows that periodisation is not to be regarded primarily as a genre consideration but as responsible to political change. The problem is: which key events may begin to act as period markers? As the Chronology suggests, not only does each country have its own key events but, given the history of political conflict, groups within single countries have based their claims to socio-cultural identity and power on rival events. In South Africa, for example, Afrikaans literature has regarded the Anglo-Boer War (1899–1902) as a key political and literary moment: out of Afrikaner defeat arose renewed commitment to the language as the shaping force of the volk. As far as African writers in South Africa are concerned, however, the date 1910 (the Act of Union which confirmed English-speakers and Afrikaners as citizens and excluded black people from political rights) or the date 1913 (the Natives Land Act which dispossessed African people of rights of tenure) may be more appropriate to mark the start of a period of important change: a period that witnessed the beginning of modern, organised opposition to white rule. The South African Native National Congress as the forerunner of the ANC was founded in 1912, and in seeking to hang the cluster of events on a key work the critic could identify Sol T. Plaatje's indictment of the Land Act, *Native Life in South Africa* (1916).

As these random examples suggest, considerations of literary periodisation are connected, emotively, to the general history of oppression, struggle and liberation and, in deciding on the selection and arrangement of the subject matter, I have kept in mind the useful insights of Christopher Heywood and Dieter Riemenschneider.[4] In discussing the question of periodisation in colonial/independence studies, both resist the temptation to emphasise disputes in settler communities as the main force of the literary-historical movement. Instead of granting, say, the Boer War status as period marker, therefore, I have allowed larger, ongoing questions of cultural, political and economic development to help me place settler communities in past time, Africanisation in future time, and all the countries of the region in the transitions of their colonial dependencies and independent destinies: flag independence has not stopped the process of history but has provoked the questions of real or mock emancipation in the new nation, real or mock citizenry in the new society. In beginning with oral tradition, I mean to remind readers that in the forms of its indigenous voices southern Africa was neither mute nor savage, and that in resilient modifications to changing circumstances oral expression remains a key component of the literary response. As far as the colonial enterprise of writing up Africa according to the metropole's own image of the dark continent was concerned, the late nineteenth century saw a flurry of activity in modes of both imperial confidence and dissent from within the ranks. The spread of higher education in the early twentieth century, particularly in South Africa, led to a surer sense of institutional literary life, and a consequence was that the creative genres as distinct from the earlier prose commentaries began to make their presence felt. By the early 1960s decolonisation was beginning to define the period and, with a new confidence in local commitments, the current phase poses questions about independence and modernisation in which Africa and the West remain complicit in each other's forms of concern.

Given that the literature continues to be marked by a to-and-fro between Africa and Europe not only in terms of language, literary conventions and critical debate but in that some of the most penetrating insights have been offered by sojourners or commentators from abroad, the qualification for being a South African writer or a Zimbabwean writer or, generally, a writer of southern Africa would seem to have less to do with birth, nationality or race than with intimate knowledge of and close identification with the life of the region. At least, this is how I have chosen to regard the matter. In deciding what writers or works are important in a politically contested field, I have granted most value to content that is committed to what may be considered generally as democratic, non-elitist activity in southern Africa. The study measures African priorities against colonial practices, however, not to effect easy endorsements or dismissals of works, but as a means of arriving at greater human understanding in the functioning of society.

Finally, I wish to return to my initial point of trying to look across the barriers of language, race and culture that, in the academic-disciplinary habit as well as in the surrounding life, can severely circumscribe fields of enquiry and experience.[5] In my own English Department (University of

Natal, Durban), for example, courses on South African literature focus on literature in English, usually written literature adjudged to be serious art. The other countries of the region rarely feature on the syllabus, and neither do those South African literatures composed originally in languages other than English. Similar practices of language exclusivity operate in departments of Afrikaans and in departments of African languages and literatures. (In the case of the latter, the texts studied will be in Zulu or Xhosa, or one of the other indigenous languages.) In countries like Zimbabwe, Zambia and Malawi, the British tradition partly as a result of Ngugi's various critical pronouncements has yielded somewhat to an African demand. But the Africa that enjoys prominence and delineation is the reasonably established literary field of West and East Africa. Having imbibed their Soyinka, Achebe, Ngugi, and their Heinemann African Writers series, many academics in southern Africa are more conversant with developments in the rest of Africa than with developments in the subcontinent. Much of what I have just said of course is understandable. Tuition in the original language is part of the university teaching intention; critical material on West and East African literature is readily available. The democratising process in this part of Africa requires, nevertheless, that we begin to hear, understand and value what Stephen Gray refers to as 'the Babel that is sprawling Southern Africa'.[6] The intention is not to venture into other people's worlds and venture out again, but to engender semantic compatibility between distinctive language-cultural systems. Of crucial consideration here is a theory and practice of translation.[7] In regarding translation not as source-text oriented but as a socio-cultural model that functions in the receiving culture, I do not argue for definitive translations when a version of any text may be regarded as bound to the use to which it is being put. Accordingly dynamic equivalence – the attempt to capture the spirit of the original in verbal re-creation – is given a lesser claim than formal equivalence: the attempt to convey the message. This is appropriate whether we are referring strictly to the translation of one language into another or, more generally, to the project that motivates the entire study: translation as an activity which, while making the insights of one culture accessible to the other, continues to respect the epistemological autonomy of the cultures between which the interchange is taking place. The principle of translation is also appropriate, of course, to the historiographic aim, which is not so much to negate artistry as to give weight to attitudes and ideas.

Notes

1. There has not been sustained debate about the writing of literary history in the countries of southern Africa, and most literary surveys make only cursory references to their own historiographical principles. Despite this, the following commentaries have helped me formulate my approach: several articles by T. T. Cloete in response to J. C. Kannemeyer's *Geskiedenis van die Afrikaanse Literatuur*, in *Tydskrif vir Letterkunde*, vol. 18, no. 1 (1980) and vol. 22, no. 1 (1982) as well as replies by Kannemeyer in *Standpunte*, vol. 33, no. 3 (1980) and in 'Die Taak van die Literêre Geskiedenis', *Geluigskrifte: Lesings en Opstelle* (Cape Town, 1989) and by G. Olivier in *Tydskrif vir Geesteswetenskappe*, vol. 21, no. 1 (1981) and vol. 22, no. 3 (1982); A. S. Gérard's 'Towards a History of South African Literature' in H. Maes-Jelinek (ed.), *Commonwealth Literature and the Modern World*, (Brussels, 1975) and 'Prospects for a National History of South African Literature' in Gérard's *Comparative Literature and African Literatures* (Pretoria, 1981); I. Glenn's review of Gray's *Southern African Literature: An Introduction*, 'Towards a Sociology of South African Literature' in *Social Dynamics*, no. 6 (1986); S. Gray's 'The Praxis of Comparative Theory: On Writing the History of Southern African Literature' in *South African Society for General Literary Studies Conference Papers* (Pretoria, 1986), 'Some Problems of Writing Historiography in South Africa', *Literator*, vol. 10, no. 2 (1989) and the Introduction to *The Penguin Book of Southern African Verse* (Harmondsworth, 1989); C. Heywood's 'The Search for Identity' in Heywood (ed.), *Aspects of South African Literature* (London, 1976); I. Hofmeyr's 'The State of South African Literary Criticism', *English in Africa*, vol. 6, no. 2 (1979); M. V. Mzamane's 'Cultivating a People's Voice in the Criticism of South African Literature', *Staffrider*, vol. 9, no. 3 (1991); and D. Riemenschneider's 'The "New" English Literature in Historical and Political Perspective: Attempts towards a Comparative View of North/South Relationships in "Commonwealth Literatures" ' in *New Literary History*, vol. 18, no. 2 (1987); and beginnings of literary-history investigation in *Alternation*, vol. 2, no. 1 (1995) and *Journal of Literary Studies*, vol. 10, nos 3–4 (December 1994). See also 'Descriptive, thematic, critical and theoretical surveys', General Bibliographies. More generally, I am indebted to the excellent essays by S. Fish ('Rhetoric') and L. Patterson ('Literary History') in F. Lentricchia and T. McLaughlin (eds), *Critical Terms for Literary Study* (Chicago, 1990).

   The approach and spirit of the present study has been anticipated in significant ways in the insights of Gray ('The proximity of writers arranged this way tends to stress the importance of common public events over individual biographies. The comparative approach is usually more sociological than aesthetic . . .', *Penguin*, p. xx), Hofmeyer ('The history of South African literature is not the tale of the literary endeavours of a small fraction of its people . . .', *English in Africa*, p. 44) and Gérard ('But in spite of the inherent divisiveness built into the cultural make-up of the country by historical circumstances, there is also a decisive element of unity which binds together all these racial and ethnic groups with their different languages and traditions', *Comparative Literature*, p. 38).

   As far as debates on literary historiography on the international scene are concerned, I wish to acknowledge especially R. Weimann's study, *Structure and Society in Literary History: Studies in the History and Theory of Historical Criticism* (Charlottesville, 1976). A summary of current thinking on the re-writing of literary history (in this particular case, American literary history) is offered by R. Reising's *The Unusable Past: Theory and the Study of American Literature* (London,

1986). Contributions to the lively debates on literary history and culture are too numerous to list here. The reader, however, is directed to the journals *Critical Inquiry* and *New Literary History* as well as to R. Young's *White Mythologies: Writing History and the West* (London, 1990) and to B. Ashcroft, G. Griffiths and H. Tiffin's *The Empire Writes Back: Theory and Practice in Post-colonial Literatures* (London, 1989). Young and Ashcroft *et al.* offer excellent summaries of debates in Western and African literary culture, respectively, and their bibliographies provide details of key works and articles pertinent to current enquiry.

2. See K. Barber's illuminating discussion of the categories 'elite', 'traditional' and 'popular', 'Popular Arts in Africa', *African Studies Review*, vol. 30, no. 3 (September 1987).

3. See, as a representative range of cultural studies, B. Bozzoli and P. Delius (eds), *History from South Africa*, special issue of *Radical History Review*, nos. 46–47 (New York, 1990), D. Bunn and J. Taylor (eds), *From South Africa: New Writing, Photographs and Art*, special issue *TriQuarterly*, no. 69 (Evanston, 1987); L. Callinocos, *Working Life 1886–1940: Factories, Townships and Popular Culture on the Rand. A People's History of South Africa* (Johannesburg, 1987); P. Kaarsholm, *Cultural Struggle and Development in Southern Africa* (London, 1991); S. Marks, 'Towards a People's History? Recent Developments in the Historiography of South Africa', in R. Samuel (ed.), *People's History and Socialist Theory* (London, 1980); F. Meintjies and M. Hlatswayo, *Worker Culture*, special issue of *Staffrider*, vol. 8, nos. 3 and 4 (Johannesburg, 1987); K. Tomaselli (ed.), *Rethinking Culture* (Belville, 1988); K. Tomaselli, *The Cinema of Apartheid: Race and Class in South African Film* (New York, 1988); K. Tomaselli and E. Louw (eds), *The Alternative Press in South Africa* (London, 1991); R. Tomaselli, K. Tomaselli and J. Muller, *Currents of Power: State Broadcasting in South Africa* (Cape Town, 1990). See also the journal *Critical Arts: A Journal of Media Studies* which has issues on popular memory, censorship, popular culture and performance, the production of popular knowledge and representations of women; the issue of *Current Writing*, vol. 6, no. 2 (October 1994) devoted to 'Democratising Literature and Culture in South Africa; the Poster Book Collective's *Images of Defiance: South African Resistance Posters of the 1980s* (Johannesburg, 1991); and studies on visual arts such as M. Manaka's *Echoes of African Art: A Century of Art in South Africa* (Johannesburg, 1987); S. Sack's *The Neglected Tradition: Towards a New History of South African Art, 1930–1988* (Johannesburg, 1988); and G. Younge's *Art of the South African Townships* (London, 1988).

4. See n. 1 above.

5. On literary education see *Proceedings of a Conference of Writers, Publishers, Editors and University Teachers of English* (Johannesburg, 1957); the proceedings of the English Academy of Southern Africa Conference, Grahamstown, 1969, in *English Studies in Africa*, vol. 13, no. 1 (March 1970); A. de Villiers (ed.), *English-speaking South Africa Today: Proceedings of the National Conference July 1974* (Cape Town, 1976); T. Moyana, *Education, Liberation and the Creative Act* [on Zimbabwe] (Harare, 1989); papers of a conference of the Association of University Teachers of Literature and Language in *Literature, Language and the Nation*, E. Ngara and A. Morrison (eds) (Harare, 1989); H. van der Merwe and D. Welsh (eds), *The Future of the University in Southern Africa* (Cape Town, 1977); L. Wright (ed.), *Teaching English Literature in South Africa: Twenty Essays* (Grahamstown, 1990). See also the annual conference proceedings of the Association of University English Teachers of Southern Africa (AUETSA) and the framework report summaries on

education in a post-apartheid South Africa in *The National Education Policy Investigation* (Cape Town, 1993).

6. Gray, Introduction, *The Penguin Book of Southern African Verse* (Harmondsworth, 1989), p. xxvi.

7. On translation in southern African literature see S. Gray's several studies [n. 1 above] and, generally, S. Bassnett-McGuire, *Translation Studies* (London, 1980); S. Bassnett and A. Lefevre (eds), *Translation, History and Culture* (London, 1990); G. W. Grace, *The Linguistic Construction of Reality* (London, 1987); A. Lefevre, *Translation, Rewriting and the Manipulation of Literary Frame* (Austin, 1992); and G. Steiner, *After Babel: Aspects of Language and Translation* (New York, 1975).

Part One
Oral Tradition: A Usable Past

Introduction to Part One

The oral tradition in southern Africa links historic times to the late stone age, not only in the re-telling and adaptation of ancient stories by sub-sequent generations, but in the mediation of the indigenous memory and voice by the written colonial record. While the transcription and translation of proverbs, mythic tales, prayers, songs and testimony had been initiated by European collectors in the mid-nineteenth century, the primary interest was linguistic, evangelical and administrative, leading to grammars, vocabularies, and collections of texts in the service of the Christian mission or 'native' government. The literary-cultural impli-cations of the various indigenous expressions, however, were not always lost on these early recorders and editors. Despite the arrogance of many travellers' accounts,[1] the argument for treating oral texts as literary phenomena was implicit in the first descriptions. By the beginning of the twentieth century, small groups of scholars in Germany, England and South Africa had developed a sense that a subject had been established,[2] and the body of published texts and criticism should by now have secured the study of oral tradition as a significant component of literature in southern Africa.[3] Yet this has not necessarily been the case. Literary discussion of the oral – whether by Western romantics like Laurens van der Post or Africanist-Marxists like Ngugi wa Thiong'o[4] – has relied on over-simplified binaries of African sympathetic magic and Western ana-lytical dissection. In spite of the obvious political purpose behind such arguments, the result has been the homogenising of the oral past: a conception of pre-colonial purity unable to sustain the modern literary intelligence schooled in moral complexities and formal intricacies. It is probably only a sensitivity to the issue of race that prevents many adherents of the written text with its opportunities for revision and refinement of argument from continuing openly to discuss the oral as the realm of the child mind. Such a view, of course, bears on the failure of anthropological study to make itself understood or felt in literary study. With anthropological-evolutionist theories having monopolised the first investigations of African culture, there remains a perception that the oral evinces not the distinctive personality or style, but the savage collective consciousness supposedly devoid of individual response or responsibility.

In reacting against the implications here of societies passing from primitive states to differentiated civilisations on the nineteenth-century European model, Ruth Finnegan attempted to define recognisably literary qualities and generic categories in oral tradition.[5] Her identification of literary effects such as heightening of style, ambiguities of tone, and moral relativism has helped to retrieve oral studies from classificatory scientific approaches. The danger attendant on accentuating textual properties, however, has been to reduce the power of the informing history and, because traditional oral expression functioned entirely in a social milieu, to end up limiting the meaning of the expressive voice. As Leroy Vale and Landeg White argue, the emphasis on 'internal structure' can detract from pertinent questions about the active association of oral form and its content with the periods of history that have given rise to its expressive voice.[6] Building on earlier comments by H. I. E. Dhlomo, A. C. Jordan, Archie Mafeje, Mazisi Kunene and others,[7] they proceed to chart a continuity of oral tradition in southern and central Africa in which 'licence' is identified as a common criterion − moral and aesthetic − granted to the *poem*, even by strong rulers. The licence permitted commentary by the bard on power relations in the surrounding life and − as Vale and White conclude − attests to the dynamic intelligence of oral man. While their concern with culturally marked utterance has the value of tying mythic to historical understanding and opening the region to its most prevalent voices, Vale and White − it seems to me − remain themselves too firmly tied to the poem's moments of production in past time. What is required is a greater attention than is usually evident in oral studies to the matter of how we recover and interpret the oral intervention in the context of the modern society. In reaching astutely and resiliently beyond its own attachments and updating itself within changing conditions, the oral voice places the critic under an obligation − I shall argue − to interpret oral tradition as retaining a contentious capacity: as a usable past.[8]

Notes

1. 'The savage custom of going naked has denuded the mind, and destroyed all decorum in the language. Poetry there is none.' R. F. Burton, *Wit and Wisdom from West Africa; or, a book of proverbial philosophy, idioms, enigma, and laconisms* (London, 1865), p. xii.

2. There was the early research of the School of Oriental Studies (later, Oriental

and African Studies) of the University of London, founded in 1916, and, in South Africa, the influence of the linguist C. M. Doke who, at the University of the Witwatersrand (Johannesburg), encouraged academic recognition of what was referred to as Bantu studies. The journal *Bantu Studies* (1921–   ), later entitled *African Studies*, remains one of the best outlets for scholarly articles, in English, on oral literature from southern Africa. (See R. F. Herbert, *Not with One Mouth: Continuity and Change in Southern African Language Studies* (Johannesburg, 1994), a critical assessment of Doke's work which spans the range of Bantu philological studies until his death in 1980.)

Other valuable resources are the Bleek and Lloyd Collection (University of Cape Town), the Grey Collection (South African Library, Cape Town) and the James Stuart Papers (Killie Campbell Africana Library, University of Natal, Durban). A wealth of recollection and testimony from Zulu respondents at the turn of the century, the Stuart material has begun to be made more accessible to scholars in the first four volumes of *The James Stuart Archive of Recorded Oral Evidence Relating to the History of the Zulu and Neighbouring Peoples*, C. de B. Webb and J. B. Wright (eds) (Pietermaritzburg, 1976–1986).

3. See the Oxford Library of African Literature series for commentary on, and collections (including English translations) of, oral literature pertinent to southern Africa: T. Cope, *Izibongo: Zulu Praise Poems* (1968); M. Damane and P. B. Saunders, *Lithoko: Sotho Praise Poems* (1974); A. C. Hodza and G. Fortune, *Shona Praise Poetry* (1979); D. P. Kunene, *Heroic Poetry of the Basotho* (1971); I. Schapera, *Praise Poems of Tswana Chiefs* (1965); H. Scheub, *The Xhosa, 'Ntsomi'* (1975) and T. E. W. Thomas, *Bushman Stories* (1950). In the same series is R. Finnegan's study *Oral Literature in Africa* (1970) which has a comprehensive bibliography of texts and criticism. Other crucial collections of texts in the study of southern African oral literature include W. H. I. Bleek, *Raynard the Fox in South Africa; or, Hottentot Fables and Tales* (London, 1864); W. H. I. Bleek and L. C. Lloyd, *Specimens of Bushman Folklore* (London, 1911); H. Callaway, *Nursery Tales, Traditions, and Histories of the Zulus* (Springvale and London, 1868; Trubner, 1970); H. Chatelain, *Folk-tales of Angola* (Boston, 1894); E. L. Ennis, *Umbundu Folk-tales from Angola* (Boston, 1962); R. Finnegan, *The Penguin Book of Oral Poetry* (London, 1978); E. Jacottet, *The Treasury of Ba-Suto Lore* (London, 1908); A. C. Jordan, [Xhosa] *Tales from Southern Africa* (Berkeley, 1973); P. Mahlangu, *Umthwakazi: Izindaba zama Ndebele Zemvelo* [The Ndebele Nation: Tales of the Origin of the Ndebele] (Cape Town, 1957; 1978); D. Rycroft and A. B. Ngcobo, *The Praises of Dingana: Izibongo zikaDingana* (Pietermaritzburg, 1988); J. M. Schoffeleers and A. A. Roscoe, *Land of Fire: Oral Literature from Malawi* (Limbe, 1985); E. Singano and A. A. Roscoe, *Tales of Old Malawi* (Limbe, 1974); H. Scheub, *African Oral Narratives, Proverbs, Riddles, Poetry and Song* (Boston, 1977); the James Stuart Readers (London, 1923–1926); G. M. Theal, *Kaffir Folk-lore: A Selection from the Traditional Tales Current among the People Living on the Eastern Border of the Cape Colony* (London, 1886). Selections of ancient and modern texts are to be found in E. (Liz) Gunner and M. Gwala (eds), *Musho! Zulu Popular Praises* (East Lansing, 1991); J. Mapanje and L. White (eds), *Oral Poetry from Africa* (London, 1983); J. Opland (ed.), *Words that Circle Words: A Choice of South African Oral Poetry* (Johannesburg, 1992); C. Style and O. Style (eds), *Mambo Book of Zimbabwean Verse in English* (Gweru, 1986); H. Tracey (ed.), *Lalela Zulu: 100 Zulu Lyrics* (Johannesburg, 1948). Critical work will be referred to in the course of Part One.

4. Van der Post, *The Lost World of the Kalahari* (London, 1958) and *The Heart of the Hunter* (London, 1961); Ngugi, *Decolonising the Mind: The Politics of Language in*

African Literature (London, 1986) and *Moving the Centre: The Struggle for Cultural Freedoms* (London, 1993).

5. Finnegan, *Oral Literature in Africa* (Oxford, 1970).

6. Vale and White, *Power and the Praise Poem: Southern African Voices in History* (Charlottesville and London, 1991). See Finnegan's *Oral Poetry: Its Nature, Significance and Social Context* (Cambridge, 1977) for formalist criticism moving towards social determinants.

7. Dhlomo, 'Nature and Variety of Tribal Drama', *Bantu Studies*, no. 13 (1939) and 'Zulu Folk Poetry', *Native Teachers' Journal, Natal*, no. 27 (1947–8), reprinted in *English in Africa*, vol. 4, no. 2 (September, 1977); Jordan's articles on Xhosa oral and written literature appeared in *South African Outlook* in the mid 1940s and are collected in *Towards an African Literature: The Emergence of Literary Form in Xhosa* (Berkeley, 1973); Kunene's observations on oral literature appear in several articles, initially in his unpublished MA dissertation, *An Analytical Survey of Zulu Poetry: Both Traditional and Modern* (University of Natal, 1962), and are restated in his introductions to his own poetry, *Zulu Poems* (New York, 1970), *Emperor Shaka the Great: A Zulu Epic* (London, 1979), *Anthem of the Decades: A Zulu Epic Dedicated to the Women of Africa* (London, 1981) and *The Ancestors and the Sacred Mountains* (London, 1982). See also A. Mafeje's important article 'The Role of the Bard in a Contemporary African Community', *Journal of African Languages*, vol. 6, no. 3 (1967) and the selection of early criticism by scholars such as Franz, Vilakazi, Grant, Fortune, Doke and Schapera in *Foundations in Southern African Oral Literature*, R. H. Kaschula (ed.) (Johannesburg, 1993). For a selection of contemporary responses see the published conference proceedings, E. Sienaert *et al.* (eds) (Natal University Oral and Documentation Centre, Durban).

8. For useful articles on modern interpretative approaches, see K. Barber and P. F. de Moraes Farias (eds), *Discourse and Its Disguises: The Interpretation of African Oral Texts* (Birmingham University, 1989).

Chapter 1
Bushman (San) Songs and Stories

Recovering voices: the Bleek and Lloyd Collection

The Bushmen have left a vivid record of paintings and stories. Using natural colours and dyes to decorate the rock faces of caves and shelters, they have bequeathed a visual art the significance and complexity of which is only now attracting detailed attention. Interpreting the rock art as symbols of shamanistic trance visions in which medicine people confronted spirits of sickness and death by evoking God's potency as embodied in animals, the archaeologists David Lewis-Williams and Thomas Dowson argue for a way of understanding the beliefs and the art from the 'Bushman perspective'.[1] It was the perspective of the colonisers and the African Bantu-speaking groups, however, that prevailed in southern African history, and Bushman paintings and stories tell not only of communions between physical and spiritual realms, but of destructive meetings with Africans and white farmers. Since the former regarded the Bushmen as little better than vermin and the latter pursued them with genocidal intent, the story of the Bushmen is one of cruelty and virtual extinction.[2]

Bushmen hunter-gatherers were organised in small, mobile, face-to-face and therefore, fairly loyal bands which were resistant to change. At one time areas in which Bushmen were to be found were widespread in southern, central and east Africa. By the seventeenth and eighteenth centuries, however, they had long given way to more aggressive people in most of their territories, surviving only in Namibia and neighbouring Botswana, in southern Angola and in a small area of Zambia, in the hinterland of the Cape, along the eastern side of South Africa, and in small pockets in the mountains of Lesotho. There is no single term used by all the Bushmen to name themselves. The word Bushman itself is a translation of the Dutch *Boschjesmans* and, as used by colonists, had pejorative associations. In consequence, some anthropologists today prefer the name San, the word the neighbouring Nama (Khoi) used for all Bushmen groups. But San was also used insultingly by the Nama for any impoverished cattleless people, and I have followed modern archaeological practice in retaining the term Bushman. Different groups are designated according to linguistic forms of the common click language that was spoken: the clicks are represented in print by the characters !, |, ||, and ≠. The extinct Cape Bushmen were called the |Xam, and the still-surviving group in the Kalahari desert are the !Kung.

In South Africa and Namibia the Bushmen co-existed with the Khoi, or Khoi-khoi (in colonial parlance, the Hottentots). The origins of the Khoi are not known with certainty, but it is probable they began as a community of Bushmen that had close contact in the Kalahari country of modern Botswana with African cattle-keepers from whom they adopted habits of pastoralism. Organised in chiefdoms, the Khoi spread into Zimbabwe, Namibia and down and across South Africa, and, as cattle-herders, could be persuaded more easily than the self-sufficient hunter-gatherer Bushmen to enter into trade and service with colonists. The Bushmen, in comparison, fiercely resisted intrusion into their hunting lands, killing herdsmen and raiding stock. In retaliation, the colony waged a war of extermination against them while bringing prisoners to Cape Town to endure life-long servitude.

By the time the German linguist Dr W. H. I. Bleek and his sister-in-law, Lucy Lloyd, arrived in South Africa in the 1850s, the |Xam, or Cape Bushmen, were no longer a stone-age people. Having initially been employed in Natal by Bishop Colenso to produce a work on the Zulu language, Bleek settled in Cape Town in the late 1860s; it came to his attention that several |Xam were working as convicts on the new break-water in Cape Town harbour. Most had been brought from the northern Cape to serve out sentences of hard labour for crimes like stock theft: crimes that spoke more of their desperate way of life brought about by the practices of the colony than of the characters of the convicts. Realising that these |Xam belonged to a culture unlikely to survive much longer, Bleek and Lloyd arranged with the governor of the colony to have some of the convicts transferred into their service, and they spent the next five years interviewing these Bushmen, first learning their language, and then devising a phonetic script for its notation. Today no one can speak the |Xam language, there is no comprehensive grammar or dictionary available, and *A Bushman Dictionary*, finally published in 1956 by Bleek's daughter, Dorothea, remains incomplete.

In three of the convicts, Bleek and Lloyd found outstanding narrators. Without any context in which to enact their stories to an audience of their own people, Dia!kwain, Han≠kasso and ||Kabbo slowly related myths, songs, prayers, tales and historical accounts to Bleek and Lloyd for transcription into phonetic script and simultaneous rendition into word-for-word English translation. The result is the 12,000-page Bleek and Lloyd prose collection which is housed in the archives of the University of Cape Town and in which the two recorded literally all the hesitations, repetitions, circling progressions, apparently a-logical digressions, and mutations of stories-within-stories that, according to researchers like Walter J. Ong, suggest the oral mind in its procedures of memorisation.[3] In the case of the convict narrators, however, it is difficult to decide whether the circularity of the tale betokens the style of the oral imagination or the patience of the tellers in accommodating themselves to the laborious process of Bleek and Lloyd's long-hand transcription and translation. The emphasis, one way or another, is probably a fine one, and presents challenges to any translator in authenticating a sense of the 'original voice'. In his book of selections from Bleek and Lloyd rendered into poetry, for example, Stephen Watson has analysed distinct styles for ||Kabbo ('he rarely gives a complete story from beginning to end; he is much more likely to introduce anything that happens to interest him, wandering from natural history to legend and back again in a kind of stream of consciousness'), Han≠kasso ('notable for the readiness with which he enlivens his narration with songs and chants') and Dia!kwain ('tends towards the serious rather than the humorous in the manner of his telling').[4] As they appear in Bleek and Lloyd, nonetheless, the |Xam texts make peculiar demands on their readers:

> The moon here is full, the moon lies (in the east) daybreak,
> she is full/great the moon lies there for the moon is living
> the moon becomes (or makes) the great moon the moon
> mounts the sky yes; for the moon is the great moon.[t]

Faced with such recordings, the practice among editors or re-creators has been to clean up the syntax, reduce some of the padding, and even impose a semblance of linearity and narrative closure. Where verse can be distinguished from prose in prayers, hymns and songs, words have been arranged on the printed page in short lines and stanzas, as in Bleek and Lloyd's substantial *Specimens of Bushman Folklore* (1911), which was published after Bleek's death and shortly before the death of Lucy Lloyd.[5] In re-working the material into lyrical and narrative poems, Watson believes that one 'could either remain close to Bleek and Lloyd's literal English version and produce a piece without poetic charge, fated to remain immured in the past; or one could re-work so as to bring the material into the present, living for those alive in the present'.[6] Accordingly, his version of the lines given above reads:

> The moon is still full, still alive
> as she hangs in the sky just before dawn.

As soon as the sun goes down in the west,
the moon in the east grows even fuller,
she climbs the sky, her face more burnished,
her belly swelling, full of moon-children . . .

Objections to procedures of re-working are likely to centre on the question of respecting a necessary boundary between the spirit of the original rendition and the conventions of modern form. This notwithstanding, Watson's argument has pertinence, and we have several scrupulous re-workings of oral material including Jack Cope's versions of Bushman songs and A. C. Jordan's English renditions of Xhosa tales. We also have numerous examples, however, of oral tales assimilated to the pattern of the well-shaped written story presented often with morality adapted to middle-class Western norms for coffee table and school markets.[7]

In oral studies, clearly, we are dealing with texts that are 'unstable', and matters of classification and interpretation remain challenging. As far as classification of Bushman literature is concerned, there were no generically distinct categories in ancient African communities corresponding in a self-consciously literary way to the Western forms of poem, narrative and drama. There were different kinds of expression for different occasions, nonetheless, and as Ruth Finnegan has argued persuasively,[8] elements recognisable in written literature are also recognisable in oral forms: the communication is expressive not merely instrumental, aestheticised not simply factual. There are elevations of style and an interest in the medium for its own sake as well as for its communicative purpose. In terms of subject, structure and manner, analogies may be perceived with written forms of panegyric, lyric, elegy, religious verse, fictional prose, and non-fictional testimony. What can be distinguished in Bushman expression are songs in which the chant-like utterances reinforce invocation, lament, dramatic performance or, in more secularised allusion, the moods of love. There are also fictional and non-fictional narratives in which character-types develop through a sequence of actions. Some narratives are mythological, others refer to events in colonial history, and in the recollections of Bleek's convict-narrators, their individual styles of testimony sometimes suggest an autobiographical element.

Mood songs. !Kaha of the Kalahari

Sacred songs were probably part of communal religious life and are said by the !Kung still to be given to particular members of the group by the great God. These include medicine songs which are often named after animals and accompany curing dances at which men, the participants, enter trance-possession states to rid the community of illness. The singing at these dances is performed by choirs of women and girls, and the songs, consisting mainly of words with no perceptible meaning, are named after various 'strong things' such as the sun, the giraffe, the elephant and the mamba, in which spiritual power is invested. There are also forms of religious ritual such as the hunting dance or the rain dance in which action proceeds through imitation, the dancers are made up as animals, and the narrative enacts the stages of a hunt, or a supplication for rain. The function of such ceremonies is to draw out sickness, to face the anxieties of lean times, and also to encourage the sharing of social harmony. Aspects of supplication are the basis, too, of hymns and prayers. As there are no priests, invocations to the spiritual powers are said to take place spontaneously as the thought comes to the person. Consonant with the scarcities of Bushman life, the topics are day-to-day material needs in which the element of prayer is more predominant than the worship associated with hymns, as in the well-documented 'Prayer to the Young Moon'[1] which was set out in English and in verse-form by Bleek and Lloyd in *Specimens of Bushman Folklore*:

> Young Moon!
> Hail, Young Moon!
> Hail, hail,
> Young Moon!
> Young Moon! speak to me!
> Hail, hail,
> Young Moon!
> Tell me of something.
> Hail, hail!
> When the sun rises,
> Thou must speak to me,
> That I may eat something.
> Thou must speak to me about a little thing,
> That I may eat.
> Hail, hail,
> Young Moon!

In characteristic fashion, the prayer opens with an invocation to the moon (or sun, or stars) and attaches life to the utter necessity of food. The language is spare of adjectives, and this translation aims for its effect in the close correspondence of the word to the thing as philosophically akin to an ancient indivisibility of the real and the mythic. Intensity relies on repetitions and parallelisms.

Only a few Bushman songs have ever been written down. One of the best-known mood songs in *Specimens* is the 'The Broken String'[(t)], told to Bleek and Lloyd by Dia!kwain. It is a lament for !Nuin-|kui-ten, an elderly shaman – a rainmaker – shot down in the 1860s by Afrikaner farmers. About to die, he told Dia!kwain's father, Xaa-ting, that he wanted to teach him the seeds of his magic, and as a mark of remembrance Dia!kwain's father composed a song of sorrow:

!k'e kan ddoa e,	People were those who
!kann !kwa ka !nuin.	Broke for me the string.
He tiken e,	Therefore,
Ti ine ikwa ua kka,	The place became like this to me,
i,	On account of it,
O !nuin a ddoa !kwa ka,	Because the string was that which broke for me.
He tiken e,	Therefore,
Ti-g |ne auki ttan-a kka,	The place does not feel to me,
Ti ka ssin |ikwei tta kka,	As the place used to feel to me,
i,	On account of it.
Ta,	For,
Ti |ku-g |ne tta bboken,	The place feels as if it stood open before me,
O !nuin a !kwa kka.	Because the string has broken for me.
He tiken e,	Therefore,
Ti auki !ne tta ǂhannuwa kka,	The place does not feel pleasant to me,
i.	On account of it.

The image of the broken string condenses several ideas. The practice of rain-making involved leading an ox (a magical rain animal) by a leather thong across the area where it was hoped rain would fall. If the thong broke during the capture and the rain animal escaped, it was believed that the drought would continue. Thus the immediate reference – the broken string of a musical instrument – places any sense of personal loss within the fate of the entire community. As a rainmaker, the dead man would have been central to the well-being of the hunter-gatherer band, and the breaking of the string symbolised a state of drought for all his people. But there is also a cosmic dimension. As long as the Bushmen heard the sounds of the stars in the vast, silent night of the desert, reciprocity existed between the human being and the universe: the breaking of these 'feeling strings', therefore, presaged disaster.

Although the song has elegiac resonance, a knowledge of the cultural context obviously increases appreciation of the range and poignancy. Roger Hewitt's research among the !Kung in the Kalahari desert, in fact, reveals a continuing tradition of songs in which highly personal reflection gains power from the concerns of the social and the spiritual life.[9] Switching from the traditional musical bow to the thumb piano, which is widespread among neighbouring African people, the young singer !Kaha from the Kalahari district of Botswana has had recorded and translated into English intense metaphorical expressions about his unique relationship to the great God. Seeing himself set apart from the nearby groups of !Kung by personal misfortune, he regards himself in the ambiguous position of being persecuted by God while called upon to be the medium of spiritual revelation to his fellow human beings:

> Terrible God deceives, torments.
> God's arms descend into my fingers.
> Yesterday God said 'Be my child and listen.
> Take what I say to the people.'
> God's arms
> God's arms
> A young soul lives in the western sky
> and is still learning.[(t)10]

Weaving into his song strange words as the inspired speech of God and regarded by the people in his district as a profoundly disturbing religious figure, !Kaha strikes a note simultaneously ancient and modern. In a contemporary world that seems to be owned by others (the Botswana government stands accused of forcing Bushmen off land containing mineral deposits and into poverty in the towns), !Kaha's songs are charged social events about solidarity, security and survival.

Creation myths, folk-tales, testimonies. ||Kabbo's story

As with the songs, narratives continue to be practised by the !Kung Bushmen. The hunter-gatherer economy traditionally facilitated conversation time, and the narration of news, anecdotes, hunting exploits and bawdy tales emphasised the 'non-specialist' nature of storytelling. The usual qualification was seniority in age, in story sessions that emphasised the activity as a communal pastime. As among the now extinct |Xam, the !Kung word for 'story' applies to a range of narratives including stories of supernatural beings, animal parables, encounters between animals and humans, and historical recollections which draw on the experiences of the narrators. In Megan Biesele's collection, which was compiled in the

course of field work among the !Kung from 1970 to 1972,[11] there are
fabular tales set in long-ago time when God walked upon the earth, and
when animals were still people. There are hunting stories, historical
stories, and simply stories (n≠wasi). Versions of creation tales occur in
both highly formalised and colloquially profane speech, and the occasion
of the storytelling session, which is characterised by much hilarity, could
in itself seem more important in its social interchange than the point of
the actual stories. Whether the reference is respectful or scatological,
however, the underlying issues are serious in their concern with fundamentals of living: sex, excrement, birth, death, hunting and gathering,
sharing food, the division of labour, the balance of sexual power. Here
is a brief story from the modern !Kung as related in the early 1970s by
Kashne n!a to Biesele. In dealing with the origins of sex, it relies on a
bawdy tale to introduce a 'feminine principle' that recurs in Bushman
oral culture according to which the practicality and good sense of the
woman acts as a check on man's propensity for hubris, recklessness, or
foolishness:

> !Gara tried screwing his wife in the nostrils. Then he tried
> her ears. Finally, he screwed her nostrils again. He was getting
> nowhere.
>   His wife looked at him, and said, 'Don't you know
> *anything*? What do you think you're doing in my nostrils
> and my ears? Can't you see there's a much better place,
> here? *This* is what you "eat", you fool.'
>   !Gara was a person who was really ignorant. He was
> definitely stupid and didn't know how things were.[(t)12]

Such idiom is not to be found in Bleek and Lloyd. In fact Lucy Lloyd,
early this century, and Laurens van der Post, in the 1950s, both claimed
that storytelling had died out among surviving Bushmen.[13] The fieldwork
of Hewitt and Biesele refutes this; Van der Post, however, would probably
argue that the invention, fantasy and cosmological significance of ancient
tales has become severely diminished in the kind of story I have just
quoted. Of course, the absence in the Bleek and Lloyd collection of the
risqué element that we encounter in Biesele's transcripts could have had
more to do with the relationship between the narrator and the transcriber
than with any shift in storytelling convention. Even had the forthright
reference been part of ||Kabbo's repertoire, it is unlikely that, as an ex-
convict in a situation of dependency, he would have let slip his somewhat
austere manner in front of the two white people of considerable authority
who had secured his release from prison.
    There are nevertheless several similarities between stories of the !Kung
and those of late nineteenth-century |Xam Bushmen. In the Bleek and

Lloyd collection there are many stories, for example, concerning an ancient people who were regarded as members of an early race (the forerunners of the Bushmen themselves) and who were associated with certain animals. It is part of the tradition that all the animals were once people, and in the parable-like form of the animal fable there is opportunity to explore tensions between true and false behaviour in the human and social world. The most important figure in the ancient race was the trickster-deity, Mantis, variously named |Kaggen, Pishiboro, ≠Gao!na, and Huwe. In many of the stories Mantis becomes the great, incorrigible disturber of peace and social order: the trickster, devilish by nature, who is at war with all human inertia. Although one of his first tasks was to give the animals their different colours and fix them with honey (for in his creative moments he is devoted to all sweetness), Mantis also gave his strange family their freedom to resist their need to obey him, to adventure in the world enlivened by mirth, darkened by shadows, and simply confounded by unpredictability. With Mantis representing the Bushmen's supreme image of the infinite in the small, many of the smaller insects, birds and animals of the desert were given particular qualities: the hamer-kop bird was charged with extra-sensory perception (in Zulu tradition, by contrast, the hamerkop is the harbinger of death); the mouse showed in its stripes the signs of differentiated being and consciousness, one able to venture into new experiences; the lynx was the lover of light; and in the graceful antelope family the Bushman's heart ranged freely between the delicate creatures and the herds of the plain. The eland was the guide to ultimate metamorphosis: creation in its highest animal form; food for survival in its greatest abundance. The stars, clouds, wind, whirlwinds, rain and, above all, the rainbow were the representations of subtle, trans-figuring powers. Guided by the hunting star Canopus, the hunter personi-fied the greatest urge of being: hunger for food of the spirit, for increasing the self through storytelling, dancing, music and dreaming (||Kabbo's name meant Dream). Seeing in a pool the reflection of a great white bird as the spirit soaring above the bonds of earth, the hunter lost all his passion for hunting game, and devoted the rest of his life to an exhausting quest that ended as he died grasping a lone white feather (truth), which came floating down to him. A version of the hunter parable is employed without conscious reference to Bushman myth by Olive Schreiner in *The Story of an African Farm* (1883), usually adjudged to be the first significant 'South African' novel.

In the early fabular period, the raw materials of life, both social and cosmological, were seen to be constantly interacting and revealing pro-found truths. In the story 'The Lynx, the Hyena and the Morning Star'[(t)], for example, Morning Star – the brightest and greatest hunter – chooses as his bride not the disproportionately large lion but the most star-like creature on earth, Lynx. An exalted element of heaven inevitably demands to be joined to an equal and opposite life on the plains. But no sooner has the logic and harmony of the union been established than all is darkened by the shadow of evil, Hyena symbolising in her carrion nature the dread power of jealousy. Lynx's ever-vigilant sister, however, warns Morning Star who, his eyes full of the fire of just anger (the arrow in the bow, the spear in the hand) descends to earth and puts Hyena to flight. Swerving to avoid Morning Star's spear, Hyena catches her hind leg on the coals of a fire, and has been condemned ever since to a lop-sided walk: a reminder of the living reality of evil. The reason for which Morning Star continues to sit with an eye so bright between night and day, therefore, is that he has learned the following lesson: the forces of darkness and evil which Hyena personifies on earth are fundamental to the universe, and are indestructible; an exercise of everlasting vigilance on the frontiers of the mind, nevertheless, can defeat evil and prevent the triumph of night over day.

As should be clear, my response to this story has shunned the register of the anthropological field-worker concerned more with the *evidence* than the *interpretation* of stories. Rather, I have deliberately imitated the approach of Laurens van der Post.[14] Whether or not we can go along with all of Van der Post's assumptions is a question to which I intend to return. My point here is that Van der Post, to a greater degree than any other commentator, has tried to enter the world of the Bushmen as a literary experience. Although he bases his understandings on the Western model of Jungian dream as the gateway of the mythic unconscious to the creative, pre-analytical richness of the human imagination and spirit, Van der Post succeeds in conveying layers of memory, allusion, metaphor and meaning in Bushman creation tales that deserve consideration along with any of the great mythologies of the world. In tracing numerous links with the stories of the Hebrews, Greeks and, more generally, Western Europe, Van der Post says of Hyena's howl that it is the perpetual, recurring Ishmael element in life. Such universalism, of course, could blur a distinctively 'Bushman perspective'; yet the value of Van der Post's empathies is to take seriously the literary culture of people who bore the brunt of colonial hostility.

Bushman songs and stories share many features with those of the Khoi.[15] Although references to an early race are very rare in Khoi story-telling, we encounter similar creatures, animal parables, and a trickster-deity (Heiseb, among the Nama Khoi). In his field research in the Kalahari, Hewitt noted that the Nahro (part hunters, part stock owners who speak a Khoi language) tell humorous tales of a fox-trickster (probably a jackal-trickster) who works as a gardener for a foolish, brutal white farmer and whose efforts are largely aimed at outwitting his employer.[16] An ancient protagonist has come to be used, therefore, as a rudimentary form of social satire, and the adaptation is a reminder that the Bleek and Lloyd collection itself may be read not only as a route back to the beliefs of a mythic age, but as a document of loss and longing within the times of colonial history. Several of the stories tell of white commandos hunting down Bushmen like animals, of the farm-worker Ruyter tied to a wagon wheel and beaten to death by his master, and of ‖Kabbo's capture, trial and imprisonment in the Cape colony. As ‖Kabbo's voice becomes perplexed about his identity in the world, his stories – like the song 'The Broken String'[t] – echo beyond his personal misfortune to evoke a dying culture and his desire for its redeeming wholeness. In '‖Kabbo Tells Me his Dream'[t] and 'Return of the Moon'[t], ‖Kabbo utters some of the most powerful testimony in our literature. These are lengthy narratives about acute homesickness and the destruction of the Bushman life in its clash with colonialism. In understanding the demise of people as synonymous with the end of their stories, ‖Kabbo confirms the central importance in Bushman tradition of the story as the definition of human and social personality:

> Thou knowest that I sit waiting for the moon to turn back for me, so that I may return to my place; that I may listen to people's stories . . . that I may sitting listen to the stories which yonder came, which are stories that come from a distance, for a story is like the wind, it comes from a far-off quarter and we feel it. Then I shall get hold of a story. . . . For I am here, I do not obtain stories; I feel that people of another place are here, they do not possess my stories. They do not talk my language. . . . [As] regards myself I am waiting that the moon may turn back for me, that I may set my feet forward in the path, having stepped around backwards. . . .[t]17

Shortly after Bleek's death in 1874, ‖Kabbo left the Bleek and Lloyd household in Cape Town to return to Bitterputs, his place on the plains of the north-western Cape, and with his own death in the following year the wind – as in Bushman mythology – erased his footprints from the earth. His words have yet to appear in any anthology of stories from southern Africa.

l

Bushman projects, Khoi projects. Draghoender's lament

Well before ||Kabbo's time, however, the Bushmen had had their meaning wrested from them as they entered the white South African psyche in the manipulative and mutating forms of frontier myth.[18] In reacting against the prevalent Dutch-colonial view of the Bushman as a scourge, early nineteenth-century British humanitarians at the Cape, such as Thomas Pringle, transformed the Bushman into a romanticised noble savage. By the mid-century the imperial scramble for Africa, backed by social Darwinist views of higher and lower races, had relegated Bushmen to their earlier colonial status as degraded members of the human family. With the rise of industrialisation in South Africa in the 1870s, and the realisation that the Bushmen had no real powers of intervention in political struggles, the romantic image of the 'little Bushman' as a proto-poet began to occupy the imaginations of several researchers and writers. The Bushman as poet had been Bleek's view: a view involving a theory of the origins of language according to which 'prefix-pronomial' languages, such as Zulu, were regarded as organically incapable of grasping poetically the constitution of things. (Among the Zulu, Bleek argued, 'not a single individual who could be called great as a thinker, inventor or poet has risen'.) In contrast, the Bushmen and the Khoi spoke a 'suffix-pronomial' language which was seen to permit speakers to endow animals with human characteristics and thus provide symbolic schemas that elevated them above the other early inhabitants of southern Africa.[19] While not necessarily endorsing Bleek, successive depictions and studies in anthropology and fiction, both 'serious' and 'popular', have consolidated the perception of the Bushman-poet. Several forms of the little hunter of the wind, the dancing, singing man of the desert, for example, occur in commercial films and television advertising: in out-pacing a band of Bushmen, a Toyota 4-wheel-drive vehicle proves its durability. In populist South African and Rhodesian fiction, the Bushmen usually play the roles of faithful trackers and retainers to white adventurers or soldiers in struggles against African 'terrorists' or, as in some of Van der Post's 'cold war' fiction, against non-individualised, non-feeling communists.[20] Bushman projects certainly require diagnostic qualification; attempts at rehabilitating the image, however, need not be treated entirely with suspicion. Van der Post's own complex intervention, for example, has both positive and negative implications. I have mentioned that his literary approach commits itself to a humane interpretation of the Bushman story including the creative potential of the culture. Although we need to guard against his temptations to romanticism, Van der Post's writings on the Bushmen remain keys to deciphering the oral tradition as texts of credible experience and continuing significance. In reacting to Van der Post, Ntongela Masilela, for instance, does not dismiss the value of interpretative sympathy. Rather, he re-reads *The Lost World of the Kalahari* (1958) as an implicit summons to the politics of cultural resistance. In calling for the Bushman and Khoi traditions to be placed at the centre of any attempt to liberate ourselves from the legacy of destructive, competing nationalisms, Masilela avoids Van der Post's tendency to flee from the twentieth century into the language and spirit of ancient times. Instead, he situates the analysis of Bushman and Khoi songs and stories firmly within current debates about the need for assessment and evaluation of a unified South Africanism derived from a common heritage.[21]

Masilela's shift of perspective is a subtle but an important one, and is exemplified, I think, by the case of Piet Draghoender's lament: a testimony relating the cruelties of apartheid to the destiny of dispossession imposed on the early inhabitants.[22] In this instance, it is the Khoi who emerge from myth into history. As early as the Renaissance voyages around the Cape, the traditions of the Khoi had been in danger of being transliterated into the European image of the dissolute Hottentot. The figure of the Hottentot Eve, for example, was sometimes lampooned because of her steatopygous appearance, at other times desired illicitly by European men because of her supposedly sluttish, exotic wiles: behaviour which was set schematically, usually by the same European men, in opposition to Western virtues of feminine grace and courtesy. With the real Saartjie Baartman billed as Hottentot Venus, exhibited in 1810 in the funfairs and circuses of Europe, subsequently dying of alcoholic poisoning and finding her eternal resting place as a curiosity in the Museum of Man in Paris, the fate of the Khoi seemed symbolically sealed.[23] Despite the humanitarian-missionary defence of the Khoi's position in the Cape colony in Dr John Philip's influential polemic *Researches in South Africa* (1828), it would take Lena – in Athol Fugard's *Boesman and Lena* (1969) – to restore human speech to the caricature of the Hottentot. Although granted equality in law with whites in the Cape in 1828, the Khoi were by then an impoverished people, and many willingly entered into the Kat River settlement, founded in 1829 by the relatively enlightened commissioner-general Andries Stockenström. Acting as a buffer district to protect white settlers from Xhosa raids the settlement, as Stockenström saw it, also served as a place to save remnants of the 'Hottentot race' from extirpation, and to civilise and Christianise them.[24] This provides the context for a shameful story of dispossession, in which the settler administration repeatedly sought to force the so-called lazy Hottentot out of the Kat River and on to the surrounding farms as cheap labour.

Under the provisions of apartheid Group Area laws in 1982, a whole community in the Kat River district was forcibly 'removed'. Born in 1906 Piet Draghoender, whose Khoi derivations had been classified by the 1980s as coloured, worked his own property in the district. Asked by an interviewer, the historian Jeff Peires, 'what happened to his neighbours?', Oom Piet (oom, uncle, in Afrikaans can be an affectionate appellation) offered an impromptu declamation of emotional force and poetic density. Captured on film, transcribed and translated into English, his lament in a mixture of biblical and colloquial Afrikaans reverberates with epic references to a past of systematic oppression as the values of the Kat River people – land, blood, freedom – found connection in present-day troubles:

die bont oorlog	the mixed war
toe was hy toe was by gevat	he was then he was then taken
en hy was weggestuur	and he was sent away
en om to baklei	and to fight
en as toe die oorlog oor is	and then then the war was over
toe vat	then he took
wat is	what is
wat is hy	what is he
hja! Mnr Stockenstroom	yes! Mr Stockenstroom
. . .	. . .
ek voel baie hartseer	so I feel very heartsore
die oorloge	these wars
my vader het vir 'n oorlog gestaan	my father has stood for a war
my oupa het vir 'n oorlog gestaan	my grandfather has stood for a war
my kinders	my children
my vader se kinders	my father's children
het vir 'n oorlog gestaan	have stood for a war
. . .	. . .
omdat die plek vrymaak	to make this place free
. . .	. . .
die Here sal dit nooit toelaat dat	the Lord will not allow you to be
jy gevat word so	taken so
en weggegooi word nie	and be thrown away
en die en die afgegee word van	and that and that be given away
van van die Here vir vir vir die	from from from the Lord for for
Vyand se	for the enemy's
sit hom in daardie varkhok	put it in that pigsty

sit hom in die varkhok	put it in the pigsty
want hy behoort aan niks	for it belongs to nothing
wat is	what is
wat is hy?	what is he?[t]25

Like !Kaha whose religious utterance spoke in the vast Kalahari of the need to understand one's story in a world that can seem to scorn simple pieties, Oom Piet articulated with agonised clarity the dilemma of a person caught between his belief in a just God and his bitter resentment of the situation in which he found himself. In explanation of the inspiration displayed by this illiterate small-holding farmer, critics have invoked Marcel Jousse's theories of the peasant moulded by the land he toils, shaped by the environment, and using the language utterly necessary to his anthropological being.[26] Probably, however, it was the injustice of apartheid that had been etched into Piet Draghoender's social self. His lament conveys the sentiments of an entire community, and the dignified oral style indicts the continuing historical wrongs perpetrated on the Khoi and their descendants. The responsibility of the researchers and re-corders of the lament should have been to ensure that Piet Draghoender's 'art statement' made its impact, in corridors of government, as the 'life statement' it was meant to be. When such common citizenry begins to function, we could perhaps consider replacing the terms Bushman or San or Khoi with that of southern African: a bland term, no doubt, but one that at least identifies the right to belonging of the first people of the entire region.

Notes

1. Lewis-Williams and Dowson, *Images of Power: Understanding Bushman Rock Art* (Johannesburg, 1989). See also Dowson and Lewis-Williams (eds), *Contested Images: Diversity in Southern African Rock Art Research* (Johannesburg, 1994).

2. See the histories referred to in the Preface, p. xxi, n. 3. Also: D. Clark, *Prehistory in Southern Africa* (Harmondsworth, 1959); R. Elphick, *Kraal and Castle: Khoikhoi and the Founding of White South Africa* (New Haven, 1977); R. Elphick and H. Giliomee (eds), *The Shaping of South African Society 1652–1820* (Cape Town and London, 1979); R. J. Gordon, *The Bushman Myth: The Making of a Namibian Underclass* (Boulder, 1992); E. Marshall Thomas, *The Harmless People* (New York, 1959); I. Schapera, *The Khoisan Peoples of South Africa* (London, 1930); P. Vinnicombe, *People of the Eland: Rock Paintings of the Drakensberg Bushmen as a Reflection of their Life and Thought* (Pietermaritzburg, 1976); E. N. Wilmsen, *Land Filled with Flies: A Political Economy of the Kalahari* (Chicago and London, 1989).

3. Ong, *Orality and Literacy: The Technologizing of the Word* (London, 1982). For studies on orality see Ong's bibliography. Of pertinence to the literary–historical approach pursued in this study is J. Vansina's *Oral Tradition as History* (London and Nairobi, 1985).

4. Watson, *Return of the Moon: Versions from the /Xam* (Cape Town, 1991), p. 15. See Watson's informative Introduction.

5. Other selections in E. W. Thomas, *Bushman Stories* (Oxford, 1950).

6. Watson, *Return of the Moon*, p. 12.

7. Cope's selection in J. Cope and U. Krige (eds), *The Penguin Book of South African Verse* (Harmondsworth, 1968); Jordan in *Tales from Southern Africa* (Berkeley, 1973). See numerous 'fireside tale' approaches by P. Savory, 'African mystifications' by V. C. Mutwa including the well-known *Indaba, My Children* (London, 1966) and, for children, the traditional tales of M. Poland.

8. Finnegan, *Oral Literature in Africa* (Oxford, 1970), pp. 1–26.

9. Hewitt, 'The Oral Literature of the San and Related Peoples', in B. W. Andrzejewski *et al.* (eds), *Literatures in African Languages*, (Warsaw and Cambridge, 1985), pp. 650–72. See also R. L. Hewitt, *Structure, Meaning and Ritual in the Narratives of the Southern San* (Hamburg, 1986).

10. Biesele, *Folklore and the Ritual of /Kung Hunter-gatherers* (Unpublished doctoral dissertation, Harvard University, 1975), p. 110. Also, later research among living Botswanan Bush people, *Women Like Meat: The Folklore and Foraging Ideology of the Kalahari Tu/'Noan* (Johannesburg, 1993).

11. N. 10 above. See transcripts of translated stories in Biesele, 'Aspects of !Kung Folklore', in R. Lee and I. DeVore (eds), *Kalahari Hunter-gatherers: Studies of the !Kung, San and Their Neighbours* (Cambridge: Mass., 1976).

12. 'Aspects of !Kung Folklore' [n.11 above].

13. Lloyd, Introduction to *Specimens of Bushman Folklore* and Van der Post (with J. Taylor), *Testament to the Bushmen* (Harmondsworth, 1984).

14. See Van der Post's *The Heart of the Hunter* (London, 1961) for extensive commentary on Bushman fables and stories. See also, *The Lost World of the Kalahari* (London, 1958), *Testament to the Bushmen*, a six-part television series co-authored with J. Taylor (Harmondsworth, 1984) and (with J.-M. Pottiez) *A Walk with a White Bushman* (London, 1986).

15. See Bleek, *Raynard the Fox*, p. 19, Introduction to Part One, n. 3.

16. Hewitt, 'The Oral Literature of the San and Related Peoples', p. 660.

17. Bleek and Lloyd collection (University of Cape Town).

18. See as representative commentaries: D. Maughan Brown, 'The Noble Savage in Anglo-Saxon Colonial Ideology, 1950–1980: "Masai" and "Bushmen" in Popular Fiction', *English in Africa*, vol. 10, no. 2 (October 1983), K. Tomaselli, 'The Cinema of Jamie Uys: from Bushveld to Bushmen', in J. Blignaut and M. Botha (eds), *Movies-Moguls-Mavericks: South African Cinema, 1979–1991* (Johannesburg, 1992); J. Uys, *The Gods Must be Crazy* (Mimosa films, 1980); L. van der Post, *The Lost World of the Kalahari* (London, 1958) and A. E. Voss, 'The Image of the Bushman in South African Writing of the Nineteenth and Twentieth Centuries', *English in Africa*, vol. 14, no. 1 (May 1987). Also, 30-second Spoornet and Toyota TV adverts (Johannesburg, 1989 and 1991).

19. Bleek, Preface, *Raynard the Fox in South Africa*.

20. See Van der Post's *A Story like the Wind* (Harmondsworth, 1974) and *A Far-off Place* (Harmondsworth, 1976) in conjunction with D. Maughan Brown, 'Laurens van der Post' in M. Chapman *et al.* (eds), *Perspectives on South African English Literature* (Johannesburg, 1992).

21. Masilela, 'The White South African Writer in Our National Situation', *Matatu: Zeitschrift für Afrikanische Kultur und Gesellschaft*, special issue Towards Liberation: Culture and Resistance in South Africa, G. V. Davis, M. Manaka and J. Jansen (eds), vol. 2, nos. 3–4 (1988).

22. See J. B. Peires, 'Piet Draghoender's Lament', *South African Outlook* (July 1984), pp. 99–104; E. Sienaert, 'Perspectives on and from an Oral Testimony: Piet Draghoender's Lament', *Mosaic*, vol. 21, no. 3 (Spring 1988), pp. 227–41; and K. G. Tomaselli and E. Sienaert, 'Ethnographic Film/Video Production and Oral Documentation. The Case of Piet Draghoender in Kat River: The End of Hope', *Research in African Literatures*, vol. 20, no. 2 (Summer 1989).

23. See S. Gray, 'The Frontier Myth and the Hottentot Eve', *Southern African Literature* (Cape Town, 1979), pp. 38–71.

24. Ordinance 50 of 1828 removed legal restrictions on Khoi, Bushmen and other free (not enslaved) people of colour in the Cape colony, and granted them equality before the law with whites. It was largely based on a report by Stockenström (*Memorandum submitted to His Honour the Lieutenant-Governor by the Commissioner-General*, 3 April 1828). Stockenström returns repeatedly to the question of the Khoi in his writings. See *The Autobiography of Sir Andries Stockenström, Vol. 1* (Cape Town, 1964), pp. 286–91.

25. Quoted in Sienaert [n. 22 above].

26. Jousse, *L'Anthropologie du geste*, 3 vols (Paris, 1978). See Sienaert [n. 22 above].

Chapter 2
African (Bantu) Songs, Stories, Praises

Separatist church songs. The 'Kamuzu' songs of Malawi

Archaeological evidence shows that negroid people living in more diversified societies than those of the Bushman and Khoi had occupied the area of the great lakes in central Africa as early as 300 BC, and that by the third century AD they had spread southwards into what is now Malawi, Zambia, Zimbabwe and South Africa. Classified according to languages and customs as Bantu, these early iron-age people smelted metals, grew crops, and made pottery. By the eleventh century the earliest Bantu-speaking inhabitants had been absorbed by later iron-age people who were related probably to the Shona in modern Zimbabwe. As they settled, they spread out into the numerous Bantu groups that constitute the African people of the subcontinent.[1]

Like Bushman and Khoi expression, African oral tradition was a means of both transmitting and recording a culture, and the written record was also started in the mid-nineteenth century when European collectors began to interview narrators in conditions of colonial constraint. We must allow that several kinds of inhibition affected the expression when the narrators had the status of servants, or subjects, and the interviewer, usually a missionary or native administrator, enjoyed the position of master. As in the case of Bleek and Lloyd's Bushman narrators, the respondents would also have been removed from their own community, in which orality had found actualisation in the purposes of the society, in conventions of expectation regarding style of delivery, and in interchange with an audience that shared customs and rituals. (We have a few descriptions by early travellers and traders of performances at the courts of the Zulu kings, Shaka and Dingana.)[2] Further, by the 1860s, the narrators themselves would have experienced forces of acculturation in the colony and, to a greater degree than Bushman and Khoi expression, African oral tradition – as it has arrived to us – reveals the interaction of tradition and innovation in forms of social utterance: elements of the past are vigorously adapted by people to the immediate situations in which they find themselves.

Such a 'living' quality can be illustrated in most kinds of oral response in southern Africa. In religious song, for example, a strong tradition continues to re-invent itself as a cultural resource that is put to various uses including the making of political statements. An account of religious song (or poetry) alone could fill a book, revealing a range that challenges the expectations and aesthetics of conventional literary scholarship. In looking at hymns, prayers, praises, possession songs, mystical songs and oracular verse, one shifts from delicate supplications to the moon and stars – which I mentioned as part of Bushman tradition – to the Xhosa Methodist hymn by a little-known schoolteacher Enoch Sontonga: 'Nkosi Sikelel' iAfrika' – Lord Bless Africa/Let her horn be raised . . . Bless it, Lord/Our nation/The African nation[t]. With several stanzas having been added to Sontonga's original opening lines by the Xhosa poet S. E. K. Mqhayi, this hauntingly beautiful hymn has gathered to its religious intention an inspirational call in African nationalism for unity and solidarity against white domination.[3] To suggest further variety in religious expression, there continues among the Sotho to be a flourishing tradition of divination praises, in which the divining words are enigmatic, allusive, associated with the throwing of bones, and developed as much for the sake of 'artful' expression on some facet of personal or social relations as for definite predictions about people's ills and misfortunes.[4] The point is that no account of religious response in Africa, even today, can easily separate traditional religion, in which the mediation of ancestors in the affairs of the living plays a crucial psychic role, and the influence of Christianity which usually co-exists with, rather than displaces, key elements of the older authorities and practices. One may refer in this respect to well-known examples of 'syncretic' hymns: in the context of Xhosa-colonial clashes in early nineteenth-century South Africa, Ntsikana utilised Xhosa structures and images in order to reinforce his Christian message; and in responding to his congregants as displaced people in the industrial city, Isaiah Shembe, in the 1920s, added a Zulu 'national' edge to his Christianised-African teachings. What these instances confirm is the all-important function of the religious utterance as a form of resistance against crises of identity and large-scale social change. This is apparent whether we are listening to traditional Zulu bow songs, to the Christian hymns of Princess Constance Magogo kaDinizulu, or to an outdoor meeting of one of the many separatist churches.

Daughter of King Dinizulu and mother of Mangosuthu Buthelezi, leader of the Inkatha Freedom Party, Princess Magogo combined a deep attachment to Zulu tradition with devotion to the Anglican church. Given her position as a royal close to the workings of contemporary politics, however, her songs have inevitably found themselves pulled into highly contentious 'contexts' especially as Inkatha, in opposing the ANC, has found it convenient to exploit Zuluness as an ethnic factor in its struggle for political power. To add to the difficulties, oral tradition in general tends to accentuate paradoxes of pre-modern and modern realities in the daily life of society. The idea of African tradition has been used by white authority in order to justify and facilitate 'European' control: apartheid was endorsed, accordingly, in portrayals of Africans as traditional, exotic, rural, city-foolish, and in retaliation many younger, educated Zulus have shunned Princess Magogo's ancient world of song. At the same time, tradition has been used by Africans themselves as a necessary means of resisting white politics of divide and rule. In South Africa the demeaning landscape of apartheid in which rural people were violently detached from their roots and torn from families and communities has created, ironically, the psychological and social conditions for a thriving continuation and renewal of oral expression. As in the cases already referred to – !Kaha's meditations, Piet Draghoender's lament, Princess Magogo's songs – the religious impulse remains potent. It is an impulse that modern political discourses in their concern for forms of democracy and Western economic systems are unlikely to be able to sweep away. The gulf between a cosmopolitan ANC leadership and illiterate migrant workers, for example, has been exploited to tragic ends in the rivalries and killings that have characterised South Africa's painful process of political transformation.

In a volatile context, even the event of a separatist church meeting can raise the difficult question of how the progressive literary critic is to value the text of the occasion. Like most forms of religious expression in Africa, separatist church activities refuse distinctions between verbal and musical elements. In dramatic interchange between the minister and the congregation, the narrative of the worship integrates scores of voices. These include Christian and traditional prayers including introductory ministerial prayer, praying in tongues, and controlled communal prayer; there is preaching that is not bound by set scripture but is led by the fervour of the Holy Spirit's ascendancy at the meeting; there are testimonies of confession and self-adulation, a profusion of hymns that are used as links to close and launch different phases of the event, and intense interlocutory sessions of healing. The content, of course, is fully meaningful only in the surrounding situation. Among congregations who in the cities are mostly drawn from the poor, the church meeting offers guidance and sustenance: group cohesion, communal emotion, a caring and curing service, and a code of morals that opposes city vices of drinking, gambling and prostitution, while reaffirming respect for age, family and custom. Party-political involvement is shunned; yet we may interpret the religious occasion as highly political in its effects. It speaks of the failure of modern political interests to serve the materially poor of the earth.[5]

In these examples of religious invocation, I may seem to have suggested that song, music and activity supersede the communicative power of words. It is true that what in Western literary education would be called the lyric – the short poem that is sung – is probably the most common form of traditional African literary expression, and that its recitation is invariably prompted by an occasion of one sort or another. Nevertheless, Bantu languages have considerable euphonic potential, and something of the exciting verbal character of traditional, indigenous-language lyrical utterance is beginning to be conveyed to English-speaking readers through skilful translations and re-creations in the written form. (Translation, of course, has been an important foundational activity in conveying the range and variety of most literature in its early stages.) The *Mambo Book of Zimbabwean Verse in English* (1986),[6] for example, opens with forty pages of striking English versions of Ndebele and Shona praises, lullabies, work songs, hunting songs, love songs, satires and children's game songs. With the exception of declamatory royal praises, such utterances are sung on informal occasions including times of leisure in the cities, as well as at rites of passage including births, initiations and marriages. Occurring throughout the region in different languages and in specific cultural codes, lyrics are frequently antiphonal: in inviting calls and responses between soloist and chorus, they utilise the formulas of traditional mores without any loss of the personal, sincere response. In Zulu society, which tradition-ally reinforces strict divisions of duty and obligation between men and women, love songs were usually sung by women and covered a range of feelings from the romance of new love to the despair of parting. Men's poetry, in contrast, included songs to do with cattle, war, hunting and work. Among the Ngoni in Malawi, war songs were accompanied by dancing with the men in the regalia of war and the women joining in the chants, the function of which was to inspire men with lust for battle. These songs are brief and often sung to 'meaningless' though rousing words (*inyo, ho, oya, ye yayo*) while among more southern groups the convention was to utter set war cries. Other kinds of 'purpose' songs have a marked political and topical intent. In ancient societies, the chief was not only praised but could be censured within limits for derelictions of duty, and among the Khoi unpopular chiefs were lectured sarcastically by women in 'reed songs'. The Chopi in Mozambique have a number of songs that, in providing for the airing of complaints in public, serve to monitor and restore harmony and justice in community relations. It is among these political songs that rapid modernisations are most evident. The organised political song, for example, featured prominently at the time of independence in African nationalist rallies in Zambia. With UNIP choirs singing between speeches, the songs contained statements of policy and aspiration ('Kaunda will politically get Africans freed from the English') at the same time as giving precise instructions for the voting, a matter of importance in campaigns among an inexperienced electorate:

> Upper roll voting papers will be green.
> Lower roll voting papers will be pink.
>
> *Chorus.*   Green paper goes in green box.
>   Pink paper goes in pink box.[t)7]

The effectiveness of the topical song in reaching its intended audience is obviously important in countries without strong alternative means of communication. Songs can be picked up and learnt by heart, transmitted orally from group to group, and form real and symbolic links between the leadership and the masses. As propaganda, comment, eulogy and slogan, the tradition has continued to adapt itself to the troubled politics of the region in the chimurenga songs of the Zimbabwe independence war and in the solidarity songs that featured at rallies during the state of emergency in South Africa in the 1980s.

The topical song sharply raises the issue of how the literary historian is to respond to political expression that adulates the leader when the leader might be regarded by some as a saviour, and by others as a tyrant. When Nelson Mandela and other ANC, PAC and SACP leaders were in gaol, their status in songs as heroes, or even martyrs, was hardly a matter of scrutiny. In Malawi, however, 'Kamuzu' songs – songs in chiChewa addressed to Dr Hastings 'Kamuzu' Banda by members of the Malawian Women's League – have been a feature since independence in 1964 of all public and state occasions.[8] Even after the June 1993 referendum, in which the majority of Malawians rejected Banda's one-party rule, the songs continued to honour a man who was widely perceived to have become ruthlessly dictatorial:

> Thanks to you, Mister President,
> we crossed the Jordan.
> You are our Uncle Number One,
> no one can separate us from you
> because you were chosen by God
> to guide us and defend us
> against the English oppressors.[t)]

What do we make of a topical song that is sung beyond the period of its own originating energy and justification? At the time of Malawian independence, the words and occasion would have had freshness; the message a national resonance. Twenty-five years later the song was regarded by many Malawians as serving not the cause of freedom but that of dictatorial conformism. Initially, thorough contextualisation would seem to be necessary to restore for the critic the explanatory and symbolic power of the event. In a society that is unashamedly patriarchal, Banda's dour presbyterianism found consonance with traditional systems of gender hierarchy, and as self-declared President-for-life he proceeded to make the Women's League his enduring power base. The apparent anomaly was not lost on the women who, living amid the realities not of poetry but of scarce resources, had their own agenda. According to traditions of praising and patronage in Africa, the praisers of the Women's League would have expected Banda, the chief, to honour reciprocal obligations towards his loyal subjects. This required that he use his all-powerful influence to favour demonstrable support with preferential access to food, housing and education. The 'Kamuzu' songs thus severely test the idea of the autonomous text, and force the critic into controversial debates that almost overwhelm the words of the songs. We are reminded, certainly, that the moral view of the critic is crucially involved in transferring the occasion to a scale of literary value. A question is: what will Malawi's new democratic government, elected in 1994, do with the 'Kamuzu' song? How does the literary historian 'place' the phenomenon? Later in Part One I shall turn to the question of how we may recover the ancient, military praise poem which, like the 'Kamuzu' song, was usually unashamedly partisan in its accounts of victories and defeats. First, however, I want to turn from songs to sayings and narratives.

Proverbs, orations, creation myths, folk-tales. Lydia umkaSetemba's recitations

These speech utterances include myths (sacred tales concerning the origins of the world, the race, the social organisation, life, death, etc.), legends (which involve human beings in stories believed to be fact, but in which fictional elements have been interwoven), oral histories (which arrange patterns of ancient and contemporary images along with genealogical data into the stories of chieftaincies and their people), and folk tales (fictionalised accounts of human and animal behaviour that comment obliquely on the society). There are also proverbs, riddles and, in public ritual, various forms of oratory. The common purposes are edification and entertainment, and the modes are dramatic, even voluble in style. In drawing on the rich store of Zulu proverbs (izaga), C. L. S. Nyembezi lists hundreds of succinct 'wisdoms' utilising imagery, paradox and irony as devices of statement-by-comparison which cover the subjects of good and bad behaviour, faithfulness and deception, friendship and enmity, fortune, bravery, marriage, age, death, and so on.[9] With references to cattle, crops and, generally, to the 'life-world' of the ancient society, many of the proverbs remain in common use both as the popular acceptance of a truth and as rhetorical ploys in their own right: *Ibel' elihle lidliwa ngumninilo* (The fine corn is eaten by the owner). Forms of oratory include the procedures of village court cases, testimonies as recorded by others of identity and purpose from migrant workers, mine workers and domestic workers and, documented in some detail, the speeches at the beer drink of the rural Xhosa which aim to reinforce social cohesion and even resist the intrusions of the modernising economy. With the sharing of beer among those present and drink offerings made to the ancestors, the occasion provides the village elder with the opportunity to offer formal, public advice and consolation to a returning migrant worker, for example, or to a widow who is released from her mourning to re-enter the activities of the community.[10]

An insight into ancient belief systems and their societal relevance is given by the vast resources of myth. A widely recorded myth concerning the origin of life, by way of illustration, involves a complication of a Khoi story about the Hare sent by Moon to grant humankind everlasting life. In his haste Hare got the message muddled, pronounced not on life but on death, and was punished by Moon who split his (hare) lip. In versions among many Bantu-speaking groups, the Supreme God – the source of all life – sent a chameleon to report that humankind would live forever. But the chameleon dilly-dallied eating berries and flies, and God dispatched the swift, canny salamander to introduce death to the world. The message is deliberately ambiguous and encourages not simple acceptance, but active interpretation. According to Mazisi Kunene, explanation concerns contradiction in life and death, in which God decides humankind must experience the unpredictability of existence as well as its multifaceted possibilities. In its nature, the chameleon thus reveals both the negative (sloth) and positive (wisdom) aspects of its slowness while the salamander's speed both hurries death and introduces decisive thought to the world.[11] Truth here is conceived as relative: a peculiarly 'modern' response. What the story seeks to define as valuable is neither a chameleon-quality nor a salamander-quality but, in combination, a chameleon-salamander quality in the human being. Arguments that characterise Africa as intuitive rather than rational, therefore, have little originary presence in African creation myths, and a modern reading of these myths is a useful check on Eurocentric/Negritude binaries regarding 'thinking' and 'feeling' races. The African creation myths confirm, rather, that somewhere in our ideological battles we all share a complex humanity.

Just as Kunene has tried to save the creation myth from 'survival' theories (that is, forms assumed to be the static products of the primitive mind), so the folk-tale has received astute attention from critics and re-creators such as Harold Scheub and A. C. Jordan.[12] While similarities of plots, motifs and characters in stories have been identified throughout the region, critics have also found configurations in the tales that are distinctive to the Zulu, Xhosa, Shona, and other groups: configurations that are linked to specific and different conditions in the different experiences of the historical life. The cannibal figures that haunt Zulu folk-tale, for example, are seen not as evidence of innate savagery, but as literary-psychological projections of the social environment in the years of trouble in the 1820s when, as a result of Shaka's military conquests, famine threatened large areas of Zulu territory. By contrast, Shona folk-tales derive from social experiences that, prior to the relatively late arrival of colonialism in Zimbabwe, were not as severe as those in early Zululand, and in consequence the folk emblems are generally less frightening, less hallucinatory than their Zulu counterparts. The Shona tale may be defined as domestic in its treatment of time-tested marriage procedures, the value of family, the individual's dependence on the village, and the position of women in the society.[13] Although trickster-figures feature in most traditions in Africa, the Zulu trickster (uChakijane) has lost some of the laughter associated with a deity of misrule, and in keeping with the harsh temper of the stories is often completely callous and selfish as, standing half inside, half outside society, he cruelly exposes the weaknesses of human nature.

Several of the Zulu stories (*izinganekwane*) recorded and translated into English in the 1860s by the Revd Henry Callaway in fact make for disturbing reading. Callaway, who travelled from England to Natal in 1858 to work under Bishop Colenso, established the mission Springvale where he set up a printing press and between 1866 and 1868 he published, in six parts, his still authoritative compilation of Zulu narratives *Nursery Tales, Traditions, and Histories of the Zulus* (1868).[14] Some of the people Callaway interviewed would still have had living memories of the spectacular events that had characterised the reigns of Shaka and Dingana: Shaka's military campaigns and his violent dispersal of rival groupings across the interior; Dingana's assassination of Shaka in 1828, and his subsequent clashes with advancing Afrikaner trekkers. In recollecting Shakan history, Callaway's respondents might also have sensed the precariousness of their own times, in which the Zulu kingdom stood threatened by the policies and designs of colonial Natal in its concern to manipulate royal power and 'control the Zulu'. As with Bleek and Lloyd, Callaway's thoroughness in copying down and translating every word told to him is both his strength and his limitation: while we have to struggle with repetitions and ellipses that sometimes threaten to subsume intelligibility, coherence and pace, we are drawn by the very density of detail into narratives that jolt the imagination in terrifying juxtapositions of the real and the fantastic.

One of the most remarked upon of these stories was performed for Callaway's benefit by Lydia umkaSetemba – also called Uskebe Ngubani – who was regarded by her Zulu contemporaries as a particularly impressive teller of tales. Assuming the role usually assigned in traditional Zulu culture to the woman, usually the grandmother, as the storyteller or educator and entertainer of young and old alike, Lydia umkaSetemba tells of Umxakaza-wakogingqwayo (the name of the central character) who passes from girlhood to womanhood, rites of passage being a common thematic and structural feature of the folk tale. She journeys from the land of her father, where her foolish, youthful vanity had encouraged him to destroy cattle stolen from neighbours, to the terrible regions of the cannibals where she is adopted and grows fat and grotesque. In the story, the cannibal king is an inverse image of her father who, in killing the cattle, had driven his community to starvation. In the region of the cannibals, therefore, the moral ugliness of the child is given concrete form, and in her return to the familiar land she encounters the trials of wizards and physical deformities – she grows a huge head packed with her vanities – before the selfless love of a prince's sister initiates Umxakaza-wakogingqwayo into her true adult beauty. After the tribulations of her journey – from the community to the veld and, as a wiser, more considerate person, back to the community – the story ends as one has grown accustomed to expect in folk-tale, with Umxakaza-wakogingqwayo's marriage to the prince.

The effect of the tale in an ancient village would have relied in part on the habit of telling stories in the atmosphere of the evening: 'the time of spirits'. What Callaway's recording indicates are concise, memorable opening and closing formulas in a three-part repetition of episodes. While character and situation develop around a single thematic 'core' cliché (sometimes in the form of a proverb, a song, or a chant for memorisation), the lesson expands into a narrative the movement of which parallels the moral journey of the heroine. The broad theme, of course, is equilibrium in behaviour and cohesion in society but, as Scheub argues in his commentary on this story and in his introduction to Jordan's re-created Xhosa folk tales (*iintsomi*),[15] the audience learns not through the dry abstraction of moral verities, but through emotional involvement in an imitative action that gives opportunity for considerable invention: in matters of character portrayal, in combinations of images and episodes, in symbols suggesting a credible psychology of creative and destructive energies vying for predominance, and in disguises and transformations as correlatives of different mental states of mind. With the basic plots of folk tales familiar to the community – it was the act of telling that introduced the unexpected twists and insights – stories tended to be stored in memory, encouraging the listeners to raid the storehouse of tradition in filling in gaps, arguing about apparent discrepancies between one rendition of a story and another, and entering as participants into what in effect were 'texts' as the generators of the experience. The tale finds its consequence in the conditions of its reception: the interchange may be regarded almost as 'post-structural'.

What I am emphasising is that the aesthetic of the folk-tale does not follow the conventions of naive realism. Instead, the stories have the potential to create, rather than merely record, the experience to be explored. Connections are not only with forms of romance and gothic, but with the contemporary South American style of magical realism: amid life's hardships, the imagination conjures up a plenitude of possibility in the emotion-saturated, surprising language of dream and desire. When we look broadly at fictional practice in the region, in fact, the folk-tale can be seen to be a kind of formative text the adaptability of which has been exploited in modern ways by, among others, A. C. Jordan and Bessie Head.[16] Jordan adds descriptive details of character and scene that the oral teller, working with stock materials, may have found unnecessary: he explains motivation and generally 'fleshes out' the absent performance with words. Head re-invents tradition in rural Botswana settings that yield present-day versions of ancient themes concerning the authority of the generations, the roles of women and men, and the tensions of conservation and change. In mentioning the journeys in folk-tales from the known to the unknown, Scheub reminds us not only how convenient early missionaries found Bunyan's *The Pilgrim's Progress* as a bridging text in Christian education, but how the mythic, the fabular, and the oral tendency of recurrence in the episode have remained important considerations in response to a range of novels in southern Africa, in which the romance mode has been required to serve a social intent. The obvious examples are the numerous 'Jim comes to Joburg' stories which in their journeys from the simple to the complicated life include Alan Paton's *Cry, the Beloved Country*.[17]

In my discussion so far I have been cautious about extrapolating salient 'oral' characteristics in the literature. Nevertheless, so long as we avoid the habit of categorising the written text as automatically more profound and analytical than its 'emotional' oral counterpart, there are useful distinctions to be made between the oral and the written in seeking to formulate an appropriate aesthetic of fictional practice in southern Africa. What we need to be vigilant about from the outset is a still wide-spread tendency in literary study to dismiss as 'not fully achieved' those stories and novels that do not comply with the formal realist criteria of the written, analytical narrative of climax and closure, in which 'rounded', psychologically-inward characters think through, rather than act out, their destinies. We might recognise, instead, that an oral 'residue' could manifest itself to effect in strong story lines, episodic plots, recurrence, copious repetitions, aggregative, additive thought, and closeness to the 'life world' that preserves several traditional values. The story might find appropriate a hyperbolic, participatory style that is empathic, subjective, and situational rather than objective or abstract. It might find appropriate also characters that are somewhat flattened into types, and dialogue that hovers between originality and the formula. The argument is that in countries where written culture is uneven and where communities in rural areas or city townships retain considerable face-to-face contacts, the oral style has real and continuing validity. The style should feature, certainly, in the articulation of an aesthetic that hopes to understand literature as having the stamp of 'African experience' in forms of stories, novels, poems, plays, and testimonies. Such an argument for the oral as serious expression, of course, contains an element of political intervention, particularly as the written is still too easily attached to the 'civilised' West, and the oral to the 'barbarous' Africa. Without following some adherents of the oral and championing the garrulous, the boringly repetitive, the ill-designed and the naive in thought simply because it is supposed to be oral and therefore authentically 'African', we do need to develop a critical language sympathetic to the style of a great deal of our literature: a style that, in the characteristics I have listed above, could be designated 'oral'.

An 'African' aesthetic: a chief is a chief by the people

In introducing a range of oral forms, I have been following Ruth Finnegan's classifications of verse and prose, and have relied for several of my examples on her comprehensive survey.[18] Her division is based on the fact that in what are widely recognised as lyrics, songs, chants, prayers, even in lengthy praise poems, elements of narrative are foreshortened by accretions of mood, laudation, invocation or apostrophe. Folk-tales and legends, in contrast, place characters in the progressions of plot where changes of mental state occur in space and time. There are views, however, which caution against distinctions between verse and prose in African literature. In remarking on the character of Bantu languages, for example, G. P. Lestrade felt he could not separate prose from verse according to laws of prosody, and regarded the difference as one of spirit rather than of form: prose tends to be less emotionally charged, less moving in content, less rhythmical in movement, less metrically balanced.[19] Kunene, for his part, argues that the only sensible division of the spoken literature is according to its function in the society where it maintains its interest by attaching itself to various social, political and religious events.[20] The gathering, accordingly, becomes the appropriate content for the performance and the total experience involves the gathering's engaging the audience in its recognition of codes and beliefs. Similarly, the performative occasion supersedes language-register and genre convention as the primary determinant of what H. I. E. Dhlomo called 'tribal drama'.[21] Locating the event in ritual and ceremony – the feast of the first fruits, initiation rites, death festivals – Dhlomo spoke inseparably of dance, song, poetry and speeches. Involvement was social, religious, and obligatory; the performances were seasonal, open to all, and the role of the audience was to participate in the action: no strict line was drawn between spectators and actors. The overall impression was that of a poetic rendition of the community's story, in which art was not distinguished from utility. As we shall see in Part Three, Dhlomo had several motives of his own in defending a usable tradition, including his need to find a theatrical model for his own plays which, in the 1930s, sought to bring lessons from the African past to bear on the segregationist politics of the day. His underlying principle of situating the text in surrounding understandings, nonetheless, remains generally valid in attempts to articulate an approach to literature from southern Africa where, in significant ways, the society continues to influence the artistic expression.

Dhlomo would have been tempted to call this principle 'African', and before turning to consider one of the crucial oral forms in the history of the region – the praise poem – it might be worth consolidating a few features of a traditional African model of language and society as it pertains to literary discussion. At the outset, we need to recognise that Bantu languages have in common exceptionally rich vocabularies with high literary potential: isiZulu and isiXhosa, for example, have vocabularies of over 30,000 words, a great proportion of which have a facility for assimilating foreign terms. One of the best concise introductions to the character of Bantu speech remains C. M. Doke's classic essay, 'The Basis of Bantu Literature' (1948), from which I am extracting my summary.[22] What Doke underlines is that, however imaginative the translation of any piece of Bantu literature, something of the picturesque forms of the expression including its vivid, concrete depictions of abstract terms is likely to be under-represented, if not lost. In Zulu, for instance, the idea 'conservation' is expressed by a phrase meaning literally 'to eat with an old-fashioned spoon', and in a language that allows for a wealth of derivative forms from a few roots, it is possible to attain fine distinctions, delicate shades of meaning and, with an elaborate verb system, a great variety of tenses, moods and implications. In Zulu a system of nouns and noun formations, in which basic structure is built up on grammatical class-gender with concordial agreement, grants immense possibilities for alliteration, onomatopoeia and balance in a 'poetry' of verse or prose.

The term 'horses', by way of illustration, is *amahhashi* characterised by the prefix *ama-* which must reappear in various fixed forms in the relevant phrase. Thus, 'his big horses ran away' is expressed as 'horses they-his they-big they-ran-away (*amahhashi akhe amakhulu abalekile*). Further features with promise for literature include a less rigid word order than in English (the changes of order can result in different shades of meaning) and the ideophone, a special word embodying an idea-in-sound which adds emotion and vividness to a description or recitation. Sometimes onomatopoeic, ideophones are also acoustic and while they resemble adverbs they are in actual use more like interjections: for example, the Shona *k'we* is the sound of striking a match; in Zulu *khwibishi* is a sudden recoil; and *pha-pha-pha-pha* in Tonga is a butterfly in the air. The ideophone is thus a rhetorical device of considerable power, and contributes to the tonal impact of Bantu speech. Finally, there are striking praise names: terms that pick out some quality of an object and are used for inanimate things, such as birds, animals and, in their fullest form, names for people as in the Zulu, 'He who hunted the forests until they murmured'[t]. Like the extended Homeric epithet, praise names grant colour and solemnity to speech. Clearly, the translator of Bantu-language literature has to make intricate decisions concerning the accuracy of the message in relation to the stylistic effect.

With cattle as a leitmotif in the literature, we are reminded that the Bantu-speaking people of southern Africa are traditionally agriculturalists: cattle represented wealth including the bride wealth, or *lobola*, paid by the man to the father of his potential wife, the food of libation, and the requirement of ritual sacrifice. In patrilineal systems, divisions of duties and obligations emphasised the family household as the centre of cohesion, in which seniority was accorded natural respect, and roles of government and domestic responsibility were allotted, respectively, to husbands and wives. Where groups of persons – clans – could trace their descent to a common ancestor, continuing contact with the ancestors, alive in memory and remaining guardians of family affairs, could provide psychological restoration. So long as magical acts were beneficial to the community they were accepted, but the religious view was neither magical nor spiritual, but was tied closely to earthly matters: the human being was judged not by the Supreme God – the source of all life and beyond human comprehension – but by fellow human beings according to the norms of social behaviour. This consonance of earthly and mystical life is summarised in the idea of the land as providing both physical and sacred roots of existence in binding the living to the ancestral living-dead. Hence, to remove Africans from their land, as in the Group Areas policies of apartheid, was an act of supreme injustice. The cardinal point in understanding traditional African ontology is thus contained in the saying, I am because we are, and since we are therefore I am. This is clearly distinct from the modern Cartesian individualism of, I think, therefore I am. In patterns of thought and necessity that continue into the industrial present, the African individual's survival and prosperity are regarded as bound to the life and destiny of the group, or community. Where organised into chiefdoms, the chief represented the unity of his community.

As political head, the chief addressed appeals brought to his court by other royals who administered divisions of the territory, while as religious head he performed rituals of sacrifice such as the annual first-fruits ceremony. Although the chief had ultimate authority, his power was restricted in that royalty was embodied in all close members of the royal family and any of them could become chief. Despite strict laws of succession, therefore, bad rule could be challenged while dissatisfied subjects could leave a chiefdom and attach themselves to another. Where the unit was political rather than confined to particular clans, such split-tings and consolidations saw some chiefdoms collapse and others – like Shaka's – expand into a kingdom. The chief's authority thus had to consider the opinions of the most powerful members of the community, and government was conducted by discussion in public meetings open to all adult males, where any man could express criticism of the chief's behaviour. Hence, the praise poet – though constrained by forms of patronage – had some licence for degrees of censure: among the southern Bantu, it is said that a chief is a chief by his birth, but is also a chief by the people. In this social organisation, the balancing of forces in the political kingdom accords with mystical design, in which God's power permeates the entire environment including the plants and animals. At the centre is the human being, who remains alert to possible manipulations of God's force for good or evil by medicine men, witches and rainmakers. In this scheme of things, traditional time was two-dimensional with a long past accumulating its experience for the present, and with almost no future. For in a society given definition by the rhythms of nature and the seasons, recurrence is predictable, and what is real is what has occurred and been experienced.

I am describing, of course, the ideal model: a model that has been marshalled, nonetheless, as myth by several writers in reaction to the ills of the colonial era. Obviously ancient chiefdoms were not seamless enti-ties, and their destruction was ensured by European settlement. A conse-quence was that older schemas found themselves having to confront a colonial enterprise characterised by linear concepts of thought, by eyes fixed energetically against the sin of sloth, and on dreams of future conquest and progress. With spiritual sanction given or denied in the rewards and punishments of a life hereafter, the Christian-colonial mind introduced its forms of messianic hope and apocalyptic vision. In the ancient order, in contrast, the concern was family-centred, generational, communal and social. Both pre-history and history were dominated by myth and legend, and telescoped into a compact oral tradition. But under the pressures of the new world, Africans suffered the loss of sanctioned authority, the fragmentation of the family, and removals from ancestral land. With urbanisation came a wedge between the religious and the secular life. The individual began to know time as a commodity to be bought and sold, and the city was experienced both as alienation and as the mobility of new relations and new opportunities. The future in its dynamism and insecurity shifted the ancient past partly into the present, partly into the unknown. In such accelerated concepts of time Christians, or indigenised Christian movements (or indeed millenarian impulses from Ethiopianism to Marxism), have attempted to establish new foundations with hopes of revelation or paradise. A result in situations of stress has been the need for the apocalyptic solution on this earth, in the reality of the present. The Western ideals of the enlightenment – the dignity of the human being, freedom – have also found place in ancient memory: in the ideologies of Negritude, African personality, African communalism, and socialism. Simultaneously, forms of democracy which might seem to be the antithesis of the old chiefdom have been dislodged from what is labelled the hypocrisy of the West and reconnected to the indigenous need for effective leadership under the constraining view that the chief must always be a chief by the people. In the physical, social and metaphysical drives and disjunctures summarised here, we can probably identify an organising concept in literature from the entire southern Africa: the society rather than the individual has remained the core upon which to construct an ethic and aesthetic of understanding and value.[23]

The praise poem: a usable past? Shaka's court to the trade-union rally

It is true that the praise poem – considered by those groups among whom it has flourished to be the highest form of traditional literary expression – is usually associated with the personalities of strong kings or chiefs, some of whom in their individual styles have been too large for their societies. There are the Zulu kings Shaka and Dingana, Mzilikazi of the Ndebele, the Sotho leader Moshoeshoe, Sobhuza of the Swazis, and Mgwana of the Ngoni, the last of whom led a group northwards to Malawi in the early nineteenth century in flight from Shaka's wars. In listing a few of the more prominent figures of royal praise, however, we are reminded that the praise poem is also the product of important societal motivations. All of these royals, for example, emerge from the troubles of the 1820s – the *mfecane* wars and migrations – when the organisation of African chiefdoms began to experience population pressures and power struggles not unconnected to colonial slave, labour and settlement practices. With the splitting of old and the consolidation of new alliances Shaka organised the Zulu into a powerful military state and scattered refugees across the hinterland: some took refuge under Moshoeshoe in his mountainous Sotho kingdom (Lesotho), others fled south among the Xhosa. New groupings included the Swazi, Goza, Ndebele and Ngoni kingdoms. At the same time Mzilikazi, a one-time ally of Shaka, rebelled against his Zulu overlord and led his Ndebele followers into the interior. In an ongoing and often desperate search for power and security, Mzilikazi overthrew the Pedi kingdom, raided the Tswana, and having withdrawn before the might of Zulu and Boer-trekker raiding expeditions, he crossed the Limpopo into the southern areas of modern-day Zimbabwe. His story, which features in Sol T. Plaatje's novel *Mhudi* (1930), gives the impetus to the narrative progression in his praises ('The Praises of Mzilikazi, Son of Matshobana')[t]:

> Mzilikazi, son of Matshobana,
> Great Bull of the Khumalo Clan,
> Who came from the land of the Zulus,
> Who fought King Shaka
> Until the skies above rumbled.
> Mzilikazi, Black Lion
> Whose roar makes men tremble
> And old men run, leaving behind their loin-skins.
> You who fathered the eater of men.
> Stabber of the heavens,
> Who fought three bulls at the same time,
> One being Shaka himself,
> The other Dingana,
> And the third was the Boers.
> You, King, who travelled the country
> Crossing it from the south
> Determined to reach the northern land.[24]

As is characteristic of these lines (translated from the Ndebele), the praise poem comprises a cumulative series of praise names applying to a single person. Sometimes the apostrophising mode is interspersed with passages of narrative, with statements and commentary. In royal praises, there were usually details of military campaigns in which the authority of the king was confirmed in relation to his lineage, subjects and victories, and in which criticism – depending on how much freedom the king was seen to allow his court poet – could be levelled at the king's conduct in battle, or at his capacities in government. Praising, as White aptly puts it, is about the power of chieftaincy. But, it is also – I shall suggest – about the insecurities and mobilities of change.

In the light of this, I want to look initially at the character and scope of the praise poem as a form that has remained resilient in its potential for renewal and relevance. The praise poem is in fact southern Africa's most characteristic form of literary expression which, prior to its written recordings in the nineteenth century, had been observed as early as the seventeenth century at the court of a Shona king.[25] (Some have speculated that royal praisings are survivals of early Egyptian and Babylonian practices.) As I see it, therefore, literary history in southern Africa must attend seriously to the tradition of praise poetry. It is a poetry of duties and obligations which especially in its ancient heroic style raises the question that has recurred in my discussion of oral expression: how do purposes and forms that might strike the reader today as backward-looking engage the contemporary moral and literary sensibility? As a start, we need to remind ourselves that in confining the praise poem to the eulogies of powerful kings, we limit its manifold social significance. Besides entrenching the rule of the leader and proclaiming his excellence, praises provided and continue to provide a focus of communal identity and solidarity, and range from encouraging the warrior in battle to acknowledging cattle for their milk as part of the necessities of everyday life. In religious service, the praise poet may act as a medium of communication between the living and the ancestors. Even the praises of past kings may not be simply commemorative, but perform purposes of invocation. The bard in his oratory, for example, can be seen to wield a mysterious creative power that conjures up the presence of exemplary past figures: 'Speak him forth!, *Musho!*,' the Zulu audience will cry in encouragement and admiration of the praiser.

There are many other formal occasions at which praises have ceremonial functions: harvest festivals, weddings, and times of initiation. Among the Sotho, where there is a strong tradition of praises, boys at the time of their initiation are expected to declaim the praises of their achievements and, in drawing on this living practice, the Sotho poet D. C. T. Bereng, who emerged in the 1920s, composed the first collection of original written poems in seSotho in the manner of praises.[26] (We shall see similar written adaptations in several other poets, notably in the work of the Xhosa S. E. K. Mqhayi.) Bereng does not merely imitate the ancient panegyric. Rather, in praising Moshoeshoe as the founder of the Sotho nation, he intersperses his descriptions of heroic battles with passages of personal reflection, thoughts and experiences which show the influences of his Christian education in the gospel and the pastor's sermon. In 'Poem on the Death of Moshoeshoe'[(t)] the great days of the Sotho king's reign are remembered as the time, in the late 1820s, when he united scattered groups which were fleeing Shaka's invaders. The historical memory, however, prompts Bereng to meditate on contemporary decline. In the 1920s Lesotho found itself wracked by disputes among an ever-increasing number of petty chieftains, and the praiser assumes the role of national prophet in warning his people to recollect and reassess the example of Moshoeshoe's wise, balanced rule:

> I shall study the history of fallen kings
> And seek the cause of their downfall.
> I shall think of administrative ways
> of various governments,
> And end up by saying,
> 'People are superior to their ruler,
> But the law is superior to the people,
> And God is superior to the law.'[t]

If the praise poem is closely associated with royal praisers, it is also popular in its composition and use. During research in KwaZulu in the 1970s, for example, Elizabeth Gunner recorded many praises by Zulu women confirming their identity, status and achievements while airing their complaints usually in traditionalist, polygamous households where tensions and rivalries had arisen among co-wives, or between a husband's mother and his wives.[27] Such statements in the form of the praise poem were regarded as socially acceptable ways of giving public expression to anger, grief or joy: the personal emotion is permitted to be told in a convention that removes itself slightly from the personal story and hints at artistic ordering of the response. The ordinary use of praises has also been recorded among the Shona in northern Zimbabwe who, unlike the southern groups that experienced the *mfecane*, have never been united under a succession of strong leaders. As a result, the Shona do not have the same emphasis as the Zulu or Sotho on royal praising; rather, the shift has been to civic values. According to A. C. Hodza and George Fortune, however, praises are fast disappearing among the Shona under the activities of education and urbanisation.[28]

In South Africa, by contrast, the praise poet has continued to function in what is sometimes an anomalous relation to the politics of power. In the Transkei (the former self-governing Bantustan created out of ancestral Xhosa territory by the engineerings of apartheid), the role of the modern praise singer has been documented by Jeff Opland as one of increasing impotence.[29] Following the example of S. E. K. Mqhayi, who in the 1920s found new critical uses for praises, bards such as D. L. P. Yali-Manisi and S. M. Z. Burns-Ncamashe spoke out in the 1970s on the need for desegregated education and opportunity. At the same time, they had to keep in mind that Kaiser Matanzima, their prime minister and effectively therefore their 'chief', was widely regarded by black people as a stooge installed by the Pretoria government. In KwaZulu – the former Zulu Bantustan – official praisers at ceremonial occasions have had to tread a difficult and skilful path between being servants and masters of the tradition. In J. C. Dlamini's praises, for example, the conventions of royal utterance with praise names and recognitions of genealogies have been used to link the achievements of the current monarch, King Goodwill Zwelithini, to the glory of Shaka, the founder of the Zulu nation. But King Goodwill has been seen also to be subject to the authority of both the South African government and his powerful uncle and chief minister, Mangosuthu Buthelezi. Whatever the skills of their oratory, therefore, contemporary royal praisers like Dlamini are going to be regarded as politically compromised by the city-based, ANC-aligned praisers who in the 1980s pushed older forms towards the content of 'the struggle'.

When we listen to Alfred Temba Qabula's 'Praise Poem to FOSATU'[t] (Federation of SA Trade Unions), it is difficult to know whether the appellation 'traditional' is adequate, or even accurate. Initially composed on paper and in the early 1980s delivered in Xhosa/Zulu at worker rallies, Qabula's eulogy addresses the trade-union movement as the protector (the chief) of its members (its subjects):

> You moving forest of Africa.
> When I arrived the children were crying,
> These were the workers, industrial workers,
> Discussing the problems that affect them in the industries
>   they work for in Africa.[t]30

Leading his large audience through abrupt changes of language-register and poetic convention, Qabula begins in the mode of apostrophe with FOSATU personified in several praise names: the moving forest of Africa, the hen that protects the chickens, the lion that roars in Pretoria. This gives way to dramatic, colloquial interchange, in which workers argue with bosses, while religious invocation – both traditional-African and Christian in the mixed references – seems not to regard itself as being at odds with the truth of economic law: 'Mvelinqangi and the ancestors have answered us, and sent to us FOSATU! . . . Teach us FOSATU about the past organisations before we came.'[t] If, as Karin Barber argues,[31] the traditional and the elite forms are both valued as symbolic capital (the former as rich cultural heritage, the latter as evidence of progress and enlightenment), then 'Praise Poem to FOSATU' is probably best classified as 'popular'. The popular is opportunistic, hybrid or syncretic in its unashamed, 'unlearned' borrowings from the past and the present as it shows its lack of respect for any demarcations between Africa and the

West. It is accessible to the indigenous people in its turning away from English to the African-language idiom of the masses, and is also peculiarly attuned to conditions of social instability. Arising from people's situations, the popular – as in Qabula's praise poem – mingles radical-political discourses with the tags of older expression as it tries to find community in the ragged experience of the city. The popular is a category which helps us to define the separatist church ceremony I described earlier. Possibly, too, the 'Kamuzu' songs from Malawi combine the traditional and the popular. By its wide, undeniable, assertive presence in Africa as a whole, the popular demands serious literary-historical consideration.

As Qabula's eulogy suggests, in expressions of praising discontinuities are as significant as continuities, and in looking at ancient royal panegyrics to the Zulu kings Shaka and Dingana, I want to return to my concern as to what, today, we might make of these older forms. In the lengthy 'Praises to King Shaka',[t] for example, we are presented with a trail of blood and achievement. The heads of rival groups are clubbed in with unquenchable relish, and the boasting seems to permit no qualification to the chauvinist ethos:

> Son of the the righteous one, he who thunders on the
>   ground,
> bird, devourer of other birds,
> great leaper who bounds over all others
> . . .
> He felled Nomahlanyana born to the king Zwide,
> he slaughtered Sikhunyana born to Zwide,
> he felled Nqubeni and Mphepha,
> He ate up Dayingubo born to Zwide.
> . . .
> Shaka! I fear to speak the name Shaka!
> For Shaka was king of the people of Mashobane.
> Raving mad he ravened among the towns
> and till dawn came the towns called to each other.
> He seized firmly the assegais of his father,
> he who was like the maned lion.[t]

The text reaches us in several Zulu-language versions recorded and collated by James Stuart and subsequently edited by others and translated into English. Stuart, who was born of British parentage in Pietermaritzburg, acquired from Zulu children a fluent command of the language. As a civil servant and magistrate in various districts of Zululand between 1888 and 1912, he made an intensive study of Zulu customs, history and oral tradition, obtaining verbatim reports from a great number of old Zulu men some of whom had served under Dingana, who reigned from

1828 when he wrested the Zulu kingship from his half-brother Shaka to 1840 when he was displaced by his own half-brother Mpande. Among the numerous praise poems recited to Stuart by practising praise poets in the early years of this century were the memorial praises of Shaka and Dingana.[32]

While Stuart's project offers invaluable data to the researcher, it has been criticised for its tendency to remove the texts from their informing contexts and to subscribe to an ideology identified as royalist, separatist, and static in its conception of a pure Zulu culture. It was a conception of Zuluness that Stuart with characteristic colonial conservatism hoped to preserve from processes of modernisation. The problem is that few commentators have attempted to re-position and re-interpret Stuart's material in any living context. Yet royal praises bear the marks of their different subjects. The 'Praises of Dingiswayo'[(t)], for example, reflect the contradictory nature of a man who was regarded as humane and enlightened, though opportunistic, in beginning to build the kingdom that Shaka would consolidate. In trying to dramatise Dingiswayo's character, respondents have set images of the homestead (the calabash, corn, marriage) in qualification with images of war: particularly the spear that reverberates like a leitmotif, and mythologises Dingiswayo as the leader who left home with a spear in his back and returned, resurrected, to lead his people in conquest.[33] After gaining Dingiswayo's military support Shaka, junior son of Senzangakhona (ruler of a small chiefdom known as the Zulu), wrested the throne from his father's nominated heir and from 1818 began to accumulate his power by conquest as chief of the Zulu. As Shaka strode beyond the station of being a chief by the people, his praises – we are led to believe by several of Stuart's respondents – resounded with his victories and seemed to eliminate any critical element by which he could be called to account. Recited at the time by specialist court poets, these royal praises certainly had the primary purpose of evoking the king's power; nevertheless, we should not be too ready to regard the praiser, even of an all-powerful king, as merely sycophantic. In the dramatic recitation of Shaka's praises, there may have been tremors in the voice or posture as the demands of image-building clashed with the praiser's own convictions, or fears. Several innovative phrases as well as ironic twists that could undercut a portrait of commemoration with a sardonic reminder of the leader's character or behaviour, for example, occur in the praises of Dingana which were attributed by several of Stuart's respondents to Magolwana kaMkhathini (referred to as the 'mother of all praisers') who served Dingana, Mpande and Cetshwayo.[34] Possibly Magolwana was an exceptionally talented imbongi (praise poet); possibly his invention was spurred, paradoxically, by a decline in the singular Shakan image of the strong king in relation to the growing complexity of black/white political arrangements. Dingana, after all, had to deal with a colonial settlement that was harbouring Zulu refugees as well as with the blustering arrival in Zulu territory of Piet Retief's trekkers.

Despite a memorial emphasis in the izibongo (praise poem), therefore, there is no ultimate rigidity to the message or form, and praises by different contributors may be consolidated, or amended, or even dropped. What does seem to distinguish royal praising from everyday forms of speech is its limited use of the common euphonic qualities of alliteration, assonance and onomatopoeia. Instead, the magnitude of the event is captured in the extended simile-like praise names which, in their meta-phoric resonance and allusiveness, contribute to the somewhat archaic, formal power of the address. The imbongi glories in the command of royal performance, and while it is easy to be swept along by the recitation of accumulated images into a past age of blood and thunder, questions persist as to whether the ancient panegyric should, or can, be recovered as anything but a curiosity. In attempting to remove the izibongo from the respective fields of anthropologists, linguists and formalist literary critics none of whom he feels has any interest in the substance of what is being advocated in the texts, Landeg White situates praises in their specific histories as records of power relations ('Where chieftaincy has lost its meaning, the Praise Poem will be in decline').[35] This at least restores content to the praises and, in illustration, he offers several cases for consideration.[36] White's largely economic interest, however, prevents his granting credence to what he himself identifies as the urgency of human response. What needs to be considered, it seems to me, is the praise poem as psychological drama in its historical circumstance. In the case of 'Praises to King Shaka'[t], such an emphasis requires not only that we restore credible human motivation to the figure of Shaka, but that we speculate on the court poet's ploys of persuasion, gestures of defiance and modes of symbolic representation. The difficulty is that the details we have of Shaka are the stuff of romance, epic, tragedy and myth. With doubts about his legitimacy as his father's heir (he was conceived before Senzangakhona had become chief) and with his mother Nandi having been driven from his father's court on account of her temper, Shaka suffered the bullying and mockery of his playmates who resented his claim to the chieftaincy. We have a study here of the great, but flawed individual – familiar to classical Greek and Renaissance dramatic inheri-tance – who grows up with a strong determination to assert himself and with a thirst for power. Having ascended to the chieftaincy by killing his father's nominated heir, Shaka by brilliant military innovation and cease-less conquest welded together the Zulu kingdom while dispersing his enemies across the South African veld as far afield as modern Zimbabwe, Zambia, Malawi and Tanzania. Overreaching himself by subjecting his warriors to endless campaigns and rigid sexual prohibitions in the service of their regiments, he met his death when he was assassinated by Dingana.

Yet even as the people in the kingdom sighed with relief, they realised that greatness had touched the Zulu.

This, at least, is one version of the Shaka story. There are many different versions in travellers' tales, diaries, popular novels by white writers, Black Consciousness poems, films and television series.[37] Seemingly too immense for any one account, Shaka emerges as both hero (the Africanist nation builder) and villain (the blood-thirsty savage of the colonial record): in other words, as the construct of his various authors' own prejudices, preferences and political agendas. In current rivalries between the ANC and the Inkatha Freedom Party, for example, Inkatha leader Buthelezi has played shrewdly on Shakan Zuluness in challenging ANC influence among Zulus, and in securing for himself a power base in KwaZulu-Natal. What the constructions of Shaka's image suggest is the convergence of literature and history according to which both the fiction-writer and the historian utilise narratives, plots, characters, settings, metaphors and ideologies in promoting their particular projects of the past. In seeking a usable past, therefore, we might decide to consider Shaka as neither hero nor villain, but as a figure more astute and sensitive than has generally been portrayed by numerous traders, adventurers, gun-runners, slavers, and lusters after Zulu women who, in the 1820s, represented the rough-neck encroachment of the British colony of Natal on to Zulu custom and territory. In subjecting Nathaniel Isaacs' *Travels* – long regarded as an authentic source of Natal history – to deconstructive textual analysis, for example, we may take note of Isaacs' advice to Henry Fynn, trader and gun-seller among the Zulu: 'Make the Zulu as bloodthirsty as you can' in order to pursuade the British government to annex Natal: a move that would have stood to benefit the fortune-seeker Isaacs.[38]

Such readings of history as narrative, of course, need to retain a purchase on the events of history as a yardstick of evaluation. Accordingly, a re-interpretation of Shaka hero and Shaka villain as Shaka human being strikes at the core of traditional white views of the *mfecane*: that Shaka's conquests were those of a savage force which defied rationality or analysis. What revisionism begins to see is a Zulu kingdom that was not entirely secure in its military might, but was having to respond to a conflictual state of affairs: Shaka, undoubtedly an exceptional being, may also be understood in relation to surrounding shifts of authority, influence and territorial occupation consequent upon the beginnings of the colonial advance into older Zulu social organisations.[39] Shaka may be regarded, therefore, as both belligerent and insecure; his wars both aggressive and defensive, expansive and conservative; and in re-locating his praises in the living past, we might want to consider whether the hyperbole and relentless catalogue of victories ('he slaughtered Sikhunyana born to Zwidi') feature simply as the documentation of a bloody age, or whether the boasting style perhaps hints at a more complicated, even devious rhetorical act concerning the obligation of the court poet to bolster the image of the kingdom at the same time as he fictionalises its immunity from intrusions on its borders. If we are prepared to grant the praiser his own humanity in a psychology of poetry and social duty in which he has to tell lies truer than the truth, we may become attuned to the resonance of several lines and phrases that persist in Stuart's variants of Shaka's praises. When the praiser announces that Shaka's name is fear – 'Shaka! I fear to speak the name Shaka!'[t] – the thrill of admiration could have been mingled almost imperceptibly with the thrill of terror as the court poet in resorting to the grand statement of public ceremony attempted to conceal the dangerous political situation from his powerful, but explicably human king. After Shaka's assassination in 1828, the colonial intrusion took root in Zululand, and in Dingana's reign the praiser Magolwana in lines consistently attributed to his invention eulogised the living-dead through the destruction of the enemy as, simultaneously, he sounded the death knell of a heroic age of action:

> Though people may die, their praises remain,
> These will remain and bring grief to them,
> Remain and lament for them in the empty houses.[t]40

The words echo eerily especially in strife-torn KwaZulu-Natal as a warning not to underestimate the complexities of people in history. The ancient royal praises are as much about processes of modernisation as about glorious chiefdoms. At least, that is how they should be understood to *live* in their reception.[41]

Notes

1. See the histories referred to in D. N. Beech, *The Shona and Zimbabwe: 900–1850* (Gwelo, 1980); P. Chidyausiku, *Broken Roots: A Biographical Narration on the Culture of Shona People in Zimbabwe* (Gweru, 1984); M. Gilfand, *The Genuine Shona: Survival Values of an African Culture* (Gwelo, 1973); M. M. Fuze, *The Black People and Whence They Came*[t] (Pietermaritzburg, 1979; 1992); W. D. Hammond-Tooke (ed.), *The Bantu-speaking Peoples of Southern Africa* (London, 1974); I. Schapera (ed.), *The Bantu-speaking Tribes of South Africa* (London, 1937); L. Thompson, *African Societies in Southern Africa* (London, 1969); L. Vail (ed.), *The Creation of Tribalism in Southern Africa* (Berkeley, 1989).

2. For example, A. F. Gardiner, *Narrative of a Journey to the Zoolu Country in South Africa* (London, 1836; Cape Town, 1966), p. 59.

3. Available in the sombre, dignified recording of the 150-voice choir of the

African Methodist Episcopal Church 'Nkosi Sikelel' iAfrika' is of course
the national anthem in Zambia and Zimbabwe and, as the official song of the
ANC, has become South Africa's national anthem sung in tandem during
the phase of national unity with 'Die Stem'. See D. D. T. Jabavu, 'The Origin
of "Nkosi Sikelel' iAfrika" ', *The Influence of English on Bantu Literature* (Alice,
1943).

4. F. Laydevant, 'The Praises of the Divining Bones among the Basotho', *Bantu
Studies*, no. 7 (1933). See R. Finnegan, *Oral Literature in Africa* (Oxford, 1970),
for a range of religious forms including funeral dirges (the still-surviving *zilengulo*
songs of the Ila and Tonga in Zambia), Ngoni songs of death in Malawi, and
the rain songs of the Ndau in Mozambique.

5. J. P. Kiernan, 'The Work of Zion: An Analysis of an African Zionist Ritual',
Africa, no. 46 (1976); 'Poor and Puritan: An Attempt to View Zionism as a
Response to Urban Poverty', *African Studies*, no. 36 (1977); 'A Thriving
"Tradition" in a Modern Context: Patterns of Oral Expression in Zionist
Discourse', in E. Sienaert *et al.* (eds), *Oral Tradition and Innovation: New Wine in
Old Bottles?* (Durban, 1991).

6. C. Style and O. Style (eds), *Mambo Book of Zimbabwean Verse in English* (Gweru,
1986).

7. Quoted in D. C. Mulford, *The Northern Rhodesia General Election 1962* (Nairobi,
1964), pp. 133–4.

8. For discussion of 'Kamuzu' songs, see L. White, 'Power and the Praise Poem',
Journal of Southern African Studies, vol. 9, no. 1 (1982), pp. 8–32. Also: L. Vail
and L. White, 'Of Chameleons and Clowns: The Case of Jack Mapanje',
Power and the Praise Poem (Charlottesville and London, 1991), pp. 278–318.

9. Nyembezi, *Zulu Proverbs* (Johannesburg, 1954; Pietermaritzburg, 1990). See also:
S. T. Plaatje, *Sechuana Proverbs with Literal Translations and their European
Equivalents* (London, 1916).

10. P. A. McAllister, 'Political Aspects of Xhosa Beer Drinking Oratory', *English in
Africa*, vol. 15, no. 1 (May 1988); 'Oratory and Innovation in Xhosa Ritual
Practice: The Case of "Making Known the Homestead" ', in E. Sienaert *et al.*
(eds), *Oral Tradition and Innovation*.

11. M. Kunene, 'South African Oral Traditions', in C. Heywood (ed.), *Aspects of
South African Literature* (London, 1976), p. 34.

12. See Scheub's Introduction to Jordan's texts in Jordan's *Tales from Southern Africa*
(Berkeley, 1973); Scheub's *The Xhosa 'Ntsomi'* (Oxford, 1975) and 'Zulu Oral
Tradition and Literature', in B. W. Andrzejewski *et al.* (eds), *Literatures in African
Languages* (Warsaw and Cambridge, 1985), pp. 505–12.

13. P. Chidyausiku, *Broken Roots* (1984); M. Gilfand, *The Genuine Shona* (1973).
See observations about domestication in Shona praise poetry, A. C. Hodza
and G. Fortune, *Shona Praise Poetry* (Oxford, 1979).

14. Callaway, *Nursery Tales, Traditions, and Histories of the Zulus* (Springvale and
London, 1868; Trubner, 1970).

15. Scheub, 'Zulu Oral Tradition and Literature' and Introduction to *Tales from
Southern Africa* [n. 13 above].

16. Jordan, *Tales from Southern Africa* [n. 13 above]; Head, *The Collector of Treasures*
(London, 1977).

17. For the influence of Bunyan's *The Pilgrim's Progress* on African-language writers, see D. B. Ntuli and C. F. Swanepoel, *Southern African Literature in African Languages* (Pretoria, 1993), pp. 20–2. Utilising like Patow the trope of innocence and experience, there are also the allegories that characterise Olive Schreiner's *Trooper Peter Halket of Mashonaland*, J. M. Coetzee's *Life & Times of Michael K* and Charles Mungoshi's rural/urban stories from Zimbabwe. A strong tradition of story telling among the Mbundu has influenced the Angolan stories of Luandino Vieira, and in Mia Couto's stories *Voices Made Night*[1] local Mozambique folk elements combine with South American magical realism to explode the constrictions of ignorance and poverty in allusively socio-psychological experiences.

18. Finnegan, *Oral Literature in Africa*, pp. 74–80.

19. Lestrade, 'Traditional Literature', in I. Schapera (ed.), *The Bantu-speaking Tribes of South Africa*, p. 307.

20. Kunene, 'South African Oral Traditions', pp. 32–4.

21. Dhlomo, 'Nature and Variety of Tribal Drama', *Bantu Studies*, no. 13 (1939).

22. Doke, 'The Basis of Bantu Literature', *Africa*, no. 18 (1948). Also by Doke: 'A Preliminary Investigation into the State of the Native Languages of South Africa with Suggestions as to Research and the Development of Literature', *Bantu Studies*, no. 7 (1933); 'The Native Languages of South Africa', *African Studies*, no. 1 (1942); *The Southern Bantu Languages* (Oxford, 1954); G. Fortune, *Ideophones in Shona* (London, 1962). More generally, R. F. Herbert, *Foundations in Southern African Linguistics* (Johannesburg, 1993).

23. See relevant studies in n. 1 above. Also: T. Asad (ed.), *Anthropology and the Colonial Encounter* (New York, 1973); A. Bergland, *Zulu Thought Patterns and Symbolism* (Uppsala, 1975); M. Bourdillon, *The Shona Peoples: An Ethnography of the Contemporary Shona with Special Reference to their Religion* (Gwelo, 1976); J. Clifford, *The Predicament of Culture: Twentieth-century Ethnography, Literature and Art* (Cambridge, Mass., 1988); J. Fabian, *Time and the Other: How Anthropology Makes Its Object* (New York, 1983); M. Fortes and G. Dieterlein (eds), *African Systems of Thought* (London, 1965); M. Gluckman, 'Social Aspects of First Fruit Ceremonies among the South-eastern Bantu', *Africa*, no. 11 (1938); M. Kunene, 'The Relevance of African Cosmological Systems to African Literature Today', in E. D. Jones (ed.), *African Literature Today, No. 11* (London, 1980); A. Kuper, *The Invention of Primitive Society* (London and New York, 1988); J. Mbiti, *African Religions and Philosophy* (New York, 1968); V. Y. Mudimbe, *The Inventions of Africa: Gnosis, Philosophy, and the Order of Knowledge* (Bloomington, 1988); E. Said, *Orientalism* (New York, 1979); A. Shutte, *Philosophy for Africa* (Cape Town, 1994); M. G. Whisson and M. West (eds), *Religion and Social Change in Southern Africa* (Cape Town and London, 1975); E. Wolf, *Europe and the People without History* (Berkeley, 1982).

24. In *Mambo Book of Zimbabwean Verse*, pp. 6–7. Mzlikazi's Praises recorded by S. J. Nordo and translated by S. J. M. Mhlabi. See: L. Vail and L. White, 'The Art of Being Ruled: Ndebele Praise-Poetry, 1835–1971', in White and T. Couzens (eds), *Literature and Society in South Africa* (Cape Town, 1984), pp. 41–58, and R. K. Rasmussen, *Migrant Kingdom: Mzilikazi's Ndebele in South Africa* (London, 1978).

25. See A. Hodza and G. Fortune, Introduction, *Shona Praise Poetry*, in which they refer to a seventeenth-century Portuguese trader's description of a powerful

feudal king, Changmere, whose court was characterised by 'cacophonous' *marombe* or praise singers. Also: E. M. Chiwome, 'The Shona Folk Song: Legitimation and Subversion', in E. Sienaert *et al.* (eds), *Oral Tradition and Innovation*, pp. 104–9.

26. Bereng, *Dithothokiso tsa Moshoeshoe le tse Ding* (Poems in Praise of King Moshoeshoe and Others, Morija, 1931). See: P. Sanders, *Moeshoeshoe: Chief of the Sotho* (London, 1975) and L. Thompson, *Survival in Two Worlds: Moeshoeshoe of Lesotho, 1786–1870* (Oxford, 1975).

27. Gunner, *'Ukubonga nezibongo'*: Zulu Praising and Praises, unpublished doctoral dissertation (University of London, 1984) as well as several articles based on the dissertation including 'Songs of Innocence and Experience: Women as Composers and Performers of *Izibongo* Zulu Praise Poetry', *Research in African Literatures*, vol. 10, no. 2 (Fall 1979) and 'A Dying Tradition? African Oral Literature in a Contemporary Context', *Social Dynamics*, no. 12 (1986). Texts recorded in Gunner and M. Gwala (eds), *Musho! Zulu Popular Praises* (East Lansing, 1991).

28. Hodza and Fortune, Introduction, *Shona Praise Poetry.* See also: G. Fortune, 'Shona Traditional Poetry', *Zambezia*, no. 2 (1971).

29. See general theme of Opland's *Xhosa Oral Poetry* (Johannesburg, 1983) and 'The Isolation of the Xhosa Oral Poet', in L. White and T. Couzens (eds), *Literature and Society in South Africa*, pp. 175–195.

30. Text in M. Chapman (ed.), *The Paperbook of South African English Poetry* (Johannesburg, 1986), pp. 294–6. Other oral 'worker' poets in A. Sitas (ed.), *Black Mamba Rising: South African Worker Poets in Struggle. Alfred Temba Qabula, Mi S'Dumo Hlatswayo and Nise Malange* (Durban, 1986). See: E. Gunner, 'Mixing the Discourses: Genre Boundary Jumping in Popular Song' and S. Kromberg, 'The Role of the Audience in the Emergence of Durban Worker *Isibongo'*, in E. Sienaert *et al.* (eds), *Oral Tradition and Innovation.* Kromberg's bibliography lists a number of articles that sparked fierce debate in the mid-1980s as to function, form and status of oral 'worker' poetry.

31. Barber, 'Popular Arts in Africa', *African Studies Review*, vol. 30, no. 3 (September 1987), pp. 1–78.

32. For Stuart, see p. 19, Introduction to Part One, n. 2. Shaka's Praises in T. Cope's *Izibongo: Zulu Praise-Poems* (Oxford, 1968), which is an edited version of D. Malcolm's English translation of Stuart's Zulu-language material. Stuart's recordings also provide the source for D. Rycroft and A. B. Ngcobo's *The Praises of Dingana: Izibongo zikaDingana* (Pietermaritzburg, 1988). Possibly Rycroft and Ngcobo's Introduction represents the best scholarly work on the ancient izibongo, including summary and bibliographical reference to the considerable debate surrounding the form. Arguments have concerned the stability of the texts and the form as epic or panegyric (could memory as the means of transmission have organised epic extensions of what was a mode of panegyric? – both C. Mutwa in *Indaba, My Children* (1966) and M. Kunene in *Emperor Shaka the Great* (1978), for example, present written epics as though they are merely copying down in translation what had been passed on to them from collective oral testimony). Other arguments concern dating by means of what Kunene and Cope refer to as loose pre-Shakan eulogies in contrast to the Shakan stanza of statement, extension, development and conclusion. Others have sought stylistic definition in cadential demarcation according to breath unit, in parallelisms and repetitions, while others again have pointed to the context

of occasion as the primary influence on intention, pace and tone. See also, C. L. S. Nyembezi, 'The Historical Background to the Izibongo of the Zulu Military Age', *African Studies*, vol. 7, nos. 2, 3, and 4 (1948).

33. See H. Scheub's perceptive analysis, 'Zulu Oral Tradition and Literature', pp. 512–17, and more generally, Scheub's 'Oral Poetry and History', *New Literary History*, vol. 18, no. 3 (1987).

34. See M. Kunene, 'Portrait of Magolwana – the Great Zulu Poet', *Cultural Events in Africa*, no. 32 (July 1967). Kunene refers to Magolwana as having served Shaka; Rycroft and Ngcobo dispute this and give Shaka's principal imbongi as Mxhamama Ntendeka, p. 32 [n. 34 above].

35. N. 26 above.

36. See earlier articles incorporated into L. Vale and L. White, *Power and the Praise Poem*. Case studies examine the songs of Lomwe people in Mozambique, protest on the Sena Sugar estate in Mozambique, the modifications at different historical moments in praises to Moshoeshoe and Lobengula, and the 'Kamuzu' songs of Malawi (to which I referred earlier in this study).

37. Accounts of early Natal/Zululand history relied largely on the observations of Henry Fynn and Nathaniel Isaacs. In the 1980s standard histories were challenged by Africanist and Marxist revisionists. At the centre of the dispute was the depiction of Shaka in relation to his dispersal of tribes (*mfecane*). See: J. Bird (ed.), *The Annals of Natal 1495 to 1845*, 2 vols (Pietermaritzburg, 1888); A. T. Bryant, *Olden Times in Zululand and Natal* (London, 1929; Cape Town, 1963); H. F. Fynn, *The Diary of Henry Francis Fynn*, eds J. Stuart and D. McK. Malcolm (Pietermaritzburg, 1950) and N. Isaacs, *Travels and Adventures in Eastern Africa*, 2 vols, ed. L. Herrman (Cape Town, 1936–7). For standard modern Natal history see E. H. Brookes and C. de B. Webb, *A History of Natal* (Pietermaritzburg, 1965) and for the first 'revisionary' reading of Shaka's wars, J. D. Omer-Cooper's *The Zulu Aftermath: A Nineteenth-century Revolution in Bantu Africa* (London, 1966) which gave the term *mfecane* contemporary African currency. Ensuing *mfecane* debate in various articles by J. Cobbing, J. Wright and C. Hamilton – see C. Hamilton (ed.), *The 'Mfecane' Aftermath: Credulity and Scepticism in Southern African Historical Debates* (Pietermaritzburg and Johannesburg, 1995). For details of Zulu nationalism see N. Cope, *To Bind the Nation: Solomon kaDinuzulu and Zulu Nationalism 1913–1933* (Pietermaritzburg, 1993). For literary revisions of Isaacs and Fynn see D. Wylie, 'Autobiography as Alibi: History and Projection in Nathaniel Isaacs' *Travels and Adventures in Eastern Africa*', *Current Writing*, vol. 3 (1991) and J. Pridmore 'The Reception of Henry Francis Fynn *c.* 1824–1992', *Current Writing*, vol. 6, no. 1 (1994). Novelistic accounts of Shaka in the colonial tradition include E. A. Ritter's best-selling *Shaka Zulu* (London, 1955) and D. R. Morris's *The Washing of the Spears: A History of the Rise of the Zulu Natal under Shaka and Its Fall in the Zulu War of 1879* (New York, 1965). For the heroic Africanist Shaka, see M. Kunene's *Emperor Shaka the Great: A Zulu Epic* (London, 1979) and several black consciousness poems of the 1970s. For attacks on the SATV series on Shaka see J. Wright and G. More, 'Shaka Zulu: The Splice of Coincidence', *Sunday Tribune*, Durban (7 December 1986) and S. Gray's 'novel', *John Ross: The True Story* (Harmondsworth, 1987) advertised as 'the real events behind the TV serial'. Also, Charles Rawden Maclean, *The Natal Papers of 'John Ross'*, ed. S. Gray (Pietermaritzburg, 1992). Several perspectives on Shaka in J. Peires (ed.), *Before and After Shaka* (Grahamstown, 1979) and for key elements in revisionist *mfecane* theory – that colonial trade intrusions into Shaka's kingdom exacerbated

tensions and contributed to territorial anxieties – see A. Smith, 'The Trade of Delagoa Bay as a Factor in Nguni Politics 1750–1835', in L. Thompson (ed.), *African Societies in Southern Africa* (London, 1969).

38. See D. Wylie [n. 37 above].

39. See A. Smith [n. 37 above].

40. Zulu-English text of 'The Praises of Dingana' in D. Rycroft and Ngcobo [n. 33 above].

41. See I. Hofmeyr's '*We Spend Our Years as a Tale That is Untold: Oral Historial Narrative in a South African Chiefdom* (Johannesburg, 1993; London, 1994), in which it is argued that crucial to an understanding of oral literature are 'material' rather than 'essential' recognitions that forms have been affected by the institutions of schools, missions and state bureaucracy including the practices of 'forced removals', the division of labour between men and women, and the 'oral' influence of modern communications technology (radio and, to a lesser extent, television).

Part Two
Writing of European Settlement: South Africa 1652–1910

Introduction to Part Two

Oral tradition can never return completely to a pre-colonial starting point, and in establishing contact as readers with its continued vitality, we are reminded that the impact of European settlement has left its mark on a great deal of African expression. We are also reminded, however, that the West – in the written word of its documentation, in its religion, ideologies, economies, institutions, moral schemas and aesthetic values – has never succeeded in subsuming the African voice. In fact, we could see colonialism as having forced the people of the continent to develop a sense of their identity as African. As I said at the outset, the categories Europe and Africa are complicit in each other's history, and an African perspective on the writing of European settlement need not involve simply dismissive argument. Rather, colonial fears and phobias need to be understood at the same time as we attempt to identify what forces of integrity there might have been in the writing.

This requires that distinctions be made within the general term 'colonial'. Some white writers are colonial in remaining nostalgically subject to the home country; others, while remaining partly subject, are able to look at the local situation. But further distinctions are important between those who looked at the local scene only to prop up preferential settler orders and those who have been willing to turn a critical eye on the motherland in its failure to live up to its own ideals in the practice of its 'civilising mission'. To use Albert Memmi's terms, some colonials are conservative, or reactionary (colonisers who *will* impose their authority through notions of conquest or occupation); others are humane, philanthropic, and troubled in conscience (colonisers who *won't* resort to the gun or sjambok in acts of annihilation and annexation).[1] Of course, the talisman of the 'colonist who won't' – the Bible – has its own ambiguity: its colonising activity is aimed at changing the entire world view of the convert to whom it is devoted.

Whether sojourners or settlers, few early colonials had a conception of home on the subcontinent, and those who 'struck root' did so usually without seriously questioning the appropriateness of the European standard in Africa. Despite this, such writing should not be ignored in any

literary-historical study. As in oral tradition, its conservatism has explanatory importance in reflecting a sense of insecurity in situations of large-
scale socio-cultural change. This may have resulted at times in colonial
commentaries of aggression and demonisation: through the medium of
print, for example, settler opinions of the frontier problem were given
the weight of fact. We should distinguish, nevertheless, between kinds of
anxiety and kinds of rant while remaining consistent to the reconstructive
purpose of seeking the creative potential of truth claims. By the 1820s,
after all, the language of dignity and rights – the inheritance of the
enlightenment – had begun to make itself heard at the Cape.

Two important aspects of European settlement in southern Africa
were the missionary enterprise among indigenous communities, and the
forming of a new group of people on the African continent, the Afrikaners, who would continue to regard themselves as European in racial
hierarchies of master and servant, but who saw their home and destiny
in Africa. In relation to European settlement, therefore, it makes sense to
discuss the start of written literature among the Xhosa, the earliest
indigenous people in southern Africa to encounter the colonial and
missionary presence in a systematic way. It also makes sense, in the
context of European settlement, to consider the beginnings of Afrikaans
expression. As I have suggested, the comparative method does not operate
on the principle that different languages necessarily preserve their discrete
literary systems. Rather, cultural translation involves the interchange of
British, Boer and Xhosa in the colonised territory. I shall begin by tracing
a few founding archetypes of the European imagination in southern
Africa and then devote more detailed commentary to the effects of British
occupation. The arrival at the Cape of the 1820 settlers led to a permanent and an influential English-speaking community in South Africa.
Turning from commentary on Xhosa and Afrikaans writing, I shall conclude this part of the study by looking at the substantial beginnings of
fictional forms for what they reveal about the story of the colony.

The focus is on South Africa. Chronologically, this is apt. By the end
of the nineteenth century, South Africa had experienced 250 years of
active colonial life. The process was more haphazard in Angola and
Mozambique where written literature emerged with regularity only in
the early twentieth century. As far as Zimbabwe, Zambia, Malawi and
Namibia were concerned, white settlement began to be established in
the 1890s. Part Three will examine the pre-independence period in some
of these countries.

Note

1. Memmi, *The Colonizer and the Colonized*[t] (London, 1990; 1957).

Chapter 1

Images of Africa, 1652–1820

Adamastor and the savage land

The Cape – the 'Cape of Storms' – first became known to Europe as a result of exploratory voyages undertaken by the Portuguese in the search for a sea route to India. Renamed the Cape of Good Hope in 1487 by Bartolomeu Dias, the Cape remained relatively neglected as the Portuguese established stop-over bases on the Mozambique coast. With shipwreck stories of gloom and horror appearing in pamphlets and keeping the popular Lisbon press busy in the sixteenth century, the Cape grew in the evil reputation it had gained in Portuguese lore when, in 1510, the viceroy Francesco de Almeida and a number of his companions, returning from India, were killed by Khoi whom they had robbed in the course of a foraging expedition from Table Bay. The clash confirmed an already-existing European iconography in which the inhabitants of Africa were depicted in stages of wild primitiveness. But it was not only the presence of people that provoked various, usually emotive observations: descriptions of the landscape veer in the records from the mirror-image of the Mediterranean paradise in climate, vegetation and, later, in viticulture to the dreary, ominous shoreline of the shipwreck story. In travel accounts, journeys across the semi-arid Karoo confirmed a vast and empty psychological and social space. In short, Africa answered Europe's requirements of the *other* place and, in the numerous early narratives of sea voyaging and travels to the interior, ideational projection ranges from that of the golden age of discovery, in which the foreign land filled with grotesqueries invites conquest by the confident Renaissance culture, to that of the age of reason: the rational, scientific observer mapping the territory, classifying the fauna and flora. The landscape and the people are thus created and re-created, and criticism influenced by post-structuralism has begun to utilise semiotics – reality as texts of power and desire – in order to interpret early colonial accounts as ideologies of the European venture, or adventure. If this is where the literature of European settlement begins, it is because the journeys and encounters struck on forms of action and codes of value that had, and still have, archetypal significance in justifying the taming and naming of the savage land according to Western Christian precept.[1]

What the literary interpretation of these records reveals is that beneath the apparently stabilising functions of myth remain doubts, uncertainties and ambiguities as to whether the white person – usually the white man – can ever 'know' Africa. The schism is already evident in the great Portuguese epic *The Lusiads* (1572)[(t)],[2] written by the national poet Luis de Camoëns in honour of Vasco da Gama, who on his victorious voyage to the East encountered the irrational pagan Bacchus-figure, Adamastor: the rocky headland of the Cape metamorphosed by Camoëns into a giant spirit of Africa. Having been exiled from the pantheon of Greek gods, Adamastor lurks in the southern waters helpless against the panache displayed by the sons of Lusus (Portugal) in their rite of passage from the hardships of maritime endeavour to the riches of the East. Nonetheless, Adamastor disturbs the moment of glory by invoking upon da Gama and all his European successors a terrible curse that has taken on increasingly menacing proportions and has echoed through the literature and history of European conquest and settlement on the subcontinent. The first English translation of *The Lusiads* by Sir Richard Fanshawe in 1655 had emphasised the unabashed advantages of European trade and, as in Camoëns's original, had depicted Adamastor as somewhat preposterous. In W. J. Mickle's version (1778) Adamastor becomes a vast and ominous spirit of a continent resisting the imperial mission. This was Roy Campbell's inspiration for his poem 'Rounding the Cape' which was written in 1926. Giving vent at the time to some of his own youthful spleen at dull colonials, Campbell has Adamastor threatening to rise from his centuries-long sleep in order to bring down destruction on the colonial house: 'The land lies dark beneath the rising crescent,/And Night, the Negro, murmurs in his sleep.'[3] Arguments continue to surround Campbell's depictions: progressive in their symbolic suggestion of Africa eventually vanquishing the European invader; regressive in that Africa continues to be seen as a dark force; patriarchally myopic in that Thetis – Peleus' wife whom Adamastor desires – is usually silenced in the story.[4] She ends as the sea lapping around the rocky Cape, and whether or not she can be recuperated by modern feminism from nature's teasing femininity and identified as culture's uncolonised repressed, the Adamastor encounter remains very much a white *man's* creation myth of agonised self-appraisal. Thus the land is hard; the great peninsula thrusts out into the southern seas inviting physical and metaphysical confrontation between the known and the unknown. Clustered around the topos are the motifs of challenge and defiance, possession and dispossession, belonging and alienation. The da Gama/Adamastor encounter in its various forms, including that of Apollo and Dionysus, appears in numerous nineteenth-century occasional colonial pieces of salutation and valediction and, periodically, in the work of almost every prominent twentieth-century South African poet. What is registered is the ambivalence of white South Africans about the European-African antinomies in their heritage and commitments.[5]

Dutch records and Afrikaner identity

This ambivalence about Africa has seemed more pronounced in English-speaking South Africans than in Afrikaners. But even though Afrikaner-dom continues to justify itself in myths of belonging to the continent, Afrikaans literature has always displayed a high degree of anxiety about ownership and control. A founding text is Jan van Riebeeck's *Daghregister* (Journal, 1651–62).[6] In the early seventeenth century, the Cape came to be used as a regular watering place by English and Dutch vessels on their way to and from the Indies, and in 1652 Van Riebeeck, in the service of the Dutch East India Company, arrived as commander at the Cape to set up a new post. During the period of his administration (1652–62), Van Riebeeck thought he was keeping a faithful record of daily occurrences, his main responsibility being to secure and ensure a regular supply of food for passing ships. What his *Journal*[t] reveals, however, is a mind continually ill at ease with itself as observations of the surrounding situation skew into psychologies of confession and self-justification. Van Riebeeck, a doctor turned factor, becomes harassed and despairing at his failure to strike deals for cattle with the Khoi on the perimeter of his 'settlement' and, with his mind in the grip of authoritarian fantasies, his record reads as an autobiography about cheating, robbing and killing the troublesome Khoi, who are depicted as the phantoms of his obsessions. Beginning to feel that he was serving a penance in a dreary outpost, Van Riebeeck cast his gaze frequently across the mountains inland beyond which, he mused and imagined, were to be found gold and other riches in the mystical and mythical interior. As it happened, the place of riches in the African interior would become a trope of the history and literature with adventure-writer H. Rider Haggard fictionalising lost cities, the mining magnate Cecil John Rhodes pursuing his quest beyond diamond and gold discoveries in South Africa to the ruins of Great Zimbabwe (the Mwene Mutapa kingdom), and hotel magnate Sol Kerzner, in a mixture of architectural bravura and dreams of metamorphosis, creating his pleasure resort, The Lost City, in the middle of the arid former Bantustan of Bophuthatswana. Van Riebeeck saw himself as a badly displaced Dutch bourgeois; his *Journal*, however, evokes the rudiments of a history in South Africa that would be characterised by suspicion, uncertainty, arrogance and pig-headedness. The poet-critic D. J. Opperman is even more specific. In seeking the beginnings of Afrikaans literature, he argues for the inclusion of early Dutch records like Van Riebeeck's *Journal* not because the language in use was yet Afrikaans, but because the spirit of the encounter had begun to capture something of the Afrikaans experience.[7]

During the years of initial Dutch settlement, this experience manifested itself in localised struggles which often involved hostilities between the Dutch East India Company and its former employees. As farming undertaken by full-time employees proved inefficient, Company servants were offered their own land. These free burghers represent the beginnings of a permanent white community. During the reign of governor Willem Adriaan van der Stel, conflict between the bourgeois entrepreneurial interests of the free burghers, many of whom had become successful farmers, and the trade monopoly of the Dutch East India Company led, in 1705, to organised protest against Van der Stel by Adam Tas whose *Dagregister* (Diary, 1668–1722),[8] conveys in elegant Dutch the spirit of independence that has subsequently been mythologised as a defining characteristic of Afrikaner identity. Refuting the seminal significance of Tas's *Diary*[t] in Afrikaans literature, however, André du Toit and Hermann Giliomee locate the beginnings of thought that conceivably could be called 'Afrikaans' in the 1820s: in reactions by Dutch colonists to British policies on the eastern frontier of the Cape colony.[9] Tas's battles, according to du Toit and Giliomee, are Dutch-European in focus, character and style. These analysts nonetheless point to the canonisation of Tas by Afrikaner nationalist historiography in its construction of the Afrikaner nation. In his introduction to the *Diary*, for example, editor Leo Fouché gives exemplary status to Tas as a voice of Afrikanerdom in comparison to governor Van der Stel whose corruption and venality are described as, *naturally*, the result of the governor's having had mixed blood in his veins.[10] This comment has been allowed to stand in the reprint published in 1970 by the Van Riebeeck Society (est. 1918), the oldest historical society in South Africa. Reacting to attempts earlier than Fouché's to appropriate Tas to the Afrikaner cause, Ian D. Colvin – the colonial journalist and Africana enthusiast – argued that the noble document of the time was not Tas's *Diary*, but Van der Stel's *Korte Deduktie* (Brief Memorial), or *Apologia*, which charged Tas and other free burghers with stealing cattle from the Khoi. The triumph of Tas's views, Colvin concluded, was a triumph of lawlessness and poor government on the frontier.[11] We are reminded by such conflicting interpretations of the need to energise the 'political unconscious' of the earliest records. Even the aims and objectives of the Africana series require political scrutiny. Certainly a literary history with any progressive intent cannot follow a current history of Afrikaans literature and be content simply to praise

Van Riebeeck's *Journal* for its accurate descriptions of the country and its people.[12] As I have suggested, Van Riebeeck constructs the Cape in the images of his own traumatised experience.

In the years preceding the Tas affair, events of crucial importance for the future development of Afrikaans had occurred with the arrival at the Cape of French and Belgian Huguenots (Calvinist Protestants), who joined the white population of mainly Dutch and German nationalities. With the use of French being discouraged, the Huguenots adopted Dutch and were absorbed by the Dutch Reformed Church which, through its rigid, puritanical doctrines, played a major role in shaping the character and outlook of the growing free-burgher population. Despite the Dutch Bible having had a powerful stabilising influence on the language in daily use, the European languages felt the proximity of Khoi and African dialects as well as the spoken Malay of slaves. (Slaves had been imported as part of the official policy of the Dutch East India Company.) The result was that a new language, Afrikaans, gradually evolved from Dutch. Virtually stripped of its inflexions, preserving only nine strong verbs, and marked by features possibly revealing Bantu influence such as a superabundance of diminutives and double negatives, Afrikaans began to be spoken between the close of the seventeenth century and the British occupation of the Cape in 1795.[13]

The significance of an *eie taal* (own language) remains central to the Afrikaner mystique of identity and destiny. It was the taal that would unite and sustain struggles against anglicisation while providing for a convenient duality of response to Europe and Africa: as a derivation of European languages, Afrikaans links Afrikaners to the supposedly superior European inheritance; as a language nurtured under the African sun, Afrikaans 'logically' has its roots in local soil. Jack Cope has noted, accordingly, that a subtle and an often unconscious dialectic has persisted since the language first bloomed into an independent literature: 'an opposition of ideas against idealism, of vision and insight against rationalisation, of the writer and poet single-handed and alone wrestling against the dark emotive forces of the self.'[14] Such an emphasis on metaphysics, however, can too easily obscure physical conditions. As farmers began to move from the settlement on the Cape peninsula to the interior in search of grazing lands, they encountered not empty spaces but African habitation. Clashes were inevitable, and the trekboers – Bible in one hand, gun in the other – shaped themselves into narrow patriarchal communities, in which Calvinism was warped into a folk religion entertaining notions of an Elect.[15] Slavery at the Cape had ensured that, in any case, master-servant relationships remained rigidly intact: a white working class did not develop, and much subsequent history in southern Africa can be explained by the myth of a white master class requiring cheap 'non-white' labour.

Against this rather dour start to Afrikaans, it is not entirely unexpected that there should have been a rebellion of the carnivalesque. A Cape-Malay slave Biron was punished in 1707 for singing a *ghoemaliedjie* (a dubious ditty, half in Malay, half in Dutch) in the streets of Cape Town. The gist of these songs was satire directed against the white master or, as the masculinity of the slave was an issue, against the ways of the white madam. Parodying the family spirit of Dutch *piekniekliedjies* (picnic songs) and based on the form of the Indonesian pantum (two four-line rhyming stanzas connected in an ironical relationship that the listener is required to posit), *ghoemaliedjies* grabbed the white person's language, assaulted it with creolised words and, in lewd puns, turned the household order upside down most graphically by the slave cuckolding the master. This tradition of misrule was expanded into the tourist spectacle of an annual 'Coon Carnival'. *Ghoemaliedjies*, which mocked the ditties sung at Dutch outings, underwent further modification in turn to re-emerge in Afrikaans culture as *volksliedjies* (folk songs): cleansed of their sexual licence, *volkslied-jies* have been promoted by nationalist language organisations as the soulful utterance of Afrikanerdom.[16]

British occupation. Barrow's travels. Lady Anne Barnard's letters

A concept of Afrikanerdom which gave exclusive connotations to the volk, or people, would begin to be consolidated towards the end of the nineteenth century. Mobilisation of the volk, however, was virtually guaranteed in advance by the British occupation of the Cape. This occurred initially between 1795 and 1802 when the Cape sea route was kept free of French interference – the forces of revolutionary France having defeated Holland – and again from 1806 onwards when British administration, policies, practices and style systematically began to replace the ramshackle functions of the by then bankrupt Dutch East India Company. In the post-Napoleonic settlement in Europe, Holland in 1814 agreed to sell the Cape colony to Britain for two million pounds. From the perspective of Afrikaans history and literature, anglicisation explains the necessity of revolt. The period from 1795 to 1834, for example, saw the increasing impact on Cape society of ideas associated with the European enlightenment: the emancipation of slaves in 1834 was the strongest example of the new influence. Many of these ideas, which involved questions of human rights, clearly did not suit the type of society that had been developed by whites, based as it was on the hereditary privilege of race. Resentment and anger in Dutch (Boer) communities of the Cape colony resulted, finally, in the mass emigration known as the Great Trek. We should not imagine, however, that only the Dutch Boers in the Cape were opposed to notions of rights and liberties. Despite the beginnings in South Africa of the new evangelical movement, few in the British settlement had sympathy for the humanitarian spirit, and the British rulers at the Cape, *ancien régime* Tories, found themselves at odds not only with the philanthropic lobby of the missionaries, but with the vigorous commercial spirit of 'ordinary' settlers. The 'ordinary' British settler, in fact, usually supported the Dutch sentiment against any extension of rights to non-white people in the colony. The popular mood is caught in Andrew Geddes Bain's lively, occasional verse. Sung to the tune 'Oh what a row', 'The British Settler' was a favourite performance at settler commemorative functions:

> Kafirs lauded and rewarded for their savage, fierce irruption,
> By the folks of Downing Street and Ex'ter Hall!
> Then no checking Boers from *trekking*, fleeing, seeing such
>   corruption;
> Hottentots and Fingoes, saucy vagrants all![17]

Bain, to whom I shall return, was writing his verse after the influx of settlers in 1820. Before that, the years of the first British occupation in the 1790s had attracted numerous travel writers who went on to describe the landscape, record its vegetation, and portray the customs of the indigenous inhabitants.[18] With cultural and scientific traditions influencing ways of seeing, there are distinctions to be made in travelogues by writers of British, French, German, Swedish, and other nationalities. The Frenchman François le Vaillant, for instance, transfigured Nerina, his Hottentot Eve, into a child of sentiment and nature. In the service of British administration, by contrast, Sir John Barrow exemplified the calm, scientific manner. What these travelogues have in common, nonetheless, is the characteristic, which I mentioned earlier, of viewing Africa through European eyes. As far as Barrow was concerned, his mission had a precise purpose (the justification of British rule in a colony settled by the Dutch), and his firm, though reasonably enlightened, response is shaken only once or twice by his encounters with Khoi, Bushmen and Xhosa. For the most part of his journey, he buries his individual self behind the generalising eye and typecasts people according to a scale of British preference and control. As the Bushmen constituted no real political threat, they are granted a rare tone of elegy. When Barrow wrote his *Travels* in 1801, the Xhosa were still a relatively rare sight, and are thus allowed the demeanour of exotic savages. The Khoi, who bore the direct marks of the heavy Dutch hand, are somewhat rehabilitated as a reminder of the more humane British way, and the chief rivals, the Dutch –

African peasants, Barrow called the farmers inland – are exaggerated into caricatures of the idle and the uncouth. As Mary Louise Pratt observes about most of these eighteenth-century travelogues, people in the land-scape are homogenised into icons or scapegoats; customs are regarded as pre-given; and the 'portraits' of life always appear amenable to domination by the national flag of the travel writer.[19] In other words, whatever its pretensions to scientific and historical investigation, the travel document is a document of ideology. In Burchell's *Travels* (1822, 1824), for example, the interchange with tribes is manipulated to the writer's advantage by his slightly amused tone (the natives are childishly duplicitous) and, as in many other travelogues, assurance is given to the colonising power that the frontier can be stabilised: colonisation is a viable enterprise. Yet the writer so often remains a 'traveller' who finds empathy with neither the land nor its people. At one point, Burchell ruminates on the problem of African species of beauty: continually on the lookout for water and greenery, he eventually gives up and, in a gesture that is slightly absurd, tries instead to harmonise sand, earth and stone into a romantic vista of the picturesque.[20] In his new preface to the second edition of his *Travels into the Interior of Southern Africa* (1806), Barrow also implied that the colony did not have a literature of habitancy; rather his stress on visitation returns us to the earliest captains' logs and explorers' reports:

> Whilst some of our public orators have held it out to be a
> terrestrial paradise, where nature spontaneously yielded all
> that was necessary . . . others have described it as a useless
> and barren peninsular promontory, connected by a sandy
> isthmus to a still more useless and barren continent.

Whereas Barrow's dreary continent required cartographical definition, the land for less restrained travellers was virgin waiting to be possessed. Lady Anne Barnard's Cape tour, in contrast, reads as an imaginative extension of domestic concern across the peninsula. A notable figure in the years of the first British occupation, Lady Anne has accrued literary status for her shrewd observations of Cape society. Born Lindsay, the eldest child of the 5th Earl of Balcarres, Lady Anne – as the intimate friend of the Prince of Wales and other important members of society – was well connected in London circles when she accompanied her husband Andrew Barnard to the Cape: to which, as a result of her influence, he had been appointed colonial secretary to the new governor, Lord Macart-ney. As Lady Macartney did not accompany her husband, Anne Barnard became the first lady in Cape Town, and with her husband was allocated the largest house in the Castle, so that she could entertain a variety of visitors. Like Barrow, Lady Anne is confidently British in her sense of how a society should evolve, and in her letters to Henry Dundas, secretary for war and the colonies, she is skilled at conveying many insights into British attitudes, behaviour and even policy in the colony. Her letters, which are scrupulous in appearing not to usurp (male) authority, mingle gossip and opinion and, through a form of rhetorical disclaimer ('I'll venture for once to launch a woman's opinion about it'), she makes her points with vigour and clarity.

The idle Boer – Lady Anne writes – is redeemable, and the Khoi should be assisted towards agricultural independence. On the difficult question of slavery, she qualifies her opinions at times with current catch-phrases such as slavery being relatively mild at the Cape. Her letters affirm, nonetheless, that colonisation should entail moral nurture and cultivation, and when British practice or policy seems inhumane, she is prepared to suggest to Dundas that he use his position to effect reform. Her sympathy for the victim usually works in tandem with a practical grasp of some of the more intractable issues of the day:

> perhaps I am about to launch a very foolish Idea – I have
> launched it by way of question in common conversation
> and always found it *Hooted at*, I think it fair to tell you this,
> but I'll launch it to *You* because I have often heard you
> say 'Speak out all your nonsense, Anne, I like to hear every
> body's ideas' – were we to give up to the Caffres that part
> of the country I mention, supposing they stipulate for it &
> supposing that we *can* according to our treaty with the Dutch
> where would be the Harm? . . . if we make peace with the
> Caffres they will gladly furnish us as usual with cattle in
> return for such articles as they want, & if they from time
> to time pillage our farmers, at 200 or 300 miles distance the
> matter will be easier adjusted than if it was 1,000.
> . . .
> the Hottentots are the free natives of the woods and may
> stipulate for fair laws between them & the dutch &
> ourselves for justice in case of breach – if we had protected
> them sooner & forced the farmers to be *just* & kind to
> them I do not believe they would now have turned against
> them.[21]

Lady Anne Barnard's limits are those of her class and are reflected in the 'middle style' of her writing: we hear a patronising humanism mixed with the guilt that characterised a genteel eighteenth-century European manner. When her sentiment and thoughts are stirred, however, the questions posed by her letters remain both thoroughly naive and thoroughly profound, and are aptly summed up by Margaret Lenta as asking whether social integration is not the crucial step towards equality.[22]

Notes

1. For a lively account of the early literature of discovery see I. Colvin's Introduction to the Mendelssohn Collection which has been reprinted conveniently as Ian D. Colvin's *Introduction to Africana being a newly-illustrated reprint of the Introduction to the 'South African Bibliography' by Sidney Mendelssohn, originally published in 1910 with a biographical sketch by Frank R. Bradlow,* A. M. Lewin Robinson (ed.) (Cape Town, 1979). Housed at the Library of Parliament, Cape Town, the Mendelssohn Collection is an invaluable resource and has been published as S. Mendelssohn, *Mendelssohn's South African Bibliography; being the catalogue of the Mendelssohn Library of works relating to South Africa . . .,* 2 vols. (London, 1910) and *A South African Bibliography to the Year 1925; being a revision and continuation of Sidney Mendelssohn's 'South African Bibliography' (1910); edited at the South African Library, Cape Town,* 4 vols. (London, 1979). The Mendelssohn Collection contains a copy of Bernardo Gomes de Brito's *Historia Tragico-Maritima* (Lisbon, 1735), a source of early Portuguese shipwreck stories, some of which Colvin discusses in his Introduction. See also, N. H. Mackenzie, 'South African Travel Literature in the Seventeenth Century', *Archives Yearbook of South African History, Vol. 2* (Pretoria, 1955).

2. G. Bullough (ed.), *The Lusiads, in Sir Richard Fanshawe's Translation* (London, 1963); Wlliam Julius Mickle (tr.), *The Lusiads; or, The Discovery of India* (Oxford, 1778); William C. Atkinson (tr.), *The Lusiads* (Harmondsworth, 1952).

3. Campbell, from the individual volume *Adamastor;* see *Selected Poems* (Johannesburg, 1991), p. 33.

4. See, respectively, M. Chapman, 'Roy Campbell, Poet: A Defence in Sociological Times', *Theoria,* no. 68 (December 1986); J. Cronin, 'Turning Around, Roy Campbell's "Rounding the Cape" ', *English in Africa,* vol. 11, no. 1 (May 1984); D. Driver, 'Women and Nature, Women as Objects of Exchange: Towards a Feminist Analysis of South African Literature', in M. Chapman *et al.* (eds), *Perspectives on South African English Literature* (Johannesburg, 1992).

5. See S. Gray, 'The White Man's Creation Myth of Africa', *Southern African Literature: An Introduction* (Cape Town, 1979) and for details of the influence on other South African poets of the Adamastor myth, M. van Wyk Smith (ed.), *Shades of Adamastor: An Anthology of Poetry* (Grahamstown, 1988). (The anthology contains an invaluable introduction.)

6. H. B. Thom (ed. and tr. from Dutch), *Journal of Jan van Riebeeck,* 3 vols (Cape Town, 1952–58).

7. Opperman, 'Wanneer begin die Afrikaanse Letterkunde?', *Naaldekoker* (Cape Town, 1974), pp. 49–60. (First published, *Die Huisgenoot,* 3 February 1939.)

8. L. Fouché (ed. and tr. from Dutch), *The Diary of Adam Tas (1705–6)* (London, 1914; Cape Town, 1970).

9. See the introductory comments to du Toit and Giliomee, *Afrikaner Political Thought: Analysis and Documents, Vol.1, 1780–1850* (Cape Town, 1983). (No further volumes have hitherto appeared in this projected series.)

10. Fouché, *The Diary of Adam Tas,* p. 11.

11. Colvin, *Introduction to the South African Bibliography by Sidney Mendelssohn . . .,* pp. liii–liv.

12. J. C. Kannemeyer, *Die Afrikaanse Literatuur, 1652–1987* (Cape Town, 1988), p. 17. See in contrast J. M. Coetzee, 'Idleness in South Africa', *White Writing* (New Haven, 1988), pp. 12–35, and J. Naidoo, 'Was the "Van Riebeeck Principle" a Plea for Peace or a Plea for Plunder?', *Tracking Down Historical Myths: Eight South African Cases* (Johannesburg, 1989), pp. 18–34.

13. For concise description of the formation of the Afrikaans language see J. Cope, *The Adversary Within: Dissident Writers in Afrikaans* (Cape Town and London, 1982), pp. 19–27. Also: E. H. Raidt, *Historiese Taalkunde: Studies oor die Geskiedenis van Afrikaans* (Johannesburg, 1994).

14. Cope, *The Adversary Within,* p. 27.

15. See W. A. de Klerk, *The Puritans in Africa: A Story of Afrikanerdom* (London, 1975), and L. Thompson, *The Political Mythology of Apartheid* (New Haven and London, 1985). Also: F. A. van Jaarsveld, *The Afrikaner's Interpretation of South African History* (Cape Town, 1964).

16. See C. Winberg, 'Satire, Slavery and the *Ghoemaliedjies* of the Cape Muslims', *New Contrast,* no. 76 (1992), pp. 78–96. (Article includes texts.) Also: I. D. du Plessis, *The Cape Malays* (Cape Town, 1974). Dutch-Afrikaans folk songs are available in *Nuwe F.A.K. Sangbundel* [Federasie van Afrikaanse Kultuurvereniginge] (Cape Town, 1961; 1969). Commentary, J. Bouws, *Die Volkslied: Deel van ons Erfenis* (Cape Town, 1969).

17. M. Chapman (ed.), *A Century of South African Poetry* (Johannesburg, 1981), pp. 47–9. ('Ex'ter Hall' – Dr John Philip and others testified on behalf of the Khoi to the Aborigines Committee at Exeter Hall, London.)

18. See as representative F. le Vaillant, *Voyage de Monsieur le Vaillant dans L'Intérieur de L'Afrique par Le Cap de Bonne-Espérance* (Paris, 1790), *Travels in Africa*[t] (London, 1790) and *New Travels*[t] (London, 1794); John Barrow, *An Account of Travels into the Interior of Southern Africa in the Years 1797 and 1798,* 2 vols (London, 1804, 1806; New York, 1968); and William J. Burchell, *Travels in the Interior of Southern Africa,* 2 vols (London, 1822–24; London, 1953).

19. 'Scratches on the Face of the Country; or, What Mr Barrow Saw in the Land of the Bushmen', *Critical Inquiry,* no. 12 (1985). See also Pratt's study *Imperial Eyes: Travel Writing and Transculturation* (London, 1992) which deals with among others the travellers Barrow, Peter Kolbe, Anders Sparrman and William Paterson. Other travel books have been published by The Van Riebeeck Society (Cape Town). Further commentary: D. Bunn, 'Relocations: Landscape Theory, South African Landscape Practice, and the Transmission of Political Value', *Pretexts,* vol. 4, no. 2 (Summer 1993), J. M. Coetzee, *White Writing* (New Haven, 1988); S. Gray, *Southern African Literature: An Introduction* (Cape Town, 1979), pp. 38–71; N. Penn, 'Mapping the Cape: John Barrow and the First British Occupation of the Colony, 1795–1803', *Pretexts,* vol. 4, no. 2 (Summer 1993); R. Ross, *Beyond the Pale: Essays on the History of Colonial South Africa* (Johannesburg, 1994); and E. R. Wolf, *Europe and the People without History* (Berkeley, 1982).

20. See J. M. Coetzee on Burchell, 'The Picturesque, the Sublime, and the South African Landscape', *White Writing,* pp. 36–44.

21. Letter 23, *The Letters of Lady Anne Barnard,* pp. 22–3.

22. M. Lenta, 'All the Lighter Parts: Lady Anne Barnard's Letters from Cape Town', *Ariel*, vol. 22, no. 2 (1991) and 'Degrees of Freedom: Lady Anne Barnard's Cape Diaries', *English in Africa*, vol. 19, no. 2 (October 1992). These 're-readings' of Barnard have found useful feminist theories of autobiography, particularly F. A. Nussbaum, *The Autobiographical Subject: Gender and Ideology in Eighteenth-century England* (Baltimore, 1989) and S. Smith, *A Poetics of Women's Autobiography* (Bloomington, 1987).

Chapter 2
The Story of Frontier, 1820s–1870s

Settler opinion, trekker opinion.
The periodical press

By the time of the second British occupation in 1806, problems of racial and frontier tension had been exacerbated by clashes between European and Xhosa communities, both of which were short of grazing lands for cattle. For fifty years after the arrival of British settlers in 1820 we have, to quote the historian Thomas Pakenham, 'the story of frontier, territorial and human, of muddle, greed and humbug, like most frontier history, and of the slow, tragic destruction of the Xhosa people'.[1] It is a period of severe conflict which can be seen also to have given rise to a significant literary 'moment'. The landing of 4,000 settlers on the eastern frontier of the Cape colony secured the permanence of the English language on the subcontinent.[2] The ideas of rights, dignity and free enterprise – the prevailing liberalism against *ancien régime* privilege – resulted in persistent challenges being levelled by ordinary bourgeois and artisan settlers at the governor of the Cape, Lord Charles Somerset. By the end of the 1820s, the eastern Cape had an active commercial centre in Grahamstown, there was a press, a periodical literature, there were schools, libraries and churches in the English tradition, and there occurred an often acrimonious exchange of opinion on issues of the frontier in editorials, pamphlets and extended polemical commentaries. The colony had provided the subject matter for at least one poet, Thomas Pringle, who has continued to attract attention in South African literature, and whose verse will be assessed after he has been mentioned as a figure involved in the struggle for a free press and in setting standards of integrity in the reporting of topical issues. In related developments, the Xhosa came under missionary influence. This led to syncretic Christian-African hymns by converts and, subsequently, to a written, intellectual literary output. The initial impetus was the radical evangelical spirit that character-ised the early years of the century; by the 1850s, however, the imperial

mood had ensured that the humanitarian ideal flickered only intermittently and weakly against the consolidation of white authority and power.
In Dutch communities, the establishment of a British presence was felt
in measures such as Somerset's language ordinances (1823–7) according
to which English replaced Dutch as the language of the courts and the
effective representation of burgher institutions was severely curtailed. In
such a climate, Afrikaner political thought began to voice its own dissatis-
factions.

The general scene reveals a close correspondence of the social event
and the literary impulse. The period between the arrival of the settlers and
the bitter Sixth Xhosa War of 1834, in fact, raises many questions that
have retained currency concerning the function and character of literature
in southern Africa. What is important is to return the texts to the living
discourse of their own time as the necessary prerequisite for understanding
their passage through the culture. Such a procedure is almost dictated by
the conditions of literary production, which saw the activities of the
1820s given shape and meaning in a history of compelling and competing
ideas. It is the substance of the ideas wrenched into the service of
communication, persuasion and mobilisation that lends a local accuracy
to the observations on 'Literature' in the first number of *The South African
Journal* (Jan.–Feb., 1824). Availing themselves of enlightened eighteenth-
century idiom, the founding editors, John Fairbairn and Thomas Pringle,
regarded serious literature as excellent in its utility value. The aim was
human improvement in the colony and, by extension, in the world
society. Literature should combine sound views with practical knowledge
and – the classical ideal tempered by the romantic revival – it should attack
despots and champion free men. Literature was liberal in its sentiments, its
style should be imbued with genuine passion while retaining its touch
with common speech.[3]

Such views, however, represented only a small fraction of the colony:
that associated in Cape Town with the liberal press which, as the decade
wore on, was seen by popular settler opinion to be in unholy alliance
with the philanthropic missionary enterprise. In 1824 George Greig, a
printer from England, had begun a weekly newspaper *The South African
Commercial Advertiser* which was described in the tradition of independent
British journalism as a 'beacon of commerce and liberty'.[4] Greig was
joined by Pringle, who had gained literary experience in Edinburgh and
who at the time was sub-librarian at the South African Library, and by
Fairbairn who had trained in medicine and teaching, and at the time was
running a private Academy together with Pringle. As editors, Fairbairn
and Pringle immediately put themselves on a course of conflict with the
autocratic rule of governor Somerset who was subject at the time to an
enquiry into his neglect of common settler interests on the eastern
frontier. With Pringle, a settler, showing sympathy for the plight of

farmers on the frontier, Somerset regarded articles on despotism and liberty in *The Commercial Advertiser* and in Pringle's *South African Journal* as a direct challenge to his authority. After publishing law reports which reflected badly on the governor and his administration, *The Commercial Advertiser* was suspended at number 18. The 'facts' concerning the suspension, however, were distributed by Greig thus giving the citizens of Cape Town evidence of the arbitrary orders of the governor. With the second number of *The South African Journal* (March–April, 1824) containing Pringle's article on the plight of settlers in Albany (the eastern Cape),[5] Somerset sent warning that the journal must cease if articles obnoxious to the government continued to be printed. The editors regarded this as censorship and, in refusing to submit, announced the cessation of publication. This action was regarded by Somerset as inopportune. With a Commission of Enquiry collecting evidence of his illiberal conduct, the governor had intended at this stage only to reprimand and warn Pringle. A stormy interview followed, Pringle stood firm, and Somerset in consequence used his influence to ruin Pringle's Academy as well as Pringle's plans to start a South African literary society. Pringle resigned his government post at the Library and, with his livelihood in Cape Town at an end, he returned to Britain in 1826 having attained little redress through petitioning the Commission of Enquiry. *The South African Journal* was never revived, but its Dutch counterpart, *Het Nederduitsch Zuid-Afrikaansche Tydschrift*, continued to be published up until 1843. Given Dutch insecurity and uncertainty in a British colony *Tydschrift*, edited by the Rev. Abraham Faure, tended to avoid reporting on many of the most heated debates. The struggle for a free press was continued by Fairbairn, and in 1828 the principle was extended by the British government to the Cape.[6] With Fairbairn remaining as editor and later as proprietor until his retirement in 1859, *The South African Commercial Advertiser* continued to advocate constitutional rights, equality for all races, and the value of private property ownership. This was the liberalism of the enlightenment that in early South Africa became known as Cape liberalism.[7]

With a *Government Gazette* offering only shipping reports and other technical details of administration, an important work on the Cape to appear before Fairbairn and Pringle's contributions was W. W. Bird's *State of the Cape of Good Hope in 1822* (London, 1823). Bird was a civil servant and his book, which was written under the pseudonym 'Civil Servant', was not permitted to be distributed at the Cape because of its jaundiced view of the colonial government. It was reviewed in *The South African Journal*, however, and together with Pringle's offending article 'On the Present State and Prospects of the English Emigrants in South Africa' indicates the nature of settler controversies in the early 1820s.[8] The general concern was the neglect towards settlers shown by London, and

Pringle alongside with Dr John Philip, superintendent-general of the London Missionary Society, became active in a settlers' relief committee on the eastern frontier, where the rest of the Pringle party continued to farm after Thomas Pringle's departure to Cape Town to take up his post at the Library. As Fairbairn and Pringle realised, settlers themselves were pawns in larger schemes of colonisation. In attempting to increase the English-speaking population in the predominantly Dutch-speaking colony and in establishing close-settlement farming as a buffer against the Xhosa on the eastern edges of the Cape, governor Somerset had gained approval for his ambitious settlement plan. While the plan helped to reduce unemployment and worker agitation in Britain, it failed to take account of the impracticalities of small-scale farming in the area known as the zuurveld (sour land). Within a short time, the majority of settlers had given up the attempt to make a living on their holdings and had moved into the towns of the eastern Cape where the wagon-building industry – set up by British enterprise – would provide the transport for the Great Trek. On the frontier, trade among Boer farmers, British settlers and the Xhosa continued to be interspersed with disputes about stock ownership and grazing space, with raids and reprisals that muddled racial, cultural and economic motives. Whereas Pringle would come to see a larger story of possession and dispossession in the frontier situation – admittedly, only after he himself had left the eastern Cape – a 'settler tradition' of literature, history, and journalism remained firmly attached to the partisan view of settler experience at the hard edge of the frontier.[9]

This settler tradition includes numerous chronicles and diaries of ordinary people such as Jeremiah Goldswain, John Montgomery and Thomas Stubbs.[10] In their accounts, limited social and political insights are often offset against vivid descriptions of the daily hardship of earning an honest living. What has to be endured, in particular, are the caprices of a distant colonial bureaucracy and the sudden, seemingly inexplicable irruptions of Xhosa warrior bands. These narratives of ordinary settlers – most of which were not meant for publication – are defined not by Barrow's authoritative measure and rule, but by an amorphous working-class sense of people as the victims of economic determinism. In defence of the integrity of these chronicles, it is notable that we rarely encounter Africa depicted as the continent of hidden riches which awaits the raiding adventurer: the 1820 settlers expected to succeed or fail by the sweat of their own brows. Neither do we encounter systematic racial or cultural prejudice. Rather, the voices speak of frustration, perplexity, the pain of family members killed in skirmishes, and livelihoods destroyed by drought and crop disease. In contrast to the sure aims of official accounts, therefore, the ideological incoherence of ordinary settler chronicles is paradoxically the saving feature of their experiential authenticity.

A similarly ill-defined world-view characterises the most graphic of

the trekker journals, the *Dagboek* (Diary, 1836–1838) of Louis Tregardt,
or Trichardt.[11] With the Bible underscoring the routines of everyday life
in homiletic wisdoms, Tregardt's observing eye remains firmly attached
to the realities of finding space in which to live and areas in which to
trade. Even as he was dying of malaria far into Portuguese territory in
present-day Mozambique, Tregardt the eccentric early trekker tried to
resist any temptation to dramatise his experience into the destiny of
isolated self-sufficiency, or the search for the Calvinist utopia. Yet it was
precisely in such ways that his story would be taken up in early Afrikaner
attempts to construct the myth of the volk as the epic of an Exodus.
Tregardt's *Dagboek*, accordingly, was turned under the hand of its editor
Gustav S. Preller into a chiliastic version of Afrikaner freedom: a version
that would justify clearing the land of other races and would eventuate
in the master narrative of apartheid. (Preller's 1938 edition, in fact,
celebrates the centenary of the Great Trek.) If we are prevented from
responding to the full poignancy of many of these early chronicles
whether Boer or British, it is because they cannot avoid their complicity
in a frontier theme of domination that has remained a crucial issue in
South Africa.

The difficulty of separating the experiential impact from its historical
consequence is even more severe when we read trekker polemic which,
as in Piet Retief's manifesto[(t)] in *The Graham's Town Journal*, defended
the Boer's right to dignity and freedom as a reactive denial of the rights
of others to dignity and freedom, at least in the same social terrain.[12]
In Retief's argument, his resentments against Tory imperiousness and
interfering missionaries are tied to Boer losses of slaves as property attendant on the emancipation act, complaints about the behaviour of vagrant
Khoi who had benefited from reforms to labour regulations, the plunder
of Caffres, and modifications to 'proper relations between master and
servant'[(t)]. As the sentiments expressed by Retief enjoyed wide sympathy
in the colony, we are left with the question of how to deal with the
truth and falsity of polemic when one group's freedom is secured at
the expense of the other's suppression. For at the crux of debates were the
big issues of slavery, emancipation, identity, justice and destiny. At the one
extreme, Dr John Philip's *Researches in South Africa* (1828) marshalled case
studies of Khoi ill-treatment in a sustained indictment of the British
government's failure to take seriously its own ideals of civil rights and to
intervene in the affairs of the Khoi:

> We ask for nothing for the poor natives more than this, that
> they should have the protection the law affords to the
> colonists. . . . [We] ask the British government, and the
> British public, whether the system of cruelty and injustice

which is now brought to light is to have their sanction?
(Preface, p. xxvi)

While the accuracy of some of Philip's evidence has been disputed by
his enemies, his moral position cannot be challenged within the Christian
humanitarian ethos, and *Researches* undoubtedly played its role in
Westminster's issuing of Ordinance 50 according to which the Khoi were
granted full equality with whites. This sent shock waves through the
colony, and Philip has remained something of a villain in orthodox white
South African historiography. At the other extreme, Dutch farmers and
British settlers found common cause in the columns of the newspapers
De Zuid-Afrikaan and *The Graham's Town Journal* in mounting a fierce
polemic in favour of slave owners and the honest industry of the ordinary
(white) man. Especially in the commentaries of Robert Godlonton, editor
of *The Graham's Town Journal*, the popular settler voice becomes populist
as the 'frontier question' is skilfully shaped to the purposes of sectional
agitation and propaganda.[13] The results have been far-reaching with many
of Godlonton's views on the lazy Khoi, the perfidious Xhosa and the
heroic settler forming the basis of a long colonial record in the histories
of G. M. Theal and, subsequently, G. E. Cory.[14]

   In seeking scales of value in the 1820s, therefore, one is forced to link
styles of persuasion firmly to an ethic of human dignity that refuses to
grant freedom on any racially selective basis. Godlonton may be classified,
accordingly, as limited in his particular brand of populist agitation; Philip
as advanced for the time in his firebrand evangelicalism. In locating
Philip in the literary scene, we may say that he shifted the discourse
from the earlier ameliorative sympathy of Lady Anne Barnard to an
uncompromisingly emancipationist argument. Other books that deserve
prominence as literature of progressive intent and ideas are the treatises
on slavery by William Wright (*Slavery at the Cape of Good Hope*, 1831)
and Thomas Miller (*Remarks on the Exact Position of the Slave Question*,
1831), both of which argue that slavery is an evil that does not admit to
amendment.[15] The argument is particularly forthright when we consider
that even Fairbairn's liberal journalism had difficulty in squaring the
concepts of rights and property: slaves should be emancipated, yet owners
should be entitled to fair compensation. Wright follows the earlier
example of Pringle's hard-hitting responses to slavery at the Cape in
using shocking details from court cases, including the punishments and
testimonies of slaves, in order to give human presence and speech to the
silenced non-being.[16] It is a procedure of utilising the public record as
autobiographical witness that has continued to be necessary in a country
where opponents of the state have been 'silenced' (that is, forbidden to
be quoted) in any other form than in their own trial proceedings in an
open court. For many years the gaoled ANC leader Nelson Mandela and

the gaoled SWAPO leader Andimba Herman Toivo ja Toivo, for example, were remembered in print only by their eloquent statements from the dock on being sentenced to long terms of imprisonment for active opposition to South Africa's race laws.[17]

In turning to Afrikaner contributions to public debate in the 1820s, consideration should be given to the speeches and testimony of those who contemplated alternatives to the trekker view of self-determination in each group's own territory. The matter is important to pursue, for the repressive policies of apartheid would later be justified, morally, in grand abstractions about separate freedoms in ethnic homelands. This became the blueprint for the massive social engineering that resulted in people being 'removed' to Bantustans. Generally Afrikaner thought, as I have suggested, had its basis in the rejection of the principle of equality. Against this, there is the mass of official correspondence and writings by Andries Stockenström who, although he was a prominent spokesman on the question of the frontier, is usually not mentioned in Afrikaans literary history. After long experience in Dutch rural government as *landdrost* in Graaff-Reinet, Stockenström was appointed commissioner-general for the eastern districts and, after his resignation in 1833, he was called as one of the major witnesses before the Aborigines Committee in London, where Philip's case for the Khoi was heard. He was subsequently appointed lieutenant-governor to implement new treaties in an attempt to bring order to the frontier. In trying to find points of coincidence between the new ideas of the enlightenment and his own conservative Dutch background, he sought to attach the practicalities of policy to a morality of equal protection. Holding the middle ground between Philip's philanthropy and settler apologists, Stockenström neither attacked nor defended the fact of settler occupation of the land, which he regarded, pragmatically, as irreversible. In trying to recognise the prejudices of both white and black, he asked how practical measures could ensure the cause of truth where 'I am to call "murder, murder" and "plunder, plunder" whatever the colour of the perpetrator's skin'.[18] Because of his morality, Stockenström fell foul of the pragmatism of white colonists; because of his pragmatism, he could not offer any higher-order morality about colonisation. He recognised, at least, that people of different races, cultures and languages needed to arrive at some *modus operandi* about co-existence. Whereas Afrikaner destiny would be predicated on the trek as an act of freedom, Stockenström's writings encourage us to consider the trek as a retreat from the complexities of social exchange.

Pringle's *African Sketches* (1834)

In considering the range of expression in the 1820s and thirties, we are reminded of how much South African literature has involved responses, both constricting and liberatory, to the 'native question'. What Stockenström's soldier-administrator's mind could not grasp was the human story informing the official problem of the frontier. It is this quality that distinguishes Thomas Pringle from most other writers of the time. In resisting unrelieved polemics, Pringle subjected the divided landscape to an intellectual and emotional quest for progressive conduct. I have already mentioned his involvement in literary activities in Cape Town. Born in Scotland in 1789, he studied at the University of Edinburgh and participated in the literary life of the city as joint editor of the *Edinburgh Monthly Magazine*, which would become famous as *Blackwood's Magazine*, before arriving at the eastern Cape with his farming family who, having felt the effects of economic depression after the Napoleonic wars, hoped to start a new life in South Africa. Inheriting the reason of the enlightenment while catching the spirit of religious revivalism and romantic idealism, Pringle was regarded by governor Somerset as 'whiggish', even Jacobin (revolutionary). It was the conditions at the Cape, however, that accentuated the streak of self-righteous aggression combined with a sharp sense of justice in a personality which, nonetheless, retained its belief in constitutional methods. Having been embroiled in the bitter recriminations of magazine wars in Edinburgh, Pringle was no stranger to controversy and threw himself into the life of the colony during his stay of six years. According to the *Cape of Good Hope Literary Gazette* of 4 September 1834, the appearance of his *African Sketches* (1834), seven years after his departure, had the potential still to arouse strong reaction:

> Pringle's new work is causing a shaking among the proud
> bones of the Colony. It has been aptly termed a *bunch of
> whipcord*; it must certainly prove lacerating to much of the
> proud flesh around us.

At the Cape, in 1834, *African Sketches* would have encountered the volatile mood spurred by the hostilities of the Sixth Xhosa War as well as resentments about the moves towards the abolition of slavery. To many colonial readers Pringle's work – parts of which had previously appeared in local periodicals – probably symbolised the author's own commitment to 'negrophilic' causes. Comprising the prose commentary *Narrative of a Residence in South Africa* and *Poems Illustrative of South Africa*, *African Sketches* does not utilise the shock tactics of the pamphleteer. Rather,

Pringle draws the reader into a struggle to understand and assess the colonial predicament, so that it is not easy merely to dismiss his views as those of a hothead, the usual defence of settler apologists against the opinions of philanthropists. In his early article, 'On the Present State and Prospects of the English Emigrants in South Africa', Pringle had offered a searching examination of ordinary people brought out to the Cape without being informed fully of the facts of settlement and then neglected by the British government.[19] There was no attempt to confuse the object of his attack, the Tory rulers, by introducing scare stories about Khoi or Xhosa. Particularly after having been influenced by the views of Philip and Stockenström, Pringle became a voice of protest against the oppression and exploitation of the native races. He is passionate, for instance, in his condemnation of the commando system: that is, reprisal raids – one of which he himself had accompanied – against indigenous people suspected of stock theft. Retaining his belief in Christianity as a regenerative force in South Africa, he showed a rare respect for the traditions and aspirations of the Bushmen, Khoi and Xhosa and, though he is harsh in his attacks on colonial policies, he is always prepared to distinguish between enlightened and despotic behaviour in individuals, whether black or white, British or Boer. As in Philip's writing, the failure of compassion and justice in Africa is regarded as the failure of the British to fulfil obligations to their own civilising mission.

In *Narrative of a Residence* his skills of reportage and re-creation combine to lend authority to his judgments because of the facts he supplies and the essential fairness and fullness of his account. At one point, he describes the arrival of a 'Caffir woman accompanied by a little girl . . ., And having an infant strapped to her back':

> She had come from the drostdy, or district town, of Uitenhage, under the custody of a black constable, who stated that she was one of a number of Caffir females who had been made prisoners by the order of the Commandant on the frontier, for crossing the line of prescribed demarcation without permission; and that they were now to be given out in servitude among the white inhabitants of this district.

The incident made a lasting impression on Pringle: an impression confirmed by many of his subsequent observations. Unlike most journals, travelogues and diaries about the Cape, the *Narrative* implicates its own narrator in evolving perceptions so that Pringle's comment, 'we back-settlers grow all savage and bloody by coming into continual conflict with savages', is modified in the course of his recollections into an acute awareness that the so-called savages are people driven to desperation and plunder by their treatment at the hands of colonists. In expanding his range of interest beyond his own experience (his clash with Somerset regarding the demise of *The South African Journal* is dramatically recounted), Pringle invests his story with a historical understanding of frontier relations. He re-tells the incident at Slachter's Nek where, in 1816, Dutch farmers who had rebelled against reforms to Khoi policy were executed by the British; he utilises Stockenström's recollections of the frontier wars to re-create the stirring speech of the Xhosa warrior-prophet Makana who, in 1819, had led a desperate millenarian-inspired attack on the British garrison in Grahamstown; and he turns the emphasis on 'customs and manners' offered by writers like Barrow towards politi-cally conscious accounts of the Bushmen, Khoi and Xhosa. As Pringle enters into characters' thoughts and alternates between physical and mental action, the huge subject of colonial occupation in South Africa makes its impact on readers with an immediacy of human depiction that suggests not so much the approach of prose commentary as that of the historical novel. In giving the reader the 'feel' of living in a colony governed by an 'unjust and mischievous policy', Pringle's *Narrative* sustains a moral coherence concerning the value of what he regarded as 'justice, kindness, Christian truth'.

Together with the *Narrative*, Pringle included the poems he had pub-lished and frequently revised during his years at the Cape, as well as several pieces written in the spirit of abolitionist propaganda after his return to Britain. There was little in Pringle's early Scottish verse to distinguish him from a dozen other minor, imitative practitioners, and his language intermittently continued to echo the generalised, meditative strain of the late eighteenth-century manner even as he aimed for the 'simple language of truth and nature . . . condensation and simplicity' associated with Wordsworth and Coleridge in the *Lyrical Ballads*.[20] (In *The South African Journal* vol. 1 and vol. 2, Fairbairn had contributed a lengthy appreciation of Wordsworth's poetry.) What gave Pringle's poetry interest and continues to give it significance is that his experience in Africa provided him with subject matter that engaged his full moral being. At times, understandably, there is nostalgia for Scotland which is seen as a kind of colony of England; at other times, Pringle identifies bonds that tie him to the Cape. In some poems, local terms and speech rhythms indicate an attempt to attach his language to the new environment:

> Powána wagh'
> Tot dat de Baas hem binnenshuis zal vraagh'.
> P.– [to F.] In boorish Dutch which means, 'Powána waits
> Till master bid him welcome to our gates.'
>
> ('The Emigrant's
> Cabin')

In other poems, the need to speak of justice overrides any experiments in language and provokes strong lines that load Pringle's sketches with authority, symbol and prophecy: 'For England hath spoke in her tyrannous mood./And the edict is writing in African blood' ('The Caffer Commando').

In reviewing the edition of Pringle's African poems issued in 1989 on the occasion of the bicentenary of the poet's birth, J. M. Coetzee charges the editors, Ernest Pereira and myself, with rewriting South African literary history in favour of historically particular writers of the liberal Left like Pringle against mythically oriented writers of the Right like Roy Campbell.[21] Noting our claim that Pringle's 'relevance' rests on his fidelity to real concerns and actual people, to Africa as a place of human and sociopolitical life rather than of masks and rituals, Coetzee sees the editors in seeking to restore Pringle to the challenge of his time having to read the poetry 'against the grain' and, in consequence, forgetting that Pringle ultimately remains an indifferent poet in his limited verbal invention. But in the context of the 'illiberal' colony, it seems worth insisting on the value of Pringle's ideas over his wordplay, and crediting him with having sanctioned the concerns of belonging and alienation, miscegenation, oppression, protest, and resistance as crucial matter for South African poetry. By restoring historical particularity to his most frequently anthologised poem 'Afar in the Desert', for example, we can appreciate the difficulties of exile when simple colonial reliances on home begin to be challenged in the poet's own divided mind by the need to commit himself to the new country:

> Afar in the Desert I love to ride,
> With the silent Bush-boy alone by my side:
> Away – away – in the Wilderness vast,
> Where the White Man's foot hath never passed,
> . . .
> A region of drought where no river glides,
> Nor rippling brook with osiered sides;
> Where sedgy pool, nor bubbling fount,
> Nor tree, nor cloud, nor rusty mount,
> Appears, to refresh the aching eye:
> But the barren earth, and the burning sky,
> And the blank horizon, round and round,
> Spread – void of living sight or sound.
>
> And here, while the night winds round me sigh,
> And the stars burn bright in the midnight sky,
> As I sit apart by the desert stone,
> Like Elijah at Horeb's cave alone,

'A still small voice' comes through the wild
(Like a Father consoling his fretful Child),
Which banishes bitterness, wrath, and fear,
Saying – MAN IS DISTANT, BUT GOD IS NEAR!

In the progressions as well as the hesitations of his text, Pringle casts around for the consolations of nostalgia and familiar expression even as the 'silent Bushboy', in mute service, seems to guarantee the colonial his myths of authority and self-sufficiency. But the gliding river and rippling brook can be named only in their absence, and Coleridge's praise of 'Afar in the Desert' ('among the two or three most perfect lyric Poems in our Language')[22] succeeds, paradoxically, in robbing the poem of its specificity. Whereas Coleridge could only imagine the exotic, Pringle had to face the impact of the unfamiliar terrain, and the poem cannot help splintering its own design.[23] It is not only lyric, but manic: it is as if Pringle's consciousness of his colonial dilemma – he must decry the system of which he is irrevocably part – cannot bear self-justification. Read in this way 'Afar in the Desert' throws the weight of alienating experience on to its final words: 'MAN IS DISTANT, BUT GOD IS NEAR!' What in many Cape chroniclers could have been pious vapourings here becomes a measure of Pringle's searching, troubled sensibility which, as God's 'still small voice' reminded Elijah, should countenance no retreats into the desert, but should learn to value good work among humankind, even in an imperfect world. This was precisely Pringle's commitment. That the Bushboy evaporates in the course of this early poem and allows the poet to imagine himself in solitude is fairly predictable within the romantic ethos and aesthetic. That the Bushboy-figure should return, recurrently, in Pringle's subsequent poems in forms of the enslaved Khoi, the defiant Bushman, and the revolutionary warrior prophet ('Wake Amakosa, wake!/ And arm yourselves for war') aptly reinforces the humanitarian ethic, and prepares us to read the poems collectively and, as Pringle desired, in conjunction with the *Narrative* as the cumulative record of his South African experience. The comment of Pringle's first editor retains a note of contemporaneity: 'With him every line has its definite object – every picture its moral purpose.'[24] With Pringle as a signatory, the Act of Emancipation was published a few months after the appearance of *African Sketches*. On the day after its publication, Pringle collapsed and died in an advanced state of tuberculosis. His remains were brought out to South Africa from London in 1970 and reinterred on the Pringle farm at Eildon in the eastern Cape.

In what I have referred to as a literary moment in the 1820s and thirties, Pringle merits attention not only because the problems with which he wrestled remain with us today, but because of the questions his work raises concerning what is meant by the colonial inheritance and

South African literature. His status is assessed not by his length of residence, for example, but by his readiness to meet local challenges. If the new ideas of the metropole remain his yardstick, he struggles to identify with the particular demands of the local environment. In refusing any easy distinctions between literary art and social commentary, or between the genre categories of imaginative and documentary forms, Pringle regards the life of the book as inseparable from the life of the world. Despite his concern to revise and perfect his craft – his notes to his 'poems illustrative of South Africa' indicate his numerous revisions – he was ready like a journalist to reprint, adapt and re-use material if he thought the cause warranted his intervention. In all this, he remains a prototype of many subsequent writers in South Africa, indeed in southern Africa.

The 1820s and the liberal tradition

The radical humanitarian edge that we find in some of the writing in Pringle's time had, however, given way by the mid-nineteenth century to the jingoistic and expansionist fantasies of the imperial vision. In hunting and missionary adventures, racist and evolutionary doctrines in the social sciences combined to give the Victorian public a picture of Africa as the dark continent that required to be 'opened up' to the twin advantages of Christianity and commerce. Despite this, some have wanted to condemn the earlier humanitarian movement as self-serving or ideologically circumscribed by bourgeois-economic views of progress and development. As a man of his time, Dr John Philip in his philanthropic activities and writings may not have conceived of an African spiritual and political revolution; nevertheless, his liberal-economic ideas gleaned from Adam Smith and the Scottish enlightenment were not meant to be merely expedient. His attempt to protect the Khoi in separate areas was envisaged not as ethnic policy, but as a temporary measure to avoid their exploitation by the technologically more advanced settlers. The objectives were equal rights and training that could empower the indigenous people to take their place in an inevitably modernising situation, in which they would be able to bargain as free, competitive human beings.[25] By the time of David Livingstone's enormously successful *Missionary Travels and Researches in Southern Africa* (1857),[26] in contrast, the British had begun to see themselves less as being guilty by association with slavery and conquest, more as the potential saviours of backward races. In short, the mission in Africa had lost the pockets of generosity we find in several earlier radical 'protestants' and, according to the temper of the Berlin Conference

(1884) which started the scramble for Africa, indigenous Africans were depicted mostly as evil and demonic. The writings of the great Victorian explorers, whether hunters or missionaries, are non-fictional quest romances, in which hero-authors struggle through enchanted or bedevilled lands towards goals of discovery (the Victoria Falls, the source of the Nile), or toward assisting in the Christian conversation of heathens and cannibals, before turning from the darkness back to the regions of light.[27] Such a trope would define the exotic adventure novel which will be discussed later. In turning from the deconstructive reading – the quest romance as overweening in its imperial assumptions – to seeking a rehabilitative potential I find very few writers in the second half of the nineteenth century to be worth attention on their own terms. The few I wish to record here are John William Colenso, his wife Frances and daughter Harriette, Olive Schreiner, Emily Hobhouse and Mahatma Gandhi, all of whom in their different ways spoke persuasively against colonial bigotry.[28]

Casting his eye over the beginnings of written poetry in South Africa, Rudyard Kipling – who was associate editor of the newspaper *The Friend* in Bloemfontein during the Anglo-Boer War and who wrote several barrack-room ballads – declared in 1907 that a hundred years of English-speaking life had produced only Pringle after whose verse we would have to scour the local newspapers.[29] In the 1980s anthologisers turned to searching the periodicals, newspapers and early selections, and the result has been the recovery of two streams of verse which could be called 'educated' and 'colloquial'.[30] The strength of the educated is to be found in its liberal seriousness (in this regard, however, no other poet in the nineteenth century matches Pringle); its limitation is to be identified in the tendency of many practitioners to muse in sub-Victorian diction on 'the spirit of the veld' (veldsingers) or, with equal fuzziness, on the subjects of God and destiny. The strength of the colloquial is a racy, down-to-earth vigour; its limitation, besides the regularity of its ballad rhythms, lies in its restricted, usually conservative social understandings with a tendency towards the racial slur. Beginning in the 1820s, the colloquial voice satirised manners in Cape Town and, in the many frontier wars, it could be relied upon to harangue the Xhosa and champion the settler. After the discovery of diamonds (1867) and gold (1886), the verse turned to digger fortunes and misfortunes and, in the Anglo-Boer War (1899–1902), it often lamented in cockney accents the fate of the ordinary soldier Tommy Atkins caught in the obscure designs of the rich and powerful. As in the case of Kipling's barrack-room ballads, an uneducated, colloquial verse was not necessarily written by uneducated people, and one of the best known of Pringle's contemporaries was Andrew Geddes Bain whose song 'The British Settler' I introduced earlier as an example of popular settler sentiment.

Having arrived at the Cape from Scotland in 1816 Bain showed his enterprise as a pioneer-explorer, a road-builder and geologist who contributed fictional articles to numerous periodicals and, in literary circles, is usually credited as being the first to capture localised speech on the stage in his dramatic sketch-in-song, *Kaatje Kekkelbek; or, Life among the Hottentots*, which was performed in Grahamstown in 1838.[31] Possibly C. E. Boniface's *The New Order of Knighthood*, which had been printed in 1832, gave Bain his idea to mingle English, Dutch (or Afrikaans) and creolised Hottentot-Afrikaans in a satiric coupling of the Hottentot Eve and the philanthropic missionary to the tune of drink and humbug. Bain's Kaatje takes her cue from the settlers' stereotype of the vagrant 'Hotnot':

> My name is Kaatje Kekkelbek,
>   I come from Katrivier,
> Daar is van water geen gebrek,
>   But scarce of wine and beer.
> Myn ABC at Ph'lipes school
>   I learnt a kleine beetje,
> But left it just as great a fool
>   As gekke Tante Meitje.[32]

The jibes are aimed at predictable targets: interfering clerics like Philip, misguided administrators like Stockenström, the Aborigines Committee. The gist of the sketch is that Kaatje remains herself, whoring, thieving, boozing, in short living like a Hotnot despite foolish attempts by philanthropists to civilise her in the European manner. Some commentators in their eagerness to find authentic speech have delighted in Kaatje as a kind of mistress of anarchy bursting with irrepressible energy beyond the bounds of middle-class respectability.[33] If his other writings are any guide, however, Bain's intention was probably to jeer at the Hottentot Kaatje at the same time as he allows her to debunk the humanitarian lobby as the other bugbear of settler society. With anger simmering after Xhosa attacks and missionary successes in emancipationist debates, Bain's sketch in 1838 would have provided a dubious cathartic release to a settler audience by confirming the prejudices of the colony. In Bain's treatment of the frontier problem, there is great delight in words, little delight in progressive ideas. Unfortunately, Kipling's comment − there is only Pringle − retains a certain justness.

At the Cape the literary scene relied heavily, as it still does in southern Africa, on the publishing opportunities of newspapers and periodicals.[34] The liberal spirit entertained by *The South African Commercial Advertiser* and the short-lived *South African Journal* was continued most forcibly in the *Cape of Good Hope Literary Gazette* (1830–35), edited by Pringle's successor at the South African Library, A. C. Jardine, who in lambasting

De Zuid-Afrikaan and *The Graham's Town Journal* gave prominence to pro-abolitionist texts by Philip, Wright, Miller and Pringle. There were a few fictional stories among which 'Wilkinson the Indian' (that is, a colonial from India) and 'Frederick', the account of an escaped slave, tried to address local issues. In their use of set-pieces to convey the sentiments of emancipation, however, neither attained the dramatic immediacy of Pringle's account of colonists' hunting down a Bushman, 'Pangola: An African Tale'.[35] The only examples of novels with a Cape setting were the anonymously written *Makanna; or, The Land of the Savage* (London, 1834) – highly improbable in its romantic 'savagery' – and E. A. Kendall's *The English Boy at the Cape* (London, 1835), a tedious list of adventures happening mostly at sea on the way to the colony. Debate about the impact of 'new ideas' on Cape life had been lively in Fairbairn and Pringle's journalism, but did not continue with the same intensity in later periodicals. By 1843 William Layton Sammons's *Sam Sly's African Journal* felt that audiences were satiated with politics and, in ranging widely over 'human interests', Sly's style was that of informal *causerie*. By the time of the long-running *Cape Monthly Magazine* (later the *Cape Quarterly Review,* 1857–1883), the colonial inheritance had become facile in its transplantation of European themes to South African settings. The magazine serialised whole novels such as the adventure romances *Kafirs and Kafirland: A Settler's Story* (1857–58) and *Jack Hawkins: A Tale of South Africa* (1867). There were also several reminiscences of the so-called Kaffir Wars: reminiscences which in their lack of analytical acumen suggest that hindsight had not lent crusty settlers and missionaries any larger view of a frontier situation in which they were part of the problem.[36]

Whether such stodgy, conservative colonialism would have regarded itself as liberal is a moot point. For the 1820s bequeaths South Africa a broad tradition of liberalism.[37] Taking its impetus from the European bourgeois revolutions, it manifested itself initially in both radically-progressive and radically-conservative forms with settlers defending their democratic rights while resisting the rights of people of colour. South African liberalism, via the Cape liberal model, has inherited both the Christian social-humanitarian aspect and the classical attachment to private institutions and property. In countering attacks by Marxist commentators on what they perceive to be middle-class, middle-of-the-road, relatively privileged economic proclivities, liberals argue that the economy is not in itself a defining value of the tradition, but that only a society with multiple centres of power can withstand the pressures of authoritarianism which is seen as endemic in South African politics whether from right-wing Afrikaner nationalism or, whatever precisely it might mean in practice, from left-wing African nationalism. Never strong in formal political terms, liberalism has had a disproportionate presence in institutional life that has laid liberals open to charges of conservatism and elitism while giving them an influential voice in key sectors of society such as the legal profession, the judiciary, the press, higher education, business, the churches, and the arts. The 1820 Settler Foundation in Grahamstown is involved in English educational projects and organises an annual national arts festival, for example, while South Africa's post-apartheid interim constitution, which was adopted in 1993, is clearly a document in the Western-liberal tradition. Many white English-speaking writers and critics in South Africa could be classified liberal, but the accents range markedly from Ken Owen's abrasive, laissez-faire insistence on individual enterprise in his column in South Africa's largest-selling newspaper, the *Sunday Times*, to the concern of authors like Alan Paton with the compassionate re-creation of human lives shattered by apartheid and urbanisation.[38] As Africanist critics have seen matters, the tenets of universalism in the liberal approach are too often euphemisms for a colonial hankering after European civilisation, culture, institutions and, implicitly, authority. Thus Es'kia Mphahlele, who regards Pringle as one of the few white writers to have had a genuine interest in exploding the myth of darkest Africa, feels bound to add that Pringle's black people in the landscape remain passive creatures of history.[39] At the nub of the civilising mission in the early nineteenth century, of course, were the missionaries with their crucial role in the development of written literature in African communities. Their influence in southern Africa was first experienced by the Xhosa.

The Xhosa legacy from Ntsikana to Mandela

It is unhelpful to separate Xhosa literary history from the history of European settlement. Both are defined by a process of acculturation, and motifs in the early Xhosa response have been reworked, in English, by subsequent African writers many of whom would not necessarily refer to themselves specifically as Xhosa. Just as writing by British settlers can be grasped properly only in relation to the conditions of colonialism operating at the Cape, so the function and forms of Xhosa literature bear the marks of frontier politics in the eastern Cape. With the registers, images and narratives suggesting a clash of worlds, Xhosa literature emerges as a literature of massive questioning that has paradigmatic significance in any understanding of the frontier.[40] It is necessary to appreciate, first, that the Xhosa-speaking people themselves are a large and diverse group divided into many clans.[41] Having little insight into the complexities and tensions of Xhosa politics, Somerset in 1818 tried to strike deals with Ngqika as a paramount chief. The concept of paramountcy, however, was alien to the culture. Ngqika belonged to one main group, the Rharhabe, and, to complicate matters further, was locked in struggle about succession with his uncle, the regent Ndlambe, who with his followers had been driven across the Great Fish river in 1811 by British forces. No chief had the power or authority to conclude agreements on behalf of the Xhosa people as a single entity and, despite Somerset's tendency to interpret broken undertakings simply as confirmation of Ngqika's duplicity, the problem went beyond the character of the apparently less than worthy Ngqika as an individual. As Makana, a supporter of Ndlambe, is reported to have said in 1819 after a battle at Amalinde, in which the British interfered on the side of the defeated Ngqika against Ndlambe thus reversing the outcome of what was in essence a dynastic feud:

> 'We lived in peace. Some bad people stole, perhaps: the nation was quiet – the chiefs were quiet. Gaika [Ngqika] stole – his chief stole – his people stole. You sent him copper; you sent him beads; you sent him horses – on which he rode to steal more. To *us* you only sent commandos.
> 'We quarrelled with Gaika about grass – no business of yours. You sent a commando you took our last cow. . . . You gave half the spoil to Gaika: half you kept yourselves. . . .'[(t)42]

Several years before his clash with the British at Amalinde, Ndlambe had witnessed a sight that must have challenged his very conception of reality. In 1811 a huge British force in redcoats, on horseback, guns blazing, had pushed across the zuurveld chasing Ndlambe beyond the Fish river in an attempt to secure the frontier between white and black. This apocalyptic image of technology crashing into the bucolic past sets the temper for the first modern Xhosa voices, those of the Christianised bard Ntsikana and the warrior-prophet Makana (or, Nxele). Both had come under forms of missionary influence: the London Missionary Society, under Dr J. T. van der Kemp, had begun work among the western Xhosa in 1799. Ntsikana and Makana – backed, respectively, by the rivals Ngqika and Ndlambe – however, epitomise two strategies of survival adopted by the Xhosa in their response to the colonial advance into their traditional world. Ntsikana claimed to be a servant of God in favour of peace and accommodation; Makana identified himself with ancient custom as a leader of resistance. The cleavage was between converts to Christianity and traditionalist countrymen: that is, between 'school' people and 'red' people, red referring to the ochre colour of the blankets that are worn.[43]

Claiming to have experienced a dramatic conversion in which his Christianity involved a direct relation to a god rather than to the ancestors, Ntsikana composed four hymns one of which – his 'Great Hymn'[(t)] – was recorded in 1828 by Dr John Philip and exists in several English translations. The lines here are from the translation by Ntsikana's biographer, the Revd John Knox Bokwe:

> He is the Great God, who is in heaven;
> Thou art Thou, Shield of truth.
> Thou art Thou, Stronghold of truth.
> . . .
> As for his chase, He hunteth for souls.
> He, Who amalgamates flocks rejecting each other.
> He, the Leader, Who has led us.
> He, Whose great mantle, we do put on.[44]

Despite the Christian content, the meaning and medium are African. The style is reminiscent in fact of the praise poem. In this case praises to God, not to the chief, are built up in a series of names recognising God as Creator and Preserver. The archaic language carries the authority of the past into the new situation and, as in traditional religion, close correspondences in metaphors and images of pastoral life are retained between the sacred and the secular in a monistic world view. In his involvement in dynastic rivalry between Ngqika and Ndlambe, Ntsikana advised his followers to discard their assegais and arm themselves spiritually by singing his song. As a result, he had to flee Ngqika's wrath after the latter had been defeated by Ndlambe. More important than Ntsikana's own literary achievement, according to A. C. Jordan, is that through his influence disciples were introduced to the arts of reading and writing and became the 'harbingers of the dawn of literacy among the indigenous people of southern Africa'.[45]

It is not Ntsikana, however, but Makana who has acquired legendary status in the literature. Leading Ndlambe's forces in a counter-attack on the British, he was prevented by military reinforcement from taking Grahamstown, and then to halt further bloodshed he delivered himself up to the British commander. Gaoled on Robben Island, he led an escape of prisoners and was drowned in the attempt, and in Black Consciousness poetry of the 1970s Makana was given iconic significance as a figure of resistance while the political prison, Robben Island, was renamed the Isle of Makana.[46] The assistance given by the colonial government to Ndlambe's rival, Ngqika, had prompted Makana to deviate from the orthodox Christianity taught to him by the missionaries and to evolve a syncretic cult in which an ancient African god was alleged to be stronger than the white man's god. Although he advocated a return to traditional religion, Makana's rousing actions and words had a millenarian impetus. It is as though the Christian concept of dramatic conversion for reward in the after-life is pushed under the political imperative into an African religious emphasis on response and solution in the secular activities of this world. Makana's millenarianism, in fact, can be seen to have anticipated the later cattle-killing, in which the Xhosa, again in a situation of political desperation, sacrificed their own means of livelihood in expectation of miraculous intervention. Having recorded Makana as a figure of resistance in his poem 'Makanna's Gathering', Pringle dramatised the warrior prophet's story in his 'Letter from South Africa, No. 2 Caffer Campaigns – The Prophet Makanna', which was incorporated into *Narrative of a Residence in South Africa*. In his letter, Pringle developed Stockenström's account of Makana's speech to the British forces into a powerful statement of dignity in defeat. (The words quoted earlier on by Makana are from Pringle's rendition.) At the same time, Pringle endorsed Makana's own view that the British were arrogant intruders into affairs about which they were ignorant.[47]

What is suggested by this set of complicated religious, cultural and political motives is the difficulty in Xhosa literature of separating tradition from modernity. For many, Christianity with its message of brotherhood and its encouragement of reading and writing promised a new meaning in life. Despite moments of apocalypse as people grasp at older solutions while confronting large-scale change, Xhosa literature is not about supernatural transformations, but about the social realities of transition. In his introductory study Jordan, in regarding the writer as a witness of the times, identifies a dialectical tension between those who saw the old order as vital to self-fulfilment and those who exhorted people to join the new Christian society where, in contrast to the dynastic past, there would be an abundance of life for all. Whatever the colonial/anti-colonial temptation simply to praise or condemn, our placing of the missionary in the traumas of the times needs to be similarly dialectical. As I have suggested, there are differences of temperament, ideals and purpose between the evangelical revival of the early nineteenth century and a later, imperial pietism. Philip's inheritance, for example, was rooted in the new middle and working classes rather than in the Tory establishment. To brand the London Missionary Society, or the Glasgow Missionary Society, as the vanguard of British imperialism, therefore, is to ignore the fact that, unlike traders, travellers or hunters, many of the early missionaries were schooled to give the term protestant substantive meaning and to take a real interest in their subjects. It is true that the colonising venture generally regarded African life as characterised by the blank page of heathenism; paradoxically, however, this meant that missionaries regarded themselves as part of a vast literacy project which extended the authority of the scriptures to local, particular, vernacular springs of creativity. The result was not only good African Englishmen, but the consciousness of early African nationalism. The indigenous accent was given a modern political cause, and two apparently contradictory questions have to be kept simultaneously in mind: did missionaries hasten the suppression of ancient communities? Did they intervene on the side of good in inevitable transition? If the 'translation' of one culture into another can be regarded as an act of dispossession, it can also be regarded as an act of empowerment.[48]

In 1823 the Glasgow Missionary Society established itself in the eastern Cape and set up a printing press at Gwali, renamed Lovedale in 1826 in honour of the secretary of the society, Dr John Love. Lovedale Missionary Institute became the main source of written literature, and the press which still operates from the town of Alice was used in the pattern that was standard throughout Africa: the indigenous language was reduced to writing, and the missionaries composed a word list and an elementary grammar in order to facilitate their dealings with the local people in the preparation of preaching and Bible translation. (In Lesotho, similar activities were performed by the Paris Evangelical Missionary Society in the 1830s, while in Zululand the foundations of Zulu linguistics were laid in the 1850s.) Some of the early contributions to a Xhosa magazine *Ikwezi* (Morning Star) were by Ntsikana's first converts, and consisted of praises to their mentor. By the time of the Seventh Xhosa War ('the War of the Axe'), in 1846, the old dynastic feuds had given way to modern, popular rebellion against the Cape authorities' determination to ensure that their version of law and order prevailed beyond the Fish river. Lovedale was closed and the principal, the Revd Govan, took with him to Europe his most promising young scholar, Tiyo Soga, who would become the first black person in southern Africa to have a university education and to enter the church ministry. Soga's hymns, scriptural translations and devotional writings, his translation of Part One of Bunyan's *The Pilgrim's Progress*, his consultancy on the revised Xhosa version of the Bible, and his journal all testify to his utter involvement in the acculturation process.

On returning to the land of the Xhosa, Soga set about trying to heal the wounds of the millenarian cattle killing of 1856 when, in a state of near despair as a result of repeated colonial military actions, the loss of land and extensive poverty, the Xhosa widely obeyed the message of a young prophetess, Nongqawuse, slaughtered their cattle and destroyed their crops in anticipation of the sun rising in the west on which appointed day fat new cattle and nutritious grain would be provided. When nothing happened, excitement was replaced by bitter disillusionment and Sir George Grey, the governor of the Cape, seized the opportunity to intersperse white settlement with the African population, thus ensuring that the severely weakened Xhosa would have to enter the Cape colony as a cheap labouring class on white farms. Soga's response was to try to distinguish what he regarded as the grosser practices of both colonial encroachment and superstitious traditional society from what he saw as best in black values and Western Christian civilisation. In seeking modern reconciliations and integrations, he raised questions concerning the destiny of the 'Kaffir race':

> I find the Negro from the days of the old Assyrians
> downwards, keeping his 'individuality' and
> 'distinctiveness'. . . . I find him enslaved – exposed to the
> vices and the brandy of the white man. . . . I find him
> exposed to all these disasters, and yet living – multiplying
> 'and never extinct'. Yea, I find him now as the prevalence
> of christian and philanthropic opinions on the rights of man
> obtains among civilised nations, returning unmanacled to
> the land of his forefathers, taking back with him the
> civilisation and the christianity of those nations.[49]

The tones are sonorous, the sentiments 'pan-African' in their echoes of American slavery, generously human in their universal applicability. The point must have been meaningless, however, to Xhosa people at grassroots who, after the cattle killing and their restrictions under colonial labour laws, had to find a usable past in the particular circumstances of their own experience. Thus the cattle killing is transformed, in oral memory, into mythic truth: the Xhosa, who were never actually defeated on the battlefield, were tricked by duplicitous Christianity (the young girl Nongqawuse, it is said, had fallen under the indirect Christian influence of 'miracles'); the Xhosa were tricked also by the guile of Sir George Grey who becomes the real villain of the tale. With the event having been reworked in several subsequent ways as justificatory myth by writers such as H. I. E. Dhlomo in his play *The Girl Who Killed to Save* (1936) and Mtutuzeli Matshoba in his Black Consciousness story 'Three Days in the Land of a Dying Illusion' (1979), the cattle killing has superseded its originary Xhosa significance and entered an 'African national consciousness' as a text of oppression and liberation.[50]

By the 1850s Britain had decided that the administration of the Cape could be more cost-efficient by granting government to settler offices. With the missionary and humanitarian movements in decline, Cape liberalism showed little conviction in defending the rights and freedom of Africans who, with the land of the Xhosa annexed to the colony in 1877, came under the political control of the Cape legislature. As African areas were incorporated and as black people – albeit largely reduced to chattels – seemed to impinge on 'European space', there was a surge of racial discrimination. With increasing conditions placed upon the African's right to vote, the Cape delegation at the national convention in 1910 felt able to forego the claims of Africans in favour of union with Natal and the two Boer republics in a South African constitution that endorsed segregationist practice. This sorry story of the Cape liberal creed – with its heady beginnings in the emancipationist debates of the 1820s – ensured that no other Xhosa writers would again achieve Soga's poise between two worlds. In several colonial yarns, the Soga figure would become a satirical type: the Christianised kaffir who, as the product of misguided humanitarian notions of integration, is left severely displaced, accepted by neither whites nor blacks in the proper functionings of the colony.[51] In response to the times, the oral bard began to reflect changes brought about by conquest: there are allusions in the poems to governors, magistrates and missionaries, and the Mfengu – who had settled in Xhosa territory as refugees from Shaka's wars and who had been used by the British as a buffer – are appealed to by the Xhosa in terms of African solidarity while scorn is reserved for African Christians who are depicted as compromised in their loyalties.[52] The writing also shifts from Soga's confidence in Christianity to a political consciousness concerning the need for education, organisation and unity.

The transition can be traced in the several journals that had been established: particularly in *Isigidimi samaXhosa* (The Xhosa Messenger), written entirely in Xhosa and edited by W. W. Gqoba who was a frequent contributor, and in John Tengo Jabavu's Xhosa/English weekly *Imvo Zabantsundu* (Native Opinion) which first appeared in 1884.[53] In two long didactic poems in Xhosa, 'Ingxoxo enkulu ngemfundo' [Great discussion on education, 1885] and 'Ingxoxo enkulu yomginwa nomkristu' [Great discussion between a heathen and a christian, 1887],[54] Gqoba utilises an allegorical mode in an attempt to vindicate Christianity even as the arguments of his characters-in-opposition strike the reader as more effective than their author's own desired conclusions. As a general feature of many of these early written works, we encounter the influence of the translated *Pilgrim's Progress* (*Uhambo lo Mhambi*). At the same time, we need to give weight to the observation that the participants in the discussions make their points in typically African fashion by introducing gnomic folk-tales and historical precedents to buttress the arguments. Well before *Isigidimi* ceased publication with the editor's death, however, young African intellectuals had begun to lose confidence in Gqoba and his journal, and voices of discontent and disillusion with the 'European way' define the argumentative prose and verse of the regular contributor Jonas Ntsiko, a blind catechist and hymn writer at the St John's Mission in Umtata. Styling himself 'Uhadi Waseluhlangeni' (The Harp of the Nation), he demanded that the editor hear the African view after Gqoba had rejected one of his articles as too hostile to the British:

> *Isigidimi* never takes up a clear stand on political matters. It
> sides with the whites, for whenever a writer voices the
> feelings of blacks, *Isigidimi* immediately makes him
> understand that he belongs to the side of the enemy.[(t)55]

The charge of lack of radicalism also began to be levelled by certain
Xhosa intellectuals at the influential politician, writer and editor of *Imvo*
J. T. Jabavu, who had connections in Cape liberal circles and was prime
mover for the establishment of a university (Fort Hare). In contrast to
the Christian liberal ideal, a voice of nascent African nationalism began
to manifest itself in the projects and writings of several of Jabavu's contemporaries and rivals including John Knox Bokwe's biography of Ntsikana
(1914). Having produced pious articles, translations of religious books,
and revisions to the Xhosa version of the Bible, Walter B. Rubusana
found his own Christian commitments increasingly secularised as he
attempted to recover African tradition, history and political rights. He
collected a great number of Xhosa proverbs and praise poems that, in
1906, were printed along with some of Gqoba's unpublished material
in the 570-page anthology *Zemk'iinkomo Magwalandini*.[56] Rubusana also
presided in 1912 at the first meeting of the South African Native National
Congress (forerunner of the ANC) and in 1914 he was part of the
delegation that was sent to London to oppose the Natives Land Act of
1913 according to which Africans were effectively dispossessed in the
land of their birth.

Several features of this early Xhosa literary activity remain important
in any delineation of South African literature. There is the composite
figure of the author-politician-journalist that still characterises many of
our writers. The newspaper and journal, as they did at the Cape in the
nineteenth century, still provide the outlet for a great deal of expression
in a country where literary audiences are small and unevenly distributed.
As encouraged in Jabavu's *Imvo*, forms of political discussion, biography,
and obituary as moral example continue to serve purposes of restructuring
African identity in demeaning colonial situations and, as Rubusana
realised, the anthology in the selection and shaping of its material can
serve as a statement of a people's living tradition. What the Xhosa writers
introduced was a discourse of African nationalism. Long regarded by the
white South African state as a trouble spot, the eastern Cape has produced
an intellectual tradition of leaders including the educationist Z. K.
Matthews, the Black Consciousness activist Steve Biko, and the politician
Nelson Mandela.[57] What we can chart here is a complex passage of
literary history that returns us not only to Ntsikana and Makana but to
their contemporaries Philip and Pringle while projecting us forward to a
humanitarian line that includes Olive Schreiner, Sol T. Plaatje and Alan
Paton. The common characteristic is a revindicated humanism which

holds its broad enlightenment to the account of particular, local causes. At its most pertinent, it is marked creatively by both the Westernism of school people and the Africanism of red people. We may identify this as the 'Xhosa legacy' in a general history of South African literature.

Notes

1. Pakenham, Review of N. Mostert's *Frontiers: The Epic of South Africa's Creation and the Tragedy of the Xhosa People, Sunday Times*, Johannesburg (12 July 1992). The 'frontier question' informs the writing of Philip, Pringle, Godlonton and other who will be examined in the course of this section. See E. Walker, *The Frontier Tradition in South Africa* (Oxford, 1930). Also: W. M. Macmillan, *Bantu, Boer and Briton: The Making of the South African Native Problem* (Oxford; rev. ed., 1963) and, in challenge to Macmillan's liberal view of race as primary factor, M. Legassick's materialist re-reading of the frontier as economic entity, 'The Frontier Tradition in South African Historiography', *Collected Seminar Papers on the Societies of Southern Africa in the 19th and 20th Centuries*, 2 vols (University of London, 1971). More generally, S. Marks and A. Atmore (eds), *Economy and Society in Pre-Industrial South Africa* (London, 1980).

2. See E. I. Edwards, *The 1820 Settlers in South Africa* (London, 1934) and G. Butler (ed.), *The 1820 Settlers: An Illustrated Commentary* (Cape Town, 1974).

3. Prospectus. *The South African Journal*, No. 1 and No. 2 available in facsimile, edited by A. M. Lewin Robinson (Cape Town, 1974).

4. No. 1, 7 January 1824 to No. 18, 5 May 1824, together with *Facts* connected with the stopping of the newspaper, available in facsimile (Cape Town, 1978).

5. 'On the Present State and Prospects of the English Emigrants in South Africa', pp. 151–160.

6. For Pringle's account of his clash with Somerset, see his *Narrative of a Residence in South Africa* (London, 1835; Cape Town, 1966). Also: A. D. Hall, 'Pringle, Somerset and Press Freedom', *English Studies in Africa*, vol. 3, no. 2 (September 1960). For surveys of early press activity in the Cape see L. H. Meurant, *Sixty Years Ago; or, Reminiscences of the Struggle for the Freedom of the Press in South Africa, and the Establishment of the First Newspaper in the Eastern Province* (Cape Town, 1885; 1963) and E. A. M. Lewin Robinson's still authoritative *None Daring to Make Us Afraid: A Study of English Periodical Literature in the Cape from Its Beginnings in 1824 to 1835* (Cape Town, 1962).

7. See R. Davenport, 'The Cape Liberal Tradition to 1910', in J. Butler *et al.* (eds), *Democratic Liberalism in South Africa: Its History and Prospect* (Middletown and Cape Town, 1987), pp. 21–34. See *Democratic Liberalism* for the liberal response to the extensive, often rancorous 'liberal'/'radical' debate that from the early 1970s up to the late 1980s preoccupied South African historiographical and cultural studies. Summary in C. Saunders, *The Making of the South African Past: Major Historians on Race and Class* (Cape Town, 1988).

8. 'State of the Cape of Good Hope in 1822', *The South African Journal*, No. 2 (March–April, 1824), pp. 136–146. Pringle [n. 6 above].

9. See particularly the editorial views of R. Godlonton in *The Graham's Town Journal* as well as Godlonton's *A Narrative of the Irruption of the Kaffir Hordes* . . . (London, 1836; Cape Town, 1965) and *Case of the Colonists of the Eastern Frontier of the Cape of Good Hope, in reference to the Kaffir Wars of 1835–36 and 1846* (Grahamstown, 1879). For Dutch opinion in *The Graham's Town Journal* and *De Zuid-Afrikaan*, see A. du Toit and H. Giliomee (eds), *Afrikaner Political Thought: Analysis and Documents, Vol. 1 1780–1850* (Cape Town, 1983).

10. Several have been published including *The Chronicle of Jeremiah Goldswain*, 2 vols, U. Long (ed.) (Cape Town, 1946), which is notable for its startling use of colloquial English. For a selection of extracts see G. Butler (ed.), *When Boys Were Men* (Cape Town, 1969).

11. *Dagboek van Louis Trichardt, 1836–1838*, G. S. Preller (ed.) (Bloemfontein, 1917; rev. ed., Cape Town, 1938). New edition, T. H. le Roux (ed.) (Pretoria, 1966). See C. Fuller, *Louis Trigardt's Trek across the Drakensberg, 1837–1839* (Cape Town, 1932).

12. Published in English translation (2 February 1837) on the eve of Retief's departure from the Cape colony. Commentary in A. du Toit and H. Giliomee (eds), *Afrikaner Political Thought*, pp. 213–15. On the Great Trek see E. A. Walker, 'A Zulu View of the Retief Massacre', *The Critic*, no. 3 (1935) and *The Great Trek* (London, 1938). Popular accounts include R.U. Kenney, *Piet Retief, the Dubious Hero* (Cape Town, 1976), J. Meintjes, *The Voortrekkers: The Story of the Great Trek and the Making of South African* (London, 1973) and J. Michener's novel *The Covenant* (London, 1980).

13. [N. 9 above]. See B. A. le Cordeur, 'Robert Godlonton as Architect of Frontier Opinion, 1850–1857', *Archives Yearbook for South African History* (Cape Town, 1960).

14. Among Theal's numerous writings are *Records of the Cape Colony*, 36 vols (London, 1897–1905) and *History of South Africa from 1828 to 1846* (London, 1904). The 'colonial view' characterises Cory's influential *The Rise of South Africa*, 5 vols (London, 1910–30); 6 vols (reprint, Cape Town, 1965).

15. Wright published in London, Miller in Cape Town.

16. Pringle's 'Letters from South Africa, No. 1 – Slavery', signed Y, was published in the *New Monthly Magazine and Literary Journal*, London (17 October 1826); conveniently reprinted in E. Pereira and M. Chapman (eds), *African Poems of Thomas Pringle* (Pietermaritzburg, 1989), pp. 140–8. On slavery, see A. E. Voss, ' "The Slaves Must Be Heard": Thomas Pringle and the Dialogue of Servitude', *English in Africa*, vol. 17, no. 1 (May 1990). Also: E. A. Eldredge and F. Morton (eds), *Slavery in South Africa: Captive Labor on the Dutch Frontier* (Boulder and Pietermaritzburg, 1995); R. Shell, *Children of Bondage: A Social History of Slavery at the Cape of Good Hope, 1652–1838* (Johannesburg, 1994); R. L. Watson, *The Slave Question: Liberty and Property in South Africa* (Johannesburg, 1991); and N. Worden and C. Crais (eds), *Breaking the Chains: Slavery and its Legacy in the 19th Century Cape Colony* (Johannesburg, 1994).

17. See Mandela, 'Black Man in a White Court' and 'The Revonia Trial', *No Easy Walk to Freedom* (London, 1965; 1990) and Toivo's 'Here I Stand' in M. Mutloatse (ed.), *Forced Landing. Africa South: Contemporary Writing* (Johannesburg, 1980).

18. Quoted in A. du Toit and H. Giliomee (eds), *Afrikaner Political Thought*, p. 139. (See 'Stockenström and the controversy about frontier politics', pp. 136–40.)

Also: C. W. Hutton (ed.), *The Autobiography of Sir Andries Stockenström, Bart.*, 2 vols (Cape Town, 1887; 1964).

19. *The South African Journal*, No. 2 (March–April 1824); reprinted as *Some Account of the Present State of the English Settlers in Albany, South Africa* (London and Edinburgh, 1824).

20. Pringle's Notes to 'The Bechuana Boy', *African Poems of Thomas Pringle*, p. 78.

21. Coetzee, *Research in African Literatures*, vol. 21, no. 3 (Fall 1990).

22. Coleridge's letter to Pringle (20 March 1828). See A. M. Lewin Robinson, 'Samuel Coleridge and Thomas Pringle', *Quarterly Bulletin of the South African Library*, vol. 6, no. 1 (September 1951).

23. See A. E. Voss on this point: 'Thomas Pringle and the Bushmen', *English in Africa*, vol. 9, no. 1 (May 1982).

24. Leitch Ritchie (ed.), *The Poetical Works of Thomas Pringle, with a Sketch of his Life* (London, 1838).

25. For liberal-Marxist arguments about Philip see A. Ross, *John Philip (1775–1851): Missions, Race and Politics in South Africa* (Aberdeen, 1986) and J. Naidoo, 'Was Dr John Philip an Advocate of "Segregation"?', *Tracking down Historical Myths* (Johannesburg, 1989).

26. Published in London. 70,000 copies were sold in the first few months of its appearance.

27. See P. Brantlinger, 'Victorians and Africans: The Genealogy of the Myth of the Dark Continent', *Critical Inquiry*, vol. 12, no. 1 (Autumn 1985).

28. John William Colenso is notable in seeing evangelicalism as communion between races and, though committed to the Christian standard, regarding the liberal-Christian task as enquiry and understanding across cultures. In fact, it was his respect for the Zulu perspective in the appropriate context that prompted his questioning religious dogma: questioning that provoked the ire of Matthew Arnold and others, and led to the Bishop's being charged with heresy. Another striking moment in Colenso's career in Natal was his decision to speak out bravely in his sermons not in support of the colony nor in vengeance after Britain's humiliating military defeat by Zulu impis at Isandlwana, but about brotherhood and truth revealed in our actions and deeds towards other people. [See biographical entry on Bishop Colenso.] Frances Colenso, wife of the Bishop, wrote 300 letters between 1865 and 1893 which, in their published form, reveal a quiet, sane personality that could transfer insights into religious and family matters to illuminating judgments on colonial bigotry. [See W. Rees (ed.), *Colenso Letters from Natal* (Pietermaritzburg, 1958).] Harriette Colenso, daughter of the Bishop, assisted on the arduous task of re-writing parliamentary Blue Books on the Anglo-Zulu War into an alternative narrative showing Britain's moral bankruptcy in instigating conflict with the Zulu king Cetshwayo as part of the drive to extend and tighten white control over the African people. [See J. Guy, *The Destruction of the Zulu Kingdom: The Civil War in Zululand 1879–1884* (London, 1979; Pietermaritzburg, 1994).] Mahatma Gandhi's writings about his years in South Africa, from 1893 to 1914, may be seen to connect his struggles against anti-Indian legislation in the Transvaal to his belief in *satyagrapha* (soul power or passive resistance), which would inspire the huge ANC campaigns of the 1950s. [See M. K. Gandhi, *Satyagrapha in South Africa* (Ahmedabad, 1928; 1972) and M. Swan, *Gandhi: The South African*

Experience (Johannesburg, 1985).] Emily Hobhouse reminded British authority in the Anglo–Boer War of its avarice and violence in wanting to control the Transvaal gold mines and of its supreme inhumanity in herding Boer women and children into concentration camps as part of its military policy. In *War without Glamour; or, Women's War Experiences written by Themselves 1899–1902* (Bloemfontein, 1924) Hobhouse's transcriptions and translations of Boer women's testimonies anticipated the editing projects that, in the 1980s, would seek to 'give voice' to the silenced, oppressed lives of black South Africa women. [See R. van Reenen (ed.), *Emily Hobhouse: Boer War Letters* (Cape Town, 1984).] Olive Schreiner will be discussed in the main text.

29. Kipling, quoted in *The Cambridge History of English Literature*, vol. 14, no. 3 (1934), p. 373.

30. Cape periodical verse in R. J. Stapleton (ed.), *Poetry of the Cape of Good Hope, Selected from the Periodical Journals of the Colony* (Cape Town, 1828) and subsequent developments in A. Wilmot (ed.), *The Poetry of South Africa* (London, 1887). Also: *Veldsingers' Verse: A Compilation of the Works of Members of the Veldsingers' Club* (London, 1910) and F. C. Slater (ed.), *The Centenary Book of South African Verse 1820–1925* (London, 1925). For details of many nineteenth-century volumes and anthologies see G. M. Miller and H. Sergeant, *A Critical Survey of South African Poetry in English* (Cape Town, 1957). For perspectives on the 'educated' and 'colloquial' streams see the introductions by G. Butler and M. Chapman, respectively, to *A Book of South African Verse* (London, 1959) and *A Century of South African Poetry* (Johannesburg, 1981). Women poets in C. Lockett (ed.), *Breaking the Silence: A Century of South African Women's Poetry* (Johannesburg, 1990).

31. Theatre at the Cape consisted of English comedies such as Sheridon's *The Rivals* and Goldsmith's *She Stoops to Conquer* which were presented by officers of the local garrison. See P. H. Laidler, *The Annals of the Cape Stage* (Edinburgh, 1926).

32. M. Chapman (ed.), *A Century of South African Poetry* (Johannesburg, 1981), pp. 51–2. Full text in M. H. Lister (ed.), *Andrew Geddes Bain. Journals of a Trader, Explorer, Soldier, Road Engineer and Geologist* (Cape Town, 1949), pp. 196–198.

33. See S. Gray, *Southern African Literature: An Introduction* (Cape Town, 1979), pp. 52–7.

34. For a survey see A. M. Lewin Robinson, *None Daring to Make Us Afraid* [n. 6 above].

35. 'Wilkinson' (16 June 1830), 'Frederick.' (vol. 3, no. 4, 1833) and 'Pongola', in T. Roscoe (ed.), *The Remembrance* (London, 1831); reprinted in *African Poems of Thomas Pringle*, pp. 159–164.

36. See for example C. Brownlee, 'The Old Peach Tree Stump: A Reminiscence of the War of 1835' (vol. 7, no. 39, 1873); reprinted with other illustrations in A. M. Lewin Robinson (ed.), *Selected Articles from the Cape Monthly Magazine (New Series, 1870–76)* (Cape Town, 1978). Also: H. H. Dugmore, *The Reminiscences of an Albany Settler* (Grahamstown, 1871). Compare the irreverence about public duty in Lady Duff Gordon, *Letters from the Cape*, edited by J. Purves (London, 1921).

37. See J. Butler *et al.* (eds), *Democratic Liberalism in South Africa* and C. Simkins, *Reconstructing South African Liberalism* (Johannesburg, 1986).

38. Owen, *These Times* (Johannesburg, 1992); Paton's writings generally.

39. Mphahlele, *The African Image* (London, 1962; rev. ed., 1974), p. 112.

40. Surveys: A. S. Gérard, 'Xhosa Literature', *Four African Literatures: Xhosa, Sotho, Zulu, Amharic* (Berkeley, 1971); D. D. T. Jabavu, *Bantu Literature* (Alice, 1921); A. C. Jordan, *Towards an African Literature: The Emergence of Literary Form in Xhosa* (Berkeley, 1973); J. Opland, *Xhosa Oral Poetry: Aspects of a Black South African Tradition* (Johannesburg, 1983).

41. C. C. Crais, *The Making of the Colonial Order: White Supremacy and Black Resistance in the Eastern Cape 1770–1865* (Cambridge: Mass., 1992); S. M. Molema, *The Bantu – Past and Present* (Edinburgh, 1920); N. Mostert, *Frontiers: The Epic of South Africa's Creation and the Tragedy of the Xhosa People* (London, 1992); J. Peires, *The House of Phalo: A History of the Xhosa People in the Days of Their Independence* (Johannesburg, 1981); J. H. Soga, *The South-Eastern Bantu* (Johannesburg, 1930); L. Switzer, *Power and Resistance in an African Society: The Ciskei Xhosa and the Making of South Africa* (Madison and Pietermaritzburg, 1993).

42. Rendered into English from Stockenström's eye-witness account by T. Pringle, 'Letters from South Africa, No. 2 – Caffer Campaigns – The Prophet Makanna', *New Monthly Magazine*, no. 17 (1827); reprinted *African Poems of Thomas Pringle*, p. 156.

43. M. Chapman, 'Red People and School People from Ntsikana to Mandela: The Significance of Xhosa Literature in a General History of South African Literature', *English Academy Review*, 10 (December 1993); A. A. Dubb, 'Red and School: A Quantitive Approach', *Africa*, no. 36 (1966).

44. Bokwe, *Ntsikana: The Story of an African Convert* (Alice, 1914). Also: J. Hodgson, 'The Genius of Ntsikana: Traditional Images and the Process of Change in Early Xhosa Literature', in L. White and T. Couzens (eds), *Literature and Society in South Africa* (Cape Town, 1984). More generally: J. Comoroff, *Of Revelation and Revolution: Christianity, Colonialism and Consciousness in South Africa, Vol. 1* (Chicago, 1991); B. Hutchinson, 'Some Social Consequences of Nineteenth-century Missionary Activity among the South African Bantu', *Africa*, no. 27 (1957); B. A. Pauw, *Christianity and Xhosa Tradition: Belief among Xhosa-speaking Christians* (Cape Town, 1975); B. G. M. Sundkler, *Bantu Prophets in South Africa* (London, 1948).

45. Jordan, *Towards an African Literature*, p. 51.

46. See M. Matshoba, 'A Pilgrimage to the Isle of Makana', *Call Me Not a Man* (Johannesburg, 1979).

47. N. 42 above.

48. For extension of this argument see L. Sanneh, ' "They Stooped to Conquer": Vernacular Translation and the Socio-cultural Factor', *Research in African Literatures*, vol. 23, no. 1 (Spring 1992). Also Sanneh's *Translating the Message: The Missionary Impact on Culture* (New York, 1989).

49. Letter in *King William's Town Gazette and Kaffrarian Banner* (11 May 1865); reprinted in *The Journal and Selected Writings* (Cape Town, 1983), p. 179.

50. See J. B. Peires, *The Dead Will Arise: Nongqawuse and the Great Xhosa Cattle-killing Movement of 1856–7* (Johannesburg, London and Bloomington, 1989).

51. For a serious treatment of the type see Perceval Gibbon's novel *Margaret Harding* (London, 1911; Cape Town, 1983).

52. See Jordan, *Towards an African Literature*, pp. 59–63.

53. For extracts from *Imvo* in the 1880s, see T. Karis and G. M. Carter (eds), *From Protest to Challenge: A Documentary History of African Politics in South Africa, 1882–1964, Vol. 1* (Stanford, 1972). The black press has played a significant role in the development of African literature, often providing the only publishing outlet for opinion. See L. Switzer and D. Switzer, *The Black Press in South Africa and Lesotho: A Descriptive Bibliographic Guide* (Boston, 1979) and T. Couzens' research in several articles including 'Widening Horizons of African Literature, 1870–1900', in L. White and T. Couzens (eds), *Literature and Society in South Africa* (Cape Town, 1984). *South African Outlook* (1922), which has been a major outlet for research on African expression, traces its beginnings, via *The Christian Express*, to the 'Lovedale tradition' of late nineteenth-century journalism.

54. See the anthology *Zemk'iinkomo Magwalandini*, edited by W. B. Rubusana (London, 1906). (Literally, Away Go the Cattle, You Cowards; metaphorically, Preserve Your Heritage. Slogan – the enemy has captured the cattle, you cowards – used to rally African warriors to battle in the nineteenth century.) See A. S. Gérard's discussion of Gqoba, 'Xhosa Literature', *Four African Literatures*, pp. 36–38.

55. See Jordan, *Towards an African Literature*, pp. 97–100.

56. N. 54 above.

57. See Z. K. Matthews, *Freedom for My People* (London, 1981; Cape Town, 1983). See biographical entries on Mandela and Biko.

Chapter 3
Anglicisation and the Afrikaans Language Movements, 1875–1930

Popular sentiment. Du Toit, Preller, Langenhoven

The beginnings of Afrikaans literature proper are linked to two overlapping revolts. The first saw the prevailing high Dutch ethos of formal communication and worship challenged by those who spoke Afrikaans. The Dutch Reformed Church, for example, regarded the new, simplified taal as a threat to all that was venerable and Christian. The second revolt was against anglicisation when, in a bitterly anti-British mood from the 1870s, Afrikaners resisted British imperial policies of confederating the two white communities, English and Afrikaans, to the advantage of English financial and political interests. Having spread out and settled in the interior after clashes with African groups, the descendants of the trekkers had by the late nineteenth century affirmed something of an Afrikaner national character and purpose. This included resisting Britain's attempt to annex the Transvaal and thus wrest the control of gold-mining from president Paul Kruger's Boer republic. The Anglo-Boer War (1899–1902), as the overwhelming threat from Britain, became the climax of the conflict, and in seeking immediately after the Boer defeat to eradicate Afrikaans as a language and to anglicise the entire South African way of life, the high commissioner, Sir Alfred Milner, whose own belief in race mythologies made him suspicious of Afrikaners, so provoked Boer reaction that the survival of Afrikanerdom was ensured. What is important from the point of view of literary developments is that Afrikaner reaction was not spontaneous, but the result of a highly successful campaign to 'build the nation from words': language, literature and ethnic identity were mobilised in a populist, liberatory rhetoric directed against high Dutch and English. Simultaneously, there was a racism in the Afrikaners' assumed European superiority: their white inheritance. It was a racism which would compromise the liberatory drive and, in its triumph, turn Afrikaans into a language of apartheid and oppression.[1]

There is likely to be little agreement on how to approach the literature. With the Afrikaner National Party having ruled South Africa uninterruptedly from 1948 to 1994, Afrikaans culture enjoyed state patronage and was granted enormous prestige. Up until the 1970s, in fact, Afrikaans writers mostly tended to avoid direct criticism of the government's apartheid policies. Afrikaans literary histories have depicted correlations between the development of the literature and the spiritual health of the Afrikaner people (the volk), in which the emphasis has been on the refinements of the Afrikaans language and style rather than on the moral consequences of living in a society of white and black politics. Accordingly, no Afrikaans literary achievement has been regarded as too small for recognition, and books found their way on to school syllabuses almost as soon as they had left the press. In the 1980s, however, a few radical revisionists began to apply deconstructive ideological critique to the Afrikaans canon, and to attack those authors who were not explicit in their opposition to racial injustice. The result is that many father figures are in the process of being castigated for their sins of commission or omission, and the path to renewal is seen by revisionists to require new canons arising from proletarian Afrikaans: that is, Afrikaans stripped of its state apparatus and representing, preferably, coloured working-class Afrikaners who use dialect forms of the language. (Coloured South Africans in the Cape were removed from the voters' roll in 1956 by the National Party's gerrymandering of the constitution.) There have also been attempts, notably by Jack Cope and André Brink, to re-read the existing tradition with the purpose of accentuating a voice of dissidence. In seeking the 'adversary within', Cope reveals his own liberal predilections as he tries to separate the 'fiercely independent spirit' in the writer's personality from its greater or lesser attachment to mystical concepts of the state, while Brink argues for our recognition of what, he believes, constitutes the real character of the dissident writer:

> [His] struggle is not just *against* what is evil in the Afrikaner,
> but *for* what he perceives to be his potential for good. In
> other words, it is not just a struggle aimed at the liberation
> of blacks from oppression by whites, but also a struggle
> for the liberation of the Afrikaner from the ideology in
> which he has come to negate his better self.[2]

Such approaches all claim a continuing if modified role for Afrikaans, and re-readings and re-positionings are obviously then necessary. As politicking after 2 February 1990 between the de Klerk government and the ANC indicated, Afrikanerdom does not regard itself as a spent force in Africa. In fact, it was a hard lesson for the black liberation movements after their unbanning to learn that they were not dealing with a defeated enemy, and that the term Afrikaner contains its own complexities, tensions, and even contradictions. As in the puritan ethos, the Afrikaner-Calvinist emphasis on sin, guilt, divine tasks, exodus from established territory to new promised lands, and belief in the sanctity of the nation over the self, has manifested itself simultaneously in its apparent obverse: a restless, questing will to power, a remarkable adaptability in retaining a grasp on the workings of the modern state. The myths of survival and Being actually reveal the fissures of economic class, and an earlier *volks-kapitalisme* (people's capitalism), which aimed at 'national-socialist' protections for Afrikaners as a group, has been transformed in the process of upwardly mobile urbanisation into an aggressive bourgeois stake in the South African economy.[3] Hankerings after the heroic age of the trekker are intertwined with an almost cynical pragmatism, and the National Party stands accused – after its long stranglehold on power – of wholesale corruption in principle and practice. All this has had its impact on the South African, and indeed southern African, scene and Afrikanerdom, whatever its imaginings about self-sufficiency, is not simply about itself. In literature and life, for example, key aspects of English-liberal and African-nationalist expression have been motivated in sharp reactions to Afrikaner dominance. This is sometimes clear in content and theme. Alan Paton's novel *Too Late the Phalarope* (1952) in its examination of psychological repression and inter-racial sex in a small Afrikaner community took its impetus from the instruments (particularly the Immorality Act) and the temper of the first years of apartheid. Mostly, however, the Afrikaner presence remains a threatening shadow in the subtext of the liberal novel of social concern, or in the black autobiography of identity. In the literature of the Afrikaans language movements in the late nineteenth and early twentieth centuries, the fervent talk of patriotism and self-determination can be recognised as a reaction to the threat of anglicisation. While we should investigate the potential of dissidence in Afrikaans, therefore, we need to question the morality of inhumane actions directed against others in the name of a people's liberation and destiny. The hard condition of the Afrikaner past may not be a sufficient justification for a spirit of volk freedom that ended up manifesting itself as a laager of the spirit.

Afrikaans was initially associated with poverty as a *kombuis taal*, or kitchen language, and in 1874 the Revd S. J. du Toit, under the pseudonym 'Ware Afrikaander' (True Afrikaner), initiated a correspondence in *De Zuid-Afrikaan* pleading for the use of Afrikaans as a written and, hence, a respectable language.[4] Together with a group of clerics and teachers in the Paarl district near Cape Town, du Toit – himself a Dutch clergyman – founded Die Genootskap van Regte Afrikaners (The Society of True Afrikaners), the aims of which were to stand for 'our Language, our Nation, our Country'[(t)].[5] Other main figures were C. P. Hoogenhout and

J. Lion Cachet. The Society published a monthly newspaper, the *Afrikaanse Patriot*,[6] which offered editorial views, correspondence, history, verse, and rules of language. It produced a dictionary, a grammar, schoolbooks and translations of the Bible, a task which was completed in 1933. Du Toit himself wrote an Afrikaans history, *Die Geskiedenis van ons Land* (The History of our Land), which asserted that the good Lord had caused it to rain so continuously when the apprenticeship of slaves ended that, to the mutual satisfaction of all, most ex-slaves were seen creeping meekly back into the service of their erstwhile owners. He also wrote a serialised novel, *Di Koningin fan Skeba* (The Queen of Sheba, 1898) – reminiscent of the standard European adventure in exotic Africa – and became embroiled in controversy as to whether the story was true or false. For, according to Afrikaans congregants, a clergyman should tell only truth, fiction being equated with lies.

After the Anglo-Boer War, it was felt that a wider movement than what would be known as the First Afrikaans Language Movement had to be established for the preservation and recognition of the taal. Some refer to this as the Second Afrikaans Language Movement.[7] It led to various developments among journalists who, in the Transvaal as well as the Cape, started using Afrikaans in their newspapers while the movement gained prestige through the support of literary figures such as Gustav S. Preller, Eugène N. Marais, Jan F. E. Celliers, J. D. du Toit (Totius) and C. Louis Leipoldt. A rationale was provided by Preller in his now famous series of articles, *Laat 't Ons Toch Ernst Wezen* (Let's Take This Matter Seriously), which appeared between April and June 1905 in his newspaper *De Volkstem* (The People's Voice).[8] In negotiations preceding the Act of Union (1910), people interested in Dutch grouped together in an academy for language, literature and art. In 1942, this became the Suid-Afrikaanse Akademie vir Wetenskap en Kuns (The South African Academy for Science and Art). In reaction to Milner's anglicisation policies, struggles were fought for the use of Dutch in schools and churches, and when Britain replaced Milner in South Africa in an attempt to reconcile English-speakers and Afrikaners, the Afrikaans lobby found a climate conducive to assertions of a patriotic Afrikaner spirit. The ex-Boer War generals Louis Botha and Jan Smuts formed political parties that would gain combined leadership in the unified white South Africa. As many Afrikaners saw matters, however, Botha and Smuts were at the beck and call of Rand mining magnates and, in 1914, General J. B. Hertzog broke away to form the National Party drawing with him small farmers and white workers who felt threatened, respectively, by English-capitalist monopolies and competition from unskilled black labour. Before Afrikaans finally gained state recognition in 1925 as an official language, a wide infrastructure of publishing outlets, cultural organisations, women's federations, and language associations had laid the basis for a nationalist literary culture.[9]

The aims were to spread the taal among ordinary people as well as to give prestige to its high literary potential. The magazines *Die Brandwag* (The Torch Commando, 1910–1922) and *Die Huisgenoot* (Home Companion, 1916–   ) reached a wide audience informing readers on educational matters, inculcating reading habits, and popularising the image of the Afrikaans family: dignified in its domesticity with the woman as capable yet selfless in her dual roles of wife and mother. Much of the fiction was historical romance (a good deal on the Boer War), much of the history was mythical in its revisionism. A narrative of national origins included re-interpretations of Slachter's Nek: the Dutch farmers who, in 1816, had resisted labour reforms to the Khoi's lot were now presented as folk heroes, and the British who had hanged them were cast as the enemies of the volk.[10] In Preller's biography *Piet Retief* (1906), which went into ten printings, and in his editions of Voortrekker documents (1918–1939), the Great Trek began to assume the significance of an exodus. With a cult of personality having been created around Retief, his death at the hands of Dingana conjured up images of God-fearing Christianity and heathen barbarism, and the Boer victory over the Zulus at Blood river in 1838 was presented as an emerging myth of a covenant with God: 'if He will be with us and protect us and give the foe into our hands, we shall ever celebrate the day as a Day of Thanksgiving like the Sabbath in His honour'[(t)].[11] Preller, who wrote mostly in Dutch, used a colourful romantic prose, in which the past became a source of inspiration to his own generation. His judgments were partisan, and by the time of the centenary celebration of the Great Trek (1938), he was being influenced by the blood and soil politics of German national socialism.

The other author who was eminent in the moulding of folk mythology was C. J. Langenhoven. Writing in Afrikaans, he produced a mass of prose and poetry, much of it extremely sentimental in tone, that made him the most popular Afrikaner writer of the Second Language Movement. His historical verse includes *Eerste Skoffies op die Pad van Suid Afrika* (First Stages on the Path of South Africa, 1921) which, in the heroic vein, deals with the episodes of Slachter's Nek and the Great Trek. Resonating with Afrikaner mythology of wagons on trek in a vast, empty land, Langenhoven's 'Die Stem van Suid Afrika' (The Voice of South Africa) was written in 1920, set to music, and adopted by the National Party government as the official anthem in the centenary year of the Great Trek, when commemoration took the form of a symbolic ox-wagon journey. The consolidation of Afrikaner nationalism belongs to the 1930s and 1940s, and its master symbols have provided the value system in the education of generations of Afrikaans schoolchildren.[12] In its iconography 'kaffirs' were the sons of Ham. But coloureds, many of whom share the blood of Afrikaners from mixed unions and who speak the taal, have continued to cause Afrikanerdom including its writers several qualms of guilt. It thus seems appropriate that one of the few Afrikaans voices to have struck the iconoclastic note in the years of the language movements should have belonged to a coloured writer, the pseudonymous Piet Uithalder (meaning, to hold forth!) whose 'Straat-praatjes' (Street chats) appeared in the *A.P.O.*, the journal of the African Political (later, People's) Organisation, which was the only news outlet owned and edited by coloured people. Uithalder's popular commentary shifts from satirical barbs directed around the time of Union at the citizens of 'European descent' to bitter attacks on the Botha-Smuts government for having introduced land-restriction acts against Africans and Indians. Similar actions against brown (coloured) people – warns Uithalder – cannot be far off (*A.P.O.*, 8 March 1913). Twisting the terms of the Afrikaans folk song 'Vat Jou Goed en Trek, Fereira' (Take your things and go . . .), he concludes that in the context of land dispossessions the coloureds are now really learning what the words of the old song are all about. According to revisionist Afrikaans critics, attention to black Afrikaners like Uithalder constitutes a necessary reconstructive move in challenging the elite, white terrain of Afrikaner literary nationalism.

Literary sensibility. Marais, Leipoldt, Totius

In the years of the language movements, however, the nationalism was not yet secure or triumphant, and several writers who are regarded as having assisted in the promotion of Afrikaans were not ideologues like Preller and Langenhoven. In encouraging popularisation as a means of reaching the bulk of the Afrikaans audience, the movement with its leadership in the middle classes of the newspapers, the schools and the church took pride in the diversity of Afrikaans literature: its capacities for genius, its abilities to absorb the different European influences to which educated writers such as Celliers, Marais, Totius and Leipoldt had been exposed. While 'nation' and 'nationalism' defined the field of interest, varieties of interpretation distinguish individualities of attitude, sentiment and style, and Marais and Leipoldt, implicitly and explicitly, began to question the very concept of nationalism. All the early writers initially sought, in Afrikaans, a language that could touch the essence of the veld, so that the quest for a language is in a sense the meaning of Marais' 'Winternag' (Winter's Night):

O cold is the slight wind
   and sere
And gleaming in dim light
   and bare,
as vast as the mercy of God,
lie the plains in starlight and shade.
   And high on the ridges,
     among the burnt patches,
the seed grass is stirring
   like beckoning fingers.[t][13]

Whereas Celliers's early poems were clearly influenced by Shelley, Marais eschews derivative romanticism, and his simplicity of diction and rhythmic nuance help to suggest in elegiac mood the memory of Boer War devastation and the need for renewal: a new respect for the delicacy and tranquillity of human wholeness in touch with the land.

In more direct ways, the Anglo-Boer War provided the inspiration for the poem 'Vergewe en Vergeet' (Forgive and Forget) by Totius (the Revd J. D. du Toit), a doctor of theology who had been educated in Amsterdam and who was a minister in the Reformed Church in Potchefstroom. Having ministered to Boer commandos, Totius offered a symbolic vision of hope: the damaged thorn tree would grow strong again, though the wound would remain forever. In 'Ragel' (Rachel) the Boer woman in the concentration camps personified suffering and endurance. Using simple Afrikaans, Totius utilised the icons of trekker mythology: the 'song of the ox wagon' in the days of the trek was a song of freedom; in war, the ox-wagon carried women and children to the camps. His meditative strain, however, permitted no bitterness and, at the height of National Party political campaigning in the 1930s, he wrote in anguish at the death of his own children, of life's mystery and despair, God's eternal meaning, and the necessity of spiritual consolation. This mystical idiom is not propagandist; neither, however, is it by any means dissident, and outside his poetry Totius sanctioned apartheid in biblical argument. My brief analysis here would not be out of place in standard Afrikaans commentaries. Initially, the critic is obliged to remain sympathetic to the victimisation of the Boer, and it is worth recollecting that at the time of the War it was not only Afrikaans writers who offered idealised portraits of a pastoral people attacked by imperial might: so did writers such as Olive Schreiner and Emily Hobhouse.[14]

The next step conducted with hindsight is to try to avoid a failure of political intellect by distinguishing clearly between myths of agrarian communities and histories of the trekker republics as racially bigoted despotisms. Such distinctions, of course, would have had no place in the populist intentions of the language movements. All too often true sympathy is manipulated into sentimentality, and real suffering restricted in its scope to the sectarian cause. This is evident in Totius's epic *Trekkerswee* (Trekkers Woe, 1915) which, in looking at the effects of urbanisation on Afrikaners, can see the city only as the loss of a people's pre-industrial innocence. Similarly, in the writing of Jacob Lub and Jochem van Bruggen, Afrikaner identity in the city is preserved in reaction to conspiracy theories about Jewish 'Hoggenheimer' capitalism using cheap black labour on the mines while Africans generally come in for disparaging treatment.[15]

Shifting from such diagnostic readings to the possibilities of progressive recovery, we have to re-read the mythologising impulse quite severely. Thus André Brink questions nationalist motives in turning Louis Tregardt, whom I discussed earlier, into a heroic trekker: his diary[(t)] was first published in 1917 by Preller and – as has been indicated – appeared again in 1938 to coincide with the centenary celebrations of the Great Trek. Instead, Brink emphasises Tregardt's eccentric individualism, his gun smuggling for the Xhosa, and his perception of himself not as a Moses in the wilderness, but as a trader looking for new markets.[16] In following the same procedure in re-reading Eugène N. Marais, one does not need to endorse the Afrikaans literary tradition in focusing on the formal achievement of 'Winternag' as the first great Afrikaans poem; rather, the line of enquiry may extend to the consequences of Marais' morphine-addicted life, his pursuit of evolutionary theories, and his pseudo-scientific investigations of the souls of white ants and apes. Such interests are not necessarily extra-literary, but can be seen to be part of Marais' liberatory, somewhat *fin de siècle* reaction to president Kruger's fundamental Calvinism in the Transvaal republic. Well versed in English literary culture Marais, as an iconoclastic journalist in the Transvaal, had only scorn for the patriarchal Kruger's evident belief that the world was flat. Accordingly, we may note that Marais' youthful patriotism at the time of the Boer War did not become doctrinaire: he accepted Afrikaner national identity, but neither racism nor politics based on colour. In short, he was not a nationalist, and his *Dwaalstories* (1927) – folk-lore tales which Marais claimed had been related to him by an old Bushman storyteller – can be interpreted as acts of faith: statements of a broad, colour-free humanism. In sharp contrast to the rigid codes of conservative Afrikanerdom, *dwaal* is to wander, to go astray, to gaze in confusion or reverie.[17]

If we pursue this sort of approach, C. Louis Leipoldt presents a particularly interesting case. Known as the founding father of Afrikaans lyric poetry Leipoldt, the well-travelled, well-read humanitarian medical doctor, seemed the antithesis of chauvinist volk culture in almost every way including his homosexuality and his support for the suffragette movement. He also wrote, as 'Pheidippides', in the English *Cape Times* and contributed articles to the *Westminster Review.*[18] In probing the problem of derivative language in English colonial verse, Leipoldt in a manner reminiscent of Browning attempted to test his own questions in the dramatic monologue, 'Oom Gert Vertel' (Uncle Gert Recounts his Story), his landmark poem on the Boer War which was published in 1911. The incident that the old man recalls concerns the extension of martial law to the British Cape colony. As a result, Boers who were living in the Cape and who took up arms against the British were classed as rebels and, if caught, liable to be hanged. (Leipoldt himself came from the Cape town of Clanwilliam.) In the poem, the younger men were restive, two joined the Boer forces while Oom Gert remained behind: 'Ach, what can you do?/ Or what can any of us do?'[(t)]. He now bears his cross, and in the climax of his story he recollects the bravery of the two youths. Having been arrested by British soldiers who, it is stressed, were only doing their duty, the young Boers are sent to the gallows in the presence of the local townspeople:

> And Johnny also took my hand and said,
> A smile around his lips: 'Good morning, Oom.
> No, Oompie, don't you cry!' Yes, as I've said,
> He always was inclined to be precocious
> And cheeky, too. 'No, Oompie, don't you cry!
> We did our duty, and it's over now.'

> And then they both talked to the minister,
> And I, as Bennie's nearest blood relation,
> Accompanied him to the gallows, there . . .
> No, boy, it's just the smoke. I'm getting old
> And your tobacco is too strong for me.
> I smoke it mild myself. Because, you see,
> It doesn't make my eye so sore.
>   Where was I?[(t)19]

Apparently artless and discursive in its conversational idiom, the blank-verse line allows for moments of lesser and greater intensity as Oom Gert tries to conceal his love for the boys, his attachment to their patriotism and, by implication, his commitment to the Afrikaner nation. One way of interpreting the accents and tone, therefore, is to stress Oom Gert's struggle to face his own bad conscience: he had prevaricated in the years of the War instead of acting on his convictions. By recognising that all the participants in this war between 'nations' were human beings whether Afrikaners or British, however, Oom Gert allows Leipoldt to hint at a theme that would increasingly direct his writing: the ultimately divisive nature of nationalist causes.

In his compassion for innocent victims on whatever side when only the narrowest commitments were expected of him, Leipoldt wrote a play

Die Heks (The Witch, 1923) using material from medieval Catholicism in a society of extreme Calvinists and even flirted with Buddhism. Combining his medical insights with a romantic view of sturdy primitiveness in *Bushveld Doctor* (1937), he gave an account in English of life as a health officer among poor white communities as he struggled to square his 'aristocratic' liberal inclinations with a belief in the basic decency of all people, and in his posthumously published novel *Stormwrack* (1980), which was written in the mid 1930s, the danger he saw for South Africa was very definitely the destructiveness of nationalism. By the 1930s Leipoldt had followed the broader South Africanism – the co-operation between the two white 'races' – that had been promoted by the Botha-Smuts influence rather than by the zealous Afrikaner sectionalism of the Hertzog faction. But his later work fails to capture the sharp observations and accents of his early poetry. Despite his dissident challenge to Afrikaner sectionalism, Leipoldt saw little need to mount an African challenge against the exclusively European concerns of Smuts' South Africanism.[20] The selective vision is a feature of most South African writing, however, and should encourage us to ponder on the difficulties attendant on the concept 'nation'. Responding to current ANC-inspired debates about the need for a new nation, the *verligte* ('enlightened') Afrikaans philosopher Johan D. Degenaar brings to his argument the problematic history of Afrikaner nation-building when he suggests that, in the racial and cultural mix of South Africa, we may be required not so much to build a nation as to create a democracy, in which the concept of nation should make way for that of a civil society.[21] This would entail Afrikaans literature being prised from its own ethnic narrative and re-interpreted within a comprehensive programme of recovery. My purpose has been to offer tentative suggestions in such a direction.

Notes

1. See W. de Klerk, *The Puritans in Africa* (Harmondsworth, 1976); A. du Toit, 'No Chosen People: The Myth of the Calvinist Origins of Afrikaner Nationalism and Race Ideology', *The American Historical Review*, vol. 88, no. 4 (October 1983); I. Hofmeyr, 'Building a Nation from Words: Afrikaans Language Literature and Ethnic Identity', in S. Marks and S. Trapido (eds), *The Politics of Race, Class and Nationalism in Twentieth-Century South Africa* (London, 1987); T. Pakenham, *The Boer War* (London, 1979); T. Sundermeier (ed.), *Church and Nationalism in South Africa* (Johannesburg, 1975); L. Thompson, *The Political Mythology of Apartheid* (New Haven, 1985); and F. A. van Jaarsveld, *The Awakening of Afrikaner Nationalism, 1868–1881* (Cape Town, 1961).

2. Brink, *Mapmakers: Writing in a State of Siege* (London, 1983), p. 20. For revisionist readings see: A. Coetzee *Letterkunde en Krisis: 'n Honderd Jaar Afrikaanse Letterkunde en Afrikaner-Nasionalisme* (Johannesburg, 1990), English translation 'Literature and Crisis: One Hundred Years of Afrikaans Literature and Afrikaner Nationalism', in M. Trump (ed.), *Rendering Things Visible* (Johannesburg, 1990); J. Cope, *The Adversary Within: Dissident Writers in Afrikaans* (Cape Town and London, 1982); M. de Jong, *'n Ander Afrikaanse Letterkunde: Marxistiese en Sociaalgerigte Teksopvattings in Afrikaans* (Pretoria, 1989) and essays in C. Malan (ed.), *Race and Literature/Ras en Literatuur* (Pinetown, 1987). On 'black Afrikaans': H. Willemse, 'Die Skrille Sonbesies: Emergent Black Afrikaans Poets in Search of Authority', in Trump. Standard histories include R. Antonissen, *Die Afrikaanse Letterkunde van die Aanvang tot Hede* (Cape Town [1946]; 2nd ed., 1961) and J. C. Kannemeyer's two-volume *Geskiedenis van die Afrikaanse Literatuur* (Cape Town, 1978, 1983).

3. See D. O'Meara, *Volkskapitalisme: Class, Capital and Ideology in the Development of Afrikaner Nationalism* (Johannesburg, 1983).

4. Prior to du Toit's intervention a few pieces of recognisable Afrikaans, as opposed to Dutch, writing had appeared at irregular intervals: e.g. L. H. Meurant's contributions to the *Kaapsche Grensblad* (Cape Border Magazine, 1844–1850) and his *Zamenspraak* (Conversation, 1861) on separate legislatures for the eastern and western Cape.

5. For an account of what is referred to as the First Afrikaans Language Movement see L. van Niekerk, *Die Eerste Afrikaanse Taalbeweging en Letterkundige Voortbrengselen* (Cape Town, 1920).

6. Facsimile edition of first volume (Cape Town, 1974).

7. See E. C. Pienaar, *Taal en Poësie van die Tweede Afrikaanse Taalbeweging* (Cape Town, 1926) and P. C. Schoomes, *Die Prosa van die Tweede Afrikaanse Taalbeweging* (Pretoria, 1922).

8. Commentary on Preller is to be found in D. J. C. Geldenhuys, *Pannevis en Preller* (Johannesburg, 1967), pp. 54–89.

9. For a perceptive account of Afrikaner cultural activities in the early twentieth century, see Hofmeyr [n. 1 above].

10. See A. Coetzee, 'The Slagter's Nek Rebellion of 1815: Idealist and Materialist Interpretations in Afrikaans Literature', in C. Malan (ed.), *Race and Literature/Ras en Literatuur*, pp. 185–96.

11. See L. Thompson, 'The Covenant', *The Political Mythology of Apartheid*, pp. 144–88.

12. In summary, legal authority is not to be questioned; whites are superior, blacks are inferior; the Afrikaner has a special relationship with God; South Africa belongs to the Afrikaner; South Africa is an agricultural country and the Afrikaner is a boer (farmer); South Africa is a hard land and the Afrikaner, accordingly, is independent, isolated, physically strong, bound to tradition; the Afrikaner is ingenuous in regarding military matters; he [sic] has a history of defeating kaffirs while it took the entire might of the British army and the tactics of farm-burning and herding women, children and the elderly into concentration camps to subdue the Boer commandos. Nonetheless, the Afrikaner numbers only 3 million on a hostile African continent and in a 'liberalistic'

and 'communistic' world (the terms are used interchangeably), his threatened status justifies whatever actions are deemed necessary for survival.

13. A. P. Grové and C. J. D. Harvey (eds), *Afrikaans Poems with English Translations* (Cape Town, 1962). This anthology provides a comprehensive selection of Afrikaans poetry in English translation. See the standard anthology, D. J. Opperman (ed.), *Groot Verseboek* (Cape Town, 1951; several reprints and revisions).

14. See Schreiner's *Thoughts on South Africa* (London, 1923; Johannesburg, 1992) and Hobhouse's *Boer War Letters*, edited by R. van Reenan (Cape Town, 1984).

15. See Lub's *Donker Johannesburg* (Pretoria, 1910) and Van Bruggen's *Ampie* trilogy (Cape Town, 1924, 1928, 1942).

16. *Mapmakers*, pp. 20–21.

17. On Marais see J. Cope, *The Adversary Within*, pp. 1–18.

18. Selection in *English in Africa*, vol. 7, no. 1 (March 1980). See particularly Leipoldt's views on language and colonial verse, 'Adam Lindsay Gordon: A Critical Study' (February 1906).

19. A. P. Grové and C. J. D. Harvey (eds), *Afrikaans Poems with English Translations*.

20. A similar loss of immediacy characterises Deneys Reitz's conversion from young Boer rebel to respected member of the Smuts government. Originally written in a school exercise book in rude Dutch by Reitz who as a youth rode with General Smuts during his commando raid into the Cape colony, *Commando* was published only in 1929, in standard English, with the excision of many bitter passages. The editing project, which was undertaken with Reitz's approval by the London publisher Faber, was meant to make a point about healing divisions between reasonable English-speaking and Afrikaans South Africans. Reitz went on to produce *Trekking On* (London, 1933) and *No Outspan* (London, 1943), both rather studied accounts of his years as high commissioner in London.

21. Degenaar, *Nations and Nationalism: The Myth of a South African Nation* (IDASA Occasional Paper, Cape Town, 1987).

The Story of the Colony. Fiction, 1880–

The heart of darkness from Rider Haggard to Wilbur Smith

By the early years of the twentieth century, it was becoming possible to define colonial fiction in its southern African manifestations.[1] In South Africa two impulses were evident, producing the tale of the colonial-sojourner for whom Africa is the exotic alternative to real existence in the metropole, and the tale of the settler on the farm in which the ordering eye, hand and gun impose authority on the savage land. The treacherous paradise – to be conquered or transcended – characterised similar colonial narratives in Rhodesia where, in the 1890s, Rhodes' British South Africa Company began to peg farms for white ownership and exploit minerals in the Ndebele and Shona kingdoms. The source material for these stories was often provided by the ready supply of reminiscences, journals and campaign narratives written by settlers, missionaries, hunters, traders and administrators, as well as the wives of various settlers. The intended readers were British. Editions of the books, in 'colonial library series', however, were shipped to the colonies where responses and reviews tended to echo metropolitan opinions. Such inter-dependence of publishing interests and realities persists particularly in the case of the novel. Whether popular like the adventure stories of Wilbur Smith, or serious like the social problem works of Nadine Gordimer, the novel has regarded – has had to regard – the international market as its primary place of sales. In South Africa, the literary novel is likely to sell only about 1,000 copies. The paradox can be observed, therefore, that the novel more than the play or, in little magazines, the poem or short story is the form through which a small foreign-educated, or foreign-influenced, authorship in southern Africa has communicated its insights in the first instance to reading publics abroad.

In surveying colonial fiction of the late nineteenth century, we can identify a very uncertain sense of place and accent, and the constant

factor is the racial–cultural prejudices, presumptions and fantasies of eurocentric and/or imperialist doctrines. Short stories, which appeared in
local newspapers and periodicals, tended to rely on predictable types,
settings were usually extraneous from rather than determining any social
function, and plots often turned on coincidence. There are hunting yarns,
tales of fortune or misfortune on the diamond diggings, and romances
set against the Anglo-Boer War. There is the hunter, his bushveld dog
and, often killed in saving his master's life, the faithful African retainer;
there are both gentlemen and bar-room diggers, remittance men who are
given second chances in the colony, and ladies with pasts who appear as
angels or whores in some Kimberley saloon. There is the administrator
who is bemused by the superstition of his native wards, the colonial
male who lets the side down and 'goes native', and practical wives who
keep house on the veld despite the unreliability of servants. Diction acts
as a social and racial marker: stiff British; colloquial working class; accentuated Jewish (usually for sharp dealers); and a kind of gibberish for
Africans who are usually cowering or clownish. Mostly, though, Africans
are mute, or absent from the action. There is the implication of egalitarian
opportunity in the colony: outside the metropolitan class–system the
enterprising person can succeed. But conventions of behaviour are rarely
open to serious investigation in terms of class, race or gender. Freedom
is usually personified as the small individual who overcomes the odds of
mining conglomerates which are mystified as wheels of fortune. Women
may be wild sports only to conform in the end to the division between
male (public) and female (domestic) activities, and men may go native
for reasons other than lust, but the British fiancée, however shallow or
priggish, is eventually favoured – by the author if not by the protagonist
– to the inevitably lax coloured woman who is referred to usually as a
'girl'.

The full-blown adventure novel was very often ethnographic in nature,
and concerned itself with quests by intrepid Victorians to the heart of
darkness: the phrase was actually coined by Sir Henry Rider Haggard.
We encounter initiations into manhood, curiosity about native tribes, the
defeat of evil witch doctors, the triumph of science, the superiority of
Christian values, and the worth of protestant industry. So successful were
his adventure romances that after the publication of *King Solomon's Mines*
(1885), Haggard was able to retire for life. Having served as a British
administrator in South Africa in the 1870s during which time he learnt
to admire Zulu culture and when Britain annexed the Transvaal republic to despise the Boer, Haggard returned to Norfolk as a gentleman
farmer and, before his death, was muttering darkly about the Jew who
was supposed to be a threat to Western, Christian civilisation. *King
Solomon's Mines* bases its story-line on the chivalric quest, in which
Victorian gentlemen, some with Nordic features, accomplish their heroic

deeds in an Africa that remains a laboratory for the proving of British manhood rather than a real place. The heroes restore a black savage to arcane rule and return home with pockets of loot. In substance, these are metropolitan concerns, and in Haggard's romances anxieties show at points where his symbols and myths touch the history that has provoked their use: the imperial confidence, for example, does not always mask the obverse fear about the decline of the West especially as it impinged upon the ethos of chauvinist, Victorian masculinity. At an unintentionally comic moment in *She* (1887), Haggard's explorers are nonplussed in penetrating the tomb (or womb?) of the white goddess only to have to confront someone who, despite her egyptological attire, sounds a little like a late nineteenth-century New Woman. The other reaction to the decline of the West is what we would now refer to as modernist: Africa is imagined, simultaneously, as horrific (the dark, destructive unconscious) and regenerative (the dark, creative unconscious). Even as he shows some reverence for African custom, Haggard indulges in colonial justifications about white – rather than indigenous – civilisations having built Great Zimbabwe (the 'ruins'). A mutual attraction across the colour line in *King Solomon's Mines* ends, in summary, with the noble black woman Foulata declaring that 'the sun cannot mate with the darkness, or the white with the black'.

All this speaks of the effects of scientific race theories on the colony, and revisionist South African criticism in the 1970s and 1980s armed itself with third-world, anti-colonialist critics like Franz Fanon and Albert Memmi, as well as with the analytical tools of structuralist-Marxism, in order to re-read colonial fiction as the grubby story of conquest, greed, arrogance, and over-weening pride. Outside university readings, unfortunately, colonial myths persist: the action-packed Rider Haggard remains a best-selling boys' adventure writer with recent editions of *King Solomon's Mines* having excised the word 'kaffir', and the 'Haggard' recipe larded with adult sex provides Wilbur Smith with his international best-seller fare: endless safaris and seductions, big game, game women, an Africa where the approved politics are thoroughly conservative. As in the case of Haggard, Smith utilises space and time as the non-socialised entities of the adventure mode, characters have only rudimentary motives and motivations, and there is little qualifying irony. The phobias of 'white culture', however, are not confined to adventure fiction in the likes of Rider Haggard or Wilbur Smith. There is a corpus of fiction that takes itself extremely seriously about the 'native question' and has been given reputable status in studies of South African literature.

Just as Haggard elevated racial and sexual determinants over and above societal causation, so did Sarah Gertrude Millin. From the 1920s to the 1950s Millin was regarded by official South African culture, as endorsed by prime minister Smuts, to be authoritative on the native question. In her best-known novel, *God's Step-children* (1924), the protagonist, the Revd Andrew Flood, breaks the bonds of white civilisation by going native, and the sins of his 'miscegenation' are visited relentlessly upon his children as the mixed blood weakens the strain and leads to enfeeblement. Attracting more attention in the United States than in South Africa when it was initially published, *God's Step-children* was successfully republished, in a joint South African/Rhodesian edition in the 1950s, in the first years of apartheid. In concealing her own shudder, Millin reserves pity for the coloured 'step-children' of the Revd Flood and, as a consequence, her practice as a novelist has received some favourable commentary.[2] It is said that she is not a virulent racist but a kind of tragic poet who, writing in a society without a strong sense of class differentiation and latching on to current European eugenicist ideas, sought her seriousness in character-study based on ethnicity. In South Africa, so the argument goes, life and destiny seemed to Millin to be *realistically* determined by colour. Another way of explaining Millin, however, might be to identify what she herself apparently could not: her own conditioning by class. As a child of poor Lithuanian immigrants, she saw the poverty of poor white and coloured on the diamond diggings; she subsequently married into Johannesburg professional society (her husband became a reasonably enlightened judge of the supreme court), and her fears of miscegenation might actually be class anxieties about dropping back into destitution transfigured, psycho-logically, into the motif of national racial dementia. The problem remains, though, that as racism in South Africa became institutionalised in the 1950s and as Rhodesian settler hysteria in the sixties grew against the wind of change, Millin's own writing – especially in *King of the Bastards* (1949), *The Burning Man* (1952) and *The Wizard Bird* (1962) – lost even its own early capacities for pity, and in its character depictions increasingly endorsed racist fears of bastards and other assorted primitives.

Several writers of the late nineteenth and early twentieth centuries were neither adventure-obsessed nor race-obsessed, but were unable to challenge prevailing manners and conventions in any telling way. Of the many novels and stories on miscegenation, Perceval Gibbon's *Margaret Harding* (1911) broke sharply from its author's own earlier *Souls in Bondage* (1904), in which race and sex had been degraded to lascivious violence, and tried to explore a relationship between a black man and a white woman. The issue is fudged, however, because Gibbon makes his black character an Oxford-educated doctor, a 'Christianised kaffir' who – backed by authorial sympathy – complains that his acculturation has led to his alienation in a world of colour where ne'er black and white shall meet. Of the numerous writers who depended for their subject matter on the customs of the indigenous people – including Francis Carey Slater and W. C. Scully – Scully typifies a brand of romantic liberalism in the colony. In his novel *Daniel Venanda: The Life Story of a Human Being*

(1923), for example, the country African meets his ruin in the sinful city of Johannesburg. Although Scully indicts the inhumanity of South African segregationist policy, the options for any change in the urban environment are hardly contemplated, and the novel ends as a plea for rural integrity. Jean Marquard accurately sums up Scully – a Cape civil servant – as passionate in his mediocrity.[3] It is a description that remains valid for a great deal of what one might still call colonial writing.

Schreiner's colonial crisis

So long as problems of race remain crucial and corrosive, we cannot simply consign a conservative tradition to the scrap heap. The stories need to be interrogated for their ideological effects. At the same time, however, we need to go beyond critiques of negation to the few writers in the nineteenth century who asked questions that cannot easily be dismissed. Among novelists there were, notably, Olive Schreiner and Douglas Blackburn. In a review, Rider Haggard thought he perceived similarities of intention and style between his romances and Schreiner's first published work, *The Story of an African Farm* (1883): 'when Naturalism has had its day . . . and the Society novel is utterly played out . . . [there are] those works of fancy which appeal, not to a class, or a nation, or even to an age, but to all time and humanity at large'.[4] For Schreiner, however, the adventure romance in its 'encounters with ravening lions, and hair-breadth escapes' was the mark of the imagination untrammelled by contact with fact. In the colony, in contrast to Piccadilly or the Strand, the artist, Schreiner maintained, must 'squeeze the colour from the brush . . . dip into the grey pigments . . . paint what lies before him'. Life must be depicted not according to the 'stage method'; rather, there is 'strange coming and going of feet. Men appear, act and re-act upon each other and pass away . . . nothing can be prophesied.'[5] As recent criticism has noted, these comments tie principles of novelistic structure in *African Farm* to Schreiner's own impressions of life in the Cape colony.[6] In her writings, she asks something that seems never to have occurred to Haggard: what must I be, and do, to live in the colony at this time?

Born on a mission station near present-day Lesotho, Schreiner lived an itinerant early life. As a result of the financial failure of her father, a missionary, she spent much of her youth and young adulthood with a sister and brother on the Kimberley diamond diggings and as a governess on isolated Karoo farms. Her dogmatically religious mother provoked her turning towards free-thought and mysticism while the Bible – especially in its parables – remained influential on her practice as a thinker and writer. Her ongoing search was for a sense of unity in what she felt to be the severe dislocations of her own experience. As she said after having had Herbert Spencer's *First Principles* (1862) brought to her notice: 'He helped me believe in the unity underlying all nature.'[7] But in the colony, her reading comprised a miscellany of scattered sources. Living as she was in other people's houses, information and books came to her from 'strangers passing through to somewhere else', and her novels cluster around a web of emotions: loss and betrayal in love, woman's alienation, guilt, and the constriction of the ardent spirit in the arid physical and mental conditions of the colony. In 1881 Schreiner travelled to England in what was to be a vain attempt to become a doctor: she had neither money nor good health. She had written a novel *Undine*, which would be published posthumously only in 1929, and had begun *From Man to Man*, the manuscript of which would never be completed and was published for the first time in 1926. These two books concern woman's identity: in *Undine* the question is whether a woman needs to *become* a man in order to participate in society; in *From Man to Man* the theme is the nature of sexual deception. Both mingle melodrama and didacticism. Despite specifically South African references, there is in the overall drive of the narratives little direct sense of colonial culture: the colony, perhaps, as the patriarchal space. Paradoxically, of course, the uncertainty of belonging is in itself a persistent colonial trait, and in *The Story of an African Farm* – which was written under the pseudonym Ralph Iron, and published to acclaim in England – the ideas of belonging and displacement, yearning and frustration, find powerful location in the setting of the Karoo:

> In one spot only was the solemn monotony of the plain
> broken. Near the centre a small, solitary 'kopje' rose. Alone
> it lay there, a heap of round iron-stones piled one upon the
> other, as over some giant's grave.

In replying to Dan Jacobson's oft-quoted comment that, in its subservience to the metropole, a colonial culture has no memory of itself,[8] Ruth First and Ann Scott – Schreiner's biographers – regard the Karoo as the motif by which Schreiner asserted the necessity of memory in her attempts to give the substance of reality to her own impressions and experiences. In terms of novelistic practice, this need not suggest any conformity to the conventions of realism, or any striving after local colour. In *African Farm* there is accurate description of landscape, there is the use of some Dutch words, and in the speech of the Dutch-Afrikaans characters, Tant' Sannie and Em, syntactical inversions and colloquialisms help capture the rhythms of the 'non-English' accent. Mostly, though, Schreiner retains standard English while she switches perspective and mode in order to inscribe, into the form, the heterogeneous, restless character of what it meant to her to be living in a colony. Adaptation of language register is not Schreiner's primary concern; rather, the use of English in the colonial situation becomes symptomatic of a radical 'inauthenticity': a mismatch of behaviour and convention. At the centre of the story are the two young, potentially free spirits, Lyndall – urgent in her desire for fulfilment as an independent woman – and Waldo, dreamy in his searches for eternal meaning. Their hopes and dreams, however, are destined to be stunted like the scrub of the landscape.

Across this blank landscape, on their way to the distant diggings, drift assorted types such as Bonaparte Blenkins – a parody of the interloper and opportunist – whose Irish blarney is sufficiently gutter-wise to impose itself as a brief and pernicious 'discourse of power' on the inhabitants of the farm. Blenkins's method is the tall story, and we realise the importance of the word 'story' in the title of the book. For the colony has to write its own story, its history, on the empty page; and the storyteller may be recognised as a key instrument of the fiction. Stories-within-stories consti-tute an exploratory technique in Schreiner's work. In *African Farm* there are, besides Blenkins's tall tales, pamphleteering speeches, lyrical sequences about unity in growth, and parodic scenes that overturn bondings and contracts and remind us of the fragility of settled existence. In a borrowing from the nineteenth-century novel Lyndall, like a fallen woman, runs away with her stranger and loses the will to live after the death of her newly-born child. But the colony with its undeveloped social life could not care less about such a 'bourgeois tragedy'. In an odd way, the colony gives Lyndall, as well as perhaps Schreiner, opportunities that would not have been available to her in the 'tamed' class-stratifications of the metrop-olis. But Schreiner – repeating the most persistent characteristic of fellow colonials – could not always recognise the entities of the life around her. What she imported from the metropole did not necessarily fit the Cape environment.

The plot of comings and goings, and the sudden juxtapositions of different planes of experience, therefore, should not be regarded primarily as matters of aesthetic challenge. In defending the book against the view that as realism its form is 'flawed', some critics have wanted to see *African Farm* as a proto-modernist novel.[9] But the style is probably the close reflection of a condition of anxiety that makes its impact precisely because it is not a grammar of pure narration: instead, Schreiner gives us the shape of historical necessity. When one story or convention is dropped for another, Schreiner is not so much pushing against the boundaries of realist art as registering her own psychic state in the frontier condition. Her realism is, consequently, a mutation of romance, even gothic: life as a conglomerate of ill-digested reading knows little of domestic calm, and the impulse is not to retain consistency of imitation, but to veer towards parable-like insertions as truth is grasped in the abstractions of allegory. Waldo provides an apt illustration. Unable to connect his religious impulsions to the sand, stone and scrub of the farm, he heads for the towns where he encounters the colony changing under the impetus of diamond discovery from an agricultural to an industrial working base. Finding only hard manual labour he returns to the farm and, on the closing page of the story, is permitted a convenient 'literary' death as he is subsumed into the landscape. This use of pastoral, however, only succeeds in accentuating by contrast the attention the story as a whole has given to the *realism* of thwarted ambition in promising young lives.

A tension between history and the ideal remains a feature of all Schreiner's work. When she returned to the Cape from England in 1889, she had been influenced by current Darwinist thinking as well as by debates on the 'woman question', and she felt the need to be involved as a public participant in South African political matters. At the same time as she produced allegorical stories – collected as *Dream Life and Real Life* (1893) – she turned to essays, speeches and pamphlets. In *African Farm*, the demands of self-identity in the uncongenial environment had led to a narrowing of the historical sense. The Boer woman, Tant' Sannie, is easily satirised; Blenkins's viciousness is dispersed in knock-about comedy; and the slightly grotesque African servants remain outside the centres of interest. There is a hint in allusions to Bushmen that the colonial enterprise had plundered the original inhabitants. But the main allegory concerning the search for the white bird of truth is not reconnected in the story to its source in Bushman mythology; rather, it is colonised as Europe's, or Schreiner's, own universal lesson. Such essentialising of historical particularity would continue to have circumscribing effects on Schreiner's understanding of the South African situation. In her defence of the Boer against British imperialism, for example, she resorted to the standard anti-imperialist images of the organic community under siege. What she added were her preoccupations with the international woman's question. In her long story 'Eighteen Ninety Nine' (written *c.*1906), she mythologised the Boer woman as the child-bearing, reverential source of continuity and life and, in linking this idea of agrarian innocence to that of woman's innate value, she argued that industrial society had devalued the woman's emotional and reproductive labour.[10] At the same time, she saw middle-class women as sex-parasites in their dependence on men in a modern society that did not train them for meaningful work. This led Schreiner to invoke myths of archetypal maternity including ideal mothering, according to which African women, but not European women, were hailed as having retained the 'hunger to bear children'. (Schreiner's only child had lived for just a few hours.) The blurring here of racial, class and gender distinctions is very clearly pre-feminist while the transfer of the European discourse on to the African woman can become unintentionally patronising, even insulting. Where the politics is advanced for its time, nonetheless, is in Schreiner's willingness to examine her own idealising tendency as she herself came to the conclusion that the European woman question had to be adjusted to the claims of South Africa, where racism as well as economic exploitation was rife in the work place. Committing herself to a South Africa without racial segregation, she resigned her vice-presidency of the Cape Women's Enfranchisement League in 1913 when the group failed to support the suffrage of black men and women along with that of white women. Her developing insight was that race is a social rather than a physical reality.

Several years before the Anglo-Boer War Schreiner had conveyed her anger at British ambitions and practices in her 'allegory story', to use her own description, *Trooper Peter Halket of Mashonaland* (1897). Turning from her initial admiration for Rhodes ('the only big man we have here')[11] she directed an animus, which had been fuelled possibly by her feelings of an unrequited love interest, at the mining magnate's vicious suppression through his British South Africa Company of the Ndebele and Shona rebellions: rebellions that had been provoked by white territorial occupation of what would be named Rhodesia. Sitting alone one night in the veld Trooper Peter − a simple Victorian youth who hopes to emulate the achievement of Rhodes and make his fortune in Africa − is visited by a Christ-like stranger who, in a 'sermon on the mount', convinces Peter of the immorality of pillage and conquest. As a result, Peter releases a black prisoner and in the confusion is shot dead by his own commanding officer. The idealising and historicising tendencies, operating in tandem, have led to some argument as to whether *Trooper Peter Halket* is a propagandist tract or a work of the imagination. But as an early reviewer − unencumbered by academic distinctions between 'poetry' and 'history' − aptly noted, if the book 'is a humanitarian pamphlet, it is also imaginative literature. . . . [A]side from its argumentative power it enthralls and impresses the reader'.[12] In using several 'mouthpiece' characters, Schreiner imbues her didacticism with human emotion, and Peter's allegory of conversion has considerable psychological verisimilitude. The inspiring example of radical Christianity is tested in the details of military conduct, and Peter, the individual, becomes representative of necessary conscience. Where the book remains colonial is in its retention of the British standard. The black prisoner is a device in the plot; the subject is British rule; and Schreiner's plea is that Britain realise the inhumanity of imperialism and re-discover its capacity for justice and compassion. Against the reality of Rhodes, she offers the ideal of Sir George Grey who − we may recall − had ensured the final destruction of the Xhosa by integrating them into the Cape colony as a severely dependent labour force. If Schreiner's moral vision was historically part of its time, however, it was more percipient than most other views in

the colony. Just as Philip and Pringle in the 1830s had identified fundamentals about power and injustice, so did Schreiner. Africa is exposed in
imperial designs as exploitable territory not only in terms of its commodi-
ties, but in terms of its people. On her grave, Schreiner said, she wanted
only the words: 'She wrote *Trooper Peter Halket*'.[13]

Blackburn's Bulalie comes to Joburg

Like Schreiner, Douglas Blackburn indicts the debased form of the civilising mission that was the colonial practice, and comes to despairing
conclusions as to what it meant to be white in South Africa. Arriving
on the Rand from south London in 1892 Blackburn, an underpaid
journalist with socialist leanings, hoped for opportunity as an ordinary
man amid the apparent mobility and excitement of gold discovery. With
the *Eastern Star* – the daily afternoon newspaper from Grahamstown –
having literally followed the gold rush to the Transvaal and set itself up
in Johannesburg as the *Star* (1887–   ), Blackburn found work and began
to offer his brand of satirical exposé journalism on the urgent issues of
the day. He had no truck with Tory imperialism and as a consequence
with mining interests, and his quarrel was not that the Kruger oligarchy
classified him as an uitlander (foreigner) thus denying him a vote. Rather,
he retained sympathy for the shambling administration of the Transvaal,
in which the pastoral, backveld mentality had been surprised by mining
developments. At the same time, he regarded it as his function to attack
nepotism and corruption wherever it occurred. The Boer government,
however, seemed to Blackburn to comprise small-time cheats in contrast
to the financial houses epitomised by the figure of Rhodes. As in the
case of Schreiner, his criticism tended to be mingled with nostalgia for
Boer society as classless and cohesive, and initially his interests did not
stretch to the problem of colour: in 1894, in fact, he rode with a Boer
commando in a campaign of genocide against neighbouring Tswana.
Having views that were not usually in consonance with editorial opinion
in the pro-British *Star*, Blackburn found himself turning increasingly to
the several fly-by-night newspapers and scandal sheets, which were a
feature of Rand life.[14] Here he unleashed his vitriolic editorials, in the
name of the decent, common white man, English or Afrikaans, against
humbug, charlatanism, crooks and sharks of all variety in the brash new
world of Johannesburg.

The image he adopted, and which inspired his first 'literary' writing,
was that of a Don Quixote conducting impossible campaigns against evil
run rampant. In considering the possibilities of fiction, he utilised the

form of the journalistic sketch – anonymously written, parading itself as plain fact – to condemn Rhodes as a warmonger in *Kruger's Secret Service, by One Who Was In It* (1900). Blackburn had been influenced here possibly by F. R. Statham's *Mr Magnus* (1896) which employed rudimentary novelistic devices to launch a ruthless attack on the exploitation of white workers by magnates such as Rhodes, the 'big man' of the title. In 1899 Blackburn had published the first novel in his 'Sarel Erasmus' trilogy, *Prinsloo of Prinsloosdorp: A Tale of Transvaal Officialdom, by Sarel Erasmus* which, together with *A Burgher Quixote* (1903) and *I Came and Saw* (1908), had the character-narrator Sarel, in deadpan, relating his own experiences as a principled person – a kind of Quixote – in the bad company of rogues and thieves:

> 'It was not without great and careful thought that I have decided, boldly and honestly, to put my full name and district to this truthful story of the struggles after righteousness of a once oprecht Burgher of the late South African Republic, with a full account of the temptations that assailed him at the hands of the clever and educated wicked, and in the end brought about his fall.'

One cannot always be certain, however, of Blackburn's satirical intention. Stephen Gray interprets *A Burgher Quixote*, in its parody of the popular phenomenon of the Boer War romance, as ultimately Quixotic in spirit: Sarel is seen as the loser from the pastoral past who only tried to humanise the chicanery of a world gone mad in war.[15] But what one encounters are scales of expediency with Sarel beaten because he is a less competent rogue than those around him. With the 'Sarel Erasmus' books utilising the popular, colloquial Transvaal tale about wily farmers, who in Blackburn's treatment are made to use an English imitation of simple Afrikaans speech, Blackburn writes an elegy to the old Transvaal even as he wants to appeal to his British readers' stereotypical view of the Boer as the cunning backvelder. The metropole, after all, remained Blackburn's primary market. Or, perhaps, the problem was more fundamental: Blackburn did not know finally how or where to locate himself in the unfolding story of South Africa. As in the case of Schreiner, his understandings of society are difficult to disentangle from his myths of the agrarian community and, in consequence, he tends to see life more securely in structures of the past than in projections of the future. Like *The Story of an African Farm*, his novels suggest the difficulty in a society, in its formative stages, of capturing a nuanced societal range: one that moves out of the romance mode with its hankerings after lost pasts into forms of the open-ended present. Yet Blackburn was writing, on the spot, as the Transvaal changed from a rural to an urban place.

In dismissing Rider Haggard's imagined Africa ('such drivel would not be worth a moment's consideration but unfortunately Mr Haggard is identified with South Africa'), Blackburn expressed his admiration for *Trooper Peter Halket*,[16] and in *Richard Hartley, Prospector* (1905) – the character's name is faintly reminiscent of Rider Haggard – he followed up his anti-heroic Boer War novel (*A Burgher Quixote*) with an elaborate undermining of the adventure fiction. Hartley, a down-on-his-luck version of Haggard's hero Alan Quatermain, runs guns through both British and Boer lines while striking deals with Tswana tribesmen, and the civilising mission becomes the butt of a sprawling 360-page exposé of economic expediency behind high-flown principles. At the end, however, one is not sure whether it is the social satire or the study of an ageing protagonist that is meant to carry the mood and direction. In his last novel, *Love Muti* (1915), Blackburn tried to work through the colonial mythos to a sense of a different society. With white Natal still shouting 'black peril' after the so-called Bambatha rebellion, when in 1906 colonial troops crushed defiance by Chief Bambatha's Zondi people to a hated poll tax, Blackburn set his story in colonial Natal and allowed his characters, Charley and the half-caste Letty, to dally in the vagaries of love. Women in Blackburn's earlier novels had tended to be Amazon Boers or sado-masochistic temptresses; Letty, for her part, certainly retains the allure of the by now proverbial Hottentot Eve, but the novel pleads for her rights as a human being in the Natal colony, even as the story ends by suggesting that the talent and success of people like Letty are more suited to the polyglot mix of Johannesburg. The conclusion, however, is something of an 'up-beat' coda, and we are reminded in retrospect that the Immorality Act, which had been an unwritten convention, would become written law in 1920 and in real life clamp down on mixed-race relationships. What we have in *Love Muti*, rather, is a straining towards the realism of survival in a working society: a direction that had been initiated by Blackburn himself in his most memorable novel, *Leaven: A Black and White Story* (1908).

Possibly completed in manuscript as early as 1897, *Leaven* transforms its comprehensive reportage – its basis is the historical event – into a searing indictment of the colonial urbanising process. The story revolves around two characters whose lives interact: Bulalie, whose name derives from the Zulu word 'to kill' and plays on Rider Haggard's character naming, is the country African who learns the vices of the city; Hyslop is the naive, non-conformist minister who comes to Natal to convert the heathen. Adopting the narrative method of free indirect speech, Blackburn confirms his skill at capturing different accents and rhythms as he slips into the minds of his characters while, at key points, stepping back into his authorial self to offer cold, ironical observations on the moral turpitude of colonial South Africa:

Bulalie knew well the ways of the police, for as long as he
could remember they had come much to his father's kraal,
for old Tambuza was a bad kafir, on whom the resident
magistrate kept strict watch and word with his young
policemen. Thrice had they taken Tambuza to Maritzburg
to be tried for stealing sheep, or taking part in a tribal fight,
and each time the old man had remained away for long,
coming back with fresh marks of the cat, looking older
and more wrathful in his speech when talking of white
men, whom he hated more than he feared.

Impatient with W. C. Scully's kind of romantic liberalism, Blackburn
avoids dichotomies between innocence and experience. Bulalie, the first
credible black figure in our fiction, is no simpleton, even during his early
life in the 'native reserves'. Scarred by sjambok lashings after being
wrongly accused of molesting a white woman, he learns on the Rand
gold mines how to manipulate a rotten system to his own petty financial
advantage. Although there is caricaturing of the philanthropic missionary
Hyslop, who is often blinded by his own earnest Christianity, Blackburn
permits his character the insight and passion roundly to condemn Natal
society from the pulpit in a sermon that rings with Bishop Colenso's
powerful evangelical voice to his Pietermaritzburg congregation.[17]

As in his other novels, Blackburn seems uncertain finally what to make
of the situation he has so convincingly evoked, and the satire gives way
to anger, or it might be to a deep pessimism. The leaven of righteousness
cannot permeate, let alone transform, the unregenerate colonial state.
What is consistently portrayed, nevertheless, is an experiential problematic
that lends the story an alarmingly contemporary edge: there is no stopping
the open-ended urbanising present. In trying to 'theorise' about the
native question, Blackburn had spoken of Kaffir socialism,[18] a radical-
conservative trap that has bedevilled South African thinking on race
relations. Following earlier British and trekker policies of segregated
reserves, the Natal native administrator, Theophilus Shepstone, had
handled the large African population in the colony by establishing substantial areas, such as the one from which Bulalie comes, where Africans
fell under 'tribal' custom. The policy was justified as necessary to protect
rural Africans from exploitation on white farms and, indeed, Natal
farmers regarded the Shepstone scheme as inimical to their interests while
Bishop Colenso, like Dr Philip before him in the Cape, saw virtue in
the idea of reserves. Of course, the obverse was that the reserves kept the
African population under demarcated control and, if custom and tradition
were preserved, proletarianisation was halted. The 'reserve native'
remained illiterate, unskilled, and, when it suited the purposes of the
colony, forced by hut and poll taxes into short-term labour contracts at

near-starvation rates. Adaptations of such proto-migrant labour policies would underpin apartheid.

When Blackburn praised Kaffir socialism, he saw himself promulgating not segregationist thinking, but the pastoral ideal. In *Leaven*, however, his imagination proved to be more complex than his theory. The realism the narrative adopts does not permit Bulalie any romantic retreat to the reserves: he had, in any case, killed his drunken father in a quarrel, in a far from idyllic setting, before setting out on what would become an 'un-picaresque' adventure in its relentless accumulation of social data and activities. Like Schreiner who granted Waldo his death as a means of avoiding the predicament of his having to earn a living in a changing world, Blackburn also seemed to require the imposition of a literary convention to enable him to conclude his novel. After a fight on the mine Bulalie, who shows no intention of succumbing to Christian conversion, is killed off by the author in a stagy Victorian bedside scene. Perhaps Blackburn, at the time, could see no way into the future for his protagonist. Despite this, urbanisation has been so fully depicted in the novel as to refute any separation of Bulalie the individual from his representative role as the black worker who cannot return to the rural past. *Leaven* explores several crucial issues: most significantly, that of Jim comes to Joburg.[19] Because this story is lived out in real life by millions in the subcontinent, it persists in the imagination, and a measure of Blackburn's achievement is that *Leaven* is far more than a founding version in our fiction: possibly no writer since Blackburn has articulated the theme in such astute, uncompromising detail.

By the time *Leaven* was distributed in South Africa, its tendentious reputation had spread ahead of it, and the anger, indignation and self-justification of local reviews suggest that the novel had succeeded in striking a raw nerve: '*Leaven* is an open, loudly-shouted, almost hysterical attack on the Natal government in particular and South African white men in general, for their treatment of the native,'[20] fulminated one critic in a response that took little heed of Blackburn's icy control of voice and tone, or his skilful intermeshing of black and white stories in the proletarian phase of colonisation. Soon after its first reception *Leaven*, along with Blackburn's other novels, was allowed to go out of print. The exception was *Prinsloo of Prinsloosdorp*, which is reasonably benign in its satire of Boer life. Until he was re-discovered in the 1980s by Stephen Gray, Blackburn had become almost a forgotten name in South African literature. When *Leaven* was reprinted in 1991, appropriately by a Natal publisher, a reviewer in the Durban *Daily News* (6 March 1992) wrote: 'Being white in Africa is a standard theme of white South African writing; I can't think of another book which questions so fundamentally the right of whites to be here.' Blackburn, for his part, returned to England where he continued to work as a journalist until his death in 1929. In *Leaven*, the story of the colony has begun to be the South African story.

Notes

1. For titles and brief descriptions of nineteenth-century fiction see A. Chennells, *Settler Myths and the Southern Rhodesian Novel* (doctoral dissertation, University of Zimbabwe, 1982); I. Hofmeyr, *Mining, Social Change and Literature: An Analysis of South African Literature with Particular Reference to the Mining Novel, 1870–1920* (Masters dissertation, University of the Witwatersrand, 1980) abbreviated in 'The Mining Novel in South African Literature: 1870–1920', *English in Africa*, vol. 5, no. 2 (September 1978); M. Rice, *From Dolly Gray to Sarie Marais: A Survey of Fiction in English Concerning the First and Second Anglo-Boer Conflicts* (doctoral dissertation, Rand Afrikaans University, 1983); J. P. L. Snyman, *The South African Novel in English, 1880–1930* (Potchefstroom, 1952).
   On colonial fiction in South Africa see D. Bunn, 'Embodying Africa: Woman and Romance in Colonial Fiction', *English in Africa*, vol. 15, no. 1 (May 1988); G. Cornwell, 'The Early South African Novel of Race', in M. Chapman *et al.* (eds), *Perspectives on South African English Literature* (Johannesburg, 1992); T. J. Couzens, ' "The Old Africa of a Boy's Dream": Towards Interpreting Buchan's *Prester John*', *English Studies in Africa*, vol. 24, no. 1 (1981) and 'The Return to the Heart of Darkness', *English Academy Review* (November 1982); S. Gray, 'Domesticating the Wilds: J. Percy FitzPatrick's *Jock of the Bushveld* as a Historical Record for Children', *English in Africa*, vol. 14, no. 2 (October 1987) and, on Wilbur Smith, D. Maughan Brown, 'Raising Goose-Pimples: Wilbur Smith and the Politics of Rage', in M. Trump (ed.), *Rendering Things Visible* (Johannesburg, 1990).
   On colonial fiction in general see P. Bratlinger, *Rule of Darkness: British Literature and Imperialism, 1830–1914* (New York, 1988); D. Dabydeen (ed.), *The Black Presence in English Literature* (Manchester, 1985); H. Ridley, *Images of Imperial Rule* (London, 1983); and C. Achebe's attack on Conrad and, by implication, on Western appropriations of Africa, 'An Image of Africa', *Research in African Literatures*, vol. 9, no. 1 (Spring 1978).
   Useful introductions to the study of South African fiction are N. Gordimer, 'The Novel and the Nation in South Africa', in G. D. Killam (ed.), *African Writers on African Writing* (London, 1973); S. Gray, 'Schreiner and the Novel Tradition', *Southern African Literature: An Introduction* (Cape Town, 1979); S. G. Liebson [Sarah Gertrude Millin], 'The South Africa of Fiction', *The State* (February 1912); K. Magarey, 'The South African Novel and Race', *Southern Review*, no. 6 (1963); E. Mphahlele, *The African Image* (London, 1962; rev. ed., 1974); D. Rabkin, 'Ways of Looking: Origins of the South African Novel', *Journal of Commonwealth Literature*, vol. 13, no. 1 (August 1978); and P. Rich, 'Romance and the Development of the South African Novel', in L. White and T. Couzens (eds), *Literature and Society in South Africa* (Cape Town, 1984).

2. Both Gordimer [n. 1 above] and Coetzee have some regard for Millin as a novelist. See J. M. Coetzee, 'Blood, Flaw, Taint, Degeneration: The Case of Sarah Gertrude Millin', *English Studies in Africa*, vol. 23, no. 1 (1980).

3. Introduction, *Transkei Stories* (Cape Town, 1984), p. xxiii. The selection, edited

by Marquard, is taken from Scully's short-story volumes *Kafir Stories* (London, 1895), *The White Hecatomb* (London, 1897) and *By Veldt and Kopje* (London, 1907). *Daniel Venanda* was published in London. Gibbon's novels were originally published in London with *Margaret Harding* republished in Cape Town (1983). Slater's large output includes the short stories *The Sunburnt South* (London, 1908) and the novel *The Shining River* (London, 1925).

4. Haggard, 'About Fiction', *Contemporary Review* (February 1887); reprinted in C. Clayton (ed.), *Olive Schreiner* (Johannesburg, 1983), p. 76.

5. Schreiner, Preface to the second edition of *The Story of an African Farm*; reprinted in the Donker (Johannesburg) editions (1975; 1986).

6. See, for example, G. Pechey, 'The Story of an African Farm: Colonial History and the Discontinuous Text', *Critical Arts*, vol. 3, no. 1 (1983).

7. Quoted by Havelock Ellis, *My Life* (London, 1940), p. 130.

8. Jacobson, Preface to the Penguin edition of *The Story of an African Farm* (1971).

9. For interesting comparisons between the methods of Schreiner and early modernists such as Woolf, Conrad, Ford and Lawrence, see R. Green, 'Stability and Flux: The Allotropic Narrative of *An African Farm*', C. Clayton (ed.), *Olive Schreiner*.

10. Schreiner, Essays on the Boer in *Thoughts on South Africa* published posthumously in 1923 (Johannesburg, 1992). *Woman and Labour* (London, 1911; 1978).

11. Like Shaka, Cecil John Rhodes has assumed symbolic significance in southern African literature. See Sarah Gertrude Millin, *Rhodes* (London, 1933) and William Plomer, *Cecil Rhodes* (London, 1933; Cape Town, 1984). Compare these two 'literary' portraits with R. I. Rotberg's authoritative biography, *The Founder. Cecil Rhodes and the Pursuit of Power* (New York and Oxford, 1989).

12. Anon., 'Olive Schreiner's New Allegory', *The New York Tribune* (21 February 1897); reprinted in C. Clayton (ed.), *Olive Schreiner*, pp. 81–2.

13. Schreiner, Letter to her brother Will (W.P.) (29 June 1896), Jagger Library (University of Cape Town).

14. A selection from *The Sentinel* (Krugersdorp) in *English in Africa*, vol. 5, no. 1 (March 1978). Other fly-by-night publications to which Blackburn contributed include *The Moon, Life: A Subtropical Journal* and the *Standard and Diggers' News*.

15. *Douglas Blackburn* (Boston, 1984), pp. 78–96.

16. Blackburn, 'The Foolishness of Rider Haggard', *Sentinel* (29 July 1896). [N. 14 above.]

17. After the British army's defeat by the Zulu at Isandlwana, Colenso avoided colonial hysteria for vengeance and preached the greater Christian message of love. See the sermon, '*What doth the Lord require of us?*' (Pietermaritzburg, 1879).

18. Blackburn, 'The Safeguard of Kafir Socialism', *The New Age* (3 October 1908).

19. For a survey of this major theme and trope see S. Gray, 'Third World Meets First World: The Theme of "Jim Comes to Joburg" in South African English Fiction', *Kunapipi*, vol. 7, no. 1 (1985).

20. Unsigned review, 'The Problem of Black and White: How a Novelist Would Treat It: Hysteria from Basutoland', *Cape Argus Weekly Review* (21 October 1908).

African or Colonial Literature: 1880s to 1960s

Introduction to Part Three

A problem of methodology and taxonomy in the literature of the independent state in Africa was summarised by Manuel Ferreira when, in the
context of Portuguese-African practice, he asked how we draw distinctions between works belonging to 'African' or 'colonial' literature. African
literary historians, he suggests, will want to forget those Europeans who
abandoned Africa, and integrate only those who opted for African
nationality. In examining the work produced by nationals, he continues,
the tendency will be to take cognisance of all expression regardless of
literary characteristics, or the nature of the content, since content is not
in itself at variance with national consciousness.[1] Admitting to the complexity of the issue Ferreira at this stage refuses, however, to adopt a rigid
stance, and some of his difficulties are picked up by Janet Carter who, in
Angolan literature of the colonial period, identifies a lack of homogeneity
which she believes renders the term 'colonial' inadequate for anything
but historical reference. She lists the traits of colonial literature: the
conviction that home and civilisation are located in Europe, that life in
the colonies is a temporary exile in an outpost surrounded by savagery,
and that the landscape and the indigenous inhabitants are both exotic and
exploitable. But instead of advocating wholesale dismissals of the colonial
past, Carter goes on to talk of texts being split between African and
colonial elements and affiliations, in which the content may be African
while the form is metropolitan or, obversely, in which forms that are
taken from indigenous traditions end up embodying a European attitude.[2]

If African and colonial fissures in the same text complicate classificatory
schema, so of course does the procedure which has been adopted in the
present study of granting literary-history writing the potential of its own
sense-making activity. In consequence, the texts in the literary-historical
narrative may be 'positioned' by the critic as either colonial or African
in support of a larger societal intention. To take the case of South
African literature in the period 1910 to 1970, we may see from one
viewpoint an ongoing colonialism whether we are looking at white or
black writers. At the same time, a different perspective might accentuate
various kinds of 'indigeneity' that qualify, or even negate, the usefulness

of the very term colonial. The early black writer Sol T. Plaatje in his novel *Mhudi* (1930), for example, found in forms of Shakespearean romance, in principles of Cape liberalism, and in the English language, benign rather than constricting influences on his 'African' purpose of investing black human beings with the power of agency in their own history.

Before turning to the question of belonging and belief in South African literature, however, I wish to look briefly at ways in which the colonial past is beginning to be re-read and re-evaluated in countries that for some time have had African independence. In the general history of colonialism, the years up to the 1960s, or 1970s, saw the emergence of black written expression about the long struggle for freedom from colonial rule. As far as white writers were concerned, ambivalence about the home place – Europe or Africa – continued to characterise conscious-ness and conscience. I shall confine myself to looking first at the two ex-Portuguese colonies of Angola and Mozambique, then at Zimbabwe where the past involves attitudes to the physical and mental landscape of what was Rhodesia. The smaller countries of Zambia, Malawi and Namibia have considerably less literary activity linking the colony to the independent state, and will be discussed mainly in Part Four where the emphasis will be on the current scene.

Notes

1. Ferreira, 'Mozambique' in A. S. Gérard (ed.), *European-Language Writing in Sub-Saharan Africa, Vol. 1* (Budapest, 1986), p. 306.

2. Carter, 'Colonial Literature in Angola: A Problem of Taxonomy in Emerging Literatures', in R. Nethersole (ed.), *Emerging Literatures* (Bern, 1990), pp. 78–96.

Chapter 1
The Colonial Past in the Independent State

Ethnography and journalism in the Portuguese colonies

The indigenous people of Angola belong to many ethnic groups of which the largest are the Mbundu in the north and, in the south, the Ovimbundu. Portuguese explorers reached the coast towards the end of the fifteenth century, but conquest and settlement occurred only in the late nineteenth and early twentieth centuries. Rich in natural resources, Angola provided Portugal with large revenues. Settlers were attracted by gains to be made from mineral and crop exploitation, and a refrain in both oral and written literature concerns the subjugation of local people to forced labour on plantations.[1] In 1961 guerilla struggle was initiated by nationalist resistance movements. A similar pattern is evident in Mozambique, a territory of numerous African groups. Peasants were forced to grow cash crops and, in 1962, nationalist activists combined to form Frelimo which led to the first effective opposition to Portuguese rule.[2]

It is important, at the outset, to identify a tendency in the two ex-Portuguese colonies that has no precise parallel in the other countries. As a result of selective assimilation policies, which became official under Salazar's New State (1926) and which were firmly discontinued only after guerilla war had begun in the early 1960s, an African and a *mestiço* (mulatto) bourgeoisie was permitted to emerge in Angola and Mozambique. One of the consequences of allowing the few who had learnt to speak Portuguese, who were gainfully employed, and who had embraced Christianity, the same rights and privileges – in theory, anyway – as Portuguese citizens was the development of a small but influential intellectual class without rigid race divisions. Based in Angola around the Europeanised city of Luanda these urban assimilados studied at Portuguese universities, absorbed modern political and cultural thought, and regarded writing as a crucial aspect of resistance to colonialism. Several writers from the Luanda districts were founding members of the Marxist guerilla movement MPLA. Politically conscious assimilados also constituted what has been called the 'generation of the 1950s' whose poems, stories and ideas can hardly be thought to be fixed in a colonial past, but are more accurately described as transitional or pre-independent, or even independent. Whether concerned with cultural revindication, social protest or combativeness, the work of Agostinho Neto, Antonio Jacinto, Costa Andrade, Luandino Vieira and others in Angola, and – in Mozambique – the work of writers such as José Craveirinha, Marcelino dos Santos and Jorge Rebelo is best regarded as part of a literature of struggle. I shall deal with such Angolan and Mozambican expression arising as it does from the independence movements in Part Four. It was only in the mid-1970s after the collapse of Salazar's Portuguese metropolitan dictatorship and its censorship, in any case, that politically inspired writer-activists from Angola and Mozambique began to appear, in print, in their home countries as well as in the rest of southern Africa. The dissemination of their writing in English translation is also a phenomenon of the 1970s and 1980s. Tied to this, there is the difficulty of placing the stories of Luis Bernardo Honwana (Mozambique) and Luandino Vieira (Angola). Honwana's stories were published in book form as early as 1964 (an English edition appeared in 1969). Vieira's collection *Luuanda*[t] appeared in typescript in 1964, but the writer was then in prison on political charges and it was only after April 1974, when a military coup toppled the Salazarist government, that Vieira's work began to be circulated in published form. Whereas a 'literature of struggle' captures the mood of the victorious guerilla campaigns, the stories of Honwana and Vieira touch the rhythms of everyday life in colonial times and remind us that despite revolutions life goes on, that problems change but do not vanish, and that people in a range of circumstances laugh, cry, hate and love. This impulse seems abundantly recoverable in any society trying to pick up the threads of its daily experience, and I shall return to discuss Honwana and Vieira in relation to what I see as a distinctive style of storytelling from Angola and Mozambique.

Formed in 1947–48, the first local literary movement in Angola, Movimiento dos Jovens Intelectuais de Angola (Movement of Young Intellectuals), had as part of its battle cry, *Vamos descobrir Angola!* (Let's discover Angola!). Taking advantage of a temporary weakening of the Salazar regime after the defeat of the Axis powers at the end of the Second World War, the Movement described its purpose as both educational – to instruct the Angolan people in the history, geography and folklore of their country – and literary: 'to recapture the fighting spirit of the African writers of the late nineteenth and early twentieth centuries' in reaction to 'exaggerated respect for the values of western culture', and with a view to promoting 'the expression of popular concerns and of genuine African nature without any concession to colonial exoticism'[t].[3] Looking at the colonial past, the key figures in the Movement – Viriato da Cruz, Neto and Andrade – would have encountered the activities of successive writers, nearly all born and raised in Europe, who had premised their work on the assumption that Angola would become more like Portugal. What they would have found valuable, in contrast, were the early efforts of the Swiss Protestant missionary Héli Chatelain and the African intellectual Joaquim Dias Cordeiro da Mata, both of whom had set about in the late nineteenth century collecting folk-tales and proverbs of the Mbundu.[4] In calling in 1959 for the recovery of indigenous languages and oral traditions, and their incorporation into written Portuguese, Neto was echoing Chatelain's letter to Mata and others 'to collaborate in developing a nascent Angolan literature'[(t)].[5] Mata had disseminated the letter under the heading, 'Angola's need for a literature of her own'[(t)]. An activity that at the turn of the nineteenth century was more widespread than the collection of folklore, or the composition in the fictional genres, was a brand of political journalism in several small journals, in which ambitious young Africans of the middle classes in Luanda contributed ideas about their own social advancement and about independence through foreign intervention.[6] The short-lived *Luz e Crença* (1902–1903), in particular, attracted a politically committed group of writers. When the relatively liberal House of Braganza lost its throne in 1910, however, the few civil liberties were replaced by military dictatorship and in the colonies compulsory labour became the rule, assimilation was curtailed, and the African press began to wither away. After the so-called pacification of the country by the Portuguese in 1922, when the last independent African groups were subdued by force of arms, thousands of settlers arrived in Angola and a 'colonial' climate was encouraged to flourish.

It is against the history of hardening Salazar repression up to the 1970s that critics today are willing to grant renewed value to the few colonial writers who managed to offer something more than the most formulaic attitudes towards Africa as the barbaric place. Since independence in 1975, not only has interest in the ethnographic past been revived (two volumes of uMbundu tales have appeared in the Lavra e Oficina series), but there has been a new edition (1979) of Assis Júnior's novel of Angolan customs, *O Segredo da Morta* (The Secret of the Dead Woman). Inspired by the journalistic activism of the late nineteenth century, António de Assis Júnior reflects the period between the end of slave traffic in Angola in 1836 and the beginning of Portuguese fascism. With traders and business people willing to use the small African bourgeoisie in economic activity, a creole society had sprung up around Luanda where cultural bivalence was common. Having initially appeared in instalments in 1929 Júnior's book, which was published as a single volume in 1934, utilises the conventions of both African folklore and European romance while basing its story on real people living in the city of Luanda. (Ximinha

Belchiar, who dies of sickness, returns to haunt those who had betrayed her when she was dying.) Instead of retreating into the convenience of colonial exotic, Júnior rejects the notion of African inferiority and proposes the reclamation of an Angolan way of life. In his determination to convey his message, he frequently deserts the novelist's stock-in-trade of character in action, and intrudes passages of ethnographic information. Twice arrested, tortured and exiled to Portugal for publishing a pamphlet against the ruthless suppression of a peasant revolution in 1917, Júnior, an attorney, stood up for African rights in isolation and, as Donald Burness argues, is deserving of recognition in any Angolan-directed literary history of Angola.[7]

In the same vein, there is the *mestiço* Oscar Bento Ribas whose novel, if novel is the correct term, *Uango-feitiço* (The Evil Spell) was written in the 1930s and published only in 1951. Less 'modern' than Júnior, Ribas puts together a rich mixture of kiMbundu folklore, ethnographic detail and allusions to classical Portuguese gods in a plea for compassion in human life.[8] To these prose writers we may add Fernando Castro Soromenho whose novels *Terra Morta* (Dead Land, 1949) and *Viragem* (The Turn, 1957) cast a disillusioned eye on the abuses that characterised the 'civilising mission', especially in its practice of forced or contract labour.[9] Among poets there is Tomás Vieira da Cruz who came to Angola as a young man, married a *mestiça*, and in his volume *Quissange, Saudade Negra* (Thumb Piano, Black Nostalgia, 1932) celebrated her in sentimental lyrics while admitting that, whatever his empathy, he would never feel other than an exile. The limitations of this colonial literature were clearly perceived by F. Morais Sarmento when he wrote that Angolan poets and prose writers had been influenced mostly by ideas and subjects from the outside and that characters are 'Blacks, Mulattoes, Colonists only because [we are told that] there are such people in Angola and never because they convince us by their reactions to local problems'[(t).10] Despite this, Luandino Vieira called both Júnior and Ribas 'compatriots' who, however imperfectly, had realised that only through an understanding of traditional Angolan life and values could African people create a future that would reflect what is best in African cultures.[11] In addition, there were the occasional activities – barely recorded – of the local musical-theatre group, N'Gola Ritmos, which long before independence had satirised colonial behaviour.

As in Angola, literary developments in Mozambique although more sporadic and on a smaller scale had by the 1950s begun to encourage a sense of identity through which writers could affirm unity and solidarity in African history against the systematic deprivations of Portuguese colonialism. Having had a more transient, more overtly business-minded European population than Angola, Mozambique only began to produce written literature in the twentieth century. As in Angola, journalism

provided the first African orientation: the black journalist João Albasini
in 1918 founded a Portuguese/Ronga bilingual weekly *O Brado Africano*
(The African Roar), which by the late 1950s was publishing a literary
supplement. As in Angola, censorship encouraged ephemeral means of
publication: periodicals were censored prior to publication; books after
publication, thus implicating publishers and authors in financial losses. By
the 1950s, writers in the Portuguese colonies were adept at deceiving
censorship and the secret police by continually re-organising themselves
and making use of immediate means of communication and dissemination
including the press, the radio, and the platforms of cultural associations.
In Angola, the Movement of Young Intellectuals in 1951 had begun the
journal *Mensagem* (The Message) which, although it would appear only
twice, placed Africans boldly at the centre of interest. The Imbondeíro
(Baobab) series in Angola also focused on local writing and, in 1960,
began publishing pamphlets of poems and stories prior to moving on to
bulkier collections and works by single authors.[12] Having attracted the
attentions of the secret police, publishing activity slowed down and, by
1963, Imbondeíro was confining itself to white authors. In Mozambique,
most writers of talent appeared with poems and short stories in the
journal *Itinerário* (1941–1955) and, between 1961 and the mid 1970s, in
A Voz de Moçambique (The Voice of Mozambique) which together with
its cultural supplement fought a running battle against closure as it tried
to offer a serious perspective on literature and the arts in the country. In
the late 1940s, co-operation in Portugal among assimilado intellectuals,
most of whom were from the *mestiço* urban elite, had led to the student
organisation Casa dos Estudantes do Império (House of Students from
the Empire) reviving the journal *Mensagem*, and producing literary essays
and ethnographic studies in pamphlet form. In giving encouragement to
creative writing, Casa also provided wider access to poems and stories
that had been published previously in periodicals by compiling several
anthologies of prose and poetry, as well as by launching the Autores
Ultramarinos (Overseas Writers) Series which issued previously unpublished books by the writers who would go on to constitute the 'generation
of the 1950s' including Neto, Dáskalos, Andrade, Santos and Vieira.[13]
Reacting to this growing cultural and political awareness among students
in Portugal, who included future MPLA leaders, the Portuguese government dissolved the Casa for short periods in 1947, from 1952 to 1957,
and again in 1961 at which point it was brought under firm state control.
With the beginning of guerilla activity in the early 1960s, it was the
radical trend initiated by Casa rather than the concentration on aesthetic
concerns as had characterised the Imbondeíro venture that would define
the direction of literature in both Angola and Mozambique.

Encouragement also came from the First International Conference of
Black Writers and Artists (19–22 September 1956, Paris). The message

was that a native literature in Angola and Mozambique should be seen
as part of a pan-African struggle for self-assertion and cultural emancipation and, given the continuing inspiration of Negritude at the time, it
is not surprising that several Angolan and Mozambican poems of the
1950s should have exalted Mother Africa in the glorification of African
values. First published in *Mensagem*, Noémia de Sousa – a mixed-race
Mozambican – led the way along with José Craveirinha – who was also
born in Mozambique of a white father and an African mother. In both
poets the influence of Negritude owes more to Aimé Césaire than to
Léopold Senghor in its accusing tone of social protest.[14] In transferring
the lyrical evocations of an idealised Africa to the collective voice of the
people, Craveirinha – a journalist who was arrested and tortured by
the Portuguese authorities for his anti-fascist activities – signalled the
Marxist-materialist base that in both countries would begin to characterise
the poetry of the independence struggles:

> Mama Saquina
> in the blinding mirage of the cosmopolitan city
> had a heart full of magic
> in the crying hour
> saying goodbye to João
> . . .
> The maganza's train put out steam and pulled away
> in the pistons its voice was saying:
> João Tavasse-went-to-the-mines
> João Tavasse-went-to-the-mines
> . . .
> And Mama Saquina hoisted up the child on her back,
> scratched maize from the earth
> and did a miracle of a hundred and fifty-five
> sacks of cotton.[t]
>
> ('Mama Saquina')[15]

The group Núcleo dos Estudantes Africanos de Moçambique, which in
1962 played a leading role in the cultural life of the country by arranging
evening classes, educational film shows and public debates on topics such
as bride price and progress, came to regard de Sousa and Craveirinha
disparagingly as 'mulatto' poets in their Euro-African 'elitist' tendency to
read their own intellectualised reactions into the minds of African people.
Instead the new aim as war gathered momentum, according to Núcleo,
was to be 'situational', 'populist', to use 'simple speech'.[16] The student-
writers of Núcleo, who included Luis Bernardo Honwana, may have
recognised in de Sousa and Craveirinha poems conceived in a style of
literary fluency. What they ignored, however, was the strength that despite

his own reservations about assimilado poetry, would be identified by first Frelimo president, Eduardo Mondlane, as the ability, gained partly from a knowledge of European history and revolutionary thinking, to analyse a political situation and express it in clear and vivid terms.[17] It is an argument to which I shall return in the later section on Angola and Mozambique.

African-language literature in the British colonies

The colonial past in Zimbabwe does not produce the ideologically coherent revolutionaries, or ever radicals, that emerged from among the assimilados in the Portuguese colonies. Some of the colonial and colonised voices, nevertheless, began to articulate what can conveniently be called African commitments in exploring key points in Zimbabwean history as the explanatory references and symbols of the literature. The early inhabitants (Bushmen) were displaced by Bantu-speaking agriculturists, and over 1,000 years ago the Shona established the Mwene Mutapa empire, which from its capital at Great Zimbabwe dominated the area from the thirteenth to the sixteenth century. In the colonial imagination of the adventure-romance, this ancient civilisation with its mythical riches and stone ruins is still traced to Egyptian, Phoenician or Arabic cultures, for Africans can be permitted no building skills, in fact no history. By the seventeenth and eighteenth centuries, a second Shona empire, the Rozwi, had risen and, in turn, fell in the 1830s to the Ndebele who had begun their migrations and conquests during Shaka's time, and who would dominate Zimbabwe until the arrival of the first European settlers late in the nineteenth century. In 1888 Lobengula, the Ndebele ruler, was persuaded by guile to grant mineral rights to Cecil John Rhodes's representative. The Ndebele in 1893 and 1896 and the Shona, in 1896–97, resisted settlement in what is popularly called the first chimurenga (war of liberation). But by 1897 white supremacy had been firmly established. Rhodes's British South Africa Company encouraged white settlement and ran Southern Rhodesia until 1923 when it became a self-governing British colony. Settlers further strengthened their position with the Land Apportionment Act (1930) which gave the small European minority the best farming land, and with the Industrial Conciliation Act (1934) which barred Africans from skilled employment. By the 1940s and 1950s some moderate white leaders were prepared to make limited concessions to encourage economic growth and gain the support of a small middle-class African elite. (This was called multiracial partnership.) Partnership in a central African federation of the countries that would become Zimbabwe, Zambia and Malawi (1953–63), however, was rejected by white supremacists and by radical nationalist African leaders, the latter regarding the federation as a sham. An African nationalist campaign gathered strength in the late 1950s as hardening white attitudes were reflected in the racist constitution of the Rhodesian Front. With leader Ian Smith unilaterally declaring the colony independent from Britain in 1965, Rhodesia was regarded internationally as illegal. The greatest pressure came not from sanctions, however, but from the second chimurenga which began in the late 1960s and ended when Smith's regime renounced UDI and, in 1979, accepted the Lancaster House agreement. This provided for a cease-fire and a rapid transition to independence under African majority rule.[18] With its reasonably developed and diversified economy, Zimbabwe – unlike Zambia and Malawi – has begun to support a lively publishing industry for literary books.[19]

An important aspect of literary development in Zimbabwe, as well as in Zambia and Malawi, has been the functioning of literature bureaux. These were established in the 1950s under colonial government with the objective of unifying the various indigenous dialects into standard written forms, promoting the reading habit, and encouraging creative writing in the local languages.[20] (Neither the Portuguese in Angola and Mozambique, nor the Germans in Namibia, saw such literacy and literary programmes as part of their colonial mission.) We are reminded immediately, however, that the promotion of expression and culture in the vernacular can have as much to do with control as with self-realisation. In South Africa, apartheid practice – we shall see – quite systematically promoted 'ethnic cultures' as a means of diverting Africans from the so-called European culture. Through editorial policy and marketing realities the African literature bureaux – the Southern Rhodesia African Literature Bureau and the Northern Rhodesia and Nyasaland Joint Publications Bureau – generally tried to influence the content, ideas and effects of indigenous-language expression. It is not only that the numerous languages spoken in Zambia and Malawi ensure minute readerships among the indigenous people; there is also the matter of wide-spread illiteracy and poverty so that even in Zimbabwe, where Shona and Ndebele comprise two widely spoken languages, the only real outlet for indigenous writing is in the schools. The results of such a situation have been widely recognised. With authors aware of the immaturity of their readers, creative writing is all too often explicit in plot while themes are simple, even naive, in purposes of edification. Novels tend to be restricted in the range of vocabulary and concepts, and indeed in length. What was even more damaging, however, was that the prevailing view of the literature bureaux – that Africans were country people who were happy with their own customs – was often faithfully reflected either out of conservative conviction, or authorial expedience, in endless tales of city sin and rural recovery. In discussing mother-tongue literature from Zambia and Malawi, for example, Daniel P. Kunene selected four Nanja writers to identify the major defects – as he saw them – of much writing in the vernacular: its sycophantic attitude to the white man, his powers, his technology and religion; the ritualistic, unquestioning acceptance of Christianity; and a mixture of self-abasement and inconsistency in the descriptions of African beliefs and mores. His conclusion was that the writing usually appeared to be an exercise in self-devaluation. The generalisation is applicable also to indigenous writing from South Africa.[21]

Clearly, the challenge for the future – as the Zimbabwean writer Charles Mungoshi understands[22] – is not only for writers who use English to incorporate elements of indigenous traditions that can still be given urgency and credibility. It is also to encourage the growth of African-language literature in the changed conditions of independence, where Shona or Ndebele is opened to the 'impurities' of urban slang, for example, and rural-city dichotomies are pressed into the adult, modern world. Despite such intent, economic practicalities remain. In independent Zambia, the National Educational Company of Zambia (NECZAM) was established, as a subsidiary of the Kenneth Kaunda foundation, to act as the foundation's publishing arm in its commitment to 'Zambianise' the production and distribution of educational material. NECZAM – with the professional help and advice of Macmillan – published in ten languages and included a sizeable proportion of fiction, drama and poetry along with its main focus on educational text books. But the economic crisis in the mid 1970s resulted in a severe curtailing of the publishing programme. While the Literature Bureau in independent Zimbabwe has continued to be preoccupied with keeping indigenous languages pure, Mambo Press, founded in 1958 and owned by the Roman Catholic Diocese of Gweru, has established impressive lists in Shona and Ndebele which range from traditional texts to new creative endeavours. To take a random example from the Ndebele section, N. S. Sigogo's *Ngenziwa Ngumumo Wilizwe* (Influenced by the Situation, 1986) skilfully analyses difficult choices some Zimbabweans had to make during the war of liberation. (This novel won first prize in the 1986 Zimbabwe Book Publishers' Association Award.) With authors of the calibre of Mungoshi writing in local language (in his case, Shona) as well as in English, there is the tentative hope, at least in Zimbabwe, of distinctly new developments in African-language literature. Under Dr Hastings Kamuzu Banda's severe rule in Malawi, such 'modernisations' were discouraged for reasons that were not only financial.

If indeed African-language literature is to have viability in any comprehensive literary history, we should not simply dismiss those aspects regarded as its 'colonial dependence'. Neither, to return to Ferreira's point, need we embrace all the writing regardless of its content because the author happens to be a 'national' of the independent country.[23] Instead, we might want to employ fresh analytical insights about the split text, or about altered contexts of reception, and thus re-energise past texts for the present generation. In this procedure we could point to the curious case of *Feso*[t] (1974; 1956) by the Shona writer Solomon M. Mutswairo, a graduate from Fort Hare who, while at school in Natal, was inspired by R. R. R. Dhlomo's Zulu-language novel *UShaka* (1937). The action of Mutswairo's historical fiction takes place in the eighteenth century and deals with the (probably legendary) invasion of the Vatapa people into the Rozwi kingdom. Seeking to invoke the historical memory of the Shona people, *Feso*, as a story of invasion and oppression, struck many readers in a climate of growing nationalism in the 1950s as an allegory of the current political situation. Several passages – especially 'O Nehanda Nyakasikana', a hymn to the ancestral spirits – began to be recited at political gatherings. After having been published and praised by the Southern Rhodesia African Literature Bureau as a story of ancient tribes, *Feso* was removed from the list of recommended reading for schools. When it appeared in English translation in 1974, *Feso* was banned.

The banning action may be seen as symptomatic of the hypersensitivity and paranoia of the censors in reacting to the fact that by 1974 nationalist guerilla activity had become a reality in Rhodesia. This notwithstanding, we can return to *Feso* as a kind of hybrid text which, in its treatment of the past, touched the temper of profound socio-cultural transition. Its hymn to the Shona spirits, for example, calls to mind the role played in the first chimurenga of 1896 by spirit mediums who, as links between the ancestors and the living, wielded charismatic power in recognising grievances and urging the Shona to rise and overthrow the white oppressors. The two mediums, Nehanda and Kagubi, were executed by the colonial authorities and, partly as a result of the revisionist, myth-making attention given to the early Ndebele and Shona rebellions in Terence Ranger's influential study,[24] the martyred Nehanda and Kagubi presences began to figure as symbols of resistance in the songs of the second chimurenga. In helping to initiate what has become a mythology of liberation, *Feso* in its references to heroic memory obviously had the potential to interact with nationalist aspirations in the air. In consequence, we could decide to interpret its peaceful close, which seems to confirm romance over history, as idealising open-endedness: the desire for a future in the 'kingdom' of an independent Africa. Our response, however, could easily remain ambiguous, for Mutswairo's second novel, *Murambiwa Goredema* (Murambiwa, Son of Goredema, 1959) does not consolidate on any progressive political intent, but follows the predictably conservative path of so many indigenous-language stories: after distressing ordeals in the Salisbury township, the hero realises the value of diligence and returns to the land where he tills the soil and cares for his family. While the question of who was allowed to work the land could have struck at the core of the Land Apportionment Act, Mutswairo does not explore the trappings of colonial power. In *Mapondera, Soldier of Zimbabwe* (1978), which was written originally in English, Mutswairo's epic hero of the 1896 Shona rebellion floats so far above his own factual biography that it is difficult to tie credible people to the grand purpose of vindicating Shona cultural nationalism. There are too few points of fruitful tension in *Mapondera* between the particularities of the action and the general scheme of a romance.

Rhodesian, Counter-Rhodesian, Zimbabwean Fiction. Cripps. Lessing. Samkange

The problematics of historical representation, as we encounter in Mutswairo's work, have continued to characterise novel writing in southern Africa. In the case of the colonial writer, this often speaks of attempts either to grasp or to avoid the intersections of Western and African historical experience. In the case of early African writers, there was often a need to respond to the assumptions of settlers that they – the natives – had no history of which to be proud, and the mingling of fact and imagination which is frequently a feature of the novels suggests a primary purpose not with creating compelling fictions, but with evaluating origins, identity and events. In numerous early Rhodesian adventure and romance sagas, for example, history as social dynamic is evaded in favour of colonial pastoral in which, as we have come to expect of this 'genre', whites domesticate the land and blacks are hostile presences on the periphery of civilised space. In adventure fiction about the independence struggles of the 1970s ('bush wars', in these stories), we are asked to consent to colonial race ideology: stock instances of settler superiority, including male sexual prowess, and African incompetence – atavistic, slothful, etc. – seek to transform historical cause into the natural justifications of myth.[25] More historical in their concern with the workings of the colony are the novels of Arthur Shearly Cripps, Doris Lessing and Stanlake Samkange.

Cripps, a radical Anglican missionary, offered his services in Southern Rhodesia after reading Schreiner's *Trooper Peter Halket of Mashonaland*, and no sooner had he arrived in 1901 than he produced his poem *The Black Christ* (1902) which he described as a 'melodramatic . . . sombre little tract of a book' that dramatised the settlers' clamour for cheap labour and 'their readiness to shut the mouths of prophetic defenders of the Africans'. In confessing to be more of a poet than a priest ('a poet meaning to me . . . a kind of prophet'), Cripps saw it as his duty to intervene through his writing in public events 'on the anti-materialist side anyhow',[26] and his novel *Bay Tree Country* (1913) used details of a forced labour scandal in 1911 to establish alternative images of Rhodesia to those condoned in settler historiography and fiction. In the Makoni district the native commissioner had resorted to coercive methods in order to raise black labour for white farmers. Basing his characters on the persons involved, Cripps depicts his settlers in heightened, melodramatic form to make his point about the 'Southern Rhodesian system, lying like a great python coiled about the villages'. With 'colonial' shortsightedness of his own, however, he could not find a place in his cast for the most impressive spokesman before the commission of enquiry: Matthew, the black Anglican catechist teacher of the district. Nevertheless, *Bay Tree Country* tears into colonial pastoral in order to present Rhodesia as a country where the wicked flourish like the green bay tree of scripture.[27]

Cripps did not write a Zimbabwean novel; neither did he write a Rhodesian novel. Like Doris Lessing's early fiction set in the colony, his is a counter-Rhodesian response. As John Reed, who coined the terms, explains: both Rhodesian and counter-Rhodesian literature are addressed outside Rhodesia and constitute an appeal to a reading public, an opinion-forming minority in Britain; the content of the appeal changes from colonial assent to colonial critique, but the appeal itself and its audience remain constantly aimed at the metropolis.[28] The reader in Zimbabwe can choose, nonetheless, to return the text to the prior demands of a local readership: something especially necessary in trying to place Lessing in the literature of southern Africa where the emphasis usually falls on her first novel *The Grass is Singing* (1950), several intelligently nuanced stories on themes of cultural displacement (collected, initially, in *This Was the Old Chief's Country*, 1951) and in her series of autobiographical novels *Children of Violence* (1952–69), the most Rhodesian, or rather counter-Rhodesian of these being *Martha Quest*. On the international scene, of course, Lessing has become a cult figure: held up as a feminist because of her novel of woman's experience *The Golden Notebook* (1962), she has since called the women's movement embarrassing and ineffectual, but remains a voyager in the realms of (woman's) consciousness. She is also regarded in certain literary quarters abroad as an authoritative commentator on almost every subject from conservation in Zimbabwe to the failure of collective ideologies – after her own early flirtation with communism – at the expense of individual growth, intelligence and destiny. Her travel book, *African Laughter: Four Visits to Zimbabwe* (1992), offers a predictable view of the African country struggling under the combined hardships of drought and neo-colonial mismanagement, and redeemed only by the folkloric charm of peasant wisdom. Whereas the earlier Lessing might have searched beneath the stereotype in her emotional and analytical response, the weary cynicism of this later 'African' Lessing suggests a thorough rejection of her own past.

Having arrived in Rhodesia with her British parents in 1925, Lessing left for England in 1949 carrying the completed manuscript of *The Grass is Singing*, which was published in London to immediate acclaim. In her twenty-five years in the colony, she had questioned the tastes and values of her British background, initially finding in African sense data shocks of new cultural recognitions – see, particularly, the story 'The Old Chief Mshlanga' – while increasingly casting a mordant eye on the attitudes and assumptions of the settler community. (Lessing was declared a prohibited immigrant in white-ruled Rhodesia.) The strength of *The Grass is Singing* lies in its powers of social observation. With icy satire Lessing sketches the petty-minded prejudices of Rhodesian life and reveals a harsh, brittle grasp of the effects of racial status on individual people. At the centre is the destructive story of the Turners: Bill cannot be simply a kindly ineffectual man, Mary his wife just another inadequate person; instead, they are shown to have absorbed an assured racial arrogance. As the mean product of an environment Lessing loathed, Mary can be permitted no sympathy in her sexual repression which is seen to be another awful manifestation of living in a stultifying, male-bigoted colony. All this may be historically precise with the Turner marriage typifying the mental and social condition of settler Rhodesia. Where imprecision occurs is when Lessing – so in command of her satire – becomes caught up in the very psychosis of race she is trying to dissect. With Mary's frustrated existence manifesting itself in fantasies of sexual submission and mastery involving the servant Moses, Moses – after he is subjected to insult and abuse – is metamorphosed into an evil presence. Without adequate psychological justification (his nature remains a mystery to readers), he kills Mary and meekly awaits his capture and eventual execution. At this crucial point of the miscegenation theme, Lessing lets slip the distancing control between her authorial self and Mary her created character, and is as incapable as Mary of dealing with the colony as an interracial entity.

In subject and attitude, *The Grass is Singing* fits into what by the 1950s was developing into a recognisable tradition of novels by whites in southern Africa. There is the matter of the colonial's mental anguish in an Africa that is regarded as testing ground (the farm setting suggests inescapable aridity); and there is the use of 'mixed sex' as focalising motif. The preoccupation is social and cultural evasion rather than rootedness. In her own life Lessing left Rhodesia, and with African society remaining peripheral to her story and the colony becoming the vague memory of her youth, Martha Quest, the protagonist in the novel that bears her name, can easily be regarded internationally as a young woman in search of a satisfying individualism. Or, we may decide to regard her quest as a colonial one by emphasising her perpetual exile: as an exemplar of the colonial's condition Martha moves away from what she experiences as a dreary social life into the mindscapes of her psychological identity. It has been suggested, in this respect, that the fragmentation of the early colonial experience guarantees the restlessness of Martha's (or Lessing's) later searches for new forms of self; also that the crude clarities of the colonial years help Martha/Lessing to see into 'the diffusion of the metropole'. Instead of European *angst* we have a continuing realism.[29] The Zimbabwean concern, however, might be Martha/Lessing's limited 'reading' of the African situation. After a decade which produced four more novels, Martha is still found to be in her state of alienation and the possibility is that, all along, Lessing's target was not really Africa, but philistinism. As she never tires of reminding us, Rhodesia was white, provincial, narrow, and boring.[30]

In arguing that Lessing's imagination was not sustained by the challenge of writing itself into a frame of African history, Zimbabwean literary criticism might find it illuminating to compare her early work with that of contemporaries among the first African elite in Rhodesia: formative figures in the rise of nationalism who in stories that are novels, or romances, or histories, set out to wrest the African cultural and historical narrative from its colonial denigration, adaptation, or neglect.[31] Perhaps the most influential work here has been Lawrence Vambe's *An Ill-Fated People* (1972) which in typical fashion fuses fact and fiction and, while invoking chimurenga as the revolutionary spirit, expresses bitter disappointment at the failure of federation to achieve an all-embracing humanism. Similarly, Stanlake Samkange in pledging himself to an African nationalist cause remains close to the liberal ideals characteristic in the 1950s of the mission-educated elite. While recognising that shifts in Samkange's attitude are symptomatic of shifts in nationalist discourse during the twenty years prior to Zimbabwean independence, critics have taken the author to task for manifesting indecisions about moderation and radicalism in a failure of truthful literary representation. A mythologising tendency in his work – we are told – undermines historical causality.[32] But this seems to me an unduly restrictive way of responding not only to the truth of fiction but also to the truth of history, especially as the point of Samkange's books is to question methods of authenticating the national story. A professional historian who for many years taught in the United States and who writes in English, Samkange in *On Trial for my Country* (1966) was possibly influenced by Schreiner's *Trooper Peter Halket of Mashonaland* as he shifts, to-and-fro, between the realism of colonial actions and an other-world vision in which Lobengula and Rhodes are put on trial for their behaviour during the events that led to the white occupation of the Ndebele kingdom.[33] *Year of the Uprising*

(1978), in its turn, links the chimurenga of 1896 to the war of independence in the 1970s. In mixing oral testimony and colonial document, Western forms of court proceedings and the subjective witness of the African indaba, *On Trial* creates an illusion of African history against which Samkange makes his moral protest about colonial conquest. Although the written record insists that the less than resourceful Lobengula failed in his dealings with the wily Rhodes, the predominant style in which the tale is told – folklorist in its formalities of address and wisdom – has the effect of resurrecting the Ndebele king as the presiding spirit. A similar reversal of the Rhodesian perspective occurs in *Year of the Uprising*, in which the early rebellion is lost only as a prelude to the later, successful struggle for a free Zimbabwe. As Baden-Powell says to Lord Gray in the narrative, ' "I am afraid that the whites here have learnt nothing from this rebellion. There will be another round, I tell you. And when that takes place, I am not sure the white man will win." '

One may ask whether Samkange is a counter-Rhodesian or a Zimbabwean writer. In *On Trial* the very fullness of his account – he gives Rhodes his say and does not offer an anti-colonial diatribe – would probably appeal to the Western-literary academic tradition of novels as complex human stories, or historical records as sober and objective. Samkange's 'Zimbabweanness', however, could be identified in a kind of historical romance that in its approximations of the oral mode implicitly undermines the superior truth associated with the written account and expansively conveys an African character in the ease of speech. Paradoxes abound, and in Samkange's novels – as I am intimating, the very term 'novel' may be a misnomer – we are left with the truth of the public voice.

The *Mambo Book of Zimbabwean Verse in English*. Constructing a tradition

In poetry, the *Mambo Book* (1986) is an attempt to create a comprehensive Zimbabwean tradition. The editors, Colin and O-lan Style, point to the limited, or specialist, nature of earlier anthologies: Snelling (1938 and 1950), whites only poetry; Finn (1968), a slim 'dipstick volume' that excludes many poems which at the time would have invited censorship; Muchemwa (1978), blacks only poetry; Kadhani and Zimunya (1981), revolutionary and war verse.[34] Instead, the editors opt for the philosophy of 'partnership' rather than 'apartheid'. In doing so they connect themselves back to the small, relatively liberal-colonial alternative to naked white supremacism that in the 1950s characterised the notion of the central African federation. Although partnership in political events was interpreted at the time by radical African nationalists as a useful contrivance to weather real change, its benign aspects encouraged some co-operation between black and white writers. As a result, the Salisbury Poetry Society (1950), the magazine *Rhodesian Poetry* and subsequent initiatives such as *Two Tone* (a quarterly of Rhodesian poetry) and *Chirimo* (a thrice-yearly review of Rhodesian and international poetry) have always had as their aims interracial co-operation. In 1961 the poet N. H. Brettell lamented the fact that 'a voice one misses is that of the Rhodesian African. To look for English poetry from him yet is perhaps too much.'[35] The term English, however, began to be given a pragmatic value in its usage, and the promising legacy of these years of poetry partnership – the legacy the editors of the *Mambo Book* want to continue and expand – was to regard translation as both an act and an art of cultural sharing. In introducing Ndebele and Shona poets to the predominantly white readers of poetry in Rhodesia and South Africa, Phillippa Berlyn, Gibson Mandishona and Douglas Livingstone had translated into English indigenous texts from both oral tradition and living African-language poets.[36] Similarly, the editors of the *Mambo Book* adopt the multiracial, multilingual outlook: the phrase 'in English', in the title, is regarded as liberatory rather than constricting, thus allowing for a tradition that happily places alongside poems originally composed in English a wide selection of translations from the Ndebele and Shona past, examples of recent oral continuities, and written representation by several African-language poets.[37] In commenting on the contribution of the translators George Fortune, Aaron C. Hodza and S. J. M. Mhlabi, the editors regard traditional oral poetry as 'transposing itself beautifully into English and standing as significant poetry in its own right', introducing a 'fresh stream of arresting similes and metaphors' and a 'wealth of Zimbabwean customs, flora and fauna' while offering the 'accumulation of the people's observations and insights'. They also see the oral past mediated by the strong, underlying principle that it is custom-built by the people, for the people, and therefore occupying a well-nigh unassailable position and saturating the work of the first written texts.

One of the best features of the *Mambo Book* is, indeed, its translations. In 'Stamping Song', for instance, the pre-colonial voice is recovered for another time (sung by Mrs Apollonia Hodza; translated by Aaron Hodza) and, as recorded in print, begins to give Zimbabwean literature its own distinctive lines of continuity:

When I was a small girl, you used to laugh at me,
That I had mucus on my nose,
What's now attracting you?
Is it because you have seen the charms of my breast?

That is so soft and so flexible?
Behind the *Mutarara* tree?
Oh see how it draws your heart as I am stamping,
See how I pound the mealie powder.[t]

The advantages of including African-language poems in translation are
evident, too, when we turn to the colonial past. One effect is to undermine for the benefit of English readers the settler myth of the empty
land that awaited its naming in the English tongue. In this respect, Wilson
B. Chivaura's wonderfully compact, morally astute Shona poems do not
give the impression in their English versions of having been colonised by
the English language. Instead, they make their contribution on their own
terms by forcefully reminding the wider readership available in English
that Africa has always had intelligence and humanity. As Chivaura puts it
in 'Confiding in a Stranger':

Don't confide in a stranger, brother,
His arrival is like a yellow breasted bird;
Its lightning flashing like the refrain of a song with distant
   rumbling thunder.
   . . .
What will you do, brother, with the stranger tomorrow,
Like a fowl looking for food in a different family?
Brother, don't prepare the cooking pot for a fowl that is
   not yours;
   The stranger in the village is the leader of a swarm of
   locusts,
Don't hurry for him.[t]

A teacher who was active in radio broadcasting, Chivaura combines
ancient wisdoms of community with a sharp awareness of change in a
modern, individualistic world. While there is an attachment to nature,
there is no idealising of bygone rural days; rather, the mind searches
through a functional use of metaphor, as in the extended simile of the
yellow-breasted bird, for apt forms of conduct in the interstices of the old
and the new.[38]
   Another effect of placing together English poetry and vernacular poetry
in English translation is to encourage comparative perspectives on the
poems as expressions of value in the multicultural situation. For the prolific Shona poet J. C. Kumbirai, the challenge is to find the liveable
relationship between ancient Shona religion and the new Christianity.
The rural scrutiny requires modifications to any established form as
Kumbirai draws on the imagery and rhythms of traditional *nhango* poetry
(ritualistic speech), didactic verse from the Book of Proverbs, and New

Testament teachings in order to confront the difficult question of what can be invested in patience and gentleness when the political strictures on Africans may demand the revolutionary response. That he was unable to arrive at any easy synthesis is the mark of his sensitivity to the volatile social climate in which he was writing between 1968 and 1983.

Kumbirai's syncretisms are a useful reminder, in fact, that several white poets of the colonial past who can still be heard to speak with some authority were also in their way syncretic in asking, implicitly, whether they could belong to Africa. One whom I have already mentioned was Arthur Shearly Cripps. Another was N. H. Brettell whose poems, on first reading, seem almost too studied in their English literary self-consciousness: 'African Student: Shakespeare for "A" Level', for example, concludes, 'Could you, or I, with honesty embrace/That golden franchise that embraced them all:/The knave, the gull, the Jew, the blackamoor'. A headmaster in rural schools for twenty-five years, Brettell came to Rhodesia in 1930 and spent the remainder of his life in independent Zimbabwe. His first volume *Bronze Frieze* (1950) sounded a memorable voice in poems of poignant contrast between the poet's native Worcester and the Rhodesian bush. It is easy now to find in the lines quoted above the liberal manner, humane, a little conservative, always ill at ease with its African subjects and subject matter, offering palliatives rather than decisive actions. This off-hand approach, however, would be unfair to Brettell; and the editors of the *Mambo Book*, who are perhaps a little self-conscious of their own European preferences in giving Brettell greater representation than the fine Chivaura, suggest at least a fruitful way of re-reading Brettell the colonial who wanted to be part of an African Zimbabwe: 'Though possessed of transcending gifts Brettell exemplifies this division in the white soul. With his technique of alternating between the English and Zimbabwean landscapes Brettell brings the divided psyche into the open and makes a deliberate feature of it.' Watching the piccanins in the slums from the window of the train, Brettell in 'Outside Kimberley' sees a solitary springbok on the plain, a creature doomed to extinction, and in the final line makes the connection that fills his elegiac musing with the uncomfortable prediction that he himself, the colonial, is the transitory one in Africa: 'Now going sad and elegant, like us, doomed family.'

In making their case for something called Zimbabwean poetry, the editors of the *Mambo Book* do not want the reader to overlook the large quantity of vivid, accessible poems by many obscure poets. (The little magazine rather than the volume by a single author has remained the most prominent outlet for poetry in Zimbabwe.) As a populariser of human attitudes and cultural diversity, poetry in independent Zimbabwe – the editors feel – should not fall victim to the kind of bitter denunciations that characterised the poems and songs of the chimurenga. But if their ideal is – commendably – reconciliation, their overriding aesthetic criterion remains a little uncomfortably formalist in its New Critical preference for poised, self-contained texts. As the editors confess in the blurb, their anthology was in planning for sixteen years and, given the dramatic changes in Zimbabwe as well as the fact that the editors are white, one is left wondering what a black Zimbabwean editor today would retain, re-arrange or drop in any tradition of Zimbabwean poetry. Probably translation would continue to be regarded as an act of communication across language and race barriers. (As is evident, I am following a similar procedure in the present study.) The most contested area, however, is likely to be the colonial past, and I am aware that in writing here on African or colonial literature I have been relying on commentaries that are almost exclusively by white critics, some of whom are residents in the countries concerned, others of whom practise abroad. What I have tried to do in this double bind of colonials' pronouncing on the colonial literature of the independent African state is, where possible, to test the outsider's opinion against the insider's view. When the American Lusophone critic Donald Burness says that 'There is the suggestion . . . that genuine maturity in Angolan literary circles will result in a revaluation of Assis Júnior and Oscar Ribas', I have searched for Angolan confirmation of what could be a contentious statement about the matter of 'genuine maturity' in particular sets of circumstance. In accordance, weight was given to Vieira's observation that Júnior and Ribas are his 'compatriots'.[39] The re-publication of Júnior's novel in independent Angola also seemed to be a sign of Angolan, in contradistinction to metropolitan, re-assessment.

The irony of my own position in all this is not lost on me. As a white South African trained in the Western-academic tradition, I have to ask myself whether a black South African critic at this juncture would think it necessary or desirable to afford the amount of coverage and discussion I have to the question of a usable colonial past. What I hope to have suggested, of course, is an African intervention in several 're-locations' of emphasis. In talking at some length on Lessing, for example, I end up considering whether Samkange is not of more interest to Zimbabwean, indeed southern African, literature; and while not dismissing Brettell, I imply that Chivaura is probably the more impressive poet in the preindependence years. A view I share with the editors of the *Mambo Book* is that, despite the language medium, we need to continue exploring points of reference between written literature and its oral antecedent. A view I do not share with Flora Veit-Wild, a white critic committed to Zimbabwe, is that black and white Zimbabwean literatures have to be treated in separate contexts on the grounds that 'apart from some institutional or personal links, cross-influences must be considered minor'.[40] Her literary history of Zimbabwean literature is devoted entirely to black writers. My comparative approach contextualised within the functioning of the whole society, in contrast, regards Zimbabwean literature as a single field, in which colonial writers are assessed in relation to their attitudes towards living in the African place. In South Africa, the first half of this century saw the questions of belonging and belief in Africa or Europe complicated in a particularly severe context of racial segregation.

Notes

1. See H. Chatelain, *Folk-tales of Angola* (Boston, 1894).

2. G. J. Bender, *Angola under the Portuguese: The Myth and the Reality* (Berkeley, 1978); D. Birmingham, *The Portuguese Conquest of Angola* (London, 1965); R. H. Chiliote, *Portuguese Africa* (New Jersey, 1967); W. G. Clarence-Smith, *The Third Portuguese Empire, 1825–1975: A Study of Economic Imperialism* (Manchester, 1985); J. Duffy, *Portugal in Africa* (Harmondsworth, 1963); P. Harries, *Work, Culture and Identity: Migrant Labourers in Mozambique and South Africa, c.1860–1910* (Johannesburg, 1994); A. F. Isaacman, *The Tradition of Resistance in Mozambique: The Zambesi Valley, 1850–1921* (Berkeley, 1976); M. Newitt, *A History of Mozambique* (Johannesburg, 1994); L. Vail and L. White, *Capitalism and Colonialism in Mozambique: A Study of Quelimane District* (London and Minneapolis, 1980); D. Wheeler and R. Pélissier, *Angola* (New York, 1971).

3. Purpose defined by Viriato da Cruz. The Movement published the first anthology of Angolan poetry, *Antologia dos Novos Poetas de Angola* (Luanda, n.d. [1950]).
   Apart from the surveys by Burness, Feirreira, Hamilton and Moser that have been listed in the General Bibliographies, see M. de Andrade, *Literatura Africana de Expressão Portuguesa* (Algiers, 1968; Liechtenstein, 1970); M. António, 'Literatura Angolana: Uma Perspectiva', *Tempo Presente*, no. 16 (August 1960); C. Ervedosa, *A Literatura Angolana: Resenha Histórica* (Lisbon, 1963), *Itinerário de Literatura Angolana* (Luanda, 1972), *Breve Resenha Histórica de Literatura Angolana* (Luanda, 1973), and *Roteiro da Literatura Angolana* (Lisbon, 1979); J. R. Júnior, *Para uma Cultura Moçambicana* (Lisbon, 1951); A. Margarido, 'Incidences Socio-économiques sur la Poésie Noire de'Expression Portugaise', *Diogène*, vol. 37 (1962) which is also available in the English and Spanish editions of the journal; G. Moser, 'The Portuguese in Africa' and 'Angola', in A. S. Gérard (ed.), *European-Language Writing in Sub-Saharan Africa, Vol. 1* (Budapest, 1986), 'African Literature in Portuguese: The First Written, The Last Discovered', *African Forum*, vol. 11, no. 4 (1967) and the special issue on Lusophone literature, *Research in African Literatures*, vol. 13, no. 3 (Fall 1982); S. Trigo, *Introduçã à Literatura Angolana de Expressão Portuguesa* (Oporto, 1977).

4. Chatelain [n. 1 above]. Mata's book of Mbundu proverbs *Filosofia Popular em Provérbios Angolenses* (Lisbon, 1891) contains under the heading 'Angola's need for a literature of her own' the transcription of a letter from Chatelain in which the missionary called on Mata and others to help in developing a nascent Angolan literature.

5. [N. 4 above.] See account of literary activities in early 1950s in Amílcar Cabral's biography, *Amílcar Cabral, Filho de África* (Lisbon, 1975) by Oleg Ignatiev.

6. See J. de Castro Lopo, *Jornalismo de Angola* (Luanda, 1964).

7. Burness, 'Literature and Ethnography: The Case of *O Segredo da Morta* and *Uango*', *Research in African Literatures*, vol. 13, no. 3 (Fall 1982). For Ribas' influence on the introduction of traditional techniques into modern prose narrative, see G. M. Moser, 'Oral Tradition in Angolan Story Writing', *World Literature Today* (1979).

8. A mulatto of precocious ability, Ribas had published two short novellas by the age of 20: *Nuvens que Passam* (Passing Clouds, 1927) and *A Resgate duma Falta* (Ransom for a Fault, 1929). Struck by blindness at the age of 21, he did not publish anything for the next two decades. *Flores e Espinhos* (Flowers and Thorns, 1948), a collection of poetry, essays and short stories, was followed by *Uango-fetiço* and the stories *Ecos da minha Terra* (Echoes of my Land, 1952). (All published in Lisbon.)

9. See G. M. Moser, 'Castro Soremenho, an Angolan Realist', *Africa Today*, vol. 15, no. 6 (1968–9).

10. Sarmento, 'Literatura sem Ambiente' (A Literature in the Void), *A Província de Angola*, Sunday supplement, no. 268 (1941).

11. Vieira, 'O Escritor na Sociedade Angolana', *Lavra e Oficina*, no. 8 (May 1979).

12. Among the writers launched by Imbondeiro was José Vieira Mateus da Graça, better known as Luandino Vieira, a pseudonym he chose to show his attachment to Luanda, the city in which he grew up. See Luandino's *Primeira Canção d. Mar* (First Song of the Sea, 1961) and *Duas Histórias de Pequeños Burgueses* (Two Petit Bourgeois Stories, 1961). Luandino's first collection of stories, *A Cidade e a Infancia* (City and Childhood, 1957), was confiscated and destroyed by the Portuguese censorship, but an enlarged edition was published in 1960 under the imprint of the Casa dos Estudantes do Império.

13. Among the writing encouraged by the Casa was poetry with the first collective manifestation of Mozambican poetry appearing in the anthology *Poesia em Moçambique* (Lisbon, 1951), edited by Orlando de Albuquerque and Victor Evaristo. For representative selections of Angolan and Mozambican poetry in English translation see the anthologies of M. Dickinson (ed.), *When Bullets Begin to Flower* (Nairobi, 1972); M. Wolfers (ed. and tr. from Portuguese), *Poems from Angola* (London, 1979); and C. Searle (ed.), *The Sunflower of Hope: Poems from the Mozambican Revolution* (London, 1982). See also P. Chabal, *Vozes Moçambicanas: Literatura e Nacionalidáde* (Lisbon, 1994).

14. See R. A. Preto-Rodas, *Negritude as a Theme in the Poetry of the Portuguese-speaking World* (Gainesville, 1970).

15. Searle [n. 13 above].

16. Communication between Luis Honwana and Manuel Ferreira in 1971–1972 reported in Ferreira, 'Portuguese Africa: The New Militancy', in A. S. Gérard (ed.), *European-Language Writing in Sub-Saharan Africa, Vol. 1*, p. 414.

17. Mondlane, *The Struggle for Mozambique* (Harmondsworth, 1969), pp. 107–12.

18. See D. Birmingham and P. M. Martin (eds), *History of Central Africa*, 2 vols. (New York, 1983); M. F. C. Bourdillon, *Myths about Africans: Myth-making in Rhodesia* (Gwelo, 1976); T. N. Huffman, *Symbols in Stone: Unravelling the Mystery*

of Great Zimbabwe (Bloomington, 1987), *Snakes and Crocodiles: Symbolic Dimensions of the Zimbabwe Ruins* (Johannesburg, 1994); A. Keppel-Jones, *Rhodes and Rhodesia: The White Conquest of Zimbabwe, 1884–1902* (Montreal, 1983); M. Meredith, *The Past Is Another Country. Rhodesia: UDI to Zimbabwe* (London, 1979); R. Palmer, *Land and Racial Domination in Rhodesia* (Berkeley, 1977); I. Phimister, *An Economic and Social History of Zimbabwe, 1890–1948: Capital Accumulation and Class Struggle* (London, 1988); T. Ranger, *The African Voice in Southern Rhodesia, 1898–1930* (Evanston, 1970), *Revolt in Southern Rhodesia, 1896–7: A Study in African Resistance* (London, 1967; 1979); W. Rayner, *The Tribe and Its Successors: An Account of African Traditional Life and European Settlement in Southern Rhodesia* (London, 1962); N. Sithole, *African Nationalism* (Cape Town, 1959); L. Vambe, 'An African's View of Federation', *Optima*, vol. 5, no. 4 (1955); C. Zvobgo, 'African Education in Zimbabwe: The Colonial Inheritance and the New State, 1899–1979', *Issue*, nos 3–4 (1981).

19. Mambo Press (founded in 1958) is owned by the Roman Catholic Diocese of Gweru and has published educational literature as well as creative writing in English and in Shona and Ndebele. Academic Books has published books for Zimbabwean schools since 1984, and since 1989 under its imprint of Baobab Books has developed a general list of titles concentrating on Zimbabwean literature, tertiary texts and books for children.

20. See W. Krog (ed.), *African Literature in Rhodesia* (Gwelo, 1966) as well as F. Veit-Wild's account of literature and education in *Teachers, Preachers, Non-Believers* (Harare, 1993). Also: Anon., 'National Educational Company of Zambia Ltd', *African Book Publishing Record*, vol. 1, no. 2 (1975); S. Muriyeriwa, 'Printing Presses and Publishing Houses in Malawi', *African Book Publishing Record*, vol. 4, no. 2 (1978); A. Plangger, 'Some Observations on Publishing in Zimbabwe, *The Zimbabwean Librarian*, nos 3–4 (1979); G. H. Wilson, 'The Northern Rhodesia-Nyasaland Joint Publications Bureau', *Africa*, no. 20 (1950).

21. D. Kunene, 'African Vernacular Writing: An Essay on Self-devaluation', *African Social Research*, no. 9 (1970) and 'Problems in Creating Writing: The Example of Southern Africa', in R. M. Dorson (ed.), *African Folklore* (Garden City, N.J., 1972). For a useful survey of African-language writing see A. S. Gérard, *African-Language Literatures: An Introduction to the Literary History of Sub-Saharan Africa* (London, 1981).

22. See F. Veit-Wild's account of Mungoshi's writing in English and in Shona, *Teachers, Preachers, Non-Believers*, pp. 267–300.

23. See p. 147.

24. See Ranger (1967) [n. 18 above].

25. See A. J. Chennells's 'The Treatment of the Rhodesian War in Recent Rhodesian Novels', *Zambezia*, vol. 5, no. 11 (1977), pp. 177–202.

26. A. S. Cripps to Edith Cripps (Rogation Tuesday, 1902) and A. S. Cripps to H. Maynard Smith (20 June 1903). Letters quoted by Cripps's biographer, D. V. Steere, *God's Irregular. Arthur Shearly Cripps. A Rhodesian Epic* (London, 1973), pp. 54–5.

27. See T. O. Ranger, 'Literature and Political Economy: Arthur Shearly Cripps and the Makoni Labour Crisis of 1911', *Journal of Southern African Studies*, vol. 9, no. 1 (October 1982).

28. 'The Emergence of English Writing in Zimbabwe', in A. S. Gérard (ed.), *European-Language Writing in Sub-Saharan Africa, Vol. 1.*

29. On the theme of Lessing and colonial exile see A. Gurr, *Writers in Exile: The Creative Use of Home in Modern Literature* (Brighton, 1981).

30. See E. Bertelsen's interview with Lessing in Bertelsen (ed.), *Doris Lessing* (Johannesburg, 1985).

31. See F. Veit-Wild for details of the early African elite in Zimbabwean literature, *Teachers, Preachers, Non-Believers.*

32. For the view that Samkange is a 'minor talent' see A. J. Chennells, 'Reading Doris Lessing's Stories in Zimbabwe', in C. Sprague (ed.), *In Pursuit of Doris Lessing* (London, 1990) and F. Veit-Wild, *Teachers, Preachers, Non-Believers.*

33. For a comparison of *On Trial* and *Trooper Peter* see A. Ravenscroft, 'Literature and Politics: Two Zimbabwean Novels', in M. van Wyk Smith and D. Maclennan (eds), *Olive Schreiner and After: Essays on Southern African Literature* (Cape Town, 1983).

34. *Mambo Book*, published in Harare. See J. Snelling (ed.), *Rhodesian Verse, 1888–1938* (Oxford, 1938) and *A New Anthology of Rhodesian Verse* (London, 1950); D. E. Finn (ed.), *Poetry in Rhodesia 75 Years* (Salisbury, 1968); K. Muchemwa (ed.), *Zimbabwean Poetry in English* (Gwelo, 1978), and M. Kadhani and M. Zimunya (eds), *And Now the Poets Speak: Poems Inspired by the Struggle for Zimbabwe* (Gweru, 1981).
    For developments in Zimbabwean poetry before independence see R. Graham, 'Poetry in Rhodesia', *Zambezia*, vol. 6, no. 2 (1978); G. Fortune (ed.), *African Languages in Schools* (Salisbury, 1964) which contains articles by G. Mandishona and S. J. Nondo on Shona and Ndebele poetry respectively; M. Hamutyinei, 'The Revival of Shona Poetry', *Nadu*, vol. 10, no. 2 (1970).

35. Brettell, Preface, *Rhodesian Poetry*, no. 6 (1961).

36. See particularly 'Eight Shona Poems', *London Magazine*, no. 10 (1965).

37. Most prominently Wilson B. Chivaura, Mordikai A. Hamutyinei, J. C. Kumbirai, Solomon H. Mutswairo and Henry Pote.

38. See A. J. C. Pongweni, *Figurative Language in Shona Discourse* (Gweru, 1989).

39. N. 7 and 11 above.

40. Viet-Wild, *Teachers, Preachers, Non-Believers*, p. 6.

Chapter 2

Belonging and Belief in South Africa, 1910–1948. Europe and Africa

From segregation to apartheid

Few writers of the years 1910 to 1970 in South Africa would have regarded themselves as colonial, although in Africanist criticism of the 1970s most white writers – whether English-speaking or Afrikaans – were typecast as being as unregenerately colonial as the white-ruled country. What we find among serious white writers, however, are struggles, hesitations, and retreats involving questions of belonging to Africa or Europe, in which collisions occur between attachments to the great English, or European, culture and attempts to establish indigenous convictions. The large issues are the relationship between the social and literary practices of the old and the new world, and between the imported language and the South African environment. Among black writers, the drift is towards African emergence even as many found themselves incorporated into white social, educational, and artistic codes. This resulted in a search for an alternative metaphysic and a political defiance that could be utilised as creative stimulants.

Such a scheme, however, requires several qualifications in South Africa's continuing colonialism, or long haul to independence, depending upon which way one looks at developments. The period between 1910, when the two British colonies and the two defeated Boer republics came together to form the Union of South Africa, and the beginning of radical black voices in the early 1970s was characterised by the dominating and domineering 'text' of apartheid.[1] This obviously was never a national text of interracial consent; rather, it remained sectarian, exclusionary, repressive, divisive and conflictual. With the Liberal Party government in Britain eager to see South Africa after the Anglo-Boer War as a united country in the empire, Westminster ignored the petitions of politically aware Africans and approved a constitution that entrenched white-minority political representation. Advantages were secured for mining interests and large-scale white agriculture while the bulk of Africans, who remained disenfranchised, were increasingly subjected to segregationist laws the object being to keep them – the 80 per cent majority – politically and economically powerless as cheap migrant labourers. On this fundamental point, English-speakers and Afrikaners were in broad agreement and a flawed South Africanism comprising the two 'white races' – to use the terminology of the day – was promoted by the Botha-Smuts government. Despite shifts in nomenclature from 'segregation', to 'apartheid', to 'separate development', the white belief, as summed up in 1917 by General Smuts, would continue to characterise official pronouncement:

> [To] apply the same institutions on an equal basis to white and black alike does not lead to the best results, and so a practice has grown up of giving the natives their own separate institutions. In land ownership, settlement, and forms of government we are trying to keep them apart. . . . The natives will, of course, be free to work in the white areas.[2]

There is an element here of double-speak even behind the avowed anti-democratic intent: separate institutions have never meant equal institutions, and the phrase 'free to work in white areas' conceals the coercive laws that confined Africans to impoverished 'reserves' (supposedly their ancestral homes in 13 per cent of the entire country) while imposing poll taxes to force males into the white areas as migrant workers. Thus the Natives Land Act of 1913 – the subject of Sol T. Plaatje's *Native Life in South Africa* (1916) – made it illegal for Africans to purchase or lease land from whites anywhere in South Africa outside the so-called reserves, and the Natives Urban Areas Act of 1923 laid down the principles of residential segregation in the cities, which were designated as the preserve of whites with Africans having no justification for being there unless needed for their work. With pass laws regulating African mobility, police checks and arrests began to define the brutality and inhumanity of the white state. Subsequent segregationist acts of the 1920s and 1930s made sexual intercourse outside marriage between whites and Africans a criminal offence (the law would later be amended to apply to whites and all non-whites), destroyed the African franchise in the Cape which had been retained in the Union constitution as a sop to the Cape liberal delegation, and continued to tighten measures against African land ownership, residential rights, and freedom of movement.

This sounds so far like a white versus black division. But splits also ran deep between the Botha-Smuts faction, which was seen to be sympathetic to big business and the international scene, and hence to English interests, and the break-away Afrikaner nationalists under General Hertzog. In Hertzog's view, the nationalism of the volk should continue to be fuelled by the problem of Afrikaner 'poor whitism' on the platteland (rural farm lands) and the problem of a semi-skilled Afrikaner proletariat in the cities. Resentment erupted in 1922 when white, mainly Afrikaans workers took to the streets of Johannesburg in opposition to an attempt by the chamber of mines – seen as Jewish-English capitalists – to use Africans at cut-rate wages in semi-skilled jobs. When the Hertzog nationalists came to power in 1923 in alliance with the Labour Party ('workers unite for a white South Africa'), a 'civilised labour policy' continued a segregationist tactic of playing semantics with the meaning of words and simply guaranteed jobs for whites by displacing non-white workers from state-controlled enterprises. A Smuts-Hertzog coalition in the 1930s continued to pursue the segregationist line. But Hertzog, who believed the coloureds were bound to whites, and Smuts, who vacillated between outright repression and policies of white trusteeship, would be rejected by extreme Afrikaner National Party members who turned from Hertzog to found the 'purified' National Party: the party that would come to power in 1948 with its vision of apartheid.

A frightening aspect of these years is the perversion of the 'visionary'. The high priest of apartheid, prime minister Dr H. F. Verwoerd, for example, spoke with messianic zeal about separate, ethnic destinies for what he called the different 'peoples' of South Africa.[3] In examining the polemic, it is sufficient to note that concepts such as justice, freedom, society, nation, civilisation, and God were debased as moral glosses that overlay a pervasive racism. Against the racist emotion, the speeches of liberals such as R. F. A. Hoernlé, the academic philosopher, and Edgar Brookes, one of seven white representatives of African interests in the white parliament, tended to rely on facts and ethics.[4] Generally, the liberal temper was 'Western' in its erudition and English articulacy. It was also cautious in trying to ameliorate conditions that could have provoked 'native unrest', and was forced into uncomfortable compromises on the question of a qualified franchise as the only practical middle way between assimilation, which was totally unacceptable to most whites, and repression, which was anathema to the Christian, humanitarian bases of the liberal spirit. In the speeches of the early African opposition – the educated elite who comprised the core of the South African Native National Congress – segregationist measures were routinely condemned without success by appeals to the Christian values that white South Africa claimed as its European inheritance.[5]

It is easy to underestimate, even caricature, the non-racial protest of these years as severely limited by its class and cultural affiliations. Even though the historian Phyllis Lewsen is sympathetic to the few liberal spokespersons who held on to ideals that were in danger of being annihilated but which remain alive today as prerequisites for change towards a more equitable, more humane society, she ends up suggesting that against the bizarre images and polemic of segregation, fact and analysis – however necessary – could not convey the anger, the impatience, the physical and mental violence of a discriminatory society impinging its overwhelming, detailed presence on the oppressed person's life. The experiential effects of apartheid, Lewsen believes, were most forcefully conveyed not in public commentary but in creative writing, and her reference to the stories of Can Themba and Es'kia Mphahlele is a reminder that by the 1960s both of these writers had fallen foul of banning orders.[6] We may also recall that it was a novel, Alan Paton's *Cry, the Beloved Country* (1948), which perhaps more than any other 'document' brought the South African racial problem to the attention of the world's conscience. Even the doyen of Afrikaans literature, N. P. van Wyk Louw, found himself being rebuked publicly by Verwoerd for raising questions in a play about the meaning of patriotism.[7] Certainly the national text of apartheid presented literary people with a provocation. For if art has anything to do with freedom of expression, creativity of thought, moral principle, or spiritual need, how does the imagination react to the vigorous entrenchment of repression? As the early years of the twentieth century saw the first sustained wave of creative literature in South Africa, I shall focus on the fictional impulse in examining several responses first by white, then by black writers in the years after Union, before turning to the impact of apartheid after 1948.

Black's satire: the popular white voice

The fact that, by the early twentieth century, local literature had achieved some magnitude was suggested in white circles by the appearance, in 1910, of Mendelssohn's *Bibliography*, a descriptive catalogue of works pertaining to South Africa in the Mendelssohn Collection (Library of Parliament); and, by the mid-1920s, critical surveys had appeared on Dutch/Afrikaans and English-language literature.[8] While delegates at the national convention were formulating the all-white constitution, Stephen Black's play *Love and the Hyphen* (first performed 1908) was enjoying a long run at the Tivoli Theatre in Cape Town, thus giving impetus to manager Arthur de Jong's intention of employing local talent in productions with a home-grown flavour. Black, a journalist and sometime professional man of the theatre, was an accurate observer of the foibles of 'South Africanism' and *Love and the Hyphen*, *Helena's Hope Ltd* (first performed 1910) and *Van Kalabas Does His Bit* (first performed 1916), along with several revue sketches, rely on vaudeville gags, knock-about routines, cross-talk and puns in comedies of manners that caricatured snobberies and pretensions in the new Union of South Africa. The types include home-born Englishmen, English-speaking (colonial) South Africans, and Dutchmen or Afrikaners, while below this European hierarchy are coloureds and Africans. Accents are exaggerated and the farce, sometimes rough in its racist appellations, could be seen as a rumbustious exorcism of colour and class tensions. As whites, especially English-speakers, held social and economic advantage in the Act of Union, they presumably felt relatively free to laugh at their own idiosyncrasies, and Black's touring performances proved enormously successful among white audiences in South Africa and Rhodesia.

As in the case of Andrew Geddes Bain almost a century before him, Black's strength lies in his exploitation of local language resources; his weakness, again like Bain, is to be found in his limited powers of social analysis. Despite the massive exclusion of black people from the Union deliberations, *Love and the Hyphen* in ridiculing social excesses does not subject the fixed orders of society to any serious questioning. In revising the play in 1928, however, Black replaced the original sparkle with a sardonic postscript that shows Sophie, a clownish Hottentot Eve in the earlier version, as a knowing woman who realises that, as a coloured, her only hope of surviving in the segregationist society is to 'try for white'. This version ends with the coloured man, Frikkie, who has been rejected by Sophie's daughter for the advantages the white world can offer her, shouting out in a bitter Malvolian disruption of the comic mood: 'You can all go to hell!' If Black violates his own dramatic structure in jumping from farce to cold fury, he conveys the temper of hardening racial attitudes, and his contribution needs to be measured against the barren field of South African theatre that he inherited.[9] According to Stephen Gray who has recovered the scripts of Black's plays, Stephen Black like several other South African English writers of the 1920s began to find himself increasingly at odds with the government in national matters of miscegenation, the poor white question, and the 'native problem' all of which are referred to in the plays.[10] As I have suggested, however, Black's understanding of these matters is not very penetrating or consistent in its concern. Having introduced the serious idea for consideration, he tends to avoid unravelling the thought in favour of iconoclastic insult and derision. This is also evident in the weekly magazine Black edited in 1929 after he had ceased his theatrical activities. *The Sjambok* ran in Johannesburg until a fourth libel action forced its closure in 1931. Regarding itself as a fierce defender of the rights of the ordinary man – those of the *white* male, while women are depicted as silly and flirtatious – *The Sjambok* launched its scurrilous, satirical journalism at authorities of various ilks usually at the level of the city councils rather than that of the Union parliament. Ideological uncertainty and sheer confusion characterise its opinion on crucial racial issues such as job reservation and 'black peril', the latter being the white fear of European womanhood raped by the hot-blooded savage. While *The Sjambok* does not entirely endorse race prejudice, neither does it feel at ease with any humane alternative and, in this, it summarises the general attitude of what we may call the popular response among white writers in the 1920s and 1930s. Catching the local flavour and the idiosyncratic homespun accent, Black stands in a line that would include Herman Charles Bosman's more astute, self-ironising South Africanism to which I shall return.

The other white line – literary elitist – was given direction by Roy Campbell, William Plomer and Laurens van der Post whose literary magazine *Voorslag* (Whiplash) Black probably had in mind when he chose the title for his own magazine venture. The term elitist here, however, requires qualification. In the three issues of *Voorslag* that fell under Campbell's editorship, the young contributors certainly saw themselves in 1926 as introducing artistic excellence to what they regarded as a philistine colony. But in their roles of satirical scourges, they were not averse to sniping at the older generation from the gutter. With *Voorslag* based near Durban, Campbell described his home town as a grocers' paradise. General Smuts was a favourite butt in the pages of the magazine, and Plomer's serialised story 'Portraits in the Nude' – a lurid satire on racial and sexual bigotry – followed up on his experimental novel *Turbott Wolfe* (1926) in shocking the proprieties of the strait-laced citizenry.[11] (For many years *Turbott Wolfe* was kept under lock and key in the Durban public library.) To literary acclaim in Britain, the 24–year old Campbell – before he returned to Durban after his student days – had published his epic poem *The Flaming Terrapin* (1924), a celebration of 'southern energies' revitalising a weary north in the post-war world. Finding his inspiration in the anti-Georgian modernist manner (in *Terrapin* his orientation was to Vorticism), Campbell as something of a show-off displayed his literary kinships and knowledge by offering readers of *Voorslag* one of the first appreciative reviews of T. S. Eliot's modernism in 'The Waste Land', a poem which Campbell saw as challenging complacency with the 'agonised searching questions of Youth'.[12]

At the time of *Voorslag*, therefore, Campbell, Plomer and Van der Post pictured themselves as romantically set apart from the common herd; simultaneously, they anticipated several of Stephen Black's aggressively 'local soil' judgments on South African literature. All agreed that Sarah Gertrude Millin, to quote Black, 'peeps at miscegenation from between the fingers of two horrified hands'. All took an interest in Afrikaans literature (Black urged Afrikaans writers to leave European models and cultivate their own turf), and all believed that ultimately South African literature had to include African expression. In introducing international modernism to the colony, the *Voorslag* trio also saw themselves as 'original Bushmen' excavating Africa and, as Plomer flamboyantly put it, daubing the marks of artistic genius on to the blank cave of the colonial mind.

Black, for his part, encouraged the publication of R. R. R. Dhlomo's stories in *The Sjambok*, but with his popular white attitude surfacing he then used the occasion to goad the two white races into closer literary union: 'are we though backed by aeons of culture, to be outstripped by the literary productions of Zulus who a few years ago were drinking each other's blood?'[13] Such a remark would not have slipped into *Voorslag*. Although Campbell had no coherent racial consciousness, both Plomer and Van der Post tied their rebellions to a firm liberal responsibility so that, in reviewing Dr Leys' book on Kenya and the colour question, Plomer provoked the arguments that would cause him to be vilified in colonial South Africa as negrophilic: 'How much longer is the colour of a man's skin to influence his rights as a man?'[14] The *Voorslag* trio disagreed with Black that Pauline Smith, whose short stories and novel appeared in the mid 1920s, had the timid accents of a Sunday school teacher and that Schreiner was merely domineering and vindictive. According to Black this was essentially because she was a woman.[15] What Black and Campbell agreed upon was the character of Plomer's *Turbott Wolfe*. As Black phrased it: 'Plomer's work is touched with genius . . . because [he] held original views particularly on sex and the native question.' Plomer – he continued – 'has been driven out of South Africa by public execration . . . the finest writer of prose this country has ever produced'.[16] By the end of 1926, all three *Voorslag* figures had left South Africa and, except for brief visits, would not return. Their own creative work raises some of the questions implicit in the *Voorslag* venture: where do high art and social responsibility intersect? What impact can the writer who flees to the 'richer culture' of the metropolis continue to have on South African affairs? The questions remain crucial particularly to Campbell's status in South African literature.

High art and social responsibility. Campbell. Plomer. Van der Post

The son of a respected family in colonial circles, Roy Campbell was sent to Oxford where he read voraciously though haphazardly in the classics, the Elizabethans and the French moderns. He was never admitted as a member of the university, and he returned to Durban in 1924 where, as the author of the precocious *Flaming Terrapin* (1924), he expected presumably to be fêted, even granted licence to insult the people of the town. After storming away partly out of pique, for he felt the 'colony' was incapable of appreciating his artistic individuality, Campbell went on to endorse some of the worst tendencies of the modernist movement:

especially its fascist rejection of the levelling effects of both liberal and social democracy in favour of a re-imagined future based on the recovery of cultural greatness the world had supposedly once owned. With *The Flaming Terrapin* utilising African sights and sounds as atavars of Nietzsche's heroic energy and *The Wayzgoose* (1928) imitating the mock-heroic forms of Augustan satire (its point was that colonials were dunces), Campbell's volume *Adamastor* (1930) revealed the European/African sources that would continue to characterise his several subsequent volumes of poems. I have already mentioned argument concerning the poem 'Rounding the Cape' (from *Adamastor*)[17]: do we regard Campbell as regressive in his depiction of the African spirit as a natural force devoid of human agency, or do we allow the poet his language of gesture and trope, in which case the Adamastor motif attracts poetic prophecy about a rehabilitated African future? Similar questions may be applied to the most frequently anthologised of the *Adamastor* poems, 'The Serf' and 'The Zulu Girl'. The latter is quoted in full:

When in the sun the hot red acres smoulder,
Down where the sweating gang its labour plies,
A girl flings down her hoe, and from her shoulder
Unslings her child tormented by the flies.

She takes him to a ring of shadow pooled
By thorn-trees: purpled with the blood of ticks,
While her sharp nails, in slow caresses ruled,
Prowl through his hair with sharp electric clicks.

His sleepy mouth plugged by the heavy nipple,
Tugs like a puppy, grunting as he feeds:
Through his frail nerves her own deep languors ripple
Like a broad river sighing through its reeds.

Yet in that drowsy stream his flesh imbibes
An old unquenched unsmotherable heat –
The curbed ferocity of beaten tribes,
The sullen dignity of their defeat.

Her body looms above him like a hill
Within whose shade a village lies at rest,
Or the first cloud so terrible and still
That bears the coming harvest in its breast.

Whether we give weight to the utterance as social or mythic, we locate ourselves ideologically in the continuing South African problem, which

I mentioned in the case of Blackburn's *Leaven*, of rural dignity signifying also proletarian dispossession, and proletarian possession signifying at the same time a rupture with tradition. Possibly, however, the intensity of Campbell's high word art in which he transfigures the scene, guarantees the poetic imagination its own special 'statement-making' power. Writing this poem in his *Voorslag* days under the influence of the race-conscious Plomer, Campbell invests the indigenous people in the landscape with a visionary power that gains succour from the past as it sweeps forward in apocalyptic liberation. In similar vein, 'The Serf' ends with the words: 'The timeless, surly patience of the serf/That moves the nearest to the naked earth/And ploughs down palaces, and thrones, and towers.' In the mid 1920s, in the context of restrictive segregationist laws, the prophetic mode of 'The Zulu Girl' and 'The Serf' may have had 'radical' social implications. Campbell's quarrel with his home country, in fact, lends a critical, social edge to the *Adamastor* volume as a whole.

Yet Campbell remains a contentious figure, whose skills of verbal magic can easily deflect the reader's attention from what should be, I think, a necessary concern with the politics of his poetry. Always ill at ease in literary Britain, Campbell for most of his adult life roamed the southern Mediterranean in Provence, Spain and Portugal, where he began to assert his identity in his 'colonial' heritage. Commentators have long noted his exceptional borrowings and translations from European poetry: the Europeanism of 'The Zulu Girl' includes the exploitation of the Madonna icon and specific references to Rimbaud's 'Les Chercheuses de Poux' (Women Hunting Lice); more generally, of course, the debt is to the romantic-lyrical tradition. But Campbell insisted equally on his debt to his youthful South African observations and to earlier South African poets: he admired especially the way Francis Carey Slater, in English, had drawn on the influences of African oral poetry in effects of hyperbole and in the tangibility of similes drawn from the surrounding 'life world'.[18] Campbell's colonial South Africanism can also be linked to his extroverted stance: when Bloomsbury shilly-shallied Campbell, the rough-neck, shouted, harangued and celebrated the physicality of existence. In his poetry the images are concrete, the verbs active, and even as he strikes the pose of the visionary, he relishes the colloquial word, and especially the insult. The damaging side of this braggadocio became evident as the radical purpose of the *Voorslag* enterprise diminished in Campbell's memory and the noble peasant emerged in his poems as the fascist-inspired symbol of agrarian continuity. In Spain, in the 1930s, the cowboy on the plain, the bullfight, the Catholic church, and General Franco all combined, in Campbell's imagination, in an iconography jealous of hierarchical authority and disdainful of all who are referred to as the Charlie Chaplins of the world: the defilers of the ancient glory. There is little that is humane in Campbell's later writing: his memoirs are bragging, bullying and preposterous in their adventures, and his satire is shrill with a 'cold war' dementia. He ended up raving about communists and – before his death in a motor accident in Portugal – he had begun to regard apartheid as a balm against the decline of the West. Given this, we might want to retain for South African literature only the striking *Adamastor* poems of Campbell's youth. Perhaps it is more instructive, however, to chart the *œuvre* as the sad case of the dislocated colonial whose romantic-symbolist imagination needs to be held warily to social account in a democratic South African response.

A commitment to the democratic ideal is precisely the quality that distinguishes Plomer's modernist imaginings from those of Campbell. In some ways less certain than Campbell that he wanted to be thought of as a South African writer, Plomer – who was born in the Transvaal – spent his early years being shipped between public school in England and his father's trading store in Zululand. As he said at a writers' conference in Johannesburg in 1956: 'So here I am, a sort of doubly displaced person . . . doubly involved, doubly detached.'[19] After having left South Africa in 1926, he studiously concealed the details of his youthful South African experiences behind the urbane manner of a British man of letters. (For many years he was a publisher's reader in London.) Plomer also carefully concealed his homosexuality, but Peter F. Alexander's biography – aimed primarily at the British market – presents Plomer of the sexual chase while P. N. Furbank, in a *TLS* review, dismisses Plomer as having remained trapped by the racial stereotypes he was wanting to debunk.[20] It is the South African perspective, ironically, that reveals continuing life in Plomer's work and, although he was revolted by the idea of a violent continent, he remained sufficiently fascinated by South Africa to keep returning to its subject matter and concerns. During his visit to Johannesburg in 1956, for example, he felt the tension of the mammoth treason trial: 156 black and white political leaders had been charged with opposing the apartheid state. In a response, he anticipated the Black Consciousness poetry of the 1970s by offering a lengthy call in 'Tugela River' for black revolutionary action. In the 1960s in the climate of hard-line apartheid, to take another example, he penned his moving elegy 'A Taste of the Fruit' for two South African writers, Nat Nakasa and Ingrid Jonker, who had defied the constricting codes, respectively, of racial discrimination and Afrikaner Calvinism only to commit suicide in the despair of their isolation. (Plomer would help to translate Jonker's poetry into English.)

Less brilliant an image-maker than Campbell, Plomer in his poems engages the reader in intelligent thought about the potential of poetry to capture and explore a consciousness of social obligation. Among his earliest literary endeavours were co-operations with the editor of the Zulu-English newspaper *Ilange laseNatali* (The Natal Sun), the writer,

educationist and politician John L. Dube. The issue involved the possibility of a national literature and, under the pseudonym P. Q. R., Plomer
published among other pieces on the race theme 'The Death of a Zulu',
an intimate, lyrical account of a Zulu woman mourning the loss of her
husband. The point of the exercise was apparent to Es'kia Mphahlele
when he remarked on Plomer's depiction of the African person as a
credible human being: in contrast, Campbell's 'The Zulu Girl', Mphahlele
felt, was obsessed with ethnicity, with the figure in the landscape as the
symbol of the group.[21] The poems published during Plomer's *Voorslag*
days (*Notes for Poems*, 1927) and his several specifically African poems of
the 1930s include satires of colonial types – the big-game hunter and the
fortune seeker – while, according to the poem 'Johannesburg', South
African society is built on the practices of the money-grubbing, frontier
mining town:

> Along the Rand in eighty-five
> Fortunes were founded overnight,
> And mansions rose among the rocks
> To blaze with girls and light.

The colloquial ballad form imitates old digger songs of the 1870s, and
swift juxtapositions of the illusory and the real permit Plomer to demythologise the romance of fortune-seeking in direct observations on greed
and oppression. An irregular syllabic count and occasionally imperfect
rhymes disrupt the easy flow of the verse leaving an impression of poetry
collapsing under the anger of denunciation into prose-like indictment.
Plomer himself, however, was not always happy with such effects and, in
recasting 'Johannesburg' as 'Conquistadors', he eliminated some of the
'crude' words (the expensive whore vanishes), elaborated on the analogy
of Spanish plunderers and the mining-town ethos, smoothed out the
rhythms and rhymes, and modified the satirist-moralist's warning on
exploitation to include generalised comment on the disillusion of age. If
literariness is increased, the result may not be totally beneficial to South
African literature. Rather the crux of Plomer's interest, it seems to me,
is that in his early African poems the unifying vision of the romantic-
symbolist explodes under the pressures of the raw experience. Social
languages in their disruptive, ordinary heterogeneity push into the enclos-
ure of the 'poetic' text: what are challenged are the poet's own colonial
hankerings after landscapes empty of the indigenous people, his own
colonial fears about Africa as savage and atavistic.

In 'The Devil-Dancers', for example, a self-ironising colonial mouthpiece, aware of its ludicrous pronouncements about the white man's
burden, upsets the tourist's version of Africa as a postcard of tribal life,

and the poem involves serious investigation about reason and action beneath the superficial image of the devil dance:

> The fretful pipes and thinly-crying strings,
> The mounting expectation of the drums
> Excite the nerves, and stretch the muscles taught
> Against the climax – but it never comes;
>
> It never comes because the dance must end
> And soon the older dancers will be dead;
> We leave by air tomorrow. How
> Can ever these messages by us be read?

The climax of the dance never comes because under the spectacle of what is in effect a show for tourists at a mining compound, there are actual mine workers whose grievances enter the larger narrative of history. In the last lines, a sanctioned 'Renaissance' conceit – the metamorphosis of the body into the spirit – is interpreted against the specificities of African retribution: 'Let us take care – that flake of flame may be/A butterfly whose bite can kill a man'. Here the poet struggles to emerge as a social commentator from the overlay of his own metaphor. We do not encounter fearful anticipation, finally, of a black devil rising from the colonial psyche to wreak irrational, inexplicable (Adamastor-type) vengeance on the white person. Rather, the closing lines are spoken as calm, logical, almost inevitable statements. Behind the masks are human, socialised beings; the action they contemplate against the colonial order is explicably part of historical causality. In contending with a psychology of hallucinatory vistas in Africa, Plomer avoids stratifying Africa into ritual and myth; instead, he demystifies the phantoms of white fears and tries to subject the experience to analytical understanding. In this, he is closer in his poetic purpose to Pringle than to Campbell.

The quest for normality in Africa was not an easy one for Plomer, and his novel *Turbott Wolfe* (1926), written when he was nineteen, testifies to his severe self-doubts about his abilities in a racist society to live up to his own liberal-humanist principles. The experimental modernism of the book, in which imagism predominates over the familiar voice, scenic juxtaposition over narrative logic, struck the accents of 'advanced' literary life at the time, and Plomer was quickly published by Leonard Woolf's Hogarth Press. The novel employs the Conradian device of the limited narrator (Turbott Wolfe tells his own story), and the overblown style of his narration as he recounts staring at his 'heart of darkness' in Africa is justified, psychologically, in that Wolfe is suffering from fever: he is hallucinating on his death bed. Yet this unhinged speaking voice is perhaps only precariously a literary device: its breathless immediacy –

conveyed in nervous, accumulated sentences and emotive repetitions – makes one, almost unthinkingly, want to pull Plomer the author into his character's story. Attracted by the African woman Nhliziyombi, Wolfe – as his name suggests, a fish in wolf's guise – avoids intimate contact and mentally transfigures the real African person into a literary noble savage, thus preserving his own European 'chastity'. Some have wanted to see in this a Freudian drama about Plomer's homosexuality. But the text empha- sises cultural concern with the fragility of the West's civilising mission, and the novel, which foreshortens linear time in poetic recurrence, manages in less than 200 pages to turn a dystopian eye on most of the figures that, by the 1920s, had begun to give South African fiction its recognisable stamp: these included bigoted colonials, ineffectual missionaries, farmers ploughing seeds of racial hatred into the earth, the man who goes native, the noble savage, and the European interloper.

Both Friston – the missionary – and Wolfe are visitors who leave people in the lurch when their grand schemes for a colour-free society crash about their own absence of conviction. Most of the characters, however, have Wolfe's measure, and whatever Mabel van der Horst's real intentions in marrying the African Zachary, she acts on Plomer's own best convictions when she says, ' "What the hell *is* the native question? . . . there is no native question. It isn't a question. It's an answer." ' To which Wolfe's only response is to talk about principles not actions, and finally it is in his lack of deeds that he reveals his largest betrayal of trust. Asked by Cabel Msomi to help Africans in the political world by lending his support to a community of people in South Africa, Wolfe – like Conrad's Decoud – can only retreat into the impotence of aesthetic self- indulgence: 'I have reached a point where life offers nothing but a few sensations, more or less indecent, which I know are only illusions.' The style tests the limits of realism; the gothic quality touches the frontiers of the European mind in Africa, and the modernist manner, which need not be bound inevitably to conserving primordial unities, parodies its own preoccupation with aesthetic rather than social commitment. Like Plomer's other African stories – 'Ula Masondo' looks critically at the 'Jim comes to Joburg' journey, 'Down on the Farm' twists the pastoral motif into unusual revelations, the short biography of Rhodes is a carica- tural denunciation of avarice and power – *Turbott Wolfe* struggles to prise the colonial mind (including, residually, Plomer's own) away from the grip of its racial and social stereotyping. In denying Plomer any success in this endeavour Furbank, in my opinion, has not taken sufficient cogni- sance of the creative tensions in the writing between the artistic temp- tation to withdraw into experiments with forms and the moral duty to confront hypocrisy, exploitation and injustice. At least, this is how Plomer impinges on the South African literary scene.

The third of the *Voorslag* trio Laurens, now Sir Laurens, van der Post has been introduced already in connection with his studies of Bushman literature and culture. Regarding himself as something of a seer, Van der Post is in great demand at business and press club functions in South Africa where his message to the country is fundamentally the same as that advocated in his best-selling ethno-mythographic story of his own 're-education' in proximity to the Bushmen, *The Lost World of the Kalahari* (1958): seek the richness of the individual imagination, nurture its originary roots — here Jung and the Bushmen are coupled — against the abstractions of rationalism, and against the group will of both nationalism and communism; conserve the environment against destructive industrialisation; amid conflict seek forgiveness and compassion. This romantic, mystical humanism has led Van der Post in his numerous writings into several naïveties regarding the superiority of intuition over analysis, but he remains too certain of his vision to enter into argument with his detractors: Africanists who see noble savages lurking behind his 'nonrational' justifications and Marxists who see his individualism as inimical to socio-economic truth, especially in its fear of mass-based political activity.[22] The quintessential Van der Post was already contained in the novel arising most immediately from his *Voorslag* experience, *In a Province* (1934).

With the title from Ecclesiastes summing up the governing liberal ideal ('If thou seest the oppression of the poor, and the violent perversity of judgment and justice in a province, marvel not at the matter'), Van der Post sets the interrelated stories of the Afrikaner Jan van Bredepoel and the African Kenon, both of whom journey from their rural 'roots' to the city, against the fact of increased African trade-union activity in the 1920s. The African Industrial and Commercial Union, known as the ICU, included a radical group made up of South African Communist Party members which had called for a militant policy of mass action. In a plot of highly charged events including strike scenes, 'agitation', and police shootings, and in elaborate discussions on principle and life, Van der Post advocates a change of heart as the prerequisite for a change in the system. As Van Bredepoel, who espouses the liberal view, tells Burgess, the communist: ' "The system is only a garment round the human heart; it doesn't give shape to the heart, it takes its own shape from the heart." ' Whereas Plomer's violent experiments with convention and mood become the correlatives of the liberal mind doubting the bases of its own belief, Van der Post retains a firm hold on the widely recognised tenets of Western liberalism. In identifying the enemies of both the human condition and art as Marxist economics, the group mentality according to which mobs always run riot, and propagandist pronouncement (Van der Post does not regard Van Bredepoel's liberalism of the heart as ideology), *In a Province* charts the field of attitude and interest that would characterise many South African novels of social responsibility. Later novelists like Alan Paton, Dan Jacobson and Nadine Gordimer would remain alert to complexities inherent in large ideas; Van der Post imposes his design.

While Bolshevik influence in the 1920s undoubtedly spurred Van der Post's strong reaction, *In a Province* revealed another societal curtailment that has implications for South African fiction. As in the cases of Schreiner, Blackburn and Plomer, Van der Post chose the novel form in circumstances that seemed unpropitious to the conventional scope of the novel as the story of character interacting with society. The Act of Union – as I have suggested – did little to encourage the potential of a single, working society, and the way Plomer coped was to veer his drama away from the industrialising process to forms of anti-pastoralism. When Van der Post attempts to enter the city, he shows virtually no understanding of its effects on people or events. Yet a 'thickening' experience could have attached itself to the abstraction of his ideas had he given more attention to the gradations of the communities he himself invokes. Van Bredepoel, for example, is nurtured in Afrikaner Calvinism, but we the readers are not permitted emotional involvement in what for him must have been a painful growth towards his liberal conviction. It is as if Van der Post, himself an Afrikaner who grew up on a farm in the Free State, wants to bury, too perfunctorily, the ghosts of his past. Similarly, there is no attempt to trace Kenon back to his community. In fact, readers are debarred from entering this character's thoughts in any illuminating way and, like a man with no cultural traditions, Kenon simply collapses into crime at the first temptation of the city. Looking back from the perspective of subsequent urbanisation after the Second World War, one is left wondering whether, demographically, the story of city life in South Africa could have been 'knowable' in the 1920s and 1930s. Such a consideration could be pursued up to the present day where fictional space continues to register the severe effects of apartheid engineering on the creation of a single, layered society. Significantly, most of the early fiction finds its locality in the country region.

Tales of rural communities. Smith. Bosman. The *plaasroman*

Through subtle forms of language transference, both Pauline Smith and Herman Charles Bosman have presented English-speaking readers with studies of rural Afrikaans communities. Smith, who spent her childhood in the Oudtschoorn district of the little Karoo, accompanied her father, a medical doctor, on his rounds to Afrikaans farming families and, having been sent to school in England at the age of twelve, she stored up in memory images of the hard simplicity of the Karoo landscape and its people. During visits to South Africa in 1905 and 1913, she kept diaries and a journal of impressions that would coalesce into her stories, collected as *The Little Karoo* (1925), and her novel *The Beadle* (1926).[23] Her earliest 'South African' children's stories were published only in 1935 as *Platkops Children*. Finding parallels between 'the slow and brooding talk of Afrikaans farmers' and the seventeenth-century English of the Authorised Version, Smith shifted prepositional phrases and direct objects to the beginning of sentences ('Every bit of news that came to her of Klaartje and Aalst Vlokman Jacoba treasured'), retained participles in a typically Afrikaans position ('And who *then* [dan] is Aalst Vlokman?') and literally translated words within a phrase ('Fetch for the beadle [vir die koster] some water') in order to create an authentic-sounding community in the Aangenaam (Pleasant) Valley, where life played out elemental, almost fatalistic passions to the rhythms of the plough, the church service, and the moods of the seasons.

The Beadle is about guilt and forgiveness. Having failed to acknowledge Andrina as his illegitimate daughter Aalst Vlokman, the beadle, knows the bitter taste of the sinner. Andrina, in contrast, has no 'saving sense of sin' and when she finds she is pregnant by the feckless Englishman from outside the valley, she shows not hatred but tolerance for his frailties, love for her child, and forgiveness towards the beadle who finally expiates his past in soul-wracking public confession. The action is tightly framed within symbolic changes in the seasons, and the moral poles of Old Testament punishment and New Testament love are personified in the contrasting figures of Andrina's two aunts who watch over the human drama. The idyllic mode is punctuated, however, by an unflinching awareness that our deeds have their consequences. With a sense of inevitability imbuing her fiction with archetypal resonances, Smith has enjoyed praise for moving the region into the wider world. More recent criticism, in contrast, has found her strength not in any universalism but in her depictions of the small, oppressive localities of Afrikaner Calvinism.[24] Certainly her short stories, which are less tempted by idyllic resolution than is the novel, connect the psychology of religious reaction unremittingly to the economic realities of poor whitism. Although there is some truth in the feminist view that Smith's criticism of patriarchy is qualified by her nostalgia for secure orders, 'The Miller' has Andries Lombard turn cruelly on his wife because she is dependent on him while, as a bywoner (a tenant farmer), he feels insecure and abandoned by God. In 'The Father' Piet Pienaar's powerlessness in the presence of the richer, smarter Andries van Reenen, and his resentment towards God for not granting him more sons, find perverse expression in the brutal way he treats his wife and only son. In 'The Schoolmaster' the generous love of a woman cannot release Jan Boetje from his haunted past – his sorrow and sin – and the music of new affection is shattered by Boetje's sudden blinding of his mules prior to his life-long penance of pulling his cart with a harness across his chest. Arnold Bennett, who coaxed the painfully shy Smith into authorship, was accurate in his famous observation that the talent is strange, austere, tender, ruthless.[25]

This does not negate the 'political' difficulty, however, that Smith's strengths in understanding the community she so vividly evoked blinded her to the place of that community in the functioning of South African society. With South Africa as a place hardly existing for her outside her childhood memories, Smith's self-enclosed Aangenaam Valley can be seen as a refuge against time, change and history, so that even though she recognised a shortage of New Testament compassion among the folk of the valley, she allowed Afrikanerdom to retain its mythos of God's Elect. As several commentators have emphasised, such a mythos has had destructive consequences, and it is not surprising that few black writers have been under illusions about Afrikaner organic communities. What this could suggest is that in future histories of South African literature, Smith will be regarded as an artist of miniature concern, the unyielding destinies of her protagonists shrinking to the small interests of their 'unmodern' predispositions. This would involve a loss, but might force us to ask other questions: particularly why so few white writers of the 1920s and 1930s felt the need to devote attention to intrusive racial issues.

Like Smith, the short-story writer Herman Charles Bosman saw little active role in his plots for black South Africans. What Bosman did, nonetheless, was to begin the process – hesitantly, at first – of debunking the myth of the pastoral Boer. Himself half Afrikaans, Bosman had strong views about an indigenous South African literature.[26] Ignoring the elite international modernism of *Voorslag*, he confirmed the common touch of Stephen Black's *The Sjambok*, in which several of his first stories were published. Bosman found value in Pringle and Schreiner (both showed 'sincere' commitment to the country's problems), he endorsed Afrikaans as 'part of Africa', and regarded it as the task of African writers to transform the gutters and the streets which they knew better than did whites into the 'imperishable grey beauty of literature' ('how can a white man get into a black man's skin – and vice versa'). In granting Pauline Smith credit for touching the 'soil' out of which an authentic South Africanism must grow, Bosman himself could not separate the 'ache' of South Africa from his thorough involvement in local literary life in its most ordinary aspects, including the muck-raking journalism to which he was always willing to contribute topical commentary. In 1930 the magazine *The Touleier* – edited by Aegidius Jean Blignaut whose 'Hottentot Ruiter' stories inspired Bosman – had Herman Malan (alias Bosman) as contributing editor, and during the following two decades there was a proliferation of Herman Malan fly-by-night scandal sheets.[27]

Eager at times to affect the image of the poetic genius – for the romance of life was inseparable in Bosman from its colloquial ironies – Bosman also took pride in knowing the bigoted, prejudiced, lazy, devious mind associated, in anecdote, with the backveld Boer raconteur. Having spent a year in 1926 teaching in the Marico district of the western Transvaal, he found his locale, characters and accents, and his 'Oom Schalk' stories began to appear regularly in the 1930s before being collected in 1947 as *Mafeking Road*. The discursive, folksy personality of the narrator, Oom Schalk Lourens, lends unity to the apparently artless unfolding of the tale: only apparently artless, however, for Bosman's skills are deliberately literary and include as models both the frontier, humorist tradition – American as well as Afrikaner – and the highly structured 'twist in the tail' that we find in O. Henry and Guy de Maupassant. The title story 'Mafeking Road', accordingly, begins with Oom Schalk – yokel or shrewd observer? – discussing the art of storytelling: what matters is the way you tell the story; what is necessary to know is what to leave out. This sets the scene for an old Boer War yarn, in which the deadpan voice of the teller belies Bosman's ironical purpose of demythologising the heroic memory. The humour works by incongruities: 'And if we had difficulty in finding the road to Mafeking, we had no difficulty in finding the road away from Mafeking.' Yet even as the myths of leadership and bravery are overturned, the mood takes on the sombre resonances of Oom Schalk's (and Bosman's) close attachment to Afrikaner history as we are offered bitter insight into Boer defeat: 'there had been very great rejoicings in England when Mafeking was relieved, and it was strange to think of the other aspect of it – of a defeated country and of broken columns blundering through the dark.' Bosman always said humour was a serious business, and the story focuses on a son's betrayal of the cause. He rides off to surrender to the British with his father in pursuit. Oom Schalk's return at the end of his story to his casual tone is deceptive. The father – Oom Schalk says – had a good story to tell, but he insisted on telling the part he should have left out, and the pathos is allowed to linger in the reader's mind. For behind the story of duty and patriotism in battle there is the more intimate, more terrible story of a father who has to live with the anguish of having shot his son as a traitor. The defence of the Marico community is to keep the story where it can be controlled: in the realm of the public theme; so when asked what 'obiit' means – the son's name on the family tree is followed by the words 'Obiit Mafeking' – the response is that it is a foreign word meaning to ride up to the English, holding your Mauser in the air, with a white flag near the muzzle. This, at least, is how I interpret Bosman's extremely elusive version of an old Boer War yarn.

Other 'Oom Schalk' stories use similar tactics of turning stock South African situations such as miscegenation, the trek into the desert, the hunting yarn, and the small-town scandal to surprisingly ambiguous purposes, in which the myth or stereotype is undercut at the same time as the insight escapes the limited region of the Marico to provoke profound considerations about the truth of the saving lie. In the few stories of black-white confrontation, however, the irony is precarious, and sometimes misfires. When Oom Schalk like a typical member of his narrow community casually insults 'kaffirs', lexical markers do not always guide the reader to placing the jibe within the prejudices of the Marico view, and I for one am sometimes left unsure where Bosman the author stands in relation to the views of his character-narrator. Bosman is also slap-dash in his treatment of women characters: they tend to remain merely fantastical veld maidens or foils to the male historical concerns. Yet the stories, which were all published locally not abroad, mostly addressed a literate, liberal readership. From 1934 to 1951 Bosman's tales appeared in *Trek* and *South African Opinion*, magazines which merged in 1946 and, in bringing to light the talents of Doris Lessing, Nadine Gordimer and Jack Cope, can be said to have reflected a liberal-humanist advance in South African writing. Perhaps Bosman just shared an average, blunted response to racial and sexual matters; perhaps he relied sometimes too easily on his literate readers' perceiving an ironical intention. For in a few key stories we do find prejudice clearly condemned. The method is usually that of *reductio ad absurdum* as in 'Unto Dust' (written relatively late, in 1949) in which apartheid's obsessions are made to bite the common earth. No one in the Marico can tell which bones belonged to the white man, which to the black, and in the sting in the tail the black man's 'yellow kafir dog' is left watching over the grave in which the folk of the community think they have buried the remains of their own kind, the white farmer Hans Welman.

After celebrating the Afrikaner National Party election victory in 1948 as a triumph over British imperialism, Bosman in his regular contribution, in 1950–51, to the liberal weekly magazine *The Forum* developed conversational pieces which, in minglings of the absurd and the mordant, began to question the mania of race-classification in the first years of apartheid.[28] The Marico characters in these sketches have lost some of the idiosyncrasies of utter regionalism, and Bosman is less indulgent than in the earlier 'Oom Schalk' stories towards their foibles and prejudices. The move seems to be, almost imperceptibly, from the Marico to South Africa. In his prison memoir *Cold Stone Jug* (1949) Bosman looked back to his four-year gaol term served after 1927 when he shot his brother-in-law in a family quarrel: the strategy of survival is recollected as bravura pitted against isolation. In his posthumously published novel *Willemsdorp* (1977), written shortly after the coming to power of Afrikaner nationalism,

Bosman gave cynical political expression to his theory of the South African dorp, or small town.[29] As in his first novel *Jacaranda in the Night* (1947), the dorp is seen as the repository of the Voortrekker inheritance: starless, Calvinistic conceptions of predestination and original sin, sectarianism, inward stress. Now race legislation, specifically the amended Immorality Act (1950) which had criminalised interracial sex between white and non-white, focuses the issues as Bosman excoriates white South African neuroses. Although characters transgress the Act, they will not face their own inner compulsions, and *Willemsdorp* suggests that at the heart of white South Africans there is a fear of living in Africa. Supremacy needs to be enforced, therefore, by laws that make a mockery of human nature. Perhaps Oom Schalk's casual insults at Africans should be regarded as part of Bosman's own crisis of white identity. What is important is that we do not limit Bosman's South Africanism to his early tales. Nor should he be classified too narrowly as a humorist.

Lacking Bosman's protean approach to the question of nationalism, Afrikaans prose writers up to the early 1960s generally retained forms of the agrarian community: at times charged with dynastic purport, at others collapsing into maudlin regrets. In writers such as D. F. Malherbe, Jochem van Bruggen, Johannes van Melle, Mikro and C. M. van den Heever, there developed a kind of novel known as the *plaasroman* (farm novel).[30] The impetus was the crisis on the platteland in which capitalist modes of farming, initiated by monied townspeople, were threatening older feudal arrangements that had been sustained by the Afrikaner peasant farmer who traded his service for space on someone else's farm. In minglings of romantic epiphany and German blood-and-soil mythologies, the fiction yearns for the restoration, amid rural poverty, of lineal memory in patriarchal, familial ownership. Whereas Schreiner's farm touches the surrounding colony, Van den Heever's farm is jealous, ancestral ground: the ghosts of the fathers hold the sons to a legacy of obligation. Lower down the rung, coloured labourers provide comic relief while they are shown welcoming their own childish, drunken dependency on the stern rule of the white overlord. The city and its agents – the merchant, the Jew, the alien Englishman – are depicted as types who are disruptive to the ideal of supra-class Afrikaner cohesion. Economics is elided into myth, and the *plaasroman* takes its ideological role in the discourse of national destiny. By the 1950s the originary, historical impetus had gelled into a set of conventions. Yet the *plaasroman* continues today to have wide appeal particularly in its re-casting of farm novels and stories into television plays. Here nostalgia for the mythic time when every Afrikaner was supposed to define his [sic] identity on the land might speak of little more than urban escapism. Or, it could delineate deep-seated fears, in a time of 'multiracial' change, about the demise of Afrikanerdom as a unifying concept. The distance between resurgences of the *plaasroman* and the restlessness of the Afrikaner Right is not a vast one.

Afrikaans, a literary language. Poetry from Van Wyk Louw to Opperman

It was the parochialism and sentimentality of '*plaasroman*' prose to which the Afrikaans poet and intellectual N. P. van Wyk Louw objected in 1958 when he pleaded with writers of fiction to show a more 'magnificent sense'[(t)] of Afrikaner potential. Referring to the *plaasroman* tradition disparagingly as a 'genial local realism'[(t)], he listed its characteristics as small sorrows, the unhappinesses of everyday, no imagination, no flights of fantasy; stylistically, it was dreary in its chronological sequences. What was required, according to Van Wyk Louw, were new themes, new structures, a new use of language.[31] As the leading figure among the Dertigers – writers, principally poets, of the Thirties who included Uys Krige, Elizabeth Eybers and W. E. G. Louw – N. P. van Wyk Louw occupies a pivotal role in Afrikaans literature.[32] In the years during which the volk was consolidated into the Afrikaner nation, Van Wyk Louw raised his powerfully confessional voice in support of the will, the deed, of the Voortrekker past. At the same time, his moralist's temperament ensured severe tensions in his poetry, poetic dramas and essays as he became increasingly disillusioned with what he saw as the philistinism and rapacious materialism of a new generation of Afrikaans bourgeois-city nationalists. What he inherited in the 1930s, politically, was a time of extremism. When Smuts' South African Party and Hertzog's Nationalists fused in the (white) 'national interest' at the time of the great depression, a group of Afrikaners – as I have said – split off to form the remodelled, or purified, National Party under the former dominee of the Dutch Reformed Church, Dr D. F. Malan. Even Malan's brand of racial politics was by-passed, however, by ideologues in the secret Broederbond including the architects of apartheid, Dr N. Diedrichs, Dr P. J. Meyer and Dr G. Cronje. With man's potential regarded as realisable only in the service of the nation and racial separation justified in the myth of the Tower of Babel, Genesis and in the Song of Moses, the National Party in 1945 adopted the doctrine of apartheid as official policy. In the company of such 'prophets' Van Wyk Louw, who like the politicians in the 1930s had been infected by Nazi thought wrapped into Calvinist theology, railed in his own prophetic tones as he held converse with God and, having grudgingly admitted three decades later that he might have sinned in his early beliefs, he went on to deliver back tortured messages to the volk even as he attempted to avoid any head-on confrontation.[33]

What he inherited in literary terms was not only the simple patriotic verses of language movement poets, but the ideal that the health of the volk was connected to a flowering of the Afrikaans language. In dismissing naïve didacticism, he grafted on to his poetry the high-flown influences of late nineteenth-century Dutch and German verse. He was attracted, equally, to the symbolist transfigurations of the European modernist movement, in which underlying views of Nietzschean renewals and aestheticisms, as opposed to economic materialism, found consonance with his nationalist beliefs. In South Africa, Roy Campbell's themes and styles of energy would be recognised as a precursor of the Dertiger manner. Van Wyk Louw also inherited a lively nationalist-inspired drama in Afrikaans that tried to apply nineteenth-century European naturalism to the issue of poor whitism among rural Afrikaners.[34] Whereas he was critical of poor-white portrayals in Jochem van Bruggen's trilogy of *Ampie* novels (1924–1942),[35] Van Wyk Louw evidently found something more satisfying in the depictions of P.W.S. Schumann's play *Hantie kom Huis-toe* (Hantie is Coming Home, 1933), and we begin to realise that when Van Wyk Louw attacked *plaasroman* prose his objections had little to do with the subject of poor whitism per se. What he objected to were portrayals through forms of bourgeois idealisation: 'a complacent idealisation of an erstwhile happy rural life in which the tenant and the landowner still knew their respective places[(t)].' The way to oppose this, however, was not to institute a critique of economic relations; rather it was to aestheticise politics, and with the proletarian drift to the cities viewed with alarm by Afrikaner ideologues, Van Wyk Louw's contribution was to seek resurgences in a folk spirit that was supposed to alleviate the dangers of class differentiation and unify the volk in its poetic image.[36]

The sublime, however, continually eluded Van Wyk Louw, and his poetic symbols re-bound beyond any possible single interpretation. As the cruelties of Nazism became known, he created a horror house of beast poems, in which the poet seeks to stare evil in the face, to purge his own soul, and to order chaos in the making of the poetic artefact. But the black leopard remains untamed to haunt the psyche, and the eagle changes from the image of heroic nobility to that of paranoia and death: 'alone and far he dines,/and even where he's not his ranging terror reigns'[(t).37] In *Raka* (1941), which is vividly written in comparatively free rhythmic couplets of four or five stresses, Raka the ape-man, dark, incapable of thought, a solitary animal, defeats the dancing, singing Koki and wins the allegiance of the tribe. By making Koki coloured, not white, Van Wyk Louw may have wanted consciously to avoid suggesting European-African dichotomies of Apollonian light and Dionysian darkness. What skews the reader's attention away from hints about the decline of the West and the resuscitation of the dark gods, however, is the poet's obsessional, almost personal accent that tears through the objective correlative of scene embodying emotion and insists on a form of dialogue with self. Having been tempted from his own darkness by the light, Van Wyk Louw is unable to shake off the gloom, and several of his works, including the verse play *Germanicus* (1956), are filled with the anguish of the artistic soul standing precariously on an abyss as huge shifts of epochs pull the heroic individual as national figure, this way and that. In the poem 'Die Hond van God' (The Hound of God), the medieval torturer glimpses in his victim the possibility of the new humanistic Renaissance at the same time as he despises the pity of it:

> But, Lord, may I not weakly bend to fit
> in with this age, this new humanity.
> Set me against it. Make a wedge of me,
> a crowbar driven in this era, so
> to break it or uplift it bodily . . .[t]

The attitudes are thoroughly ambivalent, and the mind divided against itself becomes the principle of many of the poems in a style that is metaphoric and allusive.

As apartheid took its grip in the 1950s Van Wyk Louw, who at the time was professor of Afrikaans in Amsterdam, produced his *Tristia* sequence (1962) which suggests an Eliotian shoring of cultural shards against ruin. In keeping with his Europeanising, universalising tendency – the Afrikaner, Van Wyk Louw believed, should not be parochial – the ruin is usually generalised as the 'modern condition' that requires succour from ancient (Western) cultural and spiritual sources. Every now and again, however, a jarring, localised protest at what is hypocritical in himself is extended to the South African scene. With the National Party government in 1956 having removed the historical franchise rights held by coloureds in the Cape, for example, the poem 'Nuus Berigte' (News Report) began, 'Has my country become other than I know'[t], as Van Wyk Louw returned to his bugbear: corruptions of affluence and power among the Afrikaner ruling class. The poet included himself as one of the sinners. In the cryptic 'Groot Ode' (Great Ode), in the *Tristia* sequence, the poet suddenly directs a parody at the stupidity of Afrikaner apartheid isolationism which is experienced as a freezing of the spirit. In refusing to justify Afrikaner survival in Africa at any cost, Van Wyk Louw spoke of a just survival: the socio-political details of this remain vague and certainly do not contemplate the full racial character of the population; rather, the guilt of conscience derives metaphysically from the Calvinist doctrine of original sin, a central concern in a great deal of Afrikaans literature up to the present day. Commissioned to write a play for the first festival of the Afrikaner republic in 1966, Van Wyk Louw produced *Die Pluimsaad Waai Ver* (The Wind-blown Seed Travels Far, 1972). This was a chronicle of the Anglo-Boer War revolving around the heroic figure of president Steyn of the Orange Free State republic and, while patriotic in general feeling, it refused popular anti-British stereotypes, depicted treachery among some of the burgers, and incorporated a thread of doubt as to the question it posed in the first line: what is a nation? As I have mentioned, prime minister Verwoerd delivered a public rebuke to this Milton of Afrikanerdom who replied by rejecting the charge that he lacked true patriotism. Van Wyk Louw's concern was summarised in the title of his collection of essays *Liberale Nasionalisme* (Liberal Nationalism, 1958) and in his book *Random eie Werk* (About my Own Work, 1970), in which he talks of his attempt as an Afrikaner and a poet to view life not through political-party dogma, but always with an 'uncontaminated eye' ('met 'n skoon oog'). Given that there is little sight of the South African social mixture in his verse, however, not all critics in a divisive political climate are going to be willing to extend 'truth' to Van Wyk Louw's poetry despite its verbal proficiency and its undoubted power to pull the reader into transmogrifying worlds that stretch, or even assault, the senses. In challenging the considerable status Van Wyk Louw enjoys in the Afrikaner literary establishment while trying to return his texts to the contexts of segregationist South Africa, we should at least be wary of investing all our interest in his wide European cultural reference. For the trauma that compels the prophetic voice remains in crucial aspects an insular Afrikaner affair, and it is possible to view the Dertigers as mastering the European inheritance in guard against their own sectarian commitments.[38]

Such a view may be turned also on the aesthetic formalism that continued to be sanctioned in the literary journal *Standpunte* (Points of View, 1945–1986), founded by Van Wyk Louw, as well as in D. J. Opperman's influential essays, anthologies and poetry. Where Opperman, a professor of Afrikaans, differed temperamentally from Van Wyk Louw was in not having had the earlier poet's driving Calvinist conscience. A consequence has been Opperman's willingness to play irreverently, on occasions, with contradictions between the concepts of the Afrikaner as the nationalist and the Afrikaner as the world-cultural citizen. The anthology he edited, *Groot Verseboek* (The Major Anthology of Poems, first published in 1951 and in its several revisions perennially prescribed for students) has retained the concept of the canon as a-historical high-word art. But in releasing the angel from the stone, as he described the function of the poet, Opperman to a greater degree than the Dertigers took cognisance of relationships between the symbolic and the colloquial experience. This does not necessarily undermine what, in its philosophical and literary predilections, remains a modernist programme. Opperman shared with the Dertigers preoccupations that were cultural rather than social, and aesthetic rather than political. As a result, his last important work *Komas uit 'n Bamboesstok* (Comas out of a Bamboo Stick, 1977) shows virtually no sensitivity to the new accents of Soweto protest in the 1970s that had characterised the South African scene. Instead, we have an autobiographical journey of the imagination that, after the poet's serious illness, transports us back to the clear-sightedness of child vision and, in renewal, forward in the role of adults who hope to see again, as if for the first time. In its comminglings of the ancient and the modern, the flight of ecstasy and the low word, *Komas* would satisfy the view that poetry is an alternative truth to the prose of life. Where the modernist is so often grand and arrogant, however, Opperman works towards humility, and perhaps a great deal of his poetry can be read not internationally, but locally, as a joyous reaction against the confines of Afrikanerdom.

Even in his first poems, which were written in the 1940s, Opperman seemed uncomfortable in committing himself to the compulsory themes of the volk: the love of the land, the heroic history, the national (meaning Afrikaner) destiny. His *Joernaal van Jorik* (Journal of Jorik, 1949) has attained almost cult status in the Afrikaans canon where it is seen to connect the Afrikaner's physical and spiritual destiny both to his own history and to the history of the modern age. To me, however, the poem is a hotch-potch of unresolved ideas which speaks of Opperman's own confusions as to whether he wanted to be an Afrikaner nationalist or, more broadly, an Afrikaans-speaking South African. The protagonist in the poem lands off the Cape, oddly, in a German submarine. He is a spy who has parallels in the years after the war with pro-Nazi heroes in Afrikaner circles. (Opperman evidently believed that the twentieth-century 'condition' was characterised by betrayal.) Although we are meant to see the spy becoming attached to Afrikaans versions of South Africa, the poem is unable to work through the bizarre war-time associations it has chosen to introduce. Where Van Wyk Louw draws the objective world into the subjective colourings of a mental universe, Opperman moves outwards: the romantic response is externalised into objects and scenes. Nonetheless, the city – regarded as spiritually arid – and Africa – regarded as a place of several different and valuable cultures – are universalised and aestheticised in the end into ideals of eternal meaning. In other words, the city and Africa are de-Africanised, de-historicised.

Or, perhaps the choice between the society and the poem is not as clear-cut as arguments between revisionist and standard commentary on Opperman want to make out.[39] In 1952, in *Standpunte*, Opperman published 'Kersliedjie' (Christmas Carol), a delightful version of the Bethlehem story. Three outas (humble old coloured men) follow the star to the coloured District Six in Cape Town where they pile their unpretentious gifts of biltong, sheep fat and eggs before 'God's small brown child'. In the original Afrikaans the words are 'God se klong', klong often being used as a slightly derogatory term for the young coloured person. Six years later, this highly accessible poem would create a furore when it was printed in an Afrikaans daily newspaper.[40] (Opperman's anti-modernist humility has consistently veered towards popular communication.) Virtually accused of blasphemy for presenting the baby Jesus as non-white, the poet was advised by one irate letter writer to don sackcloth, sit on an ash heap, and contemplate his sins. The real challenge to Afrikaner orthodoxy, however, is to be located probably in the final lines of the poem: 'And on her nest throughout the whole affair/a bantam clucks with a suspicious stare'[(t)]. The suggestion here is that our stories and myths are not essentially true, but the products of the fiction-making impulse. Accordingly, the related point about Opperman's Voortrekker play *Voëlvry* (Outlaw, 1968) may not be that, as the critic J. C. Kannemeyer thinks, the protagonist-figure Louis Tregardt has insufficient stature to carry the heroic theme.[41] Rather, the point could be that Tregardt, the eccentric trekker, is the right one to prick the bubble of pride and remind us – as Herman Charles Bosman does – of the real squabbling human beings behind the epic tale. Whatever the interpretation, flat-earthist attacks on writers continue to embarrass Afrikaans literary people, and Opperman has remained firmly in the canon as a more generous representative of high culture than the austere Van Wyk Louw. We are reminded, in fact, that in articles in *Standpunte* in the 1950s, while Nationalist politicians were trumpeting the purity of the volk, Opperman joined Uys Krige in considering not an exclusive Afrikaans literature, but a South African poetic line running from the socially responsible Pringle, through the cosmopolitan Leipoldt, to Campbell's vivid iconoclasm, and on to Van Wyk Louw.[42] There is reformism in this kind of thought but, as I have suggested, no radical re-imagining of black–white relations. For Africa to be much more than an exotic tribal land, we .have to turn in the first decades of segregationist South Africa to the paths followed by black writers.

Notes

1. See the essays on 'interwar' liberalism in J. Butler *et al.* (eds), *Democratic Liberalism in South Africa: Its History and Prospects* (Middletown and Cape Town, 1987); J. Cochrane, *Servants of Power: The Role of English-speaking Churches, 1903–1930* (Johannesburg, 1987); S. Dubow, *Racial Segregation and the Origins of Apartheid in South Africa, 1919–1936* (London, 1989), D. Duncan, *The Mills of God: The State and African Labour in South Africa, 1918–1948* (Johannesburg, 1994);

M. Lipton, *Capitalism and Apartheid: South Africa, 1910–1985* (Aldershot, 1985); T. D. Moodie, *The Rise of Afrikanerdom: Power, Apartheid, and the Afrikaner Civil Religion* (Berkeley, 1975); D. O'Meara, *Volkskapitalisme: Class, Capital and Ideology in the Development of Afrikaner Nationalism* (Cambridge, 1983), P. B. Rich, *White Power and the Liberal Conscience: Racial Segregation and South African Liberalism, 1921–60* (Johannesburg, 1984); D. Yudelman, *The Emergence of Modern South Africa: State, Capital and the Incorporation of Organised Labour on the South African Goldfields, 1902–1939* (Cape Town, 1984).

For commentary at the time see P. Lewsen (ed.), *Voices of Protest: From Segregation to Apartheid, 1938–1948* (Johannesburg, 1988) for speeches of M. V. Ballinger, E. H. Brookes, R. F. A. Hoernlé and D. B. Molteno who protested against segregationist policies. Also: I. D. MacCrone, *Race Attitudes in South Africa: Historical, Experimental and Psychological Studies* (London, 1937); R. E. Phillips, *The Bantu in the City: A Study of Cultural Adjustment on the Witwatersrand* (Alice, 1938); and S. T. Plaatje, *Native Life in South Africa: Before and Since the European War and the Boer Rebellion* (London, 1916; Johannesburg, 1982). Valuable source material is to be found in the holdings of the South African Institute of Race Relations (Johannesburg).

2. *Greater South Africa: Plans for a Better World. The Speeches of General the Rt. Honourable J. C. Smuts, PC, CH, KC, DTD* (Johannesburg, 1940), pp. 16–21. Also: W. K. Hancock, *Smuts*, 2 vols (Cambridge, 1968).

3. See A. Hepple, *Verwoerd* (Harmondsworth, 1967) and A. N. Pelser (ed.), *Verwoerd Speaks: Speeches, 1948–1966* (Johannesburg, 1966). Also, as representative, N. Diedricks, 'Die Fascistiese Staatfilosofie', *Die Huisgenoot* (3 November 1933) and O. Pirow, *Nuwe Order vir Suid-Afrika* (Pretoria, 1941). Cf. B. Bunting, *The Rise of the South African Reich* (Harmondsworth, 1964; rev.ed., 1969) and D. O'Meara, *Forty Lost Years: The National Party and the Politics of the South African State, 1948–1993* (Johannesburg, 1995).

4. See Lewsen [n. 1 above] as well as Hoernlé's *South African Native Policy and the Liberal Spirit* (Cape Town, 1939) and *Race and Reason* (Johannesburg, 1955). M. Legassick's interpretation of Hoernlé's equivocal liberal stance, as he sees it, gained currency among Marxist-inclined historians in South Africa in the late 1970s: 'Race, Industrialisation and Social Change in South Africa, the Case of R. F. A. Hoernlé', *African Affairs*, no. 75 (1976).

5. See T. Karis and G. M. Carter (eds), *From Protest to Challenge: A Documentary History of African Politics in South Africa, 1882–1964*, 4 vols (Stanford, 1972).

6. Lewsen, Introduction, *Voices of Protest* [n. 1 above].

7. Commissioned to write a play for the first festival of the Republic in 1966, Van Wyk Louw's response was *Die Pluimsaad Waai Ver*. Verwoerd was present at the opening performance and launched a stinging public rebuke of the poet.

8. G. Besselaar, *Zuid-Afrika in de Letterkunde* (Amsterdam and Cape Town, 1914) and M. Nathan, *South African Literature: A General Survey* (London, 1925).

9. The years between Bain's *Kaatje Kekkelbek* (1838) and Black saw home-grown theatre include only a few farces which usually veered towards the settings and accents of the Victorian stage: for example, C. E. Boniface's *Kockincoz; or, the Pettifogging Lawyers' Plot* (1843) and several odd imitations of Shakespearean tragedies gathered into the service of local events, such as Daniel Kestell's Afrikaans 'language movement' play *The Struggle for Freedom*[t] (published in English in 1881) and Harold Bolce's *A Slump in Heroes: A Transvaal War Drama*

without Warriors (?1896). Like Bain and – when he wrote in Dutch – Boniface, Melt Brink turned to slap-stick comedy in his Afrikaans-Dutch plays of which 20 were published between 1904 and 1921. (Black's plays may be said, therefore, to belong to a small tradition of knockabout comedy in which the coloured stereotype recurs.) In the 1920s Langenhoven produced plays with popular Afrikaner nationalist themes.

10. Gray, Introduction to Stephen Black's *Three Plays* (Johannesburg, 1984).

11. C. Gardner and M. Chapman (eds), *Voorslag 1–3*, Facsimile edition (Pietermaritzburg, 1985). See the Introduction for an account of the *Voorslag* venture. The sponsor Lewis Reynolds – the son of a Natal sugar-millionaire – had parliamentary ambitions and with alarm saw the magazine developing into a forum for 'radical views'. Refusing to accept greater editorial control Campbell promptly resigned after number 3. In the remaining numbers – *Voorslag* came to a halt with number 11 (May–June 1927) – it is difficult to see the point of the title.

12. Campbell, *Voorslag*, vol. 1, no. 1 (June 1926), pp. 59–62.

13. Black, *The Sjambok*, vol. 1, no. 21 (1929), p. 8.

14. Plomer, *Voorslag*, vol. 1, no. 1 (June 1926), pp. 54–6.

15. Black, on Millin, Smith and Schreiner, *The Sjambok*, vol. 1, no. 7 (1929).

16. Black, *The Sjambok*, vol. 1, no. 18 (1929).

17. See pp. 76 and p. 84 [n. 4].

18. Campbell, 'The Poetry of Francis Carey Slater' and 'Preface to *The Collected Works of Francis Carey Slater*', *Collected Works, Vol. 4* (Johannesburg, 1988).

19. Plomer, 'South African Writers and English Readers', *Proceedings of a Conference of Writers, Publishers, Editors and University Teachers of English* (Johannesburg, 1957), p. 55.

20. Furbank, 'The Man in the Misfit Mask' (3–9 March 1989).

21. Mphahlele, *The African Image* (London, 1960; rev. ed., 1974), pp. 135–6.

22. See D. Maughan Brown, 'Laurens van der Post', in M. Chapman *et al.* (eds), *Perspectives on South African English Literature* (Johannesburg, 1992).

23. The Smith manuscripts are housed at the University of Cape Town. Extracts from her journals in D. Driver (ed.), *Pauline Smith* (Johannesburg, 1983).

24. See the articles in the 'symposium' section of D. Driver (ed.), *Pauline Smith*. Also Driver's introduction and her article, 'Gods, Fathers and White South Africans: The World of Pauline Smith', in C. Clayton (ed.), *Women and Writing in South Africa: A Critical Anthology* (Johannesburg, 1989).

25. Bennett's *A.B. '. . . a minor marginal note'* (1933) is conveniently reprinted in E. Pereira (ed.), *The Unknown Pauline Smith* (Pietermaritzburg, 1993).

26. See Bosman's comments in 'An Indigenous South African Culture is Unfolding', 'The Dorps of South Africa', 'Aspects of South African Literature' and 'The South African Short Story Writer', in S. Gray (ed.), *Herman Charles Bosman* (Johannesburg, 1986). See also, I. Hofmeyr, 'Turning Region into Narrative: English Storytelling in the Waterberg', in P. Bonner, *et al.* (eds), *Holding their Ground* (Johannesburg, 1987).

27. For details see Blignaut's *My Friend Herman Charles Bosman* (Johannesburg, 1980). Blignaut's stories appear in *Dead End Road* (Johannesburg, 1980).

28. On the later stories see S. Gray, 'Herman Charles Bosman's Use of Short Fictional Forms', *English in Africa*, vol. 16, no. 1 (May 1989).

29. 'The Dorps of South Africa' [n. 26 above].

30. See J. M. Coetzee's influential articles 'Farm Novel and *Plaasroman*', 'The Farm Novels of C. M. van den Heever' and 'Simple Language, Simple People: Smith, Paton, Mikro', *White Writing* (New Haven, 1988).

31. 'Stilstand in Ons Prosa?' reprinted in *Vernuwing in die Prosa* (Cape Town, 1963). Van Wyk Louw refers to 'rustige, lokale realisme' (p.61).

32. See Van Wyk Louw, *Opstelle oor Ons Ouer Digters* (Cape Town, 1972); D. J. Opperman, *Digters van Dertig* (Cape Town, 1953) and R. Wiehahn, *Die Afrikaanse Poeziekritiek: 'n Historiese-Teoretiese Beskouing* (Cape Town, 1965).

33. For extended commentary, in English, on Van Wyk Louw, see J. Cope, *The Adversary Within* (Cape Town and London, 1982).

34. See L. W. B. Binge, *Ontwikkeling van die Afrikaanse Toneel, 1932–1950* (Pretoria, 1969) and J. van Wyk, 'Nationalist Ideology and Social Concerns in Afrikaans Drama in the Period 1930–1940', paper History Workshop, University of Witwatersrand (6–10 February 1990) and *Alterations*, vol. 2, no. 1 (1995).

35. The protagonist Ampie appears in *Die Natuurkind* (1924), *Die Meisiekind* (1928) and *Die Kind* (1942).

36. At the same time, in the 1930s, several Afrikaans women employed in the garment industry, especially the sisters Hester and Johanna Cornelius, were penning poems, plays and serials which further complicated the question of *volksunie*. Emanating from Afrikaners in trade unions that had Communist Party affiliations, 'garment-worker writing' reflects a double-voicedness beyond the control of its authors who had to try to amalgamate two apparently contradictory sets of codes: that of the Voortrekker woman as symbol of motherhood, home and family and that of the working woman in the new urban environment for whom there could be no return to an ancestral farm. Aloof on his aesthetic plain, Van Wyk Louw probably knew little, if anything, about the actual voices of poor whites. Like the nationalist writer M.E.R. (M. E. Rothmann), he contributed views in the 1930s to the Carnegie Commission on poverty; unlike M.E.R., he retained conceptions of the bourgeois and the proletarian that were cultural not social, and his volume of essays *Lojale Verset* (1939) echoes European ideas of a *religio poetae*. See E. Brink, 'Purposeful Plays, Prose and Poems: The Writings of the Garment Workers, 1929–1945', in C. Clayton (ed.), *Women and Writing in South Africa* (Johannesburg, 1989).

37. 'Eagle', in A. P. Grové and C. J. D. Harvey (eds), *Afrikaans Poems with English Translations* (Cape Town, 1962). See this anthology for a substantial section on Van Wyk Louw in translation, including the poem 'Die Hond van God' which is referred to in my argument.

38. There are useful distinctions to be made, nonetheless, among the several poets who in the 1930s saw it as their function to elevate Afrikaans into a literary language. Like his brother N. P. van Wyk Louw, W. E. G. Louw searched for the unique word while his striving for Christian redemption proceeds without his brother's tormented attachments to the Old Testament God. Elizabeth Eybers,

who since 1961 has lived in Holland, continues to produce finely wrought verses about her personal responses to love, sickness, parenthood, age and death. Having transformed an earlier generation's patriotic symbols including the Boer woman as mother of the volk and the war as a nation's suffering into internationally recognisable private experiences, Eybers shifted to depicting ironies of life in starker uses of the word. Possibly her protest was simply to have left South Africa; she does epitomise, however, a *vervynde* (refined) ideal that in this country we find in several white middle-class women poets, for whom culture means the holiday cruise to the art museums of the Mediterranean and nature means the family household. Uys Krige's contribution was to turn the troubadour's romanticism on many of the Calvinist guilts that wracked Van Wyk Louw. Born into a family which managed to combine its nationalist sympathies with creative broad-mindedness Krige, like Campbell, travelled to southern Europe, but whereas Campbell in Spain moved sharply to the right to embrace Franco's cause, Krige expressed his outrage at fascism in his angry protest poem inspired by the Spanish Civil War, 'Lied van die Fascistiese Bomwerpers' (Hymn of the Fascist Bombers). Despite its Spanish subject matter, the poem found itself being regarded as 'South African' in its anti-totalitarian effects. In seeming to strike at the pro-Nazi nationalist camp, the poem was unacceptable to all Afrikaans journals, and appeared in the liberal English-language magazine *The Forum*. Possibly Calvin's 'protestant' spirit was infusing Krige (the Catholic hierarchy in South Africa, at least, regarded the poem as sacrilegious); Krige's other writings, however, do not have the same overtly political intent, and one of the less obvious ways in which he saw himself opposing Afrikaner sectionalism was to make available, in Afrikaans translation, several Romance-language poets in the humanist tradition.

39. See A. Coetzee's revisionist commentary in 'Literature and Crisis: One Hundred Years of Afrikaans Literature and Afrikaner Nationalism', in M. Trump (ed.), *Rendering Things Visible* (Johannesburg, 1990).

40. For details of the reaction see N. J. Strydom, ''n Polemiek rondom D. J. Opperman se "Kersliedjie" ', *Tydskrif vir Letterkunde*, vol. 12, no. 4 (1974). English translation of the poem in Grové and Harvey [n. 37 above].

41. Kannemeyer, *Die Afrikaanse Literatuur, 1652–1987* (Pretoria, 1988), p. 218.

42. See Opperman's article from *Standpunte*, 'Roy Campbell en die Suid-Afrikaanse Poësie', reprinted in *Wiggelstok* (Cape Town, 1959).

Chapter 3

Belonging and Belief in South Africa, 1910–1948. Africa and Europe

Ubuntu. The case of Mqhayi

A point Plomer realised has been crucial to the purpose of writing by black South Africans: that any national literature would require a broader conception of human, social and cultural life than the South Africanism implicit in the white-minority guarantees of the Union constitution; that any South African nationalism would certainly have to be less ethnic and sectarian than Afrikaner nationalism. Under the effects of increasing disillusionment by black people with white racial politics, however, the term 'national' in black writing began to shed its earliest multiracial view, in which the inspiration had been Western, Christian and humanitarian, and became discernibly more Africanist. Accordingly, the Cape liberal ideal, as upheld by Sol T. Plaatje, was treated with considerable suspicion. In the writing of H. I. E. Dhlomo, the return to the 'source' began to draw on negritudinal concepts of African identity, pride and unity. We are talking here of difficult shifts of idea, accent and image, not of any simple turning from the West to Africa: categories which, in any case, are too broad to allow for other necessary distinctions. There were, for example, 'liberal' compulsions and 'radical' compulsions. By the 1940s Marxist insights had begun to complicate earlier preferences for moral, as opposed to economic, change. There were perceptions of being Sotho, Xhosa, or Zulu in contrast to a general African perception of being one of the oppressed majority. To add to what were complicated strands of discourse, there was the Negro American experience, one of the main purveyors being Dr J. E. K. Aggrey, the West African who, having spent twenty years studying and teaching in the United States, visited South Africa in 1921. Aggrey's message, which had been inspired by moderate Negro leaders like Booker T. Washington, was that black and white South Africans should seek racial peace and mutual co-operation. This boosted several white-black ventures such as Joint Council discussion groups that led in 1929 to the formation of the Institute of Race Relations, a fact-gathering body which opposed segregationist policies.

In the cultural sphere, several individuals and organisations of liberal persuasion, including the American Board mission, helped establish the Bantu Men's Social Centre in Johannesburg, where the black cultural elite in European and Negro derivative forms of dance, music and drama marked their class difference from popular marabi culture: the music of the slum yards and shebeens.[1]

It was in the Carnegie branch-library of the BMSC that the young Peter Abrahams would encounter a new world of Harlem renaissance voices and, more generally, it was the aspirations of a nascent 'new African' class that would characterise policy speeches by ANC leaders as well as the creative literature produced by prominent figures among the educated elite such as S. E. K. Mqhayi, Thomas Mofolo, Sol T. Plaatje, J. J. R. Jolobe, the Dhlomo brothers (H.I.E. and R.R.R.), B. W. Vilakazi and A. C. Jordan. Guiding principles can be deduced from the entries in *The African Yearly Register: Being an Illustrated National Biographical Diction-ary (Who's Who) of Black Folks in Africa*, compiled and edited in 1930 by T. D. Mweli-Skota, who at the time was general secretary of the ANC and the person identified today in the name of the black publishing house, Skotaville. The selections in the *Register* favoured the professions of the church, law, teaching and journalism; chiefs qualified for inclusion by being 'progressive' in that tribalism was firmly rejected; and figures from the past, such as Shaka and Moshoeshoe, were presented in supra-ethnic ways as heroic African nation-builders. Such markers of race and class unity had already appeared in the earliest Xhosa written expression where the influences of 'red' people – traditionalist, ancestral, communal, oral – were not so much discarded by 'school' people – urban, literate, modern – as re-examined and reworked into supportive myths: the idealis-ations of roots and continuities having a necessary function, of course, in the alienating circumstances of white domination. The philosophical and aesthetic motivations underlying a great deal of black literary activity in the years before the institutionalisation of apartheid were articulated by H. I. E. Dhlomo. In a series of critical articles in the late 1930s, Dhlomo spoke of grafting Western thoughts and modes on to an insistent 'living African tradition':

> Tradition lives! . . . Merely to go back to the past is not
> tradition. It is death. Past, present and future are not
> separate. They commingle. True tradition is rooted in the
> past, lives and speaks in the present, visualises and inhales
> the future. It is not tradition to neglect the contemporary
> scene.[2]

Here a sense of African cosmology, in which vital forces are felt to connect the experiences of the living to ancestral precept, assists in a modernising drive to confront socio-political problems of the day. The way in which tradition lives in the practice of the literary work may be seen in the representative case of S. E. K. Mqhayi.

Known as the father of modern Xhosa literature, Mqhayi inherited an ancestral legacy of obligation to chiefs as well as to two generations of Christian education. Spending his youth among traditionalist, red-blanketed people, he absorbed ancient stories and legends before training at Lovedale as a teacher. Later he would fall foul of the white authorities over the way in which Xhosa history was being taught as a story of subservience. A prolific writer of biographies, political allegories and essays, Mqhayi also wrote his autobiography and four volumes of poetry.[3] *Ityala Lamawele* (The Lawsuit of the Twins, 1914) is influenced by the Christian precept of Bunyan's *The Pilgrim's Progress* at the same time as it dramatises legal procedure among the Xhosa: the purpose is to remind us of the exemplary character of traditional justice while allegorical trans-fers hint at models of democratic behaviour for the present day. *UDon Jadu* (1929) also posits an ideal state in the land of the Xhosa: there is no racialism, no isolationism, there is social, economic and educational equality; the state is Christian but Christ is president of the ancestral spirits, and Great Britain is the political guardian. The allegory is meant to suggest Mqhayi's twin allegiances to the chief and the British king, and Xhosa tradition and Cape liberalism find easy community in a broad desire for humanism. Although he felt betrayed by Britain's failure to defend African rights at the time of Union, Mqhayi – like most of the other African politicians and writers of his generation – remained loyal to the ideals of Christianity and Western democracy. But after he had turned his back symbolically on the school to settle as a bard of his people on a lonely hill near King William's Town, Mqhayi began to see his primary task in reviving the oral panegyric as a contemporary form of both praise and criticism, the best recorded occasion being his sharp words to the Prince of Wales, during an official visit to South Africa in 1925, that Britain had not been true to its 'chiefly' responsibilities:

> Ah, Britain! Great Britain!
> You gave us Truth: denied us Truth;
> You gave us ubuntu [humanity]: denied us ubuntu;
> You gave us light: we live in darkness;
> Benighted at noon-day, we grope in the dark.[t][4]

As the lines were delivered in Xhosa, the Prince would not have under-stood anything beyond the ceremony: he thought, presumably, he was simply being honoured. Both red and school people in the audience, however, would have heard the expression of their collective disillusion-ment delivered in words that emphasised not an ethnic, but a national dimension. The past forms and sentiments provide the structuring devices according to which the present is judged: the method is not a modernistic 'shock of the new'; rather, the older rhythms set the pace and tone, and similar effects characterise the first wave of creative writing by black South Africans.

In writing by whites in the 1920s and thirties, the range – as we have seen – included the verbal art of the international modernist in poetry and, in prose, a marked accent of regionalism. The modernism sometimes parades as a flashy evasion of parochialism, at other times it reflects the limits of the reasonable speaking voice in frontier crisis. The regionalism sometimes resists history in hankerings after simpler worlds; at other times, colloquially, anecdotally, ironically, it subverts the pastoral from within its own local myopias. In black writing, we encounter not hetero-cosms of the imagination, but a consistent concern with ethical justice. As in Mqhayi's allegorical court scenes, many of the poems and novels use the dramatic forum of debate and discussion in order to explore issues of political principle, social responsibility, and cultural transition. Questions, argument, the rhetoric of public praise, judgment and socia-bility lend the flourish of human voices to crowded community life.[5] The private anxiety in inner monologue that we frequently encounter in writing by white South Africans may indicate the isolation of difficult belonging. African writers – as distinct from coloured writers – tend to take belonging for granted. They hardly need to inscribe themselves into a landscape, and descriptions of nature are relatively rare. Literariness is not really about the possibilities of richer European alternatives, and copious borrowings by the early black writers from Bunyan, Shakespeare and the Romantics, while obviously suggesting something about deriva-tive mission-school educations, are well suited to the epic scale of the themes: dynastic feuds, generational conflict, cataclysmic change, massive re-integrations. Belief is unambiguously centred on secular life, and it was Sol T. Plaatje's *Mhudi* (written in 1920, published in 1930) which thirty years before Chinua Achebe's *Things Fall Apart* (1958) saw the necessity of African literature in the colonial situation turning Western conventions to the service of African forms, perceptions and values. The savages of the white historiographical imagination had to be returned by the African writer to their ubuntu; the exotic tribal land had to be depicted sanely and recognisably in its comprehensive humanity.

The early African literary elite. Popular alternatives. Plaatje. Mofolo. Jordan. Shembe. The Lucky Stars

As one who earned his living by his pen, or at least by the persuasive power of language, Plaatje in his own way was a man of letters. Where he differed from Plomer, Opperman and others was in his close involvement in the main events of political life as well as in his view of writing, whether journalistic or imaginative, as functioning in direct relation to the political cause. His protest is not avant garde, but coherently purposeful. Mission-born and mission-educated, Plaatje joined the old Cape civil service and in becoming a court interpreter in Mafeking at the time of the Anglo-Boer War, he kept a diary of life under siege. Published in 1973 as *The Boer War Diary of Sol T. Plaatje*, the entries which began in youthful humour and literary slickness became increasingly desperate as the campaign wore on, and presented a 'black man's eye view' of what was supposed to be a white person's war: 14,000 Africans lost their lives in the fighting. The technique here of casting an unexpected perspective on the public event would go on to characterise most of Plaatje's writing. Journeying through the countryside soon after the passing of the Natives Land Act (1913), for example, he translated the journalistic fact in *Native Life in South Africa* (1916) into graphic, emotive pictures of the human anguish brought about by Africans being thrown off the land:

> The death of the child added a fresh perplexity to the
> stricken parents. They had no right or title to the
> farmlands through which they trekked: they must keep to
> the public roads – the only places in the country open
> to the outcasts if they are possessed of travelling permit.
> The deceased child had to be buried, but where, when,
> and how?

An admirer of Harriette Colenso and Olive Schreiner, Plaatje embraced Cape liberalism not merely in principle but with a keen sense of material reality, and *Native Life*, which ends as a plea to the British government to stand by its responsibility to Africans in South Africa, burns with the same anger at injustice as does *Trooper Peter Halket of Mashonaland*. When it first appeared, Plaatje's book was attacked in the white South African parliament, but led to no repeal of discriminatory legislation. The writing, however, has retained its moral power to warn of the consequences for South Africa should policies such as those embodied in the Land Act be pursued to their logical conclusion. When it was republished in 1982, *Native Life* could be seen as offering prediction and prophecy. Yet Plaatje, who in 1912 had been general-correspondence secretary of the South African Native National Congress and who had travelled to London to seek imperial veto of the Land Act, was regarded in younger African political circles by the 1920s as already somewhat detached from radical black politics and the challenges of modern urban struggles.

Certainly his novel *Mhudi*, which is described by the author as an 'epic of South African native life a hundred years ago', finds types of the past more conducive to literary creation than the sights of the present. With its rhythms, patterns and motifs effortlessly synthesising Shakespearean romance and seTswana folklore (Plaatje, a Tswana, translated Shakespeare and collected traditional tales), the story focuses on the love of Ra-Thaga and Mhudi who, after Mzlikazi's Matabele (Ndebele) attack on the Barolong community, find themselves scattered on the veld: refugees in the 1830s when African bands having fled from Shaka set up the movements, conflicts, and new alliances of the *mfecane*. In the romance mode, the journey of the two lovers proceeds from the idealised village-world of the Barolong, which is disturbed when villagers slay Mzlikazi's tax collectors, to the devastated plains and, with love triumphant, back to the new home of the Barolong community. Throughout the story, however, the romantic ideal is gently parodied as Plaatje grants Mhudi (the woman) the 'feminine principle' of good sense, humour and courage while Ra-Thaga, somewhat lax, somewhat pompous, has to learn to temper the 'male' rush to action with sensitivity and feeling. Around the romance swirls history which, as in the oral tradition, is recounted by an intermittently mentioned storyteller in the epic mode of pageantry, pomp and prediction: we follow the rise and fall of Mzlikazi who is portrayed, simultaneously, as the legendary military leader, full of sound and fury, and the vulnerable human being who is moved to tenderness in his love for his queen Umnandi. Against the vast scale of African epic, the Great Trek – Afrikaner history's central event – is diminished in importance, and in the court scene the Barolong speak the language of forgiveness and compassion in contrast to the Boers' desire for punishment. The African revisionist tendency is not allowed to go unchecked, however, and *Mhudi* absorbs the harsh knowledge that wars are won not according to planetary influence or the intervention of fate, but by superior fire power. As the Barolong enter into a treaty with the Boers to defeat Mzlikazi, prophecy and political actuality meet: one day the Barolong will regret their pact; the Boers will become their oppressors. Plaatje was too reasonable to understand the full obduracy of segregationist thinking, and it was almost inevitable that he should have ended up feeling marginalised from political life. Yet, as Tim Couzens has reminded us, *Mhudi* in its analogy of possession and dispossession resonates with the troubles of Plaatje's own day particularly in the consequences of the Land Act.[6]

There is another way, however, in which *Mhudi* provokes interest. I said in discussing Blackburn's *Leaven* that the Jim-comes-to-Joburg story would become the South African story. Similarly *Mhudi* in its concern with the occupation of the land has a national dimension while, in addition, it has a quality that is absent from *Leaven*: a celebratory play of language in which Plaatje, who was a skilled linguist, sports around with the archaisms of English:

> At last his eyes fell on the damsel who in her turn cast furtive glances at her unknown hero. 'My man, my man,' she seemed to say, 'my stranger man whom the spirits have sent to save me from loneliness, starvation, and the lion's jaw, I would willingly pass through another Matabele raid and suffer hair-breadth escapes if but to meet one like you.' And to herself she said, 'I wonder what his name is?'

Instead of subscribing to narrow measures of formal realism – as some critics have done – and condemning *Mhudi* for its 'mission-education' derivativeness as well as for its recurrence in plot, we could decide to enter into the spirit of the ancient oral world in which the action is set. This would have us grant respect not only for Plaatje's choice of diction, but for his corresponding humanism. Redeeming energies – *Mhudi* suggests – are not to be found in political solutions alone, but in rehabilitated communities where tradition lives.

African writers may not have felt the need to question whether they belonged to Africa; they have had to construct and reconstruct identities, nevertheless, amid the exigencies of large-scale social and cultural change. The relative advantages enjoyed by the early African elite – fluency in two languages (English and the vernacular), literary and religious education in two traditions, substantial involvement in African public life – also ensured that burdens and, indeed, restrictions operated on the range of their interests and sympathies. Even as segregationist legislation pushed them towards sharing disadvantages with the African masses, their educated status held them somewhat apart from the proletarian lot of urban migrations and shantytown living. The pressures of city life, as a result, are more accurately captured in popular modes of oral expression than in the written literature of Plaatje's generation. The other-worldliness that we find in the literate Christian poetry of J. J. R. Jolobe, for example, is not at all apparent in a separatist-church figure like Isaiah Shembe whose syncretic Christian-African songs and hymns of the 1920s, in Zulu, invited vocal response from the audience and refused to separate transports of the spirit from communal need in the insecure urban environment. A focus on city life also lent resilience to Reuben Caluza's songs in Zulu and English which combined ragtime with lyrics about enforced migration and the colour bar. The 1920s also saw, in popular mode, the beginnings of 'township' style plays at community venues: Esau Mthethwe's group the Mthethwe Lucky Stars, for example, performed song-and-dance sketches about slum-yard living, and struck a very different note to the literary entertainments, including the 'well-made' play, that defined the scope of the Bantu Men's Social Centre.[7]

As far as the literary elite was concerned, the challenge was how to convey the realities of acculturation in forms of the emblematic and the allegorical: what we might call the 'sermon art' as understood by the mission presses, notably Morija in Lesotho and Lovedale in the town of Alice.[8] Other outlets included newspapers aimed at African readers, such as *Ilange laseNatali* (The Natal Sun), founded in 1903 by John L. Dube, and the moderately liberal *Bantu World*, which appeared in 1932.[9] By the thirties, however, most black periodicals had fallen under white business interests, and the 'ambiguities of dependence' among the elite have been documented by social historians.[10] It is said, for example, that the 'messages' of elite stories are swayed often too predictably on the one side by Western-Christian preference, on the other by the conservative adherences to custom which characterised anthropological study and which were found convenient by the social engineers of apartheid in designating Africans as tribal creatures. As we have seen in the cases of Mqhayi and Plaatje, however, determinisms were not always utterly embracing, and under C. M. Doke's influence the University of the Witwatersrand Press and the Bantu (later African) Treasury Series did valuable work in the 1940s and fifties not only in promoting African-language literature in schools, but in publishing the commanding Zulu poet B. W. Vilakazi whose texts reveal the struggles of divided loyalties – traditional and modern – rather than acquiescence to any controlling European hand. Similarly Lovedale Press, under the energetic chaplain R. N. W. Shepherd who in 1932 was appointed director of publications, played a key role in encouraging creative endeavour by African authors in both English and Xhosa. In fact, most of the writers in these years produced work in both European and African languages as they sought unifying concepts of African concern beyond linguistic divisions: divisions that – it was feared – could entrench attitudes of ethnic affiliation. After trying for ten years to find a British publisher for *Mhudi*, Plaatje turned to Lovedale Press, and Shepherd published the book despite his disagreeing with several of the author's criticisms of Western and Christian standards. In enumerating changes between Plaatje's original manuscript and the Lovedale edition, Tim Couzens and Stephen Gray suggest that the missionary press exercised pernicious control over its authors. Their argument, however, is best seen as part of their own Africanist recovery programme in the 1970s: they offer no evidence that Plaatje was forced to alter his manuscript, and it seems doubtful that Shepherd was a more restrictive gatekeeper, or any freer of his own prejudices, than most other publishers. Instead of dwelling on the ambiguities of dependence as though conspiracies were involved, therefore, it is more productive to continue to identify what is independent and illuminating about the writers' utilisation of their African and Western commitments.[11]

A. C. Jordan's *The Wrath of the Ancestors*[t] (1980; 1940), for example, repays the kind of analysis that is also applicable to *Mhudi*. This involves the critic in having to adjust within the epic action to apparently contradictory claims of historical testimony and oral-romance. Although something of his densely-layered Xhosa style − proverbial, wide in vocabulary, expansive in its discussion scenes − is lost in translation, we can appreciate Jordan's complications of the old 'red'/'school' polarities in a grand-scale story about the inevitability of change: the theme of the questing Xhosa intellect since the mid-nineteenth century and of which *The Wrath of the Ancestors* is the culminating literary example. A more difficult but no less important matter of recovery concerns Thomas Mofolo's 'Shakespearean' *Chaka*[t], written in seSotho around 1909 and published only in 1925 when the Morija Press allowed itself to be convinced that the work was Christian in intent. (The first English translation appeared in 1931.) Having shown a mind that from the outset moved swiftly beyond simple Christian/African dichotomies, Mofolo in his Bunyanesque allegory *Moeti oa Bochabela* (The Traveller to the East, 1907) had discovered similarities, rather than differences, between modern-Western and traditional-African religious precepts, and in *Pitseng* (1910) − the title is a place name − he was critical of the discrepancy between ideal and actual Christian behaviour. *Chaka* has three interwoven strands. Mofolo, the Sotho, condemns the Zulu warrior-king whom historical memory in Lesotho blames for the country's troubles in the 1830s. Mofolo, the African, wants to retain some support for African solidarities against colonialism, and his story of Chaka, in apparent contradiction to much of its own bloody action, ends up endorsing a kind of nostalgic Zulu pride. Mofolo, the Christian, condemns what he interprets as the Zulu king's non-Christian barbarity while he rescues Chaka from colonial charges of mindless butchery by imbuing him with psychological motivations for his behaviour. Here, the play *Macbeth* probably encouraged Mofolo to study Chaka through forces that operate as projections of the Zulu king's own mental processes: the figure of the wizard appeals to the tragic flaw that, it is suggested, already resided deep in Chaka's personality. The narrative sweeps us into the past while the author, like an oral teller, intermittently punctuates the illusion in order to pass comment on the events. It is difficult to decide how to deal with this novel − or epic, or romance − that for dramatic and ideological purposes makes highly selective use of material on a controversial subject. Possibly we should treat Mofolo's *Chaka* as a huge debate, staged in splendid costumery, about the still controversial issues of ethnicity, African identity, and the Western influence.[12]

The 'new African' and the old story: H. I. E. Dhlomo. Vilakazi. Noni Jabavu

By the mid-1940s a younger generation of African political leaders had begun to signal impatience with the old guard of the ANC, which was regarded as ineffectual in its politics of principle and petition against the harsh realities of unjust laws. Founded in 1943, the ANC Youth League – its members being mostly young Africans in the professions of teaching, medicine and law – produced the Congress Youth League Manifesto (1944) which stressed the need for Africans to act on their own. Despite its criticism of co-operation with other race groups, the Youth League – which included Nelson Mandela among its leadership – generally continued to espouse the liberal, non-racial ideals traditional to the ANC, but pressed for militant tactics to achieve these aims. The representative literary figure was H. I. E. Dhlomo whose articulation of tradition as a living force in the modern situation has lent cohesion to my discussion of literature by Africans in the early years of the century. Mission-educated, Dhlomo found many of his literary outlets in journalism and, prior to his playing a role in the formation of the Youth League, had contributed to multiracial co-operative activities such as the Bantu Dramatic Society at the Bantu Men's Social Centre, where his first play was staged sometime before 1935. *The Girl Who Killed to Save: Nonquase the Liberator*, published in 1936 by Lovedale, depicted the national suicide of the Xhosa as naïvely beneficial in that it enabled the 'red' people to break out of tribal conservatism. By the time of Hertzog's segregation bills in 1936, however, Dhlomo had begun to shift from a Christian-liberal view to what we might call a liberal-democratic nationalism, and his literary dramas on the kings Dingana, Cetshwayo and Moshoeshoe are massive, rambling structures that employ Elizabethan-type poetic hyberbole and veer from stage-effective actions to lengthy static monologues. (*Moshoeshoe* was evidently staged in 1938; there is scant evidence, however, about performances of any of Dhlomo's plays.) What is propounded in the plays on the royal leaders is the rediscovery of heroic continuities in tradition; at the same time, analogies are sought with the past in order to explain current dilemmas. In *Cetshwayo*, for example, early Natal native policy, which was segregationist in intent, is debated with obvious reference to the currency of the Hertzog bills, and in *Moshoeshoe* Dhlomo, a Zulu, acknowledges the Sotho king as a leader who had the genius to transcend ethnic rivalries and promote the ideal of African unity. In the long poem *Valley of a Thousand Hills* (1941) the spirit of the 'tribal past' inspires the present generation to find roots, draw strength, and resist the discriminatory practices of the day. Romanticism, in the English-literary sense, is explored in its twin impulses: the return to the organic community as the strengthening ideal and the thirst for justice among the oppressed.

> 'You ask me whence these yearning words and wild;
> You laugh and chide and think you know me well;
> I am your patient slave, your harmless child,
> You say . . . so tyrants dreamt as e'en they fell!
> My country's not my own so I will fight!
> My mind is made: I will yet strike for Right.'

If the style of his poetry and plays in its relentless elevation remains more archaic than contemporary, this was not Dhlomo's intent, and in his several critical essays he talked of the need to engage with the down-to-earth details of the modern urbanised African's existence: the train, the police, the automobile, the cinema, trade unionism, housing and so on.[13] His plays *The Pass (Arrested and Discharged)* and *The Workers* do in fact capture a colloquial intonation in tackling the day-to-day matter of pass laws and exploitation in the work place, and his commentaries are incisive in regarding art as having a social as well as an aesthetic responsibility: the artist has an obligation to the mass of people. Although he never really identified the difficulty of making an art of ceremony serve the pulse of proletarian living, his commitment to sharp rediscoveries of African purpose and pride would find consonance with Black Consciousness programmes in South Africa in the 1970s.[14] When he attacked the aloof, academic poet B. W. Vilakazi for imitating European models – Vilakazi had contemplated fitting the rhythms of the Zulu language to the discipline of Western metres and rhymes – Dhlomo was concerned not only with literature but with an attitude to life.[15] As he himself turned in despair to alcohol, he realised that the African, however educated in the European convention, would never be accepted with due respect by most white South Africans, whether segregationists or liberals.

This was also Vilakazi's experience as an isolated African academic at a predominantly white Eurocentric university (Witwatersrand). Despite his angry reaction to Dhlomo's criticism, the key point that the African writer should seek a form suited to the expressive character of the vernacular language remains a valuable guide to some of the most impressive of Vilakazi's own poems. In his second volume, *Amal' eZulu* (Zulu Horizons, 1945), Vilakazi virtually ignored his own earlier attempts to

Europeanise the form. In 'Ezinkomponi' (In the Gold Mines) the swell of ancient praises serves the ironic purpose of condemning the roaring machines that have reduced human beings to units of sweat and toil in industrial alienation: 'How loud your roar, machines of the mine!/My hands are torn'[t]. A strain of melancholy in Vilakazi, however, ultimately blunts his engagement with the urban scene; instead, there is an other-worldly retreat. The sustained view of the city, whether by blacks or whites, would only begin to characterise writing after the Second World War when the expansion of manufacturing industry under conditions of war-time demand led to a second wave of industrialisation.

With Vilakazi, poetry in Zulu reached an intellectual peak while the robustness of the language was apparent in some of the popular modes I mentioned earlier on, such as Shembe's hymns and Caluza's songs. (Colonial conquest had been relatively late in Zululand, and as a result the songs and dances of city assertion and survival in the 1920s and 1930s retained traces of a living historical memory that invoked myths of Shakan identity and pride.) As far as literature in seSotho is concerned, the heyday is still associated with the first energies of the Paris Evangelical Missionary Society which by the 1860s had established an education system and, at Morija, a press that published a journal *Leselinyana la Lesotho* (The Little Light of Lesotho) as well as the work of Azariele M. Sekese, Everitt L. Segoete and Thomas Mofolo.[16] A notable later example of seSotho expression was that of A. S. Mopeli-Paulus, which was published under the title *Blanket Boy* (1953). Recorded, re-ordered, and put into English by Peter Lanham, this is another version of the African caught between the worlds of custom and the white man's city. In Xhosa, A. C. Jordan's *The Wrath of the Ancestors*[t] – as I mentioned – has retained its insight and complexity. Jordan, who in 1961 left South Africa without government permission to return, had also contributed articles on Xhosa literature and would later turn to re-creating, in English, selections of Xhosa folk-tales. Something of the Xhosa intellectual tradition was continued, in English, by Noni Jabavu. In her accounts of her return journeys to her family home in *Drawn in Colour* (1960) and *The Ochre People* (1963) Jabavu, who had lived in England since the age of thirteen, attempts to construct for herself an idealised 'African woman's personality' which virtually excludes the marks of her own Western upbringing and seeks stabilities in the slow rhythms and formalities of the Jabavu family living in seclusion and rural retreat near the university of Fort Hare. (Noni's father, Professor D. D. T. Jabavu, was an influential academic.) It is difficult to know how to respond to these nostalgic evocations of Xhosa traditional ways. Feminist criticism has seen an effacement of the woman's self as doubly oppressive in that Jabavu – though she was married to a white man – reverts without comment to a traditional African woman's role-model in the ancient patriarchal order.[17] Even if we interpret her observations less as those of her own registering consciousness, more as a selective re-creation out of memory and familial respect, we encounter a problem of 'exiled speech': language and perceptions 'manufactured' from the distance of another condition in another place. By the time Jabavu was published – in English, by a British publisher, in the general climate of decolonisation – the African voice in the fluency of writers like Plaatje, Jordan and Vilakazi had begun to be stifled by the controls of the apartheid mentality.[18]

With African authors' conferences having been convened in 1936 and 1937, a Literature Committee having been established (prominent members included Shepherd, D. D. T. Jabavu, Dube and Doke), with Lovedale Press and the University of the Witwatersrand Press active in the field, developments in South Africa in the 1940s must have looked promising for literary expression in the African languages. But it was the views of the educationist C. T. Loram – 'practical' instruction for the black people – that gained acceptance among many involved in African education. Accordingly, curricula focused on the Africans' supposed vernacular, rural background and, implicitly at first, on their subordinate position in the South African economy. This would provide the scaffolding for the introduction in 1953 of Bantu Education which put into practice the aims of the then minister of Native Affairs, Dr H. F. Verwoerd, who expressed his views to the Senate that 'there is no place for him [the Bantu] in the European community above the level of certain forms of labour'. Bantu Education eroded the mission schools, spread 'vernacular' and 'ethnic' education widely but thinly and, in its philosophy, reinforced the design of apartheid according to which the different African ethnic groups were regarded as having different, 'primitive' cultures that had little to do with the English language above levels of functional literacy and less to do with change in the scientific and technological world. One effect was that the monopoly the liberally-inclined Lovedale Press had enjoyed on the African educational market was broken and, as a result of state patronage, publishing in the vernacular for schools moved largely to Afrikaans publishing houses.

Occasionally a piece of creative writing had more to it than met the watchful eyes of government-controlled language boards. In 1956 T. N. Maumela's *Mafangambiti* appeared in the language tshiVenda. Ostensibly the story of a fighting bull set in the cattle-herding world of a Venda village, the book seemed to support the Bantu Education view of the African ethnic and rural reality. Republished for African secondary schools shortly before the 1976 Soweto protests against Bantu Education, the story of Mafangambiti the bull began to be seen against a militant context that is reflected in the introduction to the English version published under the original title *Mafangambiti*[(t)] by the black-run Skotaville, in 1985, in the middle of the state of emergency: the story is described as heroic, epic; the bull a symbol of Africa's will to survive, to *come back* (*Mayibuye iAfrika*, Africa come back, being the inspirational call of the ANC). Little African-language writing produced for schools under the strictures of Bantu Education, however, has had such re-evaluative potential. There are notable exceptions in the work of among others C. L. S. Nyembezi, Jordan K. Ngubane and D. B. Z. Ntuli,[19] but generally the large themes of acculturation and transition have been trivialised into trite endorsements of the exotic tribal land. As in the case of Zimbabwe, Zambia and Malawi, a challenge facing South Africa in the future is the resuscitation of African-language literature as an intelligent, adult activity: a challenge that has been accepted by writers like P. T. Mtuze − professor of African languages at Rhodes University − and Tsalali Bernard Ntokoane, both winners of Bertrams V.O. awards for African Literature, a business-sponsored competition in conjunction with Skotaville Publishers that in 1992 attracted 1,800 entries compared with the initial 600 in 1989.[20]

The founding African literary figures, some of whom I have discussed here, left an impressive body of work in both English and the indigenous languages. In their poetry, novels and more explicitly in their criticism we encounter, in embryo, debates that in the era of decolonisation in the 1950s and 1960s would begin to chart the field 'African literature' in its relations to Western tradition. The writers usually associated with this development are Senghor, Achebe, Soyinka, Ngugi and others from West and East Africa. A more comprehensive understanding would require that we add several names from South Africa.

Notes

1. See T. Couzens, 'The Continuity of Black Literature in South Africa before 1950', *English in Africa*, vol. 1, no. 2 (September 1974) and *The New African: A Study of the Life and Works of H. I. E. Dhlomo* (Johannesburg, 1985); R. F. A. Hoernlé, 'The Bantu Dramatic Society at Johannesburg', *Africa*, vol. 7 (1934); A. Irele, 'The Negritude Debate', in A. S. Gérard (ed.), *European-Language Writing in Sub-Saharan Africa, Vol. 1* (Budapest, 1986); I. Karis and G. M. Carter (eds), *From Protest to Challenge: A Documentary History of African Politics in South Africa, 1882–1964*, 4 vols (Stanford, 1971–1977); E. Roux, *Time Longer than Rope: A History of the Black Man's Struggle for Freedom in South Africa* (Madison, 1948; 1978); E. Smith, *Aggrey in Africa: A Study in Black and White* (London, 1929); P. Walshe, *The Rise of African Nationalism in South Africa* (Berkeley, 1970; Johannesburg, 1987); F. Wilson and D. Perrot (eds), *Outlook on a Century: South Africa, 1870–1970* (Alice, Johannesburg, 1973).

2. See several articles on dramatic expression conveniently reprinted in *English in Africa*, vol. 4, no. 2 (September 1977).

3. Large output in Xhosa includes *U-Samson* (Lovedale, 1907), *Ityala Lamawele* (Lovedale, 1914), *Uso-Gqumahashe* (Lovedale, 1921), *I-bandla la Bantu* (Lovedale, 1923), *U-bomi Bom-fandisi u-John Knox* (Lovedale, 1925), *Isikumbuzo zom Polofiti u-Ntsika* (Johannesburg, 1926), *Imihobe nemibongo Yokufundwa ezikolweni* (London, 1927), *Idini* (Johannesburg, 1928), *UDon Jadu* (Lovedale, 1929), *U-Aggrey um-Afrika* (London, 1935).

4. M. Chapman and A. Dangor (eds), *Voices from Within: Black Poetry from Southern Africa* (Johannesburg, 1982), p. 34. For Xhosa poems in English translation, see R. Kavanagh and Z. S. Qangule (eds), *The Making of a Servant and Other Poems* (Johannesburg, 1972).

5. Examples include W. W. Gqoba's 'debate' poems which featured in early written Xhosa expression and among early Sotho literature, Azariele M. Sekese's animal tales which in the 1880s appeared in *Leselinyana la Lesotho* and in book form as *Pitso ya Dinonyana* (Gallery of the Birds, 1928), Everitt Lechesa Segoete's allegorical novel *Monono ke Mohodi, ke Mouwane* (Riches are Like Mist, 1910) and Thomas Mofolo's various works. There is Sol T. Plaatje's historical-romance in English *Mhudi* (1930), A. C. Jordan's story of cultural transition *Ingqumbo Yeminyanya* (1940), translated into English in 1980 as *The Wrath of the Ancestors*, and Stanlake Samkange's *On Trial for my Country* (1966).

6. Couzens, Introduction, *Mhudi* (London, 1978) and 'Sol T. Plaatje and the First South African Epic', *English in Africa*, vol. 14, no. 1 (May 1987). With the 1978 edition of *Mhudi* based on Plaatje's manuscript prior to certain cuts in the originally published Lovedale edition (1930), Couzens and Gray – the recoverers of the manuscript – make a somewhat grand case about the heavy hand of missionary editorial practice when confronted by 'African orality'. See Couzens and Gray, 'Printers and Other Devils: The Texts of Sol T. Plaatje's *Mhudi*', *Research in African Literatures*, vol. 9, no. 2 (Fall 1978). In response see A. E. Voss' introduction to *Mhudi* (Johannesburg, 1989), an edition based on the 1930 Lovedale text.

7. Caluza taught music at John L. Dube's Ohlange Institute (1901), the first African educational institution in South Africa, and became nationally famous. He went on to study music in the United States before returning to a teachers' training college in KwaZulu-Natal. With the Ohlange choir he recorded his 'syncretic' music in London in 1930 and *Caluza's Double Quartet* was remastered on compact disc in 1993 (Heritage Records, West Sussex). Caluza earned only $30 for his music. For an account of the dance and music culture of the time, see D. Coplan, *In Township Tonight: South Africa's Black City Music and Theatre* (Johannesburg, 1985). A vivid account of slum-yard living, Modikwe Dikobe's *The Marabi Dance* (London, 1973) appeared initially as single sketches in Ruth First's journal *Fighting Talk* in the 1950s. Edited into book form by Lionel Abrahams and Guy Butler ('The Saga of the *Marabi Dance*', *Sesame*, no. 11, Summer 88/89), Modikwe's stories with a main thread attracted the attention in the 1970s of critics seeking 'working-class expression'. See K. Sole and E. Koch, '*The Marabi Dance*: A Working Class Novel?', in M. Trump (ed.), *Rendering Things Visible* (Johannesburg, 1990).

8. See E. Jacottet, *The Morija Printing Office and Book Depot: An Historical Survey* (Morija, 1912); J. Peires, 'Lovedale Press: Literature for the Bantu Revisited', *English in Africa*, vol. 7, no. 1 (March 1980); R. H. W. Shepherd, *Lovedale, South Africa: The Story of a Century, 1841–1941* (Alice, 1942), *Lovedale and Literature for the Bantu* (Alice, 1945), *Bantu Literature and Life* (Alice, 1955), 'The Evolution of an African Press: Lovedale's Outstanding Contribution to Bantu Literacy',

African World (November 1953), 'Recent Trends in South African Vernacular Literature, *African World* (March 1955); T. White, 'The Lovedale Press during the Directorship of R. H. W. Shepherd, 1930–1955', *English in Africa*, vol. 19, no. 2 (October 1992). An earlier view of Shepherd's contribution is to be found in an anonymous review of his book *Lovedale and Literature for the Bantu, Books for Africa*, vol. 15 (1945).

9. See T. Couzens, 'The Black Press and Black Literature in South Africa, 1900–1950', *English Studies in Africa*, vol. 19, no. 2 (September 1976) and P. Morris, 'The Early Black South African Newspaper and the Development of the Novel', *Journal of Commonwealth Literature*, no. 15 (August 1980).

10. See S. Marks, *The Ambiguities of Dependence: Class, Nationalism and the State in Twentieth Century Natal* (Baltimore, 1986), particularly the case study of John L. Dube.

11. For arguments about missionary 'gatekeeping' and the literary elite, see n. 6 and n. 8 above.

12. See the earlier discussion of Shaka, pp. 58–62. Other challenges of recovery involve John L. Dube's *Insila kaTshaka* (1933) which was translated into English as *Jeqe, the Bodyservant of King Tshaka* (Alice, 1951), a novella that in its confusions of attitude tells us more about its author's own contradictory position in black politics than about a created novelistic world (see n. 10, above). There are also numerous Jim-comes-to-Joburg novellas, most of which read like Sunday school tracts. Yet it is worth pausing at R. R. R. Dhlomo's English-language *An African Tragedy* (Alice, 1928) which confounds somewhat its own 'missionary' predispositions concerning the 'pilgrim' Robert Zulu who predictably falls into bad habits in Johannesburg. With Robert's father-in-law, a Christian, manipulating African custom, the moral difficulties set up tensions between the religious and social commentaries. See also Dhlomo's sketches of life on the gold mines which follow his editor, Stephen Black, in encouraging a low mimetic as opposed to Plaatje's 'Shakespearean' imitation as the appropriate city African style. (Several of Dhlomo's sketches first appeared in Black's *The Sjambok* in 1929.)

13. See particularly 'Drama and the African', *The New Outlook* (March 1939); reprinted in *English in Africa*, vol. 4, no. 2 (September 1977).

14. See M. Chapman's introduction, *Soweto Poetry* (Johannesburg, 1982).

15. In several of his articles on African drama Dhlomo responded to Vilakazi's 'The Conception and Development of Poetry in Zulu', *Bantu Studies*, no. 30 (1938). At the same time as Aimé Césaire and Léopold Senghor in Paris were building up Negritude which emphasises the centrality of rhythm to the essence of 'negro-hood', Dhlomo in 'African Drama and Poetry' spoke of rhythm as 'essentially African. . . . In fact, one may almost say that the greatest gift of Africa to the artistic world will be – and has been – rhythm', *South African Outlook*, vol. 69, no. 1 (April 1939). For Vilakazi's heated reply, see the issue for July 1939. Also Dhlomo's sympathetic review of Vilakazi's later volume *Amal' eZulu* (1945), *Ilanga laseNatali* (30 March 1946). See A. S. Gérard's account of the controversy and his assessment of Dhlomo and Vilakazi, *Four African Literatures* (Berkeley, 1971), pp. 230–256.

16. See Sekese's *Makhoa ea Basotho le Maele le Litsomo* (Sotho Customs, Proverbs and Tales, Morija, 1893) and Segoete's *Mefiboshethe Kapa Pheello ea Molemo ho Moetsalibe* (Mefiboshethe, or the Patience of God to the Sinner, Morija, 1910). Mofolo is

listed in the biographies. For information on Sotho, or to be exact Southern
Sotho literature, see G. H. Franz, 'The Literature of Lesotho', *Bantu Studies*,
no. 4 (1930), A. S. Gérard, *Four African Literatures*, and D. B. Ntuli and C. F.
Swanepoel, *Southern African Literature in African Languages* (Pretoria, 1993).

17. See D. Driver, 'M'a-Ngoana O Tsoare Thipa ka Bohalenga – The Child's
Mother Grabs the Sharp End of the Knife: Women as Mothers, Women as
Writers', in M. Trump (ed.), *Rendering Things Visible*, pp. 248–9. See the later
autobiography by another member of the Xhosa intellectual elite who has lived
abroad since 1961, Phyllis Mtantala's *A Life's Mosaic* (Cape Town, 1992).
(Mtantala was married to A. C. Jordan.)

18. See J. Jahn, 'The Tragedy of Southern Bantu Literature', *Black Orpheus*, no. 21
(1967).

19. Nyembezi's *Inkinsela yaseMgungundlovu* (The Auspicious Person from
Pietermaritzburg, 1961) plays skilfully on the theme of the city African (see
biographies). Ngubane's novel *Uvalo Lwezinhlonze* (His Frowns Struck Terror,
1957) is a satire on traditional marriage customs set in the early years of this
century and expresses bitterness at the destruction of Zulu culture. The novel
was banned in 1962 for several years while Ngubane, who had been assistant
editor on *Ilanga laseNatali*, sought political refuge in Swaziland. After going into
exile Ngubane, who has written on Zulu literature, taught at Howard
University in the United States and produced, in English, the bitterly anti-
apartheid, pro-Africanist *Ushaba* (Washington, 1974), which is described by its
author as an *umlando* (literally, history): the form of narrative that the Zulus
'developed over thousands of years . . . for developing the collective wisdom
or strength of the family, the clan or the nation'. See P. Nazareth, '*Ushaba* as an
African Political Novel', *English in Africa*, vol. 5, no. 2 (September 1978).
  Besides his critical writing on Zulu literature (*Limi*, June 1968) and Vilakazi,
Ntuli – professor of Zulu at the University of South Africa – has published
novels, short stories and radio plays including the collection of tales *Uthingo
Lwenkosazama* (The Rainbow, 1971) and the playscripts *Woza Nendlebe* (Lend
Me Your Ears, 1988).

20. Mtuze's novel *Ungakhe Uxelele Mntu* (Don't Tell Anybody, 1990) was the 1989
winner and in 1992 Ntokoane was awarded the prize for his seSotho novel
Borwana which is set in post-apartheid South Africa in the year 2030 and tells
of a young woman Dineo Moleke who overcomes the prejudices of a male-
dominated legal fraternity to earn the respect she deserves along with the
nickname Borwana, denoting respect for someone who succeeds against the odds.
The author is a former court interpreter and state prosecutor from the eastern
Cape.

Identity and the Apartheid State, 1948–1970

Retribalising the Bantu and the Freedom Charter

The Second World War in its ideological aspects had been a life and death struggle against the master-race doctrines of the Nazis. With the Atlantic Charter symbolising the West's commitment to non-racialism, liberty and democracy, South Africa turned firmly in 1948 to systematising segregation into the official policy of apartheid. In the war years, military demands on the manufacturing industry had led to erosions of strict segregation as African people moved to the urban areas, and in 1946 the Fagan Commission, appointed by the Smuts government, recognised the reality of industrialisation by recommending that the urban black population be regarded as a permanent part of South African cities. Malan's National Party, in contrast, declared its intentions of 'retribalising the Bantu' and with the Nazi emphasis of the race over the individual finding consonance with Afrikaner nationalist thinking, South Africa began the zealous pursuit of open discrimination against all those who were not white. International condemnation would follow. The first phase of consolidating the apartheid state resulted, in the 1950s, in one repressive measure after another designed to secure white domination. The Population Registration Act established a racial register, the Group Areas Act set out to enforce separate residential areas for the different races (broadly designated as Europeans, Africans, coloureds and Indians), and various acts legislated against mixed marriages, interracial sex, and social mixing in cinemas, restaurants, beaches, public transport, even on park benches.[1]

Fear of racial mixture and white determination to preserve racial purity were at this stage, therefore, of key psychological importance to the appeal of apartheid: an appeal that found support among most whites, whether they were Afrikaner nationalists or not. Some of the bizarre and humiliating practices of the policy, in consequence, found their way into the literature as leitmotifs after being reported with repeated variations in daily newspapers: policemen hiding in the boots of motor cars to trap 'mixed' couples in the sexual act; the scandal, which often culminated in suicide, of the staunch Afrikaner farmer or dominee caught in the maid's back room; racial classifications determined by whether a pencil remained lodged in the person's curly hair; black children removed from swings in 'Europeans Only' parks; the rough arrests of Africans who could not produce their pass books on demand.[2] As writers discovered, the facts of apartheid could confound even the most fertile imagination. When in the 1980s the satirist Pieter-Dirk Uys acknowledged the government as his tireless and demonic script writer, he was making a telling point. In 1952 the ANC in alliance with the South African Indian Congress mounted a Gandhi-inspired defiance campaign against unjust laws. The response of the state was increased repression, and the decade ended with the shooting by police of unarmed anti-pass law protesters at the township of Sharpeville, the imposition of a state of emergency, and the banning of anti-apartheid political organisations, including the ANC, the PAC and the Congress of Democrats (mainly white Marxists who, after the banning of the South African Communist Party in 1950, had no political home). After smashing underground activities by the ANC, PAC and SACP, the state imprisoned the leaders for life on charges of high treason. The experience of political imprisonment, including the life stories of martyrs, forms a sizeable component of literature in South Africa and continues to provoke debate about the very category 'literature' in relation to exemplary rhetoric such as the political testimony, the biography of the gaoled leader, or the thoughts of the prisoner killed during police interrogation. If the Act of Union was an ominous text of segregation, the Freedom Charter, which was adopted in 1955 by supporters of the defiance campaign, espoused a mixture of Western-liberal, African-humanist and vaguely socialist ideals in defining an alternative South Africa as non-racial and democratic.[3]

Literary people responded to the severe attack on human dignity and freedom in several, sometimes unexpected ways. Among English-speaking writers, some preserved Western-liberal principle in the abstract over and above detailing the nitty-gritties of living in South Africa, and there were renewed hankerings after European art worlds usually of the past. Others spoke in conscience on behalf of damaged black lives. With social pressures forcing the liberal-minded writer to examine big words such as liberty, love, justice, and truth, there was a nagging concern that the experiencing individual might be subsumed into a public domain, that the unique word might be sacrificed for the 'correct message'. A thread running through university conferences and little magazines of liberal persuasion, such as *The Purple Renoster* and *Contrast*, was the need for English in its literary and democratic heritage to nurture sensibilities in opposition to the bludgeoning apartheid pronouncement.[4] This seemed especially necessary when semantic madness had led to destitute reserves being called 'homelands' and the destruction of black communities, most spectacularly in Sophiatown and District Six, being hailed as grand successes in slum clearance. The political-literary journals *Africa South* (1956–1961) and *The New African* (1962–1970) – both would attract banning orders in South Africa – hovered between 'political' and 'artistic' agendas while radical journals like *Fighting Talk* – the mouthpiece of Congress politics until its banning under Ruth First's editorship in 1963 – took the materialist line that literature justified itself mainly in its instrumental function. Although she was producing primarily a political journal, First published pieces of creative writing and book reviews by figures such as Mphahlele, La Guma, Brutus, Paton, Fugard and Rive. Among a number of black writers, resistance to the state's retribalising policies manifested itself in a brash city idiom and style. At the same time, an autobiographical impulse in black expression suggested not so much the individuality of being as the assertion of identity in harsh, discriminatory times. The first years of apartheid hardly feature as a subject of concern in Afrikaans literature. The prose writer continued to ask who owned the farm, and when the question of colour was introduced, the advice was predictably conservative. In F. A. Venter's *Swart Pelgrim* (1952), translated into English in 1959 as *Dark Pilgrim*, for example, the African's journey to the city teaches him the conventional wisdom that he should really return to his tribe.[5] Afrikaans poets continued to journey into Europeanised metaphysical realms until, most notably, Peter Blum, Adam Small and Ingrid Jonker began to introduce to their verse localised subjects and accents.[6] The 1960s would give rise to a new generation of Afrikaans prose writers. Although their highly mannered modernism preferred the metaphysics of good and evil to the morality of race politics, their rebellion against authoritarian Calvinism may be located to some intent in the local situation.

Poetry and liberal sensibility. Butler. Miller. Clouts

The question of belonging and belief in the apartheid state arises with considerable awkwardness in poetry written in the post-war years by white liberal-minded South Africans. As Guy Butler summed up the position in the introduction to his influential *A Book of South African Verse* (1959): 'Most of our poets have tried to belong to Africa and, finding her savage, shallow and unco-operative, have been forced to give their allegiance, not to any other country, but to certain basic conceptions.' These turn out to be the standard European principles of the enlightenment which, according to Butler, are difficult to transplant to Africa particularly as Europeans in Africa have failed so often to live up to their own ideals of civilised behaviour. In formulating a moral-aesthetic about Apollonian reason and Dionysian energy, Butler – unlike several of his contemporaries who left the country – sought to strike root by imposing an English educational programme, which was fairly conservative in its liberal precepts, on to what is described as the semantic poverty and nakedness of Africa's rock. In his poem 'Myths', the African sense data threaten the poet's European inheritance which is gleaned mainly, it seems, from books:

> Reading
> Keats' *Lamia* and *Saint Agnes' Eve*
> Beneath a giant pear tree buzzing with bloom
> I glanced at the galvanised windmill turning
> Its iron sunflower under the white hot sky
> And wondered if a Grecian or Medieval dream
> Could ever strike root away from our wedges of green,
> Could ever belong down there
> Where the level sheen on new lucerne stops short.

A precarious 'African incarnation' occurs, nevertheless, when universalising parallels are perceived between the figures of Eurydice and Orpheus and two coloured wanderers on the veld: 'rivers of sorrow flowed from a battered, cheap guitar'. The authenticity of the response is to be identified, paradoxically, in Butler's very difficulties in connecting the simple openness of his own settler myth to his literary self-consciousness as a scholar-poet. Butler sees the British settlers as honest, industrious men who bequeathed to South Africa English institutions and respect for liberty; utimately, however, it is Oxford – his alma mater – rather than the Karoo as his childhood spirit of place that is made to stand in Butler's poetry as the measure of sweetness and light.

One of the few academics in the 1950s and sixties to recommend the inclusion of South African literature in university syllabuses, Butler did not argue with sustained conviction that local writing was necessarily any good, but that young South Africans – he usually meant whites – needed to find a sense of their own place. We are not talking separately, of course, of physical and moral landscapes. According to Butler, English should absorb some local names and some non-English words, but lexicologically it should remain standard. In his own writing and commentary, settler and missionary personages are given authoritative presence, and a sense of community as well as communion is found in small English-settler villages that are pictured as being remote from the hubbub of the racial scene. In 'Karoo Town, 1939'

> . . . the market price of wool
> Comes second only to the acts of God:
> Here climate integrates the landsman with his soil
> And life moves on to the dictates of the season.

A drive to recruit the townspeople for Europe's distant war, in this poem, momentarily disturbs the rhythms of the Karoo town. But, at a more fundamental level, the rhythms retain their ponderous solidity: the syntax obeys the grammar of logic, and the language – ordinary and empirical rather than unusual or imagistic – delivers English back, in assured terms, as a lesson in civility to the linguistic babel that is South Africa. Like the 1820 Foundation in Grahamstown, in whose educational activities he has been fully involved, Butler represents valuable cultural capital. Amid radical political challenge, he is frequently quoted in the English main-stream press as a confident reminder that the English heritage, supposedly about tolerance, may yet have to act as sane broker between competing Afrikaner and African nationalisms. But this is to ignore the economic principle – the settlers, after all, were very serious about commerce – and it is not surprising that materialist critics have reminded Butler that English-speaking South Africans have been thoroughly implicated in racial-capitalist structures of oppression. Or, as African critics might put it, Butler's 'English' – a kind of homogenising catch-phrase – cannot conceive of any real alternative to the imperial manner.[7] Seemingly oblivi-ous to this polemic, Butler continues to write volumes of autobiography: *Karoo Morning* (1977) has the charm of the re-created child world; *A Local Habitation* (1991) rings sonorously with Victorian piety and platitude. What we do not find in the life story are hard references to the legacy of settler-Xhosa frontier clashes. In seeking Africa, Butler has remained somewhat detached from the political actualities of the times, and in his poetry, especially, his notion of civilisation returns us, via the dream-city of Florence, to the assumptions of a classical Renaissance universalism.[8]

In all of this, Butler's work is fairly typical of a strand of 'educated' liberal writing that has never been sure where it belongs. While Butler himself on occasions is prepared to show the common touch particularly in his early war poems and, later, in several jolly colloquial ballads, the overriding impression in poetry by R. N. Currey, David Wright, Roy Macnab and others who left South Africa's rock for England's misty climes is that of intelligent, unobtrusive contemplation about living between two worlds.[9] By the 1960s this poetry of the correct English accent had begun to attach itself a little anachronistically to the old British Commonwealth which, with South Africa as a member, had shouldered the democratic task of defeating Hitler, but which was now slightly perplexed at the clamour of new (Third World) demands – dare one say it! – in non-standard English. With prime minister Verwoerd having scornfully dismissed the warning of British prime minister Harold Macmillan in 1960 that the country would have to adapt to a 'wind of change' blowing through Africa, South African whites in a referendum endorsed the long-cherished Afrikaner ideal of a republic and, after protests by African members, South Africa withdrew its application to retain membership of the increasingly multiracial, 'decolonised' Commonwealth. Among the poets to appear on the scene in the 1960s were Sydney Clouts, Ruth Miller and Douglas Livingstone. All in their own ways disrupted Butler's English.

For Livingstone, who will be discussed in Part Five, the task of the poet schooled in Western tradition was to acknowledge that he could also be a white African. Questions of belonging and belief in Livingstone's poetry would lead to severe oscillations of attitude and style. Without sacrificing 'correct' English, Ruth Miller introduces a confessional intensity to her explorations of personal relationships, loneliness and the horror of death. Interpreted autobiographically, her poetry can be regarded as a sustained response – the first in South African poetry – to what Tilly Olsen in 1972 would call the 'silences' imposed on the woman's voice by suburban mores. Miller, who died of cancer in 1969, experienced a frustrating marriage and, in her 'job description', almost typified the middle-class woman as underqualified – she worked as a typist and a teaching assistant – in comparison to society's expectation of the professionally qualified male. In turning to characteristics in her poetry that have subsequently been regarded as delineating a woman's aesthetic, we have a 'mass of testimony': Olsen's identification of what it is to be female. By involving ourselves not only in the words on the page but in the narrative of Miller's poems (Adrienne Rich's method of locating Emily Dickinson's mind), we may reconstruct the texts not as discrete objects, but as manifestations of a subjectivity with contradictions, suppressions and silent words in the spaces between the single poems: an approach that encourages us to give finer attention to the recognisably woman's preoccupations of private oppression, psychic alienation, interruptibility and awareness of chance, the last two arising, according to Jane Donovan, from domestic routine.[10] More positively, we may identify a hold on concrete reality, a reverence for the processes of nature and life, a need to speak, a need by Miller to articulate her own experience:

> Glacial Galatea knows
> Nothing unless she knows
> She was herself before Pygmalion's bold
> Stare broke truth from her in a truth as cold.

Though brittle breaks not.
Though eaten, wastes not.
Though thirsting, slakes not.
I was myself before you touched me. I.
('Galatea')

Such a 'feminisation', of course, may be more semantic than real, more
a matter of interpretation than innate style in poetry. Although we can
define her female identity experientially against the patriarchy in which
she lived, it is also possible to locate Miller's poetry specifically in South
African politics of the 1960s.

As a prominent contributor to *The Purple Renoster*, Miller can be seen in
her skilful word art as implicitly challenging the obduracy of Verwoerdian
apartheid. This was part of editor Lionel Abrahams' mission. As I suggested, keeping alive human quality and imagination in South Africa
became a liberal programme especially when censorship laws, promulgated
in 1963, directly threatened the writer in society. Usually the terms of
the protest were not spelt out in any detailed way: the blanket commitment was to 'artistic freedom' with the magazine *Contrast* declaring in its
first number in 1960 that it had no policy. Yet, in retrospect, editor Jack
Cope would say: 'I think the war and its dark political aftermath in this
part of Africa served as a powerful catalyst; the forces of reaction seem
to have activated a counter-current of energy that found its way into a
new generation of artistic expression. Not that this was necessarily committed or overtly political save in the sense that all, or nearly all, art is
relative to some overriding purpose or design.'[11] In a number of Miller's
poems, the images of strange mental worlds resonate beyond their own
immediate concern with male-female relations and thud challengingly
against the granite of the apartheid state. Images that could suggest
national oppression, nonetheless, continue to be conveyed through the
'literary' symbols of poetry. References to the burning of witches in
identifiably South African landscapes, for example, conjure up tyrannies
of contemporaneous impact. Similarly a poem like 'Voice. Silence. Echo'
alludes simultaneously to metaphysical authority and subjection and, with
Kafka-esque applicability, to the repressive climate of Verwoerdian (god-
like) control in the 1960s: 'God was listening. Was he? Can't you hear
the echo/Of his immense reply, echoing No?'

Having been given considerable encouragement by Butler and, later,
by the Grahamstown-based poetry magazine *New Coin*, Sydney Clouts
for his part ends up reminding us – ironically, against his own intention
– that the intricate imagination does not necessarily win significant spaces
in the politically repressive state. Resisting the (colonial?) temptation
anthropomorphically to possess Africa – the myth of Adamastor lurks
behind Clouts as well as behind Butler – Clouts in elliptical verbal play

finds a radical individualism that sought to be different from the moral burdens of his literary colleagues. He makes a virtue of not being able to penetrate the exterior objects of the subcontinent, the point being that Africa may therefore continue to protect its integrity from the intruding European eye: 'What I want, Zambesi's/abler darkness fools with' ('Intimate Lightning'). But such an aesthetic of the object has a philosophical parallel that is disturbing in a country which was systematically denying humanity to the (black) majority of its population: an anti-humanism of its own that, in Clouts's poetry, depopulates Africa – a few clicking Bushmen and caricatural Hotnots remain – and registers society and history only as 'commotion'. Clouts, who lived mostly in England, regarded himself as an apolitical poet. Whether he would have approved or not, his poetry is likely to have continuing interest in South Africa in contexts of ideological argument: in the crucial matter concerning the potential of the brilliant artefact to invoke ethical responsibility.

Novels against apartheid. Abrahams. Paton

Only a few publishing outlets were available in the 1950s and sixties in South Africa for books of poetry in English. The firms were fairly conservative, and regarded the school-book and coffee-table trade as more important than a list of serious literature. The situation was more favourable for Afrikaans literary publishing which, in addition to enjoying forms of state patronage, had no competition in the educational market from international publishers.[12] As far as outlets for fiction were concerned, a Dassie Book series under the auspices of the country-wide Central News Agency reprinted several works in English that had attracted favourable comment: Schreiner and Bosman appeared in the series. Contemporary political themes, however, have never been the mission of the CNA. In any case, the realities of costs in relation to a small reading public combined with the South African writer's concern to be read internationally ensured that, as I mentioned earlier, local fiction was normally filtered back to its country of origin via British and American publishers. In 1946 Peter Abrahams's *Mine Boy* was described by Faber and Faber (London) as one of the first books to draw attention to the lives of black South Africans in a white-controlled country (Abrahams had been living in Britain since 1939), and in 1948 Alan Paton's *Cry, the Beloved Country*, first published in the United States, was widely acclaimed in an English-speaking world alert to post-war ideals of justice and reconstruction. Both novels employ the story of 'Jim who comes to Joburg' and while Paton consistently regarded his primary task as pricking the conscience of fellow South Africans, Abrahams probably did not quite know to whom he was supposed to be talking.

Several confusions accompany Abrahams' ventures into fiction. Usually billed abroad not entirely accurately as an 'African writer', this coloured South African found himself as one of the earliest black writers in English to be given the licence to be any kind of radical rather than the one thing he wanted to be: a writer without colour. Having grown up in the poverty of city slums in Johannesburg, Abrahams left South Africa at the age of 20 and, in memory and through his reading, he re-created – in the dialogues and interactions of fictional types – his difficulties of personal and ideological affiliation. In his first stories of urban life in *Dark Testament* (1942), *Song of the City* (1945), and more fully in *Mine Boy* (1946), the characters are allowed rudimentary psychologies in the concrete settings of the shantytowns and the work place. There are scenes of demeaning, repetitive labour amid haphazard liberal and Marxist comments. (In the year that *Mine Boy* appeared, the African Mineworkers' Union had launched an impressively well-organised strike which the Smuts government broke at gun point.) There is a great deal of direct speech in *Mine Boy* as Abrahams tries to create a sense of people talking in the slum community, but the stock types – resilient shebeen queens, patient women, broken-spirited men – frequently descend into sentimentality, even mawkishness, while Xuma, the country African in Johannesburg, does not in the end really want sociological coherence even though the novel hints that this is what his growth is about. He wants something more simple, or perhaps more difficult: to be a man of respect. This is evidently what Abrahams himself wanted, but his portrayal of Xuma remains stagy. The subsequent novels would continue to dramatise what has remained a war of ideas in Abrahams: having grasped at the Communist Party he found it damaging to individual achievement; grasping at pan-Africanism he was unable to separate its conscientising function from its proximity to tribalism; finding liberalism too limiting to account for radical populism he then found radical populism too localised in its struggles to be sympathetic to the writer of the world community who wants to tell of freedom. Whereas Plaatje in *Mhudi* was concerned to depict the national scene through the African mind in consonance with its traditions, Abrahams in *Wild Conquest* (1951) – the novel relies heavily on *Mhudi* – shows little intimate understanding of any retrievable community. His Matabele speak like modern politicians, and the underlying purpose of the story, which is quite understandable in the first years of apartheid, is the transcendence of the individual (Abrahams?) above competing Boer (Afrikaner) and Matabele (Africanist) chauvinisms.

In *Tell Freedom* (1954) Abrahams performed his most daring autobiographical manoeuvre. His name was actually Lee de Ras (literally, 'of the Race'), he was Afrikaans-speaking, and when a teenager he had indulged in racist behaviour and petty crime. But this youthful personality is effaced in favour of the romance that presumably became a reality: the boy from the wrong side of the tracks who took the name Peter Abrahams, taught himself the 'black experience' not only in the streets of Vrededorp – the mixed-race slum area in Johannesburg – but by reading Negro authors at the BMSC and, in a breathless narrative of the man on the run, leaves South Africa far behind in his ambitions to be a successful author. Who is Peter Abrahams? In what did he believe? The key may be found in the social tragedy of racist South Africa, where to be coloured is to be reminded in humiliating ways that you are neither 'European' nor 'African'. On the population register, coloured people became the main victims of bureaucratic classification procedures with some appealing to be reclassified white and others suddenly being reclassified African. In pursuing such an 'autobiographical' approach, we begin to recognise that despite his depiction of fictional types, Abrahams addresses his own crisis of belonging and belief: a crisis that is even more intense than we generally find in white or African writing. The approach has a certain validity for other coloured writers like Richard Rive, Alex La Guma, James Matthews and Arthur Nortje. It is also worth noting in this respect that the human suffering involved in the subject of 'coloured identity' resulted in some of the more powerful plays in the first years of apartheid.[13] With the coloured identity put under the awful searchlight, something admirable does at least emerge. Behind the confusion in Peter Abrahams, there is one aspect of utter consistency: a determined anti-racism that is thrown back at the apartheid system. It is the same anti-racism that would become the governing feature in works like Rive's 'Buckingham Palace', District Six (1986) which sets out through reminiscence and memory to rehabilitate a sense of coloured community.

It is of course possible to read any fictional form as autobiography and end up ignoring methods of telling that, conventionally, are distinctive to the novel or short story. The problem of generic definition in literature from southern Africa, however, is not entirely a matter of form and artistry; rather my argument is that, where the larger issue of racial oppression is involved, the roles of artistic consciousness and social conscience have often resisted the literary critic's discrete classifications. Alan Paton's volume of autobiography Towards the Mountain (1980), for example, utilises events subjectively experienced and understood in its guiding metaphor of the pilgrim's way: the author leaves the closed world of white South Africa, and undertakes a journey of fear towards his conviction of service in a cause greater than any one individual life. Such a personal narrative also holds true for Paton's novels, short stories, and even his biographies. Hofmeyr (1964) is the drama of a private man, a liberal in Smuts' government, who must trim his personal ideals to the demands of public office; Apartheid and the Archbishop (1973) identifies

Geoffrey Clayton, archbishop of Cape Town, as a spiritual man forced by his Christian beliefs to act in the political sphere when the notorious 'church clause' (Native Laws Amendment Bill of 1957) outlawed racially mixed congregations. As criticisms of authoritarian and 'utopian' societies both of which Paton believed lose touch with human lives, as tributes to the courage of those who resisted the oppression, as lessons in humility, and as restitutions for the threatened words of dignity, compassion and love, Paton's large output of non-fictional writing underscores the intentions of his fiction.

Written before the coming to power of the nationalist government, *Cry, the Beloved Country* (1948) was motivated by the tenuous hope that, in the spirit of post-war liberty, South Africa might move towards a more open society. The novel has been attacked, in retrospect, for its paternalism, sentimentality and economic naïvety.[14] We are told that the Revd Stephen Kumalo, the country priest who travels to Johannesburg in search of his delinquent son, is given a simple, biblical language that inevitably typecasts him as a simple Zulu mind, and that the 'message' of a change of heart as the prerequisite of restoration ignores the necessity of a change in racial-capitalist structures. We are then usually reminded of the limitations of Paton's liberalism in that he cannot allow Stephen Kumalo's brother John to speak Marxist-economic sense without succumbing to caricaturing the man as a vainglorious and morally dubious African politician. The Liberal Party, founded in 1953 with Paton as a prominent member, would refuse to endorse the Freedom Charter because of socialist clauses about nationalising the mines: clauses regarded as anathema to the free principles of classical liberalism. These arguments, at least, have helped rejuvenate interest in Paton's novel. What also needs to be considered, however, is the appeal of the story to deep-seated desires and fears: the author's subscription to fundamental liberal beliefs is challenged by his own trepidation that too great a love for the beloved country can lead not to giving and sharing, but to the jealous, sectional preservation of possessions and narrow destinies: 'Cry, the beloved country, for the unborn child that is the inheritor of our fear.' With an ur-voice carrying the emotion, Paton's liberalism speaks of principles outside the specificities of history in an attempt to hold on to guiding truths; simultaneously, history involves the liberal in realisations that, as in *Cry, the Beloved Country*, there can be no dwelling in simple reverences beyond the human community. In the African reserves, nature is scarred by poverty, there is anachronism of thought, and the hard lesson is that roads will continue to lead to Johannesburg. Charity may be necessary to ameliorate suffering, but large-scale restoration requires more than comforting words, or even comforting gifts: what is necessary is practical service in the functionings of society. As the young agricultural demonstrator says to Kumalo, 'There is not even good farming without the truth.'[15]

In *Too Late the Phalarope* (1953), which was written after apartheid became official policy, the cast of mind enshrined in the Immorality Act is translated in the small Afrikaner town, Venterspan, into a terrible victory of vengeance over compassion. (In 1950 the Act had extended its prohibitions on interracial sex.) Paton employs as his narrator the kindly Tante Sophie, sister of the patriarchal Jakob van Vlaanderen and, in contrast to her measure of love and forgiveness, the story of Jakob van Vlaanderen and his son has the inevitable resonances of tragedy. In his illicit sexual act with the African woman – who in character remains little more than a plot device – the son Pieter is seen by his father to have sinned not ultimately against his marriage vows or even against the Christian God but, as his name is struck off the family Bible, against the 'iron' destiny of the Afrikaner race. While Pieter is given individual responsibility for his deeds, he is also depicted as a personality of sensitive and, in the unremittingly Calvinist context, flawed disposition, caught in the trauma of his upbringing under his father's stern laws of Afrikaner-race idolatry. Where Christian and humanitarian precepts are offended is in the father's desire to punish his son without restoring him to the family in community. But such restoration would require Jakob van Vlaanderen himself to revalue his Voortrekker inheritance. As the trembling Tante Sophie understands, her brother's will does not know how to bend, and Paton's Venterspan confirms the character of the South African dorp as described by Herman Charles Bosman: rigidity of sectarian doctrine embodied in the starless conceptions of predestination and original sin.[16]

What guarantees Paton his continuing appeal is not that, as some of his critics have claimed, he offers the bourgeois reader the comfort of change in the heart without change in the streets. There is little comfort and much desolation in the writing. Rather it is that, quite unashamedly, Paton is a compelling storyteller who conveys his social data through persuasively archetypal patternings. His characters are types that stand for attitudes in society at large; at the same time, he imbues types – in ways that Peter Abrahams does not – with sufficient individuality to lend them psychological credibility. In both *Beloved Country* and *Too Late the Phalarope* the crux of the stories involves very emotive, very fraught, father–son relationships. Journeys are framed in settings, both real and symbolic, in which the folkloric dichotomies of innocence and experience are vulnerable to modern political recognitions: 'Kumalo was too old for new and disturbing thoughts. A white man's dog, that is what they called him and his kind.' The two early novels, *Beloved Country* and *Phalarope*, emerged from central tensions of their day, in which the liberal conscience played a key oppositional role to apartheid. In the 1950s and 1960s Paton, as chairman of the Liberal Party, was often under surveillance by the secret police. In contrast, Paton's third novel *Ah, But Your Land is*

Beautiful (1981) does not engage with the radicalised political temper that characterised the late 1970s; instead, it wants to look back in temper as well as time and champion people and events of the liberal heyday in the 1950s. The story-telling impulse is still abundant, and the values are laudable. The loss, however, is the very nerve-edge of fear and sorrow, the very humility before righteousness, that constituted the peculiar power of *Cry, the Beloved Country* and *Too Late the Phalarope*.

Seeking a perspective. Jacobson. Early Gordimer

Novels written in the 1950s reveal features that were beginning to recur in fiction from South Africa. On the best-seller lists exotic Africa as a place of tribes remained prominent, Sarah Gertrude Millin produced more 'tragedies of blood', while other writers of note located miscegenation forcibly in social prejudice and legal statute. The urbanising experience began to chart the sociological city, and personal lives struggled to define themselves in large, public landscapes. As in the case of earlier novelists such as Schreiner, Blackburn and Plomer, modes of representation showed the difficulty of having to entertain, sometimes virtually simultaneously, scales of interest and understanding that were not always easily compatible: the problem of how to depict people across a 'colour bar' affected the societal range of fiction, for example, and the question of how to shift between personal worlds of domestic realism and realms of national allegory, or between individualised psychologies and typical public accounts, resulted in minglings of convention, register and ideological discourse. Formal realism was often shot through with the impulses of romance. As in the Zimbabwean novelists I have mentioned, stylistic inconsistency could be seen as either a failure of authorial control or its own kind of appropriateness under the circumstances. I want to look here at two novelists who went on to establish international reputations, Dan Jacobson and the early Nadine Gordimer. Both made their convictions about the value of personal experience in the political dimension confirm a widely-held notion of the novelistic art: individuals are not erased by, but creatively contribute to, the society in which they act out their stories. In South Africa, in the 1950s, the apartheid state by contrast had little concern for the individual citizen.[17]

Drawing threads of uncertainty into patchworks of suggestion Jacobson's allegorical stories of the 1950s, *The Trap* (1955) and *A Dance in the Sun* (1956), link their author hesitantly to something called South African literature while their ironic, sceptical narrative voices were already anticipating the generalised unease of the 'modern condition' as more existential than social in its preoccupations. Such concerns have continued to characterise Jacobson's later, fabular explorations of the fictions of our reality and the realities of our fictions. As in Schreiner's *African Farm*, *A Dance in the Sun* employs the farm setting as sterile and reductive. (The action, in fact, occurs in a dilapidated boarding house in the Karoo.) As in Plomer's *Turbott Wolfe*, Jacobson's liberal protagonists are found to be incapable of translating principle into effective action. With the organising motifs involving black-white tensions, family collapses, miscegenation, and a sense of cultural vacuum which people need to fill by desperately, obsessively telling their stories, *A Dance in the Sun* in its poetic method gives the illusion of South African inclusiveness in a small, 140-page work. We have a cast of characters that can be labelled African, Afrikaner, English-speaking South African; Fletcher is conservative, the two students are liberal-minded, and so on. Types and stereotypes, nonetheless, continually surprise us in their dependencies and dissociations. Joseph (the African), as the insulted labourer, remains in service to the white baas: in the master-slave syndrome he is a kind of albatross that Africa hangs round the crass, bullying Fletcher who in his mean frustrations ends up 'dancing in the sun', a pathetic figure on the open veld. Nasie (meaning Nation), who has fathered an illegitimate child by Joseph's sister, smashes all the furniture in Fletcher's house – Fletcher is married to Nasie's sister – before fleeing once again in his disgrace. However angry and destructive he is, Nasie – we are meant to understand – wants a home, and the most disconnected of all remain the two liberal students: one of whom, in recollecting events, gestures about his guilty complicity in South Africa's racist history, but can muster up no rage to order his impressions and memories into any coherent consideration of his own commitments to a home. A crucial question, according to Michael Wade, is at what point Jacobson, who has lived in England continuously since 1955, ceased being South African.[18] One way of answering this is to say that Jacobson's stories have always resisted being held to account for the particular problems they raise. *A Dance in the Sun*, for example, wants to escape its own hints at political parable: with the two Africans named Joseph and Mary, and with biblical parallels of flight, the concerns of home and homelessness encourage elusive, complex, universalising interpretations from the university-educated reader. But if this is seen as valuable in its non-parochialism, it can also be regarded paradoxically as a South African trait: a fear of being branded provincial; a need to be 'modern' in the style of the twentieth-century troubled consciousness.

Indeed, such a form of literary liberalism has been influential in South Africa and abroad in establishing value and scope for South African writers. It was against such expectations that Nadine Gordimer began to make her mark in the 1950s with novels that localised the lyrical mind-processes of private, white middle-class individuals in the public conflicts according to which the international community would derive its images of apartheid South Africa. It is debatable whether Gordimer has produced many political novels and stories that are not, at core, something more domestic: Freudian family romances. Her first novel, *The Lying Days* (1953), uses an immediately recognisable Western trope, the *Bildungs-roman*, in which Helen Shaw grows to reject the bigotry of the racist society for the vague liberations of Western student culture. An element of South African specificity, however, ensures that Helen's formative experiences involve black-white interchanges and that at the end of the story she cannot quite sever her troubling South African impressions from her desire to sail to the supposedly freer air of the European opportunity. In *A World of Strangers* (1958) the narrating consciousness is that of an English publisher, a bird of passage like Turbott Wolfe, who sees African township life through exotic eyes. Toby Hood imagines himself to be a Robin Hood in the jazz and jive sub-culture of the shebeens. At the same time, he is ambiguous about his commitments to the problems on which he stumbles. Finding the moneyed white suburbs banal, Hood absorbs the 'bohemian' glamour of Sophiatown, the heart of the jazz and jive mythology in the 1950s. But Gordimer, who mixed with Sophiatown literary figures such as Modisane, Nakasa and Themba, is not secure in her own ironical hold on Hood's imaginings. As a result, it is sometimes difficult to decide whether we the readers are meant to regard Hood's immersion in African 'spontaneity' as truly liberating, or whether satirical qualification is pointing us to the superficiality of his response to the South African socio-political situation. Possibly Gordimer at this stage was not herself clear about her own overriding attitude, and Hood is left half committing himself to some form of solidarity with African life while Sam, the African, hardly believes him.[19] In *Occasion for Loving* (1963) Gordimer examined the casual opportunities for sexual and politi-cal betrayal – the African man is betrayed – granted to privileged pseudo-liberal white society and, by the end of the 1960s, she had come to feel the mood of despair in anti-apartheid circles that followed the banning of black political organisations and the crushing of effective opposition by the state secret police.

This despair led to small, largely unsuccessful acts of sabotage by several young idealistic members of the Liberal Party (the Party distanced itself from their actions), and in *The Late Bourgeois World* (1966) Elizabeth van der Sandt turns her sardonic interior monologue on to her own failure to connect her smart liberal patter to any structured political activity. Her ex-husband Max, a naïve idealist in rebellion really against his privileged parents, had resorted to sabotage and, under secret-police interrogation, had betrayed his cell and later committed suicide. With the dead Max beginning to be re-evaluated somewhat in her thoughts for he had at least done something, Elizabeth is left in a decade of stasis on the verge of handling funds for a banned organisation. As she intends filtering the money through Max's grandmother's account – she remarks on the irony of colonial capitalism supporting its own demise – she is probably not taking a huge risk. The other risk – that the black activist will want to screw her – she accepts rather cynically as part of giving herself to something more real, or exciting, than her safe suburban routine. The private character has been pulled into the public demand. Yet the demand exacts its price. The action of *The Late Bourgeois World* is tightly fitted into the unity of a single day; Elizabeth's monologue, however, threatens to burst the created form and deliver Gordimer's own tirade against what in her novels has continued to serve as a convenient target of attack: 'Oh we bathed and perfumed and depilated white ladies, in whose wombs the sanctity of the white race is entombed.' Gordimer the author does not consider herself as one of these ladies, and her books usually include some white protagonists of the troubled consciousness. Yet psycho-analytical criticism might be tempted to see Elizabeth van der Sandt as a Gordimer surrogate and to ascribe her cynicism to her author's own uneasy position in South Africa where, whatever her literary and social pronouncements, she remains in her daily life-surroundings one of the privileged few: one of the privileged few on whom, in her novels – in guilt? – she expends considerable invective.

What we have in Gordimer is South African society depicted in caricatures of affluence: Afrikaners hardly appear except as state menials whose wives are likely to display bad taste in home furnishings or as exceptional jet-setters of the business elite, and as Gordimer encountered Black Consciousness in the 1970s she became less confident of giving presence and speech to African people. If this suggests honesty in not entering the skin of the other, it also delimits the depiction of the society. While her approach had the advantages of setting up a cast of good and bad characters and a self-evident scheme of moral right and wrong, the danger was the simplification of how the repressive state actually intruded on the private life so as to retain its command while adjusting itself to changing circumstances. As Gordimer is regarded internationally as the literary conscience of South Africa, questions have begun to identify as a central issue the quality of her novelistic truth. What the first novels anticipated were the difficulties of being not just a white writer, but a novelist in South Africa. What value has the domestic life – the great theme of the liberal novel – in a society that in so many spheres demands public commitments? What access can the white writer have to the 'black experience'? How does the writer, who is privileged by her race, commit herself to a future that must be African and might find her stories about the white family to be trivial in terms of revolutionary praxis? I shall return to Gordimer in the last part of this study.

Drum magazine and stories of city experience. Themba. Mphahlele. *King Kong*

The novel against apartheid has received more critical attention than have similar protests in the short story. This notwithstanding, the 1950s and 1960s witnessed various and exciting developments in short fiction and confirmed the short story as the most popular and prolific form of imaginative writing in South Africa. One of the leading practitioners was Gordimer who, in similar vein to Dan Jacobson, Jack Cope and, in Rhodesia, Doris Lessing, moved the story away from the colonial adventure yarn and the anecdotal regional tale to a sophisticated art of implication that satisfied taste in magazines abroad like *The New Yorker* and in South African magazines catering for 'literary' readers.[20] The subjects are not always obviously political with Gordimer for one often turning her scalpel on personal relationships in suburbia. The personal, nonetheless, usually reverberates against a racial dilemma, and Gordimer's early story, 'The Train from Rhodesia' (which appeared in *Trek* in 1949), is fairly characteristic of the method: a husband's persistent bargaining with a railside vendor reflects obliquely on his wife's concerns about their marriage, in which she feels that her 'self' has been invaded and dominated. External actions thus give substance to inner thoughts, and a moment of illumination is meant to occur in one of the characters or, beyond the characters, in the reader.[21] These are stories favoured in the university tutorial room: they lend themselves to analysis according to a vocabulary of subtlety and nuance. They tend to be stories, however, about silence and loneliness and, at a level perhaps not fully grasped even by the authors, the stories say something about a denial in white English-speaking South Africans of any popular attachments to a community of voices. To find stories that resonate with sound, with the bustle of people, we have to turn to the fast-talking, city-slick stories by black writers that in the 1950s began to appear in the monthly magazine *Drum* and in Rhodesia, to a lesser extent, in Lawrence Vambe's *African Parade* (1953). To make such a broad distinction is, of course, to risk generalisation. Like his novels, Paton's parable-like stories touch landscapes thick with human activity while, among black writers, Can Themba moved increasingly outside his own created myths of shebeen camaraderie into nightmares of darkness and isolation. It is nevertheless worth defining black storytelling in the 1950s as crowded with the demands of identity-making, survival techniques, and community necessity at the cutting edge of the urban experience.

Industrial expansion in the war years, as I have indicated, led to a large increase of African migration to the cities, and novels by Abrahams, Paton, and, in *A World of Strangers*, Gordimer all reflect African life finding its locality in shantytowns around Johannesburg. By the end of the 1950s the government had removed these so-called black spots and limited 'non-Europeans' (Africans, Indians and coloureds) to their own 'group areas' in soulless, uniform low-budget state housing schemes. The cruel semantics of apartheid chose for these townships quite exotic names like Meadowlands. In 1950, however, the ramshackle shops, houses and drinking dens of Sophiatown spilled towards the Johannesburg business district, and as a community perhaps more illusory than real of Africans, Indians, coloureds and poor whites, Sophiatown seemed to defy the grand designs of apartheid. Sophiatown would be 'cleared' and transformed into the white, mainly Afrikaans, working-class suburb of Triomf (Triumph). Before the bulldozers arrived, however, Sophiatown had gathered almost mythological import in the literature as a romantic, bohemian world where 'new African' teachers, nurses, lawyers, musicians and journalists, who were usually also creative writers, rubbed shoulders in shebeens with the other products of rapid urbanisation: gangsters speaking their film-star drawl and dressed in Americanised gear. In reality, Sophiatown knew wracking poverty and extortionist landlords while the many unskilled labourers and peasants fell outside the interests of its petty-bourgeois professional classes. With the term 'situation' referring to those who saw themselves above the masses even as apartheid legislation frustrated their upwardly-mobile ambitions, it was the style of the 'situation' that, both consciously and unconsciously, cocked a snook at racial classifications of Africans as essentially tribal people from distant reserves.[22]

Owned by a quirky white, individualistic entrepreneur, Jim Bailey, who evidently did not pay his black journalists over-generous wages, and staffed by 'new Africans' from Sophiatown, the magazine *Drum*, which began in 1951, tapped the spirit of jazz and tsotsi (petty gangster) talk. Appearing each month in large picture-format with a beauty queen on the cover, *Drum* combined serious journalistic crusades against prison conditions, the exploitation of African farm-workers, and the damaging consequences of racial policies, with the entertainment of soccer, sex and sin. It provided, in addition, a publishing outlet for short stories by black writers. With competitions initially encouraging entrants, over 90 stories would appear between 1952 and 1959 while in its 'African' editions *Drum* printed the first stories by several writers who would go on to make their literary reputations in West and East Africa. The commercial imperative was 'hard sell' to the amorphous though actual market of the city African, and advertisements for the latest fashions in urban living ranged from improve-yourself correspondence courses to skin-lightening creams, while owner Bailey believed that fiction too should be a hard

sell. The ideological ethos reflected messages and images about achievement and success with international inspiration in Negro America –
Langston Hughes was valued as a contributor – and African inspiration
in the decolonising ideal: Nkrumah in Ghana attracted considerable attention. On his short visit to South Africa in 1952 to report on general
conditions for a British newspaper (see *Return to Goli*, 1953), Peter
Abrahams was fêted in *Drum* as the black man who had succeeded in the
wider world. (I use the term 'man' deliberately, for *Drum* was aggressively,
even callously masculinist.) Abrahams' *Wild Conquest* was serialised in
Drum after the first issues had seen the serialisation of Paton's *Cry, the
Beloved Country*. While Paton's social conscience was respected, his
countrified parson the Revd Stephen Kumalo, as Lewis Nkosi has forth-
rightly put it,[23] was regarded as an embarrassment to the city-wise
ambitions of journalist-writers such as Henry Nxumalo – whose daring
exposés earned him the original title, Mr Drum – Can Themba, Bloke
Modisane, Nat Nakasa, Casey Motsisi, Arthur Maimane, the young Lewis
Nkosi himself, and Todd Matshikiza whose style, dubbed 'Matshikeze',
captured the modern subject and mood:

> I said to Dam-dam [Nathan Dambuza Mdedle, leader of
> the local vocal quartet the Manhattan Brothers] yesterday:
> 'Dam-dam, I bet you my last shirt you're the biggest playboy
> going on.'
>   He said: 'Blow you, Toddie-boy, I'm still looking for my
> dream girl!'
>   I said: 'What happened to the juicy berries I've seen
> hanging on you?'
>   He said: 'Skip them. You wouldn't bet your daughter on
> a donkey on the racecourse, would you? I dream at the
> pace of a racehorse. They dream at the pace of a lame
> donkey.'
>
> (*Drum*, December 1953)

Against the ethnically-based imperatives of the Afrikaner state, Sophiatown writers chose English as the medium of their challenge in minglings
of literary reference, Americanisms and tsotsi-taal, a polyglot gangster
slang. If the manner, as in 'Matshikeze', was boasting, hyperbolic and
self-aggrandising, charges of superficiality fail to contextualise the voice
as one of desperate defiance against a stressful mental and material reality,
in which the forces of politics and economics were determined to strip
black people of their humanity and secure their docility as convenient
labour. The racy, agitated, impressionistic prose, which at first angered
the writer and critic Es'kia (then Ezekiel) Mphahlele as escapist, would
later provoke his attempts to define an aesthetic of black South African

writing arising from its necessary attachment to a 'tyranny of place': 'it quivered with a nervous energy, a caustic wit . . . because our writers feel life at the basic levels of sheer survival, because blacks are so close to physical pain, hunger, overcrowded public transport, in which bodies chafe, push and pull'.[24]

When the university-educated Mphahlele, who had been banned from teaching because of his opposition to Bantu Education, arrived at *Drum* in 1955 as fiction editor, he found a literary section that offended his sense of serious African responsibility. Stories as in the Western mass media tended to be formulaic in their concern with marital infidelities, good times in the shebeens, successful and unsuccessful pimps, boxers and soccer stars. Detectives sounded as though they lived in New York rather than Sophiatown, and women were usually frivolous cheats who betrayed their reckless though basically loving men. What Mphahlele did not see clearly at the time was that the yellow press opportunities were in fact being utilised with varying degrees of resonance by several writers. Themba's 'Mob Passion', for example, may have exploited a melodramatic foreshortening in the 'Romeo and Juliet' story of two lovers in this case from different ethnic groups. But against the topical issue of tribal fights in which raw Basotho migrant workers banded together against city-slick tsotsis, Themba's lament that inter-tribal divisions are destructive to a people's humanity depicted the experiences of living in the black townships with a force of emotion and compassion that had not been felt before in fiction:

> The crowd was going back now. All the bravado gone . . .
> then that persistent wail of the anguished girl, torturing
> the innermost core of even the rudest conscience there.
> The men felt themselves before God; the women heard
> the denunciations of thwarted love. Within they were all
> crying bitterly:
>   'Jo-o! Jo-o! Jo-nana-jo!'

In the hands of Themba, Nxumalo, Motsisi and Nakasa, the journalistic sketch combined its information with fictional devices of atmosphere, character-creation and dialogue, so that an investigative report on prison conditions had powerful public impact precisely because it lodged its data subjectively in readers' emotions and imaginations. There is little generic distinction between *Drum* fiction and *Drum* journalism. In both, the 'story' of black life is paramount as the facts of the decade – mass removals, the Immorality Act, the bans on social mixing, the destruction of Sophiatown – were transformed into pot-boilers that suddenly bubbled over into serious, haunting commentaries on human motivation and behaviour. Of particular note are Themba's 'opinion pieces'.[25] Yet in

reacting against Themba's high-flown style, in which his Eng. Lit. education at Fort Hare manifested itself in the shock value of strange linguistic
coinages, Mphahlele temperamentally preferred the 'ordinary' style as
apposite to his conception of African life evaluating its humanity in the
everyday rhythms of community living. In Mphahlele's stories some incident – a family funeral, for example – provides the focus of gatherings,
conversations and reminders of the traditional respects that should be
accorded by the younger generation to their elders. Idealisations, however,
are continually undercut by the recognition that the tough conditions of
African life in the circumstances of apartheid cannot simply be wished
away.[26]

By the end of the 1950s, *Drum* had begun to lose the informing power
of its original context: the magazine, currently owned by a national,
commercial publishing group, continues today as a mass glossy which,
while it still promotes positive images of black life, no longer expands
beyond its own covers to tap the most vital currents of black experience.
Owing to the spread of literacy as well as to developments in black
politics that have resulted in several constituencies from the elite to the
grassroots, the black experience in its forms of print culture, in any case,
has become far more differentiated than it was in the 1950s. Yet the
legacy of *Drum* retains significance in South African literature. As I have
suggested, its stories gave us the resilient voice of the individual never
quite free of the community; the unselfconscious, defiant use of English
as creative communication; the flaunting of 'art' distinctions between fact
and fiction; and a sense of the big event as subject matter. All of these
characteristics have lent black writing its own humanistic strength.
Although the stories did not usually confront politics directly, the language
captured the theatrical style of a decade that dramatised black politics in
large-scale campaigns, including the defiance against unjust laws, the
signing of the Freedom Charter, and the massive treason trial: a vast
'theatre' that saw 156 leaders put on trial on charges of conspiring to
overthrow the apartheid state. *Drum* reported the events in its usual mixture of journalese and literary evocation, and provoked from Mphahlele
the kind of consideration on the truth of representation – as spectacular
or ordinary depiction – that has continued to be necessary in a country
where the public slogan has so often been felt to be more compelling
than the personal intonation.[27]

It is instructive to follow the careers of writers who were given their
first opportunities in *Drum*. Before he died in drunken despair in 1968,
in Swaziland, Themba had fashioned the myth of Sophiatown glamour
tottering on very fragile foundations. Nakasa together with the theatre-
director Barney Simon started a literary magazine *The Classic*, which was
named after a shebeen in Sophiatown: the aim was to encourage writing
by blacks, and one of the poets who would help create a 'new black

poetry' in the 1970s, Oswald Mtshali, began to publish his work in Nakasa's magazine. Nakasa, who was awarded a Nieman fellowship to study journalism abroad, left South Africa on an exit permit – that is, he was permitted to leave but not to return – and in 1965 he committed suicide in New York. Having reported the case of the boxer King Kong Dlamini, who with characteristic 'Sophiatown' bravado and recklessness descended swiftly from being a heavyweight champion in the ring to a convicted murderer,[29] Nakasa in 1959 had seen the story turned into a stage version: billed as an 'African jazz opera', *King Kong*[29] was applauded by multiracial audiences in the great hall of the University of the Witwatersrand which, because it was on university property, escaped certain provisions against interracial social mixing. With its theatrical experience reminiscent of *West Side Story* (1957), *King Kong* consolidated the data of local shebeen culture and earlier 'township' styles, such as the song and dance sketches of Esau Mthethwe's Lucky Stars, into the gaiety and sadness that, as Themba would say in drawing on Dickens, represented the 'night of the Sophiatown of my time, before the government destroyed it':

> It was the best of times, it was the worst of times; it was
> the age of wisdom, it was the age of foolishness; it was the
> season of Light, it was the season of Darkness.
>
> ('Crepuscule')

Produced by the white Union Artists with the services of black actors – who, predictably, were underpaid – *King Kong* was supposed to epitomise the dream of a better, more humane South Africa. Accordingly, its 'politics' were ameliorative rather than radical, and against the activities of decolonisation in Africa could have seemed almost quaint. Perhaps Lewis Nkosi identified the true significance of *King Kong*, however, when he said that the finished product could not have succeeded in mirroring half the conspiratorial excitement of putting on stage a play involving white-black co-operations before a mixed audience in the dark days of apartheid.[30]

Similarly *Drum* was a phenomenon which, as I have tried to suggest, can be fully appreciated only in its surrounding context. In Cape Town James Matthews and Richard Rive, both of whom had been published in *Drum*, drew inspiration from District Six, like Sophiatown a 'conglomerate' community before it too was raised to the ground and coloureds re-located in the government township of Mitchell's Plain. Rive – as I have indicated – would re-create myths of resilience and unity in '*Buckingham Palace*', *District Six*: one of several acts of literary reclamation to have occurred in the 1980s and to have offered readers the possibility not simply of remembering the fifties as the past, but of considering how stories, nourished by the ideals, emotions, aspirations and constraints of another epoch, can have continuing interest and value for people today. What should be kept in mind is that, in the eighties, the extra-parliamentary opposition of the United Democratic Front, a front for the then banned ANC, rooted its own historical memory in the mass cam-paigns of *Drum*'s heyday when, under president Albert Luthuli and leaders like Oliver Tambo, Nelson Mandela and Walter Sisulu, the ANC seemed to be on the ascendancy. Any study of the 1950s could valuably move beyond creative writing, therefore, and consider the visions of racial justice contained in commentaries by figures like Luthuli, Mandela and Trevor Huddleston. As the Anglican priest in charge of the Community of the Resurrection's mission in Sophiatown until he returned to England in 1956, Huddleston added his voice of conscience to what Verwoerd angrily regarded as a tradition of meddling clerics.[31]

Critics have noted that African writers of the 1950s, several of whom were educated at Huddleston's St Peter's School, displayed bourgeois class-elements in their hankerings after the fruits of European influence, opportunity and high culture. Themba, for example, claimed he could speak no African language and, in despising politicking, often acted as the literary dandy. The writers were regarded as sufficiently articulate, nonetheless, to be targeted as 'communists' by a government quite fren-zied in its determination to clamp down on the opinion of any black person. To speak eloquently meant presumably that you were denying your designated status as a non-being, and in 1966 a ban was imposed under the all-embracing Suppression of Communism Act on 146 black writers living abroad. As most of the *Drum* generation had by this time gone into exile, the effect was to silence their voices in South Africa where they were not permitted to be published, or even quoted. It was only in the 1980s that most of the writers I have mentioned here in connection with *Drum* began to be freely available again in their own country. The reasons for their exile, therefore, had to do with direct political harassment, but in a related way also with the fact that some of the writers lived out, as reality, their own often extravagant personae of survival. In grasping at chances to escape the demeaning strictures of apartheid, the writer aimed to realise himself abroad as a worldly citizen: as a man of culture who could appreciate Beethoven as effortlessly as penny-whistle street music. Such 'styling' had its beginnings in the shebeens of Sophiatown.

Black autobiography. Modisane. Mphahlele

The tragedy of cultural displacement is conveyed harrowingly in Bloke Modisane's *Blame Me on History* (1963), a hallucinatory rendition of Modisane's own bravado, frustration and, ultimately, despair as the destruction of Sophiatown became the metaphor for his own devastation. As an individual who moved debonairly in white literary circles, is he to blame for his own collapse and for his cruelty particularly to his wife for her reminding him that he was black? Or is he the victim of history? Modisane cannot answer his own questions. Rather *Blame Me on History* is a cathartic testimony that speaks of the overwhelming need for the writer in exile to tell his story, to explain his actions, to justify his commitments, and a spate of autobiographical writing accompanied the *Drum* writers into exile.[32] Like Mphahlele, Nakasa and others, Modisane left South Africa on an exit permit, and as his words were prohibited in South Africa, readers abroad had to provide the understanding ear. Often linking the person to particular actions rather than to a life, the philosophical assumptions are that the self comes into being only through interplay with the social world, that there is such a thing as mimetic objective circumstance according to which experience is not regarded primarily as a semantic construction, that abuses are real and damaging and require polemical response, that black histories are preserved in autobiographies, and that the ideals – which Modisane himself does not achieve – are reason and sanity as the mark of one's humanity. Among white autobiographies, Paton's approach most closely approximates what we may call 'black South African autobiography'. Clearly the 'I' is less the individualised, romantic state of consciousness than an ensemble of socio-political relations. Accents and styles, nevertheless, have individuality, and in Mphahlele's *Down Second Avenue* (1959) we encounter not the eddies of Modisane's tortured mind but an intellectual, artistic attempt to work through the hurts left by apartheid towards coherence and recovery. As we accompany the young Mphahlele in his re-created child world in the township slums, we share his adult's reflections and experience as a complex binding of the past and the present. The manner of telling shifts from the evocation of his first recollections, through emotional reaction and response in what are described as interludes, to analyses of how to reconstitute the liberated self. Critics who complain that *Down Second Avenue* does not sustain its evocative opening sequences in later discursive passages miss the character of a mind that has to give substance and thought to defining terms such as African personality, African community, and African humanity. It is not surprising that for Mphahlele the critical essay should have become a form closely allied to autobiography.

Whereas Lewis Nkosi's essays in *Home and Exile* (1965) and, later, in *Masks and Tasks* (1981) read as fragments of the writer's own personality interpreting and re-interpreting itself through its attitudes to literature, Mphahlele's *The African Image* (1962; rev. ed. 1974) and *Voices in the Whirlwind* (1968), while also following a subjective approach to the critical act, expand beyond fragmentation towards a broad cultural project that remains searching, flexible, and open to modification and change.[33] Influenced in his early years by a university education in the Western canon, Mphahlele in *The African Image* modifies his own assumptions in the course of studying black character portrayal in fiction, and begins the process of 'decolonising the mind'. (Mphahlele, not Ngugi, coined the phrase.) In tracing a line of human, as opposed to exotic, representation back to Plaatje and forward through Achebe, Mphahlele, who has sought a pan-African perspective on literature, took issue with the tendency of Negritude to idealise the return to the African source. Identifying the journey to the past not as romantic regression but as a step in understanding the present, he would pay tribute to Aimé Césaire and, in South Africa, to H. I. E. Dhlomo both of whom had treated negritudinal images not as static myths but as part of a discourse of power. Accordingly, Mphahlele defined the African personality as an inspiring construction that grasps at the hard facts of politics and economics, and undergoes continual change in its struggles with the material conditions of oppression. Marxist insights are utilised in the conception of a modernised African humanism even as Mphahlele remains insistent that any liberatory act must draw strength from the older values of reverence for the ancestors and respect for family: values that have the task of gluing damaged urban people into some sort of community. In responding favourably to the Black Consciousness poetry of the 1970s Mphahlele, who after twenty-five years mainly in West Africa and the United States was permitted to return home in 1978, tempered his praise with the warnings of his practical humanism. He did not deny what Black Consciousness poets proclaimed: that art has a functional purpose, that its language should communicate not only with a literary elite but with a wider audience, and that art should be about repossessing African history. Mphahlele added nonetheless that myths of origins, though necessary, should not confuse a generous Africanness with Africanist boasting. The African personality should take pride in its heritage, therefore, but be sufficiently humble not to imagine its language and culture as the centre of the universe. For that would be to mimic the colonial attitude.[34]

As far as Mphahlele is concerned, the role of the committed writer cannot finally be separated from a responsibility to education: African philosophy and consciousness need to form a part of syllabus reconstruction in any future South Africa that hopes successfully to withstand the onslaught of cultural imperialism in the mass and foreign media. When he attempts to dramatise his ideas of belonging and belief in fictional form, as in *The Wanderers* (1971), Mphahlele makes for tedious reading. His achievement – the intellect fired with the emotion of conviction – is to be found in his early autobiography and his essays. Possibly the most illuminating aspects of his re-interpretations and re-evaluations did not continue altogether to characterise his literary activities after his return to South Africa. As we struggle towards a broadly South African society, however, Mphahlele's writings deserve fresh attention particularly in their ability to suggest that African humanism in the practice of its moral and cultural life can offer an intelligent and a humane check on many hubristic and potentially divisive -isms, whether Westernisms or Africanisms.

The silent decade. Sestigers. Brutus, La Guma and exile. Political testimony

Acts of recovery and reassessment, as I have suggested in the case of the *Drum* generation, are particularly necessary when we turn to writing that was banned in the 1960s: the years known as the silent decade.[35] Whereas Mphahlele's African personality is recognisably human with its problems arising out of special circumstances, Verwoerdian apartheid branded Africans as essentially unlike Europeans, and the discourse of ethnicity and sectarianism not humanism, whether in its African or Western varieties, dominated public platforms. With black political organisations banned, leaders gaoled, and the secret police granted wide powers to detain and hold suspects in isolation for lengthy periods without bringing them before a court, South Africa slid into the murky world of the police state. Reports of torture in interrogation multiplied, and numbers of suspects died under mysterious circumstances while in police custody. I mentioned in Part Two that in the 1830s slaves had been given hearings in humanitarian lobbies through the publication of their court-room testimony; some of the most chilling accounts of the 1960s are to be found, no doubt, in court records and police archives, if the archives have not been destroyed. There were also several prison diaries and memoirs by detainees.[36] One of the most dramatic in its personal reflections on the mental sparring between interrogator and prisoner was *117 Days* (1965) by Ruth First, ANC and SACP activist and academic. In his introduction to the new edition of *117 Days* (1988) First's husband, SACP leader Joe Slovo, regards her book as having continuing relevance for future generations of South Africans: it is 'part of the inspiration which will inevitably lead to a society of justice and harmony . . . [for] it is a chronicle of signal bravery'.

On the surface of everyday life in the 1960s, however, it was apartheid that seemed triumphant as its enemies sat behind prison bars, or tried to revive opposition from the distance of exile, at the same time as South Africa benefited from a general Western economic boom. Alert to mounting condemnation of apartheid by 'Third-world' countries at the United Nations, alert also to the temper of decolonisation to the north and to signs of guerilla struggles in neighbouring Angola and Mozambique, Verwoerd offered his grand solution to charges that South Africa's racial policies were un-Christian and repressive. In 1961 he had called several Dutch Reformed church theologians to order for supporting a World Council of Churches rejection of the spiritual and socio-political ideal of apartheid. The 'Bantu', Verwoerd declared, would be divided into ethnic 'nations', and would enjoy 'self-determination' in the poverty-stricken reserves, renamed Bantustans, which would be given the trappings of independence while, out of economic necessity, continuing to provide the white South African industry with migrant (redubbed 'foreign') labour. Torture in prison, black lives controlled in every movement by a bullying bureaucracy including arrests on pass-law offences, the mass removals of entire black communities to their new 'group areas' sometimes in desolate dumping grounds on the veld shaped the images of terror that were shown abroad, but banned in South Africa. Like Plaatje's *Native Life in South Africa*, Cosmas Desmond's *The Discarded People* (1971) in its power of investing fact with human consequence tells a shocking story of land and people subserving the designs of massive social engineering. As Desmond, who at the time was a Franciscan priest, has continued to maintain with precise definition, African resettlement is a record of genocide.[37] Besides the gagging clauses of the Suppression of Communism Act, the 1963 Publications and Entertainments Act, which established a publications control board, provided for censorship of the word and image. Under the section that defined 'undesirability', anything deemed to be critical of apartheid policies or to transgress narrow Calvinistic sexual mores was likely to be banned. So were many international authors vaguely connected to the youth culture of the 1960s. Some of the blunders confirmed the impression of living in Kafka-esque times: *Black Beauty* was seized at customs in the belief that it promoted illegal interracial love-making, and Hardy's *The Return of the Native* was confiscated from bookshops out of fear that its title alone could subvert the apartheid order.

By the early 1980s most of the writers banned by decree in 1966 had been republished in South Africa by a few local literary publishers. Of Mphahlele's writings, for example, only *The African Image* remained generally unavailable in the country. Instead of approaching the Department of Justice for permission that would routinely have been denied to quote people 'listed' under the Suppression of Communism Act (later, the

Internal Security Act), the publishers Ad. Donker, David Philip and Ravan Press simply took the chance that the government did not have the will to pursue prosecutions in cases like those of Can Themba and Bloke Modisane where the writers had not been prominent political activists. As far as activist-figures such as Dennis Brutus, Alex La Guma, Mary Benson, Albie Sachs and Ruth First were concerned, the lifting of restrictions on their persons and, hence, on their writing formed part of president F. W. de Klerk's unbanning of anti-apartheid organisations on 2 February 1990. A flurry of publishing activity followed the 2 February announcement, and new editions of many of the works that had only been available abroad in the 1960s are now prominently displayed in South African bookshops. The task of criticism if it has anything to do with our right to pursue truth is to attend to, and understand, the writing of the silent decade in the context of both its own time and our own. According to the de Klerk government, as its own legacy continued to be attached to political assassinations and other dirty tricks, the era of apartheid has ended, and while one can agree that reconciliation not vengeance is crucial to a reconstructed future, acts of literary-historical reclamation also need to keep in mind Herbert Marcuse's words that against any surrendering of time, remembrance has to be restored to its rights as a vehicle of liberation. For to forget is also to forgive what should not be forgiven if freedom and justice are to prevail.[38] With this in mind, I want to turn briefly to the silent decade by asking the basic questions: who protested; what was the quality of the protest? The response will be partly determined, of course, by the priorities of the critic.

One form of protest, I have suggested, was the generalised artistic one of honing the vivid word in a climate of banality. In the belief that when language goes to pot ideas go to pot, this was the approach of liberal-minded literary magazines. Considerably more muted in their criticism than editorials by Lionel Abrahams and Jack Cope, or public statements by the writers Nadine Gordimer and Athol Fugard, were the literature departments in the so-called liberal universities: that is, English-speaking universities which, because of apartheid legislation that dates back to 1954, remain still largely 'white' if not in numbers then in attitudes. Here, a perceived threat to the status of the English language in the Afrikaner republic resulted in renewed, sometimes chauvinistic attachments to the metropolitan tradition with Shakespeare seen not as the creative influence he had been to Mofolo, Plaatje and Dhlomo, but as the cultural and imperial icon of Englishness. The brief of the English Academy of Southern Africa, founded in 1961, was not to promote South African literature, but to uphold the standards of written and spoken English. In Afrikaans literature, the parochial naturalism and realism of the *plaasroman* gave way, spectacularly, to an imitative Euro-modernism

among a new generation of writers many of whom had been influenced
by sojourns in France. As this writing of Sestig (Sixties) is regarded in
Afrikaans literary circles as a major achievement, it is worth pausing to
consider its relation to a protesting voice.[39]

In the work of Jan Rabie, André P. Brink, Breyten Breytenbach,
Etienne Leroux, Chris Barnard and Bartho Smit, to name the most
prominent Sestigers,[40] the existentialism of Camus and Beckett, in
fictionalised labyrinthine forms, either loses itself in its own cleverness or
jerks its concerns about good, evil, sex, anxiety and despair into mocking
rebellions by renegade sons against the dour fathers of Afrikanerdom.
Leroux's *Sewe Dae by die Silbersteins*, translated into English as *Seven Days
at the Silbersteins* (1962), for example, transforms the Afrikaans farm of
blood and soil into a modern wine estate where *nouveau riche* materialism
has run rampant in orgies of partying and in pseudo – or, is it meant to
be serious? – patter about sin, conversion, and destiny. Explaining his
practice as being an attempt to overcome the parochial Afrikaner chains
that bound him to local myths, Leroux does not want to lose what he
refers to as the grassroots of the myth, and his later novel *Magersfontein,
O Magersfontein* (1976), in which a film crew assembles to shoot a movie
based on the historic Anglo-Boer War battle, does not so much debunk
the heroic memory as satirise its bourgeois mutation. Like Van Wyk
Louw, Leroux is scornful of the modern city Afrikaner, but where the
earlier writer was tortured and confessional Leroux is comic and fantastic.
In free and racy language, he reports on promiscuous sex among the film
crew, and collapses seriousness into the floods of irreverence: the river
bursts its banks and destroys the film set. Public pronouncement is lampooned when the minister of Water Affairs delivers a fatuous speech of
the kind employed by National Party parliamentarians in the 1970s to
pacify public opinion about guerilla wars along the northern borders.
Magersfontein, O Magersfontein – translated into English in 1983 under the
same title – was hailed by the Afrikaans literati as permissive and daring. It
was banned after initially being cleared by the directorate of publications,
rebanned on appeal at ministerial level and, while banned, awarded the
prestigious Hertzog Prize by the Afrikaans Akademie. The novel is now
unbanned.

If all this says something about the psychological and cultural schizo-
phrenia that Brink identifies in the Afrikaner Calvinist mentality, the
rigmarole can lead us to overrate the element of protest.[41] Like the plays
of Bartho Smit, Leroux's novels throw out provocative but largely unanaly-
sable hints of religious – and even more elusively – political rebellion,
not revolution. This is the stuff on which lecture-room interpretation
thrives and students are expected, earnestly, to pick away at allusions and
guesses, and to find ultimate sanction in comments by the authors such
as: life is not political, it is absurd; my theme is theological terror, fear

in its abstract manifestation. Both Leroux and Smit, the latter whose plays for many years were kept off the stage by administrative fiat, remained members of the Nationalist establishment: solid citizens, but naughty boys, and one is reminded that prime minister Vorster's rebuke to André Brink's flaunting of religion and sex was to tell the author to have his hair cut! Hailed as prophets, Leroux and Smit are also apes of God. Individual compassions are sublimated to the metaphysical Idea; black people, if they appear at all, are emblems of chaos and, as with earlier Afrikaans writers, the question of the Afrikaner's relation to any wider South African community is never posed.

In the 1960s paternalistic strictures rather than censorship laws were enough to ensure that Sestigers did not unduly criticise patriotism, and it was only in the 1970s when Brink and Breytenbach moved from their earlier surrealisms to more overtly political themes that, after much agonising by the Afrikaner-dominated censorship machinery, bannings began to be imposed. After nearly a year on the shelves Brink's *Kennis van die Aand*, which was translated as *Looking on Darkness* (1974), became the first Afrikaans book to be banned. Brink and Breytenbach are best discussed in the context of the politicised 1970s. In looking back at the Sestigers, Jack Cope concluded that there was no coherent theory to the practice. With an over-emphasis on technique that was usually con-spicuous in its derivativeness and little engagement with the issues of race and politics, a sense of South African reality did not arise from the experience of the writing.[42] This is a fair assessment, and the shots aimed at Calvinist authority tend to be haphazard. In retrospect, it is the less experimental Jan Rabie who retains our interest as someone whose life commitments pushed the problem of conscience into the craft of the form. As he campaigned single-handedly against nationalism and organ-ised a petition against censorship, Rabie shifted from his Sestiger style to document, didacticism and prophetic denunciation. His novel *Ons, die Afgod* (We, the Idol, 1958) identified the year 1956 when coloureds were removed from the voters' roll as Afrikanerdom's nemesis in its betrayal of its 'brown' blood brothers, and his 'Bolandia' novels (1964–1985) with their big messages chart a history of the Afrikaner's false vision. Remain-ing himself blind to the place of Africans and English-speaking people in his scheme, Rabie saw the final indignity of his beloved Afrikaans lan-guage, which could have bound white and brown Afrikaners together, in its contemptuous rejection as the 'language of the oppressor' by the Soweto youth. Perhaps, however, his greater sorrow, which manifests itself in shrill anger, is reserved for several young Afrikaans writers of the 1980s whose attacks on the taal as complicit in state and church power Rabie can regard as only neurotic icon-bashing.[43]

Two other writers who were associated occasionally with the Sestigers also tie their concerns with form to the necessity of rejecting the Afrikaner establishment. Ingrid Jonker's confessional, imagistic poetry brusquely puts down the father figures of Afrikaans literature. Her own father, one of the Nationalist members of parliament responsible for drafting the censorship bill, disowned her after she was quoted as regarding his opinions as 'stupid nonsense'. Her rebellion, which cannot easily be called feminist as she had no coherent socio-political agenda, was shaped nonetheless by immediate social and political exigencies. In reacting against the paternalistic myth that a young Afrikaans woman's role is to be subservient and feminine, she writes:

> Free I have my own self-reliance
> from graves and from deceptive friends
> . . .
> My people have rotted away from me
> what will become of the rotten nation
> a hand cannot pray alone.
> ('I Drift in the Wind')[t]

Like Jonker, the coloured Afrikaans writer Adam Small remained an outsider. Following tentative criticism of the high metaphysical manner by the poet Peter Blum, Small infiltrated the purity of the taal with his Cape coloured dialect (*Kaaps*). His initial ideal was human brotherhood; by the 1970s, however, he had sarcastically rejected the Sestigers and he subsequently oscillated between Black Consciousness assertions and a philosophical humanism. Instability of belonging and belief may be regarded as a metaphor of his work.[44]

Both Jonker, who killed herself at the age of 31, and Small manifest a pervasive characteristic of the silent decade: a sense of exile in the home country which cannot be a home. In many writers, physically separated from home in reaction to political circumstances, the image of home set in the past, in childhood memory, or idealised as a goal of self-discovery or return leads to complicated, often contradictory claims for the universality of the local experience or for the victim's special status, as the persecuted one, living among a foreign citizenry to which the exile cannot, or does not want to belong.[45] In Dennis Brutus's poetry, memory of his imprisonment as an activist is the basis of his creativity, and his language which is nostalgic, remote and romantic in a literary way, seems itself to be exiled from any exact or secure place: 'And still I am driftwood./Still the restlessness, the journeyings, the quest' ('And I am Driftwood'). Yet as one begins to label the reminiscences, the idiom and the rhythms as dated or cliché-ridden or too generalised to identify the single being, a groundswell of feeling conveys a personality acutely conscious of its own loneliness: 'only in myself, occasionally, am I familiar'. For Alex La Guma the remedy for alienation was to try to affiliate the self to changing concepts of community. Whereas Noni Jabavu, who was not strictly a political exile, re-created a Xhosa rural world that seemed to fill her memory, La Guma – like Brutus, a political activist in exile – had most forcefully etched in his experience a coloured community that was socially, economically and politically marginalised amid the urban insecurities of group-area removals and re-locations.

In La Guma's first stories, which were written in South Africa while he was under house arrest, a minute description of place and circumstance renders his characters – types of petty criminals – almost powerless to effect change in their own lives. As far as La Guma, a committed Marxist, was concerned, however, the struggle in political and literary terms involved self-understanding not through immanent recognition, but through allegiance to ideas, actions and organisations larger than the single life. *In the Fog of the Seasons' End* (1972) has Beukes discovering his being in his existence for others. He attempts, accordingly, to define the aims of his underground political activity and to sustain himself, in new solidarities and communities, through a process of mental and social transformation that remains open-ended. As far as his character depictions are concerned, La Guma is usually more successful with comrades than with families: wives are either sentimentalised or nagging figures in the background. In *Time of the Butcherbird* (1979) La Guma, perhaps as a result of his long years in exile, seemed himself to have grown impatient with having to create character and action in the forms of a dialectic that his Marxism would have endorsed. Instead, his use of a revenge plot suggests an apocalyptic desire to obliterate the racist state. The isolated protagonist mounts an attack that only nominally connects him to any organised political group. In the hollowness of the action, La Guma perhaps signalled his own defeat in exile: the loss of his bases of creative memory; the death of his ideal of community. As a novelist, he seemed to surrender the Marxist aesthetic which in *Seasons' End* had been coherent about empowering human beings, but which in *Butcherbird* could be described in Marxist terms as excessive bourgeois melodrama.[46] The conclusion might be that *In the Fog of the Seasons' End* is the better book according to the beauty of its ideas in action. Were we to neglect *Time of the Butcherbird*, however, we would not really be able to understand the exiled voice as the expression of its condition in exile. Such a project, partly diagnostic in its analysis, is important for it forces us to situate La Guma's literary texts – his 'art' – in ethical contexts which require our remembrance, and which lend the fiction a weight that is not often evident in the writing of the Sestigers.

As in the novels of Nadine Gordimer that appeared in the 1960s, the substance behind La Guma's imagination is that of the social document: his fiction seeks correspondences with large public issues, and in restoring speech and interpretation to the silent decade we have to extend our concern beyond the genres of fiction, plays and poems to the numerous forms of document – some of which I have mentioned – that in direct, relatively unmediated ways opposed the apartheid state.[47] None of these texts, of course, should simply be allowed to stand as monuments of admiration; rather, remembrance requires that in considering forms of idealisation we try to distinguish between the projection of propaganda and the efforts by writers and spokespersons to make certain qualities seem valuable in the on-going activities of social life. Since his release from prison in 1990, for example, Nelson Mandela has been returned from hagiographic memory to a mortal politician at the hustings, but we can still re-read his speeches of the 1950s and conclude that, according to generally acceptable norms of humanity on which societies including their literatures are ultimately likely to be judged, it was Mandela – not Verwoerd – who simply and powerfully spoke truth:

> Dr Verwoerd may deceive the simple-minded Nationalist
> voters with his talk of Bantustans, but he will not deceive
> anyone else, neither the African people, nor the great world
> beyond the borders of this country. We have heard such
> talk before, and we know what it means. Like everything
> else that has come from the Nationalist Government, it
> spells nothing but fresh hardships and suffering to the masses
> of the people.
>   Behind the fine talk of 'self-government' is a sinister
> design.[48]

In granting Phyllis Lewsen her observation that it was the creative writers more than the social analysts who conveyed what it was like living in repressive times, I have implicitly been qualifying her comment. Whether a prison memoir can separate the fact from the imagination is debatable. That any of the fictional works I have discussed are free of the marks of segregationist legislation is doubtful. Novels like *Mhudi* are also intricate theoretical statements; and the literary commentary of Dhlomo and Mphahlele is simultaneously autobiographical intervention. What criticism should help us see is that in the years of the false prophets of apartheid there were alternative visions. But such identifications do not always satisfactorily answer the question I posed at the beginning of Part Three: African or Colonial Literature? What I have continued to do, therefore, is to suggest that the literature, even by displaced colonials like Roy Campbell, can be Africanised, or re-Africanised, in the processes of its interpretation.

Notes

1. See details of apartheid legislation in B. Bunting's *The Rise of the South African Reich* (Harmondsworth, 1964; rev. ed., 1969). Published in the Penguin African Library, under the general editorship of South African activist and exile Ronald Segal, Bunting's book may be supplemented by others in the series including M. Benson's *South Africa: The Struggle for a Birthright* (1966); the revised edition of *The African Patriots* (London, 1963); C. Desmond, *The Discarded People: An Account of African Resettlement in South Africa* (1971); and G. Mbeki, *South Africa: The Peasants' Revolt* (1964).

   Also: T. Lodge, *Black Politics in South Africa since 1945* (Johannesburg, 1983); S. Marks and R. Rathbone (eds), *Industrialisation and Social Change in South Africa* (London, 1982); A. Paton, *Hope for South Africa* (London, 1958); J. A. Polley (ed.), *The Freedom Charter and the Future* (Johannesburg, 1988); A. Reeves, *Shooting at Sharpeville: The Agony of South Africa* (London, 1960); J. Robertson, *Liberalism in South Africa, 1948–1963* (Oxford, 1971); A. Sampson, *The Treason Trial: The Opposition on Trial in South Africa* (London, 1958); J. H. P. Serfontein, *Brotherhood of Power: An Exposé of the Secret Afrikaner Broederbond* (London, 1979); N. Steytler, *The Freedom Charter and Beyond: Founding Principles for a Democratic South African Legal Order* (Cape Town, 1992); I. Wilkins and H. Strydom, *The Super-Afrikaners* (Johannesburg, 1979); H. Wolpe, *Race, Class and the Apartheid State* (London, 1988).

2. Probably the most critical among the mainstream press was the Johannesburg-based *Rand Daily Mail* (1902) which was closed down by its own holding company in 1985. For the controversial story of the *Mail* see J. Mervis, *The Fourth Estate: A Newspaper Story* (Johannesburg, 1989).

3. N. 1, above.

4. See for example G. Butler's writings and speeches of the time conveniently collected in *Guy Butler: Essays and Lectures, 1949–1991* (Cape Town, 1994). Also editorial comments by Lionel Abrahams (*The Purple Renoster*) and Jack Cope (*Contrast*) as well as *Proceedings of a Conference of Writers, Publishers, Editors and University Teachers of English* (Johannesburg, 1957).

5. A similar view is expressed by Arthur Fula, a coloured Afrikaans writer who has been virtually ignored in Afrikaner canon-building. See recent commentary on his novel of 1954 by H. Willemse, ' "Mens sou nie 'n Bantoe as skrywer vernoem nie" of Arthur Fula se Welwillende Afrikaans: 'n Eerste Verkenning van *Jôhannie Giet die Beeld*', *Stilet*, vol. 4, no. 2 (1992). Fula's novel was translated into English as *The Golden Magnet* (Washington, 1984).

6. See Blum's 'Kaapse sonnette' (Cape sonnets) which, while based on Guiseppe Belli's *Sonetti Romaneschi*, use 'Cape coloured' speech, *Steenbok tot Poolsee* (Cape Town, 1955).

7. For several of Butler's essays, but especially ' "The language of the conqueror on the lips of the conquered is the language of slaves" ' and the later 'English-speaking South Africa: A Cultural Whirlpool', *Guy Butler: Essays and Lectures, 1949–1991*. See M. Kirkwood on 'Butlerism', 'The Coloniser: A Critique of English South African Culture Theory', in P. Wilhelm and J. A. Polley (eds), *Poetry Today: Selected Papers from Poetry '74* (Johannesburg, 1976); N. S. Ndebele, 'The English Language and Social Change in South Africa', *Rediscovery*

of the Ordinary: Essays on South African Literature and Culture (Johannesburg, 1991); and S. Watson's Introduction to *Guy Butler: Essays and Lectures*. Also T. Morphet's review of *A Local Habitation*, 'A Good Joiner in All Respects', *Weekly Mail* (1–7 November, 1991).

8. For a reading of Butler which emphasises poems such as 'On First Seeing Florence' and 'Giotto's Campanile', see D. Maclennan, 'The Poetry of Guy Butler', in M. Chapman, *et al.* (eds), *Perspectives on South African English Literature* (Johannesburg, 1992).

9. For selections from and details of individual volumes see G. Butler (ed.), *A Book of South African Verse* (London, 1959) and M. Chapman (ed.), *A Century of South African Poetry* (Johannesburg, 1981). The introductions offer 'position papers' on South African poetry. For variations on the poetry of the correct English manner, see Francis Carey Slater's 'Dark Folk' poems in which several lamenting Xhosa mouthpieces from the mines and road gangs strike an approximation, in English, of Xhosa oral speech but do not finally divert the poet's sentiments from colonial-paternal regard for Africans as essentially rural, unsophisticated beings, *The Collected Poems of Francis Carey Slater* (Edinburgh, 1957). There is also Anthony Delius' topical satire on South Africa as a country of division between two 'white races', *The Last Division* (Cape Town, 1959).

10. Olsen, *Silences* (New York, 1978); Rich, 'Vesuvius at Home: The Power of Emily Dickinson', *On Lies, Secrets, and Silences: Selected Prose, 1966–1978* (New York, 1979); Donovan, 'Towards a Women's Poetics' in S. Benstock (ed.), *Feminist Issues in Literary Scholarship* (Bloomington, 1987).

11. 'The World of *Contrast*', *English in Africa*, vol. 7, no. 2 (September 1980). See this issue which is devoted to the 'little South African magazine'. Also, G. Gordon, 'Jack Cope and *Contrast*', *Contrast*, vol. 13, no. 1 (June 1980).

12. At least the position was more favourable for whites than for blacks. H. I. E. Dhlomo's *Valley of a Thousand Hills* (1941) was a one-off literary publication by a printing works (Knox Printers) in Durban and Peter Abrahams' slim volume *A Blackman Speaks of Freedom!* (1940) was published (Universal Printers, Durban) by supporters of Congress politics. Neither Abrahams' blunt speech ('Take up your Bible and die!/The world shall know us; we're proud we're black!') nor his understanding of poetry ('A Poet is compelled to take sides . . . Poetry must have a material base') found sympathy in Butler's *A Book of South African Verse* (1959).

13. See for example Rive's *Advance Retreat: Selected Short Stories* (Cape Town, 1983) and *'Buckingham Palace', District Six* (Cape Town, 1986); Matthews' *The Park and Other Stories* (Johannesburg, 1974; expanded ed., 1983); and Nortje's poems *Dead Roots* (London, 1973).
    We may recall that the Hottentot Eve figured in Andrew Geddes Bain's dramatic sketch *Kaatje Kekkelbek* and in Stephen Black's *Love and the Hyphen*. Lewis Sowden's *The Kimberly Train* (1958), Basil Warner's *Try for White* (1959), Athol Fugard's *The Blood Knot* (1963) and *Kanna Hy Kô' Hystoe* (1965) by the coloured Afrikaans writer Adam Small, all locate the drama of apartheid in characters 'trying for white'.

14. See as representative L. Nkosi, 'The Fabulous Decade: The Fifties', *Home and Exile and Other Selections* (London, 1965) and S. Watson, '*Cry, the Beloved Country* and the Failure of Liberal Vision', *English in Africa*, vol. 9, no. 1 (May 1982).

15. One of the most subtle recent defences of Paton is to be found in T. Morphet's

'Alan Paton: The Honour of Meditation', *English in Africa*, vol. 10, no. 2 (October 1983).

16. Bosman, 'The Dorps of South Africa', *South African Opinion* (July 1945).

17. Useful articles on the South African novel include N. Gordimer, 'English-language Literature and Politics in South Africa', in C. Heywood (ed.), *Aspects of South African Literature* (London, 1976) and 'The Novel and the Nation in South Africa', in G. D. Killam (ed.), *African Writers on African Writing* (London, 1973); S. Gray, 'Schreiner and the Novel Tradition', *Southern African Literature: An Introduction* (Cape Town, 1979); L. Nkosi, 'Fiction by Black South Africans', *Home and Exile* (London, 1965); D. Rabkin, 'Ways of Looking: Origins of the Novel in South Africa', *Journal of Commonwealth Literature*, vol. 13, no. 1 (1978); P. Rich, 'Liberal Realism in South African Fiction, 1948–1966', *English in Africa*, vol. 12, no. 1 (May 1985) and 'Romance and the Development of the South African Novel', in L. White and T. Couzens (eds), *Literature and Society in South Africa* (Cape Town, 1986). Refer to Fiction in General Bibliographies as well as to E. Mphahlele's *The African Image* (London, 1962; rev. ed., 1974). A study of a cross-section of novels published in the 1950s might include E. A. Ritter's *Shaka Zulu* (London, 1955), the best-seller about Africa as a place of magnificent barbarians, and Sarah Gertrude Millin's several 'tragedies of blood'. In contrast, miscegenation was located forcibly in social prejudice and legal statute by Abrahams, Paton, Bosman and Daphne Rooke. The last-named produced several serious examinations of South African mores including *A Grove of Fever Trees* (1950), *Mittee* (1951), *Ratoons* (1953), *Wizard's Country* (1957) and *The Greyling* (1962), all published in London. Also worthy of note is Phyllis Altman's 'sociological' perspective on the rural-urban theme, *The Law of the Vultures* (London, 1952).

18. See his review 'Jacobson's Realism Revisited', *Southern African Review of Books* (October/November, 1988). Also, C. Baxter, 'Political Symbolism in *A Dance in the Sun*', *English in Africa*, vol. 5, no. 2 (September 1978).

19. See R. Green, 'Nadine Gordimer's *A World of Strangers*: Strains in South African Liberalism', *English Studies in Africa*, vol. 22, no. 1 (1979).

20. There have been numerous anthologies of South African short stories: a representative selection in English and English translation may be obtained from J. Marquard (ed.), *A Century of South African Short Stories* (Johannesburg, 1978; rev. M. Trump, 1993) and S. Gray (ed.), *The Penguin Book of Southern African Stories* (Harmondsworth, 1985). See also: S. Gray (ed.), *Modern South African Stories* (Johannesburg, 1980); D. Hirson (ed.), *The Heinemann Book of South African Short Stories: from 1945 to the Present* (London, 1994); M. V. Mzamane (ed.), *Hungry Flames and Other Black South African Stories* (London, 1986); A. van Niekerk (ed.), *Raising the Blinds: A Century of South African Women's Stories* (Johannesburg, 1990) and, in Afrikaans, *Vrouevertellers*, 1843–1993 (Cape Town, 1994).

21. See M. Trump, 'The Short Fiction of Nadine Gordimer', *Research in African Literatures*, vol. 17, no. 3 (Fall 1986).

22. See M. Chapman (ed.), *The 'Drum' Decade: Stories from the 1950s* (Pietermaritzburg, 1989) which includes the lengthy essay, 'More Than Telling a Story: *Drum* and its Significance in Black South African Writing', as well as an extensive bibliography. Also: M. Andersson, *Music in the Mix* (Johannesburg, 1982); D. B. Coplan, *In Township Tonight! South Africa's Black City Music and Theatre* (Johannesburg, 1986); M. Nicol, *A Good-looking Corpse* (London,

1991); and the supplement to *Drum* (December/January, 1991/1992), '1951 to 1991 Then and Now: A 40 Year Perspective of Township Life as Seen through the Eyes of *Drum*'.

23. N. 14 above.

24. Mphahlele, 'The Tyranny of Place and Aesthetics: The South African Case', *English Academy Review* (1981). See also E. Mphahlele, 'South African Literature vs The Political Morality', *English Academy Review* (1983).

25. For example, 'Let the People Drink' (March 1956), 'Terror on the Trains' (October 1957), 'Why Our Living's So Tough' (June 1958) and 'Our Hungry Children' (August 1958).

26. See the series 'Lesane' (December 1956–April 1957).

27. The debate about spectacular and ordinary depictions of black life implicitly informed Plaatje's 'anti-colonial' representations of humane African societies in *Mhudi* (1930) and would provoke Chinua Achebe's sharp response to Conrad's *Heart of Darkness*, 'An Image of Africa', *Research in African Literatures*, vol. 9, no. 1 (1978). In reacting to what he referred to as 'surface' images of struggle in the 1980s, Njabulo S. Ndebele called on black writers to seek the complexity of black humanity in the 'ordinary' processes of experience, 'The Rediscovery of the Ordinary: Some New Writings in South Africa', *Journal of Southern African Studies*, vol. 12, no. 2 (April 1986).

28. Nkasa, 'The Life and Death of King Kong', *Drum* (February 1959).

29. Published text, edited by Harry Bloom, *King Kong: An African Jazz Opera* (London, 1961).

30. Nkosi, 'The Fabulous Decade: The Fifties', *Home and Exile*, p. 17.

31. See Huddlestone's *Naught for your Comfort* (London, 1956).

32. See J. Olney, *Tell Me Africa: An Approach to African Literature* (Princeton, 1973) which includes a substantial section on black South African autobiography. Also: R. Rosenblatt, 'Black Autobiography: Life as the Death Weapon', in J. Olney (ed.), *Autobiography: Essays Theoretical and Critical* (Princeton, 1980).

33. Nkosi's oft-quoted observation about black South African writers' displaying the weakness of 'journalistic fact parading outrageously as imaginative literature' appeared in 'Fiction by Black South Africans' (1964), printed in *Home and Exile*. In comments which bear on the 'spectacle'/'ordinary' debate [n. 27 above] Nkosi spoke of 'a type of fiction which exploits the ready-made plots of racial violence, social apartheid, interracial love affairs, etc., without any attempt to transcend or transmute these given "social facts" into artistically persuasive works . . .'. In contrast to what in Nkosi has remained a fairly standard view of good literature, Mphahlele has involved his readers in intricate debate about the key issue of living as a cultural being. For a perceptive critique see J. Watts, *Black Writers from South Africa: Towards A Discourse of Liberation* (London, 1989).

34. See from among Mphahlele's large critical output 'Black and White', *New Statesman* (10 September 1960), '*Fireflames*: Mtshali's Strident Voice of Self-assertion', *Rand Daily Mail* (19 December 1980), 'The Tyranny of Place and Aesthetics: The South African Case', *English Academy Review* (1981), 'South African Literature v The Political Morality', *English Academy Review* (1983), *Poetry and Humanism: Oral Beginnings* (Johannesburg, 1986) and 'Decolonising the Mind', *New Nation* (1–7 November 1991).

35. See various numbers of *Index on Censorship* including vol. 6, no. 3 (May–June 1977) which contains J. Grant's 'Silenced Generation'. Also J. M. Coetzee, 'Censorship in South Africa', *English in Africa*, vol. 17, no. 1 (May 1990); L. Silver, *A Guide to Political Censorship in South Africa* (Johannesburg, 1984); and C. Merrett, *A Culture of Censorship: Secrecy and Intellectual Repression in South Africa* (Cape Town and Pietermarizburg, 1994). Of particular pertinence to literature of the decade, I. Davies, *Writers in Prison* (Oxford, 1990) and D. Foster, *Detention and Torture in South Africa: Psychological, Legal and Historical Studies* (Cape Town, 1987).

36. See C. J. Driver, 'The View from Makana Island: Some Recent Prison Books from South Africa', *Journal of Southern African Studies*, no. 2 (1975). The article examines D. M. Zwelonke's *Robben Island* (London, 1973), Dennis Brutus's *A Simple Lust* (London, 1973), Quentin Jacobsen's *Solitary in Johannesburg* (London, 1973), Hugh Lewin's *Bandiet: Seven Years in a South African Prison* (London, 1974) and Albie Sachs's *The Jail Diary of Albie Sachs* (London, 1966; Cape Town, 1990).

37. Desmond, 'Try Apartheid's Executors for Genocide', *Weekly Mail* (29 May–4 June, 1992).

38. Marcuse, *Eros and Civilization: A Philosophic Inquiry into Freud* (New York, 1962), p. 212.

39. See R. Antonissen, 'Facets of Contemporary Afrikaans Literature', *English Studies in Africa*, vol. 13, no. 1 (March 1970); A. P. Brink, *Aspecte van die Nuwe Prosa* (Cape Town, 1967), *Aspecte van die Nuwe Drama* (Cape Town, 1974); J. C. Kannemeyer, *Opstelle oor die Afrikaanse Drama* (Cape Town, 1970); and J. Polley (ed.), *Die Sestigers* (Cape Town, 1973).

40. Smit's play *Pa Maak vir My 'n Vlieër, Pa* (Dad Make Me a Kite Please, Dad, 1964) was translated into English as *Tomorrow and Tomorrow and Tomorrow* (Johannesburg, 1970). For the other names mentioned here see the biographies.

41. Brink, 'Introduction: A Background to Dissidence', *Mapmakers: Writing in a State of Siege* (London, 1983).

42. Cope, 'Where the Sestigers Came Unstuck', in J. Polley (ed.), *Die Sestigers* (Cape Town, 1973), pp. 149–51.

43. See Rabie, 'Minder Europa, Meer Afrika', in C. Malan (ed.), *Race and Literature/ Ras en Literatuur* (Pinetown, 1987) and 'Afrikaanse Poësie Vandag', *Contrast*, vol. 14, no. 3 (July 1983).

44. See Small, 'Krisis van 'n Swart Sestiger', in J. Polley (ed.), *Die Sestigers* (Cape Town, 1973), pp. 140–48.

45. See K. Goddard and C. Wessels (eds), *Out of Exile: South African Writers Speak* (Grahamstown, 1992). (Interviews with Albie Sachs, Lewis Nkosi, Mbulelo V. Mzamane, Breyten Breytenbach, Dennis Brutus and Keorapetse Kgositsile.) More generally, A. Gurr, *Writers in Exile: The Creative Use of Home in Modern Literature* (Brighton, 1981).

46. See D. Maughan Brown, 'Adjusting the Focal Length: Alex La Guma and Exile', *English in Africa*, vol. 18, no. 2 (October 1991).

47. I have mentioned testimony of Luthuli, Mandela, Desmond, First and Huddleston. There are also the various writings of Mary Benson, in which suppressed lives are given voice, Albie Sachs's *Jail Diary* (1966) which treats the

prison as both image and actuality in impressing upon readers what happens to sensitive minds in the solitary cell, and there is the testimony on humanity and justice by Bram Fischer who, as a Q.C. from a prominent Afrikaner family, was sentenced to life imprisonment for being a leader in the outlawed South African Communist Party: *What I Did Was Right* (London, 1966).

48. Mandela, 'Verwoerd's Tribalism' (1959), *No Easy Walk to Freedom* (London, 1965; 1990), p. 78.

Part Four

Commissioned by the Nation, Commissioned by the Society. Independence, Post-independence

Introduction to Part Four

By the mid-1960s the South African authorities believed that they had cracked down on all effective opposition to apartheid rule. When voices espousing Black Consciousness began to be heard in the last years of the decade, the state initially interpreted the phenomenon as 'ethnic' and therefore not fundamentally at odds with a policy of separating races. The wind of change in the sixties, however, would influence developments in Africa as a whole, and before turning in Part Five to South Africa's long and painful interregnum, I want to look at the impact of decolonisation on literature from the independent states of the region. An implicit question has concerned the relationship between concepts of the nation and those of the society. In retaining a wariness about terms such as nation and national literature, I have been reflecting my own experience of living in a society, in South Africa, which has been fettered by the ruling words, deeds and symbols of an exclusive Afrikaner nationalism. Registering a similar wariness, the philosopher Johan D. Degenaar, whose argument has already been introduced, draws attention to the divisive rather than the cohesive potential of nationalism, and posits the rational, humane activity of the workable society as a check on the tendency of the nation to predicate itself on ethno-cultural mystique.[1]

What is evident in southern Africa, however, is that neither the 'nation' nor the 'society' has achieved any single dominance over the other. If literature in the range of its cultural expression initially accepted a commission, either willingly or under obligation, to articulate the hopes and values of the emergent nation, literature has also been ready to transfer its commission to the social charter. Loyalties, as a result, have clashed with integrities. Some writers have seen the rhetoric of nationhood as a sham while others have continued to invest value in myths of national purpose. Against intermittent resuscitations of the culture at the 'national source', there has been the cool appraisal of societal claims. In testing the synchrony of the nation as symbols in recurrent space and time against the diachrony of the society as change in the forcefield of material relations, writers in the independent states have viewed decolonisation not only as the epiphany of uhuru, but as contiguous and continuing human activity. The tensions have peculiar significance for South Africa which, in trying to turn from the oligarchy of apartheid, has begun to engage in urgent debates about the character of the new nation and the civil society. For those South Africans who desire new national narratives, the literature of decolonisation may provide something of a check on euphoria. For those who fear new national narratives, the literature of decolonisation might just help dispel atavars. Although we can categorise a 'literature of the nation' and a 'literature of the society', the responsibility since independence has been to ask how the functioning society should evaluate the expression of its own independent aspirations. Given that the histories of anti-colonial struggle and nationhood have not been identical in the several countries of the region, the questions and responses will have distinctive 'national' contours.

Note

1. *Degenaar, The Myth of a South African Nation* (IDASA Occasional Paper, Cape Town, 1987).

Chapter 1

Malawi and Zambia: The Writer in the One-party State

Banda and Kaunda

Zambia and Malawi both became independent from Britain at the same time in 1964, and under the similar circumstance of not having had to resort to protracted anti-colonial wars. It might be interesting, therefore, to compare the character and direction of literary activities in these two countries since independence. The histories of Malawi and Zambia – we may note at the outset – reveal key similarities and key differences.[1] The two countries are inhabited by several Bantu-speaking groups: the Chewa is the largest in Malawi, the Bemba in Zambia. As a consequence of there being considerable linguistic diversity in the vernacular languages, both Malawi and Zambia have found the former coloniser's language, English, to be the most serviceable means of national expression. With the Free Church of Scotland having responded to the call of the mid-nineteenth-century explorer David Livingstone, missionary endeavour in Malawi (formerly Nyasaland) provided good educational facilities. Literature in Malawi since independence has emanated largely from university-trained writers who have benefited from vigorous exchanges with British academics based at Chancellor College of the University of Malawi. In Zambia (formerly Northern Rhodesia), by contrast, missionary and cultural life did not feature prominently in a colonising venture that was prompted by Rhodes's efforts to secure mineral rights. With copper as the mainstay of the Zambian economy Britain, which took over the administration of the territory from Rhodes's Chartered Company in 1924, consolidated a pattern in which skilled mining jobs were reserved for white people while Africans gained very little in terms of economic or educational advancement. A line of rail across the copperbelt, neverthe-less, led to a degree of urbanisation, and written literature in Zambia today can be defined broadly by its 'non-university', town bias.

Although the ethnic groups in the region have no sustained history of militarism, colonial settlement led to African nationalist agitation. In

Malawi, which has remained largely rural and agricultural, poll taxes forced peasants on to colonial plantations and in 1915 the Revd John Chilembwe led a violent uprising. The report of his action, together with a biography of the leader, probably accounts for the first extended piece of writing in English by a Malawian: *A Dialogue of Nyasaland: Record of Past Events, Environments & the Present Outlook within the Protectorate*, by George S. Mwase, was discovered in the national archives by the American historian Robert I. Rotberg and, in 1967, edited into the publication *Strike a Blow and Die: A Narrative of Race Relations in Colonial Africa*.[2] The Nyasaland African Congress (NAC) led African opposition to union with Southern Rhodesia and Northern Rhodesia in the white-dominated central African federation (1953–1963). As a result NAC was banned, but re-organised itself into the Malawi Congress Party which after independence would ensure that it became the only political party in a single-party state. With Britain giving way in the early 1960s to African nationalist pressure and releasing the imprisoned leader Dr Hastings Kamuzu Banda, Malawi achieved independence under Banda's firm rule. In pursuing private enterprise and in forming ties with the apartheid government of South Africa including agreements about migrant labouring opportunities for Malawians on the Rand gold mines, Banda brought relative prosperity to sectors of his country. Revered by many of the rural peasantry as the 'father of the nation', the ageing president was resented by many urban people for his conservative, dictatorial methods. Displaying hypersensitivity and paranoia about literature, the arts and even superficial forms of Western modernity such as women's trousers, Banda's all-powerful Censorship Board (set up in 1968) banned, or prohibited for distribution, the work of several prominent Malawian writers including David Rubadiri, Felix Mnthali and Jack Mapanje, as well as work by leading African writers such as Wole Soyinka.[3] Mnthali and Mapanje served time in detention and many Malawian writers lived in exile from Banda's one-party state. Having declared himself president for life in 1971, Banda drew severe criticism from dissident Malawians and humanitarian groups abroad for abuses of human rights that led to the disappearances and deaths of political opponents. Under the pressures of international economic action, Banda reluctantly agreed in 1993 to hold a referendum in which most voters supported multi-party political activity. After the referendum there were outbursts of critical journalism in new, independent newspapers and broadsheets,[4] and as a sign of liberalisation women, though they continue to have little say in public issues, were permitted to wear the latest Western fashions. At democratic elections in 1994 Banda relinquished his 30-year grip on power, and – out of duty rather than commitment – the new democratically elected government charged the former dictator, or the grand old man of independence politics, with violations of human rights. (At the time of writing – in mid 1995 – it seemed unlikely that Banda, who is evidently senile, would ever face his accusers in a courtroom.)

Zambia, too, began its independence as a one-party state, but in 1992 president Kenneth Kaunda stepped down after suffering defeat at the ballot box. Having provided leadership in the United National Independence Party (UNIP) in the 1950s, Kaunda was involved in the massive civil disobedience campaign that brought home to Britain the point about independence, and in his various writings, including his autobiography *Zambia Shall Be Free* (1962), Kaunda has set out his commitment to peace, respect and sharing that is derived from a combination of traditional African virtues and his Christian upbringing. (Kaunda's father was the first African missionary to be sent to the Livingstonea Mission to serve his own Bemba-speaking people.) Referred to as 'Zambian humanism', Kaunda's philosophy provided the guiding principles in attempts to define a sense of nationhood. It also took the form of moral opposition to apartheid rule with a willingness to persuade South Africa, through dialogue, to abandon its racially discriminatory policies and practices. Precept alone, however, was unable to solve Zambia's economic problems. Not being self-sufficient in food and paying the price as a land-locked country for instability in the region as a whole, Zambia has not been helped by depressed markets for copper. The capitalists' retort here is that Kaunda's vaguely socialist programmes were disastrous, particularly in that the Anglo-American Corporation of South Africa was not left sufficiently unhindered to make the copper mines work to maximum efficiency and profit. With IMF structural adjustments demanding austerity measures and export-driven economies, the response by many Zambians was civil unrest, and it was fundamentally on the issue of the economy that Frederick Chiluba defeated Kaunda in an open election. True to his humanism, Kaunda became one of the first leaders in Africa graciously to accept electoral defeat. During Kaunda's lengthy rule no writers were censored by state decree, no writers ended up in prison, and as a result of his speeches on cultural nationalism, Kaunda himself gained the reputation of being a benevolent patron of the arts. Not only have differences in educational and urban opportunities in the two countries left their marks on literary expression, therefore, but perhaps more tellingly there have been two distinct climates for literature in Zambia and Malawi based, respectively, on freedom and repression. The consequences have been both predictable and unpredictable.

Zambian humanism. Stories and journalism

With Zambia having taken great public interest since independence in the question of its national identity, several works have been seen to display a 'Zambian style' that reveals the perceptible influence of Kaunda's humanism.[5] By the 1980s, however, the effects of the philosophy seemed to have become soporific, and a problem for writers was the almost paradoxical one of how to level adverse criticism at the kind leader. In Malawi, the issue of national identity permitted no criticism. As I indicated in my discussion of oral tradition, it was left to the singers of the Malawi Women's League to translate inspirational songs from the anti-colonial campaigns of the 1950s, when Banda was the people's hero, into displays of public adulation for the man who came to be regarded by some as the father and by others – notably by university-trained writers – as a tyrant. In Malawi, writers had to forego allegiances to nation-building and accept the dangerous commission of criticising the authoritarian state.

Prior to independence, literature in Zambia and Malawi had been encouraged in several indigenous languages by the colonial Northern Rhodesia and Nyasaland Joint Publications Bureau, established in 1947. Shortly after independence, the National Education Company of Zambia (NECZAM) in Lusaka was founded with the mission of publishing Zambian books in English and in local languages, and before the poor economy drastically curtailed publishing operations in the mid-1970s, NECZAM had helped launch several books which, together with articles and stories in new literary periodicals, played a role in encouraging a debate about Zambian writing in English.[6] In these works notably by Andreya S. Masiye, Fwanyanga M. Mulukita and Gideon Phiri, the Zambian quality can be defined, stylistically, by the unpretentiousness of the writing and, thematically, by the interest shown in Zambian town life. Social problems are seen to affect both rural people coming to the copperbelt and urban people adjusting to living shoulder to shoulder with other Zambians in the business district, bars and suburbs of Lusaka. The protagonists are nearly all ordinary Zambians for whom communication in English, as Kaunda had stressed, is regarded as an important means of breaking down ethnic divisions and forging new humanistic loyalties. Instead of depicting the epic clashes between Africa and the West that we associate with the first wave of post-independence literature from West and East Africa, Zambian literature in the 1960s and 1970s quickly put behind it the anti-colonial agitation of UNIP's nationalist campaigns and gave the impression of eagerly getting on with the daily routines of living in a non-racial society. Possibly this is a reminder that a fully racialistic struggle never took root in Zambia. Possibly it is also a reminder of the localised 'southern African' character of Zambia's colonial experience. Whereas West Africans, in particular, pitted their native culture against the metropolitan culture of the colonising power, the Zambian eye looked not across the waters to the West – the West was never entirely interested in the limits of this small country – but to the rail link from rural district to copperbelt town. The big journey directed the traveller not to the British or French university, but to the labour markets of Zimbabwe or South Africa. There is little cosmopolitanism in Zambian literature. Neither, however, is there the archaism that lingers not only around numerous missionary-inspired rural/city morality tales, but also around the great cultural themes of things falling apart.

Zambian writing since independence has embraced journalistic, city-wise rhythms, a style anticipated well before independence by the most memorable Bemba-language writer Stephen A. Mphashi who, in a few short novels, had satirised colonial society and the pretensions of Africans who served the system.[7] In turning the conventions of crime and detection to the intrigues and manners of copperbelt life, Mphashi revealed an accurate ear for spoken Bemba as well as for the way English is used and misused in the small mining centres. If in the work of Mphashi and others the journalistic habit – learnt from magazines and newspapers – sometimes leads to cliché and studied 'film talk', we are spared the obscurities of the imitative Eng. Lit. we find in a great deal of late-modernist African writing. In Gideon Phiri's *Ticklish Sensation*, for example, the morality tale of Jojo's growing up in the city is treated with the irreverence of a sexscapade:

> 'Sweeter than honey! How can breasts be sweet at all? How? Here there are people who ate breasts, women's breasts? Could there be such an unthinkable thing? Was I living among cannibals? Were these boys wizards, or were they not?'

The wild, joyous style in its 'send up' of colloquial Zambian English does not, however, overrule the moral intention, and the true 'tickling sensation' is experienced only at the end of the book after the young man is presumably married. Kabwe Kasoma's plays offer a developing popular theatre which, as in *Fools Marry* (1976), appeals directly to 'unsophisticated' audiences in the use of immediately recognisable comic types, set scenes rather than continuous action, and situations of drunkenness and infidelity taken from the streets and hotels of the town. Kasome's purpose is not to laugh at the difficulties of city people, but to indict the industrial copperbelt that has produced the urban conditions.[8] In Kapelwa Musonda's collection of anecdotes, *The Kapelwa Musonda File*, originally published as a weekly column in *The Times of Zambia* and first collected in 1973, the clarity of topical observation points to the moral implicit in most of this literature of non-nationalistic nation-building: that human beings through their folly, or their failure to communicate, or their wayward pursuit of selfish goals are liable to betray what is valuable in Zambian humanism.

There is similarly a national intent in Dominic Mulaisho's novel *The Tongue of the Dumb* (1971), one of the very few Zambian books to have been published outside the country. (Like Kaunda, Mulaisho appears in the Heinemann African Writers Series.) In setting up a conflict between the Christian mission and the African village, Mulaisho focuses not on the expected clash of the West and Africa, but on disunity within each community itself between the forces of order and the forces of confusion, between charity and envy. With the title in its allusion to Isaiah 35 suggesting the fierce vision of what a society could aspire to be, restoration is seen to be possible only when people put their loyalties and obedience to their fellows above the abstraction of principles. In human interchange, the tongue should not be an instrument of evil gossip, but a facilitator through communication of harmony in the societal life. The moral is not a discursive addition to the plot: Mulaisho's incident-packed action shifts swiftly between biblical intonation and conversational ease, and the stylisation of the two worlds of mission and village – neither is 'realistically' presented – benefits the conventions of voluble storytelling. *The Tongue of the Dumb* could be charged with improbabilities of incident and behaviour according to the tenets of minute textual analysis; like so much Zambian writing, however, its strength lies in the fact that its communicative character takes seriously its commission to the unity of the emergent nation. Put simply, *The Tongue of the Dumb* is a good read. When Mulaisho in his second novel, *The Smoke that Thunders* (1979), turned to the political theme of Zambia's independence struggle, he fell into a schematic trap of monsters and saints, in which campaigns of sabotage are related with all the breathlessness of comic-book heroism. The register is certainly inappropriate to the context of the depicted events, and the reader is reminded of a point made by Stewart Crehan in his argument that Kaunda's benevolent patronage has had a stifling effect on radical questioning in the arts.[9] Like Zambian humanism, Mulaisho's *The Smoke that Thunders* is ill at ease with the revolutionary stance: a stance that, in any case, would have been untrue to Zambia's own particular assertion of independence. Kaunda's moral conviction – we are reminded – was built not on guerilla war, but on campaigns of civil disobedience.

Zambian theatre. Dissent and development

In the argument mentioned above Crehan, who is looking specifically at theatre in Zambia, believes artists have been too content to work within Kaunda's old-fashioned, mission-school ideas about morality in art, and too eager not to offend the man who often made promises of state funding for developments in literature and the arts.[10] As a result, many plays at festivals organised by the Zambia National Theatre Arts Association and the National Theatre Association of Zambia have portrayed corrupt bureaucrats, dictatorial chiefs and selfish, hypocritical fathers while carefully avoiding the slightest criticism of the UNIP leadership. Plots have tended to resolve contradictions for the audiences rather than confront audiences with the need to think for themselves, thus implying – Crehan continues – the existence of a beneficent force at work in a world fundamentally governed by a religious attitude and requiring passive dependency from its subjects. If indeed this indicates something of the complacent side of Zambian humanism – translated here into its aesthetic manifestation – then there is scope for radical revisionism in forms of thought and action. We are reminded that, at the polls, Zambians were willing to forgo the past and entrust fresh possibilities, underpinned by very practical-sounding economic arguments, to ex-trade unionist and credit controller, Frederick Chiluba.

Play festivals were encouraged by the state as an important aspect of defining the nation; the commission to criticise the society, however, had long been accepted by Chakwakwe Theatre which owed much of its inspiration to the University Drama Society (Unzadrams), founded in 1966 at the University of Zambia.[11] Regarding the UNIP leadership as national bourgeoisie and Zambian humanism as the bankrupt ideology of an elite class, Chakwakwe emphasised the need to develop what it called a 'truly Zambian theatre for the people'. This would portray the progressive potential of Zambian life including the social problems of the 'ongoing Zambian revolution', the role and status of women in modern society, the conflicts between upper and lower classes, and the importance of self-reliant and organised people in struggles for just agrarian policies and practices. Under the direction of Michael Etherton and Andrew Horn, Chakwakwe in the 1970s attempted to create what Etherton referred to as 'the new aesthetic' by fusing elements in Zambian popular culture, including the songs and dances that had played a part in African nationalist mobilisation in the 1950s, with concepts of 'audience education' from European theatre, such as theatre-in-the-round, street performances, and Brechtian epic actions.[12] It is doubtful whether the fusions of African and Western modes led to a new form in which

'Zambian' elements could be discerned to be predominant. Nevertheless, Chakwakwe's use of Fwemba dances, which had arisen as a vehicle of protest in UNIP's anti-colonial campaigns, to suggest the need for the masses to dismiss the sham of Zambian flag independence was sufficient to provoke the ire of the party leadership. By the end of the 1970s Etherton and Horn, neither of whom was a Zambian citizen, had been deported, and a student production of Kasome's *Black Mamba Two*[13] – a play that showed sympathy for Kaunda's rival Simon Kapwepwe – had been banned by the university authorities who, on the campus, introduced their own forms of censoring commentary that was critical of state policy.

After neighbouring Zimbabwe had became independent in 1980, UNIP could no longer blame all economic shortcomings on the difficulties caused by war on Zambia's borders, and, although Chakwakwa's influence had been curbed by the university, many radical, independent community theatre groups began to infuse the Zambia National Theatre Arts Association with energetic, new criticisms of national themes. Among the activities were popular theatre-for-development projects and dramatised educational campaigns sponsored mainly by aid agencies such as Oxfam and the Frederick Naumann Foundation. The inspirations here were the concepts of theatre education applied by Laedza Batamani in Botswana and by the Kamirüthu community project in Kenya. Theatre-for-development projects, however, are vulnerable to state and business patronage which can be used to curb, rather than to encourage, radical dissent. The rural people at whose enlightenment a great deal of theatre-for-development is aimed, for example, may have been left with highly ambiguous responses to the play *The Solution to the Problem*. Performed by Mwanange Theatre under the sponsorship of the Wildlife Conservation Society of Zambia, the play has a district secretary explain the solution – the problem concerns the need for environmental awareness – to the assembled villagers while the local party hack repeatedly stands up to shout 'One Zambia!', the villagers being virtually compelled to answer in unison, 'One Nation'. By removing the play from its 'working space' in the village and transferring it to the stage as an 'art experience' – the path of several theatre-for-development projects – theatre practitioners of course would have been able to intervene critically in the national theme. On stage, the party hack could have been satirised, or the villagers imbued with rural wisdom. Such art adaptations notwithstanding, the difficulty for utilitarian forms of theatre, which are important in underdeveloped countries, remains how to clarify their own interventions in any debate between the unified nation and the self-analytical society. It should be interesting, in this respect, to see how Zambian theatre, indeed Zambian literature as a whole, responds in the 1990s to the post-Kaunda phase of national and social development.

Malawian writers, censorship and the 'university' style. Poetry from Rubadiri to Mapanje

Regarding Banda's nationhood as gravely flawed, writers who came to prominence through the Writers' Group, at Chancellor College (University of Malawi), gave Malawian literature of the 1970s and 1980s its distinctive character as elaborately-coded social protest.[14] This was evident particularly in the case of poetry. The work of Felix Mnthali, Steve Chimombo, Lupenga Mphande, Frank Chipasula, Jack Mapanje and others reflects the strengths and limitations of the enclosed university community, in which philosophically-thoughtful, richly ironic writing that is removed from the life and rhythms of the street or the village had to assume the burden of opposing state dictatorship. At the same time, we should note that a tradition of subtle, satirical indirection preceded the formation of the Writers' Group. In the earlier Malawian writers David Rubadiri and Legson Kayira, works by both of whom appeared in print in the 1960s, the large themes of Africa encountering the West found expression in ironic, allusive styles of approach. The first version of Rubadiri's frequently anthologised poem 'Stanley Meets Mutesa', for example, used forms of satiric discrepancy in its debt to Eliot's 'Journey of the Magi' while the later version revealed what seemed to be Rubadiri's own increasing disillusionment with the fact that he had been unable to fulfil his mission of 'trying to play the little part I can in contributing towards the reconstruction of my country'.[15] The bitterness nonetheless remains subdued and oblique as in the closing lines: 'The gates of polished reed close behind them/And the West is let in.' As Malawi's first ambassador abroad Rubadiri, who did not return home, found his literary contribution to be unacceptable to his own government. Like Rubadiri, Kayira remained outside Malawi in self-imposed exile as he came to connect his interests generally to Africa rather than specifically to his own country. His novels of the 1960s – *The Looming Shadow* (1967) and *Jingala* (1969) – employ comedies of manners in the treatment of what by then had become the standard preoccupation of modern African literature: the transition from village to urban mores. When Es'kia Mphahlele complained that Kayira did not seem to be 'sure himself where, if at all, his affiliation lies',[16] Kayira would probably have taken the comment as a good sign that he had broken out of parochialism and granted the African setting a universal recognition. Certainly *Jingala* manages to transform its African situation into a deeply felt, complexly human story – Chekhovian in a way – about change that is simultaneously a victory and a defeat.

The old man Jingala, who is symbolic of ancient Africa, has to stand aside for the younger generation. Where Kayira's long absence from Malawi does start telling against him, I feel, is in his next two novels which would be his last contributions to literature, *The Civil Servant* (1971) and *The Detainee* (1974). In trying to turn general post-independence concerns about corrupt bureaucracies to Malawian account, Kayira is unable to capture the brand of his own country's despotism. The novels read like imitations of what had already been accomplished with greater power by Achebe, Ngugi, and others.

What tangible influence writers like Rubadiri and Kayira may have had on a younger generation attached to the Writers' Group is difficult to separate from the broader influence that university study has had on most Malawian literature to have emerged since independence. The common feature is a style that has manifested itself as predominantly 'literary' rather than 'popular'. Although David Kerr and Ian White are correct to note that the dead hand of Eng. Lit. is absent from Malawian poetry, this is not entirely the case.[17] Where Steve Chimombo is at his weakest, for example, is where, as in *Napolo*, he imitates the learned, oracular voice of Okigbo, or Soyinka: 'Napolo has spoken: Life./The Chameleon stopped to consider/a joint in his leg and hesitated.' The result is an African mythological reference that, in a packed, modernist manner, often serves to obscure the point of what is being conveyed. It is refreshing, in contrast, to hear the direct 'statement poetry' with which Frank Chipasula addressed the subject of tyranny as soon as he had fled into exile. Perhaps fearing for his own safety after the appearance of his first volume *Visions and Reflections* (1973), which was immediately banned, Chipasula would remain outside the country. His second volume *O Earth, Wait for Me* (1984) was published in South Africa, and contains several haunting poems about the Malawian police state, including 'A Hanging, Zomba Central Prison', in which a political prisoner as a ritual figure resists his own execution:

> Like a stone he would not die.
> They summoned a hardcore life prisoner,
> placed a rock hammer in his hand
> and ordered him to locate the victim's heart.[18]

In the work of Felix Mnthali and Jack Mapanje, the decision whether to emphasise the 'naming word' or the 'metaphor' also has as much to do with the conditions of dictatorship as with the environment of literary education. Both poets showed a rare ability to guard their words from the state's frontal attack while leaving readers in no doubt as to their commitment to the demise of the tyrannous nation and to the re-constitution of a just society. Mnthali's range includes parodies of the political songs that celebrated Malawi's independence (see the 'Kamuzu' song quoted on p. 43) and dignified arguments in verse about the role the past will have to play in a reconstructed future. Mapanje's *Of Chameleons and Gods* (1981) utilises ironic and sometimes shocking contrasts of idea and style so that even as we hear the cryptic, riddling voice of the ancient gods, we are situated firmly in the sinister environment of Banda's Malawi. The respect the poet grants folk-lore and the mockeries he directs at modern commemorations make the salient point that a huge gulf lies between the ideals of independence and the disillusioning reality. In his adroit use of the rhetorical question, Mapanje both avoids direct condemnation of the state while refusing to flinch from the truth that he believes must be uttered. As he writes in 'A Marching Litany to Our Martyrs (3 March 1971)':

> In the name of our dear brothers dead
> Are we really marching to these tin-drums
> Rattling the skeletons beat of heroic
> Bones long laid asleep?

Both Mapanje and Mnthali were released from spells in prison without reasons being given for their detention. Published in London, Mapanje's *Of Chameleons and Gods* was not approved for circulation in Malawi; individuals, however, were permitted to own the book. Just as Chipasula had to resort to publication outside the country, Mnthali had to rely on NECZAM in Lusaka for the publication of his volume *When Sunset Comes to Sapitwa* (1980). In 1993 Mapanje, who now lives in England, published his second volume *The Chattering Wagtails of Mikuyu Prison*. These sombre yet steely poems offer their author's experience of his own detention (1987–1991) as an act of remembrance for the 'desperate voices of fractured souls': all the political detainees who over the many years suffered under Banda's autocracy.[19]

Malawi's popular voice

The anthology *The Haunting Wind: New Poetry from Malawi* (1992), edited by Anthony Nazombe and published in Malawi, together with a locally published theoretical study by Steve Chimombo, *Malawian Oral Literature: The Aesthetics of Indigenous Arts* (1992), has prompted David Kerr, who was connected to the Writers' Group in its heyday in the 1970s, to ask some pertinent questions about intellectual and literary life in Banda's Malawi.[20] The overriding concerns represented in Nazombe's anthology are – according to Kerr – death, forced partings, crises of identity, disfigurements, physical frustration that is almost masochistic, and the search for meaning in suffering. There are also 'silences' about aspects of living under dictatorship: the result probably of the deliberate exclusion of the direct political responses by writers in exile.[21] Kerr's conclusion is that the gloom of the poetry offers a more accurate barometer of the Malawian mental climate than the 'aesthetic' defined by Chimombo as *ulimbaso*: a negritudinal-inspired concept suggesting a unifying principle in ancient Malawian literature that is supposed to have defied and survived the deracinating effects of colonisation and modernisation. In dwelling on what are by now well-worn colonial and anti-colonial dualities, Chimombo shows a desire to constitute the nation as holistic and life-reverential in its Africanism: qualities that remained a mockery under Banda's rule. Kerr, for his part, would have preferred Chimombo to tackle the social task of 'tracing the dialectics of appropriation and resistance by which oral genres such as song and dance, narrative and dance, have been transformed in post-independence Malawi'.

We are reminded here of the point made earlier on in this study, in the discussion of 'Kamuzu' songs, about the difficulties of imposing intellectual-literary expectations on to popular necessity. Whether we follow Chimombo's 'African intellectual' attempt to trace a single line of tradition from ancient oral expression to modern 'university' poetry or Kerr's 'Western intellectual' penchant for critical disruption, we could end up failing to recover what must surely be a crucial aspect of Malawi's literary voice: vital, contemporary everyday speech which is neither sycophantic nor learned, but which characterises life in the daily round of the villages and the towns. It is an aspect of expression that was muffled by both the state and the university. Yet as Kerr himself reminds us, performance poetry in English and chiChewa at poetry readings, variety shows, and as fillers between plays, remains a common feature of everyday Malawian activity, and Karin Barber mentions the many popular alternatives in Malawian theatre and on radio to philosophically-inclined 'university' plays.[22] Instead of exploring issues in ideologically coherent and progressive ways, the popular social comedy or melodrama may bolster stabilities and, therefore, be safe from censorship. But the popular mode also takes audiences into its confidence and gives action and voice to the familiar situations of daily life in what up to very recently was a fearful, death-like country. In the context of popular requirement, we may recollect James Gibbs's experience at the University Drama Festival in 1976 of staging Chimombo's play *The Rainmaker* (1978).[23] This ambitious, literary attempt at dramatising the traditional rain-making cult of Chewa religion became a syncretic event involving the old and the new. During the theatrical performance, dancers from the area around the university took over the rehearsed stage action with their own 'real' rituals of identity and meaning that have survived in adapted, modern form. What-ever the intellectuals might say, it is only when the popular will rejects dictatorship that a new society in Malawi is likely to lay the foundations for a new nation. The process of democratisation now given its chance presents Malawian writers, as responsible citizens, with immense chal-lenges.

Notes

1. See D. Birmingham and P. M. Martin (eds), *History of Central Africa*, 2 vols (New York, 1983); M. Chanock, *Law, Custom, and Social Order: The Colonial Experience in Malawi and Zambia* (Cambridge, 1985); S. J. Ntara, *The History of the Chewa*[t] (Wiesbaden, 1973); B. R. Rafael, *A Short History of Malawi* (Limbe, 1980); D. T. Williams, *Malawi: The Politics of Despair* (New York, 1978).

2. Cambridge, Mass., second ed., 1970. See also S. M. Made *et al.*, *100 Years of Chichewa in Writing, 1875–1975* (Zomba, 1976).

3. See H. McIlwraithe, 'Dr Banda's Banned Books', *Index on Censorship*, vol. 8, no. 6 (1979).

4. Banda stunted journalism: the only newspapers were the government-owned *Daily Times* and *Malawi News*. After the referendum in 1993 *The Monitor* began to carry a weekly column, 'Know your History', which focuses on Banda's misdeeds and *The Nation* epitomises a new brand of journalism: powerful exposés with crude but effective graphics.

5. For an account of the 'Zambian style', see J. Reed, 'Zambian Fiction', in G. D. Killam (ed.), *The Writing of East and Central Africa* (London, 1984), 'A Zambian Literature?', *New Writing from Zambia*, no. 2 (1966); A. S. Masiye, 'Zambia's Literary Quest', *The Jewel of Africa*, vol. 2, nos. 3–4 (1970); M. R. Ward, 'Zambia', in A. S. Gérard (ed.), *European-Language Writing in Sub-Saharan Africa, Vol. 2* (Budapest, 1986).

6. See the journals *New Writing in Zambia* (1964) and *The Jewel of Africa* (1968); F. M. Mulikita's collection of stories *A Point of No Return* (1968); A. S. Masiye's novel *Before Dawn* (1971); G. Phiri's novel *Tickling Sensation* (1973); P. Zulu's volume of poetry *A Sheaf of Gold* (1971); L. Tembo's *Poems* (1972); and the anthology of stories *Voices of Zambia* (1971).
   Andreya S. Masiye had previously produced a radio play in English, *The Lands of Kazembe*, which was broadcast in 1957 and published in 1973, and which tells of the Portuguese explorer Francisco de Lacerda whose trip to the Zambezi river and negotiations with the Lunda king Kazembe are often regarded as the inauguration of modern Portuguese imperialism.

7. See D. P. Kunene's favourable review, 'An Analysis of Stephen A. Mphashi's *Uwauma Nafyala*' (He who Beats his Mother-in-Law, 1955), in B. Lindfors and U. Schild (eds), *Neo-African Literature and Culture: Essays in Memory of Janheinz Jahn* (Wiesbaden, 1976). Other writing by Mphashi includes *Uwakwensho Bushiku* (He who Leads you through the Night, 1955) and *Cekesoni aingila Ubusoja* (Jackson becomes a Soldier, 1960).

8. M. Etherton, 'The Dilemma of the Popular Playwright: The Work of Kabwe Kasoma and V. E. Musinga', in E. D. Jones (ed.), *African Literature Today No. 8*, (London, 1976). Kasoma's *Fools Marry* is a NECZAM publication.

9. Crehan, 'Patronage, the State and Ideology in Zambian Theatre', *Journal of Southern African Studies*, vol. 16, no. 2 (June 1990). Also: 'Fathers and Sons: Politics and Myth in Recent Zambian Drama', *New Theatre Quarterly*, vol. 3, no. 9 (February 1987).

10. For example, the Message from his Excellency the President of the Republic of Zambia, *Zambia Arts Festival Handbook* (1967).

11. Michael Etherton played an important role in encouraging theatre activity: see his brief article 'Zambia – Popular Theatre', *New Theatre Magazine*, no. 12 (1972) and 'Indigenous Performance in Zambia', *Theatre Quarterly*, vol. 3, no. 10 (1973), an issue which contains also D. Pownall's 'European and African Influences in Zambian Theatre'. See also *Ngoma*, vol. 3, no. 1 (1989) and several copies of the *Chakwakwa Review*.

12. *Chakwakwe Review* (1971).

13. Part of an epic trilogy on the life of Kuanda which has not been published in full.

14. See A. Calder, 'Under Zomba Plateau: The New Malawian Poetry', *Kunapipi*, vol. 1, no. 2 (1979); D. Kerr and L. White, 'New Writing from Malawi', *Afriscope*, vol. 3, no. 12 (1973); A. Roscoe, *Uhuru's Fire: African Literature East and South* (Cambridge, 1977); for extended discussion on poetry, and for useful overview, A. S. Gérard, 'Malawi', in Gérard (ed.), *European-Language Writing in Sub-Saharan Africa, Vol. 2*.

15. 'The Theme of National Identity in East African Writing', in K. L. Goodwin (ed.), *National Identity* (Melbourne, 1970). The early version was published by S. Okechukwu Mezu, 'The Origins of African Poetry', in J. Okpaku (ed.), *New African Literature and the Arts* (New York, 1970). The final version was printed by G. Okara, *et al.* (eds), *Poetry from Africa* (Oxford, 1968). For commentary see L. W. Brown, 'The Historical Sense: T. S. Eliot and Two African Writers', *The Conch*, vol. 3, no. 1 (1971) and D. E. Herdeck, *African Authors* (Washington, 1973). (Herdeck compares the two versions of Rubadiri's poem.)

16. Mphahlele, *The African Image* (London, 1962; rev. ed., 1974), p. 256. For extended commentary on Kayira, see A. Roscoe, *Uhuru's Fire*, pp. 215–25.

17. 'New Writing from Malawi', *Afriscope*, vol. 3, no. 2 (1973), pp. 54–9. The Department of English of the University of Malawi had been founded in 1964 and students' literary endeavours were encouraged by gifted expatriate teachers such as David Kerr, Lan White, James Gibbs, Angus Calder and Adrian Roscoe.

18. See A. Nazombe, 'Poetry and Liberation in Central and Southern Africa: *When My Brothers Come Home*, Frank Chipasula', in E. Ngara and A. Morrison (eds), *Literature, Language and the Nation* (Harare, 1989).

19. See Mapanje, 'Censoring the African Poem: Personal Reflections', in K. Holst Petersen (ed.), *Criticism and Ideology* (Uppsala, 1988). Also: 'Of Chameleons and Clowns: The Case of Jack Mapanje', in L. Vail and L. White, *Power and the Praise Poem: Southern African Voices in History* (Charlottesville and London, 1991).

20. Kerr, *Southern African Review of Books* (September/October 1992).

21. Malawian poets are also represented in A. Maja-Pearce (ed.), *The Heinemann Book of African Poetry in English* (London, 1990).

22. Barber, 'Popular Arts in Africa', *African Studies Review,* vol. 30, no. 3 (September 1987), pp. 44–6. According to Barber 'popular companies almost immediately found a style of theatre which was markedly different from that of the university plays' as collected for example in J. Gibbs's *Nine Malawian Plays* (Limbe, 1976).

23. Gibbs's 'Theatre in Malawi', *Odi*, vol. 2, no. 1 (1977); reprinted in *Afriscope* (November–December 1977). On development theatre see D. Kerr, 'Community Theatre and Public Health in Malawi', *Journal of Southern African Studies*, vol. 15, no. 3 (April 1989). Also: J. Linstrum, *Travelling Theatre in Malawi* (London, 1969).

Chapter 2
Angola and Mozambique. National Ideals and Pragmatic Realities

The generation of the 1950s. Neto, Jacinto, Craveirinha, de Sousa, and others

When Angola and Mozambique became independent in 1975, a burst of publishing activity ensured the return to print – in the original Portuguese and in translated editions – of a fully fledged literature of independence.[1] In poetry, fiction, testimonies and histories writers had been defining the ideology and sentiments of protest, resistance and liberation. The first phase, in the late 1940s, involved the revolt of assimilado intellectuals in conjunction with the small, but defiant, publishing activities that I mentioned in the earlier section on the Angolan and Mozambican past. The second phase, in the 1960s, saw writers of combat composing poetry in the guerilla camps and on the battlefields. The third has begun to involve critical revaluations of the heroic myths of the independence wars. Many writers had links with organisations that regarded cultural subjugation as an integral part of economic subjugation: a point which I have already introduced. As Samora Machel, Frelimo leader and first president of independent Mozambique, emphasised, colonialism was to be opposed not primarily by recourse to negritudinal revindication but by recourse to Marxist class analysis. 'The unity of the Mozambican nation and Mozambican patriotism,' Machel maintained, 'is the essential compound of, and we emphasise, anti-racism, socialism, freedom and unity'[(t)]. Ideally, there should no longer be Makonde and Shangane, Nyanja and Ronga, or any of the other numerous groups in the vast ex-Portuguese colony, but only ideologically progressive Mozambicans.[2]

Having occupied important positions in the nationalist guerilla movements – MPLA in Angola, and Frelimo in Mozambique – several writers who had been imprisoned by the Portuguese, or who had been living in exile, returned to their native countries at independence and assumed posts in the new governments. This correlation between cultural expression and political resistance signals the peculiar strengths of Angolan and Mozambican literary nationalism, but also anticipates the difficulties writers would have in adapting to the fact that the nations they had envisioned as anti-racist and socialist were unable to consolidate themselves as working societies. Instead, the two countries were pulled into the ruinous circumstances of cold-war power struggles that accentuated their own susceptibilities to internal divisiveness. In fact, civil wars continued into the 1990s, and the ongoing strife in territories where illiteracy is widespread has not been conducive to a steady literary output. Despite efforts particularly by the União dos Escritores Angolanos (Union of Angolan Writers, founded in 1975) to keep alive intellectual debate and to spread literacy and education through the publication of cheap 'pocket books', literature in Angola and Mozambique has developed little beyond its commitment to the independence struggles: a commitment that should have justified itself finally in 1975 with the downfall of the metropolitan Portuguese dictatorship. Almost twenty years later, however, it remains tempting for writers, critics and readers to return to impassioned outbursts in praise of the anti-colonial revolution rather than adjusting to the difficulties of living in countries that since independence have experienced severe problems of civil disintegration. In short, the complicated, messy histories of Angola and Mozambique could be seen to have strained the credibility of any rhetoric of liberation and, from the vantage point of the 1990s, to have caused the literature of the anti-colonial struggle with its high ideals of a socialist future to be dismissed at best as naïve, at worst as untrue. This would be to do an injustice, however, to a body of literature that has retained the insight, complexity and range to provoke interpretative questions about national ideals and pragmatic realities.

After the Portuguese withdrawal from its African territories the MPLA, which is urban-based around Luanda, predominantly Mbundu in its ethnic grouping, and supported by a radical intellectual elite, found itself opposed in Angola by rival guerilla movements, the FNLA (rural, ethnically Bakongo) and UNITA (rural, ethnically Ovimbundu). In seizing control of the state, the Marxist-Leninist MPLA became the victim of larger forces in international politics. With UNITA downplaying its ethnic loyalties in a country in which the Ovimbundu is the majority group and espousing capitalist opposition to Marxism, financial and military support was forthcoming from the United States and its willing surrogate South Africa while the MPLA, in turn, received backing from the Soviet Union and its client state Cuba. In Mozambique, Frelimo's Marxist Leninism foundered on several interrelated difficulties: an economy left bankrupt by the departing Portuguese; rigid application of European-derived revolutionary theory that in important respects was not appropriate to the ills of a poverty-stricken, underdeveloped country; the destabilising tactics of South Africa's economic and military interventions; and widespread famine in a drought-stricken territory. In trying to regulate agricultural supply, the people's government sometimes had to come down hard on the people: particularly on the rural peasantry who, in the idealised images of anti-colonial literature, are depicted as the heirs of the revolution. In country areas, the vaguely capitalist-supported Renamo movement — aided, militarily, first by Rhodesia, then by South Africa — was able to sustain a long and destructive campaign against Frelimo. By the end of the 1980s, of course, super-power rivalries had ceased to be a significant factor in the region and, like the former Soviet Union, Angola and Mozambique are being pushed into adopting forms of market economy and multiparty democracy. Having been defeated at the ballot box in elections supervised by the United Nations in 1992, UNITA refused to concede defeat to the MPLA and in continuing to wage war revealed itself not so much capitalist as Ovimbundu nationalist. By mid 1995 both UNITA and MPLA had begun to accept the fact that a peaceful future would require their mutual co-operation. Tolerance, however, is virtually non-existent, and one was reminded, tragically, of the key role independent journalism has played in Angola, in intellectual life, when the renowned journalist Ricardo de Melo — of the 'post-war' *Imparcial Fax* — was assassinated in Luanda presumably for adopting a less than laudatory view of the ruling MPLA's attempts to secure peace. In Mozambique, which is dependent almost entirely on the World Bank and the IMF, voters in 1995 elected to government a Frelimo majority with a Renamo opposition: the West's recipe for Africa — market-driven democracy — seemed not to be open to debate. As there are few resources to enable Mozambique to generate its own middle-class, economic momentum (Angola, in contrast, is potentially wealthy in oil), the result might be another nation in name rather than in actuality. It is in the context of such depressing scenarios, in which little of note has been written since the mid 1970s, that I wish to pursue the question of what status the literature of the independence struggles may be granted today. Of crucial importance to its status is the matter of its 'Africanness'.

When UNITA leader Jonas Savimbi talks wildly of restoring Angola to Africans — he probably means to the majority Ovimbundu — he is not simply threatening 'ethnic cleansing' against the Mbundu but, whether he would articulate it in this way or not, he is alluding to the Westernised influences that have infiltrated the Mbundu-based MPLA around the city of Luanda. As I have already indicated, the result has been a literary output heavily dependent upon assimilado intellectuals many of whom were of mixed race, rather than African, and were steeped in European thought, theory and style. In looking briefly at poetry by assimilado intellectuals in the 1950s, I mentioned Luis Bernardo Honwana's concern that mixed-race writers like Noémia de Sousa and José Craveirinha were more European than African, the implication being that their work was therefore inauthentic. Responding as he was to his youthful sense of

African pride, Honwana, an African assimilado, came close at the time to phrasing his difficulties in racialistic terms: most intellectuals were mulattos, not 'genuine' Africans. Although careful to see class not race as the crucial factor Eduardo Mondlane, whose argument has already been introduced, would have had some sympathy with Honwana's views that despite 'European' gains in the writing of assimilado intellectuals, something 'African' had been lost along the intellectual path, whether the writers were Africans such as Agostinho Neto (in Angola) and Honwana (in Mozambique) or mulattos like Alexandre Dáskalos, António Jacinto and Costa Andrade (from Angola) and de Sousa, Craveirinha and Marcelino dos Santos (from Mozambique). Accordingly Mondlane, as I mentioned, granted Craveirinha his European advantage: a knowledge of Western history and revolutionary thinking which contributed to his skills in analysing a political situation. At the same time, Mondlane identified what he regarded as Craveirinha's difficulties as a member of an elite class in connecting with the wider Mozambican population. An artistic-intellectual alienation – Mondlane concluded – manifested itself not only in Craveirinha, but generally in writing by those who came to be known as the 'generation of the 1950s'. The alienation was seen to have taken the form of a compensatory reliance on symbolic images of black Mother Africa and idealised, other-worldly depictions of an African past. In reminding his readers that resistance to Portuguese colonialism did not have to rely solely on radicalised European alternatives, Mondlane turned his attention to African tradition in the forceful expressiveness of the oral voice. During the guerilla wars, for example, words of ridicule, anger and solidarity, as resistance matter, had been smuggled into popular Chope songs while European images were 'bastardised' in Makonde carvings. In contrast to the firm, unambiguous responses of the indigenous culture, Mondlane identified eloquent self-pity as the predominantly 'un-African' aspect of assimilado protest: as few of these intellectuals had experienced forced labour, they tended to read their own intellectualised reactions into the mind of the African miner or labourer.[3]

Mondlane's argument is a valuable check on any temptation by the Western-trained critic to predicate Angolan and Mozambican literature entirely on the Portuguese-language writers of the relatively elite assimilado class. Nevertheless, Mondlane in his reaction to Eurocentric tendencies is too quick – I think – to underplay the mixture of Africa and Europe that gives assimilado writing its distinctive accent. What is memorable about the generation of the 1950s is its ability, in the passion of simple words, to express re-affirmations of Africa as the spiritual home and context of the future nation, while simultaneously examining the causes of the suffering inflicted upon ordinary Angolans and Mozambicans in forced labour on the Portuguese-owned plantations or, under contract, on the South African gold mines. As Antonio Jacinto writes in 'Contract Worker':

Who makes the maize grow
and the orange groves blossom
– Who?

Who provides wealth for the boss to buy
machinery, cars, women
and heads of blacks for the motors?

Who makes the white prosper,
have a big belly – have cash?
– Who?

And the singing birds
the streams meandering with joy
and the strong wind through the woods
will answer:
        – 'Contract wor-r-r-ker . . .'[t]4

The economic insights are captured in an accessible style. As this English translation tries to suggest, words act as functional naming devices even as they carry the charge of emotive associations: the questions not only invite answers in the public place, but help dramatise the life history of ordinary people under exploitative labour practices. If all this can be related to European-derived theories of politics and anti-art (clearly Brecht's rejection of 'obfuscatory' metaphor in favour of plain speech is an important principle), then the Marxism with its popular drive to rehabilitate the economically oppressed is not entirely at odds with an African humanism: a respect for the sociable potential of the native inhabitants of the land.

   In fact, Modlane's sensitivity to indigenous African claims owed a great deal to his own Marxist understandings of the ordinary person's oppression in class societies. Appropriately, some of the most striking poems by assimilados in the 1950s – like Neto's 'Kinaxixi'[t] and Jacinto's 'The Big Match'[t] – introduce intricate thought on African freedom into the apparently non-political activities of people going about the routines of their day in the streets, parks and open lots of the cities Luanda (Kinaxixi is a neighbourhood of Luanda) and Lourenço Marques (now Maputo). Having recollected the boys with whom he used to play football ('with a rag football/well tied in string')[t] Jacinto effortlessly transforms his memories of childhood into an adult's parable – African oral tale or Brechtian moral fable? – about another big match: the time when all those who now suffer in the isolation of exile, prison, or political despair will again be able to meet as equals as they did in the innocence of their young football days. Despite Modlane's observations, poetry by assimilados has never been primarily about self-pity; rather, the poetry has imbued the identifiable experiences of many Angolans and Mozambicans, whether Africans or mulattos, with consideration and feeling.

Poetry of combat, 1960–1975

It is a fact of political and literary circumstance, nonetheless, that few assimilado poets of the 1950s were read by people in the native countries, and in discarding the book for the pamphlet, and the art product in the permanence of print for the immediacy of oral performance, poets of combat such as Jorge Rebelo and Marcelino dos Santos tried to take their poems to actual people in the guerilla camps. Instead of lament there is revolutionary fervour: nothing is redundant in the vocabulary, nothing blurred in the imagery. As Rebelo puts it in 'Poem', only the simplest words are sufficiently dignified to record the suffering and hero-ism of his comrades: ' "Here my mouth was wounded/because it dared to sing/my people's freedom" '[t]. Similarly Mutimatí Barnabé João's 'I, the People'[t] – a sequence of twenty-seven poems which he bequeathed to the collective authorship of the Mozambican people – strips away romantic imagery and allusions in a manner reminiscent of attacks by European 'anti-poets' on bourgeois tradition. The trope of nature is transferred, accordingly, to the service of scientific production as revo-lutionary thinking aims to reconstruct the countryside after independence: 'To seize the wind and take its strength into Production'[t].[5]

When it conveys its point most forcefully, this poetry of utter clarity – a form of people's labour – has a vision that is concrete and realisable in the actions of Angolans and Mozambicans' moving from defeat to a new conception of the human being: ideologically clear-sighted, commit-ted to the workings of the emerging, victorious nation. Poems that are made of naming words, however, are deceptively easy to write or to orate, and the consequence has been many facile imitations of the 'combat style'. It is more difficult, of course, to imitate the earlier assimilado poetry which in its denunciations of colonialism, its compassion for the exploited worker, and its thoughts and theories of change, has attachments to wider mental landscapes than does the poetry of revolutionary solution. The conclusion, therefore, could be that as Angola and Mozambique begin to experience the complex adjustments of living societies, the assimilado literature of the 1950s will be found to be of greater durability and interest than will the more strictly-directed literature of combat. But we should desist from such an elevation of one kind of response above the other. Rather, the voices of the independence struggle, whether ideal-ised or pragmatic, are a reminder that Portuguese colonialism never defeated intelligence and creativity among Mozambicans and Angolans whose literature speaks of a power to resist evil. This is the common factor whether we are attending to assimilado poetry, the poetry of combat, or the popular Chope songs that Mondlane urged us not to forget:

> We are still angry; it's always the same story
> The oldest daughters must pay the tax
> Natanele tells the white man to leave him alone.[t]6

Without any alteration to the rhythm or tone, the phrase 'white man' in this Chope song could be replaced by any other ruling name. If such songs continue to be necessary, then the future government will have failed, and literature will have to renew its dissident intent.

Storytelling and local speech. Vieira to Couto

As I have been suggesting, we do not have to deny the validity of national aspiration as we consider commissions to the less than ideal society. What is important is a willingness to contemplate seriously the kind of self-criticism that saw the ruling MPLA endorse the publication of Pepetela's controversial novel *Mayombe* (1980). Set against the MPLA's offensive in the Cabinda region (in the Mayombe forest), the action displays Pepetela's grasp of difficult, sometimes divisive issues behind the national images of unity. Having been a commander in the guerilla movement at the time the book was written in the last years of the war, Pepetela lends his characters lengthy, highly intellectualised, and always thoroughly absorbing dialogues about regionalism, tribalism, class conflict, and the place of the *mestiço*, or mulatto, in the nationalist cause. Possibly the explicit love scenes between the guerilla leader and the fiancée of one of his younger comrades are meant to underline the point that behind ideological prin-ciples are fallible human beings. Unfortunately, the love scenes become somewhat self-indulgently 'male' in their vicariousness. What is memor-able about *Mayombe*, which was translated into English under the same title in 1983, is its ability to dramatise a theoretical debate about political cause and commitment in the 'aesthetic' equivalent of the credible human story. Another re-examination of liberation mythology – this time directed at the later civil conflict between MPLA and UNITA – occurs in Sousa Jamba's *Patriots* (1990). Written in English through the eyes of a young man who follows his 'father's wisdom' and joins UNITA, the novel, which carries its central irony in its title, is an indictment of all who would commit atrocities in the name of love for a country. In neither of these two Angolan stories has the heroic mode of revolutionary writing turned dystopian; rather, war has become the subject of sustained scrutiny. In contrast, there is the earlier novella by José Luandino Vieira, *The Real Life of Domingos Xavier*[t] (1978; manuscript completed, 1961), in which Xavier's death at the hands of the Portuguese political police (PIDE) has the effect of elevating a story of martyrdom above the constraints of realism. What we are asked to consider are the greater truths of fable: Xavier's spirit is invested in the spirit of the local community which, in its resilience, triumphs over the colonial regime.

As *The Real Life of Domingos Xavier* suggests, Vieira's purpose in the early years of the MPLA struggle was not so much critical scrutiny as the affirmation of the Angolan people's right to dignity and freedom. Despite this, his stories have the potential to travel beyond a particular phase of the national struggle towards any future civil society. This is because Vieira manages to bring to vivid life the *musseque* (shantytown) hubbub of the Angolan urban scene. In his collection of three longish stories *Luuanda*[t] (1980; 1964), the character depictions are neither heroic nor down-graded. Rather, we are placed firmly in the company of astute though vulnerable people who, in fusions of kiMbundu and Portuguese, retain their distinctive personality traits while capturing a creolised 'collective speech'. Although the subsequent civil war has accentuated ethnic tensions and should make us cautious about notions of Angolan unity, Russell G. Hamilton's comments that Vieira's 'Luanda . . . stands as a greater legacy to Angolan nation-building than any number of revindicatory, high-flown poems of cultural nationalist bent'[7] continues to have value in pointing to what Vieira's stories were attempting to achieve. Schooled in the literary influences of Brazilian neo-realism and modernism, in which the strange incident may suddenly disrupt the prosaic rhythms of life, Vieira, an MPLA activist, a former political prisoner, and in 1990 president of the Writers' Union of Angola, is at ease not only with the kiMbundu language – he himself grew up in the *messeques* of Luanda – but with the rich resources of kiMbundu oral storytelling. It is a story-telling tradition that includes fictions (*misoso*) arising from the imagination: their object, to quote Héli Chatelain, being 'less to instruct than to entertain, and to satisfy the aspirations of the mind in its capacities for the marvellous and supernatural'.[8] Utilising the opening and closing formulas of the oral tale, personifying the setting so that the natural elements seem to reinforce the mood of the human drama, and affecting the intimate, colloquial delivery of a 'community storyteller', Vieira twists the most mundane situation – an argument over the ownership of an egg, for example – into spirals of pathos and comedy that encourage our sympathy for the vanities small people employ to cope with a hard life. The biting satire is reserved for figures of authority who remain identifiable in any society: the bully, the tout, the extortionate landlord, the corrupt party official. In their creolised language and form, the stories are paradigmatic of Vieira's desire to break down divisions between Europeans and Africans as well as between the 'classes' of Angolan society. When the collection *Luuanda* first appeared in 1964, however, Vieira was a political prisoner, and in awarding his stories a prize the Portuguese Society of Writers found itself pressured by the Salazar regime into closing down. Thirty years later the stories are a reminder to the countries of southern Africa, where Vieira is becoming better known as a writer, that ordinary people will continue to need their tales of survival and dream: that societies which lose touch with the humblest voices of their communities are likely to be little more compassionate than nations which invest more in unifying symbols than in the bread and butter of civilian life.

This observation may hold, generally, for the role of storytelling in countries struggling to find new identities and values. I am not suggesting that Vieira can easily be understood in semi-literate communities. Rather, his popularising intention is signalled in his ability to turn literary erudition to the subject of ordinary life in apparently artless tales. In fact, his practice could be said to have anticipated Costa Andrade's exhortation to the Writers' Union of Angola in 1979 that writers 'lower their sights'. By this Andrade meant that even though Angolan writers had their origins in the urban middle classes and their education in elite European traditions, they should strive ideologically, imaginatively and sympathetically to take account of the real problems of the people around them. Illiteracy is high, for example, and potential readers are going to have to be found among school pupils, students and literate workers. It is the accessibility of everyday events, the voices of people talking, and the ever-absorbing relationships of African life in conditions unconducive to high literary culture that link Vieira's stories to those of the writer he encouraged in Tarrafal concentration camp, Uanhenga Xitu, who was also at the time a political prisoner. Xitu's *The World of 'Mestre' Tamoda*[t] (1989; 1974), which draws on the kiMbundu *misoso*, is a delightfully comic-serious story of the young anti-hero who returns to his village packed with big words learnt in Luanda and falls foul of the Portuguese authorities. The point is that dictatorships fear words, especially when they do not understand them, and in making his theme 'the pleasure of words' as a liberation Xitu – an African – offers a subtle but telling variation on Vieira's created language. (Vieira is mixed race.) *The World of 'Mestre' Tamoda* flouts pure kiMbundu in order to capture 'poorly spoken' Portuguese not as a colonial confirmation of *Africano* inferiority, but as an act of native defiance. The question of what kind of spoken and written Portuguese will prevail in Angola and Mozambique and what the future will hold for the indigenous languages are issues of clear concern to both Vieira and Xitu.[9] A similar concern is evident in the stories of their contemporary from Mozambique, Luis Bernado Honwana.

Born into the assimilado class, Honwana – an African-Mozambican – produced his only collection of stories, *We Killed Mangy-Dog*[t] (1969; 1967), when he was barely out of school and shortly before he was gaoled for his Frelimo activities.[10] Using standard Portuguese as his linguistic base, Honwana modifies syntax and includes phrases in his native Ronga so as to capture the inflexion of local speech. Writing in an authoritarian system, he favoured forms of parable in which some apparently non-political event illuminates a wider situation of oppression. In the title story, for example, the Senhor Administrador casts around belligerently after losing at cards for an object on which to vent his anger. With the irony proceeding by way of deflation, he orders the urchins hanging around the club to shoot a stray, mangy dog. Conditioned by the colonial ethos, the urchins deflect their own qualms about shooting the dog for no apparent reason by insulting one another according to their precise racial designations: from the white Portuguese to the native *Africano*. Like the Chope song I introduced earlier, Honwana's stories have the capacity to retain their impact in circumstances that promote untrammelled power. Their particularity identifies people who are threatened because of their race.

In encouraging the parable-like story to transfer itself from the colonial past to the independent present, however, we need not simply invoke the universality of human nature. Nor need we suggest that prejudice, exploitation and injustice are the inevitable elements of any social system. Rather it is that Honwana's stories in their penetrating understanding of people's reactions to colonial life implicitly call for a generous mind and the need for society to turn away from behaviour that is damaging to human dignity. My earlier point, nevertheless, remains valid: writers in Angola and Mozambique have not found it easy to direct their criticism at the current scene particularly as this might involve their having to question their own commitments to the new nation born of guerilla struggle and solidarity. Honwana, for example, in 1990 resigned his post as minister of culture in the Frelimo government citing a contradiction between holding high office – 'telling people what to do' – and writing fiction, 'which in most cases implies intrinsically being on the side of the dispossessed'.[11] Two writers who since independence have succeeded in retaining their loyalties to the party while turning a critical eye on social behaviour are Manuel Rui from Angola and Mia Couto from Mozambique. Rui, who served in the MPLA, has returned to academic life. So has Couto who, as a journalist, held the position as director of the Mozambican Information Agency (AIM) and editor of the official daily newspaper *Noticias*.

In subjecting folkloric elements to literary experimentation, Rui and Couto have both created styles that are reminiscent of South American magical realism. The key element is abundant invention put to social purpose. In Rui's novella *Quem Me Dera Ser Onda* (Oh, To Be an Ocean Wave!, 1982), for example, the symbol has unerring cultural resonance: the story of a pig that a Luanda family are fattening for slaughter in their seventh-floor city flat is permitted extravagance at the same time as it reflects on questions of rapid socio-cultural transition in the independent country. For Couto the symbol has eerie, realistic echoes in the story of an ox that explodes with an apparent spontaneity ('The Day Mabata-bata Exploded'). We soon learn that we are not inhabiting the realms of a grotesque folk-tale. Instead, the harsh world of a poverty-stricken childhood is brought home to the little cowherd, whose uncle will not grant him his dream of being allowed to go to school. The exploding ox is 're-situated' in the war-torn reality of Mozambique, as soldiers trample across the peasants' fields and tear away the film of folk magic with the news that the ox had been deliberately mined with explosives. The systematic violence and impoverishment of a country locked in civil strife between Frelimo and Renamo is felt everywhere in Couto's stories, and magical realism becomes a means of both coping with disaster and freeing the imagination from the poverty of life without hope. As a collection of fourteen stories Couto's *Voices Made Night*[t] (1990; 1986) is cunningly arranged to suggest the intrusion of habit and convention, whether in the form of peasant wisdom, military dictatorship, or Marxist one-party dictat, in the untidy, livable, unconquerable behaviour of people whatever their colour, class, or political persuasion. By erasing the actualities of time and place, Couto lets his criticism of peasant life, the colonial past, and the 'Frelimo' present drift towards current states of affairs: the veiled warning to Frelimo is not to fall victim to the paranoia of power that obsessed Portuguese rule. In the last story, 'The Barber's Most Famous Customer', the Portuguese political police demand to know the identity of a 'foreigner' who has reportedly been seen at the village barbershop. Eventually the PIDE produce their evidence: a photograph of the black American actor Sidney Poitier! An earlier story, however, has had sufficient similarities with the barbershop story to encourage readers to draw uncomfortable conclusions about absurdities common to the independent present and the colonial past. In 'The Tale of the Two Who Returned from the Dead' two people, presumed to be dead, baffle the official mind of the new state by turning up again very much alive and well. But death certificates have been issued and, according to bureaucratic procedure, cannot simply be removed from the record. Faced with what seems a 'mystery' of African cosmology, in which the returning people could be the spirits of the living dead, the scientific-Marxist truth of Frelimo authority is left to mutter its phraseology in Couto's wicked satire:

> *'We can't go along to the administrative cadres of the district and tell them a couple of ghosts have turned up. They'll tell us we've got ourselves mixed up in obscurantism. We could even be punished.'*[t]

Given the uncertainties of the political situation in both Angola and Mozambique, it is difficult to predict whether Rui and Couto are the precursors of what the American academic Russell G. Hamilton, in his history of Angolan literature, regards as the path of modernisation.[12] What modernisation is said to demand is a more contemplative, more aesthetically intricate literature than that produced instrumentally in the service of the struggle. But the assimalado contribution since the 1950s had already ensured that a modern, international perspective was firmly part of Angolan and Mozambican literary expression. What has also been persistent is the determination to discover the native land. As a result, there has been a continuing willingness to adapt traditional sources to hybridised languages and structures, and whether derived from Marxist-humanist or African-humanist compulsions, the literature has shown a large compassion for the ordinary people of Angola and Mozambique. Whereas Hamilton values 'cosmopolitan' modernisation, native critics like Alfredo Margarido and Costa Andrade continue to regard literature's 'instrumentality' as necessary to counter the intrusions of neo-colonialism.[13] What is certain is that in the current troubles, in which ethnic and ideological divisions have been manipulated by insiders and outsiders, literature has both an idealistic and a critical role to play. As far as literary commentary is concerned, the task may be less to anticipate future modernisations, more to re-Africanise and de-Europeanise inter-pretations of Angolan and Mozambican literature. What we are likely to see is a diminishing function for the assimilado class, an increasing func-tion for the home-based *Africano*.

Notes

1. For commentary on the independence struggle and the subsequent civil war, see H. Andersson, *Mozambique: A War against People* (London, 1992); W. Finnigan, *A Complicated War: The Harrowing of Mozambique* (Berkeley, 1992); J. Hanlon, *Mozambique: Who Calls the Shots?* (London, 1991);

T. Heriksen, *Revolution and Counterrevolution: Mozambique's War of Independence* (Connecticut, 1983); G. M. Houser, *No One Can Stop the Rain: Glimpses of Africa's Liberation Struggle* (New York, 1989); D. Knight, *Mozambique: Caught in a Trap* (London, 1989); S. Urdang, *And Still They Dance* (London, 1989).

Besides the studies mentioned in the General Bibliographies and in the relevant section of Part Three, see for the literary and cultural scene D. Burness, *Fire: Six Writers from Angola, Mozambique and Cape Verde* (Washington, 1977); R. G. Hamilton, 'Class, Race, and Authorship in Angola', in G. M. Gugelberger (ed.), *Marxism and African Literature* (London, 1985); G. Moser, 'Creating a National Literature: The Case of Mozambique', in H. Wylie (ed.), *Contemporary African Literature* (Washington, 1983); A. Neto, 'On Literature and National Culture', *Lavre e Oficina*, no. 20 (May 1978); A. Sachs, *Images of a Revolution* (Harare, 1983).

2. Quoted in I. Christie, *Samora Machel: A Biography* (London, 1988).

3. Mondlane, *The Struggle for Mozambique* (Harmondsworth, 1969), pp. 101–21. See my introduction of Mondlane's argument in the section on Angola and Mozambique in Part Three.

4. Selections of poetry, in English translation, in M. Dickinson (tr. and ed.), *When Bullets Begin to Flower* (Nairobi, 1972); C. Searle (tr. and ed.), *The Sunflower of Hope: Poems from the Mozambican Revolution* (London, 1982); and M. Wolfers (tr. and ed.) *Poems from Angola* (London, 1979). Commentary, R. G. Hamilton, 'A Country Also Built of Poems: Nationalism and Angolan Literature', *Research in African Literatures*, vol. 13, no. 3 (Fall 1982); C. Searle, 'The Mobilisation of Words: Poetry and Resistance in Mozambique', in G. M. Gugelberger (ed.), *Marxism and African Literature*. For context, see R. First, *The Mozambican Miner: A Study in the Export of Labour* (Maputo, 1977).

5. Sequence, in English translation, in Searle, 1982 [n. 4 above].

6. Quoted in Mondlane [n. 3 above]. See, from the 'non-revolutionary' perspective, H. Tracey, *Chopi Musicians: Their Music, Poetry and Instruments* (London, 1948).

7. Hamilton 'A Country Also Built of Poems' [n. 4 above], p. 324.

8. Chatelain, *Folk-tales of Angola* (Boston and New York, 1894), pp. 21, 43, 53, etc.

9. See M. Ferreira, *Que Futuro Para A Lingua Portuguesa em Africa?* (Lisbon, 1988).

10. For discussion of the class position of Honwana and his father, who wrote an autobiography, see D. Lewis, 'Assimilation and Authority in Two Mozambican Self-narratives', *Current Writing*, vol. 3, no. 1 (1991).

11. Honwana, Interview, *Weekly Mail* (3–9 April 1992).

12. Hamilton *Literatura Africana Literatura Necessária I–Angola* (Lisbon, 1981).

13. Margarido, *Estudos Sobre Literaturas das Nações Africanas de Língua Portuguesa* (Lisbon, 1980); Andrade, *Literatura Angolana (Opiniões)* (Lisbon, 1980).

Chapter 3

Zimbabwe: the Unified Nation or the Functioning Society?

Rhodesia and Zimbabwe

Like Angola and Mozambique, Zimbabwe had to resort to guerilla war against white rule, and conceptualised its nationhood on the images and principles of revolution. But pre-independent Rhodesia had been more complex in its social stratification than the two ex-Portuguese colonies: a situation that would have important consequences for literature. For one thing, the symbols of a new Zimbabwean nation have had to fight for hegemony against a 'white Rhodesian' social and cultural life which, during the long years of warfare, had continued to function strongly in many settler institutions such as schools, agricultural unions, and theatres. In addition, the relationship of African life to the settler economy was more diverse than in Angola or Mozambique. As a result, cultural expression reflects considerable heterogeneity in the range of its influences, and there is a correspondingly limited consensus among writers, black as well as white, as to the role of literature in any nation-building project. A spirit of social enquiry, which is contemplative, ironical, even sceptical, has continued to operate in tandem with commitments to Zimbabwean unity.[1]

As we have seen, conditions in Mozambique and Angola led to a fairly consistent Marxist-class understanding of the colonial past and the potential of independence. In terms of the economy, the effects on ordinary people of rudimentary extraction policies were opposed by radicals among the European-educated assimilado elite. In terms of literature, there was an intellectualised coherence of thought and aesthetics. In Zimbabwe, by contrast, the cries of freedom owed as much to African tradition as to modern analysis: the two entities, in fact, were not always clearly distinguishable, and the literature of nationhood that emerged in the war years conveyed fluid relationships between the aspirations of people in the rural trust lands and the aspirations of people in the towns. Colonial practice had sought to restrict African modernisation by preserving customary patterns of life in the reserves; the revolutionary consciousness of guerilla struggle, in opposition, drew a great deal of its justification and strength from rural issues, particularly the land issue which had seen native Zimbabweans deprived under the Land Apportionment Act (1930) of the best agricultural allotments. Younger Africans may have found opportunities for advancement in the towns but, as late as the 1970s, many were still first-generation urban sojourners with commitments to their rural-based families that could sometimes be onerous. A consequence for literature has been a greater impurity, or we could say variety, of attitude and style than we encounter in either the assimilado or combat literature from Angola and Mozambique.[2] The strength of the Zimbabwean voice is to be found in its immediacy of appeal; the difficulties are to be found in several unresolved tensions concerning the authority of leadership and the will of the people. The ideal of African nationalism with its sense of a rejuvenated cultural past remains largely untested against calls for modern socialism where the accent is on economic redistribution and change. Such tensions, however, need not point simply to ideological confusions. Instead, we may see a 'hard reality' in the fact that Zimbabwe has not found any singular definition of itself as a mythical nation, but has remained in its independence very much a working society with the attendant problems and challenges.

During the years of the wind of change, white Rhodesians – the term is politically loaded – continued to regard themselves as firmly settled in their own country. They may have retained some loyalties to their British ancestry, but their image of Britain had little to do with historical realities. To many Rhodesians, the decolonising process as insisted upon by the British government seemed, and stills seems, to have been an aberration. Rhodesians clearly saw themselves as financially independent of any distant metropolitan interference, and profits from reasonably developed agricultural and manufacturing interests were re-invested in the Rhodesian economy itself. The majority of Rhodesians, not unsurprisingly, supported the decision of Ian Smith's white supremacist Rhodesian Front to prevent the country being committed to progress towards African majority rule. In 1965 Smith, who was classified a rebel by Westminster, unilaterally declared Southern Rhodesia to be no longer a colony of Britain, but an independent state renamed simply Rhodesia: a country which, as prime minister Smith put it, would never be ruled by Africans in his life time. With UDI delaying the wind of change for fifteen years, Zimbabwe experienced its interregnum. Guerilla activity, which since 1966 had been conducted by the two African nationalist movements ZANU and ZAPU, ended when the Rhodesian Front capitulated to the combined pressure of the war and international trade sanctions. The latter was less successful than the former partly because South Africa refused entirely to abandon Smith. In 1980 British-supervised elections brought Robert Mugabe's ZANU to power. Smith continues to farm in Zimbabwe and acts intermittently as a prophet of doom about the corruption and inefficiency of the Mugabe government.

By the Mugabe government, Smith probably means almost any African-run government.[3] For white Rhodesia, particularly under UDI, developed a heightened sense of itself as a bulwark of Western Christian civilisation against what the colonial mind-set generally regarded as the childishness, ignorance, duplicity, disease and atavistic savagery of the dark continent. Beleaguered, paranoid, protected from new thought by censorship, Rhodesia, which had been declared illegal by the United Nations, developed a militaristic ethos that boasted of its kill-rate in the hot pursuit of 'terrs' (terrorists). In the towns, meanwhile, settler society in sundowners at the club, in elite schools with British-derived curricula, and in the cultural activities of flower shows, play festivals and book clubs preserved the 'unmodern', actually quite anachronistic, Rhodesian version of the superior Western manner. Numerous amateur repertory companies kept alive a nostalgic Victoriana in favourite productions such as *The Pirates of Penzance* and in boisterous, boozy sing alongs. An enthusiastic readership existed for a spate of white 'imperial' adventure novels about the so-called bush war,[4] and in very small poetry circles there was a tradition of writing a proficient verse of 'place': sometimes romantic in its love of the empty land, at other times uncomfortable and guilty about colonial attitudes to race. As we have seen, Rhodesian poetry had since the 1950s entertained the possibility of interracial co-operations. It would try during UDI to retain a sense of artistic potential as something apart from the brutalities of the war. Outside the white enclaves – there are only half a million whites in a population of 5 million – African culture in its traditional forms had never been discouraged by the colonial authorities. In fact, wood carvings, dances, rituals and ceremonies were advertised as ethnographically-primitive tourist attractions and as further confirmation of the need for paternalistic white overlordship. In addition, the Southern Rhodesia African Literature Bureau, the activities of which I mentioned in the earlier section on Zimbabwe's colonial past, continued to publish and disseminate educational and creative endeavours in the indigenous languages so long as the messages generally confirmed the settler scheme of things according to which Africans were happiest when left to their ancient ways.[5]

It is easy of course to caricature white Rhodesian life. What the independent Zimbabwe was able to find valuable, nonetheless, were institutional infrastructures that could be modified and pushed in new directions. Whereas the Portuguese in Angola and Mozambique left neither theatre companies nor a literature bureau, the National Theatre Organisation (formerly, the Southern Rhodesia Drama Association) has successfully broadened its scope and re-defined its aim as uniting all Zimbabweans, white and black, through the medium of theatre and drama. The old literature bureau outlet, while it remains 'traditional' in its guardianship of uncontaminated African languages, has become available at least for Zimbabwean priorities in the publication of educational material; European and African stylistic switching has occurred in self-critical and experimental literary works; and a 'university' tradition has subjected claims of national unity and reconciliation to lively and healthy debate. In all this, the literature of the new nation, which provided initial shocks of re-conscientisation, has remained sufficiently flexible since independence to continue to interrogate both the past document and the present circumstance. Utilised as a medium of education in the ZANU and ZAPU guerilla camps, solidarity and discussion plays, for example, have re-appeared in more professional productions with modifications that have not been afraid to level criticism at those former guerilla heroes who as members of the Mugabe government are perceived by 'new radicals' to have deviated from the ideals of the revolution. Similarly, the chimurenga (war of liberation) songs have undergone notable changes.

Chimurenga songs

During the 1970s chimurenga songs, which owe their basic structures and tones to traditional Shona and Ndebele music, sounded their opposition to Rhodesian politics and culture. In directing their derision at the settlers and uniting black Zimbabweans in defiance, celebration and tribulation, the words appealed to a heroic Shona and Ndebele past as well as to modern revolutionary thinking about material transformation. Taking on the power of a leitmotif, the excavated site of Great Zimbabwe verified the glory of an ancient indigenous civilisation, and the 'myth of liberation', which I mentioned in the earlier section on Zimbabwe, was traced back through successive spirit mediums to Murenga Sorerenzou, the progenitor of the present-day Shona people.[6] In referring recurrently to the first chimurenga of the Ndebele and Shona against the settlers in the 1890s, the songs mythologised Nehanda and Kagubi, the guides who had encouraged rebellion and in 1898 were executed by the colonial authorities. According to new chimurenga songs, which were sung by students at the University of Zimbabwe in the late 1980s, the chain of heroic voices will continue to intervene in any struggles that might be necessary in the future should rulers, including Mugabe, be tempted to betray the freedom of the people:

> Our ancestor Nehanda died
> with these words on her lips

'I'm dying for this country.'
She left us one word of advice
Take up arms
Liberate yourselves.[t]

Sung by choirs in the camps and in exile, the chimurenga songs were
unambiguous in calling for the overthrow of the Smith regime. Sung in
Zimbabwe in the war years by groups like Thomas Mapfumo and the
Acid Band, the songs managed to evade censorship in inventive uses of
idiomatic Shona, in proverbs and parables. At independence, the chimurenga songs appeared, in print, in their original vernacular lyrics together
with versions in English translation.[7] Such an exercise in publication and
translation, of course, had a strategic purpose. As in other ex-colonies in
the region, the coloniser's language has been retained as the medium of
national communication, and challenges continue to involve changing
the status of English from that of a dominating 'Western code' to that of
a facilitator in local interchange and expression. It is an exercise which
frequently takes as a common reference the figure of Nehanda either to
re-affirm the heroic example as in a Reps Theatre production, *Mhandoro*
(performed 1993), or to de-romanticise the mythic voice, as in Terri
Barnes's *To Live a Better Life: An Oral History of Women in the City of
Harare, 1930–1970* (Harare, 1992).

The de-romanticised view has emerged with some persistence since
the mid-1980s and reflects both local political disillusionments and the
influence of international women's studies which, in Zimbabwe, has
begun to examine depictions by the essentialising male gaze of women's
roles in the guerilla war.[8] In the early 1980s, however, the heroic 'male
perspective' was predominant, at least in the poetry, and in the spirit of
chimurenga previously published poets and unknown poets alike contributed to the celebratory volume, in English, *And Now the Poets Speak:
Poems Inspired by the Struggle for Zimbabwe* (1981) which, unlike the broader
selection in *Zimbabwean Poetry in English* (1978), focused solely on the
subject of the revolutionary war and conveyed sentiments of optimism
for a reconstructed future.[9] Despite the preoccupation with the struggle,
the range of response was more varied than the breathless introductory
'commendation' might have led readers to believe: a 'communion of
voices, surging forward like Musiwatunya': that is, the Victoria Falls, as
colonials would prefer. Alongside many cries of freedom, there was
Musaemura B. Zimunya's skilful use of oral-based rhythms and traditional
symbols in poems that evoke not simply hope, but hope won out of
hardship. Another accomplished poet, Kizito Muchemwa, turned a mordant eye on the icons of the colonial past. The point of the volume,
nevertheless, was the heroic moment, as in Amon Matika's 'Eve of Freedom', which I choose almost at random:

> . . . We are all free
> Zimbabwe *yavatema* No longer Rhodesia
> On my harp my *mbira* cries with songs of Freedom.

Like the chimurenga songs, many of the poems wanted to escape the stability of the printed page and live, on the spot, in their emphasis in repetition, in hyperbole, and in their large visions of victory. To me this seems appropriate, and I do not share the concern of the editors of the *Mambo Book of Zimbabwean Verse in English*, to which I referred in the earlier section on Zimbabwe, that the poetry of the chimurenga is curtailed by its single, instrumental intention. Given the circumstances of its composition in a fierce anti-colonial war, we should not expect the subtle, contemplative artefact; rather, we are invited to share in a phenomenon which, as the *Mambo* editors concede, has the worthy purpose in its context of being 'highly democratic'.[10] We are not judging a finished product but a potentiality, and when chimurenga poetry fails will be when, in its subsequent mutations, it loses its attachment to progressive political purpose and settles into the stabilities of ritual. As E. M. Chiwome astutely puts the political-aesthetic problem in tracking the tradition back to seventeenth-century Shona marombe (praise singers) and, in adapted forms, forward into the present-day: 'The celebration song when sung beyond the period of celebration, begins to look like a prayer.'[11] Up to now the chimurenga songs have not been inclined to ritualise Mugabe as the father of the nation: a point not unconnected to the fact, perhaps, that the unity pact signed in 1987 between the ruling ZANU-PF and the opposition ZAPU did not result in Mugabe's own preference for a one-party state. Instead, fresh impetus has been given to voices of dissent. In shying away from chimurenga, the editors of the *Mambo Book* have missed an important aspect of what they were seeking: Zimbabwean poetry.

The legacy of war. Mungoshi, Marechera, Zimunya

A sense of severe displacement, both mental and physical, is a feature of the writing that emerged during the war years, and we are reminded again that relationships between Zimbabwean literature and the African nationalist independence movements were more complicated than those between Lusophone writings and the MPLA or Frelimo. As I indicated in Part Three, the first generation of black Zimbabwean writers, most of whom had mission-school educations, were moderate supporters of the nationalist campaign of the 1950s at the same time as they retained respect for the multiracial ideals of the central African federation. The younger generation who came to prominence in the 1970s were mostly the products of the few schools like Goromonzi, Fletcher and St Augustine's as well as of the University of Rhodesia which, because of enlightened individual teachers, had continued to transmit rational, humane values in a period of white intransigence. The result was several literary intelligences that were fiercely independent, moodily introspective, and determined to escape ignorance and poverty through their education while fearfully aware of the Smith government's attempts in the 1970s to frustrate African advancement beyond unskilled and semi-skilled labour. Schooled in 'individualistic' notions of transforming the crude, external world into landscapes of reading and imagination, sensitive to states of exile abroad and at home in the last protracted years of colonialism, isolated from the rest of independent Africa and – in a country of relatively advanced urbanisation – already anticipating class conflicts beyond the collapse of the settler regime, writers in Zimbabwe often projected their pessimism, cynicism and interrogation beyond the colony to identify power struggles and posturings in the guerilla movements themselves.

Behind these crises of fragmented lives, of course, lies the psychological and emotional trauma of the war, or the UDI years, depending on how one chooses to view the interregnum. Certainly the war, as the intractable event, remains a key to understanding developments of the last twenty-five years in any field we may wish to call Zimbabwean literature. The fairly confident, moralistic view of peaceful progress towards a non-racial society as we find in earlier writers like Stanlake Samkange, for example, gave way in Samkange himself to a sharper African nationalist depiction in *The Mourned One* (1975) of future possibilities and actions. Among younger writers Dambudzo Marechera, in spectacular manner, and Charles Mungoshi, in melancholy introspection, are best appreciated in the context of severe personal and cultural division, and the war has continued to haunt the fiction of both Chenjerai Hove ('the war forced us back into history from the margins') and Shimmer Chinodya. In replying to a concern that writers should look to the civil society rather than back to the destruction, Chinodya says he believes that 'writers shouldn't rush to deal with current affairs, but let time give perspective to their vision'.[12] The war has served also as a catalyst for several re-valuations by white Zimbabweans: that is, whites who have committed themselves to the welfare of the African-run country. For self-confessed, ex-racist Bruce Moor-King, this has meant a violent awakening: *White Man Black War* (Harare, 1988) spits its venom at the elders of the white Rhodesian 'tribe', in particular at its big chief Ian Smith who taught the children to hate. The message is blunt: choose to be a Zimbabwean, or choose to be an enemy! For the poets Harold Farmer, Rowland Moloney and John Eppel, the struggle has involved rescuing the sustaining memory from a discredited past, and all of these writers speak in an ambiguous amalgam of nostalgia, bravado, moral evasion and determined self-scrutiny.[13] For the African poet Eddison J. Zvobgo, who was imprisoned by Smith for seven years and went on to become a cabinet minister in Mugabe's government, the challenge has been to recall the war without bitterness as a time in which Zvobgo himself was urged to re-establish links between his Shona traditions and the inevitable demands of change: 'Chivaura, brother, life is a stinging nettle' ('Come and Let Us Recite Poems Chivaura'). One of the most impressive poets in the *Mambo Book*, Zvobgo pays tribute to his poet mentor Wilson Chivaura, who was discussed earlier on, in verse that avoids the evocation of landscape for its own sake – the landscape without people being considered a trope of white writing – and communes instead with the surroundings in a simile-rich enhancement of a life-experience that fulfils itself on the wisdoms of ancient lore: a prerequisite for Zvobgo's retaining his sanity while in prison. In a great deal of the literature of war and independence, the two impulses that are held in tension, or worked into dialectical enquiry, are despair and hope.

Writing in both Shona and English Charles Mungoshi, for example, sums up the stasis of UDI in the titles of his short-story collection *Coming of the Dry Season* (1972), republished with additional stories as *The Setting Sun and the Rolling World* (1987), and in his novel *Waiting for the Rain* (1975). An author who generates powerful feeling from the use of metaphoric landscapes and idiomatic speech (the Shona folk influence) set in contrast to laconic understatement (the influence of the written story of implication and epiphany), Mungoshi could find little sense of belonging either in the rural world of his childhood or in the town world of his adulthood during the years of drought and hunger, as the poet Musaemura B. Zimunya has described the temper of UDI.[14] While biological ties held Mungoshi to his parents, the psychological ties were broken, and his various character-narrators – as in the title story 'Coming of the Dry Season' – free themselves from a dead past only to encounter an insecure present as the prelude to a terrifying future:

> One Wednesday Moab Gwati received a letter from Rusape. His mother was seriously ill. He decided to wait till he got his pay on Friday: Saturday he would go home.
> . . .
> When he felt this way Moab would walk for miles completely blind. It started always at the same emotional point, when, after a good time and he had no more money, he saw a gnarled old woman, thin as a starved cow. . . .
> He would hear over and over the small mousy voice that

was full of tears and self-pity, the voice that was a protest:
'Zindoga mwana'ngu, remember where you come from.' A
warning, a remonstrance, a curse and an epitaph. With it,
he could never have a good time in peace. Guilt, frustration
and fury ate at his nerves.

The stories in sensitive registers of thought and mood speak 'universally'
of a modern disquiet at the same time as their contours are regional. As
T. O. McLoughlin puts it, the central issue is the spiritual survival of
community and, in depicting the multiple effects of colonialism on individuals from rural areas, Mungoshi seeks succour for his own dry roots
even as he is forced to realise with uncompromising honesty that his
roots have died: there is no longer any certainty of tradition as an anchor
in the rolling world.[15]

In trying to order his perceptions of cultural scatter, Mungoshi places
great importance on the ordering capacities of writing as a craft. In
reaction to a similar dilemma – the loss of nurturing community, the
isolation of self – Marechera, who along with several other future writers
was expelled from the University of Rhodesia in 1973, adopted a style
of brash Euro-modernism in giving vent to his anger as a black exile in
England. In *The House of Hunger* (1978), *Black Sunlight* (1980), *Mindblast*
(1984) and the posthumously published *The Black Insider* (1990), Marechera
employs the metaphor of being trapped in houses of the mind. The
dominating impressions are of the voice talking obsessively rather than
the plotting of events, and of the expressive medium advanced over any
story of political commitment:

> The fighting going on throughout the country was raging
> right outside my windows throughout the city. Now and
> then a horrid THUMP and CRUMP shook the house
> and chipped down the plaster. I heard screams too, not of
> pain but apparently of an inside hilarity. Sometimes they (I
> mean 'they') sung gabbled versions of incredible national
> anthems and punctuated them with cowboy and Indian
> games of BANG-BANG YOU'RE DEAD NO I'M NOT.
> But most of the time they credibly recollected themselves
> and really got down to the grisly business of pummelling
> each other with napalm, rockets, machine guns, booby traps,
> land mines, and the trusty shaving razor.
>
> (*The Black Insider*)

Prior to his dying of AIDS, Marechera lived out his bohemian persona
by trashing all authority including that of the new Zimbabwe nation. As
a result of his narcissism, this writer has been seen as non-Zimbabwean,

non-African. But this is to ignore the desperate matter behind his masks. If he was a radical individualist who remained sceptical of the independent nation, Marechera also resented the West's several cultural impositions. There is little reverence, for example, in his style of modernism. His words explode on their own verbal excess as Marechera scoffs at the West's very pretentiousness about its high literary culture: for it is a culture – Marechera implies – that has shown little concern for the 'third world' it set out to colonise.[16]

We may regard the different styles of Mungoshi (nuanced, humane) and Marechera (flashy, rebellious), therefore, as equally valid forms of protest against the inhumanity, perhaps non-humanity, imposed upon black Zimbabweans by the designs of UDI. At the level of ideas, however, neither writer was able or willing to offer a way forward for a society in need of massive transformation. Marechera died in 1987, Mungoshi has written little since independence; and while the scepticism both writers showed about grand visions has been regarded by some as a necessary realism, Zimunya has pointed to their limitations of despair when it requires courage and hope if one is to ensure that the Zimbabwean nation functions as a just society.[17] It was in the early 1980s, soon after independence, that Zimunya himself capitulated to 'neo-colonial' despair, examples of which are rife in West and East African literature. In fearing that free Zimbabwe might produce a corrupt oligarchy, he wrote some of his worst poetry: city sketches that owed more to Eliot's European urban disillusion than to the sights, sounds and atmosphere of a medium-sized African city like Harare. What his city poems remind us, however, is that even in Zimunya's optimistic chimurenga-inspired poetry, like 'Rooster', hope had always countenanced the possibility of setbacks, reversals, and the need to continue the struggle for dignity in the general business of life. Whether recollecting his childhood – which, as in 'Cattle in the Rain', is felt in the discomfort of bare feet in the veld – or whether contemplating the danger of the war hardening the heart as in 'The Reason', Zimunya retains a conception of an African humanity that is unidealised and gathers its resources from the tough imperfections of real living. The imperfections, as features of the style, are built into the colloquial diction and irregular rhythms of a familiar speaking-voice:

> Never mind sister
> this is our home
> houses full of smoke
> and pendent soot
> full of the odour of life
> you see those umbrellas of tawny grass thatch
> from rowdy beer fires?
> They shelter our people

poor in clothes and heart
moonshine cheerful in eyes and lips
and us too.[18]

The rugged solidity in these lines from 'My Home' can easily be under-valued in comparison with the perfect unobtrusiveness of Mungoshi's writing, or the 'mind blasts' of Marechera's cult-appeal. Yet Zimunya makes the telling point that the people of Zimbabwe will have to find a new sense of community by turning away from extreme pessimism to a situation in which they can say: we can remake the world around us.

'Remaking the world'. Hove, Chinodya, Dangarembga

The idea of remaking the world is implicit in the novels of Chenjerai Hove and Shimmer Chinodya. Actions are set close to the war, and anticipations of a post-independence society are deliberately foreshort-ened. It is suggested, instead, that only by examining the minutiae of human responsiveness behind the symbols of national struggle can a new Zimbabwean consciousness emerge: a consciousness with the critical power to engage in enquiry about the character of life after the interreg-num. Like S. Nyamfukudza's *The Non-Believer's Journey* (1980), which was the first novel to turn a jaundiced eye on notions of patriotism and heroism, Chinodya's *Harvest of Thorns* (1989) contrasts official views of unity and solidarity with the reality of people – some of whom are presented as callous, others as conscience-stricken – living through the terrifying times of the independence war. Returning home at the end of the fighting, the protagonist Benjamin, an ordinary young man who was propelled into the guerilla movement more by circumstance than convic-tion, finds no traces of any utopia. Yet he is fortified in the knowledge that he has tried to regain his sense of rational discrimination about the huge events in which he had participated. In a harrowing central scene, a suspected traitor – a woman in the peasant village – is pummelled to death by guerilla soldiers as a lesson to others who, for whatever reason, might find themselves betraying their comrades. Benjamin recalls himself almost hypnotised in horror participating in the killing. Like Hove in *Bones*, Chinodya is left considering what it must have meant in the chimurenga to be a rural peasant caught between opposing forces and causes that had little meaning in the everyday hardships of village routine.

Hove focuses in *Bones* (1988) on a mother's loss of a son, and reminds us that in the great cause of nationhood women have often found themselves relegated swiftly to minor roles. Despite this, the novella has been sharply criticised for presenting the 'art' of oral cultures as holistic and unaffected by the slang of modern change. It is said, accordingly, that *Bones* has too few insights to offer the independent society and that it denies human beings the power to intervene in and change their lot.[19] Such a view, however, could be in danger of misunderstanding Hove's conventions of symbolic representation. Whereas Chinodya is strong in the realism of imitation, Hove in highly poetic language attempts to reclaim Shona culture as the vanished ideal – ideal is the operative word – from which war-damaged people may resuscitate their sensibilities:

> So now, if anybody asks me the name of one who has tasted
> all medicines in this land, I am not ashamed to mention
> your name. How could I continue to live in the same
> village? I packed my things and went away. Then when
> they gave you all sorts of names, you followed and we ended
> up in this forest where baas Manyepo is the chief. He
> growls for you to wake up, he growls for you to sleep, he
> growls for you to go and eat your afternoon meal, he growls
> for you to come and earn whatever he decides to give you.
> What can we do, Marita? We are chief's sons in a strange
> land.

The illusion of 'Shona-ness', as Dan Wylie has identified it, depends upon a complex approximation, in English, of a naïve, surprising oral immediacy captured in direct engagement with the imagery of rural life, in the use of co-ordinate sentences that have the certainty of proverbs, and in a generalising archetypal tendency that locates individual characters in collective embodiments of attitude and mood.[20] In seeking to 're-make the world', both *Bones* and *Harvest of Thorns* cut through what Lan White in his criticism of Isheunesu V. Mozorodze's war novel *Silent Journey from the East* (1989) calls the stale, bureaucratic prose of Zimbabwe's official post-independence culture, in which English as the medium of state communication has settled into public pronouncements on political correctness.[21] The fiction of Hove and Chinodya, in contrast, suggests that English in its realism or symbolism can be granted the suppleness to explore the psychological, social and moral issues of the war as the precondition of any healing in present, or even future, circumstances.

Like *Bones* and *Harvest of Thorns*, Tsitsi Dangarembga's novel *Nervous Conditions* (1988) reminds readers that the issues of socio-psychological interaction and cultural stress, which are explored by Dangarembga in the gendered family situation, will continue to have an important effect on the lives of people in any new Zimbabwean nation. (Dangarembga's manuscript, incidentally, was rejected by Zimbabwean publishers and appeared under the imprint of the Women's Press in London where, like the South African writer Ellen Kuzwayo, she received the support of director Ros de Lanerolle, the South African exile and anti-apartheid activist.) In utilising a semi-autobiographical mode in which the narrator-figure Tambudzai relates her story in the first person while retaining a measure of omniscience because she is recalling her childhood from the adult vantage point, Dangarembga returns Tambudzai to her own child-hood in the Rhodesia of the late 1960s before the war gained momentum. She thus avoids the full-scale public event and focuses instead on a difficulty that has currency for the woman writer in Zimbabwe. The dif-ficulty may be summed up in the question: when the images of war continue to preoccupy the national psyche, what is the woman's subject matter? In *Nervous Conditions* the subject of interest is a young girl's growth to maturity in the Shona extended family, where patriarchal codes designate that boys be educated and girls, even when educated, submit to their role as their husbands' wives. With character typification and ironic discrepancies between intentions and actions reminiscent of Jane Austen, Dangarembga skilfully sets her study of African mores in the frame of social comedy, and gives her story a 'universalising' life that has won *Nervous Conditions* acclaim in Western women's literary discussion. One could say in fact that the African specificity is sufficiently muted as to allow Shona patriarchy, in its mission–influenced, educated variety of Babamukura's household, to operate as an analogue of the general topic 'patriarchy'. Such an interpretation would find consonance presumably with Dangarembga's own thinking: she has said that her story, although set in the past, is about the future Zimbabwe which she anticipates as having no option but to adapt increasingly to Western conventions, attitudes and styles. The novel – a form that has so often favoured the examination of bourgeois behaviour – will gain in importance, according to Dangarembga, in choosing as its subject the crucial interface between individuals and an alienating society.[22]

While the argument has validity, *Nervous Conditions* does not end up evading its own intimate memory or temporal demand. In her Fanonist use of the phrase 'nervous conditions' – the psyche of the native under the pressures of colonialism – Dangarembga continually qualifies views that Western and African culture, including gendered behaviour, are free of particular, material cause. As a result Babamukura, who imposes his dominance in the household, is seen not only as the heavy male figure, but with a degree of sympathy as 'nervously' trapped in the colonial scheme of things: he is permitted his small, middle–class advantages because he is regarded by the white authorities as a 'good munt'. By the same token, his daughter's anorexia cannot be explained entirely by the fact that Shona codes are too narrow to cope with her Western education. For Nyasha's Western education, which she has received partly in England, has little coherence of idea, action or consequence. Its minor teenage rebellions and freedoms, such as smoking, dating, wearing mini-skirts, precocious questioning, and the haphazard reading of great books including the 'risqué' D. H. Lawrence, hardly equip the Western teenager for matters of social and political choice let alone the doubly-displaced Nyasha: the African girl caught up in the complex condition of African/colonial dependencies. More nervous even than Nyasha is the narrator, Tambudzai, whose own 'theme' cannot be confined to what she herself insists upon: the gendered character of complicity and consent. Rather, *Nervous Conditions* remains jittery about its own attempts to transfer African issues, contexts and values to Western-style dialogues, and vice versa. In such schisms of identity, the book suggests the impossibility of unlinking its woman's story from its national story. Rather, it confirms that old and new codes of behaviour are entirely complicit in each other's influence on processes of social transition. Whereas Jane Austen's observations could be called domestic, Dangarembga's are generational.

Theatre and the public sphere

In the light of Dangarembga's comments about the future of the novel, it should be interesting to consider whether developments in novel-writing in Zimbabwe, indeed in Africa as a whole, will depend on the domestic-ation of the society according to which the roles of gender and class begin to be treated with greater differentiation than the pivotal role of race. Dangarembga herself, as I have just suggested, apparently wants to lean in such a direction. The forms of expression in Zimbabwe which since independence have been most attuned to competition between national desires and societal critique, however, have been the antithesis of the novel in their accessible, public voice: namely, the dramatic per-formance of stage shows and the oratory of political speech and commen-tary. The common subject is the Mugabe government which is seen by writers – though not by the majority of the electorate – to have failed to fulfil its responsibilities. For some it has betrayed its socialist goals to creeping bourgeois capitalism; for others it has remained blinded by its own socialist sloganeering to the disadvantage of individual initiative and free enterprise. Issues include the question of land redistribution which has remained unresolved: white farmers whose expertise is necessary to the economy continue to dominate large-scale agriculture, peasants remain tillers of the soil. There is the recognition of new class divisions in the towns with an upwardly-mobile black elite showing little solidarity with its proletarian cousins, and many of Mugabe's ministers have been tainted by corruption. Privileged schools continue to offer black and white children from wealthy families an 'unreformed' Western, middle-class education, and despite its regular denunciations of apartheid, the Mugabe government never managed to sever trade links with South Africa. The first years of independence in the 1980s witnessed bitter rivalries between Mugabe's Shona-dominated ruling ZANU party and Joshua Nkomo's Ndebele-dominated ZAPU, the official opposition. As a result, the ideals and alliances of the Patriotic Front (PF), which was formed by ZAPU and ZANU in the independence war, are seen in retrospect to have been based on expediency rather than principle. Political bickering has certainly strained progressive thought and modernisation as leaders have sought traditional, ethnic legitimations of their power rather than tackling the problems of winning broad support among diverging class interests, or even among the group associations that could be thought of as constituting a civil society.[23]

The Zimbabwean 'public sphere' of the 1980s, as I have sketched it here, is reflected in an active theatre life. This includes annual drama festivals and play-of-the-year competitions run by the National Theatre Organisation (NTO). At the same time, NTO has been energetically attacked by the Zimbabwean Association of Community Theatre, ZACT (founded in 1986), for its perceived elitism in showing preference for 'well-made' plays, whether European or African. There are also several theatre-for-development projects, some organised by independent groups and critical of the government, others administered by the Ministry of Youth, Sport and Culture.[24] In returning to questions that were raised, but never really resolved, in educational plays in the ZANU and ZAPU guerilla camps, such as the relationship of leaders to the will of the people, and the place of African tradition in socio-economic transformation, Robert McLaren and Thompson Tsodzo's drama unit in the faculty of arts, University of Zimbabwe, has fused Shona/Ndebele dance spectacles and Brechtian epic structures in seeking to establish a 'Zimbabwean' didactic theatre. The drama unit has not been particularly successful, however, in analysing interrelationships of idealism and pragmatism in independent Zimbabwe; rather, 'solutions' have tended to confirm purified Marxist–Leninism in large historical scenes of gesture and celebration. In alerting audiences to what is identified as the bourgeois collapse of the revolutionary leaders in independent times, the drama unit has insisted on a path forward that could amount to little more than illusionism and mystification: a simple faith in the socialist ideal. Although he is less certain of solutions than McLaren and Tsodzo, Andrew Whaley is no less disenchanted with the direction of Zimbabwean politics and his theatre uses identifiably modernist, or post-modernist, styles in satirising the antics of power: *Platform Five* (ms., 1987) is Brechtian in dialogue scenes that prompt critical thought from the audience, while *The Nyoka*

Tree (ms., 1988) plays on conventions of television and newspaper presentation in order to mock the pronouncements of politicians.

Possibly the most penetrating theatre of political discussion has been that of Amakhosi Theatre Productions (Bulawayo) whose play *Workshop Negative* (ms., 1986), written by Cont. Mhlanga, combines action sequences in the workplace, interludes of talk, and striking choreography in popular karate-style movements in its attempts to raise questions about the post-independence policy of reconciliation. In highlighting an ex-guerilla who emerges as a profit-maker and exploiter of workers (he is presented as not very different from the old colonial bosses), *Workshop Negative* found itself condemned by playwright Stephen Chifunyise in his capacity as director of arts and crafts in the Ministry of Youth, Sport and Culture. Although on record as reminding people that drama was a valid form of criticism in ancient African societies, Chifunyise found *Workshop Negative* to be anti-government in its criticisms and therefore an affront to Zimbabwe. In arguing his case at a university forum on artistic freedom, he accused the author Mhlanga of displaying 'individual quirkiness' in his depiction of characters and therefore lapsing into bourgeois false consciousness whereas political truth would have been better served by the generality of socialist-realism: to put it bluntly, the *typical* ex-guerilla would not have become a nascent capitalist exploiter. Mhlanga, who in 1989 was elected to the chair of the Zimbabwe Writers' Union (ZIWU, founded in 1984), replied that he was reporting what he had heard among ordinary workers in the beer halls, and he endorsed the view of ZIWU that the victimisation of writers 'kills creativity and deprives society of change'.[25] Shortly afterwards Mhlanga had the dubious satisfaction of seeing the malpractices he had hinted at in the play quite blatantly exposed as several government officials were indicted by the Sandura enquiry into state corruption. Pauline Dodgson makes the interesting point in this regard that *Workshop Negative* may have helped prod the government into investigating its own offices: for wide discussion of Mhlanga's play had encouraged open talk about rumours that had been circulating for some time.[26] Although no action was ever taken against *Workshop Negative*, the play did not receive the 'government's blessing' when it toured in Botswana and other neighbouring countries. After the signing of the unity pact in 1987 between ZANU and ZAPU, however, Amakhosi Theatre – perhaps sensitive to being branded simply as anti-patriotic – responded to the diminishing of rivalries between the two former ex-guerilla allies by performing *Workshop Negative* in September 1988 with an altered ending. The revised play celebrated unity as the way to solving the problems of selfish class interests that seemed to be threatening the egalitarian ideals of the independent nation.

The Mugabe government

The content given in Zimbabwe to the terms 'nationalism' and 'social-ism', however, remains shot through with contradictions, and a feature of public life since the signing of the unity pact has not only been a resurgence of the chimurenga spirit accusing the government of capitalist tendencies, but the formation of a broad alliance consisting of black and white business, professional and church people. Taking its cue from the collapse of world communism, the alliance pictures Mugabe as the victim of discredited socialist economic policies and practices. Some members of the alliance have impeccable humanitarian-liberal credentials; others have conservative views, and are keen to link the question of human rights principally to that of property protection. The result has been considerable energy in political debate.[27] Instead of having to rely on only the ZANU 'news-speak' that since independence has dominated the state-controlled radio and television services, it became possible in the late 1980s to hear new opinions ranging from the dissident populism of Edgar Tekere, the politician who set up an anti-corruption party, to the urbane reasonable-ness of the respected former chief justice Enoch Dumbutshena. The alliance, which is constituted as the Forum for Democratic Reform Trust, has Dumbutshena as its patron and has pointed to what it regards as serious shortcomings in the arguments of both African nationalists and Marxists or, as the latter are sometimes called, African-socialists. Morgan Tsuangirai, for his part, is as sceptical of liberation rhetoric – which he believes has betrayed the masses in its un-dialectical symbol-mongering – as he is of the middle-class predilections of the Forum: 'they talk very little of the problems of hunger, inadequate shelter, poor access to education, unemployment and land redistribution'.[28] As secretary general of the 400,000-strong Zimbabwe Congress of Trade Unions, Tsuangirai looks towards a new national political culture with its growth in non-government organisations as the necessary way to oppose the govern-ment's own 'anti-liberation' attack on radical trade unions and students. The aim should be to nurture the grassroots and revitalise the activities of disaffected ordinary Zimbabweans as the strength of civil society.

What all this means for writers, most of whom come from the educated classes, is hard to say. Something of their difficulties in looking into the future is evident, perhaps, in the fact that, as my discussion has meant to suggest, there is no single direction or style that could be discerned as 'Zimbabwean', no set of ideas that is entirely coherent in relating tradition to modernity, or local affiliation to a national vision. What creative writers do seem to share, nonetheless, is the understanding that, despite Tsuangirai's confidence in grassroots renewals, the memory of the war remains tied in complicated, critical ways to concepts of a civil charter. The need to search the past as usable source, accordingly, checks any rush towards current events. Where stories set in the past touch conditions of the present day is in their wariness about the designs of authority and power. Although Mugabe's ZANU-PF won overwhelming election victories in 1990 and 1995, its pronouncements and actions are subjected as a matter of course to wide-ranging argument and debate. In literature, there is neither unalloyed idealism nor unalloyed pessimism. Instead, there are interactions in terms of content and form between the unifying drive to nationhood and the sceptical qualification regarded as necessary by the functioning society. Literature in West and East Africa since the wind of change may be identified broadly in two phases according to which myths of cultural regeneration gave way sharply to motifs of neo-colonial disillusion. In its oscillations of hope and despair, Zimbabwean literature has by contrast remained marked by the warts of experiential living. A lesson for neighbouring South Africa could be that the new state struggling to emerge since the demise of apartheid in 1990 is unlikely to be either an unmitigated national success or an unmitigated civil disaster. Just as Zimbabwean writers have been unable to shrug off the images of the war, South African writers may find that any renewal requires facing up squarely to the injustices of the apartheid past. Indeed, the pain of probing the scarred memory should not be confined to Zimbabwean literature. A similar principle and practice is necessary in the southern African region as a whole.

Notes

1. See N. J. Kriger, *Zimbabwe's Guerilla War: Peasant Voices* (Cambridge, 1992); D. Martin and Phyllis Johnson, *The Struggle for Zimbabwe: The Chimurenga War* (London and Johannesburg, 1981); T. Ranger, *Peasant Consciousness and Guerilla War in Zimbabwe* (Berkeley, 1985).

    On the socio-cultural transition from 'Rhodesia' to 'Zimbabwe' see for example, A. J. Chennells, 'The Treatment of the Rhodesian War in Recent Rhodesian Novels', *Zambezia*, vol. 5, no. 11 (1977); J. Frederikse, *None But Ourselves: Masses versus Media in the Struggle for Zimbabwe* (Johannesburg, 1982); P. Kaarsholm (ed.), *Culture and Development in Southern Africa* (London and Harare, 1988) as well as several articles including 'The Development of Culture and the Contradictions of Modernisation in the Third World: The Case of Zimbabwe', *European Journal of Development Research*, vol. 2, no. 1 (1990); D. Maughan Brown, 'Myths on the March: The Kenyan and Zimbabwean Liberation Struggles in Colonial Fiction', *Journal of Southern African Studies*, vol. 9, no. 1 (October 1982); M. Meredith, *The Past is Another Country: Rhodesia, UDI to Zimbabwe* (London, 1979); N. Sithole, *In Defence of a Birthright* (Toronto,

1975); *Roots of a Revolution: Scenes from Zimbabwe's Struggle* (Oxford, 1977); J. Todd, *The Right to Say No: Rhodesia 1972* (London, 1966; Harare, 1987).

2. Besides the works listed in the General Bibliographies, see as overviews of the literature L. Maveneka, 'Writers and the Revolution', *Moto* (August 1983); T. O. McLoughlin, 'Black Writing in English from Zimbabwe', in G. D. Killam (ed.), *The Writing of East and Central Africa* (London, 1984); J. Reed, 'The Emergence of English Writing in Zimbabwe', in A. S. Gérard (ed.), *European-Language Writing in Sub-Saharan Africa, Vol.1* (Budapest, 1986); C. Style, 'The White Man in Black Zimbabwean Literature', *Ariel*, vol. 16, no. 3 (1985), 'Zimbabwean and South African Poetry: The Parting of the Ways?', *English in Africa*, vol. 15, no. 2 (September 1988).

3. In condemning Mugabe as a communist, Smith in 1994 praised South African president Nelson Mandela.

4. See as representative John Gordon Davis's *Hold My Hand I'm Dying* (London, 1967). Commentary by Chennells [n.1 above].

5. See, as a prelude to UDI, C. T. C. Taylor, *A History of Rhodesian Entertainment, 1890–1930* (Salisbury, 1968).

6. See my discussion in Part Three on the 'invention' of the chimurenga myth with particular reference to T. O. Ranger's influential study *Revolt in Southern Rhodesia, 1896–7: A Study in African Resistance* (London, 1967; 1979). See also D. Lann, *Guns and Rain: Guerillas and Spirit Mediums in Zimbabwe* (Berkeley and Harare, 1985).

7. For a selection of chimurenga songs in English translation see A. J. C. Pongweni (ed.), *Songs that Won the Liberation War* (Harare, 1982). Also: *Chimurenga Songs. Music of the Revolutionary People's War in Zimbabwe* (Teal Records; produced by ZANU in Maputo); and, for traditional music, P. F. Berliner, *The Soul of Mbira: Music and Traditions of the Shona People of Zimbabwe* (Berkeley, 1978).

8. See R. Gaidzanwa, *Images of Women in Zimbabwean Literature* (Harare, 1985); I. Hofmeyr [n. 9 below]; I. Staunton, *Mothers of the Revolution* (Harare, 1990); F. Veit-Wild, 'Creating a New Society: Women's Writing in Zimbabwe', *Journal of Commonwealth Literature*, vol. 22, no. 1 (1987). See also Veit-Wild's attack on what she sees as Chenjerai Hove's essentialising male gaze in his widely-acclaimed novella *Bones* (1988), *Teachers, Preachers, Non-believers* (London and Harare, 1992), pp. 313–20.

9. M. Kadhani and M. Zimunya (eds.), *And Now the Poets Speak* (Harare), K. Muchemwa (ed.), *Zimbabwean Poetry in English* (Salisbury). See also C. Style and O. Style (eds), *Mambo Book of Zimbabwean Verse in English* (Gweru, 1986); and Zimunya (ed.), *Chakariri Chindunduma: Shona Poems Inspired by the Struggle for Zimbabwe* (Gweru, 1986). Commentary, I. Hofmeyr, ' "I am the new man and you are the new woman": The Iconography of the Guerilla in Some Recent Zimbabwean Poetry', *English Academy Review*, 3 (1985); and E. Ngara, 'Ideology, Craft and Commitment in Zimbabwean Freedom Poetry', *Ideology and Form in African Poetry* (London, 1990).

10. Style and Style, Introduction, p. xxvii.

11. Chiwome, 'The Shona Folk Song: Legitimation and Subversion', in E. Sienaert, *et al.* (eds), *Oral Tradition and Innovation: New Wine in Old Bottles?* (Durban, 1991).

12. Comments by Hove and Chinodya at a conference on writing in a 'new South Africa' in Johannesburg, *New Nation* (2–8 November 1990).

13. Selections in C. Style and O. Style (eds), *Mambo Book of Zimbabwean Verse in English*.

14. Zimunya, *Those Years of Drought and Hunger: The Birth of African Fiction in Zimbabwe* (Gweru, 1982).

15. See McLoughlin, 'Black Writing in English from Zimbabwe' [n. 2 above] and 'The Past and the Present in African Literature: Examples from Contemporary Zimbabwean Fiction', *Présence Africaine* (1984). Also: D. Riemenschneider, 'Short Fiction from Zimbabwe', *Research in African Literatures*, vol. 20, no. 3 (Spring 1989); F. Stratton, 'Charles Mungoshi's *Waiting for the Rain*', *Zambezia*, vol. 13, no. 1 (1986).

16. See D. Wylie, 'Language Thieves: English-language Strategies in Two Zimbabwean Novellas', *English in Africa*, vol. 18, no. 2 (October 1991). (On Marechera and Hove.)

17. N. 14 above.

18. Poems referred to appear in C. Style and O. Style (eds), *Mambo Book of Zimbabwean Verse in English*.

19. See F. Veit-Wild's attack on Hove [n. 8 above].

20. N. 16 above.

21. L. White, Review of several Zimbabwean novels, *Southern African Review of Books* (February/May 1990), p. 4.

22. T. Dangarembga, Interview, *New Nation* (2–8 November 1990), p. 9.

23. See P. Kaarsholm [n. 1 above].

24. See S. Chifunyise, 'Trends in Zimbabwean Theatre since 1980' and P. Kaarsholm, 'Mental Colonisation or Catharsis? Theatre, Democracy and Cultural Struggle from Rhodesia to Zimbabwe', *Journal of Southern African Studies*, vol. 16, no. 2 (June 1990).

25. University of Zimbabwe, 20 March 1987.

26. 'Culture and Literary Production in Zimbabwe', in A. Rutherford (ed.), *From Commonwealth to Post-Colonial* (Sydney, 1992). See *Report of the Commission of Inquiry into the Distribution of Motor Vehicles*. Under the Chairmanship of Mr Justice W. R. Sandura. Harare. March, 1989.

27. See the several articles under the theme 'Judgment Day for Zimbabwe Politics', *Africa South* (August 1992); I. Mandaza and L. Sachikonye, *The One-Party State and Democracy: The Zimbabwe Debate* (Harare, 1991); and J. N. Mayo, *Voting for Democracy: Electoral Politics in Zimbabwe* (Harare, 1992). Also: J. Herbst, *State Politics in Zimbabwe* (Berkeley, 1990); P. Kaarsholm, 'Quiet after the Storm: Continuity and Change in the Cultural and Political Development of Zimbabwe', *African Languages and Cultures*, vol. 2, no. 2 (1989); C. Stoneman (ed.), *Zimbabwe's Prospects: Issues of Race, Class, State, and Capital in Southern Africa* (London, 1988); C. Stoneman and L. Cliffe, *Zimbabwe: Politics, Economics and Society* (London, 1989). For projects on women's grassroots empowerment, which impressed Doris Lessing during her visit to Zimbabwe (*African Laughter*), see *Building Whole Communities*, 7 vols (Harare, 1991).

28. Tsuangirai, *Africa South* [n. 27 above].

Chapter 4
Namibia: Making a Literature

The 'wild south-west' of colonial imagination

A question prompted by the appearance of Dorian Haarhoff's study *The Wild South-West: Frontier Myths and Metaphors in Literature Set in Namibia, 1760–1988* (Johannesburg, 1991) is: what is Namibian Literature? Africa's most recently independent country achieved its freedom from South Africa's control in 1990, thus ending a long history of conquest and repression in the dry, sparsely populated but mineral-rich territory formerly known as South West Africa. Inhabited from prehistoric times by Bushmen and Khoi groups, including the southern Nama and the Dama who are negroid but speak a Khoi language, as well as by roving Khoi and coloured bands which had been influenced by Dutch culture in the Cape colony, Namibia has a majority of Bantu-speaking Owambo, several other Bantu African groups including the Herero, and settled whites of German and Afrikaans extraction. In 1884 Germany established the protectorate of South-western Africa, the ostensible reason being to guarantee the safety of Rhenish missionaries. In savagely suppressing the local people, German authorities gave the best farming land to white settlers. In 1915, during the First World War, South African forces defeated the German military presence and occupied the territory, and in 1920 the League of Nations confirmed South Africa as the mandatory power in South West Africa. The South African government, instead of administering its responsibility for the welfare of the local inhabitants, seized land and enforced political, economic and social discrimination against the Namibian people. (The name of the territory, as Namibia, was confirmed in 1968 by the United Nations.) Refusing to abide by a UN decision that Namibia was a trusteeship, South Africa insisted that it was the sovereign power and the dispute lasted for forty years during which time South Africa attempted to impose apartheid structures on the territory.

In thwarting moves to Namibian independence South Africa set itself in direct opposition to the UN and provoked guerilla actions by the Owambo-based SWAPO. With SWAPO greatly strengthened by the acquisition of bases in neighbouring Angola after the Portuguese withdrawal in 1975, South Africa with the backing of the United States managed to link the issue of Namibian independence to cold-war machinations involving the withdrawal from Angola of Cuban troops that were supporting the Marxist MPLA. Persuaded finally by international impatience and economic sanctions to resolve the Namibian question, South Africa accepted the inevitability of UN-supervised elections that brought Sam Nujoma's SWAPO to power in 1990 against a fairly competitive opposition which included an influential white minority. Despite its radical socialist beliefs as a guerilla movement, SWAPO as a government has shown considerable flexibility in shifting from its Marxist ideology to acceptance of a mixed economy and a multiparty democracy. In an impressive start to transforming a war-ravaged, colonially exploited country into a peaceful society, SWAPO has taken seriously its commitment to reconciliation according to which it has attempted to persuade whites that they have a future as Namibians. It has also set out to persuade the several ethnic groups that they need not fear SWAPO as an exclusively Owambo government. Writing a literary history of Namibia presents all the challenges and problems, in microcosm, that have occupied the writing of this larger study of the literatures in southern Africa. Crucial questions of intention and perspective, for example, are raised by a consideration of Haarhoff's book *The Wild South-West* which, in the mode of ideology critique, offers an overview of colonial responses to Namibia as the frontier territory, the empty space, the playground of adventure and opportunity.[1]

Just as South Africa and Rhodesia were seen by colonial scribblers as blank maps awaiting metropolitan inscription, so Namibia has a colonial literature that in German, Afrikaans and English reflects various metropolitan concerns including those of the Cape colony in the eighteenth century, Victorian Britain and the German nation in the nineteenth century and, in the twentieth century, South African dilemmas transferred to the desert landscapes of 'South-West'. We read of Afrikaners trekking from seemingly intractable problems in South Africa itself. There are also numerous South African English adventure fictions about finding manhood and treasure in the diamond-rich soil on the edges of (white) civilisation. A distinctive feature is the 'German consciousness' which, in writing by men and women, domesticated the wilds into an image of the German national-bourgeois ideal: women are cast in the role of the keepers of the culture in their home-making enterprise including the hot midday meal under the sweltering sun and the celebration of a German Christmas, while men tame the frontier with the clinical brutality shown in real life by German colonial authorities. In the early nineteenth century, for example, General Lothar von Trotha crushed Nama and Herero resistance to his administration by using quick-firing Krupp guns in an attempt to exterminate every man, woman and child. In parts of Gustav Frenssen's *Peter Moor's Journey to South-West Africa*[1] (1908; 1905) there are hints that the author, a Lutheran pastor who never visited the colony, had qualms about his government's policy of genocide. But *Peter Moor* remains typical of German colonial literature in its refusal to contemplate native Namibians as having lives that at all mattered. Resembling Olive Schreiner's *Trooper Peter Halket of Mashonaland* (1897) in its situation and setting, Frenssen's novel shows nothing of Schreiner's commitment to sympathy and justice in Africa.[2]

Several of the more recent colonial responses to Namibia have continued to experience difficulty in transferring the locus of interest from that of the metropole to that of the marginalised space. As I have said, adventure fiction presents 'South-West' as the exotic frontier zone, and although serious fiction such as J. M. Coetzee's 'Narrative of Jacobus Coetzee' (the second part of his book *Dusklands*, 1974) may destabilise the frontier myth as a text of conquest according to post-structuralist strategies, Coetzee's purpose is not to replace his decentred colonial subject with any recentred Namibian alternative. Namibia is kept even more firmly as the 'other' in what is called *grensliteratuur* (border literature): Afrikaans fiction of the 1970s that turned its attention to the war between SWAPO and the South African army.[3] Often critical of a brutal South African military code, the registering consciousnesses in these stories and novels, nonetheless, remain self-enclosed in their own anguishings about the Afrikaner identity and soul. As in *Heart of Darkness* or, more recently, numerous films about the Vietnam war, the perspective in *grensliteratuur* is either imperial or counter-imperial; rarely, however, do the indigenous people appear as anything more than the chimeras of the metropole's psyche. In devoting his study mainly to the colonial literature I have summarised here, Haarhoff has chosen an apt title, *The Wild South-West*. To turn his study into one about Namibian literature, however, he would need to have compressed the 223 pages he gives to the frontier tradition into an opening section that in a concise way could make the salient anti-imperial points. The bulk of the study should then have been allowed to grow out of what is at present a 12–page 'counter appendix' entitled 'Fighting and Writing: The Origins of Indigenous Namibian Literature'. For it is in his appendix, and in the conclusions to each chapter, that Haarhoff introduces nascent Nambian voices.

Namibian voices from Witbooi to Diescho

It is interesting to pursue the consequences of recentring Haarhoff's book. At the very outset, it is obvious that in a country of several indigenous languages (some with Bushman stems, others with Bantu stems), an official language English – as chosen by SWAPO – and a widely spoken lingua franca Afrikaans, translation studies will have to be an important aspect of making the range of the literature accessible to the researcher. Namibian literature, for example, can be seen to emerge from a classical past in the songs, stories and fables of the Bushmen and Khoi. As few, if any, literary historians are likely to have a working knowledge of the several local languages, let alone the ancient click dialects, archival work will necessarily involve renewed attention to important studies on the indigenous languages. In addition, the researcher would need to consult the Michael Scott Oral Records Project (MSORP) for transcriptions of oral history, poetry and protest songs. The first volume of the records to appear in print, *The Mbanderu*[t] (1986), based on the German recordings by Theo Sünderheimer in 1976, deals with the oral expression of the eastern Herero. (See the note for a select list of 'Namibian' works.)[4]

When we look for a rehabilitative alternative to the frontier motif, in which the 'other' may become the 'subject', a strong unifying factor is to be found in Haarhoff's observation that from the outset Namibian literature proclaimed a nascent nationalism in its exploration of the related themes of exile, home, resistance and liberation. Accordingly, a seminal text is *Die Dagboek van Hendrik Witbooi* (The Diary of Hendrik Witbooi), written between 1884 and 1893, and published in 1929. The leader of the Nama, Witbooi refused to accept German treaties of protection and led guerilla activity before being killed in battle in 1905. His body was buried secretly to prevent its falling into German hands, and Namibians subsequently began to gather annually at Gibeon, his burial place, for a special service to commemorate Witbooi's role in the early struggle for independence. Written in flamboyant, biblical Dutch prose, Witbooi's diary contains letters advocating national sovereignty for the small African state and equality among the great European nations. In breaking beyond the single life, his diary, or journal, is a resistance document in its social, communicative and rhetorical purpose. The force of the just idea is the measure of its value:

> . . . no person, nor his money will come short in our
> way to living; we do not bother anybody with questions
> about water, grass, money, and roads; but with the white

people this is different; the laws of the whites are completely incompatible and incomprehensible for us red people; these merciless laws oppress us from all sides and they contain no feeling for people.[(t)5]

As in the case of Witbooi's *Dagboek*, Namibian literature began to seek a national identity initially not in the imaginative genres, but in the public record.[6] There are the letters of Ipumbu, the Owambo ruler, to governors and native commissioners, and the courtroom address of Andimba Herman Toivo ja Toivo, trade unionist and co-founder of SWAPO, on being sentenced by the South African authorities to twenty years on Robben Island on charges of terrorism. Among 'life stories' set against the independence struggle, there is the story of Vinna Ndadi, a migrant worker who became a strike leader and fled into exile after being held in solitary detention, and the story of John Ya-Otto told by himself in *Battlefront Namibia* (1982). There is Helmut Angula's story, told in German, *Die Zweitausend Tage Des Haimbooi Ya-Haufika* (The Two Thousand Days of Haimbooi Ya-Haufika, 1988). The author, a SWAPO activist, later became SWAPO representative at the United Nations. Like Angula, the husband and wife team Magdalena and Erastus Shamena use the old coloniser's language for a liberatory purpose in their jointly authored autobiography *Wir Kinder Namibias* (We the Children of Namibia, 1984), in which their Christian voice reaches beyond their own lives to locate suffering people in the northern battle areas of the country. In similar vein, Pastor Zephania Kameeta's *Why O Lord?: Psalms and Sermons from Namibia* (1986) speaks to the Namibian oppressed in the gospel of liberation theology. It is pertinent to note that in charting a national voice, none of the texts I have mentioned here would regard itself as an art work. Neither was most of the poetry inspired by the independence struggle accredited to specialist poets. Rather, poems emerged from among teachers and students in exile from South African occupation who were placed in educational programmes at the United Nations Institute for Namibia (UNIN), in Lusaka, and in refugee schools in Angola and Zambia. Collected in *It Is No More a Cry: Namibian Poetry in Exile* (1982) and *Through the Flames: Poems from the Namibian Liberation Struggle* (1988), the poetry seeks an aesthetics of resistance not in the *form* of the expression but in the *act* of the expression, not in the intricate consideration but in the correct sentiment. As Issiek A. Zimba declaims in 'The Voice of Namibia':

March on Namibian children
march on to Windhoek,
for this is the only time to strike
hard, to strike a blow and fight
for the beloved country.

With material still to be recovered from the archives, it is obviously too soon after independence to expect a literature of nation to be subjected to scrutiny by the developing society. Literary-political debate has begun, nevertheless, to turn attention to the questions of what might qualify the writer as Namibian – birth or commitment? – and whether commitment in a functioning democracy should continue to operate as a euphemism for SWAPO affiliation. In his attempts to write a 'Namibian' poetry in English, for example, Haarhoff, who was born a white South African, has relied upon a detailed naming of local sights, a reference to the indigenous past clashing with destructive colonialism, a particularised historical sense, and a flattened accent and tone almost as if the English, slightly Afrikanerised in its syntax, has to capture in vocals the dry, unrelieved desert terrain. In 'Zacharias Lewala', the title referring to the labourer who found the first diamond, the master August Stauch

> pegged claim, staked fame
> with men doing Kolmanskop crawl
> on stomachs after spark.
> In 'Deutsche Diamanten'
> he told of the Stauch stone
> sifting Lewala
> from the carat cast.[7]

Haarhoff seeks in his writing to remove himself from his South African upbringing and to remake his identity in a physical and mental landscape that could be designated 'Namibian'. A national literature might also want to appropriate, as Namibian, revisionist commentaries and histories written in support of the country's right to freedom from colonial rule by writers who are not necessarily native Namibians, such as Ruth First (*South West Africa*, 1963) and Randolph Vigne (*Dwelling Place of our Own*, 1975). Similarly, it is apt that the important oral project I mentioned earlier has chosen to honour the memory of Michael Scott, the English priest who with the support of the South African writer-activist Mary Benson in the 1940s pleaded the cause of the Herero at the United Nations.

The question of Namibianness has also attached itself to the first novel to have been produced by a native-born Namibian, Joseph Diescho's *Born of the Sun* (1988). The author's own life finds fictionalised equivalence here in the story of Muronga who journeys from his traditional society, which is presented as idyllic in its pre-colonial rhythms and purposes, to the mines where he encounters racism and exploitation. After his politicisation, he joins the United People's Organisation which is depicted as the model of unity, experiences a harsh spell in political detention at the hands of the South African authorities and, after his release, knows the anguish of having to leave his family behind as he crosses the border to join the guerilla struggle. (In 1984 Diescho went to the United States to study Namibian history.) In drawing parallels between the fictionalised *Born of the Sun* and Ya-Otto's non-fictionalised *Battlefront Namibia*, Haarhoff refers to both books as symbolic political narratives that do not satisfy novelistic expectations.[8] What Haarhoff means is that neither author avails himself of the opportunities for individualised character exploration and, as a result, we do not hear accents of direct speech that might strike a peculiarly Namibian note. In challenging Wolfram Hartmann's contention that Diescho is a 'creator of a true Namibian literature',[9] Haarhoff finds the concept premature and, hinting perhaps at what he has tried to do in his own poetry, he predicts that only when 'writing' is separated from 'fighting', and the writer from the role of party-propagandist praise singer, will human character begin to delineate itself in a distinctively Namibian way. In conclusion Diescho's novel, which is subtitled 'A Namibian Novel', is classified at best as 'African' in its generalising, anti-colonial tendencies.

The historian Robin Hallett, however, would disagree with such a judgment.[10] Avoiding what in Haarhoff's comments sometimes suggest a hankering after a fairly standard Western realism that is Leavisian in its concreteness, particularity, and complex moral life, Hallett remains alert to the determinative context within which the new Namibian author at the present is likely to have to work: the demands of nation-building, for example, will probably precede the investigation of a differentiated civil charter. What Hallett identifies as a strength in Diescho's novel is a typicality infused with a simply-told, humanising conviction. In charting Muronga's path as one that thousands of Namibians, Zimbabweans and South Africans have had to take, 'Diescho makes his readers aware of the human realities, the human decencies behind the liberation struggle'. Such generous human recognitions – I would agree with Hallett – constitute an important 'theme' when white interests, even in the independent state, remain sufficiently powerful in education and the media to continue portraying liberation ideals as terrorist violence. In situations in which the individual feels compelled to occupy the public sphere, therefore, the 'typical' will have a crucial role to play in any aesthetics of fiction. We may agree with Haarhoff that Diescho's novel does not have gradations of sufficient precision to be identified as Namibian; we may disagree, however, that *Born of the Sun* is simply African. Rather, Diescho's two interrelated stories involving rural-urban migration and guerilla struggle confirm the tentative designation, 'southern African'.

Debates about how the Namibian experience may be represented should not ignore sceptical analysis. Neither, however, should 'Namibian-ness' ignore its own potential for reconstruction. In fact, SWAPO's declared national ideal of reconciliation presents substantial challenges for literature to connect its human concerns to the consequences of state policy: challenges which in the future might become more testing from the perspective of civil, as distinct from that of national, consciousness now that SWAPO – as a result of its massive electoral victory in 1994 – has the right to alter the Namibian constitution.

Notes

1. See H. Bley, *South West Africa under German Rule, 1894–1914* (Evanston, 1968); J. M. Bridgman, *The Revolt of the Hereros* (Berkeley, 1981); J. L. de Vries, *Mission and Colonialism in Namibia* (Johannesburg, 1978); H. Drechler, *'Let Us Die Fighting': The Struggle of the Hereros and Nama against German Imperialism, 1884–1915* (London, 1980); A. du Pisani, *SWA/Namibia: The Politics of Continuity and Change* (Johannesburg, 1986); I. Goldblatt, *History of South West Africa from the Beginning to the Nineteenth Century* (Cape Town, 1971); P. H. Katjavivi, *A History of Resistance in Namibia* (Paris and London, 1988); C. Saunders (ed.), *Perspectives on Namibia: Past and Present* (Cape Town, 1983); R. Segal and R. First (eds), *South West Africa: Travesty of Trust* (London, 1968); D. Soggott, *Namibia: The Violent Heritage* (London, 1988).

    Besides Haarhoff's book, see literary-cultural perspectives in H. Ridley, *Images of Imperial Rule* (London, 1983) which includes substantial commentary on German colonial literature; J. K. Noyes, *Colonial Space: Spatiality in the Colonial Discourse of German SWA, 1884–1915* (Reading, 1992); G. Tötemeyer, *et al.* (eds), *Namibia in Perspective* (Windhoek, 1987).

2. See G. Pakendorf, 'The Literature of Expropriation: Peter Moor's Journey to South West and the Conquest of Namibia', in G. Tötemeyer [n. 1 above].

    A select reading list of Namibian colonial literature (primary texts) might include C. J. Andersson, *Lake Ngami or Explorations and Discoveries during Four Years of Wanderings in the Wilds of South Western Africa* (London, 1865), and similar travelogues by Andersson, C. E. Bell, J. Chapman, F. Galton, P. A. Moller and, in the 1930s, H. Chilvers; F. Cornell, *A Rip van Winkle of the Kalahari and Other Tales of South West Africa* (Cape Town, 1915); W. A. de Klerk, *The Thirstland* (London, 1977); G. Frenssen, *Peter Moor's Journey to South-West Africa: A Narrative of the German Campaign*[(t)] (1908; 1905); H. Grimm, *Dina* (Berlin, 1913) and *Volk Ohne Raum* (München, 1932); T. Nash's novel *The Ex-Gentlemen* (London, 1925); and as representative of many hunter-adventure fictions, A. Scholefield's *The Eagles of Malice* (London, 1968). (See Haarhoff's Bibliography.)

3. See H. du Plessis, *Grensgeval* (Cape Town, 1985) and, in critical vein, A. Strachan, *'n Wêreld Sonder Grense* (Cape Town, 1984). For a selection of 'demythogising' military stories by SADF conscripts, *Forces Favourites* (Johannesburg, 1987).

4. A select list of nascent Namibian, as opposed to colonial, texts and studies (cf. n. 2 above) might include K. Almaes, 'Oral Tradition: The Herero in Botswana', *The Societies of Southern Africa in the 19th and 20th Centuries* (University of London, 1981); R. First, *South West Africa* (Harmondsworth, 1963); T. Hahn, *Tsuni-||Goam, the Supreme Being of the Khoi-Khoi* (London,

1881; New York, 1971); A. Heywood, *The Cassinga Event* (Windhoek, 1994);
A. Heywood and B. Lau (eds), *The Mbanderu: Their History until 1914 as Told
to Theo Sünderheimer*[t] (Windhoek, 1976); Ipumbu, Letter to the Governor,
Union Government Damaraland, Uukuambi, RCO Files, 3/1916/2 (Windhoek
State Archives); Z. Kameeta, *'Why O Lord?': Psalms and Sermons from Namibia*
(Geneva, 1986); M. Kuusi, *Ovambo Proverbs with African Parallels* (Helsinki, 1970),
Ovambo Riddles with Comments and Vocabularies (Helsinki, 1974); H. Melber
(ed.), *It Is No More a Cry: Namibian Poetry in Exile* (Basel, 1982); D. Mercer
(ed.), *Breaking Contract: The Story of Vinna Ndadi*[t] (Oakland, 1974); C. Pieterse,
'Ballad of the Cells', in C. Pieterse (ed.), *Short African Plays* (London, 1972);
M. Shamena and E. Shamena, *Wir Kinders Namibias* (Wuppertal, 1984); M.
Scott, *A Time to Speak* (London, 1958); H. Shityuwete, *Never Follow the Wolf*
(London, 1991); H. Toivo ja Toivo, 'Here I Stand', in M. Mutloatse (ed.),
Forced Landing. Africa South: Contemporary Writing (Johannesburg, 1980); L. van
der Post, *The Heart of the Hunter* (London, 1961); R. Vigne, *A Dwelling Place
of our Own* (London, 1975); H. Witbooi, *Die Dagboek van Hendrik Witbooi,
Kaptein von Witbooi-Hottentotte, 1884–1905* (Cape Town, 1929); J. Ya-Otto,
Battlefront Namibia (London, 1982).

5. See n. 4 above. (Passage transferred by Haarhoff.)

6. N. 4 above for bibliographical details.

7. Haarhoff, *Bordering* (Johannesburg, 1991) includes a section 'Crossing Kunene:
Towards a Poetic History of Namibia'.

8. Haarhoff, *The Wild South-West*, pp. 230–4.

9. Hartmann, 'Joseph Diescho: *Born of the Sun*', *Logos*, vol. 9, no. 1 (1989).

10. Hallett, Review, *Southern African Review of Books* (February–March 1989). Also:
R. Moorsom, 'Underdevelopment, Contract Labour and Worker
Consciousness in Namibia', *Journal of Southern African Studies*, vol. 4, no. 1
(October 1977).

Part Five
Writing in the Interregnum: South Africa, 1970–1995

Introduction to Part Five

Change in South Africa over the last twenty years has been dramatic. Despite the entrenchment of apartheid in the 1960s, voices of Black Consciousness firmly rejected 'black' as a racial-biological entity and by the late 1960s had begun to articulate Blackness as psychological, social and spiritual revindication: 'Black man, you're on your own.' On 2 February 1990, the liberation movements, which had been banned after the Sharpeville shooting in 1960, were unbanned. Laws based on racial discrimination have been repealed and in 1994 South Africa, which had earned the opprobrium of the world as an apartheid state, became a non-racial democracy. Such bald observations, of course, cannot account for the socio-political process operating behind the dramatic incidents. As early as the mid-1970s, for example, the demographic realities of population growth and economic necessity had begun to erode 'separate development'. In spite of controls on the movement of Africans to the cities, Africans simply continued to arrive in the cities where, legally or illegally, they could seek work. As Alan Paton's Stephen Kumalo realised forty years ago, people would continue to come to Johannesburg for that was the pattern of modernising development. Although the state attempted in various ways to regulate the growing power of African labour, substantial numbers of African workers by the early 1980s were members of trade unions. With its formation in 1985, the giant COSATU became a key force of opposition to apartheid rule. As early as 1973, massive strikes on the Durban docks had showed the potential of black labour to undermine white economic stability, and, in fact, by 1979 the state had accepted the necessity of adapting apartheid to the exigencies of the industrial expansion that was beginning to require a permanent skilled labour force based in the urban areas. Residential controls were abolished for some urban Africans while 'migrant labour' restrictions were retained against their rural counterparts whose destiny was still seen to be bound to the impoverished reserves. Such a tactic of divide-and-rule failed. Having predicted that by 1976 the 'influx' of Africans to white South Africa would have been reversed, Verwoerd was proved to have been a false prophet, and the sustained pressure of black activism pushed events on to a confrontational course.

With the factory floor finding its political voice in the 1980s, the decade of the 1970s saw the rise of militant black student opposition to white authority. The South African Students' Organisation (SASO), formed in 1969, espoused Black Consciousness (BC), and groups ranging from the political Black People's Convention to writers' associations in the townships began to regard cultural liberation as inseparable from political liberation. Inspiration arrived, somewhat haphazardly, from several sources. There was the negritudinal impulse according to which identity coalesced around images of traditional Africa as 'non-Western' in its intuition, sympathy and sense of community. There was the influence of African-American black power including its theological dimension: Christianity was cast as revolutionary in its commitment to the 'wretched of the earth'. As my use of Franz Fanon's phrase may suggest, a redemptive, humanistic Marxism linked BC to the New Left in Europe, but especially to the analyses of decolonisation by 'Third World' thinkers such as Fanon, Memmi and Cabral. What appealed to BC, for example, was Fanon's appreciation that the racially designated characteristic 'Black' had potency in the struggle to liberate the human being, mentally and economically, from colonial denigration and oppression. In bringing together existential concepts of psychological alienation and a Marxist awareness of the historical forces that have given rise to ideologies of race, Fanon's writings suggested that the praxis of social change was utterly necessary to re-definitions of identity in renewals of the word, image and symbol. Black had to be stripped, accordingly, of its negative connotations in a European sign system where it designated the 'other', the dark shape, the evil figure, and charged with positive, radical potential. Intense BC creativity in the 1970s – in new spokesmen like Steve Biko (first president of SASO); in new poetry, plays and stories; in new views of art as community-based people's resistance – gave thought and literature a distinctly Africanist energy that challenged prevailing Europeanised assumptions. Although intellectual and economic capital remained, as now, firmly in white hands Black Consciousness, at least in its public pronouncements, scorned the advice, tutelage and patronage of whites. As the poet Mongane Wally Serote put it, time had run out for the racist order; black anger had found its historical moment; whites had to learn to listen, blacks had to learn to talk.[1]

Once the state realised that Blackness for BC meant not ethnic self-determination, but the recovery of identity and pride in a programme of national liberation, the police were called to react with characteristic repression. In 1972 students who had led protests at the 'ethnic' universities, which had been established under apartheid decree, were removed from the campuses and banned. In 1974 banning orders were issued against BC leaders who had organised a Frelimo victory rally to celebrate the collapse of Portuguese colonialism in neighbouring Mozambique, and by the end of the decade the mood was apocalyptic. In an action that has come to symbolise the 1970s, school children in Soweto took to the streets on 16 June 1976 in protest against their inferior Bantu education. The immediate issue was their rejection of Afrikaans – dubbed the 'language of the oppressor' – as a medium of classroom instruction. With acts of defiance on the increase, the state banned the BC movements in 1977, and Steve Biko was battered to death in secret-police detention. Student militants, who became known as 'the children of Soweto', crossed the borders into neighbouring countries where many joined the ANC that was trying to re-organise itself in exile. The issue of Black Consciousness priorities in relation to the broader non-racialism of the ANC would feature prominently in writing by Mtutuzeli Matshoba and Mongane Serote, while Nadine Gordimer in borrowing her terms from Antonio Gramsci identified the 1970s as the beginning of South Africa's interregnum: the time when the old order was dying and the new struggled to be born.[2] It was a time of morbid symptoms: an observation graphically confirmed by post-mortem photographs of the battered Biko and television images of heavily-armed police shooting down children in ragged school uniforms. South African television began transmission early in 1976; state control, however, ensured that the story on local screens was dictated by the government's version of events: 'communistically inspired agitators' versus the 'guardians of law and order'.

Marxist commentators in South Africa have emphasised that BC had little strength among peasants and workers. Indeed, the young student and petty-bourgeois leaders, who included writers, teachers, journalists and church people, sometimes showed disdain for the country cousin in the city, who was portrayed as a satirical figure, even as a bumpkin. Nonetheless, BC's marginalisation in the 1980s as a political organisation did not negate its impact on the consciousness of disenfranchised people. In articulating its ideas of black dignity and power with clarity and vividness, BC 'elitism' generally remained sensitive to a wider forum. There is in fact no decisive break in terms of rhetoric and symbol between the negritudinal impulse of the 1970s and responses, in the 1980s, to the state's declaration of emergency rule. Many of the writers and artists who in the 1970s had endorsed BC went on to claim affiliations to the ANC. With the apartheid reaction to black activism in the 1980s taking the form of a military-backed 'total strategy' that sought to co-opt black middle-class groupings while deploying troops in the townships, the United Democratic Front (UDF) was founded in 1984 specifically to oppose 'tricameral politics': that is, the white government's granting of limited parliamentary representation to Indians and coloureds, but not to Africans. UDF mass action, which was modelled on the ANC-led civil disobedience campaigns of the 1950s, forged powerful alliances across class schisms in black communities. The appeal was broadly to the 'will of the majority' and, as it turned out, the UDF spelt a terminal crisis for the apartheid state.

Against media perceptions of ungovernable townships, in which the ugly side was the 'necklacing' (the placing of burning tyres around the necks) of suspected traitors, and against the statistics and testimonies of thousands of people in detention, the South African economy began to be effectively excluded from world money markets. When the hawkish president P. W. Botha suffered a stroke in 1989, the National Party government adopted bold and pragmatic tactics that saw a new state president, F. W. de Klerk, freeing from prison anti-apartheid leaders like Nelson Mandela and rejecting the military option in favour of tough negotiations about transition towards a non-racial future. At the height of the state of emergency in the mid-1980s, panegyrics at political funerals, the toyi-toyi (a quasi-military dance-step adapted from drills in the guerilla camps), slogan poems, and replicas of AK47 assault rifles provided an agit-prop of dramatic occasion. At the same time, the voices of apocalypse that had characterised BC's homogenising intentions – 'the people', 'the community', 'the solidarity of all the oppressed' – began to be subjected to explanatory analysis concerning different constituencies in struggles for power. While totalising narratives pictured the oppressed moving forward resolutely to a just victory, sceptical critiques asked whether marginalised 'others' like black women or the rural poor were likely to be included in any totalising narrative; indeed, whether South Africans, whatever their colour, would show the necessary wisdom and tolerance to give substance to fine-sounding ideals about a new nation.

In the last part of this study I want to consider, initially, the significance of BC creativity in the 1970s particularly in contrast to the dilemmas it posed for writers who regarded themselves as 'white Africans' strenuously committed to living in South Africa. In turning to the 1980s and continuing to focus on the art/politics issues that were integral to BC cultural activity, I shall address the question as to whether the state of emergency (1985–1990) in its priorities of political action and accountability constricted or liberated the creative imagination. It is a question which, in its various ramifications, has remained crucial to cultural debates. Did the apartheid past, as some artists and critics now imply, simply die on 2 February 1990 when de Klerk coined the term the 'new South Africa'? In consequence, do we suddenly have a 'civil imaginary' which renders resistance art nugatory and insists on universally recognisable themes about civil living? Perhaps more important than trying to anticipate what poets, playwrights and novelists will make of post-apartheid times, however, is the question of what we should expect from literary or, more broadly, cultural criticism. For if the 1970s had been the decade of the creative writer, the 1980s was the decade of the critic: not as stock-taker, but as contributor to the making of literary meaning and purpose in the movement of the society. As these comments suggest, literature – defined broadly as a form of rhetoric – can be seen as continuing its southern African tradition of locating itself firmly in the socio-political event.

Notes

1. Serote, 'Time Has Run Out' (1980), *Selected Poems* (Johannesburg, 1982). On Black Consciousness see the SASO Newsletters and miscellaneous publications (Unisa Library, Pretoria) as well as B. S. Biko (ed.), *Black Viewpoint* (Durban, 1972) and *I Write What I Like: A Selection of his Writing* (London, 1978); A. Boesak, *Farewell to Innocence: A Socio-ethical Study of Black Theology and Black Power* (Johannesburg, 1976); M. Chapman (ed.), *Soweto Poetry* (Johannesburg, 1982); R. Fatton, Jr, *Black Consciousness in South Africa: The Dialectics of Ideological Resistance to White Supremacy* (Albany, 1986); G. M. Gerhart, *Black Power in South Africa: The Evolution of an Ideology* (Berkeley, 1978); M. P. Gwala, *Black Review, 1973* (Durban, 1974); B. Hirson, *Year of Fire, Year of Ash: The Soweto Revolt, Roots of a Revolution?* (London, 1979); T. Lodge, *Black Politics in South Africa since 1945* (Johannesburg, 1983); N. C. Manganyi, *Being-Black-in-the-World* (Johannesburg, 1973); M. Motlhabi (ed.), *Essays on Black Theology* (Johannesburg, 1972); P. Randall (ed.), *Study Project on Christianity in Apartheid Society* (SPROCAS), several reports (Johannesburg, 1970–1973); T. Thoahlane (ed.), *Black Renaissance: Papers from the Black Renaissance Convention* (Johannesburg, 1975).

   For white responses to the BC challenge, see H. Adam and H. Giliomee, *The Rise and Crisis of Afrikaner Power* (Cape Town, 1984); H. Giliomee, *Looking at the Afrikaner Today* (Cape Town, 1975); J. Kane-Berman, *Soweto: Black Revolt, White Reaction* (Johannesburg, 1978); M. Lipton, *Capitalism and Apartheid: South Africa, 1910–1984* (Aldershot, 1985); S. Marks, 'Towards a People's History?: Recent Developments in the Historiography of South Africa', in R. Samuel (ed.), *People's History and Socialist Theory* (London, 1980); R. Rich, *White Power and Liberal Conscience* (Manchester, 1984); J. H. P. Serfontein, *Brotherhood of Power: An Exposé of the Secret Afrikaner Broederbond* (London, 1979); C. Simkins, *Reconstructing South African Liberalism* (Johannesburg, 1986); H. M. Wright, *The Burden of the Present: The Liberal-Radical Controversy in Southern African History* (Cape Town, 1977).

   See also, in English translation, F. Fanon, *The Wretched of the Earth* (New York, 1963), particularly Fanon's statement made at the Second Congress of Black Artists and Writers (Rome, 1959) reprinted as 'On National Culture'; O. Mannoni, *Prospero and Caliban*[(t)] (London, 1950); A. Memmi, *The Colonizer and the Colonized*[(t)] (Boston, 1967); P. Worsley, *The Third World* (London, 1964).

2. Gordimer, 'Living in the Interregnum', given as the William James Lecture, New York University (14 October 1982); first published in a slightly different version, *New York Review of Books* (20 January 1983); reprinted in *The Essential Gesture: Writing, Politics and Places* (London, 1988). (A key document of the 1970s in South Africa.)

Chapter 1

Black Consciousness and White Africans

New black poetry. Mtshali, Serote, Sepamla, Gwala

In literary discussion, Black Consciousness in the early 1970s is associated most immediately with what was called, variously, township poetry, the new black poetry and, in retrospect, Soweto poetry.[1] After the march of 16 June 1976, Soweto began to be associated symbolically with the activism of the entire decade. With the closest antecedents in South African literature being the 'fighting talk' of Peter Abrahams' poems in *A Blackman Speaks of Freedom!* (1940) and the prophecy of H. I. E. Dhlomo's *Valley of a Thousand Hills* (1941), this new black poetry began to appear in the literary journals *The Classic* and *The Purple Renoster*. After Oswald Mtshali's volume *Sounds of a Cowhide Drum* had been rejected by established publishers, notably by OUP in Cape Town, as 'not up to standard', Lionel Abrahams, the editor of *The Purple Renoster*, printed the Mtshali poems and followed *Sounds of a Cowhide Drum* (1970) with a first volume by Mongane Wally Serote, *Yakhal'inkomo* (1972). As a statement of identity, these new black poets soon began to give prominence not to their 'Christian' names, but to their ancestral names with Mtshali referring to himself not as Oswald Joseph – the names that appear on the first edition of *Cowhide Drum* – but as Mbuyiseni Oswald. The new black poetry by Mtshali, Serote, Sipho Sepamla, Mafika Gwala, and many others attached to BC-oriented writers' groups, charted not only the details of township life in its violence, poverty, alienation and desperate need for a healing community, but provoked argument and debate about the efficacy of the art product in contexts of socio-political urgency.[2]

Although speakers on SASO platforms propagated black exclusivity, the literary activities such as poetry readings that were crucial to programmes of consciousness-raising actually participated in a process of transition and change involving more than the strict principles of the BC movements. As I have just indicated, Lionel Abrahams – a white literary figure – played a leading role in encouraging new black voices, and white facilitators some of whom sensed new publishing opportunities, others of whom were sensitive to black aspirations, have continued to complicate a neat white/black dichotomy in literary production and reception. SASO may have organised conferences on literature and theatre with the fundamental idea that poetry and plays helped liberate the mind of the oppressed.[3] The new black poetry, however, spread its influence through newly-established, white-run publishers including Ravan Press (1970), David Philip (1971) and Ad. Donker (1973), and was probably always slightly removed from its preferred 'popular' audience in the black community. In its swift transfers from 'voices of the streets' to the art package of the attractively-produced poetry book, the new black poetry was a self-conscious, if hybrid, form of literary expression that with eclectic disregard for intellectual consistency gathered its strands from English romanticism, modernist imagism, American beat poetry, African-American spirituals and jazz, Christian liturgy, African oral praises, and popular township music. The choice of English as the medium of expression was justified as non-ethnic and unifying in the urban situation; English, nevertheless, had to be stripped of its cultural pretensions and forced into the agitated rhythms and intonations of Es'kia Mphahlele's 'tyranny of place'.[4] Accordingly, the township culture demanded expletives, a disregard for 'correct' syntax, ghetto Americanisms, tsotsi-taal (a slangy mixture of Afrikaans and dialogue from B-movies), the occasional use of phrases in the vernacular as 'devices' to block meaning for the non-African reader while bolstering solidarity in the African community, and naming words charged with emotive connotation such as Soweto, Biko, and Mandela.

None of this, of course, need deny fairly widely acceptable notions of the 'poetic', and readers of poetry were able to salve their consciences when accused of ignoring black opinion while sampling vibrant, accessible voices. The new black poetry enjoyed good sales. As the first publisher of new black poetry, Lionel Abrahams shared the view of many poetry readers that the early poems of Mtshali and Serote were intense lyrics in the Western mode of personal utterance.[5] Their unusual strength, however, was to be found more accurately in a mixture of alienated subjective expression and public representativeness. Without minimising a striking print-bound imagism, the voices sought power in 'oral' expansions and contractions of the line as a breath-unit. Serote's 'City Johannesburg', for example, combines its visual imagery with repetitions, parallelisms and a refrain all of which emphasise the musical score as the guiding principle of intonation and delivery:

This way I salute you:
My hand pulses to my back trousers pocket
Or into my inner jacket pocket

For my pass, my life
Joburg City.
My hand like a starved snake rears my pocket
For my thin, even lean wallet
While my stomach groans a friendly smile to hunger
Joburg City.

(*Yakhal'inkomo*, 1972)

Where Abrahams had difficulties was when the new black poetry prised itself free of Western-academic expectations concerning the value of the complex intuition, the rich simile, the ironical contrast and the surprising phrase, and turned to the belligerent statement, the panoply of negritudinal figures and attitudes, and – depending on the reader's sympathies – to the cumulative or garrulous journey along the road of the 'black experience'. As Serote declaims in the 65-page *No Baby Must Weep* (1975):

i am the man you will never defeat
i will be the one to plague you
your children are cursed
if you walk this earth, where i too walk
and you tear my clothes and reach for my flesh
and tear my flesh to reach my blood
and you spill my blood to reach my bones
. . .
let me seep into africa
let this water
this sea
seep into me own me
and break my face into its moods
break my chest
break my heart into the fathoms where no hands reach.

Such rhetorical affirmations – it was argued by some in defence of the new black poetry – struck the appropriate mood of the 1970s: the black voice had to create an emotional currency which rejected the norms of a literary academy seen to rely on the objective correlative of the well-wrought urn. If the realm of the transcendental was scorned, so was the burden of liberal conscience, and instead of seeking to prick the guilt of the white person, as in the early poems of Mtshali, black poets increasingly saw their function as drawing fellow blacks into processes of struggle and liberation. Dialectical movement rather than ironical inversion became the tenet in constructing the new black identity. Value was attached not to skill with words but to the idea, the action, the life: a defeatist attitude, however 'memorably phrased', was sufficient to condemn the poem. To speak boldly, to shape history, to saturate words with purpose was to carry the poem beyond closed form and, by implication, the closed society into the open field where the call for solidarity invited endorsement, in unison, from the reconstructed community. In 'getting off the ride' of racial and economic exploitation, for example, Gwala gives the impression of breaking the restrictions of the print-bound line as he projects his message into the speaking world:

> I ask again, what is Black?
> Black is when you get off the ride.
> Black is point of self realisation
> Black is point of new reason
> Black is point of: NO NATIONAL DECEPTION!
> ('Getting off the Ride', *Jol'iinkomo*, 1975)

As my 'aesthetic' vocabulary – saturate, open field, project the voice, call and response – may suggest, I am concurring with the view that a poem can have a wider definition than that of a verbal icon. I am not, however, necessarily deserting Western poetry for anything purely African. In fact, 'projective verse' summarises the reaction in the United States, in the 1960s, against the Poundian/Eliotian tradition of allusive detachment, and Gwala's 'Getting off the Ride' is clearly indebted to Allen Ginsberg's 'Howl' in its intellectual and aesthetic recovery of prophetic voice amid the constrictions of the bourgeois (racist) society. In drawing such parallels, I do not intend to undermine the distinctiveness of Gwala's 'new black poetry' but to reiterate that BC in the 1970s need not be regarded as representing a chauvinist rejection of the larger human story, as some critics have claimed.[6] Rather, the international scene was transferred, selectively, to the local determinant in ways that had not hitherto occurred in South Africa. Mtshali's *Sounds of a Cowhide Drum* is strongest, I think, when its Blakean songs of innocence and of experience wrench the universalising comment back to the particularised South African circumstance, as in the last line of 'Boy on a Swing': 'Mother! Where did I come from?/When will I wear long trousers?/Why was my father jailed?' Just as European anti-poets opposed romantic symbolism in the question of how the 'rich imagination' can confront Auschwitz, so James Matthews and Gladys Thomas used plain, 'uneducated' speech: an unambiguous statement-making that resulted in *Cry Rage!* (1972) becoming the first collection of poetry to be banned in South Africa. The state, which has never been too concerned about minority art, felt the need to take the poetic, or rather the anti-poetic, voice seriously.

Similarly, Serote's poetry should not have been entirely unfamiliar to the aesthetics of the poem. His most powerful compulsions, for example, dramatise a long-standing debate about the poet as active or contemplative being: his revolutionary knowledge tells him that the time for action has arrived while his sensitivity is concerned that bloodshed can easily diminish everyone's humanity. Yet as he followed the struggle from the singular focus of BC in the 1970s to the broader African nationalism of the ANC, Serote in his later poems would become derivative of his own initial responsiveness. It is apparent that, in important ways, the new black poetry was a phenomenon of the BC decade in the 1970s. Its Manichean psycho-dynamic in its language and perceptions gave poets the licence, as Mothobi Mutloatse phrased it with relish, to 'pee, spit and shit' on the literary establishment because 'we are in search of our true selves undergoing self-discovery as a people'.[7] To complain as several critics have continued to do that the new black poetry simplified class and gender differences within its conception of the 'people', or contradicted itself by pitting symbols of African purity against the necessity of modern, material change, is to ignore the peculiar strength of the 'Soweto voice'. It is a voice which with vigor and intensity defined the black person as heroic prototype in continuing struggle. The Western language, even the Western literary convention, was put to local use, and several so-called contradictions in the new black poetry may not be contradictions at all, but distinctive elements in BC thought. By refusing to conform to the paradigmatic expectations of either liberal idealists or Marxist revisionists, for example, BC can be seen to have been exploring and developing Africanism as a locus of philosophical, social and artistic value. In pursuing this line of re-interpretation, we may turn to Steve Biko's speeches as a key to reading the new black poetry, and consider too the influence of the political philosopher Rick Turner.

Biko and Turner: recasting the white state

Far from rejecting the West in favour of Africa – my entire study has implied the impossibility of maintaining such pristine identities – Biko found the necessary connection between material and psychological change in the 'third-world' perspectives of thinkers like Fanon, whose importance to BC I have already emphasised. Accordingly, the colonised who is 'othered' in the dominant discourse experiences the impact of race as both hard physical detail and linguistic assault and, in regarding BC as strategy, Biko understood what some critics of the new black poetry have not wanted to concede: that images of pan-African unity, noble Mother Africas, exemplary freedom fighters, and wise community storytellers may be mobilising devices in the second stage of a dialectic. Only when black people have rediscovered their self-esteem in their

Blackness can the quest for true humanity realise the potential of the non–racial ideal:

> The *thesis* is in fact a strong white racism and, therefore, the *antithesis* to this must, *ipso facto*, be a strong solidarity amongst the blacks on whom this white racism seeks to prey. Out of these two situations we can therefore hope to reach some kind of balance – a true humanity where power politics will have no place.
> ('Black Consciousness and the Quest for a True Humanity')

Unfortunately, Biko's analyses of racial and economic circumstance in the black world have been neglected in favour of his own fictionalisation as the martyred leader of novels, poems, plays and films. The most superficial treatment is to be found possibly in Richard Attenborough's film *Cry Freedom* which, in appealing to white international audiences, insulted the premises of BC by deflecting attention from Biko's story in a national narrative to a story of liberal guilt, anguish and awakening conscience concerning the person whose encounter with Biko would lead to his own banning, the white newspaper editor Donald Woods.[8]

In introducing Biko, I am not really digressing from the new black poetry but am suggesting that, in responding to what is a time-specific expression, we need to return the poetry to the climate of its years in the 1970s and, as a prerequisite of our understanding, indeed of our appreciation, spell out Africanism as a mind-set of continuing viability. Perhaps the new black poetry did not reach a mass audience or readership. Certainly its literary character, as well as its medium of English, would not have enabled it to compete with popular urban coping mechanisms such as *lifela* performances: competitions in which migrant workers fashion their shared city experiences into displays of extempory eloquence. In reminding us that art may have its *raison d'être* in its response to human injustice, however, the new black poetry, as a few critics were prepared to recognise at the time, helped break the hold the South African education system had on art as ahistorical, usually Europeanised, works of excellence. In taking what it wanted from the underside of empire in the Marxist-existential populism of the Fanons and the music of African-American resistance, in raiding idealising pictures of the African past for symbols of affirmation, and in treading the gutters of contemporary toughness, the new black poetry bound its 'art' to a social service that, 'after apartheid', should continue to be mustered in the form of teaching texts for new generations of South Africans. For in mediated as well as direct ways, the new black poetry has retained considerable potential for the 'raising of consciousnesses'. As I have been suggesting, for example, it discourages our halting literary and social argument at what may be termed the comforting poles of Western debate. In South Africa in the 1970s, the influence of British materialist revisionism in history writing had led to a great deal of polemic about liberalism and socialism in which insufficient modifications were granted to local conditions. The new black poetry, in contrast, forced connections between the 'international' and the 'local'. So did BC in its entire programme. If Biko was one of the influential thinkers at the time, another was the white political philosopher Richard (Rick) Turner whose work at the University of Natal, in Durban, was cut short when he was banned from teaching prior to his being assassinated at his home in 1977, the year of Biko's death. Turner's murder – a professional 'hit job' – remains unsolved. Turner had the ability to convey subtle ideas in accessible style, and in his popular *The Eye of the Needle* (1972) Marxist economic analysis and Christian redemptive ideals, as the 1960s 'new left' markers, are worked into a social theory for a just South Africa. It is a theory which is indebted in its strategic and practical manifestations to important local projects at the time on Christianity in Apartheid Society, run by Beyers Naude's Christian Institute, one of the organisations banned in 1977 along with the BC movements. As in the new black poetry, radical Western views are made to serve, rather than to dictate, the African commitment, and it is interesting to consider whether Biko would have granted Turner honorary membership of BC as a white African. The new black poets, who often equated poetry as art with speech as communication, would probably not have objected to the implication here that their poetry be understood in close consonance with other literature relevant to the times, such as the commentaries and analyses of Biko and Turner. In the commentary as well as in the poetry, we are talking of impressive imaginative acts: the recasting of the white state into forms of black empowerment.

Poetry by white Africans. Livingstone, Breytenbach and others

The question of what in a phase of black empowerment it could mean to be a white African is presented variously in the work of white writers in the 1970s and 1980s: as challenge, rancour, despair and cynicism. With the new black poetry featuring in academic discussion at a key symposium ('Africa Within Us') in 1974, liberally-inclined critics looked somewhat hesitantly at Mtshali and Serote as direct, aggressive and, whatever the commendable 'vibrancy' and 'newness', in danger of simplifying the complex range of what was referred to broadly as 'human experience'. With subject matter that was ephemeral and situational, what was the possibility of transcendence? For transcendence in its spiritual dimension was seen at the symposium to be the justification of the poetic art. Mike Kirkwood, however, strongly disagreed. In reacting to what he identified as the 'bourgeois-colonial' presumptions of the 1820 settler inheritance, he launched an attack on 'Butlerism' (his coinage). With Guy Butler in the audience as the representative 'settler' figure, Kirkwood paraded the prophets of the Third World – Memmi, Mannoni, Sartre, Fanon – and for the edification of his mainly white middle-class audience, he painstakingly explained colonial dependency (Prospero versus Caliban) as he sought to revalue the image of the colonised as agent of its own destiny. In re-defining transcendence, Kirkwood gave the term a Fanonist psycho-social intent, and art for liberation was advocated for both coloniser and colonised.[9]

Several hackles were raised but, in fact, most white poets who had come to prominence by the early 1970s were alert, in different ways, to the fact that neither English nor Afrikaans could continue serving poetry in forms of institutional 'correctness': a fairly widespread assumption in the years before the wind of change. (In this respect, see Butler's introduction to *A Book of South African Verse*, 1959.)[10] In Patrick Cullinan's poems, for example, lucid conversational tones, polished and unobtrusive, have the necessary flexibility and ironic insight to address the absurd as well as the everyday aspects of a 'frontier situation' that, by 1970, had moved firmly from the veld to the suburbs. The old theme that connects Cullinan back to Pringle – how to be here, completely, in Africa – is explored through images and archetypes that in the BC years recur in writing by whites: sundowners on the veranda as suburbia, half in fearful anticipation, half aware of its own paranoia, awaits the barbarians; the banality of domestic comfort behind burglar guards as the howl of dogs echoes through the evening streets. In the poetry of Peter Horn, a lecturer in German, forms of Brechtian moral story in the style of post-1945 East European 'new austerity' – romantic diction washed of its bourgeois-individualistic excrescences – provide the Marxist-materialist frame for studies of South African urban life. We encounter not solitary adventure, personal *angst* or unexpected epiphany as in the city poems of Arthur Nortje and Douglas Livingstone, but socio-economic space in which the oppressed are called upon by the poet – the 'organic' intellectual who wants to commit class suicide – to rise in organised resistance against the racist-capitalist oppressors. Wopko Jensma's truncated speech and rhythms ('baybee baa-baa/cryink/sommer 'n oaf off's feet') capture slum argot in the 'grey areas' of the city where, despite the Group Areas Act, the poor, whether white, coloured, Indian or African, rub shoulders in unrewarding work, boredom and desperate enjoyments. Given prominence, initially, in the semi-underground magazine *Ophir*, edited by Peter Horn and

Walter Saunders, Jensma's poems in their concern for the voices of the socially and economically impoverished victims of bureaucratic power, make their political statements in styles of the 'de-created' word. The point is to dismiss the high cultural reference: 'single 'm out . . . scrap/ flesh 'n bone, hyjack 'm to solar dust.'

There is some truth in Stephen Watson's observation that English poetry in South Africa suffers from linguistic deadness: an attribute of the fact that English established itself relatively early as the transmitter of middle-class commercial and educational communication.[11] Nonetheless, Lionel Abrahams' poetry showed the potential in the 1970s and 1980s of a 'middle-class' linguistic register to constitute ideas and emotions as sinewy, complicated, sometimes cantankerous, always unflinching in their refusal to put aside difficulty for the cliché or slogan:

> O, Doctor History, we
> thank you very much, but
> can you mend one
> broken brain?
> ('Dr History Delivers Another Political Martyr')

Similarly Douglas Livingstone, whom I mentioned briefly in Part Three, avoids prosaicness as well as the tag middle class in his unyielding view of human, social and literary life as a struggle for design amid the chaos of raw nature. In Livingstone's poems the urges, instincts and behaviour of the animal world act as vivid correlatives of human actions, dreams and disasters on what is depicted as a tough continent:

> Under the baobab tree, treaded
> death, stroked in by the musty cats,
> scratches silver on fleshy earth.
> Threaded flame has unstitched and sundered
> hollow thickets of bearded branches
> blanched by a milk-wired ivy. Choleric
> thunder staggers raging overhead.
> ('Stormshelter', 1964)

As these lines suggest, Livingstone's inheritance is Eliotian in its modernism according to which metaphors of complexity predominate over the reasonable speaking-voice. Having responded with some scepticism to decolonisation – his first poems were written in Zambia, then Northern Rhodesia, in the early 1960s – Livingstone has continued a tenuous search for the decency of our 'uncommon' humanity at levels beneath, above, and beyond what at the symposium 'Africa Within Us' he described scornfully as 'polit. lit.'.[12] This has resulted in his reachings towards the modern 'international' dimension: personal isolation and the need for love, hankerings after the redeeming moment, the synthesising myth, amid the detritus of urban 'ecology'.

A scientist in his daily life, a romantic in poetic moments, Livingstone forces his unease into tightly constructed artefacts, and a narrative of thirty years of poetry-writing proceeds through styles of psychological necessity, in which the difficulties of relationship and fulfilment involve multiple personae, oblique perspectives, and split images. Where the international meets the local circumstance is in Livingstone's registering consciousness that large public events in southern Africa have too often intruded upon the poem's capacity to speak a little outside the contingencies of history. Thus in the early 1960s, in Rhodesia, Livingstone debunked the heroic image of the colonial hunter while remaining wary of cries of Uhuru. In South Africa in the early 1970s, he commented on a lack of formal competence in the new black poetry[13] as he shaped his own intimations of living in the interregnum into the allusive evocations of change that would charactetise several poems in his collection *The Anvil's Undertone* (1978). 'Under Capricorn', for example, has the white motorist (poet) trapped in his Western technological convenience of the motor car or, by my analogy, the intricate artefact of the poem, as an older Africa rises from the earth in the hallucinatory shapes of bobbing goats. The creatures, however, transmute before the poet's eyes into the figure of an old African man who raises his clenched fists to the future:

> Another turn of the road,
> and only an old man there:
> mist coiling his thin ankles,
> headdress flapping, both arms raised
> like Moses; smiling, bowing
> from the edge of the highway,
> bleating the loud ironic
> blessings or curses of a
> temporarily deprived
> if most patient Lucifer.

All attempts by the poet to impose his own grid on the landscape fail. The goats refuse to remain goats, Lucifer may be the devil but is also the morning star: the new dawn. The point is that the classic white justification of Africa as the savage place cannot contain the suggestive power of the poet's own imagery. The story of Moses may have the stability of myth but, in the context of political crisis, Moses' action of leading people from captivity takes on the immediacies of historical possibility. (We are reminded that ANC leader Albert Luthuli used the injunction

'Let my people go' as the solidarity cry of the 1950s defiance campaign.) The ambiguities in the images perhaps indicate something of the poet's trepidation about, but recognition of, the inevitability of change. Whether the reader is prepared to grant the ambiguities a complex richness according to a modernist tenet or, also according to a modernist tenet, a political conservatism will involve more than a literary judgment: a social evaluation is inescapable. In regarding himself as a white African, Livingstone has at times caricatured revolutionary aspiration finding instead a gloomy scientist's confirmation about living on a continent trapped in ignorance, poverty and intolerance.

During the years of the state of emergency in the 1980s, Livingstone published very few poems: it was as though silence were his authentic response to the exigencies of the times. He was continuing to write, however, and *A Littoral Zone* appeared in 1991. This is a strong, dense sequence of poems which evinces the radical individualist's turning away from the political question to that of human life evolving from the pre-history of an elemental Africa. Sea, sand and rock are the deep constants against which the poet places the sometimes strident, more often vulnerable participants in the everyday business of civil living: beachgoers littering the sand after a picnic, the clearing of a polluted bay, the grandeur and comedy of small people in a large universe where God, or the gods, or the stars may, or may not, look down on the creatures of creation. There are fantasies about love and sex – Livingstone has remained a 'male' poet in the manner of raillery – and there are attempts to balance the unsteady ego against the shocks and buffetings of loss. In exploring the elusive divide between humanity's physical and psychical selves, *A Littoral Zone* has been praised by some for remaining untendentious and, in the metaphysical sense, for transcending the political struggles that in the 1980s forced white South Africa to admit to the defeat of its racist policies. Others have seen an evasion of political accountability at a time when the huge subject of human cruelty and human freedom in South Africa – it is argued – should have been the prime consideration of a humanising activity like literature. Whether or not Livingstone wants to be regarded as a political poet is not really the point. The politics of crisis have insisted on ideological interpretation, and as we track Livingstone the scientist and the poet, the internationalist and the colonial, through his commitments and ambiguities back to the contexts of the surrounding society, his identity as white African raises more questions than it can resolve. Even if we regard *A Littoral Zone* as anticipating a post-apartheid concern with ecologies of creation and destruction, there are those who are going to insist that ecology be removed from the realist/romantic dichotomy and attached to politicised interests about whose rights will prevail when a future civil government has to tackle the issue, say, of wildlife preservation at the cost of land for uprooted communities. To this the reply could be, go to the working paper not to the poem, and Livingstone's South Africanness may yet be identified in the capacity of his poetry to provoke strong debates about the responsibility of the poet in a society of scarce resources and narrow tolerances, in both economic and literary life.

I have devoted attention to Livingstone not only because his poetry is so vivid in its craft that whatever one's views on politics and aesthetics, the poems qua poems demand a serious response from the literary person, but also because his poetry returns us forcibly to difficulties of interpreting the continuing value of the white African contribution. Although they had appeared by the early 1970s, all the poets, except for Jensma, whom I have mentioned here are still active today. In the cases of Cullinan and Abrahams, the fierce political allegiances that were demanded of writers in the state of emergency have had the effect of pushing the two towards determined defences of the poetic art as a contemplative calling. While Abrahams' poetry remains gritty about its own liberal openness, his critical utterances have begun to sound quite recalcitrant about 'slogan poems',[14] and while Cullinan has felt the need to stress that South Africa is his home, he has utilised local typologies less and less and increasingly devoted his skills to generalised issues of modern unease. In making available, in English translation, the wonderfully humane poetry of the Italian Eugeno Montale Cullinan, like Abrahams, seems to be endorsing the approach of Uys Krige in the 1930s who saw his mission to bring 'sophistication' (Cullinan's repeated way of phrasing it) to the South African tribe.[15] Indeed, such a mission as supported prominently by Cullinan and Abrahams virtually became the editorial policy in the 1980s of the long-running literary journal *Contrast* (now *New Contrast*). But if there is something broadening about the sophisticated endeavour, there is also the danger of loss. Cullinan, for example, no longer seems to write from within anywhere with any completeness, and instead of recognising 'a modern sense of disquiet' in his poetry we may recognise the recurrent colonial desire to be international. What remains taboo in Cullinan's approach is the Africanisation of Africa. To be a white African is, perhaps, to live and write if not exactly in contradiction, then in paradox. Although Horn might not see the matter quite in this way, his own poetry has more and more revealed a paradox that to me was not so apparent in the 1970s. In its grasping at 'alternative discourse', BC – I have suggested – registered elisions of Africanism and Westernism, and although Horn's Marxism has always been strictly economistically European in its semantic and linguistic code, his protest tended to be seen in the early 1970s as an ally of the dominant black dissidence. Looking back, however, I am struck by Horn's reliance on European Marxist models. It is a reliance which during years of massive change in both the former Soviet bloc and in South Africa has remained constant to a fault in his poetry and, in consequence, renders him not so much white African as émigré European. As he wrote in the 1970s in 'Explaining My New Style' (or, explaining Brecht's style):

> I do not walk in the forest
> admiring flowers and trees:
> but among policemen
> who check my passport
> and my political background.

A problem of location also characterises the Afrikaans poet Breyten Breytenbach who since 1960 has lived in self-imposed exile in Paris and, while on a clandestine assignment in South Africa in 1975, was arrested on political charges and sentenced to nine years in prison. Found guilty of recruiting anti-apartheid activists, Breytenbach served seven years of his sentence. 'I am an African,' this Afrikaans dissident declares in a 'note on autobiography' at the end of *Judas Eye* (1988), his English re-creations of Afrikaans poems written while he was a political prisoner. But he hastens to add: 'I was to become Europe too.' *Judas Eye* is fairly representative, in fact, of the Breytenbach style, in which down-to-earth observations are permitted their point without displacing the predominantly surrealistic manner, a Sestiger manner:

> I dreamed:
> I'm in a prison of white walls
> where nobody knows me where voices
> go absent in corridors where lights sough
> my skull wheezes
> I saw my self:
> squat to shit in a bucket of flies
> come with summer nights
> the lights sigh white flames
> . . .
> I awoke:
> when the judas-eye looked a start at me.
> ('the dream')

By contrast, the early collection in Afrikaans, *Skryt* (Screech, 1972), has remained unusual in Breytenbach's œuvre. In this single group of poems, which is alert to student revolt in Paris and Black Consciousness in South Africa, Breytenbach seemed to want to find a new language not only to attack the religious and political intolerance of the Afrikaner volk, but to align his sympathies with the new black poetry that was beginning to emerge from his home country. As a result, his penchant for linguistic display yielded in *Skryt* to the bare utterance, to naming words in which African resettlement camps are catalogued as charges of horror, and to lists of people killed in secret-police detention. (The list as litany moving slowly down the screen, incidentally, would mark one of the more dignified moments in Attenborough's film *Cry Freedom*.) After *Skryt*, however, Breytenbach returned to the Sestiger fashion, and the challenge of reading his large output of poetry and prose as the contribution of the white African artist-activist, for so he has styled himself, clearly involves more than simply 'appreciating' his unusual extensions of Afrikaans word potential. (Such an ahistorical formalism remains fairly common in Breytenbach studies.) It also involves more than justifying his pursuits of the solitary ego at the cost of granting *content* to his dissent, survival and rehabilitation: a content that could have the effect of transforming style into the matter of literary politics.

His Vietnamese wife having been granted a visa in 1973 to accompany her husband to race-obsessed South Africa, Breytenbach recorded in the philosophical-travel narrative *A Season in Paradise*[t] (1980; 1976) all the crises and longings of the Afrikaner who has rejected his own inheritance. Realising that the demise of apartheid – a demise for which he had campaigned on public platforms – might also mean the demise of his own people the Afrikaners, Breytenbach sought a sentimental heartland in what I shall term the 'Jan Rabie' myth: at essential points deeper than the crude functionings of the apartheid state, the Afrikaner – working the land, carving a language out of the contours of the earth – was already an African (a person of Africa) who now had to be guided from the false vision of a jealous nationalism back to his Africanness. Such a myth of pastoral location did not sustain Breytenbach, however, and in 1975 he embarked on what turned out to be an amateurish mission in the service of black liberation politics. His apologies in the courtroom together with the curious show of Afrikaner *volksunie* as the secret police pleaded for leniency on behalf of their prisoner, are well documented.[16] What was traumatic for Breytenbach was the fact that, however much he was still regarded as the premier Afrikaans poet whom the literati had long dubbed a prodigal artist-son, he knew that his self-esteem no longer permitted him to be an Afrikaner. Yet in calling himself an African, he continues to have difficulties in giving substance to the concept.[17] For in crucial ways Breytenbach remains a rebel against all organisational and classificatory demands. If he despises Calvinist mores, he also despises English liberalism which, in borrowing his terms from Fanon, he typifies as bourgeois capitalist. Having spoken out strongly in support of black liberation – he is explicit in his public statements, if not in his poetry – he now expects authoritarianism as a matter of course from a future black government, and *Return to Paradise* (1993) is full of anticipatory spleen. In all this African dislocation, the anchors in his work have easily, perhaps superficially, been identified as European, or international, in familiar modernist affiliations: his poetry unfurls in the flourishing metaphors of romantic-symbolism; his prose involves us in the arty labyrinths of language games; we are invited to look into mirrors of illusion which succeed in disturbing the boundaries of art and commitment. The international, rather than the local, scene seems the apt location for Breytenbach's interpretative community: a community among whom the poet is regarded as an artist victim of all that is, or was, prejudiced and racist in South Africa. To fill the hollow core of Breytenbach's Africanness with the complex psychology of the alienated Afrikaner, nevertheless, constitutes a valuable recuperative procedure, at least as far as South African readers are concerned. For one thing, we are forced to return his style to the motor energies of the specific culture in which the plays of language may be interpreted as structuring devices imposed on unstructured time: not only the time of Breytenbach's prison years but, looking backward and forward, the time of his years in exile as the angry young (and now no longer young) man. The flights of fantasy, the sustaining memory, the intense interest in natural minutiae, free associations of thought and image, the oral impulse in the auditory character of words and swelling rhythms, fictional concealments, moments of calm in Zen detachment – these, in greater or lesser degree, have always been features of Breytenbach's writing. Yet in trying to identify the African dissident in the modernist, we might want to ask how Breytenbach's literary effects *affect* communities, outside the literary sphere, in the hard life of the South African people.

As in the case of the other white poets I have discussed, Breytenbach's need to be European and African is problematic, and from one point of view perhaps that is how it should be. For if being black is to be more hybridised in perception and humanity than the rhetoric of BC was willing to countenance, being a white African involves more than can be summarised in any uniform identity. From another point of view, however, there is to be found in white poets of the 1970s a common element which could have been at odds with their location in a country that is 'poor' in its literary investments. The element is modernism which, whether the selected mode is symbolist or anti-symbolist, whether the politics are progressive or conservative, typifies a voice highly self-conscious about speaking in the tongue of the poem, really worried about whether it is an 'art voice' or a 'politics voice'. Whatever the interpretation given to white African, the modernism positions these poets substantially in the cultural climate of the 1970s, when the demands for new perceptions and new languages were marks of a society entering its period of transition. In seeking a role, the poet grasped at the loose ends of a modernist/anti-modernist habit, and attached status either to the permanence of the lyrical craft as a bulwark against what was regarded as unsophisticated politicking, or to word weapons with which to bash in the heads of the bourgeoisie. If these two reactions can be seen, beyond ideology, as obverse sides of a similar recognition concerning the destabil-isation of word and referent, then the new black poets probably also revealed their modernist, or rather anti-modernist, compulsions as they rejected the trivial moral space of the closed form for the open field of future time. As the state of emergency in the 1980s spread its politicis-ation, some poets held even more tenaciously to the muse; others relished the insulting retort. Yet the most interesting challenge – a point to which I shall return – has been to try to move beyond reaction.

Notes

1. For representative selections see these anthologies: R. Royston (ed.), *To Whom It May Concern: An Anthology of Black Poetry* (Johannesburg, 1973), which was published abroad as *Black Poets in South Africa* (London, 1974); M. Chapman and A. Dangor (eds), *Voices from Within: Black Poetry from Southern Africa* (Johannesburg, 1982); T. Couzens and E. Patel (eds), *The Return of the Amasi Bird: Black South African Poetry, 1891–1981* (Johannesburg, 1982); S. Nbada (ed.), and *One Day in June: Poetry and Prose from Troubled Times* (Johannesburg, 1986).

    Critical commentary, M. Chapman (ed.), *Soweto Poetry* (Johannesburg, 1982); M. Chapman, 'Soweto Poetry', *South African English Poetry: A Modern Perspective* (Johannesburg, 1984); N. Gordimer, *The Black Interpreters* (Johannesburg, 1973); A. McClintock, ' "Azikwelwa" (We Will Not Ride): Politics and Value in Black South African Poetry', *Critical Inquiry*, no. 13 (Spring 1987).

2. In addition to commentary in n. 1 above, see M. Chapman, 'A Tough Task for the Critic: Mongane Wally Serote's *A Tough Tale*', *Upstream*, vol. 6, no. 3 (Winter 1988); J. Cronin, ' "Even under the Rine of Terror": Insurgent South African Poetry', *Staffrider*, vol. 8, no. 2 (1989); and E. Mphahlele, 'Mongane Serote's Odyssey: The Path that Breaks the Heels', *English Academy Review*, 3 (1985). In contrast to the generally sympathetic readings of the above critics, see S. Watson's several articles, *Selected Essays, 1980–1990* (Cape Town, 1990) and 'The Rhetoric of Violence in South African Poetry', *New Contrast*, vol. 20, no. 2 (June 1992). Also, B. Harlow, *Resistance Literature* (New York, 1987).

3. An important event was the SASO Conference on Creativity and Development (Hammanskraal, 1972). See the chronology in M. Chapman (ed.), *Soweto Poetry* [n. 1 above].

4. Mphahlele, 'The Tyranny of Place and Aesthetics: The South African Case', in C. Malan (ed.), *Race and Literature/Ras en Literatuur* (Pinetown, 1987).

5. Abrahams, ' "Political Vision of a Poet": Mongane Serote's *Tsetlo*', in M. Chapman (ed.), *Soweto Poetry*.

6. See S. Watson, 'Shock of the Old: What's Become of "Black" Poetry?' [n. 2 above].

7. Mutloatse, Introduction, *Forced Landing. Africa South: Contemporary Writings* (Johannesburg, 1980), p. 5.

8. See Woods, *Biko* (London, 1978; rev. ed., 1987).

9. Kirkwood, 'The Coloniser: A Critique of the English South African Culture Theory', in P. Wilhelm and J. Polley (eds), *Poetry South Africa* (Johannesburg, 1976).

10. In reaction to Butler's 1959 anthology see M. Chapman (ed.), *A Century of South African Poetry* (Johannesburg, 1981). The *Century* offers a representative selection of poetry in English for the period of the 1970s.

11. Watson, 'Recent White English South African Poetry and the Language of Liberalism' (1980/83), *Selected Essays, 1980–1990*.

12. Livingstone, ' "Africa Within Us". . .?', in P. Wilhelm and J. Polley (eds), *Poetry South Africa*.

13. Livingstone, 'The Poetry of Mtshali, Serote, Sepamla and Others in English: Notes towards a Critical Evaluation', in M. Chapman (ed.), *Soweto Poetry.*

14. Abrahams' attack on Jeremy Cronin's evaluation of 'worker poets' was the first of several responses by Abrahams on the debilitating effects, in the 1980s, of politics on poetry. (See Cronin and Abrahams, *Weekly Mail*, 13–19 March 1987, and 3–9 April 1987, respectively.) See *New Contrast* and *Upstream* for several of Abrahams' responses.

15. See Cullinan interviewed by M. King and S. Watson, 'A Modern Sense of Disquiet', *New Contrast*, vol. 20, no. 4 (December 1992).

16. See for example J. Cope, *The Adversary Within* (Cape Town and London, 1982), pp. 165–82.

17. See among numerous interviews and comments since the unbannings of 1990, Breytenbach's 'Land of Myths', *Sunday Tribune*, Durban (19 August 1990) and 'Lead Us from the Wasteland, Mr Mandela', *Sunday Times*, Johannesburg (21 April 1991).

Chapter 2

The Black Theatre Model. Towards an Aesthetic of South African Theatre

Black Consciousness and the popular play

The other cultural form promoted by BC through SASO cultural commissions was theatre which – like the poetry – found itself having to oscillate between 'poor' and 'rich' environments. It sought the poor in the township audience; it more often got the rich in the art-going intelligentsia. Performed by theatre groups with strong ties to student activism, such as TECON (the Theatre Council of Natal) and PET (the People's Experimental Theatre), the typical BC play of the early 1970s not unexpectedly had as its primary mission consciousness-raising. As in *Shanti*, which was first performed in 1973 and is one of the few of these plays to be committed to the printed script, the protagonists as representative figures of the oppressed are propelled through dramatic confrontations with an authority that appears in the caricatural forms of brutal state functionaries and their black 'sell outs'. The purpose is knowledge of identity in kinship with the organic, heroic black community: the people. At crucial points, actors step out of their roles – which, in any case, are 'thin' – and in declamations urge acts of resistance from what, ideally, should have been an empathic black audience. The principle was that art and life discovered common cause in the conscientising event. Actually, in popular literary discussion 'culture' rather than 'art' remains the preferred term: human exchanges, of which the poem or play are kinds, that refuse rigid distinctions between what lies within a text and what lies outside.[1]

The popularising BC play, however, did not escape being the subject of dispute within radical ranks. Marxist-revisionists, for example, identified a leader-follower approach according to which the student facilitators handed messages down to the populace: the question became whether BC discourse was not too intellectually biased to be effective as a wide medium of communication. There was also the problem of practical obstacles preventing BC theatre from finding venues in the townships. The inequalities of apartheid had ensured that theatres hardly existed in black areas: there remain literally none in African townships. In the tense mood of the 1970s, moreover, township authorities (that is, white officials) were suspicious and fearful of any gathering with political connotations, and began denying activist theatre groups the use of community halls. In contrast, the *truly* popular plays of Gibson Kente flourished before large, enthusiastic audiences of real black people in the township community. Kente, a successful impresario, utilised big casts in slick song-and-dance sequences that blend Hollywood musical and urban-African marabi rhythms. Social problems – poverty, alcoholism, sexual promiscuity, family differences between the old and the young, tensions between rural conservatism and new city ways – are removed from any precise political consideration to the level of the 'human condition'. Audiences are encouraged to reject the deviant intruder – the tsotsi, the evil witch doctor – and reassert their endurance, courage and good humour: their African ubuntu, or just their common humanity, as the prerequisites of their self-respect. Seeking new opportunities in the politicisation of the times Kente, who runs his own theatre training school and who began his career with 'township' musicals like *Manana, the Jazz Prophet* in 1963, turned in 1974 to producing the political plays *How Long, Too Late* and *I Believe,*[2] which resulted in his being treated in the same way as BC theatre groups and prohibited by township superintendents from performing in community halls. Returning to his familiar brand of 'social problem' musical, Kente resumed his theatre in the townships and, in the state of emergency in 1987, he was the only black playwright to be staged in the main, as opposed to the fringe, programme at South Africa's premier arts festival in Grahamstown. The play *Sekunjalo* (The Hour Has Come) warned against the folly of what at the time were the socialist-economic predilections of the liberation movements, with the result that young 'comrades' aligned to the UDF threatened to close down the show once it had left the protection of what was seen as the very 'white affair' of the Grahamstown festival.

Despite this, Kente continues to draw large crowds with entertainments that confirm the value of resilience in the ups and downs of life. BC theatre, in contrast, spurned the Kente formula and built stage actions around political talk interspersed with illustrative, often exemplary stories. Like the poetry, the plays veered towards the interests of the BC movement and, as township venues were denied them, theatre groups were driven to performing, in white areas, in venues such as university theatres and church halls that were exempt from certain racial restrictions. In 1965 different races had been forbidden to associate in the same places of entertainment, and plays were not permitted to employ racially mixed casts. In line with their programmes of black identity, BC theatre groups in fact did not want whites in their casts; neither did they want to perform in the main theatres in white areas: performing opportunities which, in any case, would have been denied to them. What these groups found particularly distressing in the circumstances, then, was to have to deliver their messages not to blacks but to small, reasonably discerning white audiences which, with tolerance, accepted BC consciousness-raising as an attack on their own guilty consciences. In 1977 laws against segregation in theatres were repealed: not as a sign of liberalisation, but as part of the state's new 'safety valve' approach in the easing of so-called petty apartheid. In terms of censorship, this began to mean the assessment of literary works and theatrical productions by 'committees of experts' on the publications control board according to which the absolutist view of 'danger to the safety of the state' — the criterion at the time — yielded to a more relativist view concerning the effects of a work on its likely audience. This meant in practice that black theatre, which by that time was operating in mainly white, intellectual venues, was permitted simply to continue without state harassment. (The term 'black theatre' had come to distinguish the protest brand from Kente-type 'township theatre'.) Whereas the script of Matsemela Manaka's play *Egoli: City of Gold* (1979) was banned, for example, the performance went ahead without hindrance at the Market Theatre in downtown Johannesburg before audiences which were more 'avant garde' than 'activist'.

The first black theatre to emerge from SASO cultural programmes in the early 1970s had regarded itself as serving the larger BC movement. The author of *Shanti*, Mthuli Shezi, would have described himself as an activist not a playwright. Shezi, vice-president of the Black People's Convention, was killed in 1972 in a racial confrontation with a railway official who pushed him under an oncoming train. In contrast, playwrights like Manaka, who by the late 1970s had established themselves at the Market Theatre and other 'alternative' venues, had perceptible artistic ambitions. If black plays connected to venues like the Market Theatre have not been regarded as particularly threatening by the state, however, this should not be allowed to undermine their contribution to the idea of indigenised theatre in South Africa. I shall argue, in fact, that the black theatre of the 1970s provides us with a pivot from which to articulate a tradition that has the potential to attack the static character of the closed society and contribute a dynamic dimension to social life. Of the numerous black plays performed in the late 1970s and early 1980s, *Woza Albert!* (1983) may serve as a representative case.

Devised by the two actors Percy Mtwa and Mbongeni Ngema, this two-man play took its story from a heated argument about what might happen were Jesus Christ, in a second coming, to turn his attentions to apartheid South Africa. (*Woza* means 'rise up'.) This core story — in its oral dramatisation, a core 'image' — was then worked into a stage action involving improvisation and mime: the two actors rush in and out of roles, thus giving the impression of bustling community presence. After the worker, Zulu-boy, is conscientised in the brickyard, which could be a parody of the Garden of Gethsemane, and after his racist boss is ridiculed as a product of government news-speak ('there are agitators at large'), the two actors – the BC 'organic' intellectuals who share the trials of the people – watch Zulu-boy invoke the spirits of political leaders in a grand tableau of solidarity. (Albert = Albert Luthuli, president of the ANC in the 1950s.) In envisioning a 'community of resistance', the play virtually erases distinctions between black and white activists, and rivalries between the ANC and PAC. Several issues are hinted at in the course of a tumbling action. Does organised mass resistance, for example, really need to invest faith in miracles? At points, the Christ figure is almost dismissed; at other points, Black Theology (Christ sides with the poor of the earth) flattens religious and political discourses into a singular cry of liberation. Discussion, however, remains very secondary to empathy, and if conventions of stage illusion are punctured with jokes and with quick changes of hats and coats, the thrust is towards the BC goal of unity between black actor and black community: the unity of 'the people'. Whether – as a critic says – black theatre gestures in all directions at once,[3] its black/white axis clearly conveys its intention of pitting the strength of community against the inequities of apartheid. Still, we (academic critics?) may regret that the hard-edged talk of early BC plays has given way so entirely in *Woza Albert!* to a theatricality of display, in which didacticism almost undercuts itself in its haste to return to the knock-about routine.

As should be evident from my commentary, *Woza Albert!* is a vibrant, hybridised spectacle: hybridised to the extent of being pulled into 'Western' stage time – the evening's-entertainment-with-interval – by Barney Simon, the white professional theatre director at the Market Theatre, who understood concentration spans among literary theatre-goers. *Woza Albert!* was first performed at the Market in 1981 prior to its following a familiar black theatre route: the tour to art festivals abroad as an example of a 'theatre of the oppressed'. In looking at Mtwa and Ngema's play for its South African roots, we can identify elements of traditional African performance that H. I. E. Dhlomo had in mind in 'Nature and Variety in Tribal Drama' (1948), an article which attempted to formulate an aesthetic for theatrical performance: oral improvisation, a pattern of action in the imagistic accretions of folk-tale, the ritual of ceremony, the correlation of actor and audience as sharing common knowledge and aspirations. We may also appreciate that, as Dhlomo said but did not always put into practice in his own plays, tradition has to live in the contemporary idiom. *Woza Albert!* is certainly not 'traditional' in any antiquarian sense. Rather its 'tradition' dissolves into the city experience:

Mbongeni goes on applauding. Percy reappears wearing his pink
nose and a policeman's cap. He is applauding patronisingly.
Mbongeni stares at him, stops applauding.
PERCY. Hey! Beautiful audience, hey? Beautiful musician,
     né? Okay, now let us see how beautiful his pass-book
     is! (*To appalled Mbongeni.*) Your pass!
MBONGENI (playing for time). Excuse my boss, excuse?
     What?

With its BC solidarities catching at popular swirls of conversation and
music, we are reminded that Mtwa and Ngema began their careers as
actors and singers in Gibson Kente's township plays: social problem musicals which, in turn, have their own antecedents. Kente had been connected originally to the Union Artists whose multiracial endeavours in the
1950s culminated in *King Kong*, the African jazz opera.[4] All this Africanness, of course, is impure not only in its brazen minglings of the traditional
and the contemporary, according to which the need for conservative
stability can complicate the desire for progressive change. It is also impure
in its eclectic borrowings from Western dramaturgy. Whereas Kente
favours the soap opera, black theatre turned to the *commedia dell'arte*, or
to the absurdism of Beckett's tramps, while the stage theories of Grotowski
(*Towards a Poor Theatre*) and Brook (*The Empty Space*) served the actual
poor conditions of small-cast plays with minimal props. The plays are
thus apt metaphors for an ideology of poorness: for stage actions that can
undermine the rich theatre and, in the poor condition, rediscover the
human richness of the oppressed.

   Such a model, which I shall call conveniently a 'black theatre' model,
has considerable potential. It can incorporate, simultaneously, elite and
popular structures of feeling. It can focalise and re-focalise ideas and attitudes that in stage actions may claim 'authenticity' in both African and
Western dramatic practice. Under certain necessities, the black theatre
can shed its musical scores and inhabit the barest existential space, as in
Athol Fugard's *Boesman and Lena*. Or, in looking for other opportunities,
it can load its core image with ritual and ceremony either in the recovery
of the African past or in the symbolic construction of the African identity.
Its very adaptability, however, can lead to facile self-imitation and repetition: a few dances here, a few songs there, some vehement statement-
making about victims and victimisers. The 'contemporary' vibrancy can
lapse – as in many of Manaka's plays – into the romanticised pan-African
memory; problems of urban living can give the impression of being too
easily solved in bravado and boasting. The righteousness of black anger
can lead quickly to moral collapses: Ngema's *Asinimali* (first performed,
1985),[5] for example, ends up doing violence to its own professed ideals
of ubuntu by expecting the audience's unqualified support for its spec-

tacle of revenge in the necklacing of a traitor. In the swift, recurrent actions of mime and song, the BC intention may manifest itself in the slogan rather than the exploration, and the demand for solidarity can restrict the range of representation. As I have already suggested, actor-leaders often end up 'directing' the depictions of grassroots communities in compliance with a notion of BC unity. With a plastic nose as a marker, whites (played by black actors) are made out to be such buffoons as to prompt the question of how they managed to retain power for so many years. In an argument to which I shall return, BC is seen by women's studies to have granted public prominence only to men while women were consigned to playing the support-sisters of the revolution. It is a fact that there have been relatively few opportunities in black theatre for women besides those of group singers and dancers. But while we may note in this respect BC's tendency to separate public from domestic responsibilities, we need to keep in mind that we are also talking of a politics of access to the resources of theatre according to which ownership and direction are still the preserve of white cultural authority. Theatrical opportunity has been difficult enough for black men. It is undeniable, nonetheless, that a male ethos in black theatre has led to an aggressive style of acting: bare-chested men assert themselves in pelvic thrusts which are metonymic of male camaraderie in the single-sex environments of the prison or mining compound as the common settings of many plays.

Minority and majority theatre. The performing arts councils to the worker play

How far the surface recognitions of popular modes are inimical to complex thought, and how far the popular has ensured stage-effectiveness in a polarised political situation, are subjects of ongoing debate. What I am suggesting is that the black theatre model be regarded as the basis for attempts to delineate an aesthetic of South African theatre. We are reminded, accordingly, of the large narrative behind the conventions: the performance rather than the script links the stage to conceptions of popular culture, as a way for people – living amid the shacks of city alienation and ethnic instability – to generate a sense of their belonging to a community. Theatrical activity that in South Africa falls outside such a paradigm is minority theatre. There have been the ambitions of state-subsidised arts, for example, in the form of the National Theatre Organisation (1947) and, subsequently, the performing arts councils, which were established in 1963. Here, seriousness has meant the Shakespeare production or the post-Ibsen fourth-wall drama, as the performing arts councils sought to foster 'civilisation in South Africa' with the white sector of the population targeted as the audience. The middle classes of course have to be entertained as well as instructed, and the performing arts councils have had their own version of the popular: musicals like *South Pacific*; the Gilbert and Sullivan opera; the Agatha Christie mystery; more latterly, the Andrew Lloyd Webber opera. What the mainstream theatre-goer describes as 'theatre impoverishment' in this country usually has to do with the fact that British Equity's opposition to apartheid severely curtailed the staging in South Africa of contemporary plays from abroad.[6] Outside the majority black theatre model, there has also been a sporadic verse drama, which has usually been bookish and has emanated from university circles, while there have been intermittent forays by Afrikaans writers of Sestiger stamp into surrealistic dramas about spiritual guilt.[7] When we turn to local variants of the popular, however, the theatre tradition – as I have begun to chart it – has been resilient in grounding its concerns and structures in the surrounding life. In Afrikaans drama, for example, the Euro-absurdism of Bartho Smit has provided less of a direction to younger playwrights than have the old Afrikaner family sagas of the 1930s. In the latter vein, one of the more stimulating experiments has been Pieter-Dirk Uys's *Die Van Aardes van Grootoor* (1979), first performed in 1977, which had its genesis in a popular radio serial, *Die du Plooys van Soetmelkvlei*. By parodying the women's serial, in which misfortunes somehow always right themselves, Uys takes his audience through sketches of Afrikaner history, focusing finally on the corruption of the government of the day: corruption which, it is suggested in the overblown style of the play, requires to be cleansed in a holocaust of destruction. Among recent Afrikaans playwrights, Reza de Wet and Deon Opperman have also turned the family saga into an investigation of splits and divisions in the volk's reaction to contemporary political change. As in Uys's practice, the popular intersects with the serious in the use of radio and television serials as the touchstone of 'family' recognition while the comforting myth that 'alles sal regkom' (all will come right) is subjected to corrosive irony.[8]

Popular history has continued to provide the Junction Avenue Theatre Company – one of the most astute dissident groups of the 1970s – with possibilities for a serious theatre that retains wide communicative appeal. In *Randlords and Rotgut* (first performed 1978), for example, the issue of racial and economic exploitation on the mines was embodied in the form of Victorian music hall. With creative borrowings from sources as diverse as Brechtian epic narrative and the shebeen *Drum* story, Junction Avenue as in the play *Sophiatown* (first performed 1986) has attempted to recover a heroic image of a suppressed black history while recognising class differentiation as a factor in any grand narrative of a new nation. With the Company alert to forms that since the unbannings have complicated the Manichean black/white allegory of liberation and oppression, the play *Tooth and Nail* (first performed 1989) defies synopsis – it is as if the plot of history is entirely uncertain – and shifts many characters and events into confrontations with the sign systems that constitute versions of reality: biblical lore, tribal tradition, revolutionary mystique, documentary fact. New South Africans – the play suggests – have few political certainties, and having had the past codified in monoglossial, not heteroglossial, terms will have to become competent readers of all the signs. In *Tooth and Nail*, post-modernism thus turns the black theatre model into unrecognisable shapes as the role of the artist is defined not in the rhetoric of solidarity, but in the paradoxes of detachment and commitment according to which the difficulty is the preservation of free, creative vision in a revolutionary context. Possibly the popular drive here has become elite, and instead of celebrating freedom in *Tooth and Nail* we could say that the play is characteristic of post-unbanning anxieties particularly among intellectual whites who fear the so-called people's will as anathema to subtle understanding of what life, let alone art, is supposed to be all about. It is difficult to anticipate where Junction Avenue Theatre Company, which was born into the struggles of the 1970s, will go after apartheid.[9]

A popular white form – the cabaret-like revue – has begun since the unbannings to smuggle 'bourgeois' consolations into its apparent iconoclasms. In his one-man shows Pieter-Dirk Uys having satirised the arrogance of P. W. Botha's military state in the 1980s has broadened his range to include the full spectrum of the society. Now that the ANC is unbanned – the argument goes – its leaders, like any other leaders, are grist to the satirist's mill, and in his brilliant impersonations Uys puts on stage his puppet and monster versions of the far Right and the far Left with F. W. de Klerk and Nelson Mandela, in the centre, as the two blind mice. The warning is against any authoritarianism, and the subtext has special reassurances for the mainly white suburban audiences that flock to Uys's reviews. Not only are extremists banished to the loony bin – in suburbia both de Klerk and Mandela have come to be regarded as moderates – but should a black government display the same turpitude as the old white government, this could confirm albeit in a perverse and paradoxical way that whites, in the era of apartheid, were not really the brutes they had been told they were. Rather, they were merely fallible like any rulers. Oddly, the iconoclastic Uys ends up making a good case for a cast-iron bill of rights to protect the citizenry from whatever tyrant or clown might in the future become the state president. If popular modes can be both conservative and progressive, then Uys in his chameleon roles is both. Or, perhaps he is neither. His shows, incidentally, make more money than Kente's.[10]

A clear, unambiguous message was the aim of the worker plays that began to appear in the mid-1980s under the auspices of COSATU, which at the time had strong UDF and therefore, by implication, ANC affiliations. In these plays, or dramatic sketches, the emphasis was on theatre development in which bread-and-butter issues were dramatised in factory-floor situations, the purpose being to communicate information to semi-literate workers. Other plays took as raw material large-scale strike actions, as in *The Clover Story* and *The Dunlop Play*, and constructed ambitious stage narratives concerning the trade unions' support for political activism on a nationwide scale.[11] Whether these plays can be called popular or not is worth pursuing. They did not arise spontaneously from among workers themselves where grassroots expression is likely to favour the church sermon, the hostel storytelling session or, as packaged by the internationally-travelled band Ladysmith Black Mambaso, *isicathamiya* music: soft-dance music, a mixture of African sounds and movements catching the rural/urban memories, sadnesses and joys of migrant workers. Theatre as an institution, as distinct from rituals of survival and fulfilment, has no base in African working-class life, the closest theatrical experience being the township plays of Gibson Kente. In trying to educate trade-union consciousness, therefore, theatre facilitators attached to sociological and cultural projects in the unions and the universities created the worker play of the 1980s which, in modifying the black theatre model, attempted to shift Black Consciousness towards an amalgam of Africanist-identity symbols and Marxist class analysis. With perhaps too eager a desire for new unities, the amalgam presented itself as 'worker consciousness'. Set in the alienated industrial space, these plays tended to be as strong or as weak as their 'organic' intellectual organisers and have all but ceased to exist. Most activity occurred in Durban where Ari Sitas, ex-Junction Avenue Theatre Company and lecturer in industrial sociology, played a key role through a development project, Culture and Working Life, attached to the Department of Sociology at the University of Natal. Despite or perhaps because of being 'manufactured' the plays, mostly unscripted, raise questions about political and aesthetic representation that continue to be important in the study of theatrical possibility in South Africa.

Given that black theatre is so often vivid, quick-paced, cathartic and individualistic in its reliance on colourful township types, how – asked Sitas – does one portray the gigantic mechanisms of the workplace, in which exploitation occurs not only in dramatic confrontations, but in invisible forms stretching over long periods of time? How does one, in consequence, reduce the standing of individual characters, when the 'individualised' boss or shop steward allows for inventive portraiture, and show collective heroism in the crowded existence of factory-floor life?[12] Some of the solutions were germane to the conditions of worker theatre. Performed in trade-union halls rather than professional venues with ordinary workers rather than trained actors in the roles, low costs and utilitarian views of who could be an actor permitted large casts: the crowded 'stage' was materially real, and the message – organise and act rather than, as in black theatre, react in instances of display – was reinforced by disciplining the music and dance sequences to the rhythms of the quasi-military toyi-toyi step as the metaphor of national activism. But the national arena could not be allowed to predominate over the factory, and information about everyday worker life was conveyed in non-dramatic monologues (ordinary talk) which, in telling of years spent on the production line, slowed the action to the dignified time of pride-in-endurance in contrast to black theatre's frenzy of desperate, on-the-spot, city survival. While a single person stood at centre and told the story of his working life, a 'cranky' (a paper reel of tableau pictures) unfolded across the back of the acting area thus linking the single teller to a representative history of worker struggle over many years. In the worker plays I have seen, such a theory of aesthetics, highly intricate in its formulation, did not translate consistently into performance, which veered back and forth between the 'dignity' of the worker play and the 'street-wise opportunism' of the black theatre. The truth of the practice, as distinct from the theory, was probably a more accurate indicator of the state of the society in the 1980s, in which black trade unionists were also members of an oppressed black populace. 'Workerism' and 'populism' in the substance of daily life have continued to complicate the intellectual categories of race and class.

Mda and Fugard. Literary playwrights and the black theatre model

A compelling need to capture the living substance of ideas characterises the work of probably the two most literary playwrights to have adapted the black theatre model to their purposes: Athol Fugard and Zakes Mda. Writing from Lesotho where he had his education, Mda, a student of the theatre, came to prominence in the late 1970s when his plays *Dead End* and *We Shall Sing for the Fatherland* (written in 1973) were produced in South Africa in the theatre climate of Black Consciousness. Both plays owe as much to Beckett as to African storytelling, but where the African element finally asserts itself is in the specificities of the subject matter. While he can be distinguished from most solidarity playwrights by his concern with the indeterminate, subjective consciousness, Mda refuses to inhabit an ontologically absurd universe. In *We Shall Sing* the two tramps, ex-soldiers of the wars of independence, find themselves still economically dispossessed in the independent country. Looking beyond South Africa

222

2

to the post-independent African state, Mda struggles intellectually with the problematics of race (the Africanist necessity for psychological freedom) and class (the 'bourgeois-fication' of a new elite). The dramaturgy poses, rather than tries to resolve, the difficulty. In *Dark Voices Ring* (first performed 1979), the Africanist impulse is predominant: the young man justifies his joining the guerillas while the emotional core of the play is found in the trauma of his mother who has to face the consequences of a life spent evading political conviction. In *The Hill* (first performed 1980), the emphasis has shifted to the economic principle: Mda's indictment of the stranglehold that the South African mining industry in its demands for cheap labour has over impoverished Lesotho. This could sound 'sociological'; the play, however, proceeds through a modernist action of sharply juxtaposed perspectives, in which the datum of poverty subserves human behaviour and, as is characteristic of Mda, heroics are muted. Unlike *Woza Albert!*, *The Hill* refuses the climactic unity of the freedom song. Mda has been criticised for his pessimism and commended for his toughness of vision; commended for shaping life into art and criticised for his art wanting to obscure life. His own response in his Marotholi Travelling Theatre has been to try to use his skills as intellectual and actor not merely to *show* villagers in Lesotho their situation, but – in a theatre of development – to help them become active participants in the transformation of their own life-scripts. For Mda theatre art, whether on the professional stage or in the rural clearing, has societal dedication.

While remaining less convinced than Mda that he wants a commission from society, Athol Fugard has had a commission thrust upon him. A white African of severely troubled conscience, he found his first inspirations in the 'poor theatre' environment of urban, industrial Johannesburg. In recollecting his experience as a clerk in the Native Affairs court in 1958, Fugard records how he watched with horror as pass-law offenders by the drove were shunted into gaol on petty technical offences. With images of African urban life etched in his mind, he co-operated with Sophiatown intellectuals who were attached to Union Artists, the result being his early plays *No Good Friday* (1958) and *Nongogo* (1959) both of which premiered at the Bantu Men's Social Centre. The style was reminiscent of *King Kong*, in which small people in violent surroundings assert their 'individualistic' desire to escape to other, possibly white worlds. Although assimilationist rather than radical, these township plays struck a 'bastardised' local accent that could live on the stage and, in any discussion of a black theatre model, we are reminded that Fugard is a precursor of the form. Among his most stage-effective plays are his collaborative pieces with John Kani and Winston Ntshona who, together with Fugard and the non-racial Serpent Players in Port Elizabeth, anticipated the BC theatre of the 1970s in plays like *Sizwe Bansi Is Dead* (1972) and *The Island* (1973), which were first performed at the 'alternative' Space

Theatre (Cape Town). (*The Island* was originally called *Die Hodoshe Span*.) In *Sizwe Bansi* a photograph in a pass book and, in *The Island*, a returning prisoner's horrible and hilarious stories of life on Robben Island are core images that provide the oral impulse for an improvised storytelling sufficiently anecdotal, particularly in *Sizwe Bansi*, to permit modification, even alteration, on any night in performance as a running commentary on topical events.

The plays, however, are not loosely structured. In scripting the spirit of performance into the permanence of the text, Fugard has the elements of improvisation reinforce a fundamental message: survival in harsh times. In *Sizwe Bansi* Styles's photographic studio, a place where people are allowed to dream, is suddenly inverted through a use of stage lighting into apartheid's bureaucratic nightmare: a photograph in a pass book defines the African's presence in the city with the result that Sizwe Bansi – the Jim-comes-to-Joburg figure – must die, figuratively, in order that he might live and provide for his family under the name of the dead man whose pass book is stamped with working rights. In *The Island* the play-within-the play – *Antigone* is to be performed by two prisoners – is held up in its Greek tragic anticipations prior to being collapsed into the local condition: there is no Creon who is sensitive to a conflict between divine conscience and state duty; the South African state, characterised by thugs, stamps on the oppressed who have to bond together in gestures of brotherhood. As far as BC theatre practitioners were concerned, however, the destruction of the apartheid system, not survival within its dictates, was regarded as the driving force in cultural expression: Fugard's plays according to such a tenet did not escape their Aristotelian tradition in which suffering ends up superseding radical questioning. Argument continues today about the character and quality of Fugard's commission.

Fugard has been praised in liberal circles and attacked by Marxist critics, for example, on the same issue of apparently wanting to transcend the South African locality in studies of the human condition, and the collaborative plays are not seen as entirely typical of his practice. At the same time, he has been found by some influential Africanists to be frankly insulting in depictions of black people that verge on the stereotypical.[13] Prior to his involvement in the collaborative plays with their oral residue, Fugard had turned from *No Good Friday* to economical Beckett-like settings. In *The Blood Knot* (first performed at the African Music and Drama Association, Johannesburg, 1961), games of evasion and defiance by the two coloured brothers fail to mask the fact, at least for the audience, that Morrie and Zach have absorbed into their self-images apartheid's legislative degradation of the non-white body. In *Hello and Goodbye* (first performed at the segregated Library Theatre, Johannesburg, 1965) Hester's escape from the claustrophobia of her father's Calvinist house is both brave and sad: she goes to Johannesburg where she whores for a living. But worse than this, the play suggests, is the fate of her brother Johnny who, as his crutches visibly indicate, remains crippled by the ghosts and guilts of his dead Afrikaner inheritance. In *Boesman and Lena* (first performed at the Rhodes University Little Theatre, 1969) the coloured Lena as the apotheosis of the Hottentot Eve is mentally abused by her mate, the pathetic Boesman, even as she grasps her self-esteem from the rubbish heap that signifies the life of poverty and homelessness enforced upon these coloured wanderers by the policies of apartheid. The stage set was 'poor' in its use of scraps of paper and tin.

One cannot answer with any finality whether plays like *Boesman and Lena* are 'South African' or 'universal'. Clearly, however, the characters Boesman and Lena are not representative of any bickering married couple. Their speech rhythms are accurate transliterations into colloquial English of the poor coloured-Afrikaans accent:

> BOESMAN. Quiet, hey! Let's have a *dop*.
> [Lena registers Boesman's hard stare. She studies him in return.]
> You're the hell-in. Don't look at me, *ou ding*. Blame the white man. Bulldozer!
> [Another laugh.]
> *Ja!* You were happy this morning. 'Push it over, my *baas!*' '*Dankie, bass!*' '*Weg is ons!*'

An ear for dialect is one of Fugard's strengths, and we are reminded of class markers in his own speech that locate him in the underprivileged communities for which he has consistently shown compassion and respect. (His father was working-class Irish, his mother an Afrikaans-speaking cafe owner.) Neither can *Boesman and Lena* be experienced adequately through the perceptible influences of absurdist theatre, nor Camusian existentialism, even though Fugard frequently mentions the effect of Camus's courageous pessimism on his work. Again, the universalism, or do we mean post-war European *angst*, takes its accent from the local condition: giving edge to the play are the Verwoerdian policies of racial 'clearing' and 'resettle-ment' that characterised the 1960s. Fugard accurately describes the impression on stage of *Boesman and Lena* when he says that he concerns himself with specifics: 'If there have been universals in my writing they have had to look after themselves. . . . When the fire-blackened paraffin tin or Boesman's flea-ridden mattress, or the mud between Lena's toes means something to me, things might start to happen.'[14] That Fugard is liberal in seeking value in human nature − rather than radical in seeking value in revolutionary action − is undoubtedly true. That his black characters are merely mimics is unfair: there is an important distinction to be made between the caricature and the stage-effective type, and Boesman and Lena convey very credible psychologies from behind their coloured slang. (When the play toured in South Africa in 1969, incidentally, racial prohibitions led to the two wanderers having to be played by whites with blackened faces, most memorably by Fugard himself and Yvonne Bryceland.) What *Boesman and Lena* shares with the other Fugard plays that I have mentioned so far is an action that fills the stage with its purpose: the spectacle has moral impact, and Fugard's limitations – it seems to me – lie elsewhere than in whether or not he is universal, whether or not he is revolutionary.

Concerned that he might have been short on social specifics in *Boesman and Lena*, Fugard found in Grotowski and in his African actors' storytelling skills the social commission that in *Sizwe Bansi* would manifest itself in the 'black perspective'.[15] But instead of moving forward with the possibilities of the black theatre on an open stage, he harked back to the script and the fourth wall in plays of talk rather than plays of feeling. The trouble is that Fugard is not a philosophical playwright. When he fails is when his ideas fail to be transmuted into experiential action. This is the case, I think, with *A Lesson from Aloes* (first performed 1978) and *My Children! My Africa!* (first performed 1989). In both plays there are too many words. As he elaborates on his ideas, Fugard is in danger of lapsing at one moment into abstractions, at another into good sentiments. In confirming that he is a liberal – he has felt the need frequently to justify himself in these terms – he is inclined to forget what gives his brand of liberalism its power: a deep-seated Calvinist concern with guilt that infuses his ideas with both torment and generosity. In *Playland* (first performed 1992) the subject is guilt and atonement as the African nightwatchman and the white ex-soldier meet in a dusty fairground somewhere in the Karoo. It is New Year's Eve, which is made to symbolise the eve of South Africa's post-apartheid dawn. Having spent years in prison for murdering the white 'master' whom he caught with his wife in the domestic servant's room, the night-watchman has to try to come to terms with his bitterness and even to reach tentatively to an understanding of the soldier who, as a victim of the 'total onslaught' ideology of the 1980s, has killed SWAPO guerillas in the Namibian war. The ideas of forgiveness and reconciliation could have been nobly embodied in the stage action. But the black perspective and the agony of the Calvinist, as two Fugardian strengths, are missing. As a result, the discrepancy between the two men's 'crimes' points beyond the play's own comprehensions to the ingredient that Fugard should have but has not stirred into his debate: justice. For blacks to show forgiveness might require whites to expiate their sin of racial pride, something the ex-soldier does not begin to comprehend. In the end it is perhaps worth returning to the observation that Fugard has remained caught in the ambiguity of wanting liberalisation while hedging

about liberation.[16] Times have changed since 1961, however, when Fugard
in *The Blood Knot* began to revolutionise South African theatre by putting
black experience on centre stage with a seriousness that had not hitherto
been encountered, and an astute remark by Michael Billington summarises
what may be a dilemma not only for Fugard but for other white Africans
who want to make the transition to an open society. Of *Playland* Billington notes that not only is the symbolism oppressive (funfair = white
escapism; pigeons = personal freedom) but that too strict a control is
exercised over the characters and their situation. Although the idea is that
we look to the future, the dramatic structure relies too heavily on a
'closed' stage which encourages the characters to dwell oppressively on
their own oppressive pasts.[17] What is absent is the mobility of the black
theatre model that Fugard helped initiate, but failed to develop.

Sarafina!: the seriousness of popular response

A free-flowing form is the strength of Mbongeni Ngema's widely
acclaimed *Sarafina!* (first performed 1986), the politicised Kente-style play
that forged the content of UDF activism into the song-and-dance routines
of the township musical. With the Soweto schoolgirl Sarafina anticipating
Mandela's release from prison as the utopian event that will ensure black
freedom (Mandela's photograph is used as icon), the play in its film
version in 1992 could have been seen to have fallen into the trap of
popular idealisation. Although Mandela was by then free and attended
the opening night of the slickly choreographed film, freedom in the
world of politics was continuing to prove more morally, socially, even
ethnically, divisive than the liberation rhetoric of the 1980s had been
prepared to contemplate. According to one (white) critic, *Sarafina!* the
film was myth-making at its best whereas the intellectual tradition insists
that good art is really about myth-shattering.[18] Not caring about the
expectations of good art, audiences which were mainly black packed into
cinemas to see the film. What *Sarafina!* offered, presumably, was inspiration through recognition. The schoolgirl hero undergoes a testing
experience that, in the years of the emergency, had been authenticated
in the news stories of the alternative press as the national narrative of
liberation. Against graphic images of police terror and township resistance,
Sarafina comes to know the bitter cost of struggle and the need, despite
torture and deprivation, to redouble her commitments. The dance of
unity at the end – embarrassingly reminiscent of a tribal extravaganza –
did not succeed, fortunately, in undermining a picture that is powerful

in its very one-dimensional focus on a community fighting the machinery of the state.

One may point to the irony of an intrusive white hand in the making and promotion of the film: a white South African film director, Hollywood expertise, and a R2 million subsidy from the South African government that in its pre-1990 guise was the villain of the piece. Despite this, *Sarafina!* did not make the mistake of *Cry Freedom* in turning the camera on to a white story about discovering black suffering, or adopting its cause. Rather, the screen was bequeathed to the black perspective, and the venue was the popular cinema, not the elite theatre, at prices that ordinary people could afford. In 1992 *Sarafina!* was both myth-making and myth-shattering: its remembrance was the cruelty of apartheid; its yearning was freedom; its international kudos invited world-wide assent for the black story. It is easy to be cynical about such meshing of the ideal and the opportunistic, the serious intent and the commercial temptation. At the same time, we should allow *Sarafina!* its inevitable complicity in the modern world while measuring its emotional and psychic veracity in contrast to the lucrative African song-and-dance shows that, stripped of any social comment, have over many years coined money for mainstream theatre. In 1974 Bertha Egnos's notoriously exploitative *Ipi-Tombi* (a romance of warrior chiefs and gyrating maidens), for example, played to full houses in South Africa and went on to support three touring companies abroad. (A film version appeared in 1994.) *Sarafina!* can be seen countering the effects of the *Ipi-Tombi* syndrome. It firmly removes black people from their colonial station in the musical as loin-skinned primitives and, with panache, places them on the screen as thorough-going moderns.

Theatre criticism can trouble the literary-academic mind. Where Martin Orkin's valuable study *Drama and the South African State* (1991) goes awry – it seems to me – is where, in desiring the correct idea, it is too hesitant in granting stage effect its own kind of statement. In choosing to find the creative potential of South African theatre in a black theatre model, however, modes of the popular will require our serious consideration.

Notes

1. *Shanti*, in R. 'Mshengu' Kavanagh (ed.), *South African People's Plays* (London, 1981). (See Kavanagh's introduction.) Other scripts of 'black theatre' plays in D. Ndlovu (ed.), *Woza Afrika! An Anthology of South African Plays* (New York, 1986) and in editions by single playwrights including conveniently

M. Maponya, *Doing Plays for a Change* (Johannesburg, 1995). For selections by black and white playwrights see S. Gray (ed.), *Market Plays* (Johannesburg, 1986) and *South Africa. Plays* (Johannesburg and London, 1993); T. Hauptfleisch and I. Steadman (eds), *South African Theatre: Fours Plays and an Introduction* (Pretoria, 1984).

Besides the studies listed in the General Bibliographies see, as commentary on South African theatre, articles in several issues of *Critical Arts, in English Academy Review,* 2 (1984), the *South African Theatre Journal* including the special issue 'Theatre Arts at the Crossroads', vol. 7, no. 2 (September 1993), and the special issue 'Performance and Popular Culture' of *Journal of Southern African Studies*, vol. 16, no. 2 (June 1990). Also: K. Sole, 'Identities and Priorities in Recent Black Literature and Performance: A Preliminary Investigation', *South African Theatre Journal*, vol. 1, no. 1 (May 1987) and I. Steadman, 'Stages of the Revolution: Black South African Theater since 1976', *Research in African Literatures*, vol. 19, no. 1 (Spring 1988).

2. Script of *Too Late, South African People's Plays* [n. 1 above].

3. B. Peterson, 'Apartheid and the Political Imagination in Black Theatre', *Journal of Southern African Studies*, vol. 16, no. 2 (June 1990).

4. See Part Three for commentary on Dhlomo and *King Kong*.

5. Script in *Woza Afrika!* [n. 1 above].

6. Labelled Eurocentric and elitist by 'alternative' theatre-goers, the performing arts councils, which operate as regional theatre companies, have been under severe ideological attack especially since the unbannings of the 1990s to restructure themselves as more representative of the entire South African community and to become income-generating companies.

7. In the 1950s H. W. D. Manson wrote several poetic plays in which the isolated male consciousness, as the epitome of the Renaissance ideal, sought its ontological being in mysterious, often misty settings. See as representative *Magnus* (Pietermaritzburg, 1970). While tending like Manson towards elaborate musings in blank verse, Guy Butler at least attempted to look at issues of local concern in *The Dam* (Cape Town, 1953), *Cape Charade; or, Kaatje Kekkelbek* (Cape Town, 1968), and other plays.

8. See the section on Van Wyk Louw, in Part Three, for reference to Afrikaner family dramas. In the 'tradition' there is de Wet's *Nag Generaal* (1988) and Opperman's *Stille Nag* (1989). See S. Gray on Uys's *Die Van Aardes . . .*, *English in Africa*, vol. 6, no. 2 (September 1979).

9. Scripts in *At the Junction: Four Plays by the Junction Avenue Theatre Company* (ed. M. Orkin) (Johannesburg, 1994). See F. Meintjies's interview with director of Junction Avenue, Malcolm Purkey, *Weekly Mail* (7–13 July 1989).

10. Other examples of 'white cabaret' include Johannes Kerkorrel and André le Toit of the Gereformeerde Blues Band, a kind of rock musical parody of the Afrikaner bourgeoisie and, displaying Calvinist guilt amid its iconoclasms, Gerrit Schoonhoven's *Piekniek by Dingaan*.

11. For synopses of plots and details of worker theatre in the 1980s see A. von Kotze, *Organise and Act* (Durban, 1988).

12. Sitas, 'Culture and Production: The Contradictions of Working-class Theatre in South Africa', *Africa Perspectives, New Series*, vol. 1, nos. 1–2 (1986).

13. See R. Vandenbrouke, *Truths the Hand Can Touch: The Theatre of Athol Fugard* (Johannesburg, 1985); Mshengu, 'Political Theatre in South Africa and the Work of Athol Fugard', *Theatre Research International*, vol. 7, no. 3 (1981); and L. Nkosi, 'Athol Fugard: His Work and Us', *Home and Exile and Other Selections* (London, 1965).

14. CAPAB–PACT–Phoenix Programme Notes with Phoenix Players production of *People Are Living There* and *Boesman and Lena* (1969).

15. Fugard's Notes (26 December 1968) reproduced in his introduction to *Boesman and Lena and Other Plays* (Oxford, 1978), p. xxv.

16. See D. Cohen, 'Athol Fugard and the Liberal Dilemma', *Brick*, no. 40 (Winter 1991).

17. Billington, Review, *Weekly Mail & Guardian* (19 March 1993).

18. M. Gevisser, Review of *Sarafina!*, *Weekly Mail* (2 October 1992).

Chapter 3

The Story of Community: A Resilient Tradition

Seeking a community in *Staffrider*

Throughout the 1970s a popularising discourse continued to challenge separations between art and politics while emphasising the social role of the writer and performer. In 1979 the demands of Africanism led to several black writers resigning from the Johannesburg branch of the international PEN organisation on the grounds that its avowed non-racialism was a euphemism for Eurocentric dominance in matters of selection and taste: something that was to be countered by the all-black African Writers' Association (AWA), founded in 1979. While she regretted the move, Nadine Gordimer indicated that she understood the strategic purpose; Lionel Abrahams, on the other hand, saw the term Eurocentric as a caricature of liberal values, and refused to compromise on the principle of non-racialism. In 1982 the Botswana Festival on Culture and Resistance brought writers in South Africa together with those in exile.[1] The programme looked back at the achievement of BC while simultaneously beginning to use a language of non-racialism that suggested the influence of ANC views as espoused in the Freedom Charter. White writers at the conference, including Gordimer, nonetheless came in for a rough time in being accused of remaining in South Africa and therefore benefiting from the privileges of their white skins. While non-racialism was the ideal, BC gave the edge to various forms of radicalism by both black and white commentators.

In attacking Leavisites, who in the late 1970s still had considerable purchase on university English departments, critics such as Stephen Gray, Tim Couzens and Nick Visser adopted 'African' priorities in projects to recover lost voices: with the 1930 edition virtually unattainable, Sol T. Plaatje's *Mhudi*, for example, was reprinted with a new introduction that 'placed' Plaatje as a significant founding figure, certainly as the most significant early African writer in South Africa. From a Marxist-materialist standpoint, Kelwyn Sole and Isabel Hofmeyr engaged in polemics in 'alternative' sociological journals such as *Work in Progress* concerning criteria of evaluation appropriate to South African literature.[2] Instead of identifying a number of key books as the exclusive canon – the approach of the long-running journals *Contrast* and *Standpunte* – they described literature as a discursive field: writing and speech acts that reflected and refracted the culture of the society. If such revisionist projects were sometimes in danger of being ideologically programmatic, sometimes in danger of romancing Africa, a solid start had been made not only in returning forgotten works to print where they could be read and interpreted, but in initiating critical reconsiderations of the concept 'South African literature'. By the mid-1980s it had become possible to regard the literary field as challenging, contested and, in whatever way critics might have wanted to delineate it, as a crucial aspect of our human and social understanding. In the 1970s the battles were fought not so much in university journals – academic literary exchange in South Africa came into its own in the 1980s – but in the pages of the creative magazine. To take one of several examples, rebellious young writers grouped themselves around the short-lived *Donga* (1976–78) which in Afrikaans, English and occasionally in seTswana published stories that attacked the state's military obsessions and cocked a snook at Afrikaner Calvinist morality. It was less the content of anti-militarism and sexual explicitness than its association with the BC writers' group Medupe, however, that resulted in the permanent banning of *Donga* after the eighth issue.[3]

Probably the most influential 'radical' contribution was the monthly magazine *Staffrider*, which in March 1978 began to tap the voices of protest and resistance that were emanating from many township writers' associations: the legacy of BC creativity and development. Having several years earlier swiped at 'Butlerism' Mike Kirkwood, a university lecturer, was at the time of Soweto in open rebellion against the great traditionalism of his own English Department at the University of Natal, Durban. With the backing of Ravan Press, which had emerged from the Christian Institute Programmes against apartheid, Kirkwood as part of an editorial team launched *Staffrider* with a mission that went beyond convincing the 'colonial culture' to extend its Leavisian sets of values beyond the British mainstream to include selected 'good' South African works: the approach of Jack Cope, editor of *Contrast*. Rather, Kirkwood had the idea of creating a forum for a people's community-view of literary expression. Literature – it was stressed – had a small 'l'. The base would be popular rather than elite; the strength would derive from township communities rather than from notions of established culture; the 'autobiography' of experience, in its witness of daily black life rather than the art object of solitary contemplation, would provide the model of value. The 'staff-rider' figure was emblematic (the daring black youth who defied authority by riding free – like staff – on the runner boards of the township trains), and the magazine sought to celebrate the spirit of defiance that in the

Soweto marches of 1976 had exploded the myth of the invincible white state. Combining individuality and collectivity – the same mix, incidentally, that had characterised Fugard's *Sizwe Bansi Is Dead* – the staffrider figure captured the mood of the many stories, poems, interviews and illustrations (linocuts and photographs) that filled the pages of the magazine. If the ideology was broadly Africanist, authenticity and truth (as judged by the writers' associations that selected their own work for inclusion in *Staffrider*) were inextricably bound to the fact of the writer having *lived* the black experience. The weight of the testimony in the saturation of words and images with mimetic observation, therefore, acted as a kind of norm according to which the aesthetic criterion could virtually be equated with use-value. Although *Staffrider* in its attractive format looked like an art journal and was probably read more widely among literary people than among the communities it saw as its real audience, it was consistent in defining its art – it employed the term art – as 'applied art'. The phrase is of course Achebe's, and describes the novelist as teacher: *Staffrider*, too, saw writers as having responsibilities as teachers of their people. In fact, one of *Staffrider*'s deepest insults to the ethos of Literature with a capital L was to imply that the artist was not as valuable to society as the community person who, in subscribing to democratic attitudes of sharing, accessibility and accountability, would in all probability have a worthwhile tale to tell.[4]

With the testimony of the poets Serote and Gwala already having begun to transform short lyrical poems into open fields of expression, *Staffrider* did not contribute anything particularly new to poetry: the 'children of Soweto' as a figure of speech defined utterances as heroic; Biko became the icon of praises; and Chris van Wyk, one of the more impressive voices of the late 1970s, introduced telling semantic variations to standard forms of protest: in detention 'He slipped from the ninth floor while washing/He fell from a piece of soap while slipping.'[5] It seemed as if the influence of Mtshali, Serote, Sepamla and Gwala, however, was still too close and commanding to require modification in any substantial way. Where *Staffrider* opened new potential in creative writing was in giving space to storytelling that found inspiration in the earlier *Drum* writing even as it began to delineate its own 'tyranny of place' according to which the flamboyance of Sophiatown gave way to the structural violence of the government-regulated township, Soweto. Ignoring or not knowing the conventions of the economical story of implication and epiphany, writers in *Staffrider* built up their tales in amalgamations of oral recurrence – literally, the untutored residue of close living – and newspaper reportage as the most immediate 'copy' to hand of their own experience. Determined to reject the ethnic imperatives of apartheid, and aware of limited publishing opportunities for vernacular stories which would have had to be approved for school reading, the writers sprinkled African languages into their dialogues as a gesture of commitment to the source culture while using the English of plain communication. The choice of English, in fact, revealed both the petit-bourgeois status of the writers who were schoolteachers, journalists, and so on, and the erosion of linguistic facility that, as a result of the disastrous Bantu Education system, had begun to affect the educated as well as the under-educated African speaker of English. Whereas Can Themba, educated in the relatively elite mission-school system, was prepared in the 1950s to challenge the stodginess of serviceable English by coining new and unusual turns of phrase, most *Staffrider* stories push their way through, rather than leap over, the barriers of language. It is not always easy to decide whether the dead metaphors and formulaic utterance that characterise a great deal of the writing succeed in evoking an effective 'imitation' of oral styles, or simply confirm a flattened inter-language dependency on lists of idioms and proverbs drilled into the head at school. Yet out of this unpromising situation, several narratives found their own road forward in shouldering the large subject of the black story. What has been illuminating to me, as a reader and critic, is that once I had been drawn into the accumulated content of *Staffrider*, I found myself having to re-assess several conventions of the modern written story.[6]

Matshoba: the storyteller as teacher

In any re-assessment of storytelling potential, Mtutuzeli Matshoba provides an interesting case. Like several other writers in *Staffrider*, Matshoba was given encouragement by Kirkwood, and, under the Ravan Press imprint, went on to publish a collection, *Call Me Not a Man* (1979). In reflecting life on his 'side of the fence' so that 'whatever may happen in the future, I may not be set down as a "bloodthirsty terrorist" ', Matshoba who dropped out of Fort Hare University and has worked for many years in low-key clerical and translation jobs 'writes himself' into a central debate as the observer, the counsellor, the storyteller of his rudimentary Soweto community. The question implicit in his stories, or long testimonies, is: at what point does the sectionalism of BC cease being affirming in its reconstruction of the self and become racist in its negation of ubuntu, the sharing humanity that Matshoba's own stories see as having informed the long view of the black person's struggle? In 'Three Days in the Land of a Dying Illusion', the corruption and nepotism of the modern Transkei Bantustan, which in 1976 had been set up under apartheid decree for Xhosa people, is contrasted to key moments in Xhosa history:

The baggage of the *godukas*, all *godukas*, consists of their
sweat and blood in the migrant labour-system. They work
hard for meagre incomes with which to buy little gifts and
useful implements in an attempt to make their folks' lives
a little more bearable in the forlorn wildernesses that are
said to be their homelands.
. . .

My mind was thrust back into the dubious past. Only
one thing was I certain of: Nongqause had been a daughter
of those parts. . . . In order to understand my
interpretation of past and present events in relation to each
other, I think it necessary to review the tale I heard from
my instructional voices.

In circling his stories within other stories Matshoba's narrator, who is not
really distinguishable from Matshoba himself, interprets the national suicide of 1856 not as confirmation of Xhosa defeat, but as a severe reaction
against the loss of dignity attendant upon enforced survival within the
strictures of colonisation. The lesson for his contemporaries, who according to Matshoba have sold their heritage for the crumbs of a farcical
independence, is to take the radical stand: to recover the consciousness
of their own story as prerequisite for seeing beyond current setbacks and
reclaiming their dignity. (With the Matanzima family having turned the
Transkei into a fiefdom, major-general Holomisa, who favoured co-
operation with the ANC, seized power in a military coup in 1987, and
in 1994 the Bantustans were re-incorporated into South Africa.)

In 'A Glimpse of Slavery', the famous *Drum* exposé of prison-farm
conditions in 1954, or the actuality of a repeated scandal, forms the
subject of Matshoba's lesson in sharing and solidarity as the 'educated'
storyteller finds comradeship among the humble prisoners on the boer's
farm.[7] As in Matshoba's other stories, the dramatic incident, in this case
the storyteller's escape from the farm, is not the key to the action;
rather, the prisoners' talking through the experience shapes the narrative
as a process of understanding. Similarly, 'A Pilgrimage to the Isle of
Makana' converts storytelling time – brief and paradigmatic – into historical time – syntagmatic in the journey across a landscape of learning – as
Matshoba sets off by train from Soweto to Robben Island to visit his
brother who is a political prisoner. With Makana, the warrior-prophet
of the amaXhosa, providing the inspirational myth that in BC iconology
saw the political prison renamed the Isle of Makana, and with the '76
schoolbuildings still smouldering, Matshoba charts the country as a map
of rejuvenated black history. At the same time, he tries to connect his
own BC predispositions in lengthy, contemplative passages to the ideals
of a broader non-racialism. Like the oral teller, he 'pads' his narrative

with digressions and exemplary incidents while, as in folk-tale mode, immediately recognisable types – in this story, boorish officials and resilient mother Africas – act out their roles in sharp racial confrontations. At the end, Matshoba underplays his close links to his brother so as to shift the human story away from the personal to the historical perception:

> 'Hi son,' I said into the mouthpiece.
> 'Hey't,' the service crackled back inaudibly.
> . . .
> Where could Mandela be staying on the Island.
> . . .
> *A luta continua*, I thought.

The language is direct, easily accessible, even restricted in its vocabulary and literary range. Yet the style of the journey signals Matshoba's confident occupation of the cultural ground: in terms of a Manichean aesthetic, the black other has become the subject, and the story suggests that value is determined not so much by the created properties of art as by relations embodied in social communication. The thin text has the advantage, paradoxically, of putting us in touch with the author behind the tale. While we might recognise Matshoba as a product of Bantu education, we may want to appreciate his authority in a particular time and place. As I have noted as an 'African' literary trait, the demand of the story is ethical. In responding to Matshoba's democratic intent, critics trained to revere the brilliant artefact may themselves need to undergo a kind of radical revisionism and perceive themselves as European 'others' in relation to the community storyteller. A reading of Matshoba, accordingly, does not only involve us in lessons about the black experience. For the white academic critic, there is a lesson to be learnt about the necessity for humility in the poor conditions of South African educational, cultural and literary life.

Many stories in *Staffrider* were 'thinner' than Matshoba's in their considerations of moral purpose; many were 'richer' in their presentations of ironies, subtleties and nuances. Yet Matshoba has retained the unsettling quality of attracting to his stories debates that have sharpened understandings about the potential of writing in a contested field. Three debates in particular continue to have currency.[8] First, Matshoba's stories have been analysed as revealing the limitations of the BC race-conscious vision: although he introduces economic circumstances, the thrust – we are told – remains the revindication of all the black oppressed as a unified entity. Second, Matshoba has been identified by the academic writer, Njabulo S. Ndebele, as one of the black writers who in relying on spectacular depictions of racial confrontation, failed to enter the ordinary gradations of black experience where – Ndebele continued – we would find evidence of a complex, interior humanity. Third, Matshoba has seemed to confirm the view of women's studies that BC tended to delegate subservient roles to women in the larger story of oppression and liberation. The points are not new, and are not confined to Matshoba. As I have suggested, however, the experiential story need not be expected neatly to confirm the abstract categories of race and class, especially in a situation in which race has overwhelmed class in the national psyche as the legislative and mythic marker of who was and who was not permitted to be fully human. We can go on to defend Matshoba's stories in that they were attuned to the temporal demands of black experience in the 1970s. Ndebele's case for the ordinary, nevertheless, should be allowed to remain powerful and persuasive for, like Mphahlele before him, he has had to insist that in a system designed to demean black humanity the African person requires all the humanity that is deserved. In his own stories, several of which first appeared in *Staffrider* and are collected in *Fools* (1983), Ndebele intrudes political consequence indirectly through his characters' conversations about their personal dilemmas. In 'Uncle', which is reminiscent of Mphahlele's 'Grieg on a Stolen Piano', the generous figure of the boy's uncle, as we infer, is the symbol of ubuntu, and in the title story 'Fools' the meeting of the older man – a schoolteacher – and the young activist develops obliquely in personal interchanges that have ramifications for the surrounding family life as well as for the life of political commitment. What we are drawn into is, in essence, a psychological struggle on the part of the older man to face up to his own failures of resolve and conviction: the young man who displays his 'activism' in order to conceal his vulnerability is the older man's alter ego. In Matshoba, in contrast, the actions remain firmly 'on the surface' as the storyteller guides us through the mental landscape.

The landscape, however, does not necessarily evince spectacle. Rather, Matshoba's immediate recognitions, which as I have noted are almost folkloric, subserve his considerations of discovery. In the case of Ndebele, ironically, the implicatory mode turns out to be a highly artificial construction of the ordinary. What I am suggesting is that in looking at Matshoba and Ndebele, we encounter not necessarily better or worse depictions of black life, but different conventions of representation each of which has its own challenges. What is important, therefore, is to utilise the terms 'ordinary' and 'spectacle' as categories for debate rather than as self-evident definitions. Such an approach is helpful also when we turn to the unusual stories of Joël Matlou, a *Staffrider* writer of the late 1970s whose tales were considered to be somewhat eccentric in the BC context. (They were collected only in 1991 under the title *Life at Home*.) In first drawing critical attention to Matlou, Ndebele saw the writer's ordinariness measured in the fact that his stories did not present the political event in an explicit way, but explored processes of response. At the same time,

Matlou's style may be welcomed as a version of spectacle in its quality of naïve (magical?) realism as we follow the teller through mixtures of precise observation and quirky recollections from his rural beginnings to the mines and, his humanity intact, back to a freer awareness of what it is to be alive, well and undefeated in adverse circumstance: 'everyday is a time for a wise man'. The celebration centres on small victories rather than on the certainty of new political dispensations.[9] But if Matshoba, in contrast, employs symbols of national struggle, little is certain about his own journeys of experience.

On these journeys – to turn to the third point I introduced above concerning BC's depiction of women – Matshoba's women mouthpiece-figures are treated neither more nor less sympathetically than their male counterparts. In 'Three Days', it is the woman on the bus, the Mother Africa, who asks the question that causes the men to squirm: why were they so foolish as to have accepted the hollow independence of the Bantustan? If the woman is a stock figure – the wise, resilient grandmother of folk-tale – she is also the symbol of a necessary attempt to re-establish continuities with a usable past. She may not mount a sustained attack on the patriarchal hierarchies of traditional African society according to which men bear public faces and women give practical advice. Neither, however, does she simply bolster the men's image of their own mascu-linity: ' "You enjoy being referred to as family heads. Father, father, all the time, but you forget the very tummies of the reasons for your fatherhood status." ' Somewhere in Matshoba, there is the need to be progressive almost beyond gender relations about a humanity that, as in the writing of his contemporaries Miriam Tlali and Ellen Kuzwayo, has had to learn to struggle back from the edges of disempowerment: a humanity that has made the idea of writing one's life an actual possibility.

Stories of the collective and isolated self. Tlali, Kuzwayo, Gordimer, Aucamp, Ndebele and others

Like Matshoba, Tlali and Kuzwayo are thinly educated in any literary tradition. It is the compulsion of their testimonies rather than the art of the genre that has shaped their voices into expressive forms. In the case of Tlali, the forms include the novel or, simply, a series of incidents, as in *Muriel at Metropolitan* (1975). Here, Muriel in unobtrusive though acute observations describes, and increasingly interprets, her experiences as a bookkeeper in a bustling furniture store catering for the 'black trade': racial and economic exploitation are identified in the business of the daily round. Having contributed journalistic sketches of ordinary Sowetans to *Staffrider* Tlali continued, in the 1980s, to combine reportage and dialogues in stories that focused on the problems associated with black women's urbanisation. Similarly, Kuzwayo's *Call Me Woman* (1985) – perhaps a kind of rejoinder, or complement, to Matshoba's *Call Me Not a Man* – records, autobiographically, the black woman's achievements against the adversities of city living. These include Kuzwayo's dealing creatively with the disappointments of a broken marriage – cultural dislocation is cited as a contributing factor – and intervening on the side of the oppressed in the Soweto troubles of the 1970s. (Kuzwayo's defence of the children earned her the title, the Mother of Soweto.) In seeking to salvage from the pastoral tradition of her early memories what might offer beneficial counsel amid urban alienation, Kuzwayo in her stories *Sit Down and Listen* (1990) has assumed the real and symbolic role, in the contemporary scene, of the grandmother storyteller.

Considerable interest has been invested in Kuzwayo and Tlali by women's studies which, in the 1980s, began to establish itself in South African universities.[10] As the two most prominent African women writers, Tlali and Kuzwayo have had to stand as the test cases for debates as to whether Western feminism – white, middle class, fighting for the leisure, freedom and power to be an individual – is adequate in the 'third-world' culture where Alice Walker's term womanism, adopted by Tlali, points to the strategic priority of the black woman bonding with the black man against the overall oppression of white political and domestic authority. Astute feminist readings have identified 'contradictions' in both Tlali and Kuzwayo. Contradictions in deconstruction-type analyses may signify, of course, not confusion but a text more ideologically 'stretched' than it knew, and in such a line of enquiry Tlali is seen to have reiterated the need for black women to nurture the young in domestic security while encouraging the men to fight for change. She is ready to chasten men folk, but her unwillingness to develop a critique on patriarchy in African social structures is beginning to render her as a limited subject for women's studies, which in South Africa have been directed so far by white women academics with codes imported mainly from the Western feminist debate.[11] Kuzwayo, who writes of 'living' the severity of her contradictions, may be seen to present the more interesting story.

Although she does not deny the necessity of domestic value in the broken community, Kuzwayo turns from bolstering the male's image of himself to imbuing the concept 'Motherhood' not only with spiritual immanence, but with the active, angry, political role that had her dubbed the 'Mother' in her various public confrontations with the state. Centrally involved in BC activism in the 1970s, she was detained for five months in 1977, but continued to serve on various influential committees concerned with upgrading black communities. In alluding to Kuzwayo's celebration of politically mobilised women – the Janes who not only come to Joburg but define themselves anew in the city ghettos – Nadine Gordimer has observed astutely that Kuzwayo is not Westernised; rather, she has Africanised the Western concept of the woman.[12] What this involves is Kuzwayo's 'taking the risk of essence' (call me woman) as a strategy in the fight for greater justice: accordingly, identity is tied to the reconstruction of a community that is based mentally and imaginatively on the shared history of oppression. Drawing sustenance from her rural upbringing and mission-school education, Kuzwayo allows forms of inherited loyalty to influence new, consciously-chosen alliances that complicate any discrete agendas of 'men' and 'women'. In Kuzwayo's story, for example, the language of psychological dynamism – delineated as 'women's style' in French feminist semiotics – is replaced by that of (male?) legal, economic and bureaucratic statistical reality, a reality conveyed in the prose of dense facticity that Kuzwayo, as a social worker and an activist, utilised to the advantage of Soweto:

> I now became increasingly aware of the issues of personal
> and social concern in my immediate neighbourhood.
> Some of these gradually started fully to engage my attention
> and participation. It was in the course of my involvement
> in the community that I learned of the youth work
> programme run by the recreation section of the Non-
> European Affairs Department, popularly known as NEAD,
> for the benefit of Orlando children. I visited some of the
> clubs and made my initial contribution to this programme
> on a voluntary basis.

Call Me Woman is not private destiny, but allegory: it involves the whole laborious telling of the collective self. As is characteristic of Matshoba's testimony, the ratio of the political to the personal makes the texts and textures, at first approach, somewhat alien and consequently resistant to habits of imaginative reading: at least, as these habits have come to us through Western-directed literary studies. Where feminism and womanism interact here is difficult to say, but worth pursuing beyond binary oppositions.

In considering the point at which the story of national black life ends and gendered black life begins, it is evident that, as far as *Call Me Woman* is concerned, Western feminist understandings of patrilineal and matrilineal literary traditions do not provide very useful categories within which to distinguish Kuzwayo's, or Tlali's, affiliations from those of Matshoba. If the concept patrilineal is associated in male tradition-making with dominant values that are historically uncongenial to women, and matrilineal with being ignored and undervalued in the public sphere, then both Kuzwayo and Matshoba could be regarded as matrilineal in that their forms are premised on the rejection of conventional genre-based literary norms and expression. Unlike the widely acclaimed J. M. Coetzee or Nadine Gordimer (patrilineal writers?), for example, Kuzwayo and Matshoba speak with the 'unpoetic tone'. But the argument may be recast in an almost diametrical way. If tradition – according to feminism – has reserved the difficult subject (say, national politics) for the patrilineal, the patrilineal is also expected to be anxious about politics intruding upon its 'art'. According to such a concern, Kuzwayo and Matshoba are both patrilineal and non-patrilineal. A continual worrier about the novelistic art preserving its integrity in political times, Gordimer in her preface to *Call Me Woman* praised Kuzwayo's 'true testimony' but felt compelled to add that although she has the gift of unselfconscious expression that enables her to tell her story as no one else could, Kuzwayo is not a writer. But in the Foreword that immediately follows Gordimer's remarks Bessie Head – a matrilineal writer? – has no such difficulty about the integration, in Kuzwayo, of the truth of content and the truth of form. In rejecting (patrilineal?) positions of mastery or dreams of dominance to which art genres are susceptible, Head as a writer of delicacy and skill shows greater affinities with what may be called the popularising *Staffrider* story than with the elite story-art of writers like Gordimer.

I shall return to Head's achievement, but first wish to note that in contrasting elite practice with the writing of Matshoba, or Tlali, or Kuzwayo, we encounter forms of the isolated consciousness in a–sociable, often nightmarish landscapes of crisis and collapse. While keeping a cold, sardonic eye on brittle suburbanites whose 'conviction' can seem *passé*, for example, Gordimer – like the striking newcomer in the 1970s, Peter Wilhelm – transferred dark, subjective moods to scenes of mass destruction as havoc was wreaked on war-weary villages by the militaristic imperatives of the apartheid state. In responding to the 'evidence' of the state of emergency – detentions without trial, state death-squads, etc. – Gordimer in the late 1980s would increasingly bring her powers of implication to bear on newspaper reports as the medium of relevant content. Among Afrikaans writers, the *grens* (border) stories, which I have already mentioned in the context of Namibian literature, also found their core of meaning in the isolated psyche. P. J. Haasbroek, for example, tellingly explored the Afrikaner psyche under the stress of war delirium on the Namibian and Angolan battlefields. Abraham H. de Vries, whose stories of the 1960s had looked satirically at the Afrikaner ruling elite, moved towards post-modern texts that, with the ghosts of the Sestigers still hovering in the 1980s, would become something of a vogue in Afrikaans literature. The reader is asked to grant that reality can be known only in the slippery world of language: a complex reality that despite the pronouncements of the state or the liberation movements, cannot be reduced to the simple rights and wrongs of political solutions. With Afrikanerdom sharply aware that it was beginning to lose its hold on political authority, of course, such texts – whatever their post-modern fashionableness – could be seen to be quite anxious about very definable moral and material consequences: put bluntly, what responsibility do Afrikaners bear for apartheid?[13]

As the P. W. Botha regime launched its total onslaught against the disobedience campaigns of the UDF, the evasion of history 'out there' became thoroughgoing in the intricate stories of Hennie Aucamp, for whom the private ache of personal intimacies and hurts is felt to be closer to the human heart than is the destiny of any organised community. But we could look at Aucamp in another way. In Afrikaner nationalist ideology, community has long referred to the unity of the volk and, as far as Aucamp is concerned, has become associated with a lack of toler-ance for individual behaviour and thought. The private response, there-fore, could be read as liberatory in its acknowledgement of Aucamp's own brand of political commitment: the sympathetic portrayal in many of his stories of a minority gay life in a conservative society. Like Afrikaans writers generally, however, Aucamp in the 1980s showed little anticipatory consciousness about the interests of the oppressed majority. In fact, one might observe that an absence of the concept 'community' in a great deal of white writing speaks not only of 'individualising' modes of literary representation, but of a long history of colonial displacement in Africa. In contrast, the stories of the African Njabulo S. Ndebele, the Muslim Ahmed Essop and the coloured writer Richard Rive have all utilised the well-made plot of inner motivation in order to erase isolation in favour of cultural typification. In observing people in their communities in Charterton location, in Indian Fordsburg, and in the coloured District Six, respectively, these three writers have granted restorative potential to damaged identities. Their stories – like those of Bessie Head – locate the action in the sociable setting where healing, rather than incision, reveals itself as the ancient storytelling function brought to bear on modern conditions.

Bessie Head: the telling of unexceptional tales

In Bessie Head's *The Collector of Treasures* (1977), for example, the oral sources of village gossip are shaped into subtle tales in which beauty, happiness, understanding and human compassion are affirmed in the testing situations of the old coping with the new. The structures, plots and motifs of folk-tale including good and evil types, the intrusion of the stranger into the community, and reversals occurring in wish fulfil-ment, permit Head to move easily between the 'real' and the 'fable' according to which her forms of romance do not deny, but accentuate by ironic contrast, the conditions of a society in upheaval: the women of Head's bustling Botswanan village encounter religious conflict, the burden of poverty and, partly as a result of the clashes of ancient custom and the modern way, stressful marriages. The didacticism of the oral tale is given its contemporary resonance in the story of Life who returns from Johan-nesburg to the village as a good-time girl. Although she cuckolds her village husband Lesego, who in retaliation kills her, the teller retains concern for Life as a pathetic victim of the larger southern African story: that of severe socio-economic and cultural dislocation.

> 'Lesego,' he said with deep sorrow. 'Why did you kill that fuck-about? You had legs to walk away. . . .'
> . . .
> A song of Jim Reeves was very popular at that time: *That's What Happens When Two Worlds Collide.* When they were drunk, the beer-brewing women used to sing it and start weeping. Maybe they had the last word on the whole affair.

If these stories of the village are simultaneously stories of the modernis-ing society, they are also versions of Head's own story. Born 'coloured' in racist South Africa, Bessie Head has spoken of her own hurt, resent-ment, anger and loneliness in the horror tale of her illegitimate birth.[14] The daughter of a white woman who in a liaison with an African man seemed to confirm her mental instability and was committed to an institution, Bessie was passed from white to coloured foster parents, suffered betrayal in marriage, and eventually sought her own community of belonging beyond the borders of the apartheid state in Serowe, the village of her stories. It is as though the autobiographical terror is held in check by the community utterance that fills her short stories. In contrast, the novel may have presented Head with the immense and isolated space within which to do battle with her own demons. How she copes in her novel *When Rain Clouds Gather* (1969) is to transfer the realist frame-story (the flight from South Africa of a young black activist) into the romance mode of desired harmony: useful, co-operative work in semi-arid Botswana; marriage between outsiders and Botswanan women. Similarly, *Maru* (1971) arranges its plot on folklore patternings. Like Head, Margaret is despised as a half-caste, and her arrival in the 'pure' African chiefdom sparks the archetypal conflict in the protagonist Maru between his love for Margaret and his responsibilities to the chieftaincy.

Forsaking his royal destiny, he marries the stigmatised coloured woman thus indicting racial prejudice wherever it may be found. With *A Question of Power* (1973) evoking village harmony against the turmoil of mental breakdown, Head through the character Elizabeth charts her own collapse before turning firmly from what I see as her tyranny of novelistic space to the inclusive community of her stories. *A Collector of Treasures* (1977) is followed by *Serowe: Village of the Rain Wind* (1981), in which Head brings alive portraits of communal life in her recording and interpretation of the testimonies of numerous village inhabitants. Finally, the community provides the metaphor of the nation in her history of Botswana, *A Bewitched Crossroad* (1984), in which the historical documents are human-ised in the oral mode of telling a people's story: characters act and speak in dramatic saga, and the ideal nation − non-racial, compassionate − is embodied in wise and generous rulers like Sekgoma and Khama. Head, who would have agreed with critics that she was not a feminist writer, was almost prepared to pay homage to the 'feminine' in the male when it promised women protection, care and respect. A bewitched crossroad that eluded colonial rapacity, Botswana stands as a rebuke to racist South Africa, and although Head in her own life evidently knew loneliness to the end, her stories guided her harrowing autobiographical impulse towards allegories of reconstruction and hope.

As the Bushman ‖Kabbo recognised, the demise of our cultural story is the demise of our human and social personality, and a useful way of understanding the story of community − the most resilient tradition in the whole of southern Africa − is to locate its importance in its very lack of art pretensions. As 'minor art', the story has allowed people who are less than artists to speak as more than artists, and to give expression to voices that in the realm of elite art would in all likelihood have been silenced. These include the teacher, the counsellor, the proselytiser, and the teller of the apparently unexceptional tale.

Notes

1. Report by C. Cross, *Staffrider*, vol. 5, no. 2 (1982).

2. See for example Sole's 'Problems of Creative Writers in South Africa', *Work in Progress*, vol. 1, no. 1 (1977). This journal played a key role in the 1980s in offering 'radical' analytical commentary on the South African socio-political situation. Because of financial difficulties publication ceased in 1994.

3. See W. Odendaal, '*Donga*: One Angry Voice', *English in Africa*, vol. 7, no. 2 (September 1980). This number has articles on several little magazines.

4. See Kirkwood's editorial 'About *Staffrider*', *Staffrider*, vol. 1, no. 1 (1978) which

is conveniently reprinted with representative selections from the magazine in
A. W. Oliphant and I. Vladislavić (eds), *Ten Years of 'Staffrider', 1978–1988*
(Johannesburg, 1988). Also: Kirkwood, '*Staffrider*: An Informal Discussion',
English in Africa [n. 3 above]; M. Vaughan, 'Literature and Populism in South
Africa: Some Reflections on the Ideology of *Staffrider*', *English Academy Review*
(1982), reprinted in G. M. Gugelberger (ed.), *Marxism and African Literature*
(London, 1985); Achebe's 'The Novelist as Teacher' (1965) reprinted in
G. D. Killam (ed.), *African Writers on African Writing* (London, 1973).

5. Van Wyk, *It Is Time to Go Home* (Johannesburg, 1979).

6. Selection of stories in *Ten Years of 'Staffrider'* [n. 4 above]. Writers who were
   encouraged in *Staffrider* and went on to publish individual volumes include Achmat
   Dangor, Ahmed Essop, Bheki Maseko, Joël Matlou, Mtutuzeli Matshoba,
   Mothobi Mutloatse, Mbulelo V. Mzamane, Njabulo S. Ndebele and Jayapraga
   Reddy.
   Although the short story is a widespread and an important form of expression
   in southern Africa, critical commentary remains scattered. As an introduction
   read H. Aucamp, *Kort voor Lank: Opstelle oor Kortprosatekste* (Cape Town, 1978)
   which includes the essay 'Herman Charles Bosman: Teorie en Praktyk';
   H. C. Bosman's comments on the art of storytelling which are conveyed in the
   words of his narrator Oom Schalk Lourens in several stories in *Mafeking Road*
   (Johannesburg, 1947); M. Chapman, 'The Fiction-maker: The Short Story in
   Literary Education', *Crux*, vol. 18, nos. 3–4 (October 1984) and 'More Than
   Telling a Story: *Drum* and Its Significance in Black South African Writing', in
   Chapman (ed.), *The 'Drum' Decade: Stories of the 1950s* (Pietermaritzburg,
   1989); J. Cope, 'The International Symposium on the Short Story', *Kenyon
   Review*, no. 32 (1970); N. Gordimer, Introduction to *Selected Stories*
   (Harmondsworth, 1983; originally *No Place Like: Selected Stories*, London, 1975)
   and ' "The Flash of Fireflies" ', in C. E. Mey (ed.), *Short Story Theories* (Ohio,
   1976); S. Gray, Introduction, *The Penguin Book of Southern African Stories*
   (Harmondsworth, 1985); M. Mzamane, Introduction to *Hungry Flames and
   Other Black South African Short Stories* (London, 1986) and 'The Uses of
   Traditional Oral Forms in Black South African Literature', in L. White and
   T. Couzens (eds), *Literature and Society in South Africa* (Cape Town, 1984);
   E. Pereira, 'Tall Tellers of Tales: Some Fictional Narrators and their Function
   in the South African Short Story in English', in S. Gray (ed.), *Herman Charles
   Bosman* (Johannesburg, 1986); P. A. Scanlon, Introduction to *Stories from Central
   and Southern Africa* (London, 1983); and A. van Niekerk, Introduction to *Raising
   the Blinds: A Century of South African Women's Stories* (Johannesburg, 1990).
   For selections of stories see in addition to the anthologies given above S. Gray
   (ed.), *Modern South African Stories* (Johannesburg, 1980) and *The Penguin Book
   of Contemporary South African Short Stories* (Harmondsworth, 1993); D. Hirson
   and M. Trump (eds), *The Heinemann Book of South African Short Stories: From
   1945 to the Present* (London, 1994); R. Malan (ed.), *Being Here: Modern Short
   Stories from Southern Africa* (Cape Town, 1994); J. Marquard (ed.), *A Century of
   South African Short Stories* (Johannesburg, 1978; rev. by M. Trump, 1993);
   M. Mutloatse (ed.), *Forced Landing. Africa South: Contemporary Writings*
   (Johannesburg, 1980); M. Trump (ed.), *Armed Vision: Afrikaans Writers in
   English* (Johannesburg, 1987).

7. See 'Bethal Today: *Drum*'s Fearless Exposure of Human Exploitation', *Drum*
   (March 1952). Also, 'My Success Story' by Brigadier Msuthu Khoza,
   commander of Barberton prison, who has tackled the task of reforming the

prison central to repeated horror stories in the eastern Transvaal, *New Nation* (13 May 1994).

8. See D. Driver, 'M'a-Ngoano O Tsoare Thipa ka Bohaleng – The Child's Mother Grabs the Sharp End of the Knife: Women as Mothers, Women as Writers', in M. Trump (ed.), *Rendering Things Visible* (Johannesburg, 1990); N. S. Ndebele, 'Turkish Tales and Some Thoughts on South African Fiction' (1984) and 'The Rediscovery of the Ordinary: Some New Writings in South Africa' (1984), reprinted in Ndebele, *Rediscovery of the Ordinary: Essays on South African Literature and Culture* (Johannesburg, 1991); M. Vaughan, 'Can the Writer Become a Storyteller? A Critique of the Stories of Mtutuzeli Matshoba' (1981), reprinted in A. W. Oliphant and I. Vladislavić (eds), *Ten Years of 'Staffrider'* [n. 4 above] and 'Storytelling and Politics in Fiction', in M. Trump (ed.), *Rendering Things Visible.*

9. See Ndebele, *Rediscovery of the Ordinary* [n. 8 above] and M. Kirkwood's introduction to Matlou's *Life at Home and Other Stories* (Johannesburg, 1991).

10. See as introduction to debates B. Bozzoli, 'Marxism, Feminism and South African Studies', *Journal of Southern African Studies*, vol. 9, no. 1 (1983); C. Clayton (ed.), *Women and Writing in South Africa: A Critical Anthology* (Johannesburg, 1989); D. Driver, 'Women as Sign in the South African Colonial Enterprise', *Journal of Literary Studies*, vol. 4, no. 1 (March 1988) and 'Women and Nature, Women as Objects of Exchange: Towards a Feminist Analysis of South African Literature' in M. Chapman *et al.* (eds), *Perspectives on South African English Literature* (Johannesburg, 1992); I. Hofmeyr, 'Feminist Literary Criticism in South Africa', *English in Africa*, vol. 19, no. 1 (May 1992); D. Lewis, 'The Politics of Feminism in South Africa: Natal University's Women and Gender Conference', *Staffrider*, vol. 10, no. 3 (1992); C. Lockett, Introduction to *Breaking the Silence: A Century of South African Women's Poetry* (Johannesburg, 1990). Also: *Current Writing*, vol. 2 (1990) and *Journal of Literary Studies*, vol. 9, no. 1 (April 1993).

11. See D. Lewis's attack on what she regards as the 'white' perspective [n. 10 above].

12. Gordimer, Preface to *Call Me Woman.*

13. For a selection of Afrikaans short stories in English translation see M. Trump (ed.), *Armed Vision* [n. 6 above]. Selections of Haasbroek in *Voornagvlug* (1988) and de Vries in *Soms op 'n Reis* (1987). For 'post-modernism' in the context of the state of emergency, see de Vries's *Nag van die Clown* (1989).

14. For details see S. Gardner, ' "Don't Ask for the True Story": A Memoir of Bessie Head', *Hecate*, vol. 12, nos. 1 and 2 (1986); and T. Dovey's strong response to Gardner's 'autobiographical intrusion' into a sensitive issue, 'A Question of Power: Susan Gardner's Biography versus Bessie Head's Autobiography', *English in Africa*, vol. 16, no. 1 (May 1989).

The Truth of Fiction and the Fiction of Truth: Writing Novels in the Interregnum

Gordimer, Coetzee and Soweto novels

In making a case for the short story as the resilient tradition, I am aware that in South Africa the directing hand of white literary life has granted more importance to the novel. As in Western education, the novel is seen to fashion forms of international allegiance in the latest style, and to probe the problem of words and reality as epistemological enquiry into what, in the case of many South African writers, it still means to be a white African on a black continent. In neither black nor white writing, of course, need one separate the value of genre manifestation from the value of the philosophical-cultural problematic; it is inevitable, nevertheless, that the reception accorded the short story and novel respectively should have mirrored the Western-trained intellectual's exercise over regimes of literary truth. Thus it is not the short story that, despite its appropriateness to the majority condition, has made South African writers the largest reputations. Rather, it is the novel that is thought of as the most comprehensive and complex depiction of life in its causes and variety, and that features prominently in both national and international awards. The fact that, according to sales figures, more South Africans read local short stories than local novels is besides the point: it is usually a novelist who wins a CNA Award or, abroad, a Booker Prize. Short-story writers like Matshoba and Head appear, internationally, only under special 'African Writers' imprints. Had Matshoba not initially been published locally, he would in all probability never have appeared in print. In contrast Nadine Gordimer, who is regarded first as a novelist, second as a short-story writer, André P. Brink, J. M. Coetzee, Dan Jacobson and others are considered to be mainstream internationals. Yet whatever the advantages our novelists have enjoyed in being regarded as the premier literary spokespersons, there have been peculiar demands and responsibilities attached to their pre-eminence, some of which I have mentioned already in relation to Gordimer.

Whereas the best-selling 'internationalist' Wilbur Smith has continued to purvey the South African story at home and abroad in forms of African romance, serious writers like Gordimer, Brink and Coetzee have had to retain a bifocal vision knowing that their local subject matter and preoccupations are going to be received more widely abroad than at home and, at home, by relatively few white 'literary' readers. In Brink's case, his Afrikaans narratives are translated by himself into English prior to their translation into French and other European languages. As a consequence of links that the Sestigers enjoyed with French literary life in the 1960s Brink, who absorbed the influences of the *nouveau roman*, has long been regarded in France as a very 'literary' writer, not just as a witness against the injustices of apartheid. Similarly Gordimer – who has been translated into many languages – is acknowledged, as her Nobel Prize for Literature confirms, not only as a conscience, but as an *artistic* conscience, against the cruelties of the South African state. Where the 'unschooled' Matshoba can quite unselfconsciously be less than an artist with his testimony claiming authenticity as the representation of his life condition, white novelists – who are usually privileged by race, education, income and reputation – have felt the need to be enormously self-conscious about the truth of their fiction. As artists in literary company, they have had to ensure that their forms and tropes, as I have said about Gordimer's family romances, strike consonance at least with the West's novelistic expectations. Yet, in a way, they have also had to be more than artists, even less than artists, and as the text of the South African problem impinged on the texts of their books, they had to get out of the study and appear on public platforms as special cases of the political seer.

The demand has been especially severe since the early 1970s, the beginning of the period Gordimer identified as South Africa's interregnum.[1] As she said from the public platform in New York: 'The black writer is "in history" and [history's] values threaten to force out the transcendent ones of art. The white, as writer in South Africa, does not know his place "in history" at this stage, in this time.' In articulating what could be called an aesthetic of necessity in a deep yearning for justice as the prime shaper of the experientially-loaded form, Gordimer denotes black writing of the interregnum as the representation of conditions, not the development of actions (she is quoting Walter Benjamin): a writing of participation has to be judged by the black community because in no other but the community of black deprivation is the black writer in possession of selfhood. But if the interregnum has been turned by black South Africans into epic time, the time in which the black majority gained its historical ascendancy, it has been the time of absurdity and farce for white people who have had to choose finally whether to remain responsible for the dying order or to declare themselves in favour of the order struggling to be born. How to offer oneself as a white African is no simple matter and Gordimer, the writer, cannot help expressing her anxieties that art, as she understands it, might not be regarded by black communities as having much efficacy in the interregnum. In the struggle, agit-prop has become a black art form – she observes – but whether this is the proof of solidarity or the sign of courage by someone who has perhaps survived police torture, art should not be about simple linearities, but about inner qualities of prescience and perception. A writer, in her work, may represent her 'essential gesture' as a social being for stories are about life in society, but the essential gesture must remain individual in its transformation of the experience into the art object. While loyalties to a cause, or a party line, may be important for an oppressed people, the writer – Gordimer concludes – has to retain integrity, for loyalty is an emotion, integrity a conviction adhered to out of moral values.

The concerns expressed here by Gordimer about the value of art in a political time have continued to occupy white literary circles, and – like her contemporaries among novelists in the 1970s, Brink, Coetzee, Karel Schoeman, Elsa Joubert, Wilma Stockenström, and others – Gordimer performs a predictably elitist manoeuvre in avoiding having to pursue the admittedly unresolvable difficulty of a writer's dual commitment to the troubled society and to the art of writing itself. What we are told is that in the interregnum the morality of life and the morality of art may have broken out of their categories in social flux; that the artist – an exceptional citizen, Gordimer believes – may not in consequence be able to reconcile these moralities either in the surrounding society or within the artistic temperament. But Gordimer invokes an escape clause in utilising an argument that is familiar to mainstream 'history'/'poetry' debates: the artist is not finally a politician who is expected to solve problems; rather, the artist explores the ambiguities, and thus restores dignity to the novel in forms internationally sanctioned by the freer democracies while rejoining the community of art. The only criterion that is specific to the South African situation is for the writer in rigorous conscience and social typification to ensure that private lives 'feel' public demands. The trained reader is given not the history of document, but 'history from the inside'.[2]

Or, to turn from the 'realist' Gordimer to the 'fictive' Coetzee, the discursive realm, in which language is regarded as giving events their significance, has to be wrested back from a history that, in South Africa in the 1980s, was seen to be subsuming the discourse of the imagination.[3] As far as Coetzee was concerned, the novelistic discourse in resisting history may recover purpose in its own modes of thinking. These modes involve the patternings of archetype which, in giving mythic justification to actions, are at the same time able to demythologise the actions as revelations of truth. What we have are parables which, according to Coetzee, are favoured by 'marginalised' groups that are not part of the main currents of history. (By the 1980s, such marginalised groups might have included white Africans.) The allegorical method signals not the story of collective identity but, at the highest level, meaning taking up residence in a system without becoming a term in the system. In staying with Coetzee for the time being, we encounter in his own novels attacks on forms of imperial power through his deconstructive readings – readings into the ideological fissures – of the South African literary-historical mythos. In his first book *Dusklands* (1974), the self-contained opening section about American intervention in Vietnam is set in analogous relation to part two: the deployment of the eighteenth-century colonial travel tale, in which the white hunter's will to dominance is exposed in the archetypal clash of coloniser and colonised. *Dusklands* revealed its author's intellectual interest in stylistics and modernist fictionalisations: Coetzee, who was in the United States in the 1960s, returned to South Africa in the early 1970s, and is a professor of literature and language at the University of Cape Town. In his second book, *In the Heart of the Country* (1976), the confessional monologue of an isolated spinster pulls the reader into an intense, abbreviated anti-pastoral examination of obsession and hallucination in the constricting, patriarchal colonial space: 'I live, I suffer, I am here. With cunning and treachery, if necessary, I fight against becoming one of the forgotten ones of history.' Just as the 'travelogue genre' provided the model for Coetzee's modern inscriptions in *Dusklands*, so 'intertextuality' situates *In the Heart of the Country* in ironic relation to earlier traditions of farm novels by Schreiner, Lessing and Jacobson, but perhaps more tellingly to the family sagas of the Afrikaans *plaasroman*. When we consider the claustrophobic atmosphere of Coetzee's confessional approach, we are reminded that he himself has an Afrikaans upbringing, and that his attenuated liberalism sometimes seems to have closer affinities to the Afrikaans Calvinist conscience than to the social conscience of South African English fictional responses: sympathy for the victim, for example, may be swiftly, even savagely curtailed in monologues of narcissistic self-flagellation spoken by characters who often sound like Coetzee himself, the poststructurally-aware but inwardly-tormented intellectual. In *Waiting for the Barbarians* (1980), in fact, the philanthropic liberal-humanist novel of victimisation, suffering and guilt is injected with the intensity of confession as the magistrate, whose humane but minimal concern begins to query its own moral torpor, tries in the iron times of Colonel Joll's police terror to keep alive the flickerings of consciousness, even conscience, amid relentless self-interrogation: 'I was the lie that Empire tells itself when times are easy, he the truth that Empire tells when harsh winds blow.'

In speaking as I am about Coetzee's novels in humanistic, almost mimetic terms, however, I could be accused of grounding his metafictions too firmly on an ethical story that can lead the reader who happens to be naïve about post-structuralism into giving too much credence to Lionel

Abrahams's assessment of *Barbarians* as a novel of urgent commitment.[4] The allegorical dimension is identified by Abrahams as a fairly standard literary ploy: the action occurs in an unnamed empire; the plot has wide recognition as that of the endangered state needing to create its barbarian scapegoats. Accordingly, Abrahams does not dwell on the discursive structures, the 'intertexts' of previous texts, but homes in on the impassioned voice that in its concern for justice rips through the labyrinths of words and expresses its moral conviction. This is not the fashionable view, though, in a great deal of current Coetzee criticism; rather, the author is regarded as a Lacanian-type analyst who, as Coetzee himself has suggested, places his texts in psycho-analytical relation to previous texts so as to read into the lies, silences and slippages of what has been repressed in histories that are assumed to be authoritative.[5] The danger in the post-structural approach, of course, is an endless deferral of moral consequence which, in the agonised society, can merely provoke the impatience of those for whom reality is less an elusive signifier, more a crack on the head by a police truncheon.

Yet in prising Coetzee loose from the admiring hold of theoretical intellectuals for whom literature as the 'representation of conditions' is naïve and boring, we can 'Africanise' Coetzee's stories without denying their attachments to the projects of modernity. What distinguishes Coetzee from the latter-day colonial's penchant simply to copy the Western culture, for example, is his scepticism about the master narrative of the West itself: according to his reiterated view, the ideas of the enlightenment have translated themselves in the 'third world' as imperialisms, more latterly globalisms, that through superior technology are likely to continue to impose their will on others. In retaining his suspicions of Western totalism, however, Coetzee does not offer a romantic alternative about the self-preservation, say, of indigenous cultures. There is no escape in Africa from materialism, rationalism, Western-style economics, the profit motive, and the cult of the individual. It is no use invoking lost pasts, whether Afrikaner or African: the greater responsibility is to understand, modify, and re-imagine the symbolic narratives and the maxims by which we construct and construe our 'reality'. Where the ethical core is to be found is in Coetzee's uncomfortable prediction, as identified by David Attwell, that the possibility of moral reconstruction is a movement which begins with self-abnegation within the recognition of unbridgeable historical constraints.[6] In quoting Adorno on commitment, Attwell sees Coetzee's works of art pointing to a practice from which they abstain – the creation of the just life – while anticipating ethical reciprocity at some yet to be imagined historical moment when the society, no longer hamstrung by fierce political contest, may again allow for the possibility of judgment. (Perhaps this is the point of the 'Dostoyevskian' allegory in

Coetzee's *Master of Petersburg*, which appeared after the scrapping of apartheid legislation.)

Although Coetzee has endorsed the ethical vision he finds in Gordimer's *Burger's Daughter* (1979), a novel which anticipates a time when 'human acts . . . are returned to the ambit of moral judgment, when it will "once again be *meaningful* for the gaze of the author . . . to be turned upon scenes of torture," '[7] Coetzee and Gordimer have found themselves at the opposite poles of the politics/art debate. It is Gordimer who is usually seen to grasp through the art expectation to the political life in South Africa, and Coetzee to enlist the strategies of 're-writing' primarily to understand international discourses of power rather than to assist, more immediately, in goals of liberation in his own country. We are unlikely to resolve such arguments by referring to the evidence of the works, for we are talking of ideological war in the politics of interpretation. What is interesting, nonetheless, is to recollect Gordimer's response to Coetzee's *Life & Times of Michael K* (1983).[8] At issue was the concept of allegory in its effects on a situation which, in 1984, Gordimer regarded virtually as civil strife in South Africa. It is necessary to return to the definition of allegory given earlier. It was proffered by the refugee-camp doctor in *Michael K*: allegory is meaning taking up residence in a system without becoming a term in the system. Accordingly, the simple-minded, harelipped Michael K, an extremely marginalised coloured person (the coloured representing neither white power nor African power) crawls cockroach-like (stories like cockroaches, Coetzee has said in defence of the novel, cannot be eradicated)[9] around the devastated landscape (in the interregnum several white novelists, including Gordimer, saw the future in scenes of wasteland). Refusing to be colonised by the discourse of relevance, commitment or victimisation (that is, by the discourses of history seeking to subsume novelistic imagination), Michael K – we are to believe – remains free of history's referent. Like a Derridean trace, K the signifier (who/which is only arbitrarily, not naturally, related to the signified) evades the tyranny of authority inscribed in the text of the situation. Or, we could return to Abrahams's mode of reading and grant *Michael K* the force of its own telling: the story of the single, vulnerable being in a time of the collective demand.

Neither conception of reality summarised here, however, would have been likely in the mid-1980s to have satisfied Gordimer. She pointed, instead, to the danger of allegorical form convincing the writer, Coetzee, that he was clear of the surrounding evils and their daily, grubby, tragic consequences. But like everyone else living in South Africa, Coetzee – Gordimer went on – should have realised that, given the immensity of the South African human story, he was up to his neck in the evils about which he should have had an 'inner compulsion' to write. It was Coetzee's 'inner compulsion' that Gordimer saw bursting through the allegory at the best moments to engage with victimised people; nonetheless, Coetzee – Gordimer finally felt – was squeamish about giving up his own white intellectual, social and literary authority and committing himself to the order struggling to be born. At least, this is the implication behind her observation that Coetzee denies the energy of black people to resist evil: the superb energy, to quote Gordimer, 'that is the indefatigable and undefeatable characteristic of the black people of South Africa'. However subtle and supple the interpretations of text and reality, the discourse of the interregnum in seeking to appropriate the elite culture from the standpoint of the people's life world is likely to impose narrower limits on the arbitrariness of the sign than the fictionalist may consider necessary to his role as a 'co-creator' of the world. To grant purchase to an 'aesthetic of necessity', however, is not to denigrate Coetzee's modernism since he does not retreat into a religion of art, but aches after the possibility of moral stabilities; nor is it to denigrate his post-modernism since he does not revel in the simulacra of the consumerised image, but holds the global hyper-realities to third-world account. In questioning universalising assumptions, moreover, he is aware that the unvoiced require a hearing even though he himself may be hesitant, unable, or afraid to give others the speech of their own power. In the still colonised space, for example, Michael K continued to be denied agency in his own story. Returning to Gordimer, we may consider the quality of democratic reclamation as a realisable goal in her own fiction of the interregnum.

In her response to *Michael K*, Gordimer seemed swayed more by the discourse of history than by that of the novelistic imagination. The review as a whole reveals a tension, however, in that she acknowledges Coetzee's narrative art at the same time as she queries his national vision. Possibly Gordimer was reflecting a tension in her own response as artist and spokesperson. The distinguishing trait of her novels written in the 1970s and 1980s, for example, is that of an art which, in its most powerful, conflictual, even distraught moments, has tried to incorporate massive national ideas into the yearnings of recognisable family lives. The ideas should not be regarded in terms of the simple oppositions Gordimer herself has encouraged us to pursue when, as a white writer, she claimed to have discarded liberalism for radicalism.[10] In fact, the novels *The Conservationist* (1974), *Burger's Daughter* (1979), *July's People* (1981), *Something Out There* (1984), *A Sport of Nature* (1987) and *My Son's Story* (1990) show her struggling with the psychologies of an inner life that, often against its own residual needs, feelings and beliefs, has been pressed into a principled acceptance of a radicalised milieu. The prerequisite is a willingness to grant value to the general will of 'the people'. *Burger's Daughter* grapples most comprehensively with the thrall of events. Reeling as a result of BC attacks on whites like herself, Gordimer retreated in this novel from trying to enter the black personality only to return the black presence to her narrative in the form of young activist-talk including extracts from banned SASO pamphlets. The novel was proscribed before a furore in literary circles in South Africa and abroad persuaded the publications control board that the adverse publicity of the banning was more damaging than an unbanned *Burger's Daughter.*[11]

In her use of extracts from BC documents, therefore, Gordimer in a sense compensated for her exclusion from BC by lumping the national liberation voice, in a chunk of matter, on the fragile sensibilities of her protagonist's inner life. One of the very painful scenes in the book is Rosa Burger's confrontation with the black youth, Baasie, whom she had known as a child and who now shouts at her like a pamphlet, insulting the very bases of her liberal idealism. Rosa, who bears the burden of her father's martyrdom as a member of the South African Communist Party, has to try to find her *self* by escaping the whole ideological paraphernalia of living in South Africa with commitment, whether liberal, Marxist, Afrikaner nationalist, whether the commitment is to the ties of family, or church. What sears into Rosa's being are the thousands of faceless blacks who impinge on her conscience: a conscience that insists on intervening in all the incidents – petty and horrible – that comprise the apartheid life. The more Rosa tries to erase boundaries between her private self – in her escapes to Europe – and her public self in which prison is the reality for the anti-apartheid activist, however, the more she learns about freedom paradoxically, in the very limits the white African has to offer:

> – sometimes even in the same sentence – 'my father', and the next moment you switch to 'Lionel'. –
>
> It was something curious, to you who were nosy about what you called the mores of a house of 'committed' people. In me, significant – of what? It's true that to me he was also something other than my father. Not just a public persona; many people have that to put on and take off. Not something belonging to the hackneyed formulation of the tracts and manifestos that explain him, for others . . . so I lived in my father's presence without knowing its meaning.

Following her own example in *The Conservationist*, Gordimer disrupts the grammar of the lyrical sentence as the sign of the consciousness confidently writing itself in favour of disjunctive, interior monologue interspersed with third-person free, indirect speech as though the self stumbles and begins to be written by forces beyond the self. As Schreiner and Plomer had found necessary, Gordimer in *Burger's Daughter* turned an anti-mimetic, modernist impulse into social necessity: this is a hard, ragged novel; its art and its ideas confront each other in continual unre-solved conflict. The consequence is an ethical humanism: provisional, historically contingent, socially and artistically demanding in its concern to avoid cruelty and to discover justice. If Coetzee broaches the possibility of ethical reconstruction by beginning with self-abnegation, Gordimer proceeds by an immersion in the news of the day.[12]

When she is less uncompromising than in *Burger's Daughter*, Gordimer is inclined to desert dialectical argument for symbols of desire. In *The Conservationist*, for example, criticism of the aggressive racist-economic state as typified in the latter-day colonial, Mehring, is not pursued into the grubby, everyday details of how the state succeeded for so long in entrenching its power. As I said in the earlier section on Gordimer, she has a tendency to evade the tough pragmatism of her opponents and resort to caricatural art or, in *The Conservationist*, to a self-justifying symbolism. In turning from ideas – do noble convictions alone ensure useful contributions? – to wish fulfilment, Gordimer has storms rushing in from the Mozambique channel (Mozambique was on the verge of gaining independence in 1974) to sweep away Mehring's farm in what turns out to be a dystopian version of the South African farm novel. Shifting into the redemptive mode, Gordimer saves the African farm workers, who are saved from essential primitivism only by the surface appearance of their ugly poverty, and pictures them as the inheritors of Mehring's farm: that is, inheritors of the earth, their organic birthright, as a dead African body rises from the mud to suggest the resurrected black future. Whatever is gained in *The Conservationist* in symbolist design is lost in the collapse of credible causation. In *July's People*, the future seems too painful to contemplate in any sustained interchange of ideas; instead, an art of ambiguity replaces thought as Maureen Smales, the suburban housewife uprooted from her humdrum life after a revolutionary reversal of roles, runs blindly across the African landscape towards a descending helicopter. Whether the gunship contains friend or foe is irrelevant to Maureen's single purpose of releasing herself, in danger and exhilaration, from all the constricting codes of her existence. Having left a besieged Johannesburg with her former servant July acting as guide, Maureen – the rest of the Smales family hardly feature in her story – learns little in the remote African village other than the fact that she has long lost sight of her own self-esteem in her suburban routine. The trouble is that *July's People* does not posit itself as domestic realism; in its foreshortened symbolism of a devastated future and its allusions to revolutionary activity, it gestures towards national allegory even as it remains locked in the claustrophobia of its own marital pettiness.

By the mid-1980s the revolutionary spirit had achieved fresh content closer to Gordimer's heart: the non-racialism of the UDF had superseded BC as 'policy', and instead of the pessimism that continued to pervade so many novels written by whites, *A Sport of Nature* presented the picaresque adventures of Hillela who, in utter disregard of all bourgeois convention, sleeps (screws) her way up the African high command. With canons ejaculating – Gordimer's choice of metaphor – Hillela at the end of the novel stands as the consort of the president of the Organisation for African Unity (OAU) at the independence celebrations of a new black-ruled South Africa even as the romance of the grand victory-narrative is undercut by some sardonic observations on nouveau-riche African 'Americanisation'. Whatever Gordimer's intention, *A Sport of Nature* has been adjudged a success and a failure in ways its author probably could not have foreseen. Whereas its political 'meaning' has been virtually ignored, the woman's dimension in the amoral, biological sexuality of Hillela has been regarded in some quarters – in women's glossies, for example – as a daring challenge in the mode of the airport novel to 'up-tight' middle-class morality concerning the freedom of white women to contemplate even interracial sex: a South African taboo! In other quarters, the distinctly pre-feminist depiction of Hillela, as academic feminism sees it, has been interpreted as an insult to women and confirmation that Gordimer continues to hold to her long antagonism towards feminism. Despite her own sensitivity to women's domestic oppression particularly in her short stories, Gordimer has had difficulty in regarding feminism as anything more than a dalliance of pampered Western women: the kind of women from Johannesburg's fashionable northern suburbs at whom in her novels she spits venom.[13]

A quieter novel than the bizarre *Sport of Nature*, *My Son's Story* returns to Gordimer's recurrent theme: the effects of political commitment in the family circle. Finely attuned perceptions of commitments and betrayals are filtered through the consciousness of the father, his mistress, the sullen oedipal son and, as the guide to our moral bearings, the steadfast mother. In her surprising, clandestine political involvement – for nothing in her character portrayal has prepared the reader for her actions – Aila the mother finds her self-determining purpose in a 'marriage' between her feminine, not feminist, being and her public responsibility to the liberation cause. The fact that the characters are coloured and not white hardly disturbs the recognitions of domestic romance; the fact that the son quotes Shakespeare in running allusions does not lead to a Coetzee-like intertext but merely adorns the textures of realism with some literary pretension. Meanwhile outside this low-key novel, which was presumably penned before the unbannings of early 1990, the interregnum was continuing to manifest itself in both the morbid symptoms of dying and the yearnings for renewal, and in *None to Accompany Me* (1994) Gordimer sets her story in the transitional phase of 'negotiations' prior to South Africa's first democratic election. The apocalypse has not occurred; nonetheless, the Afrikaner Right seeks by both connivance and violence to kick squatters off the land or at least to enrich itself in the last days of the old order while the protagonist, Vera Stark, involves herself in public duty on behalf of the materially dispossessed who, it is hinted, will constitute a recalcitrant post-apartheid problem for any government. In a powerful central scene Vera and a colleague are brutally robbed by a black criminal gang. What is familiar Gordimer fare is the Stark family: suburbanites who are 'internationally' liberal in attitudes to interracial mixing, extra-marital affairs, divorce, abortion and lesbianism. In the course of the novel, weak men falter and strong women move forward with none to accompany them except, in Vera's case, perhaps Zeph Rapulana, the responsible, pragmatic new black tactician who, in affirmatively correct actions, is taken on to the boards of companies – the business elite is subjected to scathing satire – but who proves to be an astute force for change: Zeph begins to flex his power in both the boardroom and the bedroom. It is significant that the balance of the public and the private has shifted towards the private – the freer civil space – in a manner reminiscent of Gordimer's novels of the 1950s. Similarly, we hear as we last did in *A World of Strangers* (1958) and *Occasion for Loving* (1963) articulate African characters among returning exiles and local activists. *None to Accompany Me*, in fact, suggests a path back to the early Gordimer. When re-read in the context of post-apartheid South Africa, for example, what renewed civil purchase may be given to the liberal, politically underdetermined Helen Shaw (*The Lying Days*) in contrast to the radical, overdetermined Rosa Burger? In reviewing Gordimer's novels of the last twenty years, one has to say that despite the crucial challenge she issued to Coetzee to accept the energy of black people to resist evil, she has not herself found it easy, as an artist, to remove her novels from their European fictional conventions and find the characters, the voices, and the forms of narration that might have proceeded beyond the 'inbetween' time: to a place 'in history' where the reconstituted community has the confidence to offer its own counsel about the novelistic imagination. What we have in this respect are several 'Soweto' novels, which were written in the aftermath of 16 June 1976, and which say to both Gordimer and Coetzee that the interregnum was, undoubtedly, about an epic time.

Despite having the energy of black people to resist evil as their thematic justification, Soweto novels such as Mongane Wally Serote's *To Every Birth Its Blood* (1981), Miriam Tlali's *Amandla* (1981), Sipho Sepamla's *A Ride on the Whirlwind* (1981) and Mbulelo V. Mzamane's *The Children of Soweto* (1982) would have been unlikely to satisfy Gordimer's other criterion that the novel delve into the 'tortuous inner qualities of prescience and perception'. Nor would they have satisfied Coetzee's preference for 'non-representational modes of thought'. In fact, Soweto novels probably confirm Gordimer's anxiety that art in the interregnum might be 'a kit of emotive phrases, an unwritten index of subjects, a typology'. For instead of pursuing truth as an individual matter in the particularities of time and consciousness, the novels of Serote, Tlali, Sepamla and Mzamane permit typicalities to predominate: individuals exist as members of imagined communities and the concerns are the organisational ones of leadership with the top usually instructing the masses, and education as a counter to the fact that the dissemination of information has been systematically denied to the oppressed. With fictionalisation itself appearing at times to be a luxury, the sweep of the action is often halted to allow for the insertion of didactic set speeches. As Mzamane says in explaining the 'aesthetic' of his trilogy of interlinked stories (novel is not really the apt term), *The Children of Soweto*: 'the events were so remarkable that the need to fictionalise does not arise . . . my simulated reports came from real newspapers. . . . My book is a record of the attempt to create a new collective consciousness for which Black Consciousness in South Africa stands. . . . I have hardly bothered to disguise the didactic purpose of my tale, which is what I imagine the traditional tale was meant to achieve'.[14]

In regarding the novelist as a teacher rather than an artist, we can presumably justify almost anything, and it is possible to conclude, particularly from the present-day vantage point, that the Soweto novel simplified the process of politics. In seeking unities in black resistance, it plastered over cleavages in liberation ideology, it invested in unambiguous choices of right and wrong, and its characterisations often favoured stereotypes rather than types, or archetypes. With the shocks of historical contingency subsumed under roll calls of honour, the path forward could have suggested flights into the realms of myth-making. Yet in positing a sympathetic reader who is asked not so much to interrogate the plot as to assent to its redemptive ideal, the Soweto novel should not be regarded automatically as falsifying truth. What was firm and remains firm in a novel like Serote's *To Every Birth Its Blood*, for example, is a determination to resist the temptations offered by the traumatic time for vengeance. Although he utilises the heroic, mobilising emblems of revolutionary romanticism, Serote fills his narrative of national liberation with humane content. His epic action ties its images of transformation to an ethics of responsibility and justice that is as scrupulous as anything we find in Gordimer or Coetzee. Where Soweto novels differed markedly from novels by white Africans is in their anticipations of hope: instead of dwelling on the morbid symptoms of the interregnum, they saw amid the blood the images of painful, inevitable rebirth. The organic metaphors suit the romance-epic mode. In *To Every Birth Its Blood*, black people are shown to have not only the energy, but the moral will to resist evil.[15]

Anxieties of influence and journalistic demands. Ebersohn, Schoeman, Joubert, Miles, Stockenström and others

In my discussion of Gordimer, Coetzee and the Soweto novels, I have tried to pursue issues that since the early 1970s have had pertinence, broadly, to novel writing in South Africa. Despite the big event of Soweto '76 having secured its remembrance by black writers in the big narrative, the novel – as I said earlier on – has remained a very white affair. Setting aside the many writers in vernacular languages whose novellas are aimed at school prescriptions, only Sipho Sepamla among African writers has continued to explore the novel as a form of expression. To reiterate further, the predisposition among novelists has been elite, self-conscious, and literary. In spite of having responded to a politics of spectacle in the reworkings of popular modes such as newspaper reportage, crime mystery and the chase of the hunted man – all of which are recurrent identifications – novelists like poets of the 1970s have displayed considerable 'anxieties of influence' in their versions of fictional truth. As in Gordimer and Coetzee so in most of the other prominent novelists whether they are writing in English or Afrikaans, we may chart tensions concerning the imaginative writer's artistic integrity in a situation calling for the commitments of political affiliation. There are also tensions between the ethical and the aesthetic demand, between the conscience of the referent as practicalist and pragmatic, and the instability of the sign: decentred, and discursive in its sense-making. At one extreme, the facts of the journalistic account have served as source and metaphor for a reality cracked at the edges. In Wessel Ebersohn's *Store up the Anger* (1980), for instance, the death of Steve Biko – a motif in several works in the later 1970s – provides the focus for a drama of interrogation, in which the spy or police thriller, the basis of Ebersohn's several popular crime books, is given the actuality of physical and psychological menace in the setting of the police torture room. At the other extreme Karel Schoeman, whose *Promised Land*[t] (1978; 1972) anticipated the recurrent white concern in the interregnum with the devastated future, slipped increasingly into moods of longing and regret. In *Promised Land* an allegorical dimension had already threatened to subsume precise political consequence under scenes of Afrikaner nostalgia for a vanished past. In the lyrical *Another Country*[t] (1991; 1984), the minutely-described social history of Bloemfontein is ultimately less significant than the disquisition of the Dutch bourgeois Versluis who overcomes his European alienation in Africa only by accepting that he will die in Africa. Interestingly

J. M. Coetzee – perhaps reflecting his own concern about belonging to Africa – has identified what he considers to be a hiatus in Schoeman's philosophical enquiry: a hiatus that has its counterpart in the social reality it represents. In learning the truth about Africa from its landscape, as if by the naming of the vegetation we can possess the spirit of the place, Versluis ignores the possibility of dialogue with Africans, and the myth of the black other takes us back to Adamastor and forward, through frontier history, to the still indeterminate white African commitment to any indigenous human culture in Africa.[16]

Such an uneasy silence about racial interchange remains a Lacanian 'gap' not only in Schoeman but – as I have intimated – in Coetzee, who might argue in his defence that white Africans are caught in a double bind. Should they enter the black consciousness, they will stand charged with colonial appropriation; should they permit the black figure its silence, as Coetzee did in *Foe* (1986) and as Gordimer did after BC questioned her authority, white Africans will stand charged with perpetuating the myth of the empty land. In most novels by whites since the 1970s, the African has remained guttural. The coloured person, in contrast, has been given voluble speech particularly by Afrikaans writers for whom the coloured – as in Jan Rabie's 'Bolandia' novels – represents a damning mark on the Calvinist conscience: the brown brother cast out of God's community by the perverted Christianity of Afrikaner nationalism. Where the African has been given speech is in Elsa Joubert's *Poppie*[t] (1980; 1978). A writer who has always taken Africa seriously, Joubert caused something of a stir in Afrikaans literary circles soon after Soweto '76 when she produced her account of the Xhosa woman Poppie – a kind of mother courage – who has survived the poverty of urban dislocation and the anguish of the 'children's revolt'. Reading like a tribute to the human spirit which has not been crushed by legalised racial discrimination, Poppie's story ranges from her life in resettlement camps to the troubles of the 1970s which engulfed her children, and the book has proved to be very popular among white Afrikaans and English-speaking readers in South Africa as well as among readers abroad. The story was turned into a stage play and produced at the premier State Theatre in Pretoria.

In responding with large doses of sentimentality to Poppie's plight as the victim of trying circumstances, readers and commentators quickly removed the story from its own political specificity to that of a parable on the universal human condition.[17] As a result, the seriousness of *Poppie* as the portrait of a life impinged upon at every turn by the cruelty of apartheid was somewhat undermined. As it transpired, the author did not help matters by supporting the widespread view that Poppie's was not a political story, but a 'pure human interest story'. Perhaps Joubert was displaying sensible caution for bannings were a constant threat in the

Soweto years, perhaps she was revealing her own subscriptions to the ideal of 'apolitical art'. Undeniably Poppie's is a powerful human-interest story. In saying this, one is alert to the criticism that in recording Poppie's testimony, Joubert, as the interviewer, the selector and shaper of the material, may well have ended up imposing some of her own middle-class, albeit reasonably enlightened values on to her subject's consciousness as it emerges in the text. Despite such a risk, Joubert's skills of narrative pace, dramatic evocation and colloquial immediacy ensure that we enter into the trials and tribulations of the achieved character. At the same time, Joubert uses authorial omniscience in sensitive and muted ways in order to place Poppie's conservative-religious understandings – she says she wants nothing to do with radical politics – in sharp, ironic contrast to the facts of bureaucratic terror. As the events of 1976 pushed against the limits of Poppie's known world, Joubert grants credible voices in the narrative to the children who justify their resistance not in the nomenclature of state television as a riot, but as a principled stand against the injustice of an entire system.

In returning to *Poppie* over a decade later, then, the challenge is to 're-politicise' the reading: to grant the book the authorisation of its own political indicators. What happened was that white readers, probably guided by superficial newspaper reviews, were as eager as Poppie in the Soweto years to flee from radical politics, and were inclined to trust Joubert's own disclaimers about political intent rather than to trust the tale itself. For Poppie's story as shaped by Joubert into national indictment suggests that the treatment of a matter as important as structural violence and oppression might require the novelist to be more than a novelist and enter the domain of investigative journalism.[18] It is something that writers in southern Africa have always had to consider, and in 1987 André P. Brink felt compelled to say: 'If the artist has come to be regarded as irrelevant by the authorities, perhaps it is because he has misrepresented the full extent of his function within this society . . . . What is feared by the government is the dissemination of factual information by the media, because whatever happens people must not be allowed to find out.'[19] Generally, the mainstream press during the emergency did not do credit to any fearless, independent tradition. As in the case of the reception of *Poppie*, tough times did not necessarily provoke tough analysis, and readers tended to be shown single acts of courage as somehow triumphing over state repression. Where fearless display was more evident was in the alternative media, especially *New Nation* and *Weekly Mail*, which recorded graphically the stories and images of police brutality and people's power that defined the emergency. It was in such a context that J. M. Coetzee felt it necessary to query the efficacy of his own novelistic imagination when, in quoting from Nietzsche, he noted in despair that 'we have art so that we shall not die of the truth. In South Africa there is now too much truth for art to hold – truth by the bucketful, truth that overwhelms and sways every act of imagination.'[20]

A similar pressure may have been at work in Christopher Hope's turning from his satires of the 'South African way of life' to the acid humour of *White Boy Running* (1988): a journalistic account of political crisis as seen by white South Africans. But with this book it was as though Hope, who has lived abroad since the mid-1970s, had looked into the wound of his home country once too often, and he has begun to find succour in the vindications of the novelistic art that have been offered to the West by East European writers like Milan Kundera: individualism, inner complexity, webs of feeling, re-makings of reality as the imagination's resistance to autocracy whether, to return the point to South Africa, autocracy manifests itself in the fervour of right-wing militarism or the fervour of left-wing revolutionism. Such ambiguity in *My Chocolate Redeemer* (1989), however, has been interpreted not only as a satire on pathological post-colonial times but, in its ridicule, as a reinscription of superior white mythology in Africa. For Stephen Gray, the journalistic imagination requires literary-historical knowledge. What is necessary is to demythologise the still authoritative colonial texts in the shaping of the surrounding society: this has been the 'metaphor of explanation' in most of Gray's writing including novels like *Caltrop's Desire* (1980), in which the protagonist is a dying colonial newspaperman. Seeing the state of emergency as a time of darkness, Gray – like Hennie Aucamp – turned in the late 1980s to giving voice and sensibility to the victims of marginalised sexuality: the homosexual body marked by the body politic. The context of local resonance for *Time of our Darkness* (1988) and *Born of Man* (1989) was P. W. Botha's onslaught against deviations from the white masculinist syndrome of patriotic South Africanism, and the pervasive 'police culture' of the time would be a target in dissident Afrikaner interrogations of the Afrikaner inheritance: an inheritance that had come to be regarded as a synonym for the South African state apparatus.

One of the more chilling responses has been John Miles's novel *Kroniek uit die Doofpot* (1991), the title taken from a Dutch proverb suggesting the 'chronicles' of our secrets released from their concealment: an apt reminder of the dirty deeds that, in the freer political climate since 1990, have begun to emerge from the dossiers of military and police 'covert operations'. Having set about in the early 1970s to rid the Afrikaans short story of its Sestiger predilections for Euro-modernist absurdity (the universe without political condition), Miles introduced an everyday, mimetic quality to the study of Afrikaner historical mythology. As far as *Kroniek* is concerned, we could argue that the police are only the by-product of the central system, and that in transferring the subject of human dignity and liberty for which many people have died to the conventions of detective thriller, Miles takes the risk of reducing what should have the public prominence of national epic to the gruesome sensation of secret interrogations in the torture room. Miles, however, compensates for any shrinkage of societal process in the implicatory power of his metaphor: the codes of the thriller are made to serve an unremittingly serious investigation. The search for justice is clarified, not obscured, as the African policeman Moliko, a new black 'everyman', is jolted out of his subservience to his white boss and, disillusioned by the malaise of the police force, begins compiling the evidence of police involvement in the slaying of prominent political activists. Fiction has to compete here with facts, and point beyond the newspaper report. Although he employs a device that in Afrikaans literature has sometimes become a convenient moral evasion – the self-consciously literary white narrator who 're-writes' events from documents in his possession – Miles avoids the temptation to turn the pragmatic claim into a post-modern language game according to which convictions of truth cannot finally be connected to a referent. Instead, the fiction of writing about written records serves to reinforce its own unavoidable core. As the documents are interpreted, the apartheid order is revealed in its spiritual bankruptcy and, symbolised by Moliko's intervention, African oral articulacy assumes the authority of chorus commentary: the white state is guilty of terrible crimes; the reader – the white, particularly the Afrikaner, reader – is complicit in the police culture which, in its arrogance and brutality, has been the monstrous guardian of white *baasskap*, or domination.[21]

In confronting the psyche of Afrikanerdom in the policies and practices of the dying apartheid state, Afrikaans writers have had to put considerable mental cost into their dissident texts. The hallucinatory, even oppressive character of J. M. Coetzee's monologues – as I have suggested – needs to be understood not only in relation to his Western demythographic habit, but to the folk-Calvinism of his Afrikaner family tradition that he is so determined to dismiss as a 'history of stubborn rejection'.[22] Attracted to Wilma Stockenström's style of enlightened response, Coetzee translated her book *Die Kremetartekspedisie* (1981) into English as *The Expedition to the Baobab Tree* (1983). Possibly Stockenström, in this prose-poetic evocation, never entirely solves the problem of how to release the woman's consciousness from its male stereotyping and return it to power in the ungendered lyrical space without replicating the male view of the intuitive, natural female: 'Only when I am asleep do I know fully who I am, for I reign over my dream-time and occupy my dreams contentedly.' Nevertheless, Stockenström creates an intensely lyrical story that in flickering images alludes to a whole history of colonised time and circumstance. In escaping structures of violence, the woman might have to melt into the organic myth of Africa with the source of its origins in ancient Bushman lore. But if this suggests nature as the regenerative 'feminine', it also suggests a supple culture that, in South Africa in the 1980s, was necessary to counteract the rigidities of the father state. Like most other Afrikaans writers Stockenström, who initially signalled her rebellion in the 1970s when she was connected to the iconoclastic *Donga* magazine, has remained part of the all-embracing Afrikaner system while consistently opposing its hegemony from within its own ranks. In her case, she has dialogised its imperative mood by introducing the feminine life principle to the choice of her diction, the implications of her imagery, and the flow of her syntax.

Brink: the internationalism of the Afrikaner rebel

The novelist who has most blatantly challenged Afrikaner power is André P. Brink who, as I mentioned in discussing the Sestigers, moved from the surrealistic, metaphysical dramas of his early novels to the political directness of *Kennis van die Aand* (translated into English as *Looking on Darkness*) which, a year after it had appeared in 1973, would be the first Afrikaans novel to be banned. Having regarded the artist in the 1960s as a 'spiritual saboteur', Brink in 1971 complained that 'No Afrikaans writer has yet tried to offer a serious political challenge to the system. . . . We have no one with enough guts, it seems, to say: No.'[23] *Looking on Darkness* held state action up to censure on several issues: racial persecution and injustice, torture by the police, and the damaging effects of apartheid including its prohibition of sex across the colour line. Details are piled up, character motivations remain slight, and it continues to be the opinion of several academic critics that Brink is short on the novelistic art, fashionable as a purveyor of dissident opinions. *Looking on Darkness*, in its Afrikaans version, remained banned until 1982 on the grounds that it was sensational and devoid of literary merit; *'n Droë Wit Seison* (1979) – translated in the same year as *A Dry White Season* – was eventually unbanned in Afrikaans because, according to the publications appeal board, it contained 'sly distortions' that would be recognised for what they were worth by the discerning reader.[24] The Afrikaner-dominated board at any one time had its perverse logic.

The directness of Brink's criticisms, I think, rankles many people in the Afrikaner establishment. What distinguishes him from other Afrikaans writers, except Breytenbach, is his willingness to speak out not only in forms of imaginative literature, but from the public platform. Like Nadine Gordimer, he regards himself as an artist of political conviction and, again like Gordimer, he ended up in the special circumstances of apartheid as having to be both an artist and a national commentator. In continuing to see similarities with Gordimer, we need not deny that there is an element of political and literary opportunism in Brink. His usual practice is to grasp outside of his own literary structures, which in their frequent use of writer-narrators hint at their 'art', and attach his stories to the more sensational events of the times. In *A Dry White Season*[t], for example, the device of having a writer of pulp romances come into possession of documents which allow him to construct Ben du Toit's story adds virtually nothing to the purpose of the novel except, and this is not explored, to offer an explanation for the popular thriller mode that is to be employed. What ensured *A Dry White Season*[t] its success and sales was not its account of du Toit's political awakening: this Afrikaans schoolteacher learns of the police killing of an African. Rather, it was the fact that Brink utilised the most emotive symbol available in the late 1970s: the black person tortured to death in the police cell. Although he claimed to have begun the novel before Steve Biko's death in 1977 and, out of respect, to have delayed completion of the manuscript until 1979, *A Dry White Season*[t] rode to world attention on the ongoing anger and publicity surrounding the death of the BC leader whose battered body had left the minister of police 'cold'.

One does not wish to deny Brink his major political subject matter, but rather to note that − like Gordimer − he has perfected a mode of novelistic 'relevance' which had him mentioned in the press as second choice to Gordimer in any Nobel Prize stakes for South African writers. What is involved, besides industrious translation, is the packaging of South African politics into familiar fictional tropes. Like Gordimer, Brink gives his readers conscience-wrenching images of life under apartheid: there are good and bad types corresponding, respectively, to those who stand against oppression and those, usually the state functionaries, who administer the vicious blows. Persecuted Africans are romanticised but do not usually provide the filtering consciousness which, except in the matter of coloured-white sexual relationships, is reserved for whites of recognisably middle-class stamp. As the Hollywood film of *A Dry White Season* found comfortably formulaic, these protagonists are jolted into political awareness by coming face to face through African victimisation with the harsh workings of the state that until then had operated beyond the sight of their domestic slumbers.

Brink in his use of bourgeois-source stories, however, is not a mere copy of Gordimer. Where her liberal values are deeply entrenched − her rejection of liberalism for radicalism, I have suggested, was a sign of anxiety rather than conversion − Brink flies from idea to idea in a panoply of Afrikaner thought and reaction. The family saga with miscegenous deeds rattling like skeletons, the coloured 'other' as the alter ego of Afrikaner guilt, the voice anguishing over its betrayal of the volk even as it endorses the good cause of racial justice, the pressure to conform leading to explosions of sexual licence in the illicit affair, the crisis of the individual who is usually male and somewhat chauvinist in his 'cultured' demeanour and who is hemmed in by church, tradition, or the latest literary '-ism': these are Brink's preoccupations which, although they have been dismissed by several Afrikaans academics, can be seen to strike uncomfortably at the psychological and social foundations of modern urbanised Afrikanerdom. Accordingly, we need not endorse a common charge and dismiss Brink's characters as predictable; rather, we should try to understand their behaviour as moulded by the dead weight of the traditions they are having to reject. A clue to the characterisation, for example, may lie in the tenet of Afrikaner nationalism that the individual deny 'individuality' in service of the God-ordained state. In granting Brink the substance of his Afrikanerdom, it is possible to identify an aptness in a style that to the English-speaking reader, anyway, can sound high-flown but which, in the Afrikaner ethos, has the necessary pitch to convey the experience measured against the calls of destiny. In translating, or more accurately re-writing, his books into English, Brink has attempted to scale down the emotion. But in doing so he risks losing the temper of cultural anxiety that characterises the Afrikaner rebel seeking solidarity with the Africa that his volk has abused. As Brink would see it, such sentiment is 'radically' different from the philanthropic sentiment at the heart of South African literary liberalism.[25]

The novel in a state of emergency

Brink's rebelliousness, I am arguing, has its articulated purposes. His is not the iconoclasm that has remained a prevalent feature of Afrikaans writers' reactions against the father-figures of their tradition. Rather, in 'breaking constantly more fetters limiting human liberty', to quote Brink, 'it is rebellion not simply directed *against* something, but aimed towards something'.[26] Like several other white writers in the 1980s, Brink – in English – wrote a 'state of emergency' novel, *States of Emergency* (1988). Like several other white writers, including Gordimer in *A Sport of Nature*, he seemed in the years of massive state repression and massive popular resistance to lose his way. Using his Sestiger skills of metaphor, allusion and analogy, he added an up-beat emphasis on post-structuralist theory according to which the writing of a love story in the middle of national crisis is supposed to keep on deconstructing itself. The result, however, is that 'public' images – of political funerals, marches, stone-throwing youths, necklacings of traitors, and police in armoured-vehicles hijacking and shooting activists – are too easily swallowed into the text of an erotic escapade. In *States of Emergency* it is as though the writer's guilty conscience seeks to avoid the political consequences of its guilt in the 'coitus interruptus' of linguistic deferral. At the same time, Karel Schoeman's 'state of emergency' novel, *Take Leave and Go*[(t)] (1992; 1990), was employing the literary motif of a middle-aged Afrikaans poet sadly taking stock of a weeping South Africa. Just as *Promised Land*[(t)] had anticipated devastation, so Schoeman's emergency resembles a Beirut option. With rain soaking the windows of the library where he is holed up with his books, the poet-figure has to learn to accept the inevitability of a new order that he is convinced will destroy the old language and seek its own texts. Although he comes to tie the recovery of his poetic potency to the change, he cannot envisage the new texts having their own richness or depth, and in retreating from the unpredictable present Schoeman the author has begun to secure his conception of stability as a text of the past: 'History is safe, because it gives you an overview,' he says in explanation of his large biographical project on Olive Schreiner.[27]

For J. M. Coetzee the state of emergency was the age of iron. Having suffered the personal loss of deaths in his own family during the late 1980s, he penned a powerful meditation on ageing and dying. In *Age of Iron* (1990), the ingenious intertextuality of his previous novel *Foe* (1986) – a palimpsest Crusoe/Roxanna tale about authors and authorities, pens and penises – is stripped to the articulated passion of Mrs Curran, the terminally-ill classics teacher who, in muted literary allusion rather than showy intertext, meets her angel of death, the Virgil to her Dante, amid the murderous death throes of Afrikaner nationalism's granite epoch. Culling her parallels from her classical repertoire, Mrs Curran with Sparta in mind asks how long before the softer ages will return. Against the violence surrounding her and her South African readers in the late 1980s, she demands in her slightly old-fashioned liberal way for the right to mourn, to die in privacy. Thus Coetzee, the arch-fictionalist, the intricate theorist, throws out his challenge to the public sphere: re-engage the individual person in her power to feel what is just and unjust. In looking sadly at the death of the child spirit in black township children who have been hardened prematurely by the demands of 'the struggle', Mrs Curran expresses her belief in goodness when the age calls for heroism, and her opinion on comradeship as a mystique of death when the age calls for bonds in the oppressed community. Her views are invested by Coetzee with considerable authority. But the very conviction of her personal story militates finally against the novel's expanding into a national metaphor: a metaphor able to countenance not only images of death, but the images of rebirth that in their heroic mode the Soweto novels had anticipated.

Among novelists who were provoked by the emergency only Richard Rive, in *Emergency Continued* (1989), tried to struggle out of the old order into the new. His early novel, *Emergency* (1964), had examined personal and political choices in the emergency declared in 1960 after the Sharpeville shootings. Although he does not hold his own liberal ideals up to scrutiny, Rive transfers his liberalism from the private commitment to the public consideration, and searches for the seeds of healing in the damaged children as the first stage towards resuscitating a climate of nurture. The implication is that when all the truth of disaster and dismemberment has been told, South Africans if they have the courage will have to look tentatively to a future community of humankind.

Where Brink's rebellion took him after *States of Emergency* was to a witty, but serious meditation on the Adamastor myth in *The First Life of Adamastor*[t] (1993; 1988). In offering a bawdy version of the dark giant whose penis, we are informed, grows longer each time he looks at a woman, Brink poses questions to himself as the Afrikaans writer: why, when the European was cursed in Africa, did he stay? Was it simply to gain the power that is now collapsing into its own greed and corruption? Or, beneath the structures of the state, are there deep-seated drives in the human psyche that will lead to endlessly recurrent Adamastor stories whoever rules in the volatile African climate? *An Act of Terror*[t] (1991) stands as the ambitious attempt to return to the beginnings of Afrikaner identity in Africa and excavate a tradition not of conquest but of dissent. Using the plot of the political thriller, Brink traces the actions of the eponymous Thomas Landman, Afrikaner convert to the ANC cause, in his attempted assassination of the state president. In the 200-page supplement to the story proper, Landman – in exile – reconstructs the history of his family, and asks what it means to live, to express, to feel, to be, this continent, this Africa. In the Afrikaans version, entitled *Die Kreef Raak Gewoond Daaraan* (The Crayfish Get Used to It), the questions are posed more abruptly: do live crayfish get used to the boiling water into which they are plunged? Does an ANC freedom fighter who has accepted armed struggle get used to the concept of violence and, more troublingly, will Afrikaners adapt to a future in a South Africa they do not control? The lengthy book reveals many of Brink's failings: notably, his inability to picture Africa as anything much more than colonial cliché. As Landman struggles heroically – the scale is epic, future-based – he encounters the land as essentialising, romantic, timeless, and Africans as symbols of ubuntu rather than as sociological beings. Having been beaten up by four black men, Landman insists that the Africans are the only people among whom he has felt safe. Yet despite the recurrent difficulties of white writers' putting credible black people in the pages of their books, *An Act of Terror* commits itself to the challenge of a new, post-interregnum South Africa and confirms that Brink has important things to say as an artist and a commentator. Although the novel can be located in the tradition of Afrikaner soul-search, it is neither sectional nor exclusive, and is a reminder that Brink in the years when Afrikaner hegemony seemed unassailable had been prepared to look beyond the laager to a vision of Afrikaans 'broadening' itself and surviving as a language not of the volk, but of all South Africans. The two examples he gave as figures who had inspired him were Mahatma Gandhi and – it must have taken some courage to say so in 1970 – the Afrikaner regarded by the establishment as a traitor, Bram Fischer. The moving statement on humanity which Fischer delivered from the dock when he was sentenced to life imprisonment as a communist is regarded by Brink as significant in his own ethical and political evolution. Fischer's ideals of racial harmony and co-operation – Brink concludes – 'did not go to jail with him'.[28]

What *An Act of Terror* does not attempt to do is to hurry Landman into any new community of Afrikanerdom: the dying community needs to be left to die. Neither is a non-racial community readily available to accept Landman. Like other white novelists in the interregnum, Brink is left to present epistemological isolation as a real condition. For black writers – as I have said – the regenerative community is almost the leitmotif: in the Soweto novels it has heroic proportions yet possibly loses some of the humane vulnerability we find in the more tentative responses of the 'teacher' and 'counsellor' narrators of the short story. With the black community posited in the Soweto novels as the metaphor of the new nation, we may reflect that the new nation will have to guard as the old Afrikaner nation did not against setting its heroic images in stone. For such an iconic act may be at odds with the relativistic, functioning demands of a complex society. While communities have value in their teachings, customs, habits and institutions of family, religion and belief, so societies have value in their technologies, constitutions and civil structures. In South Africa the politics of the working society has been obscured for too long behind identifications with nationhood, and when J. M. Coetzee concludes that no novelist has yet written the great South African novel which would be national as distinct from nationalist, he defines criteria pertaining to a viable society: the novel should contain characterisations of society at all levels during the time in which it is set; it should employ realistic techniques that make the work accessible to most of the reading public; it should make the local universal.[29] This would require not that we forget the interregnum, but that we move forward democratically towards a common citizenry as the basis of communal identification. If the challenge is artistic, it is also of course societal.

Notes

1. See Gordimer, 'Living in the Interregnum', William James Lecture, New York University (14 October 1982); reprinted in Gordimer's *The Essential Gesture: Writing, Politics and Places* (London, 1988). See also in the same selection 'The Essential Gesture', originally the Tanner Lecture on Human Values, University of Michigan (12 October 1984). Gordimer's Nobel Prize lecture, 'Writing and Being', is reprinted in *Staffrider*, vol. 10, no. 2 (1992).

2. See the general thesis of S. Clingman's influential study, *The Novels of Nadine Gordimer: History from the Inside* (Johannesburg, 1986).

3. Against the political imperatives of the state of emergency, Coetzee defended the 'imaginative' perspective at the *Weekly Mail* book week in 1987; speech subsequently published as 'The Novel Today', *Upstream*, vol. 6, no. 1 (Summer 1988).

4. Abrahams, 'Soft Man in Hard Times', *The Bloody Horse*, no. 5 (May–June 1981).

5. See for example T. Dovey, *The Novels of J. M. Coetzee: Lacanian Allegories* (Johannesburg, 1988).

6. Attwell, Introduction, *Doubling the Point: Essays and Interviews/J. M. Coetzee* (Cambridge: Mass., 1992). Also Attwell's study, *J. M. Coetzee: South Africa and the Politics of Writing* (Berkeley and Cape Town, 1993). For commentary on Coetzee's Afrikaner inheritance and his reaction to the Western economy see D. Penner, *Countries of the Mind: The Fiction of J. M. Coetzee* (New York, 1989).

7. Attwell (1992) [n. 6 above].

8. Gordimer, 'The Idea of Gardening', *New York Review of Books* (2 February 1984).

9. Coetzee, 'The Novel Today' [n. 3 above].

10. Gordimer, 'I am a white South African radical. Please don't call me a liberal. Liberal is a dirty word. Liberals are people who make promises they have no power to keep.' 'A South African Radical Exulting in Life's Chaotic Variety' (Gordimer interviewed by Michael Ratcliffe), *The Times*, London (29 November 1974). Gordimer's comments provoked Alan Paton's angry response: 'We [liberals] have no desire to climb on any anti-liberal bandwagon. Black Power, or otherwise.' See *Sunday Times*, Johannesburg (1 December 1974; 22 December 1974; and 29 December 1974). Also André Brink's support of Gordimer ('liberalism has changed its connotation – in the present day'), *Rand Daily Mail* (23 December 1974). On the subject, K. Parker, 'Nadine Gordimer and the Pitfalls of Liberalism', in Parker (ed.), *The South African Novel in English* (London, 1978) and R. Green, 'A World of Strangers: Strains in South African Liberalism', *English Studies in Africa*, vol. 7, no. 1 (1978).

11. See N. Gordimer and J. Dugard, *What Happened to 'Burger's Daughter'; or, How South African Censorship Works* (Johannesburg, 1980).

12. For an illuminating debate about 'sociological' and 'imaginative' truth in Gordimer, indeed in political fiction, see H. Adam's sociological approach, 'Reflections on Gordimer's "Interregnum"', *Indicator: Political Monitor*, vol. 1, no. 3 (1983), and T. Morphet's reply, 'In Defence of the Novelist: A Refutation

of Heribert Adam's Concept of the "Literary Fallacy" ', *Indicator*, vol. 2, no. 4 (1985).

13. In reviewing Ruth First and Ann Scott's biography *Olive Schreiner*, Gordimer said that '. . . in the South African context . . . the women issue withers in comparison with the issue of the voteless, powerless state of South African blacks, irrespective of sex. It was as bizarre then . . . as now . . . to regard a campaign for women's rights – black or white – as relevant to the South African situation. Schreiner seems not to have seen that her wronged sense of self, as a woman, that her liberation, was a secondary matter within her historical situation. Ironically, here at least she shared the most persistent characteristic of her fellow colonials (discounting the priorities of the real entities around her) while believing she was protesting against racism', *Times Literary Supplement* (15 August 1980). This seems to be Gordimer's consistent view of 'race' and 'feminism' despite several genuflections towards women's studies. When this review was modified as the Foreword to the Women's Press edition (1989) of the First and Scott biography, for example, the remarks about the women issue withering in comparison with the issue of black disenfranchisement are omitted and, added to the section on Schreiner discounting the priorities of the real entities around her, we find the following qualification: 'But then again she may have anticipated (as she did much else) the realisation, now, by South Africans of all colours in the liberation movements, that feminism South African style is an essential component in the struggle to free our country from all forms of oppression, political and economic, racist and sexist', *Olive Schreiner* (London, 1980; 1989). On the subject see D. Driver, 'Nadine Gordimer: The Politicisation of Women', *English in Africa*, vol. 10, no. 2 (October 1983) and J. Newman, *Nadine Gordimer* (London, 1988).

14. Mzamane, 'The Uses of Traditional Oral Forms in Black South African Literature', in L. White and T. Couzens (eds), *Literature and Society in South Africa* (Cape Town, 1984), p. 159.

15. Two illuminating commentaries on Serote's novel are N. Visser's 'Fictional Projects and the Irruptions of History: Mongane Serote's *To Every Birth Its Blood*', *English Academy Review*, 4 (1987) and K. Sole's ' "This Time Set Again": The Temporal and Political Conceptions of Serote's *To Every Birth Its Blood*', *English in Africa*, vol. 18, no. 1 (May 1991).

16. Coetzee, Review of *'n Ander Land*, *Die Suid-Afrikaan* (Summer 1985).

17. See D. Schalkwyk, 'The Flight from Politics: An Analysis of the South African Reception of "Poppie Nongema" ', *Journal of Southern African Studies*, vol. 12, no. 2 (April 1986).

18. One might follow J. D. Degenaar's observation at the time that the book reveals the 'structural violence' of South Africa. Letter to *Die Burger* (27 December 1978).

19. Brink, Keynote address, National Arts Festival, Grahamstown, 7–11 July 1987.

20. Coetzee, Acceptance speech, Jerusalem Award, 1987.

21. On the serious use of detective fiction in South Africa see M. Green, 'The Detective as Historian: A Case for Wessel Ebersohn', *Current Writing*, vol. 6, no. 2 (1994).

22. See his responses to his Afrikaner inheritance in D. Penner's study [n. 6 above].

23. On 'spiritual saboteur' see Brink's Sestiger manifesto and editorials in the

quarterly *Sestiger* which ran from November 1963 to August 1965. Quoted in J. Cope's chapter on Brink, 'A Driving Ferment', one of the few extended commentaries in English on Brink and to which I am indebted, *The Adversary Within: Dissident Writers in Afrikaans* (London and Cape Town, 1982). See Brink on the challenge to Afrikaans writers in *Reality* (1971) and in his essays in *Mapmakers: Writing in a State of Siege* (London, 1983).

24. Quotations from publications appeal board judgments in Cope [n. 23 above].

25. For a comparative analysis, see P. Rich, 'Tradition and Revolt in South African Fiction: The Novels of André Brink, Nadine Gordimer and J. M. Coetzee', *Journal of Southern African Studies*, vol. 9, no. 1 (October 1982).

26. For Brink's understanding of Afrikaner dissidence see his essay 'A Background to Dissidence', the introduction to *Mapmakers* [n. 23 above].

27. Schoeman, 'My Fascination with Schreiner', *Sunday Times*, Johannesburg (11 April 1993). See *Olive Schreiner: A Woman in South Africa, 1855–1881*[t] (Johannesburg, 1992; 1990) and *Only an Anguish to Live Here: Olive Schreiner and the Anglo-Boer War, 1899–1902* (Cape Town, 1992).

28. Brink, 'Mahatma Gandhi Today' (1970), *Mapmakers* [n. 23 above].

29. Coetzee, 'The Great South African Novel', *Leadership SA*, no. 2 (Summer 1983).

The State of Emergency, the New South Africa

Historical memory and the 'apartheid era'

Living in the interregnum – as I have been suggesting – need not have been only about the fears and forms of dying, but about the challenges and hopes of rebirth. In the political sphere, however, living and dying refused separate considerations. Imposed by president P. W. Botha, who was the ex-minister of defence, and his powerful national security council which in the 1980s was regarded as the main forum of government policy, the state of emergency (1985–1990) was the last desperate effort of the apartheid regime to manage the pace and perception of change. The salvage of the state from utter ruin, however, was to require a dramatic switch to 'civilian time' with Botha being outmanoeuvred from within his own cabinet and F. W. de Klerk announcing his vision of an apartheid-free South Africa. The period since the leaders of the ANC, PAC and SACP walked free from gaol has heralded an unprecedented attempt in South Africa's three hundred years of colonial history to turn away from institutionalised white racism, and the period has been traumatic in its angers, mistrusts, violence and political brinkmanship, as well as challenging of course in its redefinitions of societal potentiality. What has probably been the greatest disappointment to those committed through the dark years to the anti-apartheid struggle has been the vicious rivalries for scarce resources, patronage and power between the ANC and the Inkatha Freedom Party. The Manichean allegory of black heroes and white devils that sustained liberation rhetoric has splintered on the complex politics and politicking of redesigning a modern state. Whites were not defeated in any apocalypse and, in retrospect, the devastated landscapes of Schoeman's *Promised Land*[t] and Gordimer's *July's People* – as I have already implied – raise interesting debates about the truth of imaginative prediction. Despite *A Sport of Nature*, neither have there been pageants of victory: black South Africans have not inherited a utopia and, in a country with a severely deformed economy, many of the expectations of the freedom struggle will not easily be met. As president

Nelson Mandela has had to tell rallies packed with impatient 'young lions', the youths who sacrificed education for liberation: be patient, give us time.

Many people, nevertheless, have experienced surprising shifts of perception since the unbannings and the repeal of apartheid legislation. As increasing numbers of black children attend schools in the traditionally 'white suburbs' and as political interchange replaces the monologue of the apartheid government's voice on a broadcasting service struggling out of its own party-political habit towards broader accountability, white South Africans have had to begin to recognise black people quite simply as human beings. Perhaps black people, too, are becoming less certain in thinking of whites en bloc. The observation is almost banal; the adjustments in facets of daily life are profound, nonetheless, and range from viewing television advertisements in which black and white yuppies drink beer together in 'aspirational' ad campaigns, to the restructurings of white-controlled systems and values that have been assumed to be 'naturally' the norm. If the notion of white power has cracked, however, so has that of black experience as symbolic unity. To turn to an example from literary practice, many 'struggle plays' of the 1970s and 1980s, in which the anger of the oppressed was sanctioned as noble in any action, are now being 'placed' as expressions of their moment: expressions of a past time, the 'apartheid era', as SATV blithely phrases it. My argument, of course, has been that apartheid should not too easily be forgotten. For the task of reconstructing the post-apartheid society is going to involve acts of massive interpretation, in which the historical memory will be a crucial factor. We cannot know where we should go, what we should avoid, unless we know what has shaped us. With military intelligence proving to have been deeply complicit in murder and mayhem during the 1980s, for example, any pardons – any wiping the slate clean – should demand what Afrikaans writing has almost made its leitmotif: the confession of sin. Where literature can play a key role is not only in seeing visions in the strength of 'imagination' that defined the writing of the 1970s, but in reminding itself of its social function in argument, analysis and intervention in the public life.[1]

Poetry and prose in the 1980s: the high word to the low mimetic. Cronin, Krog, black Afrikaans poets, Goosen

To keep the text of the book in debate with the text of the world is to remind us of literature's potential as a rhetorical enterprise beyond the art genres of the poem, play and novel. What in South Africa distinguishes the 1980s from the 1970s, in fact, is critical coherence. This is the case whether we are talking of probably the most important 'new form', which is intellectual analysis itself, or the creative work of several younger writers who, in their stories and poems, give the impression of having shed the anxious allegiances to 'great art' that I detected to be character-istic of so much literature in the interregnum. The shift does not involve any actual rejection of artistry. The writers I have in mind – Jeremy Cronin will serve as an example – usually base their choice of thought, language and style on considered theories of society and literature. This notwithstanding, there is little tendency to appease great traditions abroad. One thinks, in contrast, of Gordimer's compulsion to quote foreign authorities. Interviewed in 1992, the poet Patrick Cullinan claimed to have seen nothing dramatic in developments in South African poetry since the 1960s other than that some poets were becoming more sophisti-cated and – like himself – were moving beyond the confines of South Africa to experience 'disquiet' as a world condition: a sense of alienation from God.[2] Cronin, who wrote his poems collected as *Inside* (1983) while in gaol on political charges, however, can say in contrast to Cullinan that he firmly learnt something from the oral rhythms of local black poets. In their repetitions and parallelisms, they spoke to halls of people: there was a sense of communication, of making contact.[3] In attaching his socialist commitment to the humanistic sentiments of both Marxist redemptive ideals and African ubuntu, Cronin who is prominent in the SACP has achieved a remarkably 'unauthoritative' voice in an English stripped of its layers of conquest, occupation, and even literary derivation. As he writes in easy colloquial lines imitative of the speaking voice (the title 'Motho ke Motho ka Batho Babang' means 'a person is a person because of other people'):

> By holding my mirror out of the window I see
> Clear to the end of the passage.
> There's a person down there
> A prisoner, polishing a doorhandle.
> In the mirror, I see him see
> My face in the mirror.

In a provocative comparison between Gordimer, as a writer self-conscious and self-righteous about her mission, and Cronin as a learner rather than an imposer of culture, Peter Anderson spells out the different, elusive, sometimes admittedly generalised shifts of account and attitude between the two writers.[4] Considering especially the idea of communicat-ive pacts between the writer and the audience, Anderson identifies Gordi-mer's novels as self-justifying literary acts; Cronin's poetry, in contrast, involves us in a sharing of an experience: an accessible, explicable touching of hands and thoughts. If Gordimer – as Anderson believes – is more concerned about her own impeccable credentials as artist and anti-apartheid spokesperson than about communicating to people at home, then Cronin, whose audience is at home, has regarded his challenge – as a white person of middle-class origins – to make the crossing that Gordimer has so far found to be impossible: from the anti-apartheid politics of 'enlightened opposition' in her public pronouncements and her art to the pro-liberation politics of the black majority. In poetry that in quite ordinary ways affirms the humanity of people rather than their victimisation, Cronin in *Inside* suggests a path through the bifurcated society towards an emerging culture with a common core. As Anderson notes, there are consequences for language, rhythm and voice when, instead of playing the role of splinter conscience under the hide of an oppressive system, the writer attempts to merge with the new mainstream. What is then required is not an art of parsimony, but a culture of generosity as the index of social transformation. To think of an earlier example, there is Sol T. Plaatje's *Mhudi* which in turning colonial images of black savagery into amalgamations of Western-African creativity, combined imaginative and critical insights in a consistently non-repressive use of English idiom. Similarly Cronin's poetry is both imaginative literature and literary criticism in its claims simultaneously for referential responsibility – a life grounded in material circumstance – and discursive re-interpretation: the 're-writing' of human and social obligations.

Several others also contributed 'democratising' turns of phrase and perception in the 1980s, according to which the writer's eye transmuted local images through a mind schooled on theoretical arguments about the ideology of language.[5] As in Cronin, there is a consciousness that post-structuralist decentrings of the subject can valuably deconstruct hierarchies of power while sometimes too eagerly negating the possibilities of moral agency, and the predominant 'style' is not as in the 1970s the romantic-symbolism of a-logical montage, but a low mimetic of personal and social requirement. This is what distinguishes Karen Press's 'Grieving Comrade':

> forward with the struggle, his graves a step along the way
> but I want to know where he
> went
> I want words to feed that other mouth,
> comrades of my fingers, I want a blanket for my heart.
>
> (*Bird Heart Stoning the Sea*)

Press's comments, in fact, on the collection *Signs* (1992) are apposite to a line that includes her own poetry. Nearly all the poems – she says –

create a 'formal mimesis of the process of writing', in which the poet
works within a frame of reference, verbal, emotional, analytical steeped
in the political discourse of South African struggle:

> But the ways in which this discourse appears in their poems
> are so various and so integral to the poems, that there is
> no sense of a rhetoric being pasted on to the poems. They
> are, in effect, demonstrating the extent to which this political
> discourse has become an 'organic' element of aesthetic
> practice in this country.[6]

For a number of younger writers, the burden has been to write
themselves out of a dead, white, racist and patriarchal past and to re-
inscribe themselves in a society that does not yet exist – where as Press
observes – grief is private while it is inescapably political. As in Press's
poetry, gender consciousness – added to the 'tradition' of race consciousness – is a marked feature of many younger writers of the late 1980s and
1990s, a good proportion of whom are women. Class indicators, however,
have remained amorphous: an accurate sign still of 'lived experience' in
South Africa, a public reflection being the decision of COSATU and the
SACP to support the ANC in a 'first phase' of national liberation. Among
Afrikaans writers the burden has also been to connect language to its
social derivations while deliberately limiting the 'freedom of the imagination'. Those who have not wanted to accept this burden, which entails
accepting the responsibility of being in South Africa in political crisis,
have continued to bash their great fathers: Verwoerd in politics, Van
Wyk Louw and Opperman in literature, lately Brink in sexual politics.
Accordingly, there are many extroverted displays of sexual licentiousness,
shocking depictions of homosexuality, and parodies of political commitment.[7] In contrast, the poet Antjie Krog, several black Afrikaans poets,
and the story-writer Jeanne Goosen have continued to explore the anti-
totalitarian political and sexual codes that were already evident in their
earliest work in the 1970s.

Krog became an outspoken opponent of the state's repressive measures
in the emergency especially after she had featured prominently at the
'crossing of borders' in 1989 when progressive Afrikaans writers travelled
to Zimbabwe to meet the then banned ANC,[8] and her volume in
Afrikaans, *Lady Anne* (1989), 're-writes' the letters of Lady Barnard's
Cape sojourn (1797–1803) through a consciousness that ends up rejecting
all colonialisms. In finding Lady Anne from the modern vantage point
to be unable to break sufficiently from the imperial manner, Krog quite
brilliantly, because so unobtrusively, turns European forms such as villa-
nelles, sonnets, and French ballades into illusions of non-art in earthy
dismissive lines. The style reinforces the observation that, alienated from

her Afrikaner kind, Krog might survive only by becoming Africanised. As the last generation to 'blondify' their children, the word 'blondify' being a bold contraction in the original Afrikaans, Afrikaners in the 1990s – according to Krog – must forget their claims to ancestral land, as in farm novels, and with the image taken from township street struggle, follow a new 'revolutionary rhythm':

> slowly my hand could have pulled
>   back, clasped a stone and thrown
> to that retching at the hip high
>   landscape.[t]

There is icon-bashing here, but there is no anxiety of influence: no looking back, half reverentially, to the high priests of the modernist intertext, the Dertigers.[9]

Similarly, young Afrikaans-speaking coloured poets in the western Cape, such as Frank Anthony, Patrick Petersen and Peter Snyders,[10] have tried to reject the 'resonance' of the Afrikaans literary canon which they regard as tainted by association with the Afrikaner establishment. In taking inspiration from Adam Small's use of 'Kaaps' (coloured Afrikaans dialect) these poets who are themselves educated in the petty-bourgeois class, have begun to re-connect their diction to coloured working-class speech. Whether they have merely confirmed stereotyping by an indirect route – for the drunken Kaaps coloured has always been a butt in mainstream literature – or whether they have managed to empower Kaaps as an alternative purveyor of value, remains an open question. Stripping the Afrikaans language of its official register, nevertheless, has important symbolic significance, and provides the *raison d'être* of Jeanne Goosen's award-winning novella *Ons is Nie Almal So Nie* (1990), which has been rendered into a colloquial English-language equivalent by André P. Brink, entitled *Not All of Us* (1992). In re-creating the often incoherent nationalist affiliations of lower-echelon Afrikaners in the 1950s, Goosen undercuts the high language of the establishment in an unpretentious story of people's partial recognitions in which, despite the promulgation of volk culture, the American movie remained influential in life's melodrama of love, romance and family. Although racism begins to solidify around the girl-narrator's civil-servant father, her mom – an usherette at the local bioscope – calls out pathetically to a coloured family who, in terms of the Group Areas Act, have been 'removed' from their home: 'not all of us are like that'[t]. The moment of political recognition, or more accurately human sympathy, passes; ordinary life continues, and Goosen's novella is both an implicit criticism of a whole culture as well as perhaps an unintended confirmation to its literary Afrikaans readers that not all of the volk were rabid in their nationalism. With the novella receiving high praise in Afrikaans circles, the spirit of reconciliation in 1990 was reflected in Gordimer's comment on Goosen's book that 'the time has come to garner all aspects of South African experience', as well as in the comments of Albie Sachs of the ANC that Goosen has 'captured the psyche of present-day South Africa with humanity'.[11]

Criticism and local challenges. The indigenised intellectual. Feminism. Children's literature

If Goosen's novel suggests a 'return to the ordinary', then Njabulo S. Ndebele's commentary on the black writer recovering humanity behind the slogans and stereotypes, behind the surface recognitions of race-bound life, may be finding wider application in South Africa than Ndebele himself had in mind. In the academies where in the 1980s French-derived theories of anti-humanism enjoyed prominence, we may be reminded, accordingly, of a necessary tradition of African criticism that, whether cultural or materialist, has had to pit credible humanity against the West's impressions of the heart of darkness. While writers like Cronin and Goosen were seeking to locate thought and conscience in modes of low mimetic, however, a book that during the emergency caused a considerable stir in the white mainstream press was Rian Malan's *My Traitor's Heart* (1990): subtitled 'A South African exile returns to face his country, his tribe and his conscience', this was a classic stare into the African abyss. In similar vein, Wilbur Smith was once again in 1993 on the bestseller lists with his blockbuster *River God*. Set in ancient Egypt, this epic tale involves hippopotamus-slaughtering, battles, visions, castrations, sex, gore, and colonialist trumpetings. I mention these mass interest books as a reminder that, in South Africa, the concept 'Africa' remains ideologically loaded: a site of ongoing struggle for intellectual analysis whether in the disciplines of history, sociology, literature or cultural studies. To confine critical study to the Cronins and Goosens and to ignore the need to diagnose the Wilbur Smiths – diagnosis for which the French *nouveau critique* is crucially equipped – is to curtail severely the work of intellectual and social transformation. One of criticism's democratising tasks in a society seeking to reconstruct itself, therefore, is to read all the signs in an expanded view of the text. How should the text of the Voortrekker monument be 'read' in a new South Africa? How should we record apartheid in the museum so that its evil is not cheapened in display? How might women's magazines as an example of widely read matter be employed, progressively, in syllabus reconstruction? Given the popular impact of television, how should criticism interpret the Americanisation of South Africa? As we re-enter the world, will global narratives of new opportunities also prove to be global narratives of new dependencies?[12]

In reading the signs, the challenge – as Belinda Bozzoli and Peter Delius identify it in history revisionism[13] – is the development of a scholarship that can learn from the West while recognising the continuing need to 'decolonise' its own premises and assumptions. In breaking away from colonial-imperial paradigms in the early 1970s, for example, history writing introduced new theoretical models which had been fully formed in other contexts: there were grand moves that suddenly 'explained' the functioning of South African society according to British class analysis, or whatever. In literature, similar attempts to dress the local practice in the imported garb resulted in the annoyance and frustration of several 'advanced' materialist critics when creative writers continued to hanker after individualism at the same time as embracing the collective will of community. In the 1980s, by contrast, history revisionism turned to detailed, local work, in which small voices often dramatised in 'literary techniques' have been given space to speak of their own ways of resisting authority, or preserving identities. The challenge here is for the researcher to remain as true as possible to the authenticity of the emergent voice rather than shaping the voice according to the researcher's own ideological predilections. In regarding her study of African women in Phokeng as 'domain construction' rather than theory construction,[14] for example, Bozzoli recounts the lessons in local specificity that intellectuals had to learn at the Wits History Workshops where, although intellectuals and organisations may have assisted in giving coherence and strength to popular sentiment, the ideologies of people – domestic workers, factory workers, rural peasants, etc. – were never simply the creation of those who led them. Despite debates in radical intellectual circles about Black Consciousness being replaced in the 1980s by worker consciousness, or populism replaced by socialism, what we have seen in retrospect is that BC was not so much marginalised as absorbed richly and experientially, so that it no longer needed to be articulated as philosophy. If a question for the intellectual was what happens to Marxism when it engages seriously with popular consciousness, the answer was that radical scholarship in South Africa required not only the imported scheme but a rapid apprenticeship in Africanist concerns. Such an adjustment was crucial in domain constructions being used as bases for creative theory-building: theory-building that could take its contours from the local environment.

This lesson is an accurate indication of the lesson that has informed the present literary history. In retaining its particularity in domain construction, the new society seeks the theory that can give direction to its humanist desire to shape its story. To sum up, intellectual analysis, which in South Africa is a white, Western-educated preserve, is having to return the terms of the binaries, Africa and the West, to conceptual interrogation and choose a commitment to a primary field of action. Instead of holding up the model of the global intellectual, we are going to have to train 'indigenised' intellectuals – Frantz Fanon is a useful indigenised example – who can recognise that a decisive moment in struggle is the move from undiscriminating nationalism, black or white, to social and economic awareness. At the same time, the indigenised intellectual has to recognise that one cannot foreclose the decolonising phase in which, to quote Fanon, 'new people are created even in the untidy affirmation of an original idea'.[15] While the deconstruction of centres is an important activity, therefore, so in any programme of reconstruction is the anchor of ethical consequence, and it is not surprising that other strong forms of expression in South Africa continue to be autobiography and biography, in which 'personality' is rehabilitated in the sum of its social relations.[16]

In literary study, the indigenised challenge – as I have been suggesting – can be traced to the intellectual and creative energies that attached themselves if not necessarily to BC itself, then to its radicalised milieu. In questioning the separation of art and politics and the superiority of the written to the spoken word, for example, critics in the 1970s – notably Kelwyn Sole, Isabel Hofmeyr, Stephen Gray, Tim Couzens and Mike Kirkwood – found literary spaces outside the confines of the university system in which to begin the task of convincing others of their belief that literatures and cultures from other parts of the world were not automatically better than the local products. The point was that critical value could be seen as transitive: a relation between the work and the reader within the determinants of a context. As far as Couzens and Gray were concerned, the recovery of forgotten texts struck a chord with the interests and ambitions of new local literary publishers and, as I have already mentioned, works that had been long out of print were returned to publication in the course of painstaking empirical research and flourishes of romantic Africanism. Sometimes the excitement of recovery lost sight of the message being recovered, and several rather dubious colonials were allowed to air their bigotry all over again. As a result, criticism has had to try to distinguish the enlightened from the reactionary voices of the past, sometimes even within the single text. The importance of such activity for scholarship, of course, was that works were put before readers for investigation while new anthologies of poems and stories broadened the field and made it less elitist.

By the end of the 1970s critical commentary, particularly in giving credence to the new black poetry, had begun to articulate a language of literary revisionism. In regarding peripheries as the centres of experience, the local enterprise found consonance in the 1980s with the general intention of post-structuralism in forms of structuralist-Marxism, feminism, reader reception, and more recently what has been called post-coloniality.

More pointedly, perhaps, the democratising procedure was not ideo-logically averse to the notion and practice of 'participatory culture' that was inseparable from the mass-based politics of the emergency years: the posters, the freedom songs, the popular testimonies of commitment. As the present study has tried to do, it is possible now to talk reasonably unselfconsciously about the virtues not only of the traditional and the elite in literature: categories both sanctioned in the academy, albeit in anthropological and artistic ways, respectively. It is also possible to include as literature the more amorphous category of the popular, in which the expression in question may be opportunistic, rough-edged, even inimical to the propensities of the 'artistic vision'. We are also able to consider, as 'fluid', those equations that in academic-literary study have traditionally elevated art over culture, the private over the public, and the individual over the type. Hybridism has come now to be regarded as a condition of the European-African encounter. In consequence, disjuncture, radical 'inauthenticity', the mundane and functional, the process, and the hollow space may all assume the validity of structures of consciousness in their modes of expression. In setting up an aesthetic scale, we may want to identify the political import over and above the formal property. When accountability is placed above free rights, civil education above the tran-scendental spirit, the non-fictional fact above the fictional imagination, the practice of the critic above the practice of the literary creator, even the policy document above the art work, it is possible to summarise in bald terms some of the challenges to the 'literary' that in the 1980s was posed by the social demand. Among those who have contributed to such acts of 'local' reconsideration has been – as I said – Stephen Gray, not only in his strictly editorial work, but in his reconceiving of the editor as a creator, and of the critic as a novelist in reformulations of history as imaginative literature. (See particularly Gray's *Southern African Literature: An Introduction*, 1979.) In similar vein, J. M. Coetzee's *White Writing* (1989) utilises both post-structural readings 'against the grain' and the novelist's mode of archetypal arrangement in subjecting the master ideas of colonial self-justification to the Africanist reminder that the landscape was never empty. Coetzee's almost bleak conclusion is that until white writers are able to recognise the ordinary people whom Njabulo S. Ndebele wants to rediscover, they will continue to display the 'concerns of people no longer European, not yet African'.

Two critics who with considerable purpose have continued to struggle out of their European derivativeness and seek the common voice that Cronin has sought in his poetry are – I think – Kelwyn Sole and Isabel Hofmeyr. By the end of the eighties, both were offering some of the most illuminating insights into democratising practices in the circumstances of South African social and literary life. Where their Marxist perceptions remain valuable are in procedures like Bozzoli's domain construction:

procedures which in their concern with the minute gradations of non-essentialising activities are the very opposite of system-building. In pursuing BC discourse through its temptations to revolutionary romanticism and back to the core of its challenge, Sole has kept a rigorous, analytical eye on all attempts to erase distinctions in local complexities and put in their place comforting but simplifying unities. The rigour, however, is combined with the reminder that democracy requires not only the intellectuals' insights but their humility. This entails not sneering at BC poets: the tactic of the poet-critic Stephen Watson. Rather, a new South Africa will need to take seriously previously peripheralised and neglected forms in the explanation of the whole culture.[17] Here, Sole restates a position he shared in the 1970s with Hofmeyr, and in writing the present study I am aware how critics in South Africa have had to keep re-inventing wheels. In calling for a broadening of the concept literature, I am repeating one of Hofmeyr's key arguments in 1979 for a history of South African literature that should include 'the modes and discourses of all South Africa, be that discourse oral, be it in newspapers, archives, magazines and pamphlets, in a comprehension of the text as embodying social relationships'.[18] While I agree with the objective, I do not claim to have accomplished the task: an enormous task. As I said in the introduction, the convention of literature as elite, imaginative expression has informed modern expectation in Africa as well as in the West and, like any convention, is not easy to ignore. Perhaps one does not want to ignore convention, but effect modifications along the way. I hope the present study points towards 'modes and discourses of all South Africa', indeed of all southern Africa. What I want to turn to here, however, is Hofmeyr's intervention from the local perspective in the other important discourse of revisionism that, like BC, has the potential to assist in far-reaching changes of perception and value in any future South African society: feminism.[19]

In seeking a rationale for women's studies, Hofmeyr tries to look beyond its current fixation – in literature, anyway – on the undoubtedly necessary task of recovering and re-interpreting women creative writers.[20] The essays in Cherry Clayton's *Women and Writing in South Africa* (1989), for example, remain focused on the traditional art genres. At the same time, Hofmeyr avoids the other current debate as to whether white feminists can distance themselves sufficiently from their own ideological conditioning which is said to be Western and middle class, in order to understand the material fact of African women's oppression. The question is whether white researchers of African women's lives are more interested in their own academic power than in the position, in the patriarchy, of the actual women who are the subject of their enquiry. Instead of pursuing the standard lines, Hofmeyr calls for a particularised sense of the contexts in which women in Africa, white or black, have mobilised ideas about gender, thus manipulating the supposedly all-oppressive male discourse and, in the process, empowering themselves in surprising ways. Women in a new South Africa are not pictured in poses of victimisation. Neither is emphasis given to recurrent domestic psycho-dramas: the selection of themes in Cecily Lockett's anthology, *Breaking the Silence: A Century of South African Women's Poetry* (1990), favours not only the gynocritical, but the gynaecological.

Suggesting rather that feminism look broadly at women's intellectual activity, Hofmeyr identifies a crucial intersection between the text of the book and the text of the world: the point at which discourse leaves the realm of contemplation to define its field of action. One is reminded, accordingly, that the many feminist analyses of Miriam Tlali's stories or Ellen Kuzwayo's autobiography – analyses which refine and further refine the representation of selfhood – may require, as their supplement, the sociological treatise. As the authors (sociologists, not literary critics) of ' "A Bit on the Side"?' recognise,[21] the material bases of poverty and economic marginalisation that in the African situation give substance to the categories woman, mother, children, and home, may enable us to view the trajectory of struggle in terms other than the well-established 'reactive' BC versus woman model: the primacy of the male revolutionary hero; the domestic support role of wife and mother. Rather, sociological modifications require us to see a gendered campaign, in which women outside their depictions in the novel, outside the reception of their texts in literary studies, were drawn into conflict because they were mothers and because the conflict had moved into the area they regarded as their own responsibility: the area in which they had to defend their children and their homes. In justifying motivations and principles rooted in localisms, women's struggles are not a 'bit on the side' but, in character, plot, theme and symbolism, are central to the narrative of any society that espouses non-oppression. According to such a 'pro-active' view, important areas of women's intellectual activity range from the analyses of human rights documents to the analyses of the influential women's voices that comprise the editorials in the glossy magazines. In respect of the latter, questions might include whether the woman editor is coherent, progressive, and non-sexist; whether she is a victim of the (usually) male ownership/ advertising structure; whether, even in conditions of relative control, her 'stories' are able to suggest modes of resistance in the male-dominated society. The implication of such questions is that, in the education of new South Africans, spaces should be won on school and university curricula for the intelligent reading of 'popular' women's experience.

Should the writing and criticism of children's literature be regarded specifically as women's activity? In the patriarchy, the children's story has largely been the domain of the woman storyteller from the time of the ancient African village to that of the modern city. The question is only raised here, however, to suggest that critics, whether male or female, could usefully follow the examples set by Andreé–Jeanne Tötemeyer, Jay Heale and Elwyn Jenkins[22] and explore a field that so far has been severely under-researched, but that could be a valuable educational means of cultivating a future generation of South Africans less racist, less sexist, generally less intolerant of others, than previous generations. In surveying children's writing from Bushveld stories, which endorsed the masculinist ethos of the British public school, to the dystopian inversion of 'South African school culture' in Michael Bransby's attacks on stifling, repressive behaviour, Jenkins warns of the dangers of romanticism, such as Bushmen stories re-created as quaint, primitive tales about little people. But he also perceives the marks of the interregnum on several contemporary teenage stories, in which 'the young people are ready for change while the adults are bogged down with caution'. In his criticism of the literary institution which, whether black or white, male or female, has shown little interest in children's literature, Jenkins condemns South African criticism generally as 'poorer for its ignorance of children's literature' in which we may find many of the challenges confronting any South African writer, or more importantly any future South African citizen. The point is taken. This critic can only gesture in assent.

The liberated zone: politics and polemics

My own response to critical debate in the 1980s is embodied in the present study which presumably bears the marks of both my having lived in the interregnum and my trying to envisage what it might mean to live in a new South Africa. In 1978 I began studying South African literature by considering, specifically, the poetry of Douglas Livingstone. Given the virtual neglect of local writing at the time, a question that seemed important to someone trained, as I was, in the 'great tradition' concerned Livingstone's 'modern' standing. The question that now seems important – the one I have addressed in the section on Livingstone – concerns the problems and possibilities of poetry by a white African in a period of massive social change. In responding to the politicisation of the interregnum, I tried to extend a language of aesthetics from that of 'the writer as crafter of artefacts' to that of 'the writer as register of the shocks of the time', and pursued the text into the contexts of its reception in relation especially to the new black poetry, or Soweto poetry, of the 1970s.[23] As the state of emergency began to impose its burden on writers and critics, there seemed to be a responsibility to take a long, hard look at what could be said to constitute a South African reality.

What value should be accorded the 'free artist', what the 'committed cultural worker', when the former contemplated vision and the latter organised consciousness-raising activities?

In an article, 'The Liberated Zone: The Possibilities of Imaginative Expression in a State of Emergency' (1988), I attempted to summarise and assess the polemics of the emergency as criticism was forced out of the study with a vengeance, and found itself buffeted in the streets.[24] To take an example, Jeremy Cronin had spoken enthusiastically of a new phenomenon of the mid-1980s: worker poets who, benefiting from 'organic' intellectual interventions in what were called cultural locals attached to trade unions, began to deliver inspirational messages at political and union rallies. Alfred Temba Qabula's recitation of traditional praises, national solidarities, and socialist factory-floor advice has already been introduced in the section on oral literature, and as part of the same activity I spoke earlier in Part Five about worker plays. Although Cronin translated his own socialist preferences into an astute language of 'oral aesthetics' (the poets 'swoop back and forth . . . between the plain-spoken and the oratorical, between the international and the local'), he was concerned primarily to locate value in the occasion of the poems which were originally performed at collective gatherings, May day rallies, and funeral services for fallen comrades. What the poems suggested to Cronin was a particular conception of humanity according to which the truly heroic was the ordinary, the everyday of the (black) South African working class. Although he did not make explicit claims about the 'art' of the poetry, it was impossible for Cronin, as for any of us, to remove the value of the idea from the value of its expression, and his commentary provoked an angry response from Lionel Abrahams who felt that art, as universally appreciated, was being reduced to the sloganeering of a political programme. But if the business of poetry – as Abrahams claimed – was to pursue the high and the deep, then Cronin – alert to post-structuralist investigations of all speech as ideology – had little difficulty in pinpointing Abrahams's 'liberal humanist' preference for the romantic-idealist aesthetic. In throwing back the Marxist challenge, Cronin asked: whose high, the high of the crane operator, or the mystical dreamer? and whose deep, that of the exploited miner or the obscurant melancholic?[25]

As I have already observed, there is nothing obscurantist about Abrahams's own poetry, but in the charged atmosphere of the 1980s Abrahams the critic, like many of us at the time, became emotively attached to defending his version of 'standards'. The ensuing polemics, which were important in reminding us that criticism at its most testing has always had a social mission, sounded the rancour of embattled positions. The positions were often simplified and caricatured: high-word poets were depicted as gathering truculently in 'communities of art' and cultural workers as gathering self-righteously in 'communities of activism'. The poets of contemplation accused the cultural workers of new authoritarian-isms in condoning the formation of cultural desks that paraded UDF/ANC party banners. For their part, the poets of contemplation exercised authority as gatekeepers on certain little magazines. In reply to the cultural activists' charge that the poets of contemplation were Eurocentric, elitist, and conservative in their professed liberalism, the poets of contemplation defended the exploratory value of language removed from cliché and slogan at the same time as Mzwakhe Mbuli rose to prominence in the arena of political action as a 'people's poet'. In thrilling performances before sympathetic audiences, Mzwakhe filled the air with large words of mobilisation: words which on the printed page could have been accused of flattening the gradations of any human situation including that of the struggle. In the place of the poets, Stephen Watson mooned around in his long-lined verses while in his essays he aimed goading, angry attacks at 'politicisation': that is, politics in art becoming authoritarian with the collapse of ethical contemplation – his aesthetic justification of the poetic art – into mindless action-speech that merely imitated, rather than ques-tioned, the brutalities of political conflict.[26] Whether 'revitalised' language necessarily guarantees us valuable ideas was an issue that was not followed through with any rigour, and Watson's best thoughts about the morality of the word were often vitiated by his intemperate style. My own view at the time was that in the overwhelming context of state repression the authority of the experience as the locus of power had superseded its transformation into the art object. In an effort to curtail Mzwakhe's appearances at rallies and funerals, for example, the police periodically hauled him into detention: it was not the meaning of his words that were at stake, but his 'performative' contribution to the occasion. Interpreted as having attacked, even insulted, the art of the imagination, I was subjected to several angry rejoinders in which the concepts 'fictionalis-ation' and 'reference' were set in false oppositions: the former was supposed to ensure creativity in the elusive language-based realities of post-modernism; the latter promised – it was said – only static facticity in the socialist-realist style. As I hope the present study has suggested, fictionalisation and reference are both rhetorically circumscribed in dis-course, so that any 'fact' or any 'fiction' assumes interpretative significance in a narrative order. In turning the underlying premise of this literary history on to the polemics of the 1980s, we can interpret the struggle in the body politic as a massive struggle for the authority of the sign.

Soon after the unbannings Albie Sachs of the ANC, for example, provoked heated and public debate by popularising the arguments that, in the late 1980s, had featured prominently in little magazines and local academic journals.[27] (As South African universities became research con-scious in the 1980s, there was an increase in the number of academic journals and a large increase in academic criticism.) In calling for a moratorium on 'culture as a weapon of the struggle' (the cultural workers' cry), Sachs in 1990 possibly hoped to suggest that the unbanned ANC was not the bogey it had been depicted as over so many years in South Africa, but was open to the variousness of a common humanity. Having recently returned from many years in exile, however, he misjudged the severity of the verbal war in the cultural zones: cultural workers felt betrayed while the contemplative artists who had seen the emergency as inimical to good art felt they had been vindicated from within the liberation movement itself. The result was further polarisation, and Sachs a year later had to tell a largely white 'art audience' at the Grahamstown National Arts Festival that he envisioned a new South Africa which would be able to appreciate both the toyi-toyi dance and Beethoven. Many in art circles, nevertheless, continued to derive justification from Sachs in wanting to consign the agit-prop of the emergency to the dustbin of history as they anticipated an end to the cultural boycott: the return to South Africa of imported theatre, ballet, and symphony orchestras. Stephen Watson, for his part, thought Sachs's 'puerility' was superseded only by that of a society which could get into a state of euphoria about artists being given the sanction to write on love, or painters to paint brightly coloured pictures.[28]

Watson's reaction, of course, endorsed his own views about the value of the artist-sage. The question for the literary historian, however, is what standing should be granted to the expression of the emergency which, whether it was politics or art, took on the full might of the state in the struggle for the sign. The mid-1980s, for example, were characterised by a proliferation of worker poems and the mobilising messages of 'instant' praise singers. Political funerals were framed in the alternative media as huge spectacles where fallen comrades received orations to their martyrdom, and where flags of banned organisations signalled their defiance of the police lined up on the perimeter of the cemetery or stadium. Freedom songs incorporated traditional African lyrics, Christian liturgy and revolutionary slogans in a broad language and imagery of 'people's democracy', and the prayer as well as the life story was reinforced as truth in ritualised dance, banner-waving, and chants of call-and-response: *Amandla* (Power) . . . *Awethu* (to the People). Expression in the state of emergency included the short hagiographic biography, reminiscent of the first Xhosa writing in which the obituary in the newspaper served the function of political conscientisation. The voice of immediacy, in the street or outside the courtroom, authenticated its own experience of detention or torture. Wooden or wire AK47s symbolised struggle and victory, while derelict township lots were adorned in the colours of the liberation movements as 'freedom parks'. Perhaps of especial importance, 'stories' of the emergency appeared in alternative newspapers like *New Nation*, *Weekly Mail*, *South* and *Vrye Weekblad*, all of which began publication under the threat of closure. In trying to penetrate beneath the event to its analysis, these weekly newspapers usurped the moral authority of the mainstream press and, in helping to create a radicalised language, disseminated images and ideas that began to purvey the values of a 'new nation' to a relatively small, but politically attuned readership. What the new nation would require was not the flight of its skilled white sector, but an increasing role for its black counterpart, and in trying to look beyond the 'liberated zone' I suggested, in 1989, that in literature and education we might have to move through the 'epic' phase of the emergency towards a 'theory of reconstruction'. Accordingly the past, even the near past, should not be consigned to the dustbins of history, but would need to be continually recovered and re-interpreted as usable, in the search for new canonisations derived from African challenges and demands.[29]

In advancing such a dialectic of past significance and present meaning in this study as a whole, I have relied — as I indicated at the outset — neither entirely on a model of politically committed reference nor entirely on the challenge of deconstructive analysis. Where the former pictures narrativity as secondary to objectivity and the latter reverses this order of priority in making the referent secondary or even illusory, the approach here has been to recognise the dependency of objectivity upon its signification without devaluating the mimetic ground in any communicative action. In applying the method to the expression of the emergency, we may — despite Albie Sachs — permit the series of expressive 'actions' between 1985 and 1990 to confirm 'culture as a weapon of struggle'. Within such a paradigm, the state displayed a spectacle of crisis as P. W. Botha tried to retain control of an apartheid order that by the late 1970s was already something of a chimera. Many of its fundamental laws, as I have said, had become unenforceable: signifiers without referents. By challenging the state, the UDF became a 'motif' in the imagination of the streets and, in the shadow of police terror, embodied in song and insignia the principles of redemption and hope. Political funerals, as theatres of resistance, were frequently banned, but continued to be 'staged' and assumed the significance of morality pageants in which leaders delivered messages and the crowd discovered revolutionary solidarity in the toyi-toyi and the freedom song:

U Nelson Mandela ubuyile	Nelson Mandela has returned
Sizohlangana simbane	We'll meet in order to see him
Chorus: Sizohlangana simbane	We'll meet in order to see him
Uyabalik' uBotha	Botha is fleeing
Uyabalik' uBotha	Botha is fleeing
Nezinya zakhe.	Together with his dogs.
(Chorus joins)[30]	

Such forms of expression are cut in the war zones, not in the contemplative space, and clearly cannot be fully understood as texts removed from the hyper-reality of the emergency: a simulacrum that remained, simultaneously, a mimetic entity. We are not even considering single performance events, but components in the entire process of transformation. In a situation in which it was difficult to decide where mimesis ended and discourse began, Mzwakhe, Qabula, Archbishop Tutu and other rhetorical presences, as well as numerous assembled singers at gravesides, emerged as persuasive forces of intervention in the content of the emergency. Whether we call them cultural workers or just socially engaged human beings, they offered the conviction of their counsel, communication, inspiration and prophecy. As the 'image' of resistance began to lodge itself in the world imagination, the state reacted with increasing desperation. In one notorious incident which has entered the folklore of struggle as the 'Trojan Horse', police concealed themselves in the back of a truck and, at close range, opened fire on a group of stone-throwing township youths. The incident provides the material for one of Abraham H. de Vries's short stories.[31] By the end of 1987 it was becoming apparent to many people, if not to Botha himself, that South Africa had crossed some point of no return on the long, hard road of its interregnum: the old order could not be resuscitated. Usually cautious about overstepping the provisions of the law – even the unjust law – many English-speaking mainstream newspapers asserted their editorial independence and printed full-page advertisements marking the 75th anniversary of the still banned ANC. In 1988 Mandela's biography appeared under the imprint of a local publisher, and Mandela's willingness to talk to the South African government was conveyed, from his prison cell, with increasing insistence by influential foreign contacts. By the time United States banks curtailed further credit to South Africa in a pragmatic action that had its symbolic import, Botha although he continued to bluster must have known that he had lost the war of perceptions.

For the emergency – I have suggested – was not only about the material objectives of repression. Like Makana's confrontation with British forces in 1819, like the national suicide of the Xhosa in 1856, like many other events that are also texts requiring interpretation, the state of emergency was about ideas, rhetoric, images, and symbols: about the South African story. Looking back to the mid-1980s, the issue for the literary critic is not whether or not Mzwakhe's oral utterances, or Tutu's sermons, have the 'art' to transcend their own moment. What the expression of the emergency continues to remind us is that, in dangerous times throughout the South African story, many people who in other circumstances would have been less than artists have had to become more than artists. Without the protection of ambiguity, irony or even the expensive package of the literary book, they have had to find the words to speak out boldly against injustice. In a study like the present one, which has defined literature broadly as the rhetorical act of writing and speaking and which has tested the quality of forms against the quality of ideas, it would be inconsistent not to argue for the recording and evaluation of emergency expression as an important aspect of our literary culture. It is expression that, in its remembrance, should provide a healthy check on amnesia.

Southern African Literatures: literary history and civil society

Since the demise of apartheid in 1990, the question of civil society in South Africa has prompted several debates. Will majority-rule mean people's power or neo-colonial control, what is the force of ethnicity (is it in the blood or in the mind?), and will internationalism involve World Bank 're-colonisation'? In trying to anticipate where creative writing might go 'after apartheid', there have been calls for both the variousness of the ordinary life and the invention of post-modernity.[32] Common elements have been identified as psychological interiority in the gradations of civil living and – currently fashionable as a check on any ethnic absolutism – cultural diffusion in a 'black Atlantic' creolisation of Africa and the West. But as television will become a widespread carrier of civil plots, dreams and values mostly of United States bourgeois-soap derivation, the issues of how not to stifle the 'South African' accent and how not to forget that we are part of Africa are likely to remain points of contention: particularly as the English language with its inherited 'Western' codes will be the most practicable means of national communication. How to nurture a 'non-oppressive' Afrikaans, how to nurture the African languages not only as repositories of past cultures but as mediums of contemporary thought, are likely to become increasingly important questions for literary studies, and may point to what remains a form of considerable potential for both education and entertainment in poor conditions: the radio.

In researching this book, I found a sombre check on any desertion of locality and memory in the post-independence writing from the neighbouring southern African countries. In Zimbabwe, the spectre of the war still challenges literature's commitment to civil living while in Angola and Mozambique calamitous post-independence histories can almost suggest, in retrospect, that the assimilado poetry of the freedom struggle – so coherent, so idealistic in its Western intellectualism – was not local enough: that the textures of the African Angola and the African Mozambique still await their authors. At the same time, local traditions have been manipulated into authoritarian controls: Malawi is the obvious case. Or, as in Joseph Diescho's 'Namibian' novel, localisms have had to yield in necessary ways to nation-building based on modernisation. In hesitating to anticipate what writers should or should not write about in the future, I have not shied away from a conception of the future in literary history. In casting the eye to usable pasts, in seeking insights from the southern African region as a whole, I have tried in the course of the study to broaden and deepen the idea of 'revolution' so as to incorporate the idea of an evolutionary drive towards a modernising society: a society in which internationalism is most likely to be given substance by southern Africa's being true to its own most immediate and urgent concerns.

My own contribution – should this study find itself the subject of literary, social or educational debate – has been to keep alive a tension between deferrals of reverence and the need to rehabilitate identities, practices and aesthetic possibilities in the context of a just idea. The enquiry is about progress in the intersections of the large work and the small, in the intersections of the traditional, the popular, and the elite. Without diminishing 'difference', it has been important to examine the potential of a common humanism, whether in the utterance of an ancient Bushman or a contemporary metafictionalist. It has also been important, in an intellectual climate currently favouring decentred subjects, to recover an 'African' justification for the accessibility and sociability of communication as well as for the moral agency necessary to effect change. In short, the rhetorical enterprise has been closely determined by the pragmatic situation at hand: it is ends – specific goals in local contexts – that have governed the invocation of theory. What the scars of the emergency have left on the study is a concern for a social contract between writer and citizen that is humanising and democratising in its obligations. It seems a concern that, despite borders of language, race, or even nation, is applicable to the entire region of southern Africa.

Notes

1. In 1994 the new minister of justice, Dullah Omar, pushed for the establishment of a truth commission, the aim being disclosure of the past with the view to justice and national reconciliation.

   Several books have offered analyses of a new South Africa in which liberal/ Marxist paradigms as well as African thought systems have been redefined in the post-apartheid, more generally post-'cold war', climate. See as representative: H. Adam and K. Moodley, *The Opening of the Apartheid Mind: Options for the New South Africa* (Berkeley, 1993) republished in South Africa as *Negotiated*

Revolution: Society and Politics in Post-Apartheid South Africa (Johannesburg, 1993); A. du Toit (ed.), *Towards Democracy: Building a Culture of Accountability in South Africa* (Cape Town, 1991); D. L. Horowitz, *A Democratic South Africa? Constitutional Engineering in a Divided Society* (Berkeley, 1991); M. Lipton and C. Simkins (eds), *State and Market in Post-Apartheid South Africa* (Boulder, 1993); N. Mandela, *Nelson Mandela Speaks: Forging a Democratic, Non-Racial South Africa* (London and New York, 1993); M. Ottaway, *South Africa: The Struggle for a New Order* (Bloomington, 1993); A. Shutte, *Philosophy for Africa* (Cape Town, 1993); C. Simkins, *Reconstructing Liberalism* (Johannesburg, 1986); N. Steytler, *The Freedom Charter and Beyond: Founding Principles for a Democratic South African Legal Order* (Cape Town, 1992); J. Suckling and L. White (eds), *After Apartheid* (London, 1988); F. Wilson and M. Ramphele, *Uprooting Poverty: The South African Challenge* (Cape Town, New York, London, 1989). See the issues of *Theoria* on 'Development and Ethics', no. 78 (October 1991) and 'The State and Civil Society', no. 79 (May 1992).

2. 'A Modern Sense of Disquiet' (Cullinan interviewed by Michael King and Stephen Watson), *New Contrast*, vol. 20, no. 4 (December 1992).

3. Cronin, ' "Even under the Rine of Terror": Insurgent South African Poetry', *Staffrider*, vol. 8, no. 2 (1989). ['Rine' imitates flattened, Afrikanerised South African accent associated here with the police culture of the apartheid state.]

4. Anderson, 'Essential Gestures: Gordimer, Cronin and Identity: Paradigms in White South African Writing', *English in Africa*, vol. 17, no. 2 (October 1990). On Cronin see also P. Horn, 'The Self-presence of the Poet Inside: Jeremy Cronin's *Inside*', *Staffrider*, vol. 10, no. 3 (1992).

5. For reviews of current publications see particularly *Current Writing* and the *Southern African Review of Books*. A representative selection of poetry might include Tatamkulu Afrika's *Nine Lives* (Cape Town, 1991); Ari Sitas's *Tropical Scars* (Johannesburg, 1989); Kelwyn Sole's *The Blood of Our Silence* (Johannesburg, 1987) and *Projections in the Past Tense* (Johannesburg, 1992); Ingrid de Kok's *Familiar Ground* (Johannesburg, 1988); *Signs: Three Collections of Poetry: Francis Faller, Verse-Over; Sally-Ann Murray, Shifting; Joan Metelerkamp, Towing the Line* (Cape Town, 1992); Karen Press's *Bird Heart Stoning the Sea* (Cape Town, 1990); and Lesego Rampoleng's *Horns for Hondo* (Johannesburg, 1990).
    Among new titles of fiction are Menán du Plessis' *A State of Fear* (Cape Town, 1983) and *Longlive!* (Cape Town, 1989); Mandla Langa's *A Rainbow on the Paper Sky* (London, 1989); Ivan Vladislavić's *Missing Persons* (Cape Town, 1989); Maureen Isaacson's *Holding Back Midnight* (Johannesburg, 1992); Mike Nicol's *This Day and Age* (Cape Town, 1992); Koos Prinsloo's *Slagplaas* (Cape Town, 1992); Zoë Wicomb's *You Can't Get Lost in Cape Town* (London, 1987); and, in autobiographical mode, Sindiwe Magona's *To My Children's Children* (Cape Town, 1990). (Other titles will be mentioned in the course of the chapter.)

6. Press, 'Pushing the Boundaries. Review of *Signs*', *New Contrast*, vol. 2, no. 3 (September 1992). (For full title of *Signs*, see n. 5 above.)

7. See J. Rabie's attack on Afrikaans writing of the 1980s, 'Afrikaanse Poësie Vandag', *Contrast*, vol. 14, no. 3 (July 1983). See Prinsloo's stories in *Slagplaas* [n. 5 above].

8. See A. Coetzee and J. Polley (eds), *Crossing Borders: Writers Meet the ANC* (Johannesburg, 1990).

9. For a perceptive review of *Lady Anne* see B. J. Toerien, *New Contrast*, no. 71 (Spring 1990).

10. See Anthony's *Robbeneiland My Kruis My Huis* (Kasselsvlei, 1983); Petersen's *Amandla Ngawethu* (Genadendal, 1985); and Snyder's *'n Ordinary Mens* (Cape Town, 1982). For commentary, R. Rive, 'Culture, Colouredism, Kaaps', in J. F. Smith *et al.* (eds), *Swart Afrikaanse Skrywers* (Bellville, 1986) and H. Willemse, 'Die Skrille Sonbesies: Emergent Black Afrikaans Poets in Search of Authority', in M. Trump (ed.), *Rendering Things Visible* (Johannesburg, 1990).

11. The remarks on reconstruction and reconciliation were made in the context of the New Nation Writers' Conference in Johannesburg (December 1991), a conference that brought South African writers into contact with their counterparts from southern and the rest of Africa. Reports on the conference in the weekly *New Nation* newspaper between 29 November and 19 December 1991.

12. In South Africa cultural studies was formulated as an academic discipline in 1984 when, utilising the theoretical insights of the Frankfurt school and – from the British tradition – Raymond Williams and the influence of the Birmingham school, the Centre for Cultural and Media Studies (as it is now called) was established at the University of Natal (Durban). Under the directorship of Keyan Tomaselli, the emphasis has been on journalism and the visual media. Influenced by economistic-Marxism in the late 1980s, the move now is to a symbolic-representational understanding; nonetheless, a literary-cultural response has been to attack what is regarded as South African cultural studies' neglect of the persuasive power of rhetoric: see, in this respect, G. Willoughby, 'Keyan Tomaselli and the Task of Cultural Criticism: A Review Article on *The Cinema of Apartheid*', *Journal of Literary Studies*, vol. 6, no. 4 (December 1990). As director of CCMS, Tomaselli and his colleagues have published several studies: K. Tomaselli and E. Louw (eds), *The Alternative Press in South Africa* (Bellville and London, 1991); K. Tomaselli, *The Cinema of Apartheid: Race and Class in South African Film* (New York, 1988); K. Tomaselli, (ed.), *Rethinking Culture* (Bellville, 1988); R. Tomaselli, K. Tomaselli and J. Muller, *Currents of Power: State Broadcasting in South Africa* (Cape Town, 1990). The term 'popular culture' is notoriously slippery in South Africa and has meant many things from the heroic expression of the black oppressed to the mass circulation of American film. Given the large-scale Americanisation of South African cinema and television – it is cheaper evidently to buy than to produce TV material – one may point in introduction to examples of indigenised, or at least Western/African hybridised culture including the increasing blend of African and Western voices on Radio Metro (one nation, one station), Afrikaans satire-rock groups like Johannes Kerkorrel and the Gereformeerde Blues Band, several Africanised music sounds like Ladysmith Black Mambazo, local TV productions such as *Konings* and *Egoli, Place of Gold* (soaps like *Loving* with South African costumery) and, with the serious intention of addressing issues of health and poverty *Soul City*, the 'heart of darkness' approach to South African military adventurism in *The Stick* and Brechtian qualification to the crime thriller in the film *Mapantsula* and the television serial *The Line*. (*The Line* sparked controversy: Inkatha claimed to be unfairly depicted as train killers and after heated debate, the serial was screened on a Saturday evening as a single film thus hurrying viewers to its conclusion that amid the violent rivalries of the early 1990s non-violence was the only option.)
  As memory of apartheid there is the Poster Book Collective's *Images of Defiance: South African Resistance Posters of the 1980s* (Johannesburg, 1991) and,

as a reminder of tradition 'living' in the modern circumstance, Gcina Mhlophe's storytelling performances. There are several 'white cabaret' shows of which Pieter-Dirk Uys provides the model. (See I. Glenn, 'South African Satire', *New Contrast*, no. 77, 1992.)

Easier access to publication was initiated in 1987 by the Congress of South African Writers (COSAW) which, during the emergency, mobilised cultural communities in the struggle against apartheid and, since the unbannings, has attempted to spread writing skills while ensuring that cultural programmes are linked to democratic insights and the democratisation of cultural and art institutions. In the debates, the terms 'art' and 'culture' tend to be used interchangeably: see extracts from speeches by Mongane Serote, ANC Department of Arts and Culture (*New Nation*, 2–8 August 1991) and the ANC's Barbara Masekela, 'Democratic Culture', *The New African* (1 October 1990). See also: D. Bunn and J. Taylor (eds), *From South Africa: New Writing, Photographs and Art*, special issue of *Triquarterly*, no. 69 (1987); W. Campschreur and J. Divendal (eds), *Culture in Another South Africa* (London, 1989); K. Holst Petersen and A. Rutherford (eds), *On Shifting Sands: New Arts and Literature from South Africa* (Sydney and Portsmouth, NH, 1991); and, taking cognisance of the information in its 92 end notes – history *with* footnotes – M. Chapman's 'The Liberated Zone: The Possibilities of Imaginative Expression in a State of Emergency', *English Academy Review*, 5 (1988).

The focus is on 'cultural' as opposed to 'literary' studies in *Current Writing*, vol. 6, no. 2 (1994), which has the thematic title of 'Democratising Literature and Culture in South Africa', and in the several issues of *Critical Arts: A Journal for Media Studies*. See also the issues of *Staffrider* devoted to 'Worker Culture' (vol. 8, nos. 3–4, 1991). The new Ministry of Arts, Culture, Science and Technology faces a struggle between the ANC Department of Arts and Culture which sees culture being mobilised in programmes of national reconciliation and the National Arts Coalition which favours the 'freedom' of artists from any state-directed programme, however 'democratic' in its intentions.

13. Bozzoli and Delius, 'Radical History and South African Society', special issue of *Radical History Review* entitled 'History from South Africa', nos. 46–7 (1990).

14. Bozzoli, *Women of Phokeng: Consciousness, Life Strategy, and Migrancy in South Africa, 1990–1993* (Johannesburg, 1991).

15. See Fanon, 'On National Culture', *The Wretched of the Earth*[t] (London, 1961).

16. Instructive examples include autobiographies by Mary Benson, Emma Mashinini and Sindiwe Magona, and biographies by Tim Couzens on H. I. E. Dhlomo, and by Brian Willan on Sol T. Plaatje.

17. As representative of Sole's criticism see 'Problems of Creative Writers in South Africa: A Response', *Work in Progress*, vol. 1, no. 1 (1977); 'Culture, Politics and the Black Writer: A Critical Look at Prevailing Assumptions', *English in Africa*, vol. 10, no. 1 (May 1983); 'The Role of the Writer in a Time of Transition', *Staffrider*, vol. 11, nos.1, 2 and 3 (1993); 'Democratising Culture and Literature in a "New South Africa": Organisation and Theory', *Current Writing*, vol. 6, no. 2 (1994). See also the polemic between Sole and D. Attwell on the question of 'political supervision', *Pretexts*, vol. 2, no. 1 (Winter 1990).

18. Hofmeyr, 'The State of South African Literary Criticism', *English in Africa*, vol. 6, no. 2 (September 1979).

19. See Chapter 3, n. 10 (page 384) for a select list of South African feminist commentary.

20. Hofmeyr, 'Feminist Literary Criticism in South Africa', *English in Africa*, vol. 19, no. 1 (May 1992).

21. Shireen Hassim, Jo Metelerkamp and Alison Todes, ' "A Bit on the Side"?: Gender Struggles in the Politics of Transformation in South Africa', *Transformation*, no. 5 (1987).

22. Totemeyer, 'Towards Interracial Understanding through South African Children's and Youth Literature', in I. Cilliers (ed.), *Towards Understanding/Op Weg na Begrip: Children's Literature for Southern Africa* (Cape Town, 1988); Heale, 'South African Children's Books in English', in M. Hölscher (ed.), *Doer-Landy/Far Far Away* (Cape Town, 1980); Jenkins, *Children of the Sun: Selected Writers and Themes in South African Children's Literature* (Johannesburg, 1993).

23. See my 'Soweto Poetry', *South African English Poetry: A Modern Perspective* (Johannesburg, 1984).

24. *English Academy Review*, 5 (1988); reprinted in M. Chapman, *et al.* (eds), *Perspectives on South Africa English Literature* (Johannesburg, 1992). For reaction see M. van Wyk Smith, ' "Which Liberated Zone Would That Be?" ', *Current Writing*, vol. 5, no. 1 (1993) and S. Watson, letter to *Southern African Review of Books* (April–May 1989). See also the follow-up article, Chapman, 'The Critic in a State of Emergency: Towards a Theory of Reconstruction', *Theoria*, no. 74 (October 1989) and, with modification, *On Shifting Sands* [n. 12 above].

25. Cronin, 'Poetry: An Elitist Pastime Finds Mass Roots', *Weekly Mail* (13–19 March 1987) and replies by L. Abrahams and F. Asvat (3–9 April 1987). Further, Cronin's reply to Abrahams (16–23 April 1987) and K. Sole's letter (30 April–7 May 1987). The publication under review was *Black Mamba Rising: South African Worker Poets in Struggle. Alfred Temba Qabula, Mi S'Dumo Hlatswayo and Nise Malange*, edited by A. Sitas (Durban, 1986). For extended commentary see Sitas, 'Traditions of Poetry in Natal', *Journal of Southern African Literary Studies*, vol. 16, no. 2 (June 1990).

26. See several essays on poetry in Watson's *Selected Essays, 1980–1990* (Cape Town, 1990) and his poetry in *In This City* (Cape Town, 1986).

27. What became known as the 'Albie Sachs' debate was started by Sachs's in-house ANC discussion paper, 'Preparing Ourselves for Freedom' (1989) which was published, in part, in the *Weekly Mail* in February 1990. For the text and several responses see I. de Kok and K. Press (eds), *Spring is Rebellious: Arguments about Cultural Freedom by Albie Sachs and Respondents* (Cape Town, 1990). Other responses in D. Brown and B. van Dyk (eds), *Exchanges: South African Writing in Transition* (Pietermaritzburg, 1991) and T. Morphet, 'Cultural Settlement: Albie Sachs, Njabulo Ndebele and the Question of Social and Cultural Imagination', *Pretexts*, vol. 2, no. 1 (Winter 1990). See also L. Abrahams, 'Start the Utopia without Me', *New Contrast*, vol. 21, no. 4 (December 1993) and N. S. Ndebele, 'Redefining Relevance', *Pretexts*, vol. 1, no. 1 (Winter 1989).

28. Watson, *Exchanges* [n. 27 above].

29. See 'The Liberated Zone' for details of 'emergency' expression and 'The Critic in a State of Emergency' for the argument about reconstruction [n. 24 above].

30. See several recorded songs by H. C. Groenewald and S. Makopo, 'The Political Song: Tradition and Innovation for Liberation', in E. Sienaert *et al.* (eds), *Oral Tradition and Innovation: New Wine in Old Bottles?* (Durban, 1991).

31. See *Nag van die Clown* (Cape Town, 1989).

32. A summary of different views may be gained from D. Attwell's introduction to the issue of *Current Writing* devoted to post–colonialism, vol. 5, no. 2 (1993) and, in its echoing many of N. S. Ndebele's comments on the ordinary, A. W. Oliphant's 'The Renewal of South African Literature', *Staffrider*, vol. 9, no. 4 (1991). More generally: P. Gilroy, *The Black Atlantic: Modernity and Double Consciousness* (London, 1993).

Part Six
Further References

Chronology

Literature and Historical–Cultural Events in Southern Africa

The ordering in a single chronology of works and events from ten countries presents difficulties. The sequence within each year's entry is determined by the relative state of literary production: thus South Africa – most highly developed – is followed by Zimbabwe, after which countries are listed alphabetically from Angola to Zambia.

Note: D = Drama, F = Fiction, NF = Non-Fiction, P = Poetry, J = Journal, Magazine, Periodical
Dates for plays refer to first performances

A = Angloa, B = Botswana, L = Lesotho, M = Malawi, Mz = Mozambique, N = Namibia [South West Africa = SWA], SA = South Africa, S = Swaziland, Za = Zambia, Z = Zimbabwe

DATE	LITERATURE	HISTORICAL/CULTURAL EVENTS
c. 1 million years ago		Stone-age people at Makapansgat
25,000–27,000 years ago		Earliest dated rock painting in Namibia
14,000 years ago	click-language creation myths, prayers, stories, etc.	Bushmen hunter-gatherers widely distributed
2,300 years ago		Bushmen bands in Botswana become pastoralists; now known as Khoikhoi
1,750 years ago		Iron-using farmers, ancestors of present-day Bantu-speaking people, established south of Limpopo river

DATE	LITERATURE	HISTORICAL/CULTURAL EVENTS
1,000 years ago	Bantu–language creation myths, prayers, songs, stories, etc.	Shona in Zimbabwe establish powerful Mwena Mutapa empire with capital Great Zimbabwe
AD 1200–1400		Bantu–speaking iron-age settlement, Zimbabwe
1300		Gradual changes in pottery related to arrival in region of Nguni and Sotho-Tswana Bantu-speaking people
1400		Bushmen and Khoi as dominant societies in Cape
1450–1500	Portuguese shipwreck stories	Bushmen and Khoi in contact with first Europeans
		Portuguese establish trade routes around Cape, reach Angola, Christianise ruling family of the Kongo and engage in trade and missionary work
		Da Gama lands on Mozambique Island and by 1531 Portuguese have established inland trading settlements
1500s	Descriptions of the Cape by Drake, Houtman, Hakluyt, Herbert, Terry and others	
1572	Camoëns, The Lusiads (P)	
1600		Inland trade between Cape peninsular Khoi and African chiefdoms
1652	Van Riebeeck, Daghregister	Van Riebeeck establishes Dutch East India Company station at the Cape
		Free burghers farm on Khoi land. Quarrels between Dutch and Khoi
		Slaves arrive at Cape
1668	Tas, Dagregister	

DATE	LITERATURE	HISTORICAL/CULTURAL EVENTS
1688		French Huguenot refugees increase settler numbers at Cape
		Beginning of settler community in what would become Cape Town
		Trekboer class emerges as Dutch farm further into interior
1713		Smallpox decimates Khoi
1730s		Slave trading in Mozambique
		Cape Khoi reduced to labour status
Up to 1750		Nguni territory occupied by small chiefdoms
1778		Dynastic feuds among Xhosa (Nguni groups)
		Trekboer–Xhosa clashes
		Great Fish river becomes eastern boundary of white settlement
1795	Travel writing by British, French and other European administrators and visitors continues during the nineteenth century	First British occupation of the Cape
	Letters of Lady Anne Barnard to Henry Dundas from Cape (1793–1803)	
1799		London Missionary Society arrives at the Cape
1806		Britain re-occupies the Cape
1807		Britain bans slave trading
1811		British–Xhosa hostilities on eastern frontier of the Cape. Grahamstown established

DATE	LITERATURE	HISTORICAL/CULTURAL EVENTS
1815–1828	Royal Zulu praise poetry Shaka's praises	*Mfecane*, or dispersal of African communities by military might of Shaka's Zulu
	Dingana's praises	Mzilikazi flees to eastern Transvaal and his Ndebele mount attacks on other African communities
		Ngoni disposed to present-day Malawi
		Moshoeshoe consolidates Basotho nation
		Shaka assassinated in 1828 by Dingana who becomes king of the Zulu
1818		South African Library, Cape Town
1820	Ntsikana's Xhosa-Christian hymns Bennie begins translation of Bible into Xhosa	Arrival of British settlers including poet Pringle
1822	Barrow, *Travels in the Interior of Southern Africa* Settler chronicles, diaries	Productions of *The Rivals* and *She Stoops to Conquer* in Cape Town Governor Somerset's Language Proclamation declares official use of English in the Cape colony with effect from 1827
1823	Missionary production of Xhosa grammars, dictionaries, etc.	Agents of Glasgow Missionary Society reach Cape; Bennie and Ross set up first printing press at what would be Lovedale
1824	Fairbairn and Pringle, *The South African Commercial Advertiser* and *The South African Journal* Pringle's African poems appear in journals Faure, *Het Nederduitsch Zuid-Afrikaansche Tijdschrift* Fynn's *Diary* (colonial source of early Natal history including accounts of Shaka)	
1826	Bennie, first Xhosa grammar De Lima's newspaper *De Verzamelaar*	Bennie establishes Lovedale Mission Institute (originally Ncera, 1824)

DATE	LITERATURE	HISTORICAL/CULTURAL EVENTS
1828	Philip, *Researches in South Africa*	Ordinance 50 grants Khoi and other free non-whites legal equality with settlers
1829		South African College, forerunner of University of Cape Town
1830s	Mzlikazi's royal praises	Rozwi empire of Shona, which had arisen by 17th century, falls to Ndebele who had come from the south and who would dominate Zimbabwe until the arrival of white settlers
1830	*Cape Literary Gazette* *Die Zuid-Afrikaan* (J)	
1831	*The Graham's Town Journal* Bennie, English–Xhosa dictionary	
1833		Moshoeshoe welcomes French missionaries to his kingdom
1834	Pringle, *African Sketches* (NF and P; SA)	Emancipation of slaves Sixth frontier war between settlers and Xhosa
1835	Godlonton, *A Narrative of the Irruption of the Kaffir Hordes . . .* (SA) Retief, *Manifesto* (SA) Trekker journals	Boers begin Great Trek from Cape colony into interior; clashes follow with African groups including Dingana's Zulu who in 1838 are defeated at Blood river
1836		After Portugal's slow colonisation of Angola during which slave trade flourished, slave trafficking officially suppressed but continued illegally; similarly in Mozambique where Portuguese governor had been appointed in 1752 while Arab-Swahili slaving was major factor in Mozambique economy
1837	Xhosa journalism inaugurated by Wesleyans	
1838	Bain, *Kaatje Kekkelbek; or, Life among the Hottentots* (D; SA)	
1849		Portuguese settlers arrive in Angola

DATE	LITERATURE	HISTORICAL/CULTURAL EVENTS
1850s		Bushman rock art tradition ends as last Bushmen in the Cape are killed by colonists or, convicted of crimes like stocktheft, are taken into captivity
		Cape Public Service introduces oral examinations in English and Science on British civil service model
		British missionary activity in Malawi, includes Livingstone as first white person to see 'Victoria Falls'
1854		Establishment of Boer republic, Orange Free State
		David Livingstone visits Luanda
1855	Colenso, Zulu grammar	
1856		Apocalyptic cattle killing breaks Xhosa resistance to colonialism
1857	Bible in seTswana	
	Soga, *Journal* (SA)	
	Livingstone, *Missionary Travels and Researches in Southern Africa*	
1859	Bible in Xhosa	
1860		Boer republics north of Vaal river unite in South African Republic (later, Transvaal)
1860s	Sketches of native customs, geography and local colour by Portuguese colonials and *mestiços* in Angola	
1861	Casalis, *The Basutos*, English translation of *Les Bassoutos* (1859) which includes examples of oral literature	New press and book depot set up at Morija (Lesotho)
	Colenso, Zulu–English dictionary	
	Leselinyana la Lesotho (J)	
1864	Bleek, *Hottentot Fables and Tales*	Bleek and Lloyd in 1860s begin interviewing Bushmen convicts, transcribe click language and translate into English Cape (/Xam) Bushman myths, songs and stories
	Bleek and Lloyd begin notes on Bushman oral traditions and testimonies	

DATE	LITERATURE	HISTORICAL/CULTURAL EVENTS
1866	Soga, Xhosa translation of Bunyan's *The Pilgrim's Progress* (Pt 1) (Completed in 1926 by son J. H. Soga) Colenso's Natal sermons	Beginning of premier Afrikaans university at Stellenbosch
1867	Digger broadsheets, pamphlets and news items	Discovery of diamonds near Kimberley results in 10,000 diggers on Vaal river and massive start to migrant labour
1868	Callaway, *Nursery Tales, Traditions, and Histories of the Zulus* (a substantial collection of oral literature, Zulu and English translations) New Testament in seSotho	Shortly before Moshoeshoe's death British annex Basutoland (Lesotho) Rhenish missionaries in German SWA appeal to Prussia for protection against local African population
1872	Bunyan's *The Pilgrim's Progress* translated anonymously into seSotho	Cape colony granted 'responsible' (settler) government Khama III, chief of Bamangwato, unites his people and negotiates with European arrivals in present-day Botswana
1873		Beginning of University of Cape Town
1874	Series of articles by S. J. du Toit promotes Afrikaans (First Language Movement, 1875–1900)	
1875	Xhosa translation of *Aesop's Fables*	Genootskap van Regte Afrikaners
1876	Xhosa *Indaba* succeeded by bilingual monthly *The Kafir Express* and shortly afterwards by *Isigidimi samaXhosa* and, in English, by *The Christian Express*	
1877	Chalmers, biography of Tiyo Soga (SA)	
1878	Complete Bible in seSotho	

DATE	LITERATURE	HISTORICAL/CULTURAL EVENTS
1879	Numerous written contributions by Sothos on customs, proverbs and allegorical stories including dramatised animal satires by Moteame and Sekese	Anglo–Zulu war which saw the defeat of the Zulu kingdom and in 1897 the annexation of Zululand by the self-governing British colony of Natal
		Dr Langham Dale, vice-chancellor of the University of Cape Town, advocates retaining prestige of English race in South Africa through education on the 'European standard' while pursuing duty of elevating the 'degraded savage' of Africa to civilised life
1880	Several small journals by Angolan Africans prior to arrival of more Portuguese settlers in early 20th century	Rhodes forms De Beers Mining Company
1883	Bible in Zulu Colenso translates *The Pilgrim's Progress* into Zulu Schreiner's unpublished *Undine* (F); publication of *The Story of an African Farm* (F; SA)	
1884	Jabavu founds *Imvo Zabantsundu* (J, SA) Matthew's gospel translated into Ndebele Witbooi, *Dagboek* (1884–1905) (N)	
1885	Haggard, *King Solomon's Mines* (F) and beginning of African adventure-romance fiction by Haggard, Mitford and others	Cape Town to Kimberley railway
1886		Gold discovered in the Transvaal; industrialisation and beginning of Johannesburg
1887	Haggard, *She* (F) *The Star* newspaper moves from Grahamstown to Johannesburg	
1881	Bird edits *Annals of Natal*	
1889		German forces land in SWA

DATE	LITERATURE	HISTORICAL/CULTURAL EVENTS
1890		Rhodes forms British South Africa (BSA) Company which sets out to exploit minerals in Ndebele and Shona kingdoms in present-day Zimbabwe
1891	Mata, book of kiMbundu proverbs *Filosofia Popular em Provérbias Angolenses* (A)	Britain declares Nyasaland a protectorate and local Africans forced to work on settler coffee plantations to pay taxes to colonial authorities
1892	Couper, *Mixed Humanity: A Story of Camp Life in South Africa* (F)	
1893		Gandhi arrives in Natal
		Beginning of Ndebele and Shona resistance to Rhodes's mining settlements; resistance – known as Zimbabwe's first chimurenga – put down in 1897 by BSA Company
1894	Chatelain, *Folk-tales of Angola*	
1895	Lorimer and Zidoke, Zulu translation of *The Pilgrim's Progress*	
1896	*Ons Klyntji* (J) (promotes Afrikaans)	Central News Agency (CNA) opens in SA
1897	Schreiner, *Trooper Peter Halket of Mashonaland* (NF; SA)	
1899	Blackburn, *Prinsloo of Prinsloosdorp: A Tale of Transvaal Officialdom . . .* (F)	Outbreak of Anglo–Boer War (1899–1902)
	Sontonga composes hymn 'Nkosi Sikelel' iAfrika'	BSA Company proclaims Northern Rhodesia
1900	Flourish of Afrikaans writing known as Second Language Movement (1900–1930)	
	Plaatje, *Boer War Diary* (SA)	
1901	Dube, views on Christianity and education in African life (SA)	Dube establishes Ohlange, first educational institute run by Africans
	Cripps, *The Black Christ* (P; Z)	
1902	Johannesburg *Rand Daily Mail*	

DATE	LITERATURE	HISTORICAL/CULTURAL EVENTS
1903	Dube founds *Ilange laseNatali* (first African-run newspaper in Zulu) Gandhi starts *Indian Opinion* (J) Blackburn, *A Burgher Quixote* (F; SA)	John Clark of St Andrews (Scotland) appointed first professor of English literature at University of Cape Town; introduces practical method of close reading in opposition to historical periodisation
1904		Herero and Nama rise against German colonialism in SWA
1905	Marais' 'Winternag' as beginning of new Afrikaans literary consciousness Mqhayi begins contributing Xhosa praise poems to *Izwe Labantu* Series of articles by Preller pointing to Afrikaner interest in promoting not Dutch but Afrikaans	Afrikaans Taalgenootskap Schreiner calls for unionisation of all mine workers
1906	Rubusana's Xhosa anthology *Zemk'iinkomo Magwalandini*	Bambatha rebellion in which Natal colony savagely puts down African protest against poll tax
1907	FitzPatrick, *Jock of the Bushveld* (F; SA) New Testament in Shona	
1908	Black, *Love and the Hyphen* (D; SA) Blackburn, *Leaven: A Black and White Story* (F; SA) Jacottet, *Treasury of Ba-Suto Lore* Frenssen, *Peter Moor's Journey to South West Africa*[t]	Indians in South Africa launch massive anti-pass campaign
1909		Delegation of African and coloured politicians protest in London at racial character of draft South Africa Act Establishment of Suid-Afrikaanse Akademie (renamed in 1942 Die Suid-Afrikaanse Akademie vir Wetenskap en Kuns)

DATE	LITERATURE	HISTORICAL/CULTURAL EVENTS
1910	Black, *Helena's Hope, Ltd.* (D; SA) *Die Brandwag* (J; SA) Cory, *The Rise of South Africa* (1910–30) (NF) Mendelssohn, *South African Bibliography* Segoete, *Mono ke Mohodi ke Mouwane* (F; L)	Union of South Africa with Louis Botha as prime minister Select committee in the white SA parliament suggests limits on African landownership Limited non-white franchise retained in the Cape province
1911	Bleek and Lloyd, *Specimens of Bushmen Folklore* Leipoldt, *Oom Gert Vertel en Ander Gedigte* (P; SA) Schreiner, *Woman and Labour* (NF; SA)	
1912		South African Native National Congress. (In 1927 name changed to ANC)
1913	Cripps, *Bay-tree Country* (F; Z) *The Pilgrim's Progress* in Ndebele	Natives Land Act (SA) African women in Orange Free State choose gaol rather than carry passes
1914	Bokwe, biography of Ntsikana (SA)	National Party (SA) Boer generals plan coup in SA; Botha crushes rebellion Outbreak of First World War Union Defence Force invades German SWA Hertzog Prize for Afrikaans literature
1915	Totius, *Trekkerswee* (P; SA) Mwase, *A Dialogue of Nyasaland . . .* (NF)	
1916	*Die Huisgenoot* (J; SA) Plaatje, *Native Life in South Africa* (NF)	Constitution of University of Cape Town South African Native College (later Fort Hare)
1918	*O Brado Africano* (J; Mz)	Formation of Afrikaner Broederbond Van Riebeeck Society – historical society – founded in SA

DATE	LITERATURE	HISTORICAL/CULTURAL EVENTS
1919		On Botha's death Smuts becomes SA prime minister
1920	Caluza, Zulu-English songs	SA granted League of Nations mandate over SWA
	Langenhoven, didactic Afrikaans writing including 'Die Stem van Suid Afrika'	70,000 African mine workers strike for more pay
	Shembe, Zulu-Christian hymns	Beginning of systematic Portuguese-colonial rule in Mozambique in which majority of local population subjected to forced labour
	Zulu school drama organised by Fr B. Huss at Mariannhill Catholic mission in Natal	
	Ribas, *Uango-feitiço* (F; A)	
1921	*Bantu Studies* (J; SA)	
	Jabavu, *Bantu Literature . . .* (NF; SA)	
1922	*South African Outlook* (J) (previously *The Christian Express*)	Rand Revolt in which troops crush striking white mine workers
1923		Natives (Urban Areas) Act extends segregation to towns (SA)
		Southern Rhodesia becomes self-governing British colony
1924	Campbell, *The Flaming Terrapin* (P; SA)	Britain assumes administration of Northern Rhodesia
	Millin, *God's Step-Children* (F; SA)	
	Stuart, Zulu readers	
	Van Bruggen, *Ampie* trilogy (1924–1942) (F; SA)	
1925	Nathan, *South African Literature: A General Survey*	Afrikaans becomes an official language in SA
	Plomer, *Turbott Wolfe* (F; SA)	
	Slater edits *Centenary Book of South African Verse*	
	Smith, *The Little Karoo* (F; SA)	
1926	Malherbe, *Die Meulenaar* (F; SA)	'Civilised' labour policy reserves skilled work for white South Africans
	Mofolo, *Chaka* (F; L)	
	Smith, *The Beadle* (F; SA)	Dictatorial Salazar government in Portugal; rigid censorship policies would be extended to colonies in 1933
	Voorslag (J; SA)	

DATE	LITERATURE	HISTORICAL/CULTURAL EVENTS
1927	Mbata and Mdhladhla's collection of Zulu oral narratives *uChakyana* . . .	Native Administration Act extends controls over Africans in SA
	The Outspan (J; SA)	Carnegie Foundation funds commission into 'poor white' problem in SA
	Plomer, *I Speak of Africa* (F; SA)	
	Plomer, *Notes for Poems* (P; SA)	
1928	Sekese, *Pitso ya Dinonyana* (F; L)	
1929	Macmillan, *Bantu, Boer and Briton* (NF; SA)	Hertzog government in SA gives votes to white women and removes economic qualification for white men as part of attempt to boost white vote and remove Cape African franchise
	Mthethwa's Lucky Stars stage township plays	
	Reitz, *Commando* (written in rude Dutch *c.* 1990) (NF; SA)	
	The Sjambok (J; SA)	Federasie van Afrikaanse Kultuur-vereeniginge (FAK)
	Slater, *Drought: An African Parable* (P; SA)	
	Assis Júnior, *O Segredo da Morta* (published, 1934) (F; A)	
1930	Campbell, *Adamastor* (P; SA)	Land Apportionment Act in Southern Rhodesia
	Plaatje, *Mhudi* (F; SA)	
	Schumann's Afrikaans plays in 1930s	Negritude cultural movement launched in Paris by Senghor, Césaire and Dumas
	Soga, *The South-Eastern Bantu* (NF; SA)	
	Zenani's Xhosa *iintsomi* (imaginative narratives)	
1931	Mweli-Skota, *The African Yearly Register* . . . (Who's Who of Black Folks)	
	Bereng, seSotho praises of King Moshoeshoe (L) ·	
1932	Da Cruz, *Quissange, Sandade Negra* (P; A)	
1933	Complete Bible in Afrikaans	
	Ntara, *Mbiri ya Nthondo* (F; M)	
1934	Mikro, *Toiings* trilogy (F; SA)	Malan breaks from Hertzog-Smuts coalition (United Party) to form 'Purified' National Party
	Totius, *Passieblomme* (P; SA)	
	Van der Post, *In A Province* (F; SA)	Southern Rhodesian Industrial Conciliation Act discriminates against African majority

DATE	LITERATURE	HISTORICAL/CULTURAL EVENTS
1935	Dekker, *Afrikaanse Literatuurgeskiedenis* Mqhayi, Xhosa translation of *Aggrey of Africa* Slater, *Dark Folk* (P; SA) Van der Heever, *Somer* (F; SA) Vilakazi, *Inkondlo kaZulu* (P; SA)	Shuter and Shooter in Pietermaritzburg begins publishing books in Zulu University of Witwatersrand Bantu Treasury series
1936	Bennie's Xhosa anthology *Imibengo* (F, NF, P) Jolobe, *Umyezo* (P; SA)	Native Representation Act in SA removes Cape African franchise South African Broadcasting Corporation (SABC)
1937	Cloete, *Turning Wheels* (F; SA) R. Dhlomo, *UShaka* (F; SA) *Die Transvaaler* (J) edited by H. F. Verwoerd Van Wyk Louw, *Die Halwe Kring* (P; SA)	African Authors' Conference in Johannesburg issues 'proposals for the development of Bantu Literature' (in *South African Outlook*, no. 67, 1937)
1938	*The South African Forum* (J)	Centenary celebrations of Great Trek
1939	Hoernlé, *South African Native Policy and the Liberal Spirit* (NF) *The Pilgrim's Progress* in seTswana *Trek* (J; SA) Van Wyk Louw, *Loyale Verset* (NF; SA)	Start of Second World War (Smuts leads divided South Africa into War) Geoffrey Durrant arrives from Cambridge and influences university English education in South Africa with close readings of literary texts
1940	Jordan, *Ingqumbo Yeminyanya* (tr. *The Wrath of the Ancestors*, 1980) (F; SA)	Bus boycotts in Johannesburg African townships Southern Rhodesian government establishes first schools for Africans
1941	De Kiewiet, *A History of South Africa: Social and Economic* H. Dhlomo, *Valley of a Thousand Hills* (P; SA) *Itinerario* (J; Mz) Van Wyk Louw, *Raka* (P; SA)	

DATE	LITERATURE	HISTORICAL/CULTURAL EVENTS
1943	Mqhayi, *Inzuzo* (P; SA) Van Melle, *Bart Nel* (published in Dutch in 1936) (F; SA)	Leading middle-class Africans in SA outline black political demands in document *African Claims* Formation of ANC Youth League
1945	*Standpunte* (J; SA) Vilakazi, *Amal' eZulu* (P; SA)	UNO refuses to allow SA to incorporate SWA India articulates world opposition to SA's racial policies Increase in Portuguese settlers to Angola African rail strike in Northern and Southern Rhodeaia Postwar increase in African townships and shantytowns as work-seekers come to Johannesburg
1946	P. Abrahams, *Mine Boy* (F; SA) Campbell, *Talking Bronco* (P; SA) Jolobe, *Poems of an African*[t] (SA)	Strike by African mine workers crushed by SA police
1947	Bosman, *Mafeking Road* (F; SA) Khaketla, *Moshoeshoe le Baruti* (F; L) *Vandag* (J; SA)	National Theatre Organisation (SA) Movimiento dos Jovens Intelectuais (A)
1948	Paton, *Cry, the Beloved Country* (F; SA) follows Abrahams and, earlier, Blackburn, Plomer, Scully, R. Dhlomo and Van der Post in focusing on 'Jim comes to Joburg' Roux, *Time Longer than Rope: The Black Man's Struggle for Freedom in South Africa* (NF)	[Reunited] National Party wins white SA election and begins implementing policy of apartheid ANC Youth League proposes militant programme of action; among members are Buthelezi, Mandela, Mugabe, Tambo and Sobukwe Northern Rhodesia and Nyasaland Joint Literature Bureau
1949	Bosman, *Cold Stone Jug* (NF; SA) Opperman, *Joernaal van Jorik* (P; SA) Brettell, *Bronze Frieze* (P; Z) Soremenho, *Terra Morta* (F; A)	Beginning of apartheid laws which would include Group Areas Act, Immorality Act, Population Registration Act and Suppression of Communism Act

DATE	LITERATURE	HISTORICAL/CULTURAL EVENTS
1950	*Rand Daily Mail* takes bold investigative approach to apartheid Lessing, *The Grass is Singing* (F; Z) *Antologia dos Novas Poetas de Angola*, the first anthology of Angolan poetry Poetry of de Sousa and Craveirinha begins to appear in journals (Mz)	Communist Party of South Africa disbanded ahead of state action South Africa attempts to impose apartheid on SWA Verwoerd becomes minister of Native Affairs Opening of University in Salisbury (Southern Rhodesia) Southern Rhodesia Subversive Activities Act imposes censorship on books, periodicals and newspapers
1951	P. Abrahams, *Wild Conquest* (F; SA) Campbell, *Light on a Dark Horse* (NF; SA) *Drum* (J; SA) Opperman, first edition of *Groot Verseboek* (P; SA) Rooke, *Mittee* (F; SA) *Tydskrif vir Letterkunde* (J; SA) Lessing, *This Was the Old Chief's Country* (F; Z) *Mensagem* (J; A) Anthology *Poesia em Moçambique*	
1952	Butler, *The Dam* (D; SA) Butler, *Stranger to Europe* (P; SA) *Msaho* (J; Mz) Paton, *Too Late the Phalarope* (F; SA) Yali-Manisi, *Izibongo Zeenkosi zamaXhosa* (P; SA)	ANC launches defiance campaign in SA
1953	Gordimer, *The Lying Days* (F; SA) *African Parade* (J; Z) Mopeli-Paulus, *Blanket Boy* (F; L) (*Blanket Boy's Moon*, 1984)	National Party wins white election in SA with mandate to remove coloured people from common voters' role Bantu Education Act Non-racial Liberal Party and Congress of Democrats formed in SA

DATE	LITERATURE	HISTORICAL/CULTURAL EVENTS
1953 (*Cont.*)		Central African federation of two Rhodesias and Nyasaland
		Southern Rhodesia Literature Bureau
1954	P. Abrahams, *Tell Freedom* (NF; SA)	Male hostels in Witwatersrand African townships see increase in mainly Zulu migrant workers and tensions between urban and rural inhabitants
	H. Dhlomo, *Dingana* (D; SA)	
	Nyembezi, collection of Zulu proverbs	
	Mofokeng, *Leetong* (F; L)	
1955	Antonissen, *Die Afrikaanse Letterkunde van Aanvang tot Hede* (NF; SA)	Freedom Charter adopted at Congress of the People
	Blum, 'Kaapse sonnette' in *Steenbok tot Poolsee* (P; SA)	SA government begins removals from Sophiatown
	Ritter, *Shaka Zulu* (NF; SA)	
	Dos Santos (Kalungano), negritude black poetry in *O Brado* (Mz)	
	Mpashi, *Uwakwensho Bushiku* and *Uwaumu Nafyala* (F; Za)	
1956	*Africa South* (J; SA)	Treason trial of 156 SA activists all of whom are eventually acquitted
	Huddleston, *Naught for your Comfort* (NF; SA)	Coloured people removed from common voters' roll in SA
	Jacobson, *A Dance in the Sun* (F; SA)	University English conference at University of Witwatersrand raises issue of teaching local SA literature; anxious about status of English in Afrikaner-dominated state
	The Purple Renoster (J; SA)	
		First international conference of black writers and artists in Paris encourages African perspective in Angola and Mozambique
1957	Jordan's articles on Xhosa literature in *Africa South* (1957–59)	University College of Rhodesia and Nyasaland established
	Mutswairo, *Feso* (F; Z)	Ghana gains independence
	Soromenho, *Viragem* (F; A)	
	Paralelo 20 (J; Mz)	
	Masiye, *The Lands of Kazembe* (D, radio; Za)	

DATE	LITERATURE	HISTORICAL/CULTURAL EVENTS
1958	Cele, Zulu translation of Haggard's *King Solomon's Mines*	Verwoerd becomes prime minister of SA
	Gordimer, *A World of Strangers* (F; SA)	Extension of Universities Act prepares for separate 'non-white' universities in SA
	Jolobe, Xhosa translation of Haggard's *King Solomon's Mines*	
	Van der Post, *The Lost World of the Kalahari* (NF; SA)	Banda in Nyasaland campaigns against federation
	Chitepo, *Soko Resini Musoro* (P; Z)	
	Moçambique 58, a literary supplement to Notícias (J)	
1959	Butler edits *Book of South African Verse*	Anti-apartheid movement founded in London after Luthuli appeals for international boycott of SA
	Delius, *The Last Division* (P; SA)	
	King Kong (D; SA)	Pan Africanist Congress formed by Sobukwe
	Mdedle, Zulu translation of *Macbeth*	Mambo Press in Southern Rhodesia as Catholic mission press; scope broadened in 1962 under Fr Traber who was deported in 1970 and Mambo's newspaper *Moto* banned in 1974
	Mphahlele, *Down Second Avenue* (NF; SA)	
	Nyembezi, Zulu translation of Haggard's *She*	
	Shona dictionary	Campaigns for African rights in Northern and Southern Rhodesia
	Sithole, *African Nationalism* (NF; Z)	
		Kaunda imprisoned and United Independence Party banned; on his release he leads massive civil disobedience campaign
		Banda's Nyasaland African Congress party banned and Banda imprisoned; NAC reorganised as Malawi Congress Party which continues protests
1960	J. Cope, *The Tame Ox* (F; SA)	Sharpeville shooting in PAC anti-pass campaign
	Nyembezi, *Lafa Elihle Kakhulu* (Zulu translation, *Cry, the Beloved Country*)	ANC and PAC banned, leaders flee into exile and set up military wings
	Nyembezi & Nxumalo, *Inqolobane Yesizwe*, volume of Zulu customs and traditions	British prime minister Macmillan delivers 'wind of change' speech to SA parliament; SA withdraws from Commonwealth
	Petersen, *Die Kinders van Kain* (P; SA)	

DATE	LITERATURE	HISTORICAL/CULTURAL EVENTS
1960 (*Cont.*)	SABC introduces radio service in 9 (South African) African languages resulting in new activities in the writing of radio plays and serials	Banda released from prison and invited to independence talks in London
	Imbondeíro imprint publishes new Angolan writers including Vieira	
	De Lemos, *Poemas do Tempo Presente* (P; Mz)	
1961	*Contrast* (J; SA)	SA becomes republic on white mandate
	Fugard, *The Blood Knot* (D; SA)	
	Nyembezi, *Inkinsela yaseMgungundlovu* (F; SA)	Mandela proposes adoption of armed struggle
	Small, *Kitaar my Kruis* (P; SA)	Luthuli, president of ANC, receives Nobel Peace prize
	Tydskrif vir Geesteswetenskappe (which since 1922 had combined with natural sciences as *Tydskrif vir Wetenskap en Kuns*) (J; SA)	Cottlesloe conference results in World Council of Churches and SA churches including sections of Afrikaner Dutch Reformed church rejecting spiritual justifications for apartheid; Verwoerd pressures Afrikaner theologians to recant; Revd Beyers Naudé resigns as moderator and minister to direct Christian Institute which rejects apartheid as 'false gospel'
	Van der Post, *The Heart of the Hunter* (NF; SA)	
	A Voz de Moçambique with cultural supplement (J)	
		CNA Literary Prize (SA)
		English Academy of Southern Africa
		Beginning of armed struggle in Angola
1962	La Guma, *A Walk in the Night* (F; SA)	
	Leroux, *Sewe Dae by the Silbersteins* (F; SA)	
	Luthuli, *Let My People Go* (NF; SA)	
	Mphahlele, *The African Image* (NF; SA)	
	Smit, *Putsonderwater* (D; SA)	
	Van Wyk Louw, *Tristia* (P; SA)	

DATE	LITERATURE	HISTORICAL/CULTURAL EVENTS
1962 (*Cont.*)	Chidyausiku, *Nyadzidzinokunda Rufu* (NF; Z) Kaunda, *Zambia Shall be Free* (NF)	
1963	First, *South West Africa* (NF; SA) Jonker, *Rook en Oker* (P; SA) Kente, *Manana, the Jazz Prophet* (D; SA) Modisane, *Blame Me on History* (NF; SA) Ervedosa, *A Literatura Angolana: Resenha Histórica* (NF; A) Vieira's stories *Luuanda* appear in Angola and, although the author was in political detention, stories awarded prize by Portuguese Society of Writers which was then dissolved by Salazar government	'90-day' detention in SA Rivonia trial of Umkhonto we Sizwe leaders SA Publications and Entertainments Act with severe censorship provisions State subsidised performing arts councils in SA Mugabe, secretary general of ZANU, returns to Southern Rhodesia and is detained Terence Ranger, influential history lecturer, deported from Southern Rhodesia Núcleo dos Estudentes Africanos de Moçambique, a student debating society
1964	Barnard, *Pa Maak vir My 'n Vlieër, Pa* (D; SA) Breytenbach, *Die Ysterkoei Moet Sweet* (P and F; SA) Livingstone, *Sjambok, and Other Poems from Africa* (SA/Z) *New Coin Poetry* (J; SA) Paton, *Hofmeyr* (NF; SA) Rabie, 'Bolandia' novels (1964–85) (F; SA) Smith, *When the Lion Feeds* (F; SA/Z) *Two Tone* (J; Z) Craveirinha, *Chigubo* (P; Mz) Honwana, *Nós Matámos a Cão Tinhoso* (We Killed Mangy-Dog) (F; Mz) Poems from Mozambique and other Frelimo-inspired cultural activities in the 1960s *New Writing from Zambia* (J)	Malawi gains independence University of Malawi, where English Department under British expatriates would encourage literary activities Frelimo launches armed resistance in Mozambique Zambia gains independence

DATE	LITERATURE	HISTORICAL/CULTURAL EVENTS
1965	First, *117 Days* (NF; SA)	Rhodesian government of Smith declares UDI from Britain
	Mandela, *No Easy Walk to Freedom* (NF; SA)	
	Nkosi, *Home and Exile* (NF; SA)	
	Small, *Kanna Hy Kô'Hystoe* (D; SA)	
	Rubadiri's poems (M) in *Transition, Black Orpheus* and *Présence Africaine*	
	Santos, *Quinaxixe* (P; Mz)	
1966	Clouts, *One Life* (P; SA)	Verwoerd assassinated
	Fugard, *Hello and Goodbye* (D; SA)	Cape Town's District Six declared white area
	Gordimer, *The Late Bourgeois World* (F; SA)	ZANU and ZAPU launch armed struggle in Zimbabwe
	Mutwa, *Indaba, My Children* (NF; SA)	Botswana gains independence
	Omer-Cooper, *The Zulu Aftermath* (NF; SA)	Lesotho gains independence
	Sachs, *Jail Diary* (NF; SA)	SWAPO launches armed struggle in Namibia
	Chivaura, *Mulinhimira Wedetembo* (P; Z)	University of Zambia
	Samkange, *On Trial for my Country* (F; Z)	
	Kachingwe, *No Easy Task* (F; M)	
1967	Ranger, *Revolt in Southern Rhodesia, 1896–7* (NF; Z)	Censorship and Entertainments Control Act in Rhodesia would include among its bannings Samkange's *Origins of Rhodesia*, Sithole's *Obed Mutezo*, Vambe's *An Ill-fated People* and Mungoshi's *Coming of the Dry Season*
	Kayira, *The Looming Shadow* (F; M)	
		Literature Bureau in Zambia taken over by NECZAM (National Education Company of Zambia); publishing activity by NECZAM
1968	Brutus, *Letters to Martha and Other Poems from a South African Prison*	'Resettlements' of Africans under SA apartheid social engineering leads to massive human suffering
	Cope and Krige edit *The Penguin Book of South African Verse*	Ndebele replaces Zulu as school subject in Rhodesia
	Cope, *Izibongo: Zulu Praise-Poems*	

DATE	LITERATURE	HISTORICAL/CULTURAL EVENTS
1968 (*Cont.*)	*Dictionary of South African Biography* (ongoing)	Malawian Censorship Board
		Swaziland gains independence
	Miller, *Selected Poems* (SA)	Student protests in Paris and on USA campuses
	Chirimo (J; Z)	
	Samkange, *Origins of Rhodesia* (NF; Z)	
	Mendes, *Véspera Confiada* (P; Mz)	
1969	Cope, *The Dawn Comes Twice* (F; SA)	South African Students' Organisation (SASO) with Biko as first president espouses Black Consciousness
	Fugard, *Boesman and Lena* (F; SA)	
	Wilson and Thompson edit *The Oxford History of South Africa*, 2 vols (1969, 1971)	
	Kusile Mbongi Zohlanga, first anthology of Ndebele poetry	
	Kayira, *Jingala* (F; M)	
	Mondlane, *The Struggle for Mozambique* (NF)	
	Mulukita, *A Point of No Return* (F; Za)	
1970	Finnegan, *Oral Literature in Africa* (NF)	Millions of Africans in SA declared citizens of ethnic Bantustans
	Kunene, *Zulu Poems* (SA)	
	Livingstone, *Eyes Closed against the Sun* (P; SA)	Beginning of small literary publishers in SA, Donker, Ravan, David Philip
	Marks, *Reluctant Rebellion: The 1906–8 Disturbances in Natal* (NF; SA)	Human rights violations in Malawi
		Writers' Group, University of Malawi
1971	Desmond, *The Discarded People* (NF; SA)	UN revokes SA's mandate in SWA and renames territory Namibia
	Du Plessis, *Siener in die Suburbs* (D; SA)	
	Gérard, *Four African Literatures* (NF)	Residential Property Owners (Protection) Bill, a Rhodesian version of SA Group Areas Act
	Jensma, *Sing for our Execution* (P; SA)	Banda declares himself Malawi's president for life and opens diplomatic relations with apartheid SA
	Kgositsile, *My Name Is Afrika* (P; SA)	

DATE	LITERATURE	HISTORICAL/CULTURAL EVENTS
1971 (*Cont.*)	McClure, *The Steam Pig* (F; SA)	
	Mtshali, *Sounds of a Cowhide Drum* (P; SA)	
	Walshe, *The Rise of African Nationalism in South Africa* (NF)	
	Mulaisho, *The Tongue of the Dumb* (F; Za)	
1972	Biko, writings and speeches; collected as *I Write What I Like* (1978)	Black Peoples's Convention in SA co-ordinates Black Consciousness Activities
	Breytenbach, *Skryt: Om 'n Sinkende Skip Blou te Verf* (P; SA)	MDALI (Music, Drama, Arts and Literature Institute), a Black Consciousness initiative in SA
	Fugard, *Sizwe Bansi Is Dead* (D; SA)	Nasionale Afrikaans Letterkuidige Museum en Navorsingsentrum, Bloemfontein (Documentation of Afrikaans language and literature)
	Jordan, *Towards an African Literature: The Emergence of Literary Form in Xhosa*	
	La Guma, *In the Fog of the Seasons' End* (F; SA)	The Space Theatre, Cape Town
	Matthews and Thomas, *Cry Rage!* (P; SA)	Death of Salazar in Portugal
	Schoeman, *Na die Geliefde Land* (F; SA)	
	Serote, *Yakhal'inkomo* (P; SA)	
	Turner, *The Eye of the Needle* (NF; SA)	
	Mungoshi, *Coming of the Dry Season* (F; Z)	
	Rhodesian Poetry (J)	
	Vambe, *An Ill-fated People: Zimbabwe before and after Rhodes* (NF)	
1973	Brink, *Kennis van die Aand* (F; SA)	National English Literary Museum and Documentation Centre, Grahamstown
	Currey, *The Africa We Knew* (P; SA)	
	Dikobe, *The Marabi Dance* (F; SA)	Massive strikes by African workers in SA
	Eybers, *Kruis of Munt* (volumes since 1936) (P; SA)	Mass expulsion of students from University of Rhodesia ('pots and pans demonstrations') include writers Marechera, Nyamfukudza and Zimunya
	Gordimer, *The Black Interpreters* (NF; SA)	

DATE	LITERATURE	HISTORICAL/CULTURAL EVENTS
1973 (*Cont.*)	Royston edits first anthology of new black poetry in SA, *To Whom It May Concern*	
	Phiri, *Tickling Sensation* (F; Za)	
1974	Coetzee, *Dusklands* (F; SA)	SA Publications Act continues rigid censorship
	English in Africa (J; SA)	
	Gordimer, *The Conservationist* (F; SA)	Kirkwood advocates radical Marxist/Third-world populist analysis of SA literary-culture
	Lewin, *Bandiet: Seven Years in a South African Prison* (NF)	Market Theatre, Johannesburg
	Ipi-Tombi, commercially popular African musical (SA)	Mugabe escapes from 10-year detention to continue war as president of ZANU
	Neto's collected poems *Sagrada Esperança*, tr. *Sacred Hope* (A)	End of Portuguese metropolitan dictatorship
	'Popular Publications' series in Malawi by White Fathers' Montfort Press (1957) include *Tales of Old Malawi*	
	Craveirinha, *Kiringana ua Karingana* (P; Mz)	
1975	Gordimer, *Selected Stories* (from 1949 to mid-1970s) (SA)	Poet Breytenbach gaoled under SA 'terrorism' laws
	Roberts, *Outside Life's Feast* (F; SA)	Inkatha, a mainly Zulu political and cultural organisation with roots dating back to 1928, founded by Buthelezi
	Serote, *No Baby Must Weep* (P; SA)	
	Tlali, *Muriel at Metropolitan* (F; SA)	Angola and Mozambique attain independence and experience continuing civil war – in Angola MPLA seize power and are opposed by UNITA (USA, Soviet Union, SA involvement); in Mozambique Renamo supported by Rhodesia and later by SA oppose Frelimo
	Mungoshi, *Ndiko Kupindana Kwamazuva* (F; Z)	
	Mungoshi, *Waiting for the Rain* (F; Z)	
	Rhodesian Literature Bureau publishes shortened Shona version of Haggard's *King Solomon's Mines*	
	Andrade, *Poesie com Armas* (P; A)	Union of Angolan Writers, Angolan Authors' Series and Angolan Work and Workshop Series
	Hamilton's literary history of Angola, *Voices from an Empire*	
	'Mutimatí Barnabé João', *Eu, o Povo* (P; Mz)	

DATE	LITERATURE	HISTORICAL/CULTURAL EVENTS
1975 (*Cont.*)	Three-volume anthology, *No Reino de Caliban: Antologia Panorâmica de Poesia Africana de Expressão Portuguesa*	
1976	Aucamp, *Dooierus* (F; SA)	16 June, Soweto school children march in protest against Afrikaans as medium of instruction; hundreds killed as protests against socio-political repression spread across SA
	Coetzee, *In the Heart of the Country* (F; SA)	
	Leroux, *Magersfontein, O Magersfontein* (F; SA)	
	Sepamla, *The Blues Is You in Me* (P; SA)	Mambo Writers' Series encourages 'Zimbabwean' voices
	Vambe, *From Rhodesia to Zimbabwe* (NF; Z)	Muchemwa, first black editor of *Two Tone* (Z)
	Riu, *11 Poemas em Novembro* (P; A)	
	Gibbs edits *Nine Malawian Plays*	
1977	Butler, *Karoo Morning* (NF; SA)	Biko dies in police detention and Black Consciousness movements banned
	Dhlomo's theatre criticism of 1940s recovered in *English in Africa* (SA)	
	Gwala, *Jol' iinkomo* (P; SA)	Attacks in journals and at conferences on 'Eurocentric' bias in SA university syllabuses by liberal-Africanist and Marxist-class analyses
	Head, *The Collector of Treasures* (F; B/SA)	
	Mann, *First Poems* (SA)	Editor Qoboza gaoled as SA state closes down *The World* (Johannesburg)
	Webb and Wright begin editing *The James Stuart Archive* (SA)	
	The World under Qoboza's editorship becomes most widely read newspaper by black South Africans	
	Fereira, *Literaturas de Expressão Portuguesa* (NF; A, Mz)	
	Poesia de Combate-2, anthology of combat poems (Mz)	
1978	Branford edits first *Dictionary of South African English* (ongoing)	Botha succeeds Vorster as SA prime minister and launches 'total onslaught' against enemies of apartheid
	Cullinan, *Today Is Not Different* (P; SA)	
	Essop, *The Hajji and Other Stories* (SA)	Cassinga massacre in which SA attacks SWAPO camp in Angola

DATE	LITERATURE	HISTORICAL/CULTURAL EVENTS
1978 (*Cont.*)	Jacobson, *Through the Wilderness: Selected Stories* (SA)	Introduction of Amstel Playwright of the Year Award in SA
	Joubert, *Die Swerfjare van Poppie Nongema* (F/NF; SA)	
	Kannemeyer, first vol. of 2-vol. *Geskiedenis van die Afrikaanse Literatuur*	
	Marquard edits anthology *A Century of South African Short Stories*	
	Staffrider (J; SA)	
	Marechera, *The House of Hunger* (F; Z)	
	Samkange, *Year of the Uprising* (F; Z)	
1979	Brink, *'n Droë Wit Seisoen* (F; SA)	SA introduces major changes in labour field in face of mounting strike actions
	Bundy, *The Rise and Fall of the South African Peasantry* (NF)	
	Gordimer, *Burger's Daughter* (F; SA)	Association of University English Teachers of Southern Africa
	Gray, *Southern African Literature: An Introduction*	President dos Santos, former MPLA, begins leading Angola away from hard-line Marxist–Leninism
	Kunene, *Emperor Shaka the Great* (P; SA)	
	Manaka, *Egoli: City of Gold* (D; SA)	
	Matshoba, *Call Me Not a Man* (F; SA)	
	Mda, *We Shall Sing for the Fatherland* (D; SA/L)	
	Opperman, *Komas uit 'n Bamboesstok* (P; SA)	
	Pakenham, *The Boer War* (NF; SA)	
	Poland, *The Mantis and the Moon: Stories for the Children of Africa* (SA)	
	Wolfers edits anthology (tr. from Portuguese) *Poems from Angola*	
	Mulaisho, *The Smoke that Thunders* (F; Za)	

DATE	LITERATURE	HISTORICAL/CULTURAL EVENTS
1980	Coetzee, *Waiting for the Barbarians* (F; SA) Ebersohn, *Store up the Anger* (F; SA) First and Scott, *Olive Schreiner: A Biography* (SA) Gray, *Caltropp's Desire* (F; SA) Mda, *The Hill* (D; SA) Paton, *Towards the Mountain* (NF; SA) Uys, several political cabarets in the 1980s (SA) Kahari, *The Search for Zimbabwean Identity: An Introduction to the Black Zimbabwean Novel* Marechera, *Black Sunlight* (F; Z) Nyamfukudza, *The Non-Believer's Journey* (F; Z) Pepetela, *Mayombe* (tr. English) (F; A) Vieira, *Luuanda* (tr. English) (F; A)	ZANU–PF with Mugabe as president wins British-supervised elections in Zimbabwe Independent Zimbabwe takes strong public line against apartheid while retaining censorship laws Zimbabwean indigenous-language writing continues to be channelled through Literature Bureau concerned with 'purity' of Shona and Ndebele Activities of former Southern Rhodesian Drama Association widen in National Theatre Organisation Southern Africa Development Coordination Conference formed to counter SA economic influence
1981	Bosman, posthumous *Collected Works* (F, P; SA) Chapman edits anthology *A Century of South African Poetry* Gordimer, *July's People* (F; SA) Mtwa, Ngema and Simon, *Woza Albert!* (D; SA) Serote, *To Every Birth Its Blood* (F; SA) Stockenström *Die Kremetartekspedisie* (F; SA) Wilhelm, *At the End of a War* (F; SA) Kadhani and Zimunya edit anthology *And Now the Poets Speak: Poems Inspired by the Struggle for Zimbabwe* Mapanje, *Of Chameleons and Gods* (P; M)	

DATE	LITERATURE	HISTORICAL/CULTURAL EVENTS
1982	Cope, *The Adversary Within: Dissident Writers in Afrikaans* (NF) Gordimer, 'Living in the Interregnum' (NF; SA) Slabolepszy, *Saturday Night at the Palace* (D; SA) Pongweni edits anthology *Songs that Won the Liberation War* (Z) Zimunya, *Those Years of Drought and Hunger: The Birth of African Fiction in Zimbabwe* Zimunya, *Thought-Tracks* (P; Z) Searle edits anthology (tr. from Portuguese) *The Sunflower of Hope* (P; Mz) Ya-Otto, *Battlefront Namibia* (NF)	Poet Breytenbach released from political imprisonment after seven years of his nine-year sentence (SA) Culture and Resistance Festival, Botswana
1983	Aucamp, *House Visits*[t] Brown, et al., *LIP from Southern African Women* (F; NF) Coetzee, *Life & Times of Michael K* (F; SA) Cronin, *Inside* (P; SA) Fugard, *'Master' Harold and the Boys* (D; SA) Fugard, *Notebooks, 1960–1977* (SA) Maponya, *The Hungry Earth* (D; SA) Miles, *Blaaskans* (F; SA) Ndebele, *Fools and Other Stories* (SA) O'Meara, *Volkskapitalisme: Class, Conflict and Ideology in the Development of Afrikaner Nationalism* *Upstream* (J; SA)	Political activist and poet Cronin completes seven-year prison sentence on political charges (SA) Zimbabwe International Book Fair and Writers' Workshop
1984	Breytenbach, *The True Confessions of an Albino Terrorist* (NF; SA) Chapman, *South African English Poetry: A Modern Perspective* (NF)	SA tricameral parliament gives limited and separate voting rights to Indians and coloureds

DATE	LITERATURE	HISTORICAL/CULTURAL EVENTS
1984 (*Cont.*)	Livingstone, *Selected Poems* (SA) Schoeman, *'n Ander Land* (F; SA) Stockenström, *Monsterverse* (P; SA) Tutu, *Hope and Suffering: Sermons and Speeches* (SA) Willan, *Sol Plaatje: A Biography* (SA) Chidyausiku, *Broken Roots: A Biographical Account of the Culture of the Shona People in Zimbabwe*	United Democratic Front (UDF) formed and protests against 'tricameral' politics SA police shoot African demonstrators in eastern Cape SWAPO co-founder Toivo ja Toivo released from Robben Island after 20 years of his 24-year sentence under SA 'terrorism' act Zimbabwe Writers' Union (ZIWU)
1985	Couzens, *The New African: A Study of the Life and Times of H.I.E. Dhlomo* (SA) Durban Workers' Cultural Local co-ordinates worker plays Hope, *Kruger's Alp* (F; SA) Kuzwayo, *Call Me Woman* (NF; SA) Manaka, *Echoes of African Art: A Century of Art in South Africa* Matthee, *Fiela se Kind* (F; SA) Mzwakhe Mbuli, people's poet, comes to prominence at political gatherings *The World of Can Themba* makes Themba's writings readily available in SA Drama Group at University of Zimbabwe active in dramatisation of Katiyo's *A Son of the Soil*, called *Mavambo: First Steps, Katshaa! The Sound of the AK* (1986), *Samora Continua!* (1987) and *Samora Continua! Two* (1988)	Botha declares state of emergency in SA Civil unrest in SA sparks economic crisis Congress of South African Trade Unions (COSATU) Ongoing strife in Natal between ANC and Inkatha Under editor Qoboza *City Press* achieves largest black readership in SA End Conscription Campaign (ECC) challenges white military call up and organises Art for Peace exhibition Several apartheid laws openly ignored: Hillbrow in Johannesburg becoming 'unofficial' mixed-race suburb; books still banned on sale in SA bookshops
1986	Benson, *Nelson Mandela* (NF) Clingman, *The Novels of Nadine Gordimer* (SA) *The Clover Story* (D; SA) Cope, *Selected Stories* (SA) Ngema, *Sarafina!* (D; SA)	SA military raids on ANC bases in Zimbabwe, Zambia and Botswana as Commonwealth Eminent Persons group arrives for negotiations and recommends economic sanctions in view of little progress towards dismantling apartheid

DATE	LITERATURE	HISTORICAL/CULTURAL EVENTS
1986 (*Cont.*)	Rive, *'Buckingham Palace', District Six* (F; SA)	Repeal of several apartheid laws including section of Immorality Act, Mixed Marriages Act, and Prohibition of Political Interference Act; Pass laws repealed
	Van Heerden, *Toorberg* (F; SA)	
	Mhlanga, *Workshop Negative* (D; Z)	
	Sigogo, *Ngenziwa Ngumumo Wilizwe* (F; Z)	Zimbabwe Association of Community Theatre
	Style and Style edit *Mambo Book of Zimbabwean Verse in English* (tr. from siNdebele and chiShona by Hodza, Fortune and others)	Civil strife in Lesotho
		Machel of Mozambique dies in plane crash
	Couto, *Voices Made Night*[t] (F; Mz)	Zambia adopts IMF austerity programme
	Kameeta, *'Why O Lord?': Psalms and Sermons from Namibia*	
1987	Gordimer, *A Sport of Nature* (F; SA)	Secret meetings between SA government and gaoled ANC leader Mandela
	The Long March (D; SA)	
	Smith, *Rage* (F; SA)	Afrikaner dissidents meet ANC in Senegal
	Whaley, *Platform Five* (D; Z)	COSATU Cultural Day
		Congress of SA Writers (COSAW) formed
		Culture in Another SA Conference, Amsterdam
		Alternative newspapers *New Nation*, *South*, *Weekly Mail* and *Vrye Weekblad* targeted by directorate of Media Relations; mainstream newspaper *The Sowetan* warned
		Grahamstown National Arts Festival 'fringe' events capture mood of state of emergency
		Poet Mapanje detained by Banda
		President Chissano, ex-Frelimo, commits Mozambique to IMF austerity measures
		Civil war continues in Mozambique and Angola

DATE	LITERATURE	HISTORICAL/CULTURAL EVENTS
1988	Breytenbach, *Judas Eye* (P; SA)	Dissident Afrikaans writers meet ANC in Harare
	Coetzee, *White Writing* (NF; SA)	
	Haasbroek, *Voornavlug* (F; SA)	
	Hope, *White Boy Running* (F; SA)	
	Meer, *Higher than Hope*, biography of Mandela (SA)	
	Meli, *A History of the ANC: South Africa Belongs to Us*	
	Dangarembga, *Nervous Conditions* (F; Z)	
	Hove, *Bones* (F; Z)	
	Mungoshi, *The Setting Sun and the Rolling World* (F; Z)	
	Whaley, *The Nyoka Tree* (D; Z)	
	Diescho, *Born of the Sun: A Namibian Novel*	
	Katjavivi, *A History of Resistance in Namibia*	
1989	De Vries, *Nag van die Clown* (F; SA)	Collapse of eastern bloc and world communism
	Fugard, *My Children! My Africa!* (D; SA)	After Botha suffers stroke de Klerk leads National Party SA government
	Krog, *Lady Anne* (P; SA)	
	Miles, *Kroniek uit die Doofpot* (F; SA)	Corruption in Mugabe government which sees cabinet ministers disgraced
	Peires, *The Dead Will Arise: Nongqawuse and the Great Xhosa Cattle-Killing Movement of 1856–7* (NF; SA)	
	Lewis-Williams and Dowson, *Images of Power: Understanding Bushman Rock Art*	
	Chinodya, *Harvest of Thorns* (F; Z)	
1990	Coetzee, *Age of Iron* (F; SA)	De Klerk unbans liberation movements and releases more political prisoners including Mandela; negotiations begin towards new non-racial, democratic SA
	Goosen, *Ons Is Nie Almal So Nie* (F; SA)	
	Sachs, 'Preparing Ourselves for Freedom' (NF; SA)	
	Watson, *Selected Essays* (SA)	

DATE	LITERATURE	HISTORICAL/CULTURAL EVENTS
1990 (*Cont.*)		Inkatha relaunched as an open political party
		Performing arts councils in SA come under pressure to focus on representative, not white-elite, SA community
		Superpowers and SA withdraw from Angola; MPLA wins election which UNITA refuses to recognise; civil war continues
		Efforts to end civil war in Mozambique and move to multiparty democracy
		Namibia wins independence
1991	Brink, *An Act of Terror* (F; SA) Ndebele, *Rediscovery of the Ordinary: Essays on South African Literature and Culture*	Gordimer awarded Nobel Prize for literature Kaunda relinquishes power after defeat in multiparty elections which focus on Zambia's severe economic difficulties
1992	Fugard, *Playland* (D; SA)	
1993	Veit-Wild, *Teachers, Preachers, Non-Believers: A Social History of Zimbabwean Literature* Zeleza, *A Modern Economic History of Africa. Vol. 1* (M)	Mandela and de Klerk share Nobel Peace Prize as severe strife complicates SA's move to democracy
1994	Alexander, *Alan Paton* (NF; SA) Coetzee, *The Master of Petersburg* (F; SA) Cullinan, *Selected Poems* (SA) Gordimer, *None to Accompany Me* (F; SA) Gray, *Selected Poems* SA Mandela, *Long Walk to Freedom* (NF; SA) Political commentary and criticism in Malawian press	Non-racial, democratic elections in SA bring ANC-majority government of national unity to power with Mandela as president SA rejoins world community including OAU and Commonwealth; Dutch Reformed Church continues painful move away from apartheid National Arts Coalition lobbies for policy on arts funding in new SA free of government interference Peace talks in Angola fail to secure end to civil war

DATE	LITERATURE	HISTORICAL/CULTURAL EVENTS
1994 (*Cont.*)		Banda's life-presidency ends in Malawi: multiparty elections; democratic ethos leads to new freedom of expression particularly in local press
		Cease-fire in Mozambique civil war; multiparty elections
		SWAPO gains increased electoral support in Namibia
1995	Brink, *Sandkastele* (F; SA)	SA formulates non-apartheid policies in education, health and labour; SABC continues process of reform; ACTAG (Arts and Cultural Task Group) recommends to Ministry of Arts, Culture, Science and Technology a new arts policy which includes scrapping the performing arts councils and making funding available not only for 'elite' art, but for development projects
	Fugard, *Valley Song* (D; SA)	
	Schoeman, *Die Uur van die Engel* (in *Stemme* trilogy) (F; SA)	
	Singh, new film version of Paton's *Cry, the Beloved Country*	
	D. Tambo, *People of the South* (guest show, SATV)	
	Uys, *You ANC Nothing Yet* (one of many satirical-political cabarets in SA)	
		Run-up to SA local government elections sees increasing violence in KwaZulu-Natal between ANC and Inkatha supporters
		SA constitutional court abolishes death penalty; bill passed to establish SA Truth Commission
		SA rugby team wins world cup at home and receives widespread non-racial support; Mandela in Springbok rugby jersey as guest of honour
		Mandela's *Long Walk to Freedom* – best-seller in SA and abroad – wins Alan Paton Literary Award and CNA Literary Award
		International Conference on Children's Literature, Pretoria
		ZANU-PF easily wins election in Zimbabwe. Mugabe's attempt to ban participation of gay support group at Zimbabwe International Bookfair results in attack by bookfair participants including Gordimer on insensitivity of Zimbabwe government to human rights
		Cease-fire in Angola

General Bibliographies

Note: Place of publication, Johannesburg (J), Cape Town (CT), London (L), New York (NY)

i) Bibliographies, dictionaries

Adey, D., R. Beeton, M. Chapman and E. Pereira (eds) *Companion to South African English Literature* (J, 1986). (Comprehensive A–Z.)

Benson, E., L. W. Conolly, G. D. Killam (eds) *Encyclopaedia of Post-colonial Literatures in English* (L, 1994). (Several entries on writers from southern Africa.)

Boehmer, E. *Colonial & Postcolonial Literature* (Oxford, 1995). (Critical and chronological selections.)

Coldham, G. *A Bibliogaphy of Scriptures in African Languages*. 2 vols (L, 1966).

—— *Dictionary of South African Biographies* (Pretoria, 1968–). (Ongoing.) (Prominent public figures.)

—— *Dictionary of South African English* (CT, 1978; subsequent editions). (Ongoing.)

Dubbeld, C. *Reflecting Apartheid: South African Short Stories in English with Sociopolitical Themes, 1960–1987: A Select and Annotated Bibliography* (Johannesburg, 1990).

Goddard, K., *et al. A Bibliography of South African Literature in English* (Grahamstown, 1995).

Grové, A. P. (ed.) *Letterkundige Sakwoordeboek vir Afrikaans* (Pretoria, 1988). (No translation available, but essential A–Z on Afrikaans writing.)

Jahn, J. *Who's Who in African Literature* (Tübingen, 1972).

Killam, G. D. (ed.) *Dictionary of Literary Biography* (Columbia) (Ongoing. Volume on South African writers, 1995.)

Mendelssohn, S. *South African Bibliography* (L, 1910). (Ian Colvin's introduction reissued separately, CT, 1979.)

Moser, G. M. *A Tentative Portuguese-African Bibliography: Portuguese Literature in Africa and African Literature in the Portuguese Language* (Penn. State, 1970).

Musiker, R. *Companion to South African Libraries* (J, 1986). (Details of Africana libraries, collections and documentation centres.)

Pichanick, J., A. J. Chennells and L. B. Rix, *Rhodesian Literature in English, A Bibliography* (1890–1974/1975) (Gwelo, 1977).

Richter, B. and S. Kotzé *A Bibliography of Criticism of Southern African Literature in English* (Bloemfontein, 1983).

Scott, P. E. *Southern Bantu Literature: A Preliminary Bibliography of Some Secondary Sources* (Grahamstown, 1977).

Scheub, H. *Bibliography of African Oral Narratives* (Madison, 1971). (References to southern Africa.)

Switzer, L. and D. Switzer *The Black Press in South Africa and Lesotho: A Descriptive Bibliographic Guide to African, Coloured and Indian Newspapers, Newsletters and Magazines, 1836–1976* (Boston, 1979).

Switzer, L. *Fire with Your Pen!: A Century of the Subaltern Press in South Africa* (J, 1995).

Torien, B. J. *Afrikaans Literature in Translation: A Bibliography* (CT, 1993).

ii) Descriptive, thematic, critical, theoretical surveys

Andrzeyejewski, B. W., S. Pilaszewicz and W. Tyloch (eds) *Literature in African Languages: Theoretical Issues and Sample Surveys* (Warsaw and Cambridge, 1985). (Includes articles on San, Zulu, Xhosa, Southern Sotho and Tswana literature including extensive biographies.)

Barnett, U. A. *A Vision of Order: A Study of Black South African Literature in English (1914–1980)* (L, CT, 1983).

Beuchat, P.-D. *Do the Bantu Have a Literature?* (J, 1963).

Brink, A. P. *Mapmakers: Writing in a State of Siege* (L, 1983).

Burness, D. (ed.) *Critical Perspectives on Lusophone Literatures from Africa* (Washington, 1980).

Butler, G. *Guy Butler: Essays and Lectures. 1949–1991* (CT, 1994).

Campschreur, W. and J. Divendal (eds) *Culture in Another South Africa* (L, 1989).

Chapman, M., C. Gardner and E. Mphahlele (eds) *Perspectives on South African English Literature* (J, 1992). (Comprehensive selection of essays.)

Chimombo, S. *Malawian Oral Literature: The Aesthetics of Indigenous Arts* (Zomba, 1992).

Clayton, C. (ed.) *Women and Writing in South Africa: A Critical Anthology* (J, 1989).

Coetzee, A. *Letterkunde en Krisis: 'n Honderd Jaar Afrikaanse Letterkunde en Afrikaner-nasionalisme* (J, 1990). Translated into English as 'Literature and Crisis: One Hundred Years of Afrikaans Literature and Afrikaner Nationalism', *Rendering Things Visible*, edited by M. Trump (see below). (Revisionist study.)

Coetzee, A. and J. Polley (eds) *Crossing Borders: Writers Meet the ANC* (J, 1989).

Coetzee, J. M. *White Writing: On the Culture of Letters in South Africa* (New Haven, 1988). (English and Afrikaans revisionism.)

Cope, J. *The Adversary Within: Dissident Writers in Afrikaans* (CT, L, 1982).

Daymond, M. J. (ed.) *Feminists Reading South Africa: Writing, Theory and Criticism* (NY, 1995).

Daymond, M. J., J. U. Jacobs and M. Lenta (eds) *Momentum: On Recent South African Writing* (Pietermaritzburg, 1984).

Department of African Languages (University of South Africa) 'A Brief Survey of Modern Literature in the South African Bantu Languages', *Lime*, no. 6 (Pretoria, 1968). (A 68-page survey.)

Dorson, R. M. (ed.) *African Folklore* (Garden City, N.J., 1970).

Dowson, T. A. and J. Deacon (eds) *Voices from the Past: /Xam Bushmen and the Bleek and Lloyd Collection* (CT, 1994). (Commentary on Bleek and Lloyd's research.)

February, V. A. *Mind Your Colour: The 'Coloured' Stereotype in South African Literature* (L, 1981).

Ferreira, M. *Literaturas Africanas de Expressão Portuguesa*, 2 vols (Lisbon, 1977). (Authoritative on Angola and Mozambique, but not available in English translation. See Ferreira in Gérard, *European-Language Writing*, below.)

Finnigan, R. *Oral Literature in Africa* (Oxford, 1970). (Substantial reference to southern Africa.)

Gaidzanwa, R. *Images of Women in Zimbabwean Literature* (Harare, 1985).

Gérard, A. S. *Four African Literatures: Xhosa, Sotho, Zulu, Amharic* (Berkeley and Los Angeles, 1971). (Comprehensive survey.)

—— *African-Language Literatures: An Introduction to the Literary History of Sub-Saharan Africa* (L, 1981). (Sections on South Africa, Malawi, Zambia and Zimbabwe.)

—— *Comparative Literature and African Literatures* (Pretoria, 1983; Gérard *et al.*, rev. ed., 1993).

Gérard, A. S. (ed.) *European-Language Writing in Sub-Saharan Africa*, 2 vols (Budapest and Cambridge, 1986). (Includes articles on South Africa English and Afrikaans, Angola, Mozambique, Zimbabwe, Zambia and Malawi as well as entries on oral tradition, Negritude and Black Consciousness. See also for details of Portuguese-language criticism of Angolan and Mozambican literature.)

Gerwel, J. *Literatuur en Apartheid* (CT, 1983).

Gray, S. *Southern African Literature: An Introduction* (CT, 1979). (Selective, mythological perspective.)

Groenewald, H. C. (ed.) *Oral Studies in Southern Africa* (Pretoria, 1990).

Guma, S. M. *The Form, Content and Technique of Traditional Literature in Southern Sotho* (Pretoria, 1967).

Haarhoff, D. *The Wild South-West: Frontier Myths and Metaphors in Literature Set in Namibia, 1760–1988* (J, 1991).

Hamilton, R. G. *Voices from an Empire: A History of Afro-Portuguese Literature* (Minneapolis, 1975). See also Hamilton's updated history in Portuguese, *Literatura Africana Literatura Necessaria I–Angola* (Lisbon, 1981).

Heywood, C. (ed.) *Aspects of South African Literature* (L, 1976).

Jabavu, D. D. T. *Bantu Literature: Classification and Reviews* (Alice, 1921).

Jordan, A. C. *Towards an African Literature: The Emergence of Literary Form in Xhosa* (Berkeley, 1973). (Key essays first published in 1940s.)

Kaarsholm, P. *Cultural Struggle and Development in Southern Africa* (L, 1991). (Special interest in Zimbabwe.)

Kannemeyer, J. C. *Geskiedenis van die Afrikaanse Literatuur*, 2 vols (CT, 1978, 1983). Abbreviated single volume, *Die Afrikaanse Literatuur 1652–1987* (CT, 1988) and, in English translation, *History of Afrikaans Literature* (Pietermaritzburg, 1993). (Standard, comprehensive survey.)

Kaschula, R. H. (ed.) *Foundations in Southern African Oral Literature* (J, 1993). (Selection of formative essays from *Bantu Studies*, later renamed *African Studies*.)

Killam, G. D. (ed.) *The Writing of East and Central Africa* (L, 1984). (Includes reference to Malawi, Zambia and Zimbabwe.)

Krog, W. (ed.) *African Literature in Rhodesia* (Gwelo, 1966).

Kunene, D. and R. A. Kirsch, *The Beginning of South African Vernacular Literature* (Los Angeles, 1967).

Lewin Robinson, A. M. *None Daring to Make Us Afraid: A Study of English Periodical Literature in the Cape from its Beginning in 1824 to 1835* (CT, 1962).

Mahlasela, B. E. N. *A General Survey of Xhosa Literature from Its Beginnings in the 1800s to the Present* (Grahamstown, 1973).

Malan, C. (ed.) *Race and Literature/Ras en Literatuur* (Pinetown, 1987). (Selection of key essays.)

Moser, G. M. *Essays in Portuguese-African Literature* (Penn. State, 1969).

Moyana, T. *Education, Liberation and the Creative Act* (Gweru, 1989). (On Zimbabwe.)

Mphahlele, E. *The African Image* (L, 1962; rev. ed., 1974). (Authoritative African perspective.)

Nathan, M. *South African Literature: A General Survey* (L, 1925). (First comprehensive treatise covering English, Dutch and Afrikaans languages and, in addition to fiction, poetry and drama, subjects of travel, history, biography, ethnology, sociology and politics.)

Nazareth, P. *Literature and Society in Modern Africa* (Nairobi, 1972). (Pertinent to southern Africa.)

Ndebele, N. S. *Rediscovery of the Ordinary: Essays on South African Literature and Culture* (J, 1991).

Nethersole, R. (ed.) *Emerging Literatures* (Bern, 1990).

Nkosi, L. *Home and Exile and Other Selections* (L, 1965).

Ntuli, D. B. and C. F. Swanepoel, *Southern African Literature in African Languages: A Concise Historical Perspective* (Pretoria, 1993). (Valuable complement to Gérard.)

Nyembezi, C. L. S. *A Review of Zulu Literature* (Pietermaritzburg, 1961).

Pahl, H. W., D. N. Jafta and J. J. R. Jolobe, *Xhosa Literature: Its Past and Future* (Alice, 1971).

Petersen, K. H. and A. Rutherford (eds) *On Shifting Sands: New Art and Literature from South Africa* (Sydney and Portsmouth, New Hampshire, 1991). (Coincides with unbannings of 2 February 1990.)

Pieterse, C. and D. Munro (eds) *Protest and Conflict in African Literature* (L, 1969). (Includes articles on several writers from southern Africa.)

Riemenschneider, D. (ed.) *History and Historiography of Commonwealth Literature* (Tübingen, 1983).

Roscoe, A. *Uhuru's Fire: African Literature East to South* (Cambridge, 1977). (Aspects of Malawian and South African literature.)

Rutherford, A. (ed.) *From Commonwealth to Post-colonial* (Sydney, 1992). (Sections pertinent to the present study.)

Shava, P. V. *A People's Voice: Black South African Writing in the Twentieth Century* (L, 1989).

Shepherd, R. W. *Lovedale and Literature for the Bantu: A Brief History and Forecast, Lovedale Press* (Alice, 1945; NY, 1970).

—— *Bantu Literature and Life* (Alice, 1955).

Trump, M. (ed.) *Rendering Things Visible: Essays on South African Literary Culture of the 1970s and 1980s* (J, 1990).

Van Wyk Smith, M. *Grounds of Contest: A Survey of South African English Literature* (CT, 1990). (Brief overview.)

Van Wyk Smith, M. and D. Maclennan (eds) *Olive Schreiner and After: Essays on Southern African Literature* (CT, 1983).

Veit-Wild, F. *Teachers, Preachers, Non-Believers: A Social History of Zimbabwean Literature* (L, Harare, 1992). (Study of black Zimbabwean literature with focus on fiction.)

Vilakazi, B. W. *The Oral and Written Literature in Nguni* (Doctoral dissertation, University of the Witwatersrand, J, 1945). (Remains comprehensive and authoritative on Zulu literature.)

Wade, M. *White on Black in South Africa: A Study of English-Language Inscriptions of Skin Colour* (NY, 1993).

Watson, S. *Selected Essays, 1980–1990* (CT, 1990).

Watts, J. *Black Writers from South Africa: Towards a Discourse of Liberation* (L, 1989).

White, L. and T. Couzens (eds) *Literature and Society in South Africa* (CT, 1984). (Essays on oral and written literature.)

iii) Fiction

Chennells, A. *Settler Myths and the Southern Rhodesian Novel* (Doctoral dissertation, University of Zimbabwe, Harare, 1982).

Christie, S., G. Hutchings and D. Maclennan *Perspectives on South African Fiction* (J, 1980).

Gardner, J. H. *Impaired Vision: Portraits of Black Women in the Afrikaans Novel, 1948–1988* (Amsterdam, 1991).

Gorman, G. E. *The South African Novel in English since 1950: An Information and Resource Guide* (Boston, 1978).

Guenther, M. G. *Bushman Folktales: Oral Traditions of the Nharo of Botswana and the /Xam of the Cape* (Stuttgart, 1989). (Commentary and anthology.)

Hewitt, R. L. *Structure, Meaning and Ritual in the Narratives of the Southern San* (Hamburg, 1986).

Hofmeyr, I. *'We Spend our Years as A Tale That is Told': Oral Historical Narrative in a South African Chiefdom* (J, 1994). (Studies role of oral narrative in historical memory of a community.)

Kahari, G. *The Search for Zimbabwean Identity: An Introduction to the Black Zimbabwean Novel* (Gwelo, 1980).

—— *Aspects of the Shona Novel and Other Related Genres* (Gweru, 1986).

—— *The Rise of the Shona Novel: A Study in Development, 1890–1984* (Gweru, 1990).

Klima, V. *South African Prose Writing in English* (Prague, 1971).

Leveson, M. *The Image of the Jew in South African English Fiction* (J, 1994).

Msimang, C. T. *Folktale Influence on the Zulu Novel* (Pretoria, nd [1980]).

New, W. H. *Among Worlds: An Introduction to Modern Commonwealth and South African Fiction* (Erin, Ont., 1975).

Ngara, E. *Art and Ideology in the African Novel: A Study of the Influence of*

Marxism on African Writing (L, 1985). (Specific references to fiction in southern Africa.)

Oboe, A. *Fiction, History and Nation in South Africa* (Padua, 1994).

Parker, K. (ed.) *The South African Novel in English: Essays in Criticism and Society* (L, 1978).

Snyman, J. P. L. *The South African Novel in English, 1880–1930* (University of Potchefstroom, 1952). (Early descriptive survey of fiction by white writers.)

Von Wielligh, G. R. *Boesmanstories*, 4 vols. (CT, 1919–1921). (Ethnographic commentary and anthology.)

Zimunya, M. *Those Years of Drought and Hunger: The Birth of African Fiction in Zimbabwe* (Gweru, 1982).

In Afrikaans see N. P. van Wyk Louw's *Vernuwing in die Prosa* (CT, 1961) and André P. Brink's *Aspecte van die Nuwe Prosa* (CT, 1967).

iv) Poetry

Alvarez-Péreyre, J. *The Poetry of Commitment in South Africa*[t] (L, 1979; 1984).

Chapman, M. *South African English Poetry: A Modern Perspective* (J, 1984).

Chapman, M. (ed.) *Soweto Poetry* (J, 1982).

Coplan, D. '*In the Time of the Cannibals*': *The Word Music of South Africa's Basuto Migrants* (Chicago, L, 1994).

Finnigan, R. *Oral Poetry: Its Nature, Significance and Social Context* (Cambridge, 1977).

Gordimer, N. *The Black Interpreters* (J, 1973). (Second half on new black poetry from South Africa.)

Miller, G. M. and H. Sergeant *A Critical Survey of South African Poetry in English* (CT, 1957).

Ngara, E. *Ideology and Form in African Poetry* (L, 1990). (Sections on Zimbabwean and South African poetry.)

Opland, J. *Xhosa Oral Poetry: Aspects of a Black South African Tradition* (J, 1983).

Preto-Rodas, R. *Negritude as a Theme in the Poetry of the Portuguese-Speaking World* (Gainesville, 1970).

Roscoe, A. and M. Msiska *The Quiet Chameleon: Modern Poetry from Central Africa* (L, 1992). (Articles on Zimbabwean and Malawian poets.)

Sundkler, B. G. M. *Bantu Prophets in South Africa* (L, 1948).

Vail, L. and L. White *Power and the Praise Poem: Southern African Voices in History* (Charlottesville and L, 1991).

Van Wyk Smith, M. *Drummer Hodge: The Poetry of the Anglo-Boer War, 1899–1902* (Oxford, 1978).

Wild, F. *Patterns of Poetry in Zimbabwe* (Gweru, 1988).

Wilhelm, P. and J. Polley (eds) *Poetry South Africa: Selected Papers from Poetry '74* (J, 1976).

In Afrikaans see D. J. Opperman's *Digters van Dertig* (CT, 1953) and N. P. van Wyk Louw's *Opstelle oor ons Oor Digters* (CT, 1972).

v) Drama

Banham, M. (ed.) *Cambridge Guide to African and Caribbean Theatre* (Cambridge, 1994). (Substantial sections on theatre in the countries of southern Africa.)

Bosman, F. C. L. *The Dutch and English Theatre in South Africa, 1800 till Today* (Pretoria, 1951).

Etherton, M. *The Development of African Drama* (L, 1982). (Pertinent to southern Africa.)

Gunner, E. (ed.) *Politics and Performance: Theatre, Poetry and Song in Southern Africa* (J, 1994). (Expanded and enlarged edition of special issue of *Journal of Southern African Studies*, vol. 16, no. 2, June 1990.)

Kavanagh, R. *Theatre and Cultural Struggle in South Africa* (L, 1985).

Laidler, P. H. *The Annals of the Cape Stage* (Edinburgh, 1926).

Linstrum, J. *Travelling Theatre in Malawi* (L, 1969).

Mda, Z. *When People Play People: Development Communication through Theatre* (J, 1993).

Mwansa, D. (ed.) *Zambian Performing Arts: Currents, Issues, Policies and Directions* (Lusaka, 1974).

Orkin, M. *Drama and the South African State* (Manchester, J, 1991). (Comprehensive textual study.)

Schwartz, P. *The Best Company: The Story of Johannesburg's Market Theatre* (J, 1988). (Anecdotal, journalistic.)

Zinyemba, R. *Zimbabwean Drama: A Study of Shona and English Plays* (Gweru, 1986).

In Afrikaans see L. W. B. Binge's *Ontwikkeling van die Afrikaanse Toneel 1832 tot 1950* (Pretoria, 1969), J. C. Kannemeyer's *Opstelle oor die Afrikaanse Drama* (CT, 1970) and André P. Brink's *Aspecte van die Nuwe Drama* (CT, 1974).

vi) Scholarly journals

Current journals in the field of southern African literary-cultural studies include *African Studies, Alternation, Critical Arts, Current Writing, English Academy Review, English in Africa, English Studies in Africa, Journal of Contemporary African Studies, Journal of Literary Studies, Insig, Literator, Pretexts, South African Journal of African Languages, South African Theatre Journal, Southern African Journal for Folklore Studies, Stilet, Tydskrif vir Geesteweetenskappe* and *Tydskrif vir Letterkunde* (all South Africa). Southern Africa features regularly in journals devoted to African studies including the *African Literature Today* series, *Index on Censorship, Journal of Commonwealth Literature* and *Wasafiri* (UK), *Research in African Literatures, Transition* and *World Literature Today* (USA), *Ariel* (Canada), *Kunapipi* (Denmark) and *Matatu* (Germany). Substantial reviews in *Southern African Review of Books* and *Die Suid Afrikaan* (South Africa).

Individual Authors

Notes on biography, important works and criticism

Note: The following lists presume English-speaking readers. For titles of works in the other languages of southern Africa see the Chronology and refer to relevant bibliographies, surveys and studies recorded in the General Bibliographies

ABRAHAMS, Lionel (1928–), born in Johannesburg where he lives. Contribution includes editing Bosman's stories and publishing the new black poetry of the 1970s. Founder of the now defunct literary journal *The Purple Renoster* in 1957, he has published autobiographical stories *The Celibacy of Felix Greenspan* (J, 1977) and collections of poems including *Journal of a New Man* (J, 1984), *The Writer in the Sand* (J, 1988) and *A Dead Tree Full of Live Birds* (CT, 1995). Selection of writing in *Lionel Abrahams: A Reader* (J, 1988).

ABRAHAMS, Peter (1919–), born in Vrededorp, Johannesburg, and left SA for Britain in 1939 prior to settling in Jamaica. Early volume of poetry *A Blackman Speaks of Freedom!* (Durban, 1940) was followed by journalistic sketches, stories and novels including *Mine Boy* (L, 1946), *The Path of Thunder* (L, 1948) and *Wild Conquest* (L, 1951). Novels about Africa include *A Wreath for Udomo* (L, 1956). Autobiography *Tell Freedom* (L, 1954).

> See: Gray, S. 'The Long Eye of History: Four Autobiographical Texts by Peter Abrahams', *Pretexts*, vol. 2, no. 2 (Summer 1990).
> Ogungbesan, K., *The Writing of Peter Abrahams* (L, 1979).
> Wade, J-P., 'Peter Abrahams' *The Path of Thunder*: The Crisis of the Liberal Subject', *English in Africa*, vol. 16, no. 2 (October 1989).
> — 'Song of the City and Mine Boy: the "Marxist" Novels of Peter Abrahams's, *Research in African Literatures*, vol. 21, no. 3 (Fall 1990).
> Wade, M., *Peter Abrahams* (Edinburgh, 1972).

AUCAMP, Hennie (1934–), born in the Cape, lectures in education at University of Stellenbosch. Several volumes of Afrikaans short stories since 1964; selection in English translation, *House Visits* (CT, 1983).

BAIN, Andrew Geddes (1797–1864), born in Scotland, came to SA in 1816. Occasional and satirical verse on settler life in Cape periodicals; text of dramatic sketch *Kaatje Kekkelbek; or, Life among the Hottentots* included in M. Lister (ed.), *Journals* (CT, 1949).

BARNARD, Lady Anne (Lindsay) (1750–1825), born in Scotland and hostess to many social figures in London until, at age 43, she accompanied her husband, the colonial secretary, to the Cape colony. Her letters to Henry Dundas, secretary for war, and her other writings are collected in A. M. Lewin Robinson (ed.), *The Letters of Lady Anne Barnard to Henry Dundas from the Cape and Elsewhere, 1793–1803; together with her Journal of a Tour into the Interior and Certain other Letters* (CT, 1973) and *The Cape Journals of Lady Anne Barnard*, edited by A. M. Lewin Robinson (CT, 1995).

> See: Lenta, M., 'All the Lighter Parts: Lady Anne Barnard's Letters from Cape Town', *Ariel*, vol. 2, no. 2 (1991).
> — 'Degrees of Freedom: Lady Anne Barnard's Cape Diaries', *English in Africa*, vol. 19, no. 2 (October 1992).

BENSON, Mary (1919–), born in Pretoria, an active opponent of apartheid, was banned and placed under house arrest by the SA government before leaving to live in exile in London. Writing includes political biographies on Luthuli (L, 1963) and Mandela (L, 1986; updated 1990), a history of the ANC *The African Patriots* (L, 1962) which was updated and reissued as *South Africa: The Struggle for a Birthright* (L, 1966; 1985), a novel *At the Still Point* (L, 1969) and the autobiography *A Far Cry: The Making of a South African* (L, 1989).

> See: Chapman, M., ' "A Certain Responsibility": Interview with Mary Benson', *Current Writing*, 3 (October 1991).

BERENG, David (D.C.T.) (1900–1973), born in Lesotho, studied at Lovedale; a regent of Quacha district, Lesotho. Volume of praise poetry *Dithothokiso tsa Moshoeshoe le tse Ding* (Moshoeshoe's Praises and Others. Morija, 1931).

BIKO, Bantu Stephen (Steve) (1946–1977), born in eastern Cape, was educated at the Roman Catholic Mariannhill in KwaZulu-Natal and, while a medical student at the University of Natal in Durban, broke with the predominantly white National Union of SA Students (NUSAS) to form SASO (South African Students' Organisation) of which he was elected first president in 1969. Active in Black Consciousness politics, he was restricted, banned and arrested under terrorist legislation by the SA government and died gruesomely in police detention. The subject of many articles and creative works including the play *Steve Biko: The Inquest* (Durban, nd); Donald Woods's biography *Biko* (L, 1978; rev. 1987) and Richard Attenborough's film *Cry Freedom* (1983). Selection of his speeches and writings, *I Write What I Like* (L, 1978).
Woods, D., *Biko* (L, 1978).

> See: Lötter, H. P. P., 'The Intellectual Legacy of Stephen Bantu Biko (1946–1977)', *Acta Academica*, vol. 24, no. 3 (September 1992).
> Pityana, B., et al. (eds), *Bounds of Possibility: The Legacy of Steve Biko and Black Consciousness* (L, 1992).

BLACK, Stephen (?1880–1931), born in Cape Town, was a crime reporter on a daily newspaper before forming his own acting company. The scripts of his social comedies, including *Love and the Hyphen* (first performed 1908), are available in *Three Plays*. Founded the satirical magazine *The Sjambok* (1929–1931). A selection of his reportage in *English in Africa*, vol. 8, no. 2 (September 1981).

See: Gray, S., Introduction, *Three Plays* (J, 1984).

BLACKBURN, Douglas (1857–1929), born in London, was a journalist in Johannesburg mainly on satirical fly-by-night broadsheets. Strongly anti-imperialist views inform his several novels including *Kruger's Secret Service, by One Who Was In It* (L, 1900), *Prinsloo of Prinsloosdorp: A Tale of Transvaal Officialdom, by Sarel Erasmus* (L, 1899), *A Burgher Quixote* (L, 1903; CT, 1984), *Richard Hartley, Prospector* (L, 1905), *I Came and Saw* (L, 1908), *Leaven: A Black and White Story* (L, 1908; Pietermaritzburg, 1991) and *Love Muti* (L, 1915). A selection of his journalism in *English in Africa*, vol. 5, no. 1 (March 1978).

See: Gray, S., *Douglas Blackburn* (Boston, 1984).

BLEEK, Wilhelm (W.H.I.) (1827–1875), born in Berlin where he trained as a philologist; with Bishop Colenso sailed for Natal colony in 1853 to compile a Zulu grammar. For governor Sir George Grey in the Cape he acted as official interpreter and collected folk material, resulting in first of many publications, *Reynard the Fox in South Africa: Hottentot Fables and Tales* (L, 1863). Enjoyed patronage from South African Library and Cape parliament and devoted himself to recording and preserving Bushman language and lore, working with breakwater prisoners as informants. Together with his sister-in-law Lucy C. Lloyd, first to research indigenous languages on a scientific basis. Research continued after Bleek's death by Lloyd who published a selection of the collected material (Bleek and Lloyd Collection, University of Cape Town) as *Specimens of Bushman Folklore* (L, 1911).

See: Dowson, *Voices from the Past* (Gen. Bib.).

BOKWE, John Knox (1855–1922), born in eastern Cape, was a Presbyterian minister, a journalist and composer; worked mainly at Lovedale where he edited the newspapers *The Kafir Express* and *Isigidimi samaXhosa*; in 1897 he joined John Tengo Jabavu in editing *Imvo Zabantsundu*. Religious writing in Xhosa, and biography *Ntsikana: The Story of an African Convert* (Alice, 1914).

BOSMAN, Herman Charles (1905–1951), was born in the Cape, and in the mid-1920s taught briefly in the Marico district of the Transvaal, the setting of his 'Oom Schalk' short stories which appeared in several literary journals and were first collected in *Mafeking Road* (J, 1947). The semi-fictional prison account *Cold Stone Jug* (J, 1949), the posthumously published novel *Willemsdorp* (J, 1977) and later sketches from the *Forum* appear with short stories, poems and novels in *The Collected Works of Herman Charles Bosman*, 2 vols (J, 1981).

See: Gray, S. (ed)., *Herman Charles Bosman* (J, 1986).

Gray, S., 'Herman Charles Bosman's Use of Short Fictional Forms', *English in Africa*, vol. 16, no. 1 (May 1989).

BRETTELL, Noel Harry (N.H.) (1908–1991), born in England, emigrated to Rhodesia in 1930 where he taught in rural schools; after retirement farmed in Zimbabwe. Poetry collections include *Bronze Frieze* (L, 1950) and posthumously published *Selected Poems* (CT, 1994).

BREYTENBACH, Breyten (1939–), born in western Cape, has lived since 1962 in Paris as professional painter and writer. Active spokesperson against apartheid, he was arrested during clandestine visit to SA in 1975 and imprisoned for seven years. Numerous Afrikaans books of poems many of which have been translated into English including *And Death White as Words* (L, CT, 1978), *In Africa Even the Flies are Happy* (L, NY, 1978) and *Judas Eye* (L, 1988). Prison autobiography, *The True Confessions of an Albino Terrorist* (J, L, 1984), surreal novel *Memory of Snow and of Dust* (L, J, 1989), philosophical-travel writing, *A Season in Paradise* (L, NY, 1981) and *Return to Paradise* (L, CT, 1993), and literary-political commentary, *End Papers: Essays, Letters, Articles of Faith, Workbook Notes* (L, NY, 1986).

See: Jacobs, J., 'Breyten Breytenbach and the South African Prison Book', *Theoria*, no. 68 (December 1986).
Lazarus, N., 'Longing, Radicalism, Sentimentality: Reflections on Breyten Breytenbach's *A Season in Paradise*', *Journal of Southern African Studies*, vol. 12, no. 2 (April 1986).

BRINK, André P. ['André' in English versions of his fiction] (1935–), born in the Free State (SA) and after spell in Paris in 1960s lectured Afrikaans at SA universities; currently professor of English at University of Cape Town. Numerous Afrikaans novels translated by Brink into English include *Looking on Darkness* (L, 1974), *An Instant in the Wind* (L, 1976), *Rumours of Rain* (L, 1978), *A Dry White Season* (L, 1979), *A Chain of Voices* (L, 1982), *States of Emergency* (L, 1988), *An Act of Terror* (L, NY, 1991), *The First Life of Adamastor* (L, 1993) and *On the Contrary* (L, 1993). Collection of essays, articles and speeches, *Mapmakers: Writing in a State of Siege* (L, 1983). Afrikaans critical studies include *Aspekte van die Nuwe Prosa* (CT, 1967) and *Aspekte van die Nuwe Drama* (CT, 1974).

See: Cope, *The Adversary Within* (Gen. Bib.).

BRUTUS, Dennis (1924–), born in Zimbabwe, educated at universities in SA, and taught in high schools prior to his imprisonment on Robben Island for his active opposition to apartheid. Left SA as political exile in 1966; writings banned and forbidden to be quoted in SA until 1990. Currently professor of poetry at Northwestern University, USA. Volumes of poems include *Letters to Martha and Other Poems from a South African Prison* (L, 1968) and selections from several individual volumes in *A Simple Lust* (L, 1973) and *Stubborn Hope* (L, 1979).

See: Goodwin, K., 'Dennis Brutus', *Understanding African Poetry: A Study of Ten Poets* (L, 1982).
Tejani, B., 'Can the Prisoner Make a Poet?: A Critical Discussion of

Letters to Martha by Dennis Brutus', E. D. Jones (ed.), *African Literature Today, No. 6* (L, 1973).

Also: Egudu in Heywood, (ed.), *Aspects of South African Literature* (Gen. Bib.).

BUTLER, Guy (1918–), born in the Karoo (SA), student at Rhodes and Oxford universities before serving in the allied forces in the Second World War. University lecturer for 30 years, mostly as professor of English, Rhodes University, Grahamstown. See writings, *Guy Butler: Essays and Lectures*. Active in educational and cultural movements relating to the 1820 settlers as reflected in his books *When Boys Were Men* (CT, 1969) – extracts from SA diaries 1795–1870 – and *The 1820 Settlers* (CT, 1974). Selection from his several volumes of poetry in *Selected Poems* (J, 1975; enlarged 1989); has written plays including *Cape Charade; or, Kaatje Kekkelbek* (CT, 1968) and volumes of autobiography, *Karoo Morning* (CT, 1977), *Bursting World* (CT, 1983) and *A Local Habitation* (CT, 1991). Important editing work includes the Oxford *Book of South African Verse* (Oxford, 1959).

Read, J. (ed.), *Guy Butler: A Bibliography* (Grahamstown, 1992).

See: Hutchings, G., 'Ghost at a Window Pane: The War Poetry of Guy Butler', *English in Africa*, vol. 15, no. 2 (October 1988).

Watson, S., Introduction, *Guy Butler: Essays and Lectures 1949–1991* (CT, 1994).

Also: Kirkwood in Wilhelm and Polley (eds), *Poetry South Africa*, and Bradbrook in Van Wyk Smith and Maclennan (eds), *Olive Schreiner and After* (Gen. Bib.).

CALLAWAY, Henry (1817–1890), born in England, was a medical doctor who later in his life was ordained in the Anglican church; in 1854 travelled to SA to work among the Zulu under Bishop Colenso; established mission with printing press near Pietermaritzburg; became first Bishop of 'Kaffraria' in 1873; took ill and returned to England in 1873. Translated psalms and published *Nursery Tales, Traditions, and Histories of the Amazulu* (Springvale, 1868) and the four-part *The Religious System of the Amazulu* (Springvale, L, 1868–1870; 1884).

CAMPBELL, Roy (1901–1957), born in Durban, was the prodigious son of a prominent colonial family. After early poetry had attracted attention abroad during his unsuccessful spell at Oxford, he returned to Durban and in 1926 edited the literary journal *Voorslag* before leaving SA permanently to spend the rest of his life as a professional writer in England, Spain and Portugal. Several volumes of poetry including *The Flaming Terrapin* (L, 1924), *Adamastor* (L, 1930) and *Talking Bronco* (L, 1946); numerous translations of French, Spanish and Portuguese poetry, journalistic and social criticism, and two volumes of autobiography, *Broken Record* (L, 1934) and *Light on a Dark Horse* (L, 1951). Various editions of his work include *Selected Poems* (J, 1981) and the four-volume *Collected Works* (J, 1985, 1988).

Alexander, P. F., *Roy Campbell: A Critical Biography* (Oxford, 1982).

See: Chapman, M., 'Roy Campbell, Poet: A Defence in Sociological Times', *Theoria*, no. 68 (December 1986).

Cronin, J., 'Turning Around, Roy Campbell's "Rounding the Cape" ', *English in Africa*, vol. 11, no. 1 (May 1984).

Smith, R., *Lyric and Polemic: The Literary Personality of Roy Campbell* (Montreal, 1972).

CHIMOMBO, Steve (1945–), born in Malawi, studied in Malawi and Leeds; returned from England in 1972 and lectures in English at University of Malawi. Long poems *Napolo* (1975) and *Python Python* (1992) collected as *Napolo and Python* (L, 1994). Also play *The Rainmaker* (Limbe, 1978) and critical study *Malawian Oral Literature: The Aesthetics of Indigenous Arts* (Zomba, 1992).

See: Roscoe and Msiska, *The Quiet Chameleon* (Gen. Bib.).

CHINODYA, Shimmer (1957–), born in Gweru, educated at Universities of Zimbabwe and Iowa; works in ministry of education. Novels include *Dew in the Morning* (Gweru, 1982) and *Harvest of Thorns* (Harare, 1989; L, 1990).

See: Veit-Wild, *Teachers, Preachers, Non-Believers* (Gen. Bib.).

CHIPASULA, Frank Mkalawile (1949–), born in Malawi, received mission education and studied at University of Malawi; founder and organiser of Zomba Writers' Group; lived in exile from Banda's regime; professor of literature in the USA. Several volumes of poetry include *Visions and Reflections* (Lusaka, 1972) and *O Earth, Wait for Me* (J, 1984). Editor of *When My Brothers Come Home: Poems from Central and Southern Africa* (Middletown, 1985).

See: Nazombe in Rutherford (ed.), *From Commonwealth to Post-Colonial* (Gen. Bib.).

CHIVAURA, Wilson B. (1927–1968), born in Chimhoyi, Zimbabwe; teacher, producer and announcer in broadcasting. Poems in Shona in *Madetembedzo Akare Namatsva* (1959) and *Mutinhimira Wedetembo* (1966) and, translated into English by himself and others, in several journals and anthologies in Zimbabwe and overseas including *London Magazine*.

CLOUTS, Sydney (1926–1982), born in Cape Town, worked most of his adult life as a librarian in London. Poems in *One Life* (CT, 1966) and in the posthumous volume *Sydney Clouts: Collected Poems* (CT, 1984).

See: Glenn, I., 'Sydney Clouts Our Pen-Insular Poet', *English Academy Review,* 3 (1985).
Memorial issue of *English in Africa,* vol. 11, no. 2 (October 1984).
Also: Chapman, *South African English Poetry* (Gen. Bib.).

COETZEE, John Maxwell (J.M.) (1940–), born in Cape Town, returned to SA in 1971 after several years in Britain and USA, and is professor of English at the University of Cape Town. Novels are *Dusklands* (J, 1974), *In the Heart of the Country* (L, J, 1976), *Waiting for the Barbarians* (L, J, 1980), *Life & Times of Michael K* (L, J, 1983), *Foe* (L, J, 1986), *Age of Iron* (L, J, 1990) and *The Master of Petersburg* (L, 1994). Literary criticism in *White Writing: On the Culture of Letters in South Africa* (New Haven, 1988).
Goddard, K. and J. Read (eds), *J. M. Coetzee: A Bibliography* (Grahamstown, 1990).

See: Attwell, D., *J. M. Coetzee: South Africa and the Politics of Writing* (Berkeley, 1993).

Attwell, D. (ed.), *Doubling the Point: Essays and Interviews* (Cambridge, Mass., 1992).

Dovey T., *The Novels of J. M. Coetzee* (J, 1988).

Huggan, G. and S. Watson (eds), *Critical Perspectives on J. M. Coetzee* (L, 1995).

Penner, D., *Countries of the Mind: The Fiction of J. M. Coetzee* (Westport, 1989).

COLENSO, Frances (Mrs) (1816–1893), born in England, accompanied her husband Bishop Colenso to SA and, between 1865 and 1893, wrote letters on life and times in colonial Natal which have been collected, with commentary, by W. Rees in *Colenso: Letters from Natal* (Pietermaritzburg, 1958).

COLENSO, John William (1814–1883), born and educated in England, arrived in Natal colony in 1853 as newly ordained bishop of the diocese and devoted energy to work among the Zulu whose perspective influenced his numerous anti-colonial writing as well as his controversial biblical criticism that saw him tried for heresy in his absence, and excommunicated from the Anglican church; on successful appeal his position as Bishop was confirmed but the church continued to withhold its support. In addition to Zulu-English grammars and a dictionary, Colenso published numerous accounts of life in Natal, sermons including *'What doth the Lord require of us?'* (Pietermaritzburg, 1879) and the massive study of British government Blue Books, *The Course of Political Events in Zululand from October 1881 to June 1883: Official, Colonial and Zulu Statements Analysed and Compared* (Bishopstowe, nd.).

Guy, J., *The Heretic: A Study of the Life of John William Colenso, 1814–1883* (J, 1983).

COPE, Jack (1913–1991), born in KwaZulu-Natal, farmed before pursuing career as a full-time writer. Several novels including *The Fair House* (L, 1955) and *My Son Max* (L, 1978); selection from several volumes of short stories in *Selected Stories* (CT, 1986); poetry including translations of Bushman meditations. Founding editor of the long-running literary journal *Contrast* (now *New Contrast*); commentary *The Adversary Within: Dissident Writers in Afrikaans* (CT, L, NY, 1982).

COUTO, Mia (1955–), born in Beira, became involved in Frelimo independence struggle at the beginning of his career as a journalist; lives in Maputo and has returned to university to qualify as an environmental biologist after having established himself as director of the Mozambique Information Agency (AIM) and the official newspaper *Notícias*. Two collections of short stories have been translated into English, *Voices Made Night* (L, 1990; 1986) and *Every Man Is a Race* (L, 1994). Other writing: journalism *Cronicando* (Lisbon, 1989), the novel *Terra Sonâmbula* (Lisbon, 1992) and the stories *Estórias Abensonhadas* (Lisbon, 1994).

CRAVEIRINHA, José (1922–), born in Maputo, was a journalist in colonial times and contributor to early Mozambican cultural journal, *O Brado Africano*. A fierce critic of Portuguese colonialism, he was arrested in 1966, and suffered torture and hardship in Machava gaol. Now lives in Maputo and works in Library of Economy, University of Eduardo Mondlane. Volumes of poetry include *Kigubo* (1964) and *Karingana ua Karingana* (1974); selections translated into English in many journals and anthologies of Mozambican poetry.

CRIPPS, Arthur Shearly (1869–1952), born in England and educated at Oxford, came to what was then Mashonaland (part of present-day Zimbabwe) as a missionary in 1907. Poetry includes *The Black Christ* (L, 1901) and novels include *Bay-tree Country* (L, 1913; reprinted in Brown and Chennells, below). A selection of his work appeared in 1976.

>   Steere, D. V., *God's Irregular. Arthur Shearly Cripps. A Rhodesian Epic* (L, 1973).

>>   See: Brown, G. R. and A. J. Chennells, Introduction, *Arthur Shearly Cripps: A Selection of his Prose and Verse* (Gwelo, 1976).
>>   Ranger, T. O., 'Literature and Political Economy: Arthur Shearly Cripps and the Makoni Labour Crisis of 1911', *Journal of Southern African Studies*, vol. 9, no. 1 (October 1982).

CRONIN, Jeremy (1949–), born in the Cape, educated at the University of Cape Town, was sentenced to imprisonment in 1976 for active opposition to apartheid. His volume of poems *Inside* (J, 1983; enlarged edition, L, 1987) was published on his release. Prominent in SA Communist Party politics.

CULLINAN, Patrick (1932–), born in Pretoria, educated at Oxford, lectured English in Cape Town. Volumes of poetry include *Today Is Not Different* (CT, 1978) and *White Hail in the Orchard* (CT, 1984). *Selected Poems, 1961–1994* (CT, 1994).

DANGAREMBGA, Tsitsi (1959–), born in Mtoko, Zimbabwe, into intellectual family; educated at mission school and largely white prestigious school in Harare; studied medicine in Cambridge but felt out of place in Britain and returned to Zimbabwe where she studied psychology at University of Zimbabwe. In 1980 she began course at Academy for Film and TV in Berlin. Has written a play *She No Longer Weeps* and acclaimed novel *Nervous Conditions* (L, 1988).

>   See: Veit-Wild, *Teachers, Preachers, Non-Believers* (Gen. Bib.).

DE SOUSA, Noémia (1927–), born in Maputo, was active anti-fascist in Lisbon in 1950s. Went into exile permanently in France in 1964. Poems including English translations scattered in journals and anthologies.

DESMOND, Cosmas (1935–), born in London, was ordained in the Franciscan Order in 1959 and went straight to SA to work among African mineworkers. Travels around the country to investigate conditions among African people 'resettled' under apartheid policies led to *The Discarded People: An Account of Resettlement in South Africa* (L, 1971). Listed as a banned person, Desmond was not permitted to be quoted in SA. After unbannings of February 1990, he again became a prominent commentator. Lives permanently in SA.

DHLOMO, Herbert (H.I.E.) (1903–1956), born in KwaZulu-Natal, educated Adams mission, was journalist on *Bantu World* (Johannesburg) and *Ilanga laseNatali* (Durban). Long poem *Valley of a Thousand Hills* (Durban, 1941) is included with other poems, stories and playscripts in *H. I. E. Dhlomo: Collected Works* (J, 1985). Selection of literary criticism in *English in Africa*, vol. 5, no. 2 (September 1977).

> Couzens, T., *The New African: A Study of the Life and Works of H. I. E. Dhlomo* (J, 1985).

> See: Mootry, M. K., 'Literature and Resistance in South Africa: Two Zulu Poets', *African Literature Today, No. 6*, edited by E. D. Jones (L, 1973). (Dhlomo and Vilakazi.)
> Peterson, B., ' "The Black Bulls" of H. I. E. Dhlomo: Ordering History out of Nonsense', *English in Africa*, vol. 18, no. 1 (May 1991).

DHLOMO, Rolfes (R.R.R.) (1906–1971), born in KwaZulu-Natal, worked as a mine clerk before becoming journalist; assistant editor *Bantu World* and, in 1943, editor *Ilanga laseNatali* (Durban). Most of his creative work is in Zulu including historical novels of Zulu leaders, *UDingane* (Pietermarizburg, 1936) and *UShaka* (Pietermaritzburg, 1937). In English he wrote novella *An African Tragedy* (Alice, 1928) and stories in the literary journal *The Sjambok* which are collected in *English in Africa*, vol. 2, no. 1 (March 1975).

DIESCHO, Joseph (1955–), born in rural Namibia, worked on mines before involvement with SWAPO. In 1984 he went to USA to study history. One novel *Born of the Sun: A Namibian Novel* (NY, 1988).

DOS SANTOS, Marcelino (1929–), pseudonym Kalungano, born in northern Mozambique. Educated University of Lisbon; one of founder militants of Frelimo; after independence minister of economic planning. Reputation as a poet established in 1950s. Poems in English translation in journals and anthologies.

DU TOIT, Stephanus (S.J.) (1847–1911), born in Belgium, minister of religion in Paarl; prominent in Afrikaans language movement; founded Genootskap van Regte Afrikaners (Association of True Afrikaners, 1875); prolific contributor to early Afrikaans newspapers including *De Zuid-Afrikaan* and *Die Afrikaanse Patriot*; wrote an Afrikaans grammar (1876), a history of the Afrikaans language movement (1880) and what he described as a historical novel, *Di Koningin fan Skeba* (1898).

DUBE, John L. (1871–1946), born near American Board Mission station in KwaZulu-Natal where he began his schooling; an ordained minister; first president of what was to become the ANC. Founded the first Zulu newspaper *Ilange laseNatali* (1903); historical novel in Zulu translated as *Jeqe, the Body-servant of King Tshaka* (Alice, 1951; 1933) and biography in Zulu *uShembe* (Pietermaritzburg, 1935).

EYBERS, Elisabeth (1915–), born in Klerksdorp, has lived in Holland since 1961; numerous volumes of Afrikaans poetry since 1936; in English translation, *The Quiet Adventure* (J, 1948).

FIRST, Ruth (1925–1982), born in Johannesburg, studied social science at University of Witwatersrand. A journalist, writer and political activist, she was arrested and detained without trial in 1963 prior to being forced into exile in Britain.

Taught at universities including the Centre for Southern African Studies in Maputo where she was killed by a letter bomb planted presumably by SA agents. Writing includes the first serious political study of Namibia *South West Africa* (L, 1963), *117 Days* (L, 1965; 1988) which is her account of her political imprisonment, and, together with Ann Scott, the biography *Olive Schreiner* (L, 1980). Editor of Nelson Mandela's speeches *No Easy Walk to Freedom* (L, 1965; 1990); also editor of radical newspapers *The Guardian* and *New Age* (both of which were banned) and the literary-political journal *Fighting Talk* from 1954 until its banning in 1963.

FUGARD, Athol (1932–), born in eastern Cape, attended school in Port Elizabeth where together with the Serpent Players he experimented with early scripts in non-racial conditions of 'poor theatre'. First plays with black actors and Sophiatown intellectuals examined township life: *No-Good Friday* (1958) and *Nongogo* (1959). Followed by *The Blood Knot* (1961), *Hello and Goodbye* (1966), *People are Living There* (1968) and *Boesman and Lena* (1969). With John Kani and Winston Ntshona, Fugard devised in workshop *Sizwe Bansi Is Dead* (1972) and *The Island* (1973). The scripts of the plays listed so far are most conveniently available in *Boesman and Lena and Other Plays* (Oxford, 1978) and *The Township Plays* (Oxford, 1993). Other plays in single editions include *A Lesson from Aloes* (Oxford, 1981), *'Master' Harold and the Boys* (CT, 1993), *My Children! My Africa!* (J, 1990), which is published with selected shorter plays, and *Playland* (J, 1992). Fugard's comments on his own dramatic practice appear in his introductions to collections of his plays and most extensively in his *Notebooks, 1960–1977*, edited by M. Benson (J, 1983).

Read, J. (ed.), *Athol Fugard: A Bibliography* (Grahamstown, 1991).

See: Gray, S. (ed.), *Athol Fugard* (J, 1982).
    Vandenbrouke, R., *Truths the Hand Can Touch: The Theatre of Athol Fugard* (J, 1986).
    Walder, D., *Athol Fugard* (L, 1984).
    — Introductions to *Selected Plays* (Oxford, 1987) and *The Township Plays* (see entry above).

GOOSEN, Jeanne (1940–), born in the Cape, worked in various occupations including journalism. Has published poetry and produced her own plays including *Kombuis-blues*. Novella *Ons Is Nie Almal So Nie* (1990), translated as *Not All of Us* (CT, 1992).

GORDIMER, Nadine (1923–), born near Johannesburg, has consistently opposed racial injustice in novels and short stories that span over forty years. First stories in 1949; international acclaim acknowledged in 1991 Nobel Prize for Literature. A selection from the first five volumes of stories is contained in *Selected Stories* (L, 1975) and subsequent collections include *A Soldier's Embrace* (L, 1980), *Something Out There* (L, 1984) and *Jump and Other Stories* (L, NY, CT, 1991). Novels are *The Lying Days* (L, 1953), *A World of Strangers* (L, 1958), *Occasion for Loving* (L, 1963), *The Late Bourgeois World* (L, 1966), *A Guest of Honour* (L, 1971), *The Conservationist* (L, 1974), *Burger's Daughter* (L, 1979), *July's People* (L, J, 1981), *A Sport of Nature* (L, 1987), *My Son's Story* (L, CT, 1990) and *None to Accompany Me* (L, 1994). Critical study on black writing, *The Black Interpreters* (J, 1973), and selection of critical articles, *The Essential Gesture: Writing, Politics and Places* (L, 1988).

Driver, D., A. Dry, C. MacKenzie and J. Read (eds), *Nadine Gordimer: A Bibliography* (Grahamstown, 1993).

See: Clingman, S., *The Novels of Nadine Gordimer: History from the Inside* (J, 1986).
Cooke, J., *The Novels of Nadine Gordimer: Private Lives/Public Landscapes* (Baton Rouge, 1985).
JanMohamed, A. R., 'Nadine Gordimer: The Degeneration of the Great South African Lie', *Manichean Aesthetics: The Politics of Literature in Colonial Africa* (Amherst, 1983).
King, B. A. (ed.), *The Later Fiction of Nadine Gordimer* (NY, 1993).
Newman, J., *Nadine Gordimer* (L, 1988).
Smith, R. (ed.), *Critical Essays on Nadine Gordimer* (Boston, 1990).
Wade, M., *Nadine Gordimer* (L, 1978).
Wagner, K., *Rereading Nadine Gordimer* (J, 1994).

GQOBA, William Wellington (W.W.) (1840–1888), born in eastern Cape, attended Lovedale; taught and worked as Christian preacher. From 1884 to 1888 he edited *Isigidimi samaXhosa* and was a regular contributor to his own journal.

GRAY, Stephen (1941–), born in Cape Town, educated at Universities of Cape Town, Cambridge and Iowa, was professor of English in Johannesburg; now full-time writer. Numerous editorial projects on Plaatje, Bosman, Black and Fugard; editor Penguin books of SA poetry and short stories; critical study *Southern African Literature: An Introduction* (CT, 1979). Volumes of poetry include *Hottentot Venus and Other Poems* (CT, 1979), *Love Poems: Hate Poems* (CT, 1982), and *Selected Poems, 1960–92* (CT, 1994); novels include *Caltrop's Desire* (CT, 1980) and *Time of Our Darkness* (L, 1988). Autobiography, *Accident of Birth* (J, 1993).

GWALA, Mafika (1946–), born in KwaZulu-Natal, worked as schoolteacher and research writer; currently in England. Volumes of poetry, *Jol'iinkomo* (J, 1977) and *No More Lullabies* (J, 1982).

See: Chapman, *Soweto Poetry* and *South African English Poetry* (Gen. Bib.).

HAGGARD, Sir Henry Rider (1856–1925), born in London, arrived in Natal colony in 1875 as colonial civil servant; returned to England in 1881 and studied for the bar. Novels of adventure set in Africa include *Cetewayo and his White Neighbours* (L, 1882), *King Solomon's Mines* (1885), *Allan Quatermain, Jess, She* (L, all 1887) and *Nada the Lily* (L, 1892).
Cohen, M., *Rider Haggard: His Life and Work* (L, 1960).

See: Couzens, T., 'The Return to the Heart of Darkness', *English Academy Review* (1982).
Gilbert, S. M., 'Rider Haggard's Heart of Darkness', *Partisan Review*, no. 50 (1983).
Katz, W., *Rider Haggard and the Fiction of Empire* (Cambridge, 1988).

HEAD, Bessie (1937–1986), born in KwaZulu-Natal, was a primary school teacher and journalist before leaving SA for Botswana on an exit permit in 1963; worked as a teacher and gardener; later a full-time writer in Serowe. Published novels *When Rainclouds Gather* (L, 1969), *Maru* (L, 1971) and *A Question of*

Power (L, 1973). Interviews with local inhabitants, *Serowe: Village of the Rainwind* (L, 1981). Short stories, *The Collector of Treasures* (L, 1977) and the posthumous collection *Tales of Tenderness and Power* (J, 1989; L, 1990); historical novel *A Bewitched Crossroad* (J, 1984) and posthumously published early novel and stories, *The Cardinal* (CT, 1993). Autobiographical writings, *A Woman Alone*, edited by C. MacKenzie (L, 1990) and biographical writings, *A Gesture of Belonging*, edited by R. Vigne (L, 1991).

Gardiner, S. and P. E. Scott (eds), *Bessie Head: A Bibliography* (Grahamstown, 1986).

See: Abrahams, C. ed., *The Tragic Life: Bessie Head and Literature in Southern Africa* (Trenton, 1990).

Clayton, C., ' "A World Elsewhere": Bessie Head as Historian', *English in Africa*, vol. 15, no. 1 (May 1988).

MacKenzie, C., 'Short Fiction in the Making: The Case of Bessie Head', *English in Africa*, vol. 16, no. 1 (May 1989).

Marquard, J., 'Bessie Head: Exile and Community in Southern Africa', *London Magazine*, vol. 18, nos 9–10 (1978/79).

Stead Eilersen, G., *Bessie Head, Realist and Dreamer: Her Life and Writings* (L; CT, 1994).

Wilhelm [Clayton], C., 'Bessie Head: The Face of Africa', *English in Africa*, vol. 10, no. 1 (May 1983).

HOFMEYR, Isabel (1953–), born in Potchefstroom, educated at the University of the Witwatersrand where she is professor of African Literature. Numerous critical articles on SA literary-cultural topics; book-length study *'We Spend our Years as A Tale That is Told': Oral Historical Narrative in a South African Chiefdom* (J, L, 1994).

HONWANA, Luis Bernardo (1942–), born in Maputo, was active in Frelimo while still at school; sentenced to three years in prison and released in 1967 after which he travelled abroad before returning to Mozambique in order to serve as minister of culture in the independent government; in 1990 withdrew from party politics. Collection in translation *We Killed Mangy-Dog and Other Mozambique Stories* (L, 1969; 1967).

HOVE, Chenjerai (1956–), born in Mazvihwa, Zimbabwe, trained as a teacher. Editor with Mambo Press and Zimbabwe Publishing House. Volumes of poetry *Up in Arms* (Harare, 1982) and *Red Hills of Home* (Gweru, 1985). Novels *Bones* (Harare, 1988) and *Shadows* (Harare, 1991); journalism/stories, *Shebeen Tales: Messages from Harare* (Harare, L, 1994).

JABAVU, John Tengo (1859–1921), born in eastern Cape, an educator, a politician and newspaper editor, he was first editor of Xhosa/English weekly *Imvo Zabantsundu* which was financed by Cape (white) liberals as forum of African opinion. Increasingly compromised in white politics which betrayed African nationalist aspirations. Established African college which became Fort Hare (1916).

JABAVU, Noni (1919–), born in eastern Cape into the Xhosa intellectual class, has spent most of her life abroad. Reminiscences, *Drawn in Colour* (L, 1960) and *The Ochre People: Scenes from a South African Life* (L, 1963).

JACINTO, Antonio (1924–), born in Luanda, was a leader in Angolan movement for cultural nationalism. As an MPLA militant, he was arrested by Portuguese secret police and spent four years in Tarrafal concentration camp until 1972 when he was allowed to live in Lisbon where he worked as an accountant. Escaped from Portugal in 1973 and joined MPLA; after independence appointed minister of education and culture. Volume of poems (1961) and poems in numerous anthologies in Portuguese and in English translation.

JACOBSON, Dan (1929–), born in Johannesburg, spent his schooldays in Kimberley and later studied at University of the Witwatersrand leaving SA soon afterwards for Israel and Britain. Since 1954 he has lived in London and has continued to return to SA concerns in numerous short stories and novels. Representative SA stories in *Through the Wilderness: Selected Stories* (L, 1978). Strong SA focus in early novels *The Trap* (L, 1955), *A Dance in the Sun* (L, 1956) – republished in single edition (CT, 1985) – *The Price of Diamonds* (L, 1957; J, 1986) and *The Beginners* (L, 1966). Other novels include *The Rape of Tamar* (L, 1970) and *The Confessions of Josef Baisz* (L, 1977). Autobiographical writing *Time and Time Again* (L, 1985); commentary *The Electronic Elephant: A Southern African Journey* (L, 1994).

> See: Baxter, C., 'Political Symbolism in *A Dance in the Sun*', *English in Africa*, vol. 5, no. 2 (September 1978).
> Roberts, S., *Dan Jacobson* (Boston, 1984).
> Wade, M., 'Jacobson's Realism Revisited: *The Trap* and *A Dance in the Sun*', *Southern African Review of Books* (October/November, 1988).

JAMBA, Sousa (1966–), born in central Angola, fled to Zambia in 1976 and in 1985 joined UNITA; worked as reporter-cum-translator with UNITA news agency before going to Britain in 1986 to study journalism. Novels *Patriots* (L, 1990) and *A Lonely Devil* (L, 1993).

JENSMA, Wopko (1939–), born in the Cape, was of itinerant occupation in the 1970s when he produced volumes of poetry *Sing for our Execution* (J, 1971), *Where White is the Colour Where Black is the Number* (J, 1974) and *I must show you my clippings* (J, 1977).

JOLOBE, James (J.J.R.) (1902–1976), born in eastern Cape and attended University of Fort Hare; taught at Lovedale, and his career in ministry culminated in his appointment in 1970 as moderator of Presbyterian Church of SA. Numerous volumes of poetry in Xhosa. He translated poems into English from his own volume *Umyeso* (1936) as *Poems of an African* (Alice, 1946).

JONKER, Ingrid (1934–1965), born in the Cape, lived mostly in Cape Town; ended her own life by drowning. Important volumes of Afrikaans poetry (1963 and 1966). In English translation, *Selected Poems* (L, 1986).

JORDAN, Archibald (A.C.) (1906–1968), born in eastern Cape, left SA on an exit permit in 1961 to take up a Carnegie fellowship, and at the time of his death was professor of African Languages and Literature at the University of Wisconsin, USA. Novel in Xhosa *Ingqumbo Yeminyanya* (Alice, 1940) translated into English by author and [daughter] Priscilla P. Jordan as *The Wrath of the Ancestors* (Alice, 1980). Author of series of critical articles on Xhosa literature in 1940s collected as *Towards an African Literature: The Emergence of Literary Form in Xhosa* (Berkeley, 1972) and re-created Xhosa folk tales, in English, published posthumously as *Tales from Southern Africa* (Berkeley, 1973).

> See: Riordan, J., '*The Wrath of the Ancestors*', *African Studies*, vol. 20 (1961).
> Scheub, H., 'An Approach to a Xhosa Novel', *Contrast*, vol. 6, no. 3 (1970). (Analysis of *The Wrath of the Ancestors*.)

JOUBERT, Elsa (1922–), born in the Cape, has written travel books and several novels, a number of which have been translated into English including *To Die at Sunset* (L, 1982; 1963), *The Last Sunday* (L, 1989; 1983) and *Poppie* (L, 1980; 1978).

> See: Schalkwyk, D., 'The Flight from Politics: An Analysis of the South African Reception of "Poppie Nongema" ', *Journal of Southern African Studies*, vol. 12, no. 2 (April 1986).

JÚNIOR, Antonio de Assis (1878–1960), born in Angola, was a journalist, lawyer and novelist; an assimilado who suffered deportation, he compiled a KiMbundu-Portuguese dictionary (1941) which had been predated by ethnographic novel *O Segredo da Morta* (Lisbon, 1934; Luanda, 1979).

> See: Burness, D., 'Literature and Ethnography: The Case of *O Segredo da Morta* and *Uanga*', *Research in African Literatures*, vol. 13, no. 3 (Fall 1982).

‖KABBO (?–1874), a /Xam Bushman narrator whose narratives were recorded between 1871 and 1873 by W. H. I. Bleek and Lucy Lloyd; texts in /Xam and English transcription in Bleek and Lloyd's *Specimens of Bushman Folklore* (L, 1911).

!KAHA (1947?–?), !Kung Bushman singer and shaman who lives in Ghanzi district of Botswana. Songs recorded by M. Biesele and texts presented in her *Folklore and Ritual of !Kung Hunter-gatherers* (Doctorial dissertation, Harvard University, 1975).

KANI, John and Winston Ntshona. *See* FUGARD, Athol.

KAPELWA MUSONDA, pen-name of William Saidi, a journalist on the *Times of Zambia* whose column has been published as *The Kapelwa Musonda File* (Lusaka, 1973). Under Saidi, short stories and a novel *The Hanging* (Lusaka, 1979).

KASOMA, Kabwe, born in Zambia, writer of popular plays including *Distortion* (Lusaka, 1974) and *Fools Marry* (Lusaka, 1976).

> See: Etherton, M., 'The Dilemma of the Popular Playwright: The Work of Kabwe Kasoma and V. E. Musinga', *African Literature Today, No. 8*, edited by E. D. Jones (L, 1976).

KAUNDA, Kenneth (1924–), born at Lubwa, son of an African missionary, was central to anti-colonial campaign in Zambia. Founded Zambian African National Congress which in 1960 became United National Independence Party (UNIP). With Kaunda as president, UNIP ruled independent Zambia from 1964 until 1992. Exponent of doctrine 'Zambian humanism' in his various books, *Zambia Shall Be Free* (L, 1962), *A Humanist in Africa* (L, 1966) and *Humanism in Zambia and a Guide to Its Implementation* (Lusaka, 1967).

See: Kandeke, T., *Fundamentals of Zambian Humanism* (Lusaka, 1977).

KAVANAGH, Robert Mshengu (1944–), born in Durban, studied at the Universities of Cape Town, Oxford and Leeds, played an active part in the development of SA theatre in the 1970s through his participation in Experimental Theatre Workshop '71 and is currently influential in Zimbabwean theatre through activities at the University of Zimbabwe. Editor of *South African People's Plays* (L, 1981); author of *Theatre and Cultural Struggle in South Africa* (L, 1985).

KAYIRA, Legson (1942–), born in Malawi, mission educated, wandered north to Khartoum carrying Bible and *The Pilgrim's Progress* and remained abroad in USA. Novels *The Looming Shadow* (L, 1968), *Jingala* (L, 1969), *The Civil Servant* (L, 1971) and *The Detainee* (L, 1974).

See: Roscoe, *Uhuru's Fire* (Gen. Bib.).

KENTE, Gibson (1932–), has toured townships throughout SA from late 1960s to 1990s presenting his stage spectacles including *Beyond a Song, Taximan and the Schoolgirl* and *Manana, the Jazz Prophet*. More politically contentious were *How Long* (1973), *I Believe* (1974), *Too Late* (1975) – the script of which appears in *South African People's Plays* (see entry on Kavanagh) – and *Sekunjalo* (1987).

See: Orkin, *Drama and the South African State* (Gen. Bib.).

KIRKWOOD, Mike (1943–), born in the West Indies, educated at University of Natal where he lectured in English prior to his playing a key role in founding the magazine *Staffrider* (1978). Director of Ravan Press in the late 1970s and early 1980s; now lives in England. Has published poetry; attacked 'Eurocentric' SA literary-academic scene in editorials and policy of *Staffrider* while promoting a literature of 'black community'.

KRIGE, Uys (1910–1987), born in western Cape, educated Stellenbosch University; travelled in France and Spain; war correspondent with SA forces in North Africa in Second World War. Poems, plays in Afrikaans; translations into Afrikaans of English, French, Spanish and Italian literature. Autobiographical experiences in *The Way Out* (L, 1946) and, in English translation, the stories *The Dream and the Desert* (L, 1953).

KROG, Antjie (1952–), born in Kroonstad, studied at Universities of Orange Free State and Pretoria; lives in Kroonstad. Several volumes of poetry in Afrikaans since 1970 including the acclaimed *Lady Anne* (CT, 1989).

KUMBIRAI, Joseph (J.C.) (1922–1986), born at mission in Mvuma; teacher and Catholic priest; lecturer in African languages, University of Zimbabwe. Poems in Shona widely anthologised, broadcast, and published in magazines in Zimbabwe.

See: Chiwome, E. M., 'Commitment and Language in Joseph Kumbirai's Poetry', *Research in African Literatures*, vol. 22, no. 1 (Spring 1991).

KUNENE, Mazizi (1930–), born in Durban, educated at University of Natal where he lectures after having spent over 30 years abroad during which time he was professor of African Literature and Language, University of California. English poetic re-creations of Zulu historical and mythic narratives include *Emperor Shaka the Great* (L, 1979). Various articles on traditional African cosmology.

KUZWAYO, Ellen (1914–), born in the Free State farming district (SA), was educated at mission schools and qualified as a schoolteacher before turning to social work. Has lived most of her adult life in Soweto. Autobiography *Call Me Woman* (J, 1985) was followed by short stories *Sit Down and Listen* (L, CT, 1990).

See: Driver in Trump (ed.), *Rendering Things Visible* (Gen. Bib.).

LA GUMA, Alex (1925–1985), born and educated in Cape Town, left SA in 1966 after a period of house arrest under apartheid laws. Forbidden to be quoted in SA until 1990, La Guma died in Cuba where since 1970 he had been ANC representative. Novella *A Walk in the Night* (Ibadan, 1962) was reissued with a selection of his short stories (L, 1968). Other novels are *And a Threefold Cord* (L, 1964), *The Stone Country* (L, 1967), *In the Fog of the Seasons' End* (L, 1972) and *Time of the Butcherbird* (L, 1979).

See: Abrahams, C., *Alex La Guma* (Boston, 1985).
     Coetzee, J. M., 'Alex La Guma and the Responsibilities of the South African Writer', *New African Literature and the Arts, Vol. 3*, edited by J. Okpaku (NY, 1973).
     Coetzee, J. M., 'Man's Fate in the Novels of Alex La Guma', *Studies in Black Literature*, vol. 4, no. 4 (Winter 1974). [The bibliographical information on the original journal is in error; it should be vol. 5, no. 1 (Spring 1974).]
     Maughan Brown, D., 'Adjusting the Focal Length: Alex La Guma and Exile', *English in Africa*, vol. 18, no. 2 (October 1991).

LANGENHOVEN, Cornelis (C.J.) (1873–1932), folk poet, essayist involved in Afrikaans language movement in 1920s. Enormous output collected in 16 volumes.

LEIPOLDT, C. Louis (1880–1947), born in the Cape, turned from journalism to medicine – as medical inspector of schools and child specialist – and from medicine to literature producing numerous journalistic and medical publications. In Afrikaans, several volumes of poetry including *Oom Gert Vertel en Ander Gedigte* (CT, 1911) and, in English, *The Ballad of Dick King and Other Poems* (CT, 1949), the autobiographical *Bushveld Doctor* (L, 1937; CT, 1980) and the posthumously published novel *Stormwrack* (CT, 1980).

LEROUX, Etienne (1922–1990), pseudonym of Stephanus Le Roux; born in the Cape, farmed in the Free State; published eleven Afrikaans novels several of which have been translated into English including *Seven Days at the*

Silbersteins (J, L, 1968; 1964), *One for the Devil* (L, 1968; 1968), *The Third Eye* (L, 1969; 1966) and *Magersfontein, O Magersfontein* (J, 1983; 1976).

> See: Cope, *The Adversary Within* and Coetzee, *One Hundred Years of Afrikaans Literature* (Gen. Bib.).

LESSING, Doris (1919–), born in Persia of English parents, arrived in Southern Rhodesia in 1925 where her father had been allocated a farm by the colonial government. Worked as civil servant in Salisbury (Harare) and was influenced by radical, communist discussion groups in Salisbury during Second World War. Left Rhodesia in 1949 and, in England, devoted herself to writing full time. Novel *The Grass Is Singing* (L, 1950) written while she was in Rhodesia was followed by stories *This Was the Old Chief's Country* (L, 1951). *Martha Quest* (L, 1952), the first and most 'Rhodesian' of a five-volume saga with general title *Children of Violence*, was followed in the series by *A Proper Marriage* (L, 1954), *A Ripple in the Storm* (L, 1958), *Landlocked* (L, 1965) and *The Four-gated City* (L, 1969). Numerous other 'international' novels including *The Golden Notebook* (L, 1962). Of specifically southern African interest, observations and commentary *African Laughter: Four Visits to Zimbabwe* (L, 1992).

> See: Bertelsen, E., 'Doris Lessing's Rhodesia: History into Fiction', *English in Africa*, vol. 11, no. 1 (May 1984).
> Bertelsen, E. (ed.), *Doris Lessing* (J, 1985).
> Style, C., 'Doris Lessing's "Zambesia" ', *English in Africa*, vol. 13, no. 1 (May 1986).

LIVINGSTONE, Douglas (1932–), born in Malaya of British parents, arrived in SA in 1942 and trained in Salisbury (Harare) as a marine bacteriologist; worked in Zambia and returned to SA in 1964 where he continues to practise his scientific career. Volumes of poems are *The Skull in the Mud* (Dulwich, 1960), *Sjambok and Other Poems from Africa* (L, 1964), *Eyes Closed against the Sun* (L, 1970), *A Rosary of Bone* (CT, 1975), *The Anvil's Undertone* (J, 1978) and *A Littoral Zone* (CT, 1991). Translations (with Phillipa Berlyn) of Shona poems by Wilson Chivaura and others. *Selected Poems* (J, 1984).
Ullyatt, A. G., (ed.), *Douglas Livingstone: A Bibliography* (Pretoria, 1979).

> See: Chapman, M., *Douglas Livingstone: A Critical Study of his Poetry* (J, 1981).
> Also: Chapman, *South African English Poetry* (Gen. Bib.).

LLOYD, Lucy C. See BLEEK, W. H. I.

LOUW, Nicholaas P. van Wyk (1906–1970), born in western Cape, lectured at University of Cape Town, established chair of Afrikaans in Amsterdam, and from 1958 professor of Afrikaans at University of Witwatersrand. Founded literary journal *Standpunte* (1945). First volume of poetry in 1935 followed by several others including *Tristia* (CT, 1962). *Raka* (1941) translated into English (CT, 1968) and selection of his poems in English, *Oh Wide and Sad Land* (CT, 1975). Plays *Germanicus* (CT, 1956) and *Die Pluimsaad Waai Ver* (CT, 1972); literary and cultural essays include volumes *Lojale Verset* (CT, 1939), *Liberale Nasionalisme* (CT, 1958); criticism includes *Vernuwing in die Prosa* (CT, 1961) and *Opstelle oor Ons Over Digters* (CT, 1972).

Olivier, G., *N. P. van Wyk Louw* (CT, 1992).

See: Cope, *The Adversary Within*, and Coetzee, *One Hundred Years of Afrikaans Literature* (Gen. Bib.).

LUTHULI, (Chief) Albert (1898–1967), born in southern Rhodesia and educated at mission schools in Natal; teacher who became active in anti-apartheid politics; president-general of ANC during turbulent 1950s; banned by SA government; awarded Nobel Peace Prize, 1961. Autobiography, *Let My People Go* (L, 1962); speeches in E. S. Reddy (ed.), *Luthuli* (Durban, 1991).

MAGOGO kaDINIZULU, Princess Constance (1900–1984), born in KwaZulu-Natal, member of the Zulu royal family, produced Zulu traditional music which sometimes revealed her simultaneous devotion to the Anglican church; sound recordings by H. Tracey in 1940s and 1950s (International Library of African Music, AMA TR9 and AMA TR10) and stereo LP disc 'The Zulu Bow Songs of Princess Magogo' by Tracey in early 1970s (Gallo Music of Africa Series, no. 37: SGALP 1678).

See: Rycroft, D., 'Princess Constance Magogo kaDinizulu, 1900 to 1984', *Africa Insight*, vol. 15, no. 4 (1985).

MAGOLWANA kaMKHATHINI, warrior and chief imbongi of King Dingana of the Zulu, hailed as the 'mother of all praisers'. Also served Mpande and Cetshwayo after Dingana's death.

See: Kunene, M., 'Portrait of Magolwana, the Great Zulu Poet', *Cultural Events in Africa*, vol. 32, no. 1 (1967).
Rycroft, D. K. and A. B. Ngcobo, Introduction, *The Praises of Dingana: Izibongo zikaDingana* (Pietermaritzburg, 1988).

MANAKA, Matsemela (1956–), founder member of Soyikwa African Theatre Group, has been active in black theatre since mid-1970s. Several plays most of which are unscripted; *Egoli: City of Gold* (J, nd. [1981]) and *Pula* (J, 1990).

MANDELA, Nelson Rolihlahla (1918–), born in eastern Cape, educated at Fort Hare and the University of the Witwatersrand, practised law in Johannesburg in 1952 while active in ANC politics. Arrested several times and in 1964 sentenced to life imprisonment on charges of treason as ANC military wing was uncovered by SA police. Released in February 1990 after 27 years in gaol and entered negotiations with government which led to ANC winning SA's first non-racial elections. In 1993 awarded Nobel Peace Prize jointly with president F. W. de Klerk; inaugurated as new state president May 1994. Speeches collected in R. First (ed.), *No Easy Walk to Freedom* (L, 1965; 1990), *Nelson Mandela: The Struggle Is My Life* (L, 1986), and *Nelson Mandela Speaks: Forging a Democratic, Non-Racial South Africa* (L, NY, 1993). *Long Walk to Freedom: The Autobiography of Nelson Mandela* (J, NY, 1994).
Benson, M., *Nelson Mandela* (L, 1986).
Meer, F., *Higher than Hope* (J, 1988).

See: Chapman, M., 'Mandela, Africanism and Modernity: A Consideration of *Long Walk to Freedom*', *Current Writing*, vol. 7, no. 2 (1995).

MAPANJE, Jack (1944–), born in southern Malawi, attended mission school and completed his education at Universities of Malawi and London. Lectured in English at Malawi and founder member of Zomba Writers Workshop. Detained by Banda's government (1987–1991). Currently in England. Volumes of poetry, *Of Chameleons and Gods* (L, 1981) and *The Chattering Wagtails of Mikuyu Prison* (L, 1993).

See: Ngara, *Ideology and Form*, and Vail and White, *Power and the Praise Poem* (Gen. Bib.).

MARAIS, Eugène N. (1871–1936), born near Pretoria, edited newspapers in the Transvaal republic in opposition to president Kruger; left for London to study medicine and law, and on outbreak of Anglo-Boer War joined Boer cause. Spent latter years of his life, in addition to writing, as unofficial country doctor and lawyer until his suicide. Poetry in Afrikaans; selection in English translation *Gedigte/Poems* (J, 1956). *Dwaalstories en Ander Vertellings* (CT, 1927), essays translated in *The Road to Waterberg* (CT, 1972) and writing on nature includes *The Soul of the White Ant*[1] (L, 1937 and 1971; 1934).
Rousseau, L., *The Dark Stream: The Story of Eugène N. Marais* (J, 1982).

See: Brink, *Mapmakers* (Gen. Bib.).

MARECHERA, Dambudzo (1952–1987), born in Rusape, Zimbabwe, educated at mission school and University of Rhodesia where in 1973 he was expelled with other student demonstrators; spell at Oxford; returned to Zimbabwe in early 1980s as freelance writer. Novels *The House of Hunger* (L, 1978), *Black Sunlight* (L, 1980) and the posthumous *The Black Insider* (Harare, 1990). Plays and other pieces in *Mindblast* (Harare, 1984) and collected poems in *Cemetery of the Mind* (Harare, 1992).
Veit-Wild, F., *Dambudzo Marechera: A Source Book on his Life and Works* (L, 1992).

See: Gaylard, G., 'Dambudzo Marechera and Nationalist Criticism', *English in Africa*, vol. 20, no. 2 (October 1993).
Mzamane, M. V., 'New Writing from Zimbabwe: Dambudzo Marechera's *The House of Hunger*', in E. D. Jones (ed.), *African Literature Today, Vol. 13* (L, 1983).
Veit-Wild, F., 'Words as Bullets: The Writings of Dambudzo Marechera', *Zambezia*, vol. 14, no. 2 (1987).
Wylie, D. See HOVE, C.

MASIYE, Andreya (1922–), born in Zambia, educated at mission schools, worked in radio broadcasting. Has written in Njanja and English including the radio play *The Lands of Kazembe* first broadcast 1957 (Lusaka, 1973) and the novel *Before Dawn* (Lusaka, 1971).

MATSHOBA, Mtutuzeli (1950–), born in Soweto where he lives; attended school at Lovedale and dropped out of Fort Hare; works in translation services. Stories published in volume *Call Me Not a Man* (J, 1979); playscript *Seeds of War* (J, 1981).

See: Ndebele, N. S., 'Turkish Tales and Some Thoughts on South African Fiction', *Staffrider*, vol. 6, no. 1 (1984).

Vaughan, M., 'The Stories of Mtutuzeli Matshoba', *Staffrider*, vol. 4, no. 3 (1981).

Williams, J., ' "A New Act of Mediation": The Screenplays of Mtutuzeli Matshoba', *Current Writing*, vol. 4, no. 1 (1992).

MATTHEWS, James (1929–), born in western Cape, has worked in journalism and publishing. Stories first appeared in *Drum* magazine in 1950s and collected as *The Park and Other Stories* (CT, 1983). Poetry persistently banned in 1970s includes (with Gladys Thomas) *Cry Rage!* (J, 1972), *Pass Me a Meatball, Jones* (CT, 1977) and *No Time for Dreams* (CT, 1981).

MBULI, Mzwakhe (1959–), born in Sophiatown, works as a professional poet and musician performing locally and internationally with his band; rose to prominence as oral poet at political rallies and funerals in 1980s. Three albums of his poems, *Change Is Pain* (J, 1986), *Unbroken Spirit* (J, 1989) and *Africa* (J, 1993); books of poems *Before Dawn* (J, 1989).

MDA, Zakes (1948–), born in eastern Cape, attended school in Johannesburg before leaving SA with his politically conscious family for Lesotho where he worked as a teacher and then a lecturer in drama at the University of Lesotho. Plays produced in SA and USA, and Mda's travelling theatre company involved in development projects in Lesotho. Scripts of *Dead End* (1979), *We Shall Sing for the Fatherland* (1979), *Dark Voices Ring* (1979), *The Hill* (1980) and *The Road* (1982) collected in *The Plays of Zakes Mda*. Subsequent plays in *And the Girls in Their Sunday Dresses: Four Works* (J, 1993). Study *When People Play People: Development Communication through Theatre* (J, 1993).

See: Holloway, M., 'Social Commentary and Mediation in Zakes Mda's Early Plays', *English Academy Review*, 6 (December 1989).

Horn, A., Introduction to *The Plays of Zakes Mda* (J, 1990).

MILES, John (1938–), born in Port Elizabeth, lectures in Afrikaans at the University of the Witwatersrand. Short stories *Liefs Nie Op Straat Nie* (CT, 1970); several novels since 1973 include *Kroniek uit die Doofpot* (J, 1991).

MILLER, Ruth (1919–1969), born in the Cape, lived her adult life in Johannesburg where she worked as a typist and teacher. Volumes of poetry *Floating Island* (CT, 1965) and *Selected Poems* (L, 1968); extended selection in the posthumously published *Ruth Miller: Poems, Prose, Plays*.

See: Abrahams, L., Introduction to *Ruth Miller: Poems, Prose, Plays* (CT, 1990).

Chapman, M., 'Ruth Miller: Breaking Silences?', *English Academy Review*, 7 (December 1990).

Metelerkamp, J., 'Ruth Miller: Father's Law or Mother's Lore', *Current Writing*, vol. 4, no. 1 (1992).

Also: Chapman, *South African English Poetry* (Gen. Bib.).

MILLIN, Sarah Gertrude (1889–1968), born in Lithuania, came to SA as a small child, grew up near the diamond diggings and was educated in Kimberley; married Philip Millin who later became a judge of the SA supreme court. Spent most of her adult life in Johannesburg and wrote prolifically from mid-1920s to mid-1960s during which time she was widely acclaimed as a literary personality – perhaps more so abroad than in her own country, though she had close friends in influential people like prime minister Jan Smuts. Novels include *God's Step-Children* (NY, L, 1924; J, 1986), *Mary Glenn* (NY, L, 1925), *The Herr Witchdoctor* (J, 1941), *King of the Bastards* (NY, 1949), *The Burning Man* (NY, L, 1952) and *The Wizard Bird* (J, L, 1962). Biographies of Rhodes (NY, L, 1933) and Smuts (L, NY, 1936) and autobiography *The Measure of My Days* (J, NY, L, 1955).

Whyte, M., *Bibliography of the Works of Sarah Gertrude Millin* (CT, 1952).
Levy, F., *The Works of Sarah Gertrude Millin 1952–1968* (J, 1969).
Rubin, M., *Sarah Gertrude Millin: A South African Life* (J, 1977).

See: Coetzee, J. M., 'Blood, Flaw, Taint, Degeneration: The Case of Sarah Gertrude Millin', *English Studies in Africa*, no. 23, no. 1 (1980).

Green, M., 'Blood and Politics/Morality Tales for the Immorality Act: Sarah Gertrude Millin in Literary History and Social History', *English in Africa*, vol. 18, no. 1 (May 1991).

Also: Rabkin in Parker (ed.), *The South African Novel* (Gen. Bib.).

MNTHALI, Felix (1933–), born in Zimbabwe of Malawian parents, was educated in Malawi and in Canada; professor of English at University of Malawi and latterly University of Botswana. Volume of poetry *When Sunset Comes to Sapitwa* (Lusaka, 1980; L, 1982).

See: Roscoe, *Uhuru's Fire* (Gen. Bib.).
Roscoe and Msiska, *The Quiet Chameleon* (Gen. Bib.).

MODISANE, William (Bloke) (1923–1986), born in Sophiatown, became a journalist on *Drum* magazine in the 1950s. Left SA illegally in 1959; banned under the all-embracing Suppression of Communism Act in 1966 and lived in London where he worked in broadcasting; died in Germany. Autobiography *Blame Me on History* (L, 1963; J, 1986).

See: Coste, J., 'The Masks of Modisane', *World Literature Written in English*, vol. 19 (1971).

Ngwenya, T. H., 'The Ontological Status of Self in Autobiography: The Case of Bloke Modisane's *Blame Me on History*', *Current Writing*, 1 (1989).

MOFOLO, Thomas (1877–1948), born in Lesotho, attended Bible school at Morija mission and qualified as a teacher; worked at Morija book depot. Wrote *Moeti oa Bochabela* (Morija, 1908), *Pitseng* (Morija, 1910) and *Chaka*, which was completed in 1910 and first published in seSotho and in English translation in 1925: most convenient edition in English (L, 1981).

See: Gérard, A. S., 'Rereading *Chaka*', *English in Africa*, vol. 13, no. 1 (May 1986).

Kunene, D. P., *Thomas Mofolo and the Emergence of Written Sesotho Prose* (J, 1989).

Malaba, M., 'The Legacy of Thomas Mofolo's *Chaka*', *English in Africa*, vol. 13, no. 1 (May 1986).

MONDLANE, Eduardo (1920–1969), born in southern Mozambique, taught himself English and went on to study social science at University of the

Witwatersrand. After harassment by Portuguese colonial police, he completed studies in the USA. Central to founding of Frelimo of which he was elected president; assassinated in Dar-es-Salaam. Political study, *The Struggle for Mozambique* (L, 1969).

MOPELI-PAULUS, Adwell (A.S.) (1913–), born near Lesotho, trained as a teacher at mission schools; active in Sotho politics. Has written novels and historical narratives in seSotho; his autobiographical story, written in English by Peter Lanham, was published by Lanham and Mopeli-Paulus as *Blanket Boy* (NY, 1953) and as *Blanket Boy's Moon* (CT, 1984).

MOTSISI, Casey (Kid) (1932–1977), born in Western Native Township (Soweto), began to train as a teacher but in 1950s moved to journalism on *Drum* magazine. Regular column 'On the Beat'. Selection of his writings, *Casey & Co.* (J, 1978).

MPHAHLELE, Ezekiel (later, Es'kia) (1919–), born in Pietersburg area and educated at the University of SA, was banned from teaching in state schools in 1950s because of his opposition to Bantu education and worked as fiction editor on *Drum* magazine prior to leaving SA in 1957. Sought freedom from apartheid in Nigeria and other African countries including Zambia (1968–70); lived for many years in USA where he was professor of English at the Universities of Denver and Pennsylvania. Permitted to return to SA in 1978, he became professor of Comparative and African Literature at the University of the Witwatersrand until his retirement; continues to be active in literary education and regular contributor to the monthly magazine *Tribute*. Autobiography to 1957, *Down Second Avenue* (L, 1959) continued in *Exiles and Homecomings* (J, 1983) and *Afrika My Music, 1957–1983* (J, 1984); autobiographical novel *The Wanderers* (NY, 1971; CT, 1984) and southern African novel *Chirundu* (J, 1979). Several volumes of short stories: selection together with poetry in *The Unbroken Song* (J, 1981). Critical study *The African Image* (L, 1962; rev. ed., 1974), collection of critical essays *Voices in the Whirlwind* (NY, L, 1972) and numerous articles in literary journals. Letters, *Bury Me at the Marketplace*, edited by N. Chabani Manganyi (J, 1984).
    Woeber, C. and J. Read (eds), *Es'kia Mphahlele: A Bibliography* (Grahamstown, 1989).

        See: Barnett, U. A., *Ezekiel Mphahlele* (Boston, 1976).
            Obuke, O. O., 'South African History, Politics and Literature: Mphahlele's *Down Second Avenue*', E. D. Jones (ed.) in *African Literature Today, No. 10* (L, 1979).
            English in Africa, vol. 13, no. 2 (October 1986). (Several articles on Mphahlele.)
        Also: Watts, *Black Writers* (Gen. Bib.).

MQHAYI, Samuel Edward Krune (S.E.K.) (1875–1945), born in eastern Cape, lived his early years among traditional Xhosas before attending school and training as teacher at Lovedale; later proofreader for Lovedale Press; retired to traditional family home in Ciskei where he died. Numerous poems including collection *Inzuzo* (J, 1943), biographies of Bokwe and Ntsikana, autobiography *U-Mqhayi wase-Ntab'ozuko* (Alice, 1939), novel *Ityala Lamawele* (Alice, 1914) and allegory *UDon Jadu* (Alice, 1929).

See: Kuse, W. F., 'Mqhayi through the Eyes of his Contemporaries', *South African Outlook*, no. 109 (1975).
Also: Opland, *Xhosa Oral Poetry* (Gen. Bib.).

MTSHALI, Mbuyiseni Oswald (1940–), born and educated in KwaZulu-Natal, worked as a messenger in Johannesburg prior to publishing his first poems in the late 1960s; studied at Columbia University, returned to SA in 1979 as arts critic and then English teacher. Currently in USA. Volumes of poetry *Sounds of a Cowhide Drum* (J, 1971) and *Fireflames* (Pietermaritzburg, 1980).

See: Chapman, *Soweto Poetry* and *South African English Poetry* (Gen. Bib.).

MTWA, Percy (1954–), born near Johannesburg, worked as a stores clerk before being given a role as singer/dancer by Gibson Kente. Devised *Woza Albert!* (1981) together with Mbongeni Ngema and Barney Simon. See the playscript, Mtwa, Ngema, Simon, *Woza Albert!* (L, 1983). Script of Mtwa's *Bopha!* (1985) in D. Ndlovu (ed.), *Woza Afrika!* (NY, 1986). (See entry, NGEMA.)

See: Orkin, *Drama and the South African State* (Gen. Bib.).

MULAISHO, Dominic (1933–), born in Zambia, received mission education, trained as a teacher before studying economics at the then University College of Rhodesia and Nyasaland; works as a civil servant. Novels *The Tongue of the Dumb* (L, 1971) and *The Smoke that Thunders* (L, 1979).

MUNGOSHI, Charles (1947–), born in Manyene, Zimbabwe, educated at mission school, editor with Literature Bureau 1975–1981; director, Zimbabwe Publishing House, and writer-in-residence, University of Zimbabwe. Novels in Shona include *Ndiko Kupindna Kwamazuva* (Harare, 1975); short stories in English, *Coming of the Dry Season* (Nairobi, 1972) and *Some Kinds of Wounds* (Gweru, 1980); selection in *The Setting Sun and the Rolling World* (L, 1989). Novel *Waiting for the Rain* (L, 1975) and poems *The Milkman Doesn't Only Deliver Milk* (Harare, 1981).

See: Veit-Wild, *Teachers, Preachers, Non-Believers* (Gen. Bib.).

'MUTIMATÍ BARNABÉ JOÃO', thought to be pseudonym of poet and artist Antonio Quadros. Sequence of 27 poems *Euo,o Povo* supposed to have been found in knapsack of Mutimatí, a Frelimo guerilla. Poems published by Frelimo (Maputo, 1975); English translation in anthology *The Sunflower of Hope*, edited by C. Searle (L, 1982).

MUTSWAIRO, Solomon M. (1924–), born in Mozowe, Zimbabwe, educated at Fort Hare and Howard University, USA, where he taught; first writer-in-residence, University of Zimbabwe. Novels include – in Shona – *Feso* (1957) with English translation available in D. E. Herdeck, S. M. Mutswairo, *et al.* (eds), *Zimbabwe Prose and Poetry* (Washington, 1974) and *Mapondera: Soldier of Zimbabwe* (Washington, 1978). Also *Chaminuka: Prophet of Zimbabwe* (Washington, 1983) and *Nweya wa Nehanda* (Harare, 1988).

MZAMANE, Mbulelo V. (1948–), born near Johannesburg, educated at Universities of Botswana and Sheffield, has lectured in USA and currently rector Fort Hare. Short stories, *Mzala* (J, 1980) reissued as *My Cousin Comes to Jo'burg and*

Other Stories (L, 1981); trilogy of stories *The Children of Soweto* (J, 1982). Articles of criticism in several journals.

NAKASA, Nathaniel (Nat) (1937–1965), born in Johannesburg, was a journalist on *Drum* magazine and the *Rand Daily Mail*. Founder editor in 1963 of short-lived literary journal *The Classic*. Left SA on exit permit and committed suicide while studying journalism in New York. Selection of his writings, *The World of Nat Nakasa* (J, 1975).

NDEBELE, Njabulo S. (1948–), born near Johannesburg, studied and lectured in Lesotho; further university training at Cambridge and Denver. Prominent in literary-cultural debate in the 1980s; founder member of the Congress of South African Writers (COSAW). Several lecturing posts; currently rector of the University of the North. Stories, *Fools and Other Stories* (J, 1983); selection of critical writings, *Rediscovery of the Ordinary: Essays on South African Literature and Culture* (J, 1991), also published as *South African Literature and Culture: Rediscovery of the Ordinary*.

> See: Morphet, T., 'Cultural Settlement: Albie Sachs, Njabulo Ndebele and the Question of Social and Cultural Imagination', *Pretexts*, vol. 2, no. 1 (Winter 1990).
> Pechey, G., Introduction to Ndebele's *South African Literature and Culture: Rediscovery of the Ordinary* (L, 1994).

NETO, Agostinho (1922–1979), born near Luanda, worked in colonial health service before saving money to study medicine at Coimbra University where he became active in anti-colonial politics. After having been briefly imprisoned, he returned to Angola in 1959 and set up medical practice. Frequent arrests and detentions by Portuguese secret police. Elected president of MPLA and led political and armed struggle; president of MPLA-ruled Angola in 1975. Poetry has appeared in many countries, editions and languages since late 1950s. *Sagrada Esperança* (1974) translated into English as *Sacred Hope* (Dar-es-Salaam, 1974).

> See: Amuta, C., 'The Poetic Essence of National Liberation: Agostinho Neto's *Sacred Hope*', *The Theory of African Literature: Implications for Practical Criticism* (L, 1989).

NGEMA, Mbongeni (1955–), born in Durban, worked as unskilled labourer before acting breaks with, among others, Gibson Kente. Script of play *Asinamali* (1985) in D. Ndlovu (ed.), *Woza Albert!* (NY, 1985). Musical *Sarafina!* (1986) became successful Hollywood film. (See entry, MTWA.)

NKOSI, Lewis (1936–), born in KwaZulu-Natal, joined newspaper *Ilange laseNatali* in 1955 and the following year moved to *Drum* magazine in Johannesburg. Left SA in 1961 to study journalism in USA; banned in 1966 under the all-embracing Suppression of Communism Act. University study in England; has lectured at universities in Poland, Zambia and currently in USA. Play *The Rhythm of Violence* (L, 1964), novel *Mating Birds* (L, 1986) and selections of criticism, *Home and Exile* (L, 1965), *The Transplanted Heart* (Benin City, 1975) and *Masks and Tasks* (L, 1981).

NTSIKANA kaGabha (1760–1821), born in eastern Cape, was converted to

Christianity and urged followers to give up traditional Xhosa customs. Composed hymns. 'Great Hymn' translated into English by Rev. J. Philip and, again, by T. Pringle (1827); literal translation by J. K. Bokwe published by Lovedale (1876); subsequently reprinted in several anthologies including S. Gray's *Penguin Book of Southern African Verse* (L, 1989).

Bokwe, J. K., *Ntsikana: The Story of an African Convert* (Alice, 1914).

See: Dargie, D., 'The Music of Ntsikana', *South African Journal of Musicology*, no. 2 (1982).

Also: Hodgson in White and Couzens (eds), *Literature and Society* (Gen. Bib.).

NTSIKO, Jonas (*c*.1860–*c*.1915), born in eastern Cape, poet, hymn writer, teacher and Christian preacher. Wrote articles in Xhosa-language journal *Isigidimi samaXhosa* under pseudonym 'uHadi Waseluklangeni' (Harp of the Nation); hymns in *Xhosa Hymn Book* (Grahamstown, 1881).

NYAMFUKUDZA, Stanley (1951–), born in Wedza, Zimbabwe, was expelled from University of Rhodesia in 1973 along with other student demonstrators; spell in prison before continuing studies at Oxford; in Zimbabwe works in a furniture factory. Novel *The Non-Believer's Journey* (L, 1980).

NYEMBEZI, Cyril (C.L.S.) (1919–), born in KwaZulu-Natal, educated at Mariannhill mission and several SA universities; editor of Zulu books for publishers in Pietermaritzburg and instrumental in fostering Zulu literature. Numerous novels in Zulu including *Inkinsela yaseMgungundlovu* (Pietermaritzburg, 1961). In English, *Zulu Proverbs* (J, 1954; Pietermaritzburg, 1990) and *A Review of Zulu Literature* (Pietermaritzburg, 1961).

OPPERMAN, Diederik (D.J.) (1914–1985), born in KwaZulu-Natal, educated at University of Natal becoming teacher, journalist and, later, professor of Afrikaans at University of Stellenbosch. Numerous volumes of poetry since 1945 include *Komas uit 'n Bamboesstok* (CT, 1979); plays include *Voëlvry* (CT, 1968). Editor of literary journal *Standpunte* since 1946 for many years, and, since 1951, editor of comprehensive anthology of Afrikaans verse, *Groot Verseboek*. Study of Dertigers, *Digters van Dertig* (CT, 1953).

Kannemeyer, J. C., *D. J. Opperman* (CT, 1986).

See: Coetzee, *One Hundred Years of Afrikaans Literature* (Gen. Bib.).

PATON, Alan (1903–1988), born in Pietermaritzburg, was principal of Diepkloof reformatory for young African offenders before his involvement in the Liberal Party until its disbandment in 1968 following government legislation against mixed-race political parties. Novel *Cry, the Beloved Country* (NY, L, 1948) was followed by the novels *Too Late the Phalarope* (NY, L, 1953) and, much later, *Ah, But Your Land Is Beautiful* (CT, 1981). Other writings include short stories *Debbie Go Home* also published as *Tales from a Troubled Land* (NY, 1961), the biographies *Hofmeyr* (L, 1964) and *Apartheid and the Archbishop* (L, 1973), and numerous political and literary articles selections of which are to be found in E. Callan (ed.), *The Long View* (NY, 1968) and C. Gardner (ed.), *Knocking on the Door* (CT, 1975). Autobiographies, *Towards the Mountain* (NY, 1980) and *Journey Continued* (NY, L, CT, 1988).

Alexander, P. F., *Alan Paton: A Biography* (CT, 1994).

See: Callan, E., *Alan Paton* (Boston, 1969; rev. ed., 1982).
    Cooke, J., ' "A Hunger of the Soul": *Too Late the Phalarope* Reconsidered', *English Studies in Africa*, vol. 22, no. 1 (1979).
    Watson, S., '*Cry, the Beloved Country* and the Failure of the Liberal Vision', *English in Africa*, vol. 9, no. 1 (May 1982).
    Morphet, T., 'Alan Paton: The Honour of Meditation', *English in Africa*, vol. 10, no. 2 (October 1983).
    Nash, A., 'The Way to the Beloved Country: History and the Individual in Alan Paton's *Towards the Mountain*', *English in Africa*, vol. 10, no. 2 (October 1983).

PEPETELA, pen-name of Arthur Carlos Pestana (1941–), born in Luanda area, studied in Angola, Portugal, France and Algeria where he was founder member of the Centre for Angolan Studies. In late 1960s he joined MPLA and served on the central front; after independence deputy minister of education. On steering committee of Union of Angolan Writers. Written in Portuguese in 1971 his novel *Mayombe: A Novel of the Angolan Struggle*[t] appeared in Luanda and Lisbon in 1980 with English translation in 1983 (L). Other writing includes children's story *Nguga's Adventures*[t] (L, 1980; 1972).

PHILIP, The Reverend (Dr) John (1775–1851), born in Scotland, was appointed general superintendent of London Missionary Society at the Cape and played leading role in movement for emancipation of the Khoi. Reports of British and Boer practices against indigenous inhabitants of the Cape in *Researches in South Africa: Illustrating the Civil, Moral, and Religious Condition of the Native Tribes*, 2 vols (L, 1828; NY, 1969).
    Ross, A., *John Philip (1773–1851): Missions, Race and Politics in South Africa* (Aberdeen, 1986).

PHIRI, Gideon (1942–), born in Zambia where he lives. Two novels *Tickling Sensation* (Lusaka, 1973) and *Victims of Fate* (Lusaka, 1974).

PLAATJE, Solomon (Sol T.) (1876–1932), born near Kimberley, joined the Cape civil service and moved to Mafikeng (Mafeking) as court interpreter shortly before the outbreak of the Anglo-Boer War and the siege of the town. Between 1902 and 1908, edited the seTswana-English weekly *Koranta ea Bechuana* before establishing newspaper *Tsala ea Batho* in Kimberley. As general correspondence secretary of the South African Native National Congress (forerunner of the ANC), he accompanied delegation to London to petition British government against denial of African rights in Union of South Africa (1910) including dispossessions under 1913 Natives Land Act. Wrote works on seTswana language including *Sechuana Proverbs* (L, 1916) and translated Shakespeare's *A Comedy of Errors* and *Julius Caesar* into seTswana. Non-fictional works include *The Boer War Diary of Sol T. Plaatje*, edited by J. L. Comaroff (NY, 1973), which was also published as *Mafeking Diary* (J, 1989), and *Native Life in South Africa* (L, 1916; J, 1982). Historical-romance *Mhudi: An Epic of South African Native Life a Hundred Years Ago* (Alice, 1930; L, 1978; J, 1989) was first published over 10 years after it had been written.
    Willan, B., *Sol Plaatje: A Biography* (J, 1984).

See: Couzens, T., Introduction to *Mhudi* (L, 1978).
    Couzens, T., 'Sol T. Plaatje and the First South African Epic', *English in Africa*, vol. 14, no. 1 (May 1987).

Couzens, T. and S. Gray, 'Printers and Other Devils: The Texts of Sol T. Plaatje's *Mhudi*', *Research in African Literatures*, vol. 9, no. 2 (Fall 1978).

Gray, S., 'Plaatje's Shakespeare', *English in Africa* vol. 4, no. 1 (March 1977).

Plaatje centenary issue of *English in Africa*, vol. 3, no. 2 (September 1976).

Voss, T., Introduction to *Mhudi* (J, 1989).

Voss, T., 'Sol Plaatje, the Eighteenth Century, and South African Cultural Memory', *English in Africa*, vol. 21, nos 1 and 2 (1994).

PLOMER, William (1903–1973), born in Pietersburg, educated in England, returned to SA in 1920s during which time, together with Campbell and Van der Post, he edited the literary journal *Voorslag* (1926) before sailing for Japan and returning to England where he became a respected man of letters, a director of and reader to the publishing firm Jonathan Cape. SA novel *Turbott Wolfe* (L, 1925; J, 1980) was followed by 'English' novels including *Museum Pieces* (L, 1952). Early SA writing in *Notes for Poems* (L, 1927) and volumes of stories, *I Speak of Africa* (L, 1927) and *The Child of Queen Victoria* (L, 1933). Selections most conveniently available in *Selected Stories* (CT, 1984) and *Selected Poems* (J, 1985). Also biography *Cecil Rhodes* (L, 1933; CT, 1984). Autobiographies *Double Lives* (L, 1943) and *At Home* (L, 1958) revised and combined as *The Autobiography of William Plomer* (L, 1975): SA sections published as *The South African Autobiography* (CT, 1984).

Alexander, P. F., *William Plomer: A Biography* (Oxford, 1990).

See: Lockett, C., '*Turbott Wolfe*: A Failed Novel or a Failure of Criticism?', *UNISA English Studies*, vol. 25, no. 1 (May 1987).

Thompson, E., 'Nature and History in William Plomer's African Poetry', *Theoria*, no. 80 (October 1992).

Van der Post, L., 'The *Turbott Wolfe* Affair', Introduction to the 1965 edition reprinted in *Turbott Wolfe* (J, 1980).

Wade, M., 'William Plomer, English Liberalism and the South African Novel', *The Journal of Commonwealth Literature*, vol. 8, no. 1 (June 1973).

Also: Rabkin in Parker (ed.), *The South African Novel* (Gen. Bib.).

PRELLER, Gustav S. (1875–1943), born in Pretoria, was a journalist in the Transvaal republic on *De Volkstem* and, in 1920s and 1930s, continued to be active in Afrikaans-language and nationalist causes producing numerous polemical and hagiographic writings including biography *Piet Retief* (Pretoria, 1906); edited *Dagboek van Louis Tregardt* (Pretoria, 1917), and editions of testimonies *Voortrekkermense, I–V* (Pretoria, 1918–1938).

PRINGLE, Thomas (1789–1834), born in Scotland, educated in Edinburgh, worked in Scottish record office while nurturing journalistic and literary ambitions; in 1817 co-editor of first few numbers of Blackwood's new *Edinburgh Monthly Magazine*. Economic recession and failure of editorial enterprises led Pringle and his family to emigrate to the Cape in 1820. After farming on eastern frontier, he moved to Cape Town as librarian of Government (later South African) Library. After clashes with governor Somerset over principle of free press, Pringle returned to London in 1826 and remained active in Anti-Slavery Society until his death. Together with countryman John Fairbairn, he founded and edited the short-lived *South African Journal* (1824) and contributed to Fairbairn's newspaper *The Commercial Advertiser* as well as to British journals including the *New Monthly Magazine*. Autobiographical prose commentary *Narrative of a Residence in South Africa* published jointly with *Poems Illustrative of South Africa* as *African Sketches* (L, 1834). Later editions of his African poems include J. R. Wahl (ed.), *Poems Illustrative of South Africa* (CT, 1970) and, most recently, E. Pereira and M. Chapman (eds), *African Poems of Thomas Pringle*.

> See: Calder, A., 'Thomas Pringle (1789–1834): A Scottish Poet in South Africa', *English in Africa*, vol. 9, no. 1 (May 1982).
> Klopper, D., 'Politics of the Pastoral: The Poetry of Thomas Pringle', *English in Africa*, vol. 17, no. 1 (May 1990).
> Pereira, E. and M. Chapman, Introduction, *African Poems of Thomas Pringle* (Pietermaritzburg, 1989).
> Shklyazh, I. M., *Thomas Pringle: A South African Democrat* (Moscow, 1986).
> Voss, A. E., 'Thomas Pringle and the Image of the "Bushman" ', *English in Africa*, vol. 9, no. 1 (May 1982).

QABULA, Alfred Temba (1942–), born in eastern Cape, worked as migrant labourer and, later, as factory-hand in Durban where he became involved in trade-union activity; presently at Culture and Working Life Project, University of Natal. Rose to prominence as oral poet at trade-union rallies in 1980s. Has published poems, together with Mi Hlatswayo and Nise Malange, in *Black Mamba Rising* (Durban 1986); autobiography *A Working Life; Cruel beyond Belief* (Durban, 1989).

RABIE, Jan (1920–), born in western Cape where, after sojourn in Europe in 1960s, he has continued to live as full-time writer. Four Afrikaans historical novels – 'Bolandia' sequence – include the translation into English of *Waar Jy Sterwe* (1966) as *A Man Apart* (L, 1969). Last Bolandia novel *Ark* (CT, 1977). Attack on Afrikaner nationalism, *Die Evolusie van Nasionalisme* (CT, 1960). Also early poems (1956) and collected stories (1980).

REBELO, Jorge (1940–), born in Mozambique, educated at Coimbra University (Portugal); joined Frelimo during armed struggle and became editor of their English-language journal, *Mozambique Revolution*. After independence he occupied senior party posts including minister of information. Poems in English translation in journals and anthologies.

RUBADIRI, David (1930–), born in Malawi, educated Makerere University (Uganda). Active in nationalist politics in the 1950s, he was appointed Malawi's first ambassador to USA and UNO, but had work banned by Banda's government and lived in exile from Banda's Malawi. Novel, *No Bride Price* (Nairobi, 1967), and poems in several journals and anthologies.

> See: Roscoe, *Uhuru's Fire* (Gen. Bib.).

RUBUSANA, Walter B. (1858–1916), born in eastern Cape, studied at Lovedale; teacher and, in 1884, ordained minister. Active in what would become ANC; accompanied Dube and Plaatje to London in 1914 to protest against

Natives Land Act. Wrote religious tracts, political articles, and edited anthology of Xhosa writing *Zemk'iinkomo Magwalandini* (L, 1906).

RUI, Manuel (1941–), born in Huambo, studied law at Coimbra University (Portugal); arrested in 1974 on charges of political activity for MPLA. Since independence he has held senior party posts in legal and information services and, in late 1970s, returned to academic life. Has published volumes of poems, literary criticism, children's stories, and the works of fiction *Sim Camarada!* (Lisbon, 1977) and *Qem Me Dera Ser Onda* (Lisbon, 1982).

SAMKANGE, Stanlake (1922–), born at Chipata, Zimbabwe, and educated at mission schools in Rhodesia and SA; university education at Fort Hare and Indiana; founded college of education in his home country and, having left Rhodesia shortly before UDI, held academic post in African history at Northwestern University, USA. Published historical novels *On Trial for my Country* (L, 1966), *The Mourned One* (L, 1975) and *Year of the Uprising* (L, 1978). Historical works, *Origins of Rhodesia* (NY, 1968) and *On Trial for that UDI* (Harare, 1986).

> See: Ravenscroft in Van Wyk Smith and Maclennan (eds), *Olive Schreiner and After*, and Veit-Wild, *Teachers, Preachers, Non-Believers* (Gen. Bib.).

SCHOEMAN, Karel (1939–), born in the Free State (SA), works as senior librarian in Cape Town. Several Afrikaans novels have been translated into English, *Promised Land* (L, 1979; 1972), *Another Country* (L, 1991; 1984) and *Take Leave and Go* (L, 1992; 1990). Biography (tr. from Afrikaans) *Olive Schreiner, A Woman in South Africa* (J, 1992) and *Only an Anguish to Live Here: Olive Schreiner and the Anglo-Boer War 1899–1902* (CT, 1992).

SCHREINER, Olive (1855–1920), born near Lesotho on mission station, spent itinerant early life on Kimberley diamond diggings and as governess on isolated Karoo farms; sailed for England in 1881 in search of publisher for novel *The Story of an African Farm* (L, 1883; J, 1986) which, like the posthumously published *Undine* (L, 1929; NY, 1972) and *From Man to Man* (L, 1926; 1982), reflected her concerns with the 'woman question' and repressive social mores. Having mingled with Victorian intellectual-literary personalities, she returned to SA in 1889 and her subsequent writings include allegorical dream-stories and public-political commentaries, with combination in *Trooper Peter Halket of Mashonaland* (L, 1897; J, 1992). Selection from *Dreams* (L, 1890), *Dream Life and Real Life* (L, 1893) and *Dreams and Allegories* (L, 1923) in C. Clayton (ed.), *The Woman's Rose* (J, 1986). Views on coming union of SA provinces in *Closer Union* (*The Transvaal/ Leader* newspaper, 1908), essays on SA race problems in *Thoughts on South Africa* (L, 1923; J, 1992) and commentary on the woman question in *Woman and Labour* (L, 1911; 1978).
First, R. and A. Scott, *Olive Schreiner: A Biography* (L, 1989).

> See: Berkman, J. A., *The Healing Imagination of Olive Schreiner: Beyond South African Colonialism* (Cambridge, Mass., 1989).
> Clayton, C. (ed.), *Olive Schreiner* (J, 1983).
> — Introduction, *The Story of an African Farm* (J, 1986).
> Murray, S., Introduction, *Trooper Peter Halket of Mashonaland* (J, 1992).

Pechey, G., '*The Story of an African Farm*: Colonial History and the Discontinuous Text', *Critical Arts*, vol. 3, no. 1 (1983).
Also: Murray in Chapman *et al.* (eds), *Perspectives* (Gen. Bib.).

SEPAMLA, Sipho (1932–), born near Johannesburg, trained as a teacher; subsequently prominent in literary activities. Poetry volumes *Hurry Up to It!* (J, 1975), *The Blues Is You in Me* (J, 1976), *The Soweto I Love* (CT, 1977), *Children of the Earth* (J, 1983) and *Selected Poems* (J, 1984). Novels *The Root Is One* (J, 1979), *A Ride on the Whirlwind* (J, 1981), *Third Generation* (J, 1986) and *A Scattered Survival* (J, 1989).

See: Chapman, *Soweto Poetry* and *South African English Poetry* (Gen. Bib.).

SEROTE, Mongane Wally (1944–), born in Sophiatown, worked in advertising and studied fine art in the USA; returned to southern Africa in 1979 and lived in self-imposed exile from SA in Botswana and later in London where he became active in ANC cultural department; returned to SA after 1990 and is ANC member of parliament. Several volumes of poetry *Yakhal'inkomo* (J, 1972), *Tsetlo* (J, 1972), *No Baby Must Weep* (J, 1975), *Behold Mama, Flowers* (J, 1978), *A Tough Tale* (L, 1987), *Third World Express* (CT, 1992) and *Come and Hope with Me* (CT, 1994). *Selected Poems* (J, 1982) and a novel *To Every Birth Its Blood* (J, 1981). Essays, *On the Horizon* (J, 1990).

See: Mphahlele, E., 'Mongane Serote's Odyssey: The Path That Breaks the Heels', *English Academy Review*, 3 (1985).
Chapman, M., 'A Tough Task for the Critic: Mongane Serote's *A Tough Tale*', *Upstream*, vol. 6, no. 3 (March 1988).
Also: Mzamane (poetry), Visser (novel) in Chapman *et al.* (eds), *Perspectives*, Watts, *Black Writers*, Chapman, *Soweto Poetry* and *South African English Poetry* (Gen. Bib.).

SHEMBE, Isaiah (*c.*1868–1935), born in Natal colony, was a preacher who, in the early twentieth century, wrote hymns in Zulu. Collected in *Izihlabelelo zamaNazaretha* (Hymns of the Nararites, 1940).
Dube, J. L. *uShembe* (Pietermaritzburg, 1963).

See: Gunner, E., 'New Wine in Old Bottles: Imagery in the Izibongo of the Zulu Zionist Prophet, Isaiah Shembe', *Journal of the Anthropological Society of Oxford*, vol. 13, no. 1 (1982).
Oosthuizen, G. C., *The Theology of a South African Messiah: An Analysis of the Hymnal of 'The Church of the Nazarites'* (Leiden, 1967).
Vilakazi, A., *et al.* (eds), *The Revitalisation of African Society* (Johannesburg, 1986).

SLATER, Francis Carey (1876–1958), born in eastern Cape, bank manager in Grahamstown; retired early to devote himself to his writing. Selection of poetry including 'Dark Folk' poems and 'Drought: A South African Parable' (1929) in *Collected Poems* (Edinburgh, 1957). Editor of first substantial anthology of SA poetry, *The Centenary Book of South African Verse (1820–1925)* (L, 1925).

SMALL, Adam (1936–), born in western Cape, studied at Universities of Cape Town, London and Oxford, lectures in philosophy and head of Department of Social Work at University of Western Cape. Since 1957 several volumes of Afrikaans 'Cape coloured' patois poems including *Kitaar my Kruis* (CT, 1961). Play, *Kanna Hy Kô' Hystoe* (CT, 1965) presented in USA as *Kanna He Is Coming Home*.

SMIT, Bartho (1924–1987), born in Potchefstroom, educated at University of Pretoria; after spell in Europe in 1960s worked in publishing. Several plays some of which have been translated into English including *Putsonderwater* (1962) as *Well-without-Water* (J, 1968) and *Christine* (1971) in T. Hauptfleisch and I. Steadman (eds), *South African Theatre* (Pretoria, 1984).

SMITH, Pauline (1882–1959), born in the Karoo, left SA in 1895 to attend school in England; returned for brief spells which are recorded in her '1905 diary' and in her 'journal, 1913–1914'. Children's stories published posthumously as *Platkops Children* (L, 1935; CT, 1981); short stories, *The Little Karoo* (L, 1925; CT, 1990) and novel *The Beadle* (L, 1926; CT, 1981). Selection of other writing in E. Pereira (ed.), *The Unknown Pauline Smith* (Pietermaritzburg, 1993).

> See: Coetzee, J. M., 'Pauline Smith and the Afrikaans Language', *English in Africa*, vol. 8, no. 1 (March 1981).
> Driver, D. ed., *Pauline Smith* (J, 1983).
> Gardiner, M., 'Critical Responses and the Fiction of Pauline Smith', *Theoria*, no. 60 (May 1983).
> Haresnape, G., *Pauline Smith* (Boston, 1969).

SMITH, Wilbur (1933–), born in Zambia, educated in SA, followed his first international best-seller *When the Lion Feeds* (L, 1964) with numerous novels of African high adventure including *Rage* (L, 1987).

> See: Maughan Brown in Trump (ed.), *Rendering Things Visible* (Gen. Bib.).

SOGA, Tiyo (1829–1871), born in eastern Cape, was educated at Lovedale and in Scotland; qualified as Presbyterian minister and opened a mission among the Xhosa. Wrote hymns, collected oral material, translated first part of Bunyan's *The Pilgrim's Progress: uHambo Lomhambi* (Alice, 1866), a task completed by his son J. H. Soga (L, 1926). Writings in D. Williams (ed.), *The Journal and Selected Writings of Reverend Tiyo Soga* (CT, 1983).
> Chalmers, J. A., *Tiyo Soga* (Edinburgh, 1877).
> Williams, D., *Umfundisi: A Biography of Tiyo Soga, 1829–1871* (Alice, 1978).

SOLE, Kelwyn (1951–), born in Johannesburg, educated Universities of Witwatersrand, London and Cape Town; lecturer in English at Cape Town. Several articles on socio-cultural issues in SA; volumes of poetry *The Blood of our Silence* (J, 1988) and *Projections in the Past Tense* (J, 1992).

SONTONGA, Enoch (*c.*1860–1904), born in eastern Cape, teacher in Methodist mission schools, wrote songs for his pupils. Compositions lost except for first stanza and chorus of 'Nkosi Sikelel' iAfrika' (composed 1897). By 1927 stanzas 2–8 provided by S. E. K. Mqhayi, published by Lovedale in 1934 with D. D. T. Jabavu's English translation, 'Lord Bless Africa' as *The Bantu National Anthem*.

STOCKENSTRÖM, Wilma (1933–), born in the Cape, educated at University of
Stellenbosch; has published several volumes of Afrikaans poetry including
Monsterverse (CT, 1984) and novels include (in English translation) *The
Expedition to the Baobab Tree* (L, 1983; 1981).

STUART, James (1848–1942), born in England, was magistrate in Natal colony and
dedicated collector of Zulu oral traditions. Recordings in early twentieth-
century school readers and in papers in Killie Campbell Africana Library
(Durban) which are sources of several subsequent publications including
T. Cope's *Izibongo: Zulu Praise Poems* (L, 1968) and D. K. Rycroft and A. B.
Ngcobo's *The Praises of Dingana* (Pietermaritzburg, 1988). Multi-volume
series based on original manuscript material: C. de B. Webb and J. B. Wright
(eds), *The James Stuart Archive of Recorded Oral Evidence Relating to the History
of the Zulu and Neighbouring Peoples* (Pietermaritzburg, 1976–1986).

THEMBA, Daniel Canodoise (Can) (1924–1968), born in Pretoria, educated at Fort
Hare, taught English before joining *Drum* magazine in 1950s as a journalist.
After leaving SA and being declared a banned person, he lived until his death
in Swaziland. Selections of short stories and journalistic pieces which first
appeared in *Drum* are available in *The Will to Die* (L, 1972; CT, 1982) and
The World of Can Themba (J, 1985).

> See: Chapman, M., 'Can Themba, Storyteller and Journalist of the 1950s:
> The Text in Context', *English in Africa*, vol. 16, no. 2 (October
> 1989).

TLALI, Miriam (1933–), born near Johannesburg, attended school in Western
Native Township (Soweto), contributed regular interviews with Sowetans
in *Staffrider* magazine in the late 1970s. Novel, or thinly fictionalised series
of autobiographical sketches, *Muriel at Metropolitan* (J, 1975) was followed
by the novel *Amandla!* (J, 1981) and by selection of stories, sketches,
reminiscences and commentary in *Mihloti* (J, 1984) and in *Footprints in the Quag*
(CT, 1989), which was also published as *Soweto Stories* (L, 1989).

> See: Hunter, E., ' "A Mother Is Nothing but a Backbone": Women,
> Tradition and Change in Miriam Tlali's *Footprints in the Quag*',
> *Current Writing*, vol. 5, no. 1 (1993).
> Also: Lockett in Clayton (ed.), *Women and Writing* (Gen. Bib.).

TOTIUS, pseudonym of Jacob Daniël du Toit (1877–1953), born in the Cape,
studied theology in Amsterdam; minister of religion in the Transvaal and in
charge of theology school, University of Potchefstroom. Translation of Bible
into Afrikaans. Several volumes of poetry including *Ragel* (1913), *Trekkerswee*
(1915) and *Passieblomme* (1934).

> See: Merwe Scholtz, M. (ed.), *Die Lewende Totius* (CT, 1977).

TURNER, Richard (Rick) (1941–1978), born in Cape Town, educated in Cape
Town and Paris; returned to SA in early 1970s and lectured in political
philosophy at University of Natal (Durban), while involved in anti-apartheid,
wages investigation into African labour. Banned by the state; killed by
unknown assassins presumed to be state agents. Published *The Eye of the
Needle: Towards a Participatory Democracy in South Africa*.

See: Morphet, T., Introduction, *The Eye of the Needle* (J, 1972; 1980).
' "Brushing History against the Grain": Oppositional Discourse in
South Africa', *Theoria*, no. 76 (October 1990). (On Turner and
Biko.)

TUTU, Mpilo Desmond (Archbishop) (1931–), born near Johannesburg, trained as
a teacher and taught at a high school before obtaining his licentiate in
theology at St Peter's Theological College in 1960. Ordained as priest in 1960;
studied abroad; Anglican dean, Johannesburg, 1975–76; Nobel Peace Prize,
1984; Archbishop of Cape Town, 1986. Prominent public spokesman on
social justice in 1970s and 1980s. Speeches, sermons, writings in *Hope and
Suffering* (J, 1983) and *The Rainbow People of God: South Africa's Victory over
Apartheid* (L, NY, 1994).

See: De Boulay, S., *Tutu: Voice of the Voiceless* (L, 1988).
Tlhagale, B. and I. Mosala, (eds) *Hammering Swords into Ploughshares:
Essays in Honour of Archbishop Mpilo Desmond Tutu* (J, 1986).

UKXONE, a Bushman narrator and singer from the central Kalahari in Botswana;
elderly in 1950s and probably no longer alive. Songs recorded by Marshall
expeditions in 1950s; accounts of his songs and many narratives in E. Marshall
Thomas's *The Harmless People* (NY, 1959).

UYS, Pieter-Dirk (1945–), born in Cape Town, based in Johannesburg and tours
SA with his theatrical entertainments including *Snow White and the Special
Branch*, *Adapt or Dye* and *Total Onslaught*. Scripts of several of his plays have
been published including *Paradise Is Closing Down* and *God's Forgotten* in
Theatre One (J, 1978) and *Theatre Two* (J, 1981), respectively, both edited by
S. Gray, and *Die van Ardes van Grootoor* (J, 1979).

VAMBE, Laurence (1917–), born at Mashonganyika in Catholic mission; teacher
and keen interest in priesthood during education partly in SA; later went
to London while involved in Zimbabwean nationalist politics. Returned to
Zimbabwe in 1979 and played active role in Harare business community.
Wrote *An Ill-Fated People: Zimbabwe before and after Rhodes* (L, 1972) and *From
Rhodesia to Zimbabwe* (L, 1976). Edited the magazine *African Parade*.

See: Veit-Wild, *Teachers, Preachers, Non-Believers* (Gen. Bib.).

VAN DEN HEEVER, Christiaan (C.M.) (1902–1957), born in concentration camp
during Anglo-Boer War; teacher, journalist, in 1933 professor of Afrikaans
at University of the Witwatersrand. Several farm novels including *Op die Plaas*
(1926), *Droogte* (1930), *Groei* (1933), *Somer* (1935) which was translated into
English as *Harvest Home* (J, 1945) and *Laat Vrugte* (1939).

See: Coetzee, J. M., 'Farm Novel and *Plaasroman* in South Africa', *English
in Africa*, vol. 13, no. 2 (October 1986).

VAN DER POST, Laurens (1906–), born in a Free State farming district (SA),
worked as a journalist in Durban where he met Campbell and Plomer
whom he joined in 1926 as contributor to and editor of the literary journal
Voorslag. Left SA with Plomer for Japan in 1926 and, except for intermittent
returns to his home country, has remained in London where his service to

British commonwealth life, including distinguished duty in the Second World War, has earned him a peerage. Numerous novels including *In a Province* (L, 1934), *The Face beside the Fire* (L, 1953), *Flamingo Feather* (L, 1955) and *A Story Like the Wind* (L, 1972). Long fascination with the Bushmen in ethno-mythographic accounts such as *The Lost World of the Kalahari* (L, 1958) and *The Heart of the Hunter* (L, 1961). Autobiographical *Yet Being Someone Other* (L, 1982).

See: Carpenter, F., *Laurens van der Post* (Boston, 1969).
    Lloyd, D. W., 'Transformation of the Colonial Narrative: Laurens van der Post's *The Lost World of the Kalahari*', *English Academy Review*, no. 10 (December 1993).
Also: Maughan Brown in Chapman *et al.* (eds), *Perspectives* (Gen. Bib.).

VIEIRA, Luandino (adopted name of José Vieira Mateus da Graça) (1935–), born to a peasant family in Portugal, was brought to Angola as a small child and grew up in Luanda townships. Began working at age of 15 selling car parts; became active in anti-colonial politics and in 1961 sentenced to 14 years' imprisonment mostly in Tarrafal concentration camp where he began to write stories some of which appeared initially in clandestine editions. In 1972 he was allowed to live under restricted residence in Lisbon; returned to Angola on fall of Salazar and since independence has occupied senior MPLA posts in information. President of Union of Angolan Writers which he helped to found. Novels include *The Real Life of Domingos Xavier*[t] which was written in Portuguese in the early 1960s and published in English translation in 1978 (L); six collections of stories include *Luuanda*[t] which, in its original Portuguese, dates back to the early 1960s and which appeared in English translation in 1980 (L).

See: *Luandino: José Luandino Vieira e a Sua Obra* (Lisbon, 1980).

VILAKAZI, Benedict Wallet Bambatha (B.W.) (1906–1947), born in KwaZulu-Natal, attended school at Mariannhill Mission and SA universities; lectured in Zulu at University of Witwatersrand. With C. Doke compiled *Zulu-English Dictionary* (J, 1958). Selection from poetry volumes in Zulu, *Inkondlo kaZulu* (1935) and *Amal' eZulu* (1945) published in English rendition by D. McK. Malcolm and L. Friedman as *Zulu Horizons* (CT, 1962). Complete *Amal' eZulu* rendered into English by Friedman as *Zulu Horizons* (J, 1973). Several key writings on Zulu literature including 'The Conception and Development of Poetry in Zulu', *Bantu Studies*, vol. 12, no. 4 (1938), and *The Oral and Written Literature in Nguni* (J, 1945).

See: Mootry, M. K., see entry DHLOMO, H. I. E.
    Ntuli, D. B. Z., *The Poetry of B. W. Vilakazi* (Pretoria, 1984).

WATSON, Stephen (1954–), born in Cape Town, lectures in English at the University of Cape Town. Volumes of poetry, *Poems 1977–1982* (J, 1982), *In This City* (CT, 1986), and poetic renditions of traditional Bushman songs and stories, *Return of the Moon* (CT, 1991). Prominent contributor to literary debate in 1980s: *Selected Essays: 1980–1990* (CT, 1990).

WILHELM, Peter (1943–), born in Johannesburg, editor of a business journal. Poetry *White Flowers* (J, 1977); novels *The Dark Wood* (J, 1977), *The Healing*

Process (J, 1988) and *The Mask of Freedom* (J, 1994); and collections of short stories, *L.M. and Other Stories* (J, 1975), *At the End of a War* (J, 1981) and *Some Place in Africa* (J, 1987).

WITBOOI, Hendrick (1840–1905), born in northwestern Cape, migrated north to Namibia under patriarchal rule of clan; settled at Gibeon in 1860s. Mission educated and convert to Christianity, he actively opposed German colonialism and, after period of successful guerilla activity, was shot while on campaign. Diary in Dutch, *Die Dagboek van Hendrick Witbooi, Kaptein van Witbooi-Hottentotte, 1884–1905* (CT, 1929).

XITU, Uanhenga, pen-name of Agostinho Mendes de Carvalho (1924–), born in Mbundu district, Angola; active in MPLA politics and imprisoned in Tarrafal concentration camp in 1960s. Wrote novels *Manana* (1974) and *'Mestre' Tamoda* (1974), the latter translated into English as *The World of 'Mestre' Tamoda* (L, 1989).

ZIMUNYA, Musaemura B. (1949–), born in Mutare, Zimbabwe, educated Universities of Zimbabwe and Kent; lecturer in English at Zimbabwe. Volumes of poetry, *Zimbabwe Ruins* (Harare, 1981), *Thought-Tracks* (L, 1982), *Kingfisher, Jikinya and Other Poems* (Harare, 1982) and *Country Dawns and City Lights* (Harare, 1985). Critical study of Zimbabwean fiction, *Those Years of Drought and Hunger: The Birth of African Fiction in Zimbabwe* (Gweru, 1982). Co-editor, with M. Kadhani, of anthology *And Now the Poets Speak: Poems Inspired by the Struggle for Zimbabwe* (Gweru, 1981); editor of *Chakarira Chindumduma: Shona Poems Inspired by the Struggle for Zimbabwe* (Gweru, 1986).

ZVOBGO, Eddison T. (1935–), born in Mtilikwe, Zimbabwe, educated Roma University, Lesotho, and Taft, USA. Teacher who, under UDI, was detained for long period, during which he qualified as lawyer; after independence became cabinet minister in the Mugabe government. Writes poetry in Shona and English with poems in journals in Zimbabwe, SA and USA.

Index

Note: Bracketed page numbers refer to entries in the Chronology or in the section on Individual Authors. Entries in Notes at the end of individual chapters are indicated by 'n' directly after the page number, e.g. 33n

'The Big Match', 285–6
'Contract Worker', 285
Jack Hawkins: a Tale of South Africa, 102
Jacobson, Dan, 134, 187, 233–4, 237, 385, 388, (493)
   A Dance in the Sun, 233–4, (455)
   Through the Wilderness: Selected Stories, (464)
   The Trap, 233
Jacottet, Edouard
   Treasury of Ba-Suto Lore, (448)
Jamba, Sousa, (493)
   Patriots, 288
Jane comes to Joburg, see *Jim comes to Joburg*
Jardine, A. C., 101–2
Jenkins, Elwyn, 423
Jensma, Wopko, 340–1, 344, (493)
   Sing for our Execution, (460)
Jim comes to Joburg, 48, 133, 142, 144n, 185, 186, 209, 218n, 219n, 223, 228, 229, 362, 378, (453)
Jolobe, J. J. R., 204, 209, (456), (493)
   Poems of an African, (453)
   Umyezo, (452), (453)
Jonker, Ingrid, 182, 223, 251, (493)
   'I Drift in the Wind', 251
   Rook en Oker, (458)
Jordan, A. C., 24, 46, 47, 48, 105, 106, 204, 214, 215, (455), (493–4)
   Ingqumbo Yeminyanya, 217n, (452)
   Towards an African Literature: The Emergence of Literary Form in Xhosa, (461)
   The Wrath of the Ancestors, 211, 214, 217n, (452)
Joubert, Elsa, 387, (494)
   Poppie, 398–9
   Die Swerfjare van Poppie Nongema, (464)
Junction Avenue Theatre Company, 357–8, 359
Júnior, Antonio de Assis, 152, 167, (494)
   O Segredo da Morta, 151–2, (451)

Kaapsche Grensblad, 127
||Kabbo, 22, 23, 28, 29, 31, 32, 382, (494)
   '||Kabbo Tells Me His Dream', 31
   'Return of the Moon', 31
Kachingwe, Aubrey
   No Easy Task, (459)
Kadhani, M. and Musaemura B. Zimunya
   And Now the Poets Speak: Poems Inspired by the Struggle for Zimbabwe (eds), 163, 299, (465)
The Kaffir Express, (445)
Kafirs and Kafirland: A Settler's Story, 102
Kagubi, 158, 298
!Kaha, 27, 35, 41, (494)
Kahari, George P.
   The Search for Zimbabwean Identity: an Introduction to the Black Zimbabwean Novel, (465)
Kameeta, Zephania
   '*Why O Lord?*': *Psalms and Sermons from Namibia*, 319, (468)
Kani, John, (494)
   Die Hodoshe Span, 362
   The Island, 361–2
   Sizwe Bansi is Dead, 361–2, 364, 371
Kannemeyer, J. C., 198
   Geskiedenis van die Afrikaanse Literatuur, (464)
Kapelwa Musonda, (494)
   The Kapelwa Musonda File, 269–70
Karoo, 75, 134, 188, 224
Kashne n!a, 28
Kasoma, Kabwe, 269, (494)
   Black Mamba Two, 272
   Fools Marry, 269
Katiyo, Wilson
   Mavambo: First Steps, (467)
   A Son of the Soil, (467)
Katjavivi, Peter H.
   A History of Resistance in Namibia, (469)
Katshaa! The Sound of the AK, (467)
Kaunda, Kenneth, 267, 268, 270, (456), (470), (494–5)
   Zambia Shall Be Free, 267, (458)
Kavanagh, Robert Mshengu (McLaren) (495), see also McLaren, Robert
Kayira, Legson, 273–4, (495)
   The Civil Servant, 274
   The Detainee, 274
   Jingala, 273–4, (460)
   The Looming Shadow, 273, (459)
Kendall, E. A.
   The English Boy at the Cape, 102
Kente, Gibson, 352, 355, 358, 359, (495)
   How Long, 352
   I Believe, 352
   Manana the Jazz Prophet, 352, (458)
   Sekunjalo, 352
   Too Late, 352
Kerkorrel, Johannes, 367n
Kerr, David, 274, 275, 276